THE MAJOR METAPHYSICAL POETS OF THE SEVENTEENTH CENTURY

OSCAR WILLIAMS (1900-1964) was the editor of over a dozen major anthologies of poetry including *Master Poems of the English Language,* a distinguished compilation of the most dynamic works of our literary heritage with individual critical essays by the most prominent British and American poets and critics. A poet in his own right, he lectured at leading colleges throughout the country as well as at the Library of Congress.

THE MAJOR METAPHYSICAL POETS OF THE SEVENTEENTH CENTURY

John Donne, George Herbert,
Richard Crashaw, and
Andrew Marvell

AN ANTHOLOGY

Edited by
Edwin Honig and Oscar Williams

WSP

WASHINGTON SQUARE PRESS, INC.
New York
1968

Library of Congress Catalog number: 66-24831

Printed in the United States of America

❦

ACKNOWLEDGEMENTS

The texts for the poems in this book are those of the most authoritative editions available:

THE POEMS OF JOHN DONNE,
edited by H. J. Grierson. London, Oxford University Press, 1929.

THE WORKS OF GEORGE HERBERT,
edited by F. E. Hutchinson. Oxford University Press, 1945.

THE POEMS ENGLISH, LATIN, AND GREEK
OF RICHARD CRASHAW,
edited by L. C. Martin. Oxford, Clarendon Press, 1927.

POEMS AND LETTERS OF ANDREW MARVELL,
edited by H. M. Margoliouth. Oxford, Clarendon Press, 1952.

CONTENTS

INTRODUCTION   *1*

A NOTE ON THE TEXT   *33*

John Donne   *37*

Songs and Sonnets   40
Epigrams   89
Elegies   93
Epithalamions   127
Satyres   141
Letters to Severall Personages   161
An Anatomie of the World   206
Of the Progresse of the Soule   223
Epicedes and Obsequies   238
Epitaphs   255
Infinitati Sacrum   257
Divine Poems   273
Translations from Latin Poems   317

George Herbert   *321*

The Temple   323
The Church-porch   *323*
The Church   *337*
The Church Militant   *486*
English Poems Not Included in THE TEMPLE   495
Poems from Walton's LIVES   500

Richard Crashaw   *505*

Steps to the Temple   508
Divine Epigrams   514
The Delights of the Muses   571
Carmen Deo Nostro   611
*A Letter from Mr. Crashaw to the
Countess of Denbigh   692*
Poems from Manuscripts   695

Andrew Marvell   *709*

Poems   711
Satires of the Reign of Charles II   823

BIBLIOGRAPHY   *867*

INDEX OF FIRST LINES   *879*

INDEX OF TITLES   *892*

Introduction

"Poor intricate soule! Riddling, perplexed, lab-
yrinthicall soule!"   — *John Donne*

"He that lies boyling on a Gridiron in others eies,
lies in his own Conceit upon a Bed of Pleasure."
— from *The Story Books of Little Gidding*

English metaphysical poetry is the richest and most wide-
ranging in the language. The features of the metaphysical
style are well known: analytic and self-conscious, colloquial in
tone, dramatic in emphasis. It is also notorious for wild image-
ry, hyperbole, scrupulous intellectual construction, elaborate
and ingenious working out of tropes. Although medieval in
dialectic, metaphysical poetry is celebrated for its sensitivity
to the new learning of the Renaissance and for adapting the
poetic novelties of Continental poetry into English. When the
style was most vigorous in the seventeenth century, it brought
forth the best erotic poetry and the best devotional poetry as
well as the finest lyrics, satires, pastorals and visionary medita-
tions of that era—perhaps the best of any era.

The metaphysical temper goes beyond the seventeenth cen-

1

tury and pervades some of the best poetry written since: the odes of Keats, the nature poetry of Wordsworth, the ballads of Coleridge, and the poems of Hopkins, Dickinson, Eliot, Stevens, Ransom, Hart Crane, and Dylan Thomas. Besides following this sporadic and recurrent development in English poetry, the metaphysical style also shows up in the Renaissance poetry of France, Spain, Italy, Germany, and Holland, and even appears in the past seventy-five years among the symbolist and surrealist poets.

The rediscovery of the metaphysicals (the seventeenth-century poets and the poetic temperament both) is part of the modern appropriation of all aspects of the baroque, the bizarre, the difficult, the primitive, and the off-beat. In this century of the hydrogen bomb and Malraux's museum without walls, the metaphysicals have been taken over as our "true" ancestors. To read them reveals not only what we were but, even more, what we have become. For, like the metaphysicals, we are undergoing total revolutions in our thinking about the universe and mass societies and about the biological and psychological composition of human life. Like the metaphysicals we feel threatened by annihilation both as individuals and as a race. We also know the "ecstacy" and the "drug" of religious enthusiasm and the difficult "peace" of stoical rationality. We have the same programmatic lunatics and the same extremist "solutions" in the arts with all their fanatic energy and ephemerality. From this we know what the metaphysicals felt, just as they too might have understood what we feel.

I

The four chief metaphysical poets flourished in the century between Donne's birth (1572) and Marvell's death (1678). But until our time their literary fate has been oddly dismal. Although a vogue for metaphysical poetry existed in the first two decades of the seventeenth century, when Donne's verse was being admired and imitated by wits, lawyers, and diplomats, this type of poetry was usually underrated for being obscure, highbrow, and affected. Historically, the matter turns into a contention between the advocates of the plain style and the ornamentalists with a philosophical bent. In the early view the plain-stylists, like Dryden, Pope, and Johnson, were the natural enemies of the ornamentalists, who would include Donne and Marvell as well as Spenser and Shakespeare. The bias against the ornamentalists has apparently never been stamped out. In the modern period the symbolists were victimized as the seventeenth-century metaphysicals had been. After being briefly admired, the symbolists were criticized for inflating language and for failing to be the clean-cut adapters of "the prose tradition" which Ezra Pound later discerned for modern poetry in the writing of Flaubert.

Like the modern poetic innovators, historians are often rationalists, conservatives, doctrinaires. As apologists for the classical norm of literary decorum, they cannot sanction those who deviate from it; hence they grudgingly admit the metaphysicals into the canon of English poetry only because the influence of the metaphysicals on the development of recent poetry has been so considerable. These historians are always neatening categories, smoothing out matters of influence and literary diet, prescribing healthful meals for writers and readers alike.[1] They name and nickname eras, groups, and periods according to historical occasions, most of which are accidental. But labels stick, and the writers are misshapen under the pressure of curious nicknames. Nicknaming a group of poets may help to point at what they were trying to do and what they may have had in common, but usually it minimizes the special merits of the individuals being classified.

The term "metaphysical poets" was used (and, almost always, then as now, used derogatorily) by Samuel Johnson, who seems to have adapted it from John Dryden, in order to designate the faults of the mid-seventeenth-century poets derived from Donne. The relevant criticism appears in Johnson's *Life of Cowley*. He says first that "about the beginning of the

---

[1] An especially pompous piece of critical rationalization on Donne, written by C. S. Lewis, ends with this square-jawed mouthful: "It would hardly be too much to say that the final cause of Donne's poetry is the poetry of Herbert, Crashaw, and Marvell; for the very qualities which make Donne's kind of poetry unsatisfying poetic food make it a valuable ingredient." "Donne and Love Poetry in the Seventeenth Century," from *Seventeenth Century Studies Presented to Sir Herbert Grierson*, ed., W. R. Keast, (Oxford, 1938), pp. 64–68.

seventeenth century appeared a race of writers that may be termed metaphysical poets." He then adds that "whatever is improper or vicious (among them) is produced by a voluntary deviation from nature in pursuit of something new and strange"; and "that the writers fail to give delight, by their desire of exciting admiration." Earlier, in his *Discourse Concerning Satire* (1693), Dryden had written that Donne "affects the metaphysics, not only in his satires, but in his amorous verse, where nature only should reign; and perplexes the minds of the fair sex with nice speculations of philosophy, when he should engage their hearts, and entertain them with the softnesses of love."

Dryden and Johnson found Donne reprehensible for offending against literary decorum, both in subject and in style. This attitude echoes the earlier criticism of Donne's friend and great contemporary, Ben Jonson. Responsible for a poetic lineage as illustrious as Donne's, Jonson censured Donne's elegy on Prince Henry for its "obscureness." He also said that Donne deserved hanging for not keeping regular accent in his verse. Both remarks occur in Jonson's *Conversations* with William Drummond of Hawthornden; and Drummond himself alluded derogatorily to poets who use "Metaphysical Ideas and Scholastical Quiddities."

The asperity of these comments originates among critics who venerated plain diction and thought Donne the arch malefactor among those who were distorting poetry by willful and eccentric mannerisms. In this view the metaphysicals were adding something equally bad to the older literary offenses of deliberate archaism, artificiality of address, decorative metaphor—the offenses of Spenser and Sidney and the Petrarchans which Donne had rebelled against. To complicate the matter, these were offenses which the plain-stylist Ben Jonson himself did not escape in his florid masques and heady comedies. The particular style Donne had invented, the style which suited his genius so well that he could express all he wanted of his complicated personality in it, was not always appropriate to those who adopted it, even when they were notably different from Donne. This applies variously to Herbert, Crashaw, and Marvell and to other metaphysicals who evolved styles of their own along similar lines—mainly Thomas Traherne and Edward Taylor.

These are observant, devout, often religiously enthusiastic poets. Yet, despite his deeply serious concerns, one would never think of associating such attributes with Donne. Unlike Donne, the other metaphysical poets do not express the full complexity of their lives in their poetry; they express their thoughts, their scruples, their beliefs and consciences. In Blake's terms Donne is the poet of experience, the others, poets, most often, of lost innocence. Despite their indebtedness to him, Donne's followers write best when they do not imitate him, when, in fact, they are least metaphysical. As has been shown, they are poets who were as often influenced by Jonson as by Donne. This is not surprising; Donne and Jonson were seminal influences on seventeenth-century poetry, and Jonson, particularly, had more to do with shaping the course of English poetry than even Shakespeare or Milton, whose influence during their century was comparatively negligible.

Like the romantics, the metaphysicals are poets thrown together under an inappropriate name. What have they in common? What has Byron's "Don Juan" in common with Shelley's "Epipsychidion"? No more than Herbert's "The Collar" has with Marvell's "Upon Appleton House." Yet romanticism is often a useful term, helping to highlight certain striking predilections in nineteenth-century poetic practice. Similarly, the term metaphysical seems more meaningful when contrasted with Petrarchan and neo-classical modes in English poetry. But to let the term bemuse one is to forget that the subject is the poets and their poetry, not the curious historical circumstances which bestowed the name upon them.

Moreover, the adjective is more useful than the noun, since it designates one of several attributes appearing in the poetry and one that several poets have in common. Such a term as meditative,[2] designating another attribute, may suggest something more inclusive than metaphysical for a poetry that is religious, personal, and introspective. The term metaphysical is relative in another way. Although pointing to a dominant style in English poetry that ended with Dryden, the term may be historically applicable to the work of only one poet, John Donne, in the same way that the baroque styles bearing their

[2] See Louis L. Martz, *The Poetry of Meditation* (New Haven, 1954).

names are typical of the works of Góngora and Marino. Metaphysical would thus refer to the temperamental predisposition which makes a poet write the way he does. Viewed in this way, Marino and Góngora would be more truly metaphysical than Herbert. So too, for similar reasons, would the Puritan Emily Dickinson, the Jesuit Victorian Gerard Manley Hopkins, or the heterodox Dylan Thomas seem closer to Donne.

Metaphysical, then, refers to the extreme position of a very personal kind of poetry, where ideas and intellect drive the poetic imagery in a language that is sinewy, supple, and ambivalent. It is also the name for a condition of poetry—not only in English, since it crops up in other literatures too—when the poetry goes inward, becomes least public, least professional, most speculative. So we may say that if Traherne and Taylor, undiscovered until recently, are metaphysicals, then so are Dickinson and Hopkins, who were as unknown in their own time as Traherne and Taylor were before them. This indicates that there is a metaphysical temperament (often buried or slighted because of shifts in taste), which transcends other distinctions and links together poets of a special intelligence, psychological complexity, and high linguistic inventiveness, who may be removed from one another by centuries, by language, and by quite different cultures and beliefs.

Questions of literary nomenclature are seldom resolved to everyone's satisfaction. Often, in fact, too much general agreement about a term means that the life has gone out of it and that nobody is much interested in the literature it designates. The continual discussion of the meaning of terms, when this is not a futile airing of nonliterary prejudices, may show the order an age wishes to give a literary work or works in its own organization of valuable ideas. The poems, dramas, and novels do not change; what changes is the order of preference in which they are cast by successive ages. The metaphysical poem may be a genre, but before the term existed there were poems of that description answering to other names.

II

Yet the rationalistic animus against the metaphysicals remains deeply rooted. Sir Herbert Grierson, the man who did most to revive interest in Donne and the metaphysical poets in our time, is himself a victim of the prejudice which buried the metaphysicals for over two hundred years. Grierson denies Donne the "highest seriousness" because his metaphysical wit lacked "the entire artistic sincerity that Shakespeare conveys in the greater of his sonnets and Drayton once achieved."[3] Grierson seems paradoxically to praise Donne for his wide-ranging humanism, wit, and intellectual curiosity while censuring him for lacking either a great philosophic system, which would "unite" his poetic thought, or a single, driving force safeguarded by Church doctrine, which would derive from humility instead of curiosity, in the simpler manner of George Herbert.

What philosophical and unifying originality of thought had Shakespeare (not to mention Drayton)? Even Dante and Virgil, the poets Grierson thinks the greatest, did not create systems of thought but employed those of others. In any event, Grierson seems to want another kind of poet—at least with part of his mind—while his criticism falls in line with Dryden's and Jonson's. The worried historian in Grierson, searching for light and order, is chafed by Donne's dark thought, pirouetting ideas, and linguistic ebullience; he yearns for the comfort of something like Herbert's poetry, a poetry of belief. This leads to other surprising lapses, as when Grierson speaks of Donne's "subtle and fantastic misapplication of learning" in the same breath that he notes Donne's power, which none of his school possessed, "the range of personal feeling which lends such fullness of life to Donne's strange and troubled poetry."[4] Donne was surely aware of his own crotchets, having once spoken of them ironically in a letter as "the worst voluptuousness, which is an Hydroptique, immoderate desire of humane learning and languages." But it is odd that Grierson, his defender, should use Donne's words against him. It is also odd that a learned scholar would indict a learned poet for being a man of learning instead of a humbler being.

In Donne we have the fullest conceivable use made of personal event and style. His poetry gives as much of a

[3] Introduction to *Metaphysical Lyrics and Poems of the Seventeenth Century* (Oxford, 1959), p. xx.

[4] *Ibid.*, pp. xxff.

biographical sense of his life and character as we can get, not only because Donne uses the actual details and events of his life, but also because he treats erotic and devotional themes with psychological accuracy, not merely exploiting them because they are popular. We know, therefore, what he thought, how he felt about love, marriage, and religion, and we know what troubled him. The other metaphysicals turn out a more official version of the self, though not for that reason a less valuable or less authentic profile of their lives. Marvell put his strongest passions into verse, conspicuously (as in "Appleton House" and the garden poems), on occasion. Crashaw, obsessed by his fancies and hopes, sometimes made traumatic objects of religious symbols. Herbert deliberately cultivated the obedient side of his nature, the dutiful as against the natural man. The poets are all *personal* in different ways, but Donne's voice seems the most openly urgent, the most emphatic, and the most insistent on getting the whole man into the poetry. In his poetry Donne could say everything he wished. His prose (his sermons and letters), though remarkable for its intensity, seriousness, and persuasiveness, is different—perhaps because it was composed for definite occasions and hence has a public tone rather than the deep intimacy of his best poems.

III

The world first had Donne's and Herbert's published books of poems in the same year, 1633, although their works had circulated among friends in manuscript and a little had even occasionally been printed. Donne was Herbert's senior by twenty-one years; he had been a friend of the Herbert family, particularly of Herbert's mother. He had written poems to the Herberts—to Edward and to Magdalen, and a Latin one to George—and had been a frequent guest at the family estate. It is clear that Donne's poetic influence on George Herbert was extensive; under the circumstances it would have been strange had it not been so. Yet when the two poets are compared, their differences from one another are usually stressed—Donne's wit and tough intellectual gambits, Herbert's devoutness and simple ardor. These may be their primary traits, but at times Herbert is as witty and dispassionately intellectual as Donne

and Donne's devoutness and ardor as impressive as Herbert's.
Yet each poet expresses these secondary traits differently. The
difference is dramatic, as when Donne's "The good-morrow" is
put alongside the sonnets Herbert sent to his mother from
school when he was seventeen. The poems perfectly express
the basic temperaments, even at an early age, of the two poets.
The relevant lines from Donne are:

> If ever any beauty I did see,
> Which I desir'd, and got, t'was but a dreame of thee.
>
> . . .
>
> What ever dyes, was not mixt equally;
> If our two loves be one, or, thou and I
> Love so alike, that none doe slacken, none can die.

And the lines from Herbert:

> My God, where is that ancient heat towards thee,
>   Wherewith whole showls of *Martyrs* once did burn,
>   Besides their other flames? Doth Poetry
> Wear *Venus* Livery? only serve her turn?
>
> . . .
>
> Why doth that fire, which by thy power and might
>   Each breast does feel, no braver fuel choose
>   Than that, which one day Worms may chance refuse?

There is, first, a difference of theme, Donne's celebration of
erotic love and Herbert's pointed abjuring of it; but also there
is a difference of feeling, of predisposition, which the com-
parison of these lines reveals. The taste for martyr's blood and
the enthusiastic *contemptu mundi* attitude which Herbert
shows directly oppose Donne's deliberately blasphemous and
heretical glorification of woman and love in the place of God
and eternity. But it is not enough to say that Herbert's devout-
ness and simplicity set him off from Donne's witty womaniz-
ing. Donne can be as devout and simple as Herbert; in his
"Holy Sonnets" there is as much passionate humanity put into
the effort of realizing God as we find in Herbert. Each poet's
voice is similarly, deliberately, pitched to dramatic utterance,

and this voice recounts from poem to poem the daily inward behavior and conflicts of the soul with the self. One remembers best the opening lines from some of Donne's well-known poems:

> For Godsake hold your tongue, and let me love,
> (The Canonization)

> I am two fooles, I know,
> For loving, and for saying so
> In whining Poëtry;
> (The triple Foole)

> 'Tis true, 'tis day; what though it be?
> O wilt thou therefore rise from me?
> Why should we rise, because 'tis light?
> Did we lie downe, because 'twas night?
> (Breake of day)

> Some that have deeper digg'd love's Myne then I,
> Say, where his centrique happinesse doth lie:
> I have lov'd, and got, and told,
> But should I love, get, tell, till I were old,
> I should not finde that hidden mysterie;
> (Love's Alchymie)

> He is starke mad, who ever sayes,
> That he hath beene in love an houre,
> (The broken heart)

> Come, Madam, come, all rest my powers defie,
> Until I labour, I in labour lie.
> (Going to Bed)

And these are the similarly well-known beginnings of Herbert's poems:

> Full of rebellion, I would die,
> Or fight, or travell, or denie
> That thou hast ought to do with me.
> (Nature)

Kill me not ev'ry day,
Thou Lord of life; since thy one death for me
  Is more then all my deaths can be,
                              (Affliction II)

I struck the board, and cry'd, No more.
      I will abroad.
    What? shall I ever sigh and pine?
My lines and life are free; free as the rode,
                              (The Collar)

My comforts drop and melt away like snow:
I shake my head, and all the thoughts and ends,
Which my fierce youth did bandie, fall and flow
Like leaves about me: or like summer friends,
                              (The Answer)

The harbingers are come. See, see their mark;
White is their colour, and behold my head.
But must they have my brain? must they dispark
Those sparkling notions, which therein were bred?
                              (The Forerunners)

The metaphysicals were fond of making personal invento-
ries of their inner conflicts, and their dramatization of these is
so much a part of the poem's structure that the absence of
dramatic method would make metaphysical poetry inconceiv-
able. But the quieter and simpler reflective idiom of Herbert
influences Vaughan's poetry as well as Marvell's garden poetry.
This is the poetry of reflection, meditation, speculation, and
praise. Herbert probably learned something from Ben Jonson
in this vein, as did the others. But the typical Donneian dia-
logue of conflict, as in the "Holy Sonnets," seems to express a
passion shared more by Crashaw and Marvell than by Vaughan
and Herbert, although the latter can write a poem, like "The
Pulley," reminiscent of Donne in device, but in idiom com-
pletely his own.
  These are tricky matters; it is not easy to characterize or
identify the idioms of these poets. One must be wary of many
things: of literary classifications that heap them all together;
of the antipathies of competitive poets who come later, under

a new literary dispensation; and especially of the poets' con-
temporaries, off on a campaign of malicious abuse. One must
differentiate among the biases; otherwise no reading is refresh-
ing or renewing, but only resounds with the old categorical
prejudices still grinding away against one another.

IV

We need an example of how theme, device, and method
work among the metaphysical poets. Since many of their
themes are conventional—love of woman, fear of death, praise
of spiritual beauty, religious renunciation—one can choose a
fairly comprehensive example, such as Marvell's *carpe diem*
theme, in which many other themes come together. This will
show the way typical ideas are turned into poetry by the craft
and temperament that are called metaphysical.

It is impressive that the argument and tone of Marvell's
"To his Coy Mistress" should form the pattern, with devious
and disguised elaborations, of a good number of his other
poems. In a sense such poems are variations on the tonal idea
of his best-known poem. In "Daphnis and Chloe," for example,
Daphnis' surprising monologue, in which he refuses Chloe's
offer of herself at last, is a magnificent argument, given the
circumstances of their long abstinence and ideal attachment.
But then, in the last three stanzas, the high-flown sentiment is
so realistically reversed that it is difficult to take Daphnis'
dramatic plea seriously in view of his suddenly revealed phi-
landerings:

> Last night he with *Phlogis* slept;
> This night for *Dorinda* kept;

It is true that Chloe is given her due for having been "coy" too
long. But this is not precisely what Daphnis has been telling
her. How long, we want to know, has he been playing the field
while pretending to be Chloe's true love? When the parting
hour arrives, it "must all his Hopes devour, / All his Labour,
all his Art." Thus, Chloe's coyness is matched by Daphnis'
duplicity until their idealized love-anguish turns into a piece of
comic opera.

Idealized love is also the subject, ironically treated, in "The Definition of Love." Critic after critic has taken the poem quite literally, despite the bravura of the first stanza:

> My Love is of a birth as rare
> As 'tis for object strange and high:
> It was begotten by despair
> Upon Impossibility.

That so pure an ideal can be framed so that it is immediately reduced to the grossest terms should be warning enough of the underlying irony. After this initial grimace, the poem follows the conventions of platonic love to show the extravagantly difficult condition of "two perfect loves." But what now becomes clear is that the character of Fate is being depicted, and not love. And so the concluding astronomical metaphor demonstrates love immobilized on the rack of Fate:

> Therefore the Love which us doth bind.
> But Fate so enviously debarrs,
> Is the Conjunction of the Mind,
> And Opposition of the Stars.

It is a beautiful last quatrain, cold and imperturbable as the great spinning earth and the spent emotion which conduct the irony through the poem. Also underlying is the hidden metaphor of the twin compasses, the most imitated of Donne's conceits, from "A Valediction: Forbidding Mourning." Marvell speaks of "Where my extended Soul is fixt" by Fate that will not let "Two perfect Loves . . . close: . . . And therefore her Decrees of Steel / Us as the distant Poles have plac'd"; and further,

> As Lines so Loves *oblique* may well
> Themselves in every Angle greet:
> But ours so truly *Paralel*,
> Though infinite can never meet.

A comparison with the Donne poem would emphasize the poets' different attitudes towards love, hence their different treatments of the theme. "A Valediction" and "The Definition" are poems of wit that use geometrical and scientific details for metaphoric purposes. But Donne's tone is basically serious and personal, dealing with the comfort a husband offers his wife whom he has to leave temporarily. Marvell's tone is abstract and critical of all love as being dominated by "tyrannic" Fate, and he resorts to the language of platonic love ironically in order to argue its deceptiveness and impossibility.

Marvell's "Mourning" is similar; the poet is apparently celebrating the devotion of Chlora to her dead husband. Yet the diction and poetic devices, insisting upon the conjunction of tears, eyes, water, oceans, skies, showers, soon make one doubt the sincerity of the surviving spouse's grief. By contrast, Crashaw's "The Weeper," a longer, serious, ecstatic religious poem in which the same conjunction of words appears, does not betray itself or fall into bathos, but sustains its tone throughout.

In "The Gallery" and "A Dialogue between the Soul and the Body" Marvell again depends upon the *carpe diem* theme, using tonal irony to convert a conventional subject into something new and unexpected. In the first the poet, addressing Chlora, likens his soul to a picture gallery where all the faces have turned into various portraits of his beloved. But there really are only two kinds: one where "Thou art painted in the Dress / Of an Inhumane Murtheress;" and "on the other side, th' art drawn / Like to *Aurora* in the Dawn; / When in the East she slumb'ring lyes, / And stretches out her milky Thighs. . . ." It is Chlora herself who has "invented" them,

> Either to please me, or torment:
> For thou alone to people me,
> Art grown a numerous Colony;

Yet in the final stanza, the poet admits that he likes his first view of her best, the picture which first captivated him with that "same posture" and that same "look" of

> A tender Shepherdess, whose Hair
> Hangs loosely playing in the Air,
> Transplanting Flow'rs from the green Hill,
> To crown her Head, and Bosome fill.

But the nostalgia seems anticlimactic because the description here reflects the picture of Chlora given earlier ("*Venus* in her pearly Boat"), another picture invented by Chlora herself. The question, Which is more enchanting, the shepherdess or Venus? would be a hard one to answer. Though the poet himself prefers the earliest picture, the conventional Chlora-as-shepherdess, we see that this too is as much a product of her "fertile Shop of cruel Arts" as is the Venus or the Aurora pose. The point is that the speaker himself has no version of her image but that which she by her own artifice has created for him. He has done nothing to imagine her in his own terms. We are left with the impression that once having fallen for her guilefulness, the poet-as-frustrated-lover can now do no more than become a sorry collector of Chlora's continual artifices. He is obviously fated to end as her victimized picture collector.

A similar theme, advanced and resolved in the short, hyperbolic "The Fair Singer," is treated more lightly. The lady's fatal attractiveness is based upon a double appeal—the beauty of her eyes and the beauty of her voice. The speaker's heart and mind are captivated; he cannot fight, but neither can he win her. In the end she will leave him deviceless,

> And all my Forces needs must be undone,
> She having gained both the Wind and Sun.

But in "A Dialogue between the Soul and Body" an unexpected turn comes with the final exchange between the two antagonists in the second half of the poem. Normally, in such poems we expect the soul's argument to be overpowering and provide the last word, as in fact it is and does in another Marvell poem with a similar title, "A Dialogue Between the Resolved Soul, and Created Pleasure." But in this instance the soul complains that the body's health is the soul's disappointment:

> Constrain'd not only to indure
> Diseases, but, whats worse, the Cure:
> And ready oft the Port to gain,
> Am Shipwrackt into Health again.

The body is the more sympathetic advocate; it has the better of the argument *and* the last word. As a result, the question of whether there is any possibility of a victory of one over the other is held in abeyance, since the body and the soul prove interdependent.

> But Physick yet could never reach
> The Maladies Thou me dost teach;
> Whom first the Cramp of Hope does Tear:
> And then the Palsie Shakes of Fear.
> The Pestilence of Love does heat:
> Or Hatred's hidden Ulcer eat.
> Joy's chearful Madness does perplex:
> Or Sorrow's other Madness vex.
> Which Knowledge forces me to know;
> And Memory will not foregoe.
> What but a Soul could have the wit
> To build me up for Sin so fit?
> So Architects do square and hew,
> Green Trees that in the Forest grew.

The cryptic poem "The unfortunate Lover" is probably a statement in mythical terms of Marvell's most definitive view of the *carpe diem* theme. Ostensibly this aspect of the subject concerns the birth and death of love, but the real theme appears to be a strange satire on romantic love. If we consider the poem alongside another, "The Match," an ingenious, mannered, and polished emblematic fable, the working out of "The unfortunate Lover" may then become clearer.

Readers of "The Match," "To his Coy Mistress," and half a dozen other Marvell poems know that the poet is a master of hyperbole; his elaborate, highly wrought metaphors, which often carry a whole poem, actually work as they are intended to. The difference between workable and unworkable hyperbole is that the one transforms feeling into a verbal-visual artifice inviting an intellectual grin while the other betrays the poet into muddying the feeling or catches him up as he tries to escape from the feeling.

"The Match" is built upon a pair of effective hyperboles. That it is a love poem, expressing a complimentary tribute to Celia and the speaker, who is the lover, hardly emerges until the last two stanzas of the ten-stanza poem. Marvell is mainly interested in working out the emblematic abstractions for which the lovers seem to serve as convenient excuses. One involves Nature, the other, Love. The culmination of Nature's hoarding of "her choisest store" turns out to be "one perfect Beauty," Celia. This is the burden of the first four quatrains. The burden of the next four is that Love is equally zealous in building up a treasury of light and heat compacted into one. The speaker then admits,

> Thus all his fewel did unite
>   To make one fire high:
> None ever burn'd so hot, so bright;
>   And *Celia* that am I.

Then the final stanza aptly resolves the hyperboles:

> So we alone the happy rest,
>   Whilst all the World is poor,
> And have within our Selves possest
>   All Love's and Nature's store.

The poem is a slight, sophisticated, and not highly ambitious construction; since Marvell's devices seldom misfire, his aims appear to be modest, whereas other poets, failing in this way, seem overly ambitious. We get unexpectedly vivid pictures of Nature (as an aging woman) and Love (as an aging man) piling up storehouses of the things they will need when they can no longer be active or effective. The abstractions are thus humanized, and being humanized are shown, somewhat like the Greek gods, to be nothing more than extraordinary specialists whose zeal makes them vulnerable, laughable, *allzumenschlich*. So Nature is an old shopkeeper, perhaps a Pandora grown old, carefully putting away her hoarded things in boxes. And Love, similarly, like an old Vulcan storing his "magazine," keeps

> the several Cells repleat
>   With Nitre thrice refin'd;
> The Naphta's and the Sulphurs heat,
>   And all that burns the Mind.

By implication, if love is all perfume and heat in the proportions that Nature and Love are here shown to be generating,

then human love is a matter to be taken lightly and not serious-
ly. The poem enlightens by hyperbole without directly attack-
ing its subject; the poem slights its subject by magnifying the
conventions which inform it, thus showing love to be pleasant-
ly ludicrous.

There is no doubt that Marvell uses hyperboles satirically,
but what often happens, as in the "Coy Mistress," where the
satire turns from pleasant to serious, is that the subject is
completely transformed in rising to another plane. This sort
of transformation occurs again in the enigmatic poem, "The
unfortunate Lover," but it occurs almost immediately instead
of gradually as in "The Match." The result is a piece of un-
mitigated, sadistic absurdity, almost clinical in treating its
subject—the onanist disguised as lover.

"The unfortunate Lover" is a Marvell-created myth on the
nature of love. The focus is double: love viewed as a fate-im-
posed and as a self-imposed martyrdom. The poem includes
its own commentary on the narrative, using classical mythology
obliquely, for its own purposes. The unfortunate lover is the
"he" of the narrative and is also a synecdoche for the experi-
ence of love as distinct from any particular aspect, such as "In-
fant Love" or "Tyrant Love." The "poor Lover" of the eleventh
line ("That my poor Lover floting lay") is the mythical indi-
vidual foisted on the vagrant, sad, characterless "he," who thus
becomes something of a prototype, like the *my-hero* or *our-hero*
figure in nineteenth-century novels. The revealing note about
the hero of Marvell's fable comes toward the very end, with
the line, "he in Story only rules." This prototype of the lover,
then, is a fictional being, an abstract and not a human charac-
ter at all.

The introductory first stanza proposes that the pleasur-
able aspect of love, as, for example, "Infant Love," is illusory,
short-lived, impossible to sustain. The tone here is bitter-sweet
nostalgia:

> Alas, how pleasant are their dayes
> With whom the Infant Love yet playes!
> Sorted by pairs, they still are seen
> By Fountains cool, and Shadows green.
> But soon these Flames do lose their light,
> Like Meteors of a Summers night:

> Nor can they to that Region climb,
> To make impression upon Time.

The rest of the poem, except for the last stanza, tells how the unfortunate situation came about. It deals with a nameless hero, born "in a Shipwrack" at sea, of a Venus- or Aphrodite-like mother who is rather grossly "split against the Stone, / In a *Cesarian Section*." Thus the strife begins.

Starting in water, a wrecked figure, buffeted by winds and thunder, this hero is destined to become a melancholiac, seeing nothing but what appears "As at the Fun'ral of the World." To add to the gloomy picture, the infant is given over to black cormorants (related to the mythical semi-human vultures, the harpies), who

> . . . fed him up with Hopes and Air,
> Which soon digested to Despair.

The lines echo that other gross physical image in "The Definition of Love": "My Love is of a birth as rare / As 'tis for object strange and high: / It was begotten by despair / Upon Impossibility." The habits of the melancholiac continue to be described in physical terms:

> Thus while they famish him, and feast,
> He both consumed, and increast:

In this condition, the hero is wittily described as "Th' *Amphibium* of Life and Death." Having put, or found, him at his worst, Fate in the guise of "angry Heaven" petulantly calls for "a spectacle of Blood," to reduce him further. What follows is a gory contest between the unfortunate lover and Fortune. The outcome is fairly predictable, except that one does not expect him to turn into an avatar of Prometheus:

> See how he nak'd and fierce does stand,
> Cuffing the Thunder with one hand;
> While with the other he does lock,
> And grapple, with the stubborn Rock. . . .

Concerning this old, punishable, and suffering Titan's fight with Zeus again, Marvell drily remarks, as if quoting the god himself, "And all he saies, a Lover drest / In his own Blood does relish best." (Here "relish" must be taken as an intransitive verb, in the sense of "please.")

The sardonic view toward the sacrificed hero in these lines is sustained into the final stanza; but in the last lines of the poem, as if to mitigate the horror for the sensitive reader, Marvell seems to say, "This is only a story, unrelated to real life." (The traditional way of enforcing the realism of a fiction is for the narrator to say, "This story is true." But it is often just as effective to say the opposite, "Don't be frightened, there's not a word of truth in it.") If one turns back to the first stanza now, one can see that Marvell is really saying the opposite—the fiction is real. The "dying" lover of the first stanza, who "leaves a Perfume here, / And Musick within every Ear;" is indeed the mythical hero whose course we have been following, the pattern of all lovers in their "pleasant" days, "Sorted by pairs, they still are seen / By Fountains cool, and Shadows green." So the unfortunate lover, in fact as well as in fiction, turns out to be a masochistic monster: "And all he saies, a Lover drest / In his own Blood does relish best."

If this seems too clinical a view to attribute to the author of "To his Coy Mistress," one should not forget the ghoulish realism to be found in the more famous poem:

> Thy Beauty shall no more be found;
> Nor, in thy marble Vault, shall sound
> My echoing Song: then Worms shall try
> That long preserv'd Virginity:
> And your quaint Honour turn to dust;
> And into ashes all my Lust.
> The Grave's a fine and private place,
> But none I think do there embrace.

Marvell's realism is persuasive and poetically justified—and not simply an attack on the reader's credulity, as it often is among such metaphysicals as Cowley and Crashaw. The urbane Marvell would not have been capable of such inept antifeminism as that appearing in Abraham Cowley's "On the Death of Mr. Crashaw":

Nay with the worst of Heathen dotage We
(Vaine men!) the monster Woman Deify;
Find Stars, and our Fates there in a Face,
And Paradise in them by whom we lost, it, place.

Marvell would have shared Cowley's distrust of womanizing
in poetry, but would have been temperamentally against
wanton misrepresentations in the name of a cause or a modish
proverbialism. Marvell is unlike Crashaw in this too—Crashaw
whose religious zeal has strangely sexual connotations, as when
writing of the Christ child and Mary (in a commentary on
Luke 11, "Blessed be the paps which Thou hast sucked,") the
poet deliberately confuses one biological function with another:

Suppose he had been Tabled at thy Teates,
Thy hunger feeles not what he eates:
Hee'l have his Teat e're long (a bloody one)
The Mother then must suck the Son.

It is the same Crashaw whom fervor sometimes leads into
making such a coy declaration as "I would be married, but I'de
have no Wife, / I would be married to a single Life." Or, else-
where, in his enthusiasm for the martyrdom of "our crucified
Lord Naked, and bloody," he allows heavy wit to destroy the
credibility of the emotion:

Th' have left thee naked Lord, O that they had;
This Garment too I would they had deny'd.
Thee with thy selfe they have too richly clad,
Opening the purple wardrobe of thy side.
O never could bee found Garments too good
For thee to weare, but these, of thine owne blood.

Marvell may have known these lines of Crashaw's when he
wrote of his unfortunate lover "drest in his own blood." But
Marvell's line is a conceit which holds its subject at arm's
length to define it; Crashaw's hyperbole betrays the poet's
willed involvement with a subject on which he believed that
no expense of wit or passion could be thought misspent. By
contrast with Crashaw's, Marvell's enthusiasm emerges in
quiet surroundings—in the garden world of the mower and
the Bermudas, or the sumptuous English estate around Apple-

ton House, with its mysterious rivers and forests that exist unaffected by the poet's wonder or praise.

V

The difference between Marvell and Crashaw is more than a difference in taste or temperament; moreover, it emerges from something they share—the cultivation of sensibility by a whole era breaking away from Neoplatonism and Petrarchanism, which often involved a deliberate confusion of earthly and divine love. This confusion was often noted by conscientious critics among the religious and the poets themselves. As Ben Jonson, according to Drummond, remarked of Donne's poem, "The *anniversarie* was profane and full of blasphemies . . . that if it had been written of the Virgin Marie it had been something." The same criticism is made by one of his recent editors:

> In the two series of sonnets composed during 1617 and 1618, and entitled 'La Corona' and 'Holy Sonnets,' he confessed in his approach to God the same remorse for past infidelity as he had shown to his wife at the time of his marriage.[5]

What the criticism seems not to recognize is that the question of the praise of an ideal—woman or God—is often part of the search of the emotions for a subject which every poet must sooner or later find and appropriate for himself. Jonson, if he were not so envious of Donne's reputation, would have been guided by this knowledge. Nor is it hypocritical of Donne to practice what his editors and Jonson charge him with. One remembers the Donne statement, sympathetically quoted by Grierson, "I had my first breeding and conversation with men of a suppressed and afflicted religion, accustomed to the despite of death and hungry of an imagined martyrdom."[6] If this is true, it would not be hard to imagine such a poet deliberately merging the adoration of God with the adoration of his mistress, the passion of love with the passion for death, and

[5] Hugh I'Anson Fausset, Introduction to *Poems by John Donne*, Everyman's Library (London, 1931), p. xxi.

[6] *Op. cit.*, p. xvii.

the hope for a sanctuary in love with the soul's salvation. Far from being a new thing, this meshing of hopes and appetites goes back to an old tradition of rescuing profane texts, such as the Song of Songs, for the exegetical purposes of theologians. The same sort of merging is found in troubadour poetry, various forms of Neoplatonic dialogue, pulpit literature, and the medieval *débat*; and the metaphysical poets were keenly aware of these traditions. Moreover, the spiritual-carnal identification is part of the rich, speculative movement which invades all phases of humanistic learning with "anatomies" of the emotions and the character of beauty and goodness. The moral, psychological, and theological explorations of the age had not yet been dissipated, although literature was turning toward the new science and the plain style, which were soon to make old-fashioned the medievalism of Marvell's and Donne's speculative sympathies as well as Herbert's and Crashaw's devotional enthusiasm.

Metaphysical poets take it for granted that the aspiration for the love of God is equivalent, as an emotional experience, to the aspiration for the love of woman. At the beginning of his career, Herbert gainsays this vehemently; and Crashaw, following Herbert's example, does so too. But their animadversion still proves the vitality of the tradition which they were partly impugning, because they recognized its strength and its usefulness. If, for example, one compares such a poem as "To Roses in the Bosome of Castara" by William Habington, a minor metaphysical, with Crashaw's devoutly intended "Prayer. An Ode, Which Was Præfixed to a little Prayer-book giuen to a young Gentle-Woman," the same Petrarchan conventions are put to work in each poem, though for quite different purposes. These are Habington's lines:

> Yee blushing Virgins happy are
> In the chaste Nunn'ry of her brests,
> For hee'd prophane so chaste a faire,
> Who ere should call them *Cupids* nests.
>
> Transplanted thus how bright yee grow;
> How rich a perfume doe yee yeeld?
> In some close garden, Cowslips so
> Are sweeter then i' th' open field.

In those white cloysters live secure
From the rude blasts of wanton breath,
Each houre more innocent and pure,
Till you shall wither into death.

Then that which living gave you roome,
Your glorious sepulcher shall be,
There wants no marble for a tombe,
Whose brest hath marble beene to me.

Crashaw begins:

Loe here a little volume, but great Book!
A nest of new-born sweets;
　　Whose natiue fires disdaining
　　To ly thus folded, & complaining
　　Of these ignoble sheets,
　　Affect more comly bands
　　(Fair one) from thy kind hands
　　And confidently look
　　To find the rest
Of a rich binding in your BREST.

And he concludes:

O fair, ô fortunate! O riche, ô dear!
O happy & thrice happy she
　　Selected doue
　　Who ere she be,
　　Whose early loue
　　With winged vowes
Makes hast to meet her morning spouse
And close with his immortall kisses.
Happy indeed, who neuer misses
To improue that pretious hour,
　　And euery day
　　Seize her sweet prey
All fresh & fragrant as he rises
Dropping with a baulmy Showr
A delicious dew of spices;
O let the blissfull heart hold fast

Her heaunly arm-full, she shall tast
At once ten thousand paradises;
   She shall haue power
   To rifle & deflour
The rich & roseall spring of those rare sweets
Which with a swelling bosome there she meets
   Boundles & infinite
   Bottomles treasures
Of pure inebriating pleasures.
Happy proof! she shal discouer
   What ioy, what blisse,
How many Heau'ns at once it is
To haue her GOD become her LOVER.

One does not have to look far in Donne to find examples of the same thing. It is seen in the beginning of "The Extasie," the love poem written on a figurative and rhetorical pattern of religious mysticism:

Where, like a pillow on a bed,
 A Pregnant banke swel'd up, to rest
The violets reclining head,
 Sat we two, one anothers best.
Our hands were firmely cimented
 With a fast balme, which thence did spring,
Our eye-beames twisted, and did thred
 Our eyes, upon one double string;
So to' entergraft our hands, as yet
 Was all the meanes to make us one,
And pictures in our eyes to get
 Was all our propagation.
As 'twixt two equal Armies, Fate
 Suspends uncertaine victorie,
Our soules, (which to advance their state,
 Were gone out,) hung 'twixt her, and mee.
And whil'st our soules negotiate there,
 Wee like sepulchrall statues lay;
All day, the same our postures were,
 And wee said nothing, all the day.

There is the love poem, "The Canonization," elaborately worked out to conclude with the extravagant but logically sustained resolution of lovers made saints:

>   . . . all shall approve
> Us *Canoniz'd* for Love:
>
> And thus invoke us; You whom reverend love
>   Made one anothers hermitage; . . .

And there are the lines in "The Relique," mixing funereal wit and marital devotion:

> When my grave is broke up againe
> Some second ghest to entertaine,
> (For graves have learn'd that woman-head
> To be to more then one a Bed)
>   And he that digs it, spies
> A bracelet of bright haire about the bone,
>   Will he not let'us alone,
> And thinke that there a loving couple lies,
>
>   .   .   .
>
> If this fall in a time, or land,
> Where mis-devotion doth command,
> Then, he that digges us up, will bring
> Us, to the Bishop, and the King,
>   To make us Reliques; then
> Thou shalt be a Mary Magdalen, and I
>   A something else thereby; . . .

The reverse of the process—the comparison of sacred things with earthly things—is exploited in the "Holy Sonnets." In Sonnet XVIII, Christ is invoked to reveal His Spouse, whom the poet describes as a mystery woman "open to most men."

> Dwells she with us, or like adventuring knights
> First travaile we to seeke and then make Love?
> Betray kind husband thy spouse to our sights,
> And let myne amorous soule court thy mild Dove,
> Who is most trew, and pleasing to thee, then
> When she'is embrac'd and open to most men.

And there is the famous "Batter my heart" sonnet (XIV), where the poet invokes the Godhead and asks to be taken, as a woman or a "usurp'd town":

> Yet dearely 'I love you,' and would be loved faine,
> But am betroth'd unto your enemie:
> Divorce mee, 'untie, or breake that knot againe,
> Take mee to you, imprison mee, for I
> Except you'enthrall mee, never shall be free,
> Nor ever chast, except you ravish me.

A clinical, sentimental, ultraromantic, and rhetorical poetry marks the excesses of the metaphysical style; it is evident in Crashaw, Cowley, and the early Dryden, but rarely again in English until Shelley and Poe. Yet such a poetry appears on the Continent often during the late Renaissance, particularly in Spain and Italy, where rhetorical traditions prevail and continue to infiltrate the expression of even great poets into our own time. (This may be why the sumptuous metaphorical poetry of García Lorca often sounds embarrassing to English readers and hence does not really come through in translation.) The excesses of Góngora and, even more, those of Marino—a lesser but more influential poet, some of whose poems Crashaw translated—tend systematically to distort all the rhetorical effects which ideaplay and wordplay allow. This shows up particularly where the metaphors of spiritual and carnal love are fused. A recent scholar has put the matter cogently:

> Marino and the poets who, in following him, gave
> seventeenth-century Italian poetry its characteristic
> shape chose ... [to cry for madder music, stronger
> wine] and in their work Baroque appears as over-
> blown Renaissance. In their secular verse as in their
> religious verse ... the aim is a rarefied sweetness
> made sweeter by the occasional intrusion of horror,
> an enticing sexuality made more enticing by a touch
> of perversity, a facile religiosity made more facile by
> sensuality.[7]

[7] Fred J. Warnke, *European Metaphysical Poetry* (New Haven, 1961), pp. 50–51.

Such effects suggest the programmatic experiments of the French symbolists: Baudelaire's *Les fleurs du mal*, which mixes Christian love with explorations in masochism and flamboyant sensuality, Rimbaud's derangement of the senses, all the *poètes maudits* and their conscientiously applied diabolisms. The metaphysicals' apparent blasphemy in confusing erotic and devotional genres may have been intended playfully, as obviously in their different ways Donne, Crashaw, and Marvell intended it; but there is always someone to find the practice in bad taste or take it amiss, no matter how beguiling the poetry may be. Poetry, one must remember, *is* play and an expression of feeling, not a recipe for action or belief. To make poetry more portentous than it is robs it of its value.

VI

The incongruent and the contradictory, as well as the paradoxical and the astounding, deeply engage the metaphysical esthetic of the seventeenth century. The principle of thinking in terms of polar opposites has always been sanctioned by the leading cultural traditions—the Christian, the Hebraic, the Greco-Roman, and by many of the Asiatic cultures. The opposition of the real and the ideal are reconciled in Christ's parables in the Gospels. The same kind of thinking in the Renaissance goes with a quest for unity, to make the facts of personal experience in the real world accord with the visions and dogmas of faith in the supernatural. The simultaneous presence of sexual love and religious devotion, or the habit of expressing the search for one in the language of the other, would seem less crude or shocking to a seventeenth-century Englishman, or to any European brought up in the Catholic tradition, than it does to the inheritors of the Protestant ethic. The habit came of an old religious view and from an old poetic tradition. It helped to frame an urgent emotion, and it was a way of thinking about the world which poets, theologians, and naturalists had in common. But with their strong need to exhibit contradictions they felt in their blood, the poets were quicker to seize on paradoxes and to dramatize the basic incongruity of things which could not have rational resolutions. Having something of this in mind, Professor Robert M. Adams observes the strange effects of the carnal-spiritual identification in the poetry of Crashaw:

> . . . the poet unites feelings and thoughts about things which have, indeed, some points of genuine similarity, but between which common sense maintains a degree of antipathy. And the special quality of his fusion is that he does not try to gloss over the latent antipathy, for to sense it is to sense the depth of the feelings that override it. The poet loves God as a baby loves its mother's breast and as a martyr loves the final spear-thrust, he loves God as a gaping wound and a voluptuous mouth, in sophisticated paradox and childish innocence. . . . The unity of opposites, of pain with pleasure, life with death, fruition with denial, assertion with surrender, is his favorite theme. It always involves a degree of incongruity, often of incongruity unresolved, a sense of strain and grotesquerie.[8]

Whatever else they may have been, the metaphysicals were all intellectuals who took their religion seriously. As poets they were essentially amateurs. This does not mean that they were inferior poets, but that they all had vocations other than the writing of poetry and were not professionally engaged in publishing it or in exchanging influential notices of one another's verse. They were university men with public careers; Donne, Herbert, and Crashaw held religious offices, Marvell had a diplomatic post. The consequences of their amateur status were striking. Unlike the professional Ben Jonson, who prepared and edited his own works for publication, these poets, except for Crashaw, did not see their poetry in book form. Publishing poetry was the exception, not the rule; poetry was circulated privately in manuscript among a circle of friends and admirers. This made for an élite audience of sympathetic readers; the situation allowed the poet to do his best without fear of censorship or legal penalty. On the other hand, because

---

[8] "Taste and Bad Taste in Metaphysical Poetry: Richard Crashaw and Dylan Thomas," in *Seventeenth Century English Poetry*, edited by W. R. Keast (New York, 1962), p. 268.

the poet depended upon patronage, he was often compelled to write complimentary verses which did not engage his entire faculties, although Crashaw's poem to the Countess of Denbigh and Donne's "Anniversaries" on the death of Elizabeth Drury are among these poets' masterpieces.

No one now doubts that Donne was the greatest poet writing in what we have come to call the metaphysical style, and that he influenced, though not always personally, all other metaphysical poets. George Herbert was the only one of those represented here who knew him. Through Herbert, Donne's influence spread. It spread further for a few decades after his death, when five editions of his published poems had established a wider audience. Crashaw and Marvell both drew upon Herbert and Donne, although both were too young to have known the older poets, and there is no evidence of their having met one another.

Like Donne, Marvell traveled abroad, and this shows up in his poems and in the interests which come out of them. His experiences in France, Italy, Spain, Holland, Russia, Sweden, and Denmark are reflected in particular references, and in the customs, issues, and ideas of people described in his poems. One feels the same kind of alertness to the times, to the excitement of events (as in his Odes on Cromwell), which is so attractive in Donne as well as in Shakespeare and Jonson. This is not the appeal of Herbert and Crashaw (even though Crashaw traveled and lived abroad, and was influenced by Continental poetry), who are both more insular, certainly more subject to religious doctrine. Herbert was torn between the wide cultural interests he naturally possessed as an aristocrat with an interrupted academic career and the provincialism he accepted with his religious vocation as a country parson. His poetry is devout and quiet, and the best of it, like "The Collar," "Forerunners," "Affliction," "Love," is spirited and deeply moving, the work of a man whose struggles with himself led to the discovery of the unique source of his poetic imagination. The wit and natural inventiveness in his work, as in the celebrated "Easter Wings," is balanced by a disciplined and simplified diction turning to parable and allegory. In his poetry there is the same savory sharpness of idiom that one finds in the King James Bible—perhaps one reason why Herbert has always appealed to clergymen. He was also the favorite of two significant, original metaphysicals of the nineteenth century, Emily Dickinson and Gerard Manley Hopkins.

Crashaw has in common with Herbert an emblematic use of parable and allegory. The popularity of emblem books in the sixteenth and seventeenth centuries, widely used by the Jesuits as instructional material, affects the poetry of the period as well. Francis Quarles, a very popular poet of the time, was known for his glosses of Biblical texts accompanied by pictorial illustrations. He called his emblems "talking pictures," and scholars have demonstrated that the emblem book was the generic source for certain metaphysical imagery, the meditative poem, and the mystical exercise in verse. (An analogous modern appropriation of pictorial materials is in the imagistic use of the cinema made by T. S. Eliot, Hart Crane, Dylan Thomas, and other poets.) Perhaps the most distinguished poem in this tradition is "The Dark Night of the Soul" (*La noche oscura del alma*), by St. John of the Cross. A convert to Catholicism, Crashaw was much taken by the Spanish mystics and incorporated the emblematic images both of Spanish poetry and those of Quarles. In his best-known poem, "The Weeper," the imagery is full of emblematic content.

> Haile *Sister Springs,*
> Parents of Silver-forded rills!
> Ever bubling things!
> *Thawing Christall! Snowy Hills!*
> Still spending, neverspent; I meane
> Thy faire Eyes sweet *Magdalene.*
>
> . . .
>
> When sorrow would be seene
> In her brightest Majesty,
> (For shee is a Queen)
> Then is shee drest by none but thee.
> Then, and onely then shee weares
> Her richest Pearles, I meane thy Teares.

Rhetoric as the structure of argument and decoration as the motive for metaphor frequently appear in Crashaw's poetry. Both were part of the medieval heritage of pulpit oratory notable in most metaphysical poetry. Through other sources —the early Church fathers and the rhetoric books of Quintilian and Tertullian—the same uses appear in Ben Jonson's poetry and criticism. Fundamentally, imagery and metaphor give color to ideas and concepts, particularly moral ones; out of these figures emerges the portrayal of ideas or the making of conceits, of which the language, when it is most inventive and close to common speech, is fullest. And the metaphysicals at their best are exemplary users of common speech.

But the seventeenth-century metaphysicals were perhaps more alike in what they were against than in what they were for. If, for example, there were an explicitly stated esthetic of classical decorum and of the Petrarchan use of poetic subject and artifice, our four poets could be said to have worked against such an esthetic. Donne and Marvell mocked the poetry of imitation with its idealized and empty love compliments, typical of the Petrarchan style. In effect, they made their conceits parody the Petrarchan clichés and so converted worn-out hyperboles into something new and entirely their own. Herbert and Crashaw were anti-Petrarchan in a more limited sense; they opposed on principle the vapid subjects of the earlier love poetry and sought to replace them with subjects of religious faith lit up by their personal vision and experience.

A variety of styles and subjects that derive from Donne marks the poetry of Herbert, Crashaw, and Marvell. Conscious of Donne, as all three were at the beginning, each learned how to pursue different and vivid lines of his own. Verbal ingenuity, ideaplay and wordplay, particularly about serious subjects, is the most striking similarity in the mature style of these poets. And it is just such pursuits which subsequently involved all four in an offense against rules of classical decorum, and caused them to be downgraded by literary historians who favor plain against complex styles. C. S. Lewis provides a modern case in point when he finds it incredible that Donne, against the classical precept that art should be instructive as well as entertaining, could have dared to state that he "would have no such readers as he could teach."

The colloquial and passionately dramatic voice quickens the work of these poets, mainly in the kind of address we call lyrical: when the poet is speaking to himself. This voice, distinct and different for each, goes with their unique styles, and, in the history of English poetry, establishes a mode unequalled in poignancy, strength, and intimacy of feeling. The mode follows straight through to the later metaphysicals—Dickinson, Hopkins, and Eliot. What brings Donne, Herbert, Marvell, and Crashaw together and identifies them as a group is that they were the first to share this mode in English poetry. Naturally enough, this fact also starts a convention in the literature; for the offense against the old decorum, which unites the metaphysicals more firmly than any of them could have imagined, has now become, despite the prejudices of literary historians, a decorum in itself. The metaphysicals have entered into the mainstream of literature. Whenever a new poet arrives who has the same exuberant sense of language and imagistic invention, his existence fortifies the poetry of the metaphysicals beyond the proscriptions of the Drydens, Jonsons, and Lewises. And such a poet comes to validate a tradition in our poetry in the only way it can be truly validated, by adding to it new life and new art.

—*Edwin Honig*

A Note on the Text

The complete English verse of each poet is printed here; the poems written in Latin or Greek and the poems of doubtful authorship are excluded. The verse in this volume is based on the definitive Oxford University Press editions of each of the four poets. Questions about textual details should be referred to the Oxford editions since space limitations have made the inclusion of notes impossible.

The original spelling and punctuation have been retained. While some may think this increases the difficulty of reading a poetry that is often inherently complex, the editors feel there are only two possible alternatives: a completely modernized version or a text which preserves the original as much as possible. Partially modernizing the text leaves the unanswerable question, "Why this and not that?" It may also wrongly suggest that seventeenth-century poets were basically familiar with modern usage but just could not avoid making a "mistake" or lapsing into their native tongue now and then. In other words, presenting a partial modernization would seem like offering a faulty translation as equivalent to the original.

Since half measures won't do, why not go all the way and completely modernize the texts? The answer is that in effect one would thus be "translating" not only the language but also the attitudes toward writing and spelling of the seventeenth century. Consistency in these matters is a modern idea developed partly through the needs of large-scale printing. It is also true that when the poem is presented in modern dress, the reader tends to forget that word meanings have changed. To disguise seventeenth-century practice is to deprive the reader of a closer understanding of the period.

Some editors argue that given the careless mistakes of seventeenth-century printers and the uncertain manuscripts from which much printing was done, a modernized version may actually be as reliable as the earliest text—and even more readable. But ambiguities and inconsistencies were not always the fault of careless printers; since a uniform standard for spelling, capitalization, and punctuation did not exist, poets themselves could play with various spellings and overlook inconsistencies. A modern reader should be allowed to see how different poets work within this more flexible framework. It seems arbitrary to be given the editors' interpretation without having had the chance to resolve for oneself the alternatives occasioned by such differences.

A few general hints about differences in usage may be of help. Seventeenth-century punctuation is frequently much heavier than modern. Commas may indicate only slight pauses, semi-colons may be used where we use commas, and colons where we use periods. Apostrophes indicating contractions and possessive case are often left out, though regularly used as elision marks, while capitals and italics are frequently used to set off a word or words and to indicate a quotation or a proper name.

Some letters and words are used interchangeably. Common examples are *v* and *i*, *v* and *u*, initial *I* and initial *J*, *then* and *than*, *whither* and *whether*. Final letters are sometimes omitted as in *of* for *off*, *hast* for *haste*, *judg* for *judge*. The *ed* past participle ending is pronounced as a separate syllable; thus where *blest* is one syllable, *blessed* is two.

Finally as to the problem of choosing between different versions of some of Crashaw's poems, the practice here has been to include both versions in those instances where Crashaw revised his own poems and the versions are substantially different.

John Donne
1571(?)-1631

John Donne

JOHN DONNE was born a Roman Catholic in London in late 1571 or early 1572. His father, a prosperous ironmonger, died in 1576. His mother, Elizabeth, was the daughter of the dramatist, John Heywood, sister of Jasper Heywood, a Jesuit missionary priest, and grandniece of Sir Thomas More, who suffered martyrdom. Donne's younger brother Henry, accused of having harbored a priest, died in Newgate prison. Donne was educated by tutors and briefly at Oxford and Cambridge; he withdrew from the university before he could be asked to sign the Thirty-Nine Articles of the Church of England. By 1592 he was a law student at Lincoln's Inn. Somewhat before that, as Izaak Walton states in his *Life of Dr. John Donne* (1640), Donne, unable to get to the Holy Land, went to Italy and Spain and became "perfect in their languages."

A passionate and sensual man, Donne is the subject of a legend that the *Songs and Sonets* he wrote in his early twenties, together with the first three *Satires* and some of the *Elegies*, point to the debaucheries, the indulgence of "the emancipated instincts," from which he was to withdraw so penitently in his later work. Earthiness or earthliness, at any rate, seems fortunately in his case to have belonged to a temperament that was rich enough never to deny but to be strengthened by it. Walton says, "In the most unsettled days of his youth, his bed was not able to detain him beyond the hour of four in the morning; and it was no common business that drew him out of his chamber till past ten; all which time was employed in study; although he took great liberty after it."

Because so much of his writing is personal, biographers customarily follow Donne's life through the poems, the letters, and the sermons. In London he became the center of a circle of wits, law students, young diplomats, rich courtiers, who read his poems in manuscript and tried to imitate them. His close friend Henry Wotton is supposed to have persuaded him to join the group of young volunteers who went with Raleigh and Essex to Cadiz in 1596 and to the Azores in 1597 in search of the Spanish treasure fleet. The next year he became private secretary to Sir Thomas Egerton, Keeper of the Great Seal. To get and keep this position, Donne probably had to profess conformity to the Church of England. But his public career ended abruptly on his secret marriage in 1601 to Ann More, in spite of the opposition of her father, Sir George More. Donne was jailed and lost his job before his father-in-law recovered from his rage. Subsequently he lived in poverty with his wife and growing family, dependent on the small charities of others and forced into a kind of sycophancy before the wealthy nobility; this was common enough among talented men at the time but seems particularly humiliating in Donne's case.

In this period he wrote a pamphlet attacking the Jesuits, *Ignatius, his Conclave;* other prose works: *The Pseudo-Martyr,* and a defense of suicide, the *Biothanatos;* also a series of poems in the form of epistles to his friends. He wrote the great poems, "Anatomy of the World" and "Of the Progress of the Soul" (sometimes called "The First and Second Anniversaries"), on the death of Sir Robert Drury's young daughter. Sir Robert gave Donne's family a place to stay in London, and Donne accompanied him abroad in the autumn of 1611, the occasion of Donne's famous poems to his wife Ann, "A Valediction Forbidding Mourning" and "Sweetest Love, I Do Not Go." Sickness and poverty dogged him for years; but his inability to decide between a public career and the taking of holy orders was partly resolved in 1615 when he was ordained an Anglican minister. Two years later his wife died while giving birth to their twelfth child; this blow and his temperamental indispositions turned him toward the writing of devotional poetry almost exclusively. "La Corona" and the "Holy Sonnets" were written in 1617 and 1618, the "Hymn to Christ" the following year. Donne was appointed Dean of St. Paul's in 1621. His sermons, which occupied most of his literary attention until his death, are among the richest in English pulpit oratory, dealing almost exclusively with decay and dying. A few days before his own death in 1631 he posed for his portrait wearing a shroud.

SONGS
AND
SONNETS

The good-morrow

I wonder by my troth, what thou, and I
Did, till we lov'd? were we not wean'd till then?
But suck'd on countrey pleasures, childishly?
Or snorted we in the seaven sleepers den?
T'was so; But this, all pleasures fancies bee.   5
If ever any beauty I did see,
Which I desir'd, and got, t'was but a dreame of thee.

And now good morrow to our waking soules,
Which watch not one another out of feare;
For love, all love of other sights controules,   10
And makes one little roome, an every where.
Let sea-discoverers to new worlds have gone,
Let Maps to other, worlds on worlds have showne,
Let us possesse one world, each hath one, and is one.

My face in thine eye, thine in mine appeares,   15
And true plain hearts doe in the faces rest,
Where can we finde two better hemispheares
Without sharpe North, without declining West?
What ever dyes, was not mixt equally;
If our two loves be one, or, thou and I   20
Love so alike, that none doe slacken, none can die.

Song

Goe, and catche a falling starre,
   Get with child a mandrake roote,
Tell me, where all past yeares are,
   Or who cleft the Divels foot,
Teach me to heare Mermaides singing,   5
   Or to keep off envies stinging,
        And finde
        What winde
Serves to advance an honest minde.

If thou beest borne to strange sights,   10
   Things invisible to see,
Ride ten thousand daies and nights,
   Till age snow white haires on thee,
Thou, when thou retorn'st, wilt tell mee
All strange wonders that befell thee,   15
        And sweare
        No where
Lives a woman true, and faire.

If thou findst one, let mee know,
   Such a Pilgrimage were sweet;   20
Yet doe not, I would not goe,
   Though at next doore wee might meet,
Though shee were true, when you met her,
And last, till you write your letter,
        Yet shee   25
        Will bee
<Falfe>*, ere I come, to two, or three.

Womans constancy

Now thou hast lov'd me one whole day,
To morrow when thou leav'st, what wilt thou say?
Wilt thou then Antedate some new made vow?
        Or say that now
We are not just those persons, which we were?   5

* Brackets indicate elements missing from or not clear in original
material.

Or, that oathes made in reverentiall feare
Of Love, and his wrath, any may forsweare?
Or, as true deaths, true maryages untie,
So lovers contracts, images of those,
Binde but till sleep, deaths image, them unloose?   10
        Or, your owne end to Justifie,
For having purpos'd change, and falsehood; you
Can have no way but falsehood to be true?
Vaine lunatique, against these scapes I could
        Dispute, and conquer, if I would,   15
        Which I abstaine to doe,
For by to morrow, I may thinke so too.

The undertaking

I have done one braver thing
    Then all the *Worthies* did,
And yet a braver thence doth spring,
    Which is, to keepe that hid.

It were but madnes now t'impart   5
    The skill of specular stone,
When he which can have learn'd the art
    To cut it, can finde none.

So, if I now should utter this,
    Others (because no more   10
Such stuffe to worke upon, there is,)
    Would love but as before.

But he who lovelinesse within
    Hath found, all outward loathes,
For he who colour loves, and skinne,   15
    Loves but their oldest clothes.

If, as I have, you also doe
    Vertue'attir'd in woman see,
And dare love that, and say so too,
    And forget the Hee and Shee;   20

And if this love, though placed so,
  From prophane men you hide,
Which will no faith on this bestow,
  Or, if they doe, deride:

Then you have done a braver thing   25
  Then all the *Worthies* did;
And a braver thence will spring,
  Which is, to keepe that hid.

The Sunne Rising

Busie old foole, unruly Sunne,
  Why dost thou thus,
Through windowes, and through curtaines call on us?
Must to thy motions lovers seasons run?
    Sawcy pedantique wretch, goe chide   5
    Late schoole boyes, and sowre prentices,
  Goe tell Court-huntsmen, that the King will ride,
  Call countrey ants to harvest offices;
Love, all alike, no season knowes, nor clyme,
Nor houres, dayes, moneths, which are the rags of time. 10

    Thy beames, so reverend, and strong
    Why shouldst thou thinke?
I could eclipse and cloud them with a winke,
But that I would not lose her sight so long:
    If her eyes have not blinded thine,   15
    Looke, and to morrow late, tell mee,
  Whether both the'India's of spice and Myne
  Be where thou leftst them, or lie here with mee.
Aske for those Kings whom thou saw'st yesterday,
And thou shalt heare, All here in one bed lay.   20

    She'is all States, and all Princes, I,
    Nothing else is.
Princes doe but play us; compar'd to this,
All honor's mimique; All wealth alchimie.
    Thou sunne art halfe as happy'as wee,   25

In that the world's contracted thus;
  Thine age askes ease, and since thy duties bee
  To warme the world, that's done in warming us.
Shine here to us, and thou art every where;
  This bed thy center is, these walls, thy spheare.   30

The Indifferent

I can love both faire and browne,
Her whom abundance melts, and her whom want betraies,
Her who loves lonenesse best, and her who maskes and
        plaies,
Her whom the country form'd, and whom the town,   5
Her who beleeves, and her who tries,
Her who still weepes with spungie eyes,
And her who is dry corke, and never cries;
I can love her, and her, and you and you,
I can love any, so she be not true.   10

Will no other vice content you?
Wil it not serve your turn to do, as did your mothers?
Or have you all old vices spent, and now would finde out
        others?
Or doth a feare, that men are true, torment you?   15
Oh we are not, be not you so,
Let mee, and doe you, twenty know.
Rob mee, but binde me not, and let me goe.
Must I, who came to travaile thorow you,
Grow your fixt subject, because you are true?   20

Venus heard me sigh this song,
And by Loves sweetest Part, Variety, she swore,
She heard not this till now; and that it should be so no
        more.
She went, examin'd, and return'd ere long,   25
And said, alas, Some two or three
Poore Heretiques in love there bee,
Which thinke to stablish dangerous constancie.
But I have told them, since you will be true,
You shall be true to them, who'are false to you.   30

Loves Vsury

For every houre that thou wilt spare mee now,
      I will allow,
Usurious God of Love, twenty to thee,
When with my browne, my gray haires equall bee;
Till then, Love, let my body raigne, and let   5
Mee travell, sojourne, snatch, plot, have, forget,
Resume my last yeares relict: thinke that yet
      We'had never met.

Let mee thinke any rivalls letter mine,
      And at next nine   10
Keepe midnights promise; mistake by the way
The maid, and tell the Lady of that delay;
Onely let mee love none, no, not the sport;
From country grasse, to comfitures of Court,
Or cities quelque choses, let report   15
      My minde transport.

This bargaine's good; if when I'am old, I bee
      Inflam'd by thee,
If thine owne honour, or my shame, or paine,
Thou covet most, at that age thou shalt gaine.   20
Doe thy will then, then subject and degree,
And fruit of love, Love I submit to thee,
Spare mee till then, I'll beare it, though she bee
      One that loves mee.

The Canonization

For Godsake hold your tongue, and let me love,
  Or chide my palsie, or my gout,
My five gray haires, or ruin'd fortune flout,
    With wealth your state, your minde with Arts improve,
      Take you a course, get you a place,   5
      Observe his honour, or his grace,
Or the Kings reall, or his stamped face
  Contemplate, what you will, approve,
  So you will let me love.

Alas, alas, who's injur'd by my love?   10
   What merchants ships have my sighs drown'd?
Who saies my teares have overflow'd his ground?
   When did my colds a forward spring remove?
    When did the heats which my veines fill
    Adde one more to the plaguie Bill?   15
Soldiers finde warres, and Lawyers finde out still
   Litigious men, which quarrels move,
   Though she and I do love.

Call us what you will, wee are made such by love;
   Call her one, mee another flye,   20
We'are Tapers too, and at our owne cost die,
   And wee in us finde the'Eagle and the Dove.
    The Phœnix ridle hath more wit
    By us, we two being one, are it.
So to one neutrall thing both sexes fit,   25
   Wee dye and rise the same, and prove
   Mysterious by this love.

Wee can dye by it, if not live by love,
   And if unfit for tombes and hearse
Our legend bee, it will be fit for verse;   30
   And if no peece of Chronicle wee prove,
    We'll build in sonnets pretty roomes;
    As well a well wrought urne becomes
The greatest ashes, as halfe-acre tombes,
   And by these hymnes, all shall approve   35
   Us *Canoniz'd* for Love:

And thus invoke us; You whom reverend love
   Made one anothers hermitage;
You, to whom love was peace, that now is rage;
   Who did the whole worlds soule contract, and drove   40
    Into the glasses of your eyes
    So made such mirrors, and such spies,
That they did all to you epitomize,
   Countries, Townes, Courts: Beg from above
   A patterne of your love!   45

The triple Foole

I am two fooles, I know,
For loving, and for saying so
   In whining Poëtry;
But where's that wiseman, that would not be I,
   If she would not deny?   5
Then as th'earths inward narrow crooked lanes
Do purge sea waters fretfull salt away,
   I thought, if I could draw my paines,
Through Rimes vexation, I should them allay,
Griefe brought to numbers cannot be so fierce,   10
For, he tames it, that fetters it in verse.

   But when I have done so,
Some man, his art and voice to show,
   Doth Set and sing my paine,
And, by delighting many, frees againe   15
   Griefe, which verse did restraine.
To Love, and Griefe tribute of Verse belongs,
But not of such as pleases when'tis read,
   Both are increased by such songs:
For both their triumphs so are published,   20
And I, which was two fooles, do so grow three;
Who are a little wise, the best fooles bee.

Lovers infinitenesse

If yet I have not all thy love,
Deare, I shall never have it all,
I cannot breath one other sigh, to move;
Nor can intreat one other teare to fall.
And all my treasure, which should purchase thee,   5
Sighs, teares, and oathes, and letters I have spent,
Yet no more can be due to mee,
Then at the bargaine made was ment,
If then thy gift of love were partiall,
That some to mee, some should to others fall,   10
   Deare, I shall never have Thee All.

Or if then thou gavest mee all,
All was but All, which thou hadst then,
But if in thy heart, since, there be or shall,
New love created bee, by other men,　　　　15
Which have their stocks intire, and can in teares,
In sighs, in oathes, and letters outbid mee,
This new love may beget new feares,
For, this love was not vowed by thee.
And yet it was, thy gift being generall,　　　　20
The ground, thy heart is mine, what ever shall
　　Grow there, deare, I should have it all.

Yet I would not have all yet,
Hee that hath all can have no more,
And since my love doth every day admit　　　　25
New growth, thou shouldst have new rewards in store;
Thou canst not every day give me thy heart,
If thou canst give it, then thou never gavest it:
Loves riddles are, that though thy heart depart,
It stayes at home, and thou with losing savest it:　　　　30
But wee will have a way more liberall,
Then changing hearts, to joyne them, so wee shall
　　Be one, and one anothers All.

Song

Sweetest love, I do not goe,
　　For wearinesse of thee,
Nor in hope the world can show
　　A fitter Love for mee;
　　　　But since that I　　　　5
Must dye at last, 'tis best,
To use my selfe in jest
　　　　Thus by fain'd deaths to dye;

Yesternight the Sunne went hence,
　　And yet is here to day,　　　　10
He hath no desire nor sense,
　　Nor halfe so short a way:

Then feare not mee,
But beleeve that I shall make
Speedier journeys, since I take   15
   More wings and spurres then hee.

O how feeble is mans power,
   That if good fortune fall,
Cannot adde another houre,
   Nor a lost houre recall!   20
     But come bad chance,
And wee joyne to'it our strength,
And wee teach it art and length,
   It selfe o'r us to'advance.

When thou sigh'st, thou sigh'st not winde,   25
   But sigh'st my soule away,
When thou weep'st, unkindly kinde,
   My lifes blood doth decay.
     It cannot bee
That thou lov'st mee, as thou say'st,   30
If in thine my life thou waste,
   Thou art the best of mee.

Let not thy divining heart
   Forethinke me any ill,
Destiny may take thy part,   35
   And may thy feares fulfill;
     But thinke that wee
Are but turn'd aside to sleepe;
They who one another keepe
   Alive, ne'r parted bee.   40

The Legacie

When I dyed last, and, Deare, I dye
   As often as from thee I goe,
   Though it be but an houre agoe,
And Lovers houres be full eternity,
I can remember yet, that I   5
   Something did say, and something did bestow;

Though I be dead, which sent mee, I should be
Mine owne executor and Legacie.

I heard mee say, Tell her anon,
    That my selfe, (that is you, not I,)   10
    Did kill me, and when I felt mee dye,
I bid mee send my heart, when I was gone,
But I alas could there finde none,
    When I had ripp'd me,'and search'd where hearts did
        lye;   15
It kill'd mee againe, that I who still was true,
In life, in my last Will should cozen you.

Yet I found something like a heart,
    But colours it, and corners had,
    It was not good, it was not bad,   20
It was intire to none, and few had part.
As good as could be made by art
    It seem'd; and therefore for our losses sad,
I meant to send this heart in stead of mine,
But oh, no man could hold it, for twas thine.   25

A *Feaver*

Oh doe not die, for I shall hate
    All women so, when thou art gone,
That thee I shall not celebrate,
    When I remember, thou wast one.

But yet thou canst not die, I know;   5
    To leave this world behinde, is death,
But when thou from this world wilt goe,
    The whole world vapors with thy breath.

Or if, when thou, the worlds soule, goest,
    It stay, tis but thy carkasse then,   10
The fairest woman, but thy ghost,
    But corrupt wormes, the worthyest men.

O wrangling schooles, that search what fire
    Shall burne this world, had none the wit
Unto this knowledge to aspire,   15
    That this her feaver might be it?

And yet she cannot wast by this,
    Nor long beare this torturing wrong,
For much corruption needfull is
    To fuell such a feaver long.   20

These burning fits but meteors bee,
    Whose matter in thee is soone spent.
Thy beauty,'and all parts, which are thee,
    Are unchangeable firmament.

Yet t'was of my minde, seising thee,   25
    Though it in thee cannot persever.
For I had rather owner bee
    Of thee one houre, then all else ever.

Aire and Angels

Twice or thrice had I loved thee,
Before I knew thy face or name,
So in a voice, so in a shapelesse flame,
Angells affect us oft, and worship'd bee;
    Still when, to where thou wert, I came,   5
Some lovely glorious nothing I did see.
    But since my soule, whose child love is,
Takes limmes of flesh, and else could nothing doe,
    More subtile then the parent is,
Love must not be, but take a body too,   10
    And therefore what thou wert, and who,
        I bid Love aske, and now
That it assume thy body, I allow,
And fixe it selfe in thy lip, eye, and brow.

Whilst thus to ballast love, I thought,   15
And so more steddily to have gone,
With wares which would sinke admiration,
I saw, I had loves pinnace overfraught,

Ev'ry thy haire for love to worke upon
Is much too much, some fitter must be sought;   20
For, nor in nothing, nor in things
Extreme, and scatt'ring bright, can love inhere;
Then as an Angell, face, and wings
Of aire, not pure as it, yet pure doth weare,
So thy love may be my loves spheare;   25
Just such disparitie
As is twixt Aire and Angells puritie,
'Twixt womens love, and mens will ever bee.

Breake of day

'Tis true, 'tis day; what though it be?
O wilt thou therefore rise from me?
Why should we rise, because 'tis light?
Did we lie downe, because 'twas night?
Love which in spight of darknesse brought us hether,   5
Should in despight of light keepe us together.

Light hath no tongue, but is all eye;
If it could speake as well as spie,
This were the worst, that it could say,
That being well, I faine would stay,   10
And that I lov'd my heart and honor so,
That I would not from him, that had them, goe.

Must businesse thee from hence remove?
Oh, that's the worst disease of love,
The poore, the foule, the false, love can   15
Admit, but not the busied man.
He which hath businesse, and makes love, doth doe
Such wrong, as when a maryed man doth wooe.

The Anniversarie

All Kings, and all their favorites,
All glory of honors, beauties, wits,

The Sun it selfe, which makes times, as they passe,
Is elder by a yeare, now, then it was
When thou and I first one another saw: 5
All other things, to their destruction draw,
    Only our love hath no decay;
This, no to morrow hath, nor yesterday,
Running it never runs from us away,
But truly keepes his first, last, everlasting day.   10

    Two graves must hide thine and my coarse,
        If one might, death were no divorce:
Alas, as well as other Princes, wee,
(Who Prince enough in one another bee,)
Must leave at last in death, these eyes, and eares,   15
Oft fed with true oathes, and with sweet salt teares;
    But soules where nothing dwells but love
(All other thoughts being inmates) then shall prove
This, or a love increased there above,
When bodies to their graves, soules from their graves   20
    remove.

    And then wee shall be throughly blest,
        But wee no more, then all the rest;
Here upon earth, we'are Kings, and none but wee
Can be such Kings, nor of such subjects bee;   25
Who is so safe as wee? where none can doe
Treason to us, except one of us two.
    True and false feares let us refraine,
Let us love nobly, and live, and adde againe
Yeares and yeares unto yeares, till we attaine   30
To write threescore: this is the second of our raigne.

A Valediction: of my name, in the window

            My name engrav'd herein,
    Doth contribute my firmnesse to this glasse,
        Which, ever since that charme, hath beene
            As hard, as that which grav'd it, was;
    Thine eye will give it price enough, to mock   5
            The diamonds of either rock.

'Tis much that Glasse should bee
As all confessing, and through-shine as I,
   'Tis more, that it shewes thee to thee,
   And cleare reflects thee to thine eye.   10
But all such rules, loves magique can undoe,
      Here you see mee, and I am you.

    As no one point, nor dash,
Which are but accessaries to this name,
   The showers and tempests can outwash,   15
   So shall all times finde mee the same;
You this intirenesse better may fulfill,
      Who have the patterne with you still.

    Or if too hard and deepe
This learning be, for a scratch'd name to teach,   20
   It, as a given deaths head keepe,
   Lovers mortalitie to preach,
Or thinke this ragged bony name to bee
      My ruinous Anatomie.

    Then, as all my soules bee,   25
Emparadis'd in you, (in whom alone
   I understand, and grow and see,)
   The rafters of my body, bone
Being still with you, the Muscle, Sinew, and Veine,
      Which tile this house, will come againe: 30

    Till my returne, repaire
And recompact my scattered body so.
   As all the vertuous powers which are
   Fix'd in the starres, are said to flow
Into such characters, as graved bee   35
      When these starres have supremacie:

    So since this name was cut
When love and griefe their exaltation had,
   No doore 'gainst this names influence shut;
   As much more loving, as more sad,   40
'Twill make thee; and thou shouldst, till I returne,
      Since I die daily, daily mourne.

When thy inconsiderate hand
Flings ope this casement, with my trembling name,
  To looke on one, whose wit or land,   45
  New battry to thy heart may frame,
Then thinke this name alive, and that thou thus
    In it offendst my Genius.

        And when thy melted maid,
Corrupted by thy Lover's gold, and page,   50
  His letter at thy pillow'hath laid,
  Disputed it, and tam'd thy rage,
And thou begin'st to thaw towards him, for this,
    May my name step in, and hide his.

        And if this treason goe   55
To an overt act, and that thou write againe;
  In superscribing, this name flow
  Into thy fancy, from the pane.
So, in forgetting thou remembrest right,
    And unaware to mee shalt write.   60

        But glasse, and lines must bee,
No meanes our firme substantiall love to keepe;
  Neere death inflicts this lethargie,
  And this I murmure in my sleepe;
Impute this idle talke, to that I goe,   65
    For dying men talke often so.

Twicknam garden

Blasted with sighs, and surrounded with teares,
  Hither I come to seeke the spring,
  And at mine eyes, and at mine eares,
Receive such balmes, as else cure every thing;
  But O, selfe traytor, I do bring   5
The spider love, which transubstantiates all,
  And can convert Manna to gall,
And that this place may thoroughly be thought
True Paradise, I have the serpent brought.

'Twere wholesomer for mee, that winter did 10
   Benight the glory of this place,
   And that a grave frost did forbid
These trees to laugh, and mocke mee to my face;
   But that I may not this disgrace
Indure, nor yet leave loving, Love let mee 15
   Some senslesse peece of this place bee;
Make me a mandrake, so I may groane here,
   Or a stone fountaine weeping out my yeare.

Hither with christall vyals, lovers come,
   And take my teares, which are loves wine, 20
   And try your mistresse Teares at home,
For all are false, that tast not just like mine;
   Alas, hearts do not in eyes shine,
Nor can you more judge womans thoughts by teares,
   Then by her shadow, what she weares. 25
O perverse sexe, where none is true but shee,
   Who's therefore true, because her truth kills mee.

A Valediction: of the booke

I'll tell thee now (deare Love) what thou shalt doe
   To anger destiny, as she doth us,
   How I shall stay, though she Esloygne me thus,
And how posterity shall know it too;
     How thine may out-endure 5
     Sybills glory, and obscure
     Her who from Pindar could allure,
   And her, through whose helpe *Lucan* is not lame,
And her, whose booke (they say) *Homer* did finde, and
     name. 10

Study our manuscripts, those Myriades
   Of letters, which have past twixt thee and mee,
   Thence write our Annals, and in them will bee
To all whom loves subliming fire invades,
     Rule and example found; 15
     There, the faith of any ground
     No schismatique will dare to wound,

That sees, how Love this grace to us affords,
To make, to keep, to use, to be these his Records.

This Booke, as long-liv'd as the elements,   20
    Or as the worlds forme, this all-graved tome
    In cypher writ, or new made Idiome,
Wee for loves clergie only'are instruments:
        When this booke is made thus,
        Should againe the ravenous   25
        Vandals and Goths inundate us,
    Learning were safe; in this our Universe
Schooles might learne Sciences, Spheares Musick, Angels
        Verse.

Here Loves Divines, (since all Divinity   30
    Is love or wonder) may finde all they seeke,
    Whether abstract spirituall love they like,
Their Soules exhal'd with what they do not see,
        Or, loth so to amuze
        Faiths infirmitie, they chuse   35
        Something which they may see and use;
    For, though minde be the heaven, where love doth sit,
Beauty a convenient type may be to figure it.

Here more then in their bookes may Lawyers finde,
    Both by what titles Mistresses are ours,   40
    And how prerogative these states devours,
Transferr'd from Love himselfe, to womankinde,
        Who though from heart, and eyes,
        They exact great subsidies,
        Forsake him who on them relies,   45
    And for the cause, honour, or conscience give,
Chimeraes, vaine as they, or their prerogative.

Here Statesmen, (or of them, they which can reade,)
    May of their occupation finde the grounds:
    Love and their art alike it deadly wounds,   50
If to consider what 'tis, one proceed,
        In both they doe excell
        Who the present governe well,
        Whose weaknesse none doth, or dares tell;

In this thy booke, such will their nothing see,   55
As in the Bible some can finde out Alchimy.

Thus vent thy thoughts; abroad I'll studie thee,
    As he removes farre off, that great heights takes;
    How great love is, presence best tryall makes,
But absence tryes how long this love will bee;   60
        To take a latitude
        Sun, or starres, are fitliest view'd
        At their brightest, but to conclude
Of longitudes, what other way have wee,
But to marke when, and where the darke eclipses bee?   65

Communitie

Good wee must love, and must hate ill,
For ill is ill, and good good still,
    But there are things indifferent,
Which wee may neither hate, nor love,
But one, and then another prove,   5
    As wee shall finde our fancy bent.

If then at first wise Nature had
Made women either good or bad,
    Then some wee might hate, and some chuse,
But since shee did them so create,   10
That we may neither love, nor hate,
    Onely this rests, All, all may use.

If they were good it would be seene,
Good is as visible as greene,
    And to all eyes it selfe betrayes: 15
If they were bad, they could not last,
Bad doth it selfe, and others wast,
    So, they deserve nor blame, nor praise.

But they are ours as fruits are ours,
He that but tasts, he that devours,   20

And he that leaves all, doth as well:
Chang'd loves are but chang'd sorts of meat,
And when hee hath the kernell eate,
    Who doth not fling away the shell?

Loves growth

I scarce beleeve my love to be so pure
    As I had thought it was,
    Because it doth endure
Vicissitude, and season, as the grasse;
Me thinkes I lyed all winter, when I swore,   5
My love was infinite, if spring make'it more.

But if this medicine, love, which cures all sorrow
With more, not onely bee no quintessence,
But mixt of all stuffes, paining soule, or sense,
And of the Sunne his working vigour borrow,   10
Love's not so pure, and abstract, as they use
To say, which have no Mistresse but their Muse,
But as all else, being elemented too,
Love sometimes would contemplate, sometimes do.

And yet no greater, but more eminent,   15
    Love by the spring is growne;
    As, in the firmament,
Starres by the Sunne are not inlarg'd, but showne.
Gentle love deeds, as blossomes on a bough,
From loves awakened root do bud out now.   20

If, as in water stir'd more circles bee
Produc'd by one, love such additions take,
Those like so many spheares, but one heaven make,
For, they are all concentrique unto thee;
And though each spring doe adde to love new heate,   25
As princes doe in times of action get
New taxes, and remit them not in peace,
No winter shall abate the springs encrease.

Loves exchange

Love, any devill else but you,
Would for a given Soule give something too.
At Court your fellowes every day,
Give th'art of Riming, Huntsmanship, or Play,
For them which were their owne before;   5
Onely I have nothing which gave more,
But am, alas, by being lowly, lower.

I aske no dispensation now
To falsifie a teare, or sigh, or vow,
I do not sue from thee to draw   10
A *non obstante* on natures law,
These are prerogatives, they inhere
In thee and thine; none should forsweare
Except that hee *Loves* minion were.

Give mee thy weaknesse, make mee blinde,   15
Both wayes, as thou and thine, in eies and minde;
Love, let me never know that this
Is love, or, that love childish is;
Let me not know that others know
That she knowes my paines, least that so   20
A tender shame make me mine owne new woe.

If thou give nothing, yet thou'art just,
Because I would not thy first motions trust;
Small townes which stand stiffe, till great shot
Enforce them, by warres law *condition* not.   25
Such in loves warfare is my case,
I may not article for grace,
Having put Love at last to shew this face.

This face, by which he could command
And change the Idolatrie of any land,   30
This face, which wheresoe'r it comes,
Can call vow'd men from cloisters, dead from tombes,
And melt both Poles at once, and store
Deserts with cities, and make more
Mynes in the earth, then Quarries were before.   35

For this, Love is enrag'd with mee,
Yet kills not. If I must example bee
To future Rebells; If th'unborne
Must learne, by my being cut up, and torne:
Kill, and dissect me, Love; for this   40
Torture against thine owne end is,
Rack't carcasses make ill Anatomies.

Confined Love

Some man unworthy to be possessor
Of old or new love, himselfe being false or weake,
  Thought his paine and shame would be lesser,
If on womankind he might his anger wreake,
      And thence a law did grow,   5
      One might but one man know;
      But are other creatures so?

Are Sunne, Moone, or Starres by law forbidden,
To smile where they list, or lend away their light?
  Are birds divorc'd, or are they chidden   10
If they leave their mate, or lie abroad a night?
      Beasts doe no joyntures lose
      Though they new lovers choose,
      But we are made worse then those.

Who e'r rigg'd faire ship to lie in harbors,   15
And not to seeke new lands, or not to deale withall?
  Or built faire houses, set trees, and arbors,
Only to lock up, or else to let them fall?
      Good is not good, unlesse
      A thousand it possesse,   20
      But doth wast with greedinesse.

The Dreame

Deare love, for nothing lesse then thee
Would I have broke this happy dreame,
      It was a theame

For reason, much too strong for phantasie,
Therefore thou wakd'st me wisely; yet   5
My Dreame thou brok'st not, but continued'st it,
Thou art so truth, that thoughts of thee suffice,
To make dreames truths; and fables histories;
Enter these armes, for since thou thoughtst it best,
Not to dreame all my dreame, let's act the rest.   10

As lightning, or a Tapers light,
Thine eyes, and not thy noise wak'd mee;
     Yet I thought thee
(For thou lovest truth) an Angell, at first sight,
But when I saw thou sawest my heart,   15
And knew'st my thoughts, beyond an Angels art,
When thou knew'st what I dreamt, when thou knew'st
Excesse of joy would wake me, and cam'st then,   [when
I must confesse, it could not chuse but bee
Prophane, to thinke thee any thing but thee.   20

Comming and staying show'd thee, thee,
But rising makes me doubt, that now,
     Thou art not thou.
That love is weake, where feare's as strong as hee;
'Tis not all spirit, pure, and brave,   25
If mixture it of *Feare, Shame, Honor,* have.
Perchance as torches which must ready bee,
Men light and put out, so thou deal'st with mee,
Thou cam'st to kindle, goest to come; Then I
Will dreame that hope againe, but else would die.   30

A Valediction: of weeping

    Let me powre forth
My teares before thy face, whil'st I stay here,
For thy face coines them, and thy stampe they beare,
And by this Mintage they are something worth,
     For thus they bee   5
     Pregnant of thee;
Fruits of much griefe they are, emblemes of more,
When a teare falls, that thou falst which it bore,
So thou and I are nothing then, when on a divers shore.

On a round ball 10
A workeman that hath copies by, can lay
An Europe, Afrique, and an Asia,
And quickly make that, which was nothing, *All*,
     So doth each teare,
     Which thee doth weare, 15
A globe, yea world by that impression grow,
Till thy teares mixt with mine doe overflow
This world, by waters sent from thee, my heaven dissolved
   so.

     O more then Moone, 20
Draw not up seas to drowne me in thy spheare,
Weepe me not dead, in thine armes, but forbeare
To teach the sea, what it may doe too soone;
     Let not the winde
     Example finde, 25
To doe me more harme, then it purposeth;
Since thou and I sigh one anothers breath,
Who e'r sighes most, is cruellest, and hasts the others
   death.

Loves Alchymie

Some that have deeper digg'd loves Myne then I,
Say, where his centrique happinesse doth lie:
     I have lov'd, and got, and told,
But should I love, get, tell, till I were old,
I should not finde that hidden mysterie; 5
     Oh, 'tis imposture all:
And as no chymique yet th'Elixar got,
     But glorifies his pregnant pot,
     If by the way to him befall
Some odoriferous thing, or medicinall, 10
   So, lovers dreame a rich and long delight,
   But get a winter-seeming summers night.

Our ease, our thrift, our honor, and our day,
Shall we, for this vaine Bubles shadow pay?

Ends love in this, that my man, 15
Can be as happy'as I can; If he can
Endure the short scorne of a Bridegroomes play?
That loving wretch that sweares,
'Tis not the bodies marry, but the mindes,
Which he in her Angelique findes, 20
Would sweare as justly, that he heares,
In that dayes rude hoarse minstralsey, the spheares.
Hope not for minde in women; at their best
Sweetnesse and wit, they'are but *Mummy*, possest.

The Flea

Marke but this flea, and marke in this,
How little that which thou deny'st me is;
It suck'd me first, and now sucks thee,
And in this flea, our two bloods mingled bee;
Thou know'st that this cannot be said 5
A sinne, nor shame, nor losse of maidenhead,
    Yet this enjoyes before it wooe,
    And pamper'd swells with one blood made of two,
    And this, alas, is more then wee would doe.

Oh stay, three lives in one flea spare, 10
Where wee almost, yea more then maryed are,
This flea is you and I, and this
Our mariage bed, and mariage temple is;
Though parents grudge, and you, w'are met,
And cloysterd in these living walls of Jet. 15
    Though use make you apt to kill mee,
    Let not to that, selfe murder added bee,
    And sacrilege, three sinnes in killing three.

Cruell and sodaine, hast thou since
Purpled thy naile, in blood of innocence? 20
Wherein could this flea guilty bee,
Except in that drop which it suckt from thee?
Yet thou triumph'st, and saist that thou
Find'st not thy selfe, nor mee the weaker now;

'Tis true, then learne how false, feares bee;   25
Just so much honor, when thou yeeld'st to mee,
Will wast, as this flea's death tooke life from thee.

The Curse

Who ever guesses, thinks, or dreames he knowes
Who is my mistris, wither by this curse;
      His only, and only his purse
      May some dull heart to love dispose,
And shee yeeld then to all that are his foes;   5
   May he be scorn'd by one, whom all else scorne,
   Forsweare to others, what to her he'hath sworne,
   With feare of missing, shame of getting, torne:

Madnesse his sorrow, gout his cramp, may hee
Make, by but thinking, who hath made him such: 10
      And may he feele no touch
      Of conscience, but of fame, and bee
Anguish'd, not that 'twas sinne, but that 'twas shee:
   In early and long scarcenesse may he rot,
   For land which had been his, if he had not   15
   Himselfe incestuously an heire begot:

May he dreame Treason, and beleeve, that hee
Meant to performe it, and confesse, and die,
      And no record tell why:
      His sonnes, which none of his may bee,   20
Inherite nothing but his infamie:
   Or may he so long Parasites have fed,
   That he would faine be theirs, whom he hath bred,
   And at the last be circumcis'd for bread:

The venom of all stepdames, gamsters gall,   25
What Tyrans, and their subjects interwish,
      What Plants, Mynes, Beasts, Foule, Fish,
      Can contribute, all ill which all
Prophets, or Poets spake; And all which shall
   Be annex'd in schedules unto this by mee,   30
   Fall on that man; For if it be a shee
   Nature before hand hath out-cursed mee.

The Message

Send home my long strayd eyes to mee,
Which (Oh) too long have dwelt on thee;
Yet since there they have learn'd such ill,
    Such forc'd fashions,
    And false passions,   5
      That they be
      Made by thee
Fit for no good sight, keep them still.

Send home my harmlesse heart againe,
Which no unworthy thought could staine;   10
But if it be taught by thine
    To make jestings
    Of protestings,
      And crosse both
      Word and oath,   15
Keepe it, for then 'tis none of mine.

Yet send me back my heart and eyes,
That I may know, and see thy lyes,
And may laugh and joy, when thou
    Art in anguish   20
    And dost languish
      For some one
      That will none,
Or prove as false as thou art now.

A nocturnall upon S. Lucies day, Being the shortest day

Tis the yeares midnight, and it is the dayes,
Lucies, who scarce seaven houres herself unmaskes,
The Sunne is spent, and now his flasks
Send forth light squibs, no constant rayes;
    The worlds whole sap is sunke: 5
The generall balme th'hydroptique earth hath drunk,
Whither, as to the beds-feet, life is shrunke,

Dead and enterr'd; yet all these seeme to laugh,
Compar'd with mee, who am their Epitaph.

Study me then, you who shall lovers bee　　　　10
At the next world, that is, at the next Spring:
　　For I am every dead thing,
　　In whom love wrought new Alchimie.
　　　　For his art did expresse
A quintessence even from nothingnesse,　　　　15
From dull privations, and leane emptinesse:
He ruin'd mee, and I am re-begot
Of absence, darknesse, death; things which are not.

All others, from all things, draw all that's good,
Life, soule, forme, spirit, whence they beeing have;　　20
　　I, by loves limbecke, am the grave
　　Of all, that's nothing. Oft a flood
　　　　Have wee two wept, and so
Drownd the whole world, us two; oft did we grow
To be two Chaosses, when we did show　　　　25
Care to ought else; and often absences
Withdrew our soules, and made us carcasses.

But I am by her death, (which word wrongs her)
Of the first nothing, the Elixer grown;
　　Were I a man, that I were one,　　　　30
　　I needs must know; I should preferre,
　　　　If I were any beast,
Some ends, some means; Yea plants, yea stones detest,
And love; All, all some properties invest;
If I an ordinary nothing were,　　　　35
As shadow, a light, and body must be here.

But I am None; nor will my Sunne renew.
You lovers, for whose sake, the lesser Sunne
　　At this time to the Goat is runne
　　To fetch new lust, and give it you,　　　　40
　　　　Enjoy your summer all;
Since shee enjoyes her long nights festivall,
Let mee prepare towards her, and let mee call
This houre her Vigill, and her Eve, since this
Both the yeares, and the dayes deep midnight is.　　　　45

Witchcraft by a picture

I fixe mine eye on thine, and there
   Pitty my picture burning in thine eye,
My picture drown'd in a transparent teare,
    When I looke lower I espie;
      Hadst thou the wicked skill   5
By pictures made and mard, to kill,
How many wayes mightst thou performe thy will?

But now I have drunke thy sweet salt teares,
   And though thou poure more I'll depart;
My picture vanish'd, vanish feares,   10
    That I can be endamag'd by that art;
      Though thou retaine of mee
One picture more, yet that will bee,
Being in thine owne heart, from all malice free.

The Baite

Come live with mee, and bee my love,
And we will some new pleasures prove
Of golden sands, and christall brookes,
With silken lines, and silver hookes.

There will the river whispering runne   5
Warm'd by thy eyes, more then the Sunne.
And there the'inamor'd fish will stay,
Begging themselves they may betray.

When thou wilt swimme in that live bath,
Each fish, which every channell hath,   10
Will amorously to thee swimme,
Gladder to catch thee, then thou him.

If thou, to be so seene, beest loath,
By Sunne, or Moone, thou darknest both,
And if my selfe have leave to see,   15
I need not their light, having thee.

Let others freeze with angling reeds,
And cut their legges, with shells and weeds,
Or treacherously poore fish beset,
With strangling snare, or windowie net: 20

Let coarse bold hands, from slimy nest
The bedded fish in banks out-wrest,
Or curious traitors, sleavesilke flies
Bewitch poore fishes wandring eyes.

For thee, thou needst no such deceit,   25
For thou thy selfe art thine owne bait;
That fish, that is not catch'd thereby,
Alas, is wiser farre then I.

The Apparition

When by thy scorne, O murdresse I am dead,
And that thou thinkst thee free
From all solicitation from mee,
Then shall my ghost come to thy bed,
And thee, fain'd vestall, in worse armes shall see;   5
Then thy sicke taper will begin to winke,
And he, whose thou art then, being tyr'd before,
Will, if thou stirre, or pinch to wake him, thinke
          Thou call'st for more,
And in false sleepe will from thee shrinke,   10
And then poore Aspen wretch, neglected thou
Bath'd in a cold quicksilver sweat wilt lye
          A veryer ghost then I;
What I will say, I will not tell thee now,
Lest that preserve thee'; and since my love is spent,   15
I'had rather thou shouldst painfully repent,
Then by my threatnings rest still innocent.

The broken heart

He is starke mad, who ever sayes,
     That he hath beene in love an houre,
Yet not that love so soone decayes,
     But that it can tenne in lesse space devour;

Who will beleeve mee, if I sweare 5
That I have had the plague a yeare?
  Who would not laugh at mee, if I should say,
  I saw a flaske of *powder burne a day*?

Ah, what a trifle is a heart,
  If once into loves hands it come! 10
All other griefes allow a part
  To other griefes, and aske themselves but some;
They come to us, but us Love draws,
Hee swallows us, and never chawes:
  By him, as by chain'd shot, whole rankes doe dye, 15
  He is the tyran Pike, our hearts the Frye.

If 'twere not so, what did become
  Of my heart, when I first saw thee?
I brought a heart into the roome,
  But from the roome, I carried none with mee: 20
If it had gone to thee, I know
Mine would have taught thine heart to show
  More pitty unto mee: but Love, alas,
  At one first blow did shiver it as glasse.

Yet nothing can to nothing fall, 25
  Nor any place be empty quite,
Therefore I thinke my breast hath all
  Those peeces still, though they be not unite;
And now as broken glasses show
A hundred lesser faces, so 30
  My ragges of heart can like, wish, and adore,
  But after one such love, can love no more.

A Valediction: forbidding mourning

As virtuous men passe mildly away,
  And whisper to their soules, to goe,
Whilst some of their sad friends doe say,
  The breath goes now, and some say, no:

So let us melt, and make no noise, 5
   No teare-floods, nor sigh-tempests move,
T'were prophanation of our joyes
   To tell the layetie our love.

Moving of th'earth brings harmes and feares,
   Men reckon what it did and meant, 10
But trepidation of the spheares,
   Though greater farre, is innocent.

Dull sublunary lovers love
   (Whose soule is sense) cannot admit
Absence, because it doth remove 15
   Those things which elemented it.

But we by a love, so much refin'd,
   That our selves know not what it is,
Inter-assured of the mind,
   Care lesse, eyes, lips, and hands to misse. 20

Our two soules therefore, which are one,
   Though I must goe, endure not yet
A breach, but an expansion,
   Like gold to ayery thinnesse beate.

If they be two, they are two so 25
   As stiffe twin compasses are two,
Thy soule the fixt foot, makes no show
   To move, but doth, if the'other doe.

And though it in the center sit,
   Yet when the other far doth rome, 30
It leanes, and hearkens after it,
   And growes erect, as that comes home.

Such wilt thou be to mee, who must
   Like th'other foot, obliquely runne;
Thy firmnes makes my circle just, 35
   And makes me end, where I begunne.

The Extasie

Where, like a pillow on a bed,
    A Pregnant banke swel'd up, to rest
The violets reclining head,
    Sat we two, one anothers best.
Our hands were firmely cimented   5
    With a fast balme, which thence did spring,
Our eye-beames twisted, and did thred
    Our eyes, upon one double string;
So to'entergraft our hands, as yet
    Was all the meanes to make us one,   10
And pictures in our eyes to get
    Was all our propagation.
As 'twixt two equal Armies, Fate
    Suspends uncertaine victorie,
Our soules, (which to advance their state,   15
    Were gone out,) hung 'twixt her, and mee.
And whil'st our soules negotiate there,
    Wee like sepulchrall statues lay;
All day, the same our postures were,
    And wee said nothing, all the day.   20
If any, so by love refin'd,
    That he soules language understood,
And by good love were growen all minde,
    Within convenient distance stood,
He (though he knew not which soule spake,   25
    Because both meant, both spake the same)
Might thence a new concoction take,
    And part farre purer then he came.
This Extasie doth unperplex
    (We said) and tell us what we love,   30
Wee see by this, it was not sexe,
    Wee see, we saw not what did move:
But as all severall soules containe
    Mixture of things, they know not what,
Love, these mixt soules doth mixe againe,   35
    And makes both one, each this and that.
A single violet transplant,

The strength, the colour, and the size,
(All which before was poore, and scant,)
   Redoubles still, and multiplies.   40
When love, with one another so
   Interinanimates two soules,
That abler soule, which thence doth flow,
   Defects of lonelinesse controules.
Wee then, who are this new soule, know,   45
   Of what we are compos'd, and made,
For, th'Atomies of which we grow,
   Are soules, whom no change can invade.
But O alas, so long, so farre
   Our bodies why doe wee forbeare?   50
They'are ours, though they'are not wee, Wee are
   The intelligences, they the spheare.
We owe them thankes, because they thus,
   Did us, to us, at first convay,
Yeelded their forces, sense, to us,   55
   Nor are drosse to us, but allay.
On man heavens influence workes not so,
   But that it first imprints the ayre,
Soe soule into the soule may flow,
   Though it to body first repaire.   60
As our blood labours to beget
   Spirits, as like soules as it can,
Because such fingers need to knit
   That subtile knot, which makes us man:
So must pure lovers soules descend   65
   T'affections, and to faculties,
Which sense may reach and apprehend,
   Else a great Prince in prison lies.
To'our bodies turne wee then, that so
   Weake men on love reveal'd may looke;   70
Loves mysteries in soules doe grow,
   But yet the body is his booke.
And if some lover, such as wee,
   Have heard this dialogue of one,
Let him still marke us, he shall see   75
   Small change, when we'are to bodies gone.

Loves Deitie

I long to talke with some old lovers ghost,
　Who dyed before the god of Love was borne:
I cannot thinke that hee, who then lov'd most,
　Sunke so low, as to love one which did scorne.
But since this god produc'd a destinie,   5
And that vice-nature, custome, lets it be;
　I must love her, that loves not mee.

Sure, they which made him god, meant not so much,
　Nor he, in his young godhead practis'd it;
But when an even flame two hearts did touch,   10
　His office was indulgently to fit
Actives to passives. Correspondencie
Only his subject was; It cannot bee
　Love, till I love her, that loves mee.

But every moderne god will now extend   15
　His vast prerogative, as far as Jove.
To rage, to lust, to write to, to commend,
　All is the purlewe of the God of Love.
Oh were wee wak'ned by this Tyrannie
To ungod this child againe, it could not bee   20
　I should love her, who loves not mee.

Rebell and Atheist too, why murmure I,
　As though I felt the worst that love could doe?
Love might make me leave loving, or might trie
　A deeper plague, to make her love me too,   25
Which, since she loves before, I'am loth to see;
Falshood is worse then hate; and that must bee,
　If shee whom I love, should love mee.

Loves diet

To what a combersome unwieldinesse
And burdenous corpulence my love had growne,
　But that I did, to make it lesse,

And keepe it in proportion,
Give it a diet, made it feed upon   5
That which love worst endures, *discretion.*

Above one sigh a day I'allow'd him not,
Of which my fortune, and my faults had part;
    And if sometimes by stealth he got
    A she sigh from my mistresse heart,   10
And thought to feast on that, I let him see
'Twas neither very sound, nor meant to mee.

If he wroung from mee'a teare, I brin'd it so
With scorne or shame, that him it nourish'd not;
    If he suck'd hers, I let him know   15
    'Twas not a teare, which hee had got,
His drinke was counterfeit, as was his meat;
For, eyes which rowle towards all, weepe not, but sweat.

What ever he would dictate, I writ that,
But burnt my letters; When she writ to me,   20
    And that that favour made him fat,
    I said, if any title bee
Convey'd by this, Ah, what doth it availe,
To be the fortieth name in an entaile?

Thus I reclaim'd my buzard love, to flye   25
At what, and when, and how, and where I chuse;
    Now negligent of sport I lye,
    And now as other Fawkners use,
I spring a mistresse, sweare, write, sigh and weepe:
And the game kill'd, or lost, goe talke, and sleepe.   30

The Will

    Before I sigh my last gaspe, let me breath,
    Great love, some Legacies; Here I bequeath
    Mine eyes to *Argus*, if mine eyes can see,
    If they be blinde, then Love, I give them thee;
    My tongue to Fame; to'Embassadours mine eares;   5
        To women or the sea, my teares.

Thou, Love, hast taught mee heretofore
By making mee serve her who'had twenty more,
That I should give to none, but such, as had too much
    before.   10

My constancie I to the planets give;
My truth to them, who at the Court doe live;
Mine ingenuity and opennesse,
To Jesuites; to Buffones my pensivenesse;
My silence to'any, who abroad hath beene;   15
   My mony to a Capuchin.
Thou Love taught'st me, by appointing mee
To love there, where no love receiv'd can be,
Onely to give to such as have an incapacitie.

My faith I give to Roman Catholiques;   20
All my good works unto the Schismaticks
Of Amsterdam; my best civility
And Courtship, to an Universitie;
My modesty I give to souldiers bare;
   My patience let gamesters share.   25
Thou Love taughtst mee, by making mee
Love her that holds my love disparity,
Onely to give to those that count my gifts indignity.

I give my reputation to those
Which were my friends; Mine industrie to foes;   30
To Schoolemen I bequeath my doubtfulnesse;
My sicknesse to Physitians, or excesse;
To Nature, all that I in Ryme have writ;
   And to my company my wit.
Thou Love, by making mee adore   35
Her, who begot this love in mee before,
Taughtst me to make, as though I gave, when I did but
    restore.

To him for whom the passing bell next tolls,
I give my physick bookes; my writen rowles   40
Of Morall counsels, I to Bedlam give;
My brazen medals, unto them which live

In want of bread; To them which passe among
    All forrainers, mine English tongue.
Thou, Love, by making mee love one   45
Who thinkes her friendship a fit portion
For yonger lovers, dost my gifts thus disproportion.

Therefore I'll give no more; But I'll undoe
The world by dying; because love dies too.
Then all your beauties will bee no more worth   50
Then gold in Mines, where none doth draw it forth;
And all your graces no more use shall have
    Then a Sun dyall in a grave.
Thou Love taughtst mee, by making mee
Love her, who doth neglect both mee and thee,   55
To'invent, and practise this one way, to'annihilate all
    three.

The Funerall

Who ever comes to shroud me, do not harme
    Nor question much
That subtile wreath of haire, which crowns my arme;
The mystery, the signe you must not touch,
    For 'tis my outward Soule,   5
Viceroy to that, which then to heaven being gone,
    Will leave this to controule,
And keepe these limbes, her Provinces, from dissolution.

For if the sinewie thread my braine lets fall
    Through every part,   10
Can tye those parts, and make mee one of all;
These haires which upward grew, and strength and art
    Have from a better braine,
Can better do'it; Except she meant that I
    By this should know my pain,   15
As prisoners then are manacled, when they'are condemn'd
    to die.

What ere shee meant by'it, bury it with me,
    For since I am
Loves martyr, it might breed idolatrie,   20

If into others hands these Reliques came;
        As 'twas humility
To afford to it all that a Soule can doe,
        So,'tis some bravery,
That since you would save none of mee, I bury some of   25
        you.

The Blossome

        Little think'st thou, poore flower,
        Whom I have watch'd sixe or seaven dayes,
And seene thy birth, and seene what every houre
Gave to thy growth, thee to this height to raise,
And now dost laugh and triumph on this bough,   5
        Little think'st thou
That it will freeze anon, and that I shall
To morrow finde thee falne, or not at all.

        Little think'st thou poore heart
        That labour'st yet to nestle thee,
And think'st by hovering here to get a part   10
In a forbidden or forbidding tree,
And hop'st her stiffenesse by long siege to bow:
        Little think'st thou,
That thou to morrow, ere that Sunne doth wake,   15
Must with this Sunne, and mee a journey take.

        But thou which lov'st to bee
        Subtile to plague thy selfe, wilt say,
Alas, if you must goe, what's that to mee?
Here lyes my businesse, and here I will stay: 20
You goe to friends, whose love and meanes present
        Various content
To your eyes, eares, and tongue, and every part.
If then your body goe, what need you a heart?

        Well then, stay here; but know,   25
        When thou hast stayd and done thy most;
A naked thinking heart, that makes no show,
Is to a woman, but a kinde of Ghost;

How shall shee know my heart; or having none,
        Know thee for one? 30
Practise may make her know some other part,
But take my word, shee doth not know a Heart.

   Meet mee at London, then,
    Twenty dayes hence, and thou shalt see
Mee fresher, and more fat, by being with men, 35
Then if I had staid still with her and thee.
For Gods sake, if you can, be you so too:
       I would give you
There, to another friend, whom wee shall finde
As glad to have my body, as my minde. 40

The Primrose, being at Mountgomery Castle, upon the hill, on which it is situate

    Vpon this Primrose hill,
     Where, if Heav'n would distill
A shoure of raine, each severall drop might goe
To his owne primrose, and grow Manna so;
And where their forme, and their infinitie 5
     Make a terrestriall Galaxie,
     As the small starres doe in the skie:
I walke to finde a true Love; and I see
That 'tis not a mere woman, that is shee,
But must, or more, or lesse then woman bee. 10

    Yet know I not not, which flower
     I wish; a sixe, or foure;
For should my true-Love lesse then woman bee,
She were scarce any thing; and then, should she
Be more then woman, shee would get above 15
     All thought of sexe, and thinke to move
     My heart to study her, and not to love;
Both these were monsters; Since there must reside
Falshood in woman, I could more abide,
She were by art, then Nature falsify'd. 20

Live Primrose then, and thrive
  With thy true number five;
And women, whom this flower doth represent,
With this mysterious number be content;
Ten is the farthest number; if halfe ten   25
    Belonge unto each woman, then
    Each woman may take halfe us men;
Or if this will not serve their turne, Since all
Numbers are odde, or even, and they fall
First into this, five, women may take us all.   30

The Relique

When my grave is broke up againe
  Some second ghest to entertaine,
  (For graves have learn'd that woman-head
  To be to more then one a Bed)
    And he that digs it, spies   5
A bracelet of bright haire about the bone,
    Will he not let'us alone,
And thinke that there a loving couple lies,
Who thought that this device might be some way
To make their soules, at the last busie day,   10
Meet at this grave, and make a little stay?

If this fall in a time, or land,
  Where mis-devotion doth command,
  Then, he that digges us up, will bring
  Us, to the Bishop, and the King,   15
    To make us Reliques; then
Thou shalt be a Mary Magdalen, and I
    A something else thereby;
All women shall adore us, and some men;
And since at such time, miracles are sought,   20
I would have that age by this paper taught
What miracles wee harmelesse lovers wrought.

First, we lov'd well and faithfully,
  Yet knew not what wee lov'd, nor why,
  Difference of sex no more wee knew,   25

Then our Guardian Angells doe;
Comming and going, wee
Perchance might kisse, but not between those meales;
Our hands ne'r toucht the seales,
Which nature, injur'd by late law, sets free: 30
These miracles wee did; but now alas,
All measure, and all language, I should passe,
Should I tell what a miracle shee was.

The Dampe

When I am dead, and Doctors know not why,
And my friends curiositie
Will have me cut up to survay each part,
When they shall finde your Picture in my heart,
You thinke a sodaine dampe of love   5
Will through all their senses move,
And worke on them as mee, and so preferre
Your murder, to the name of Massacre.

Poore victories! But if you dare be brave,
And pleasure in your conquest have,   10
First kill th'enormous Gyant, your *Disdaine*,
And let th'enchantresse *Honor*, next be slaine,
And like a Goth and Vandall rize,
Deface Records, and Histories
Of your owne arts and triumphs over men,   15
And without such advantage kill me then.

For I could muster up as well as you
My Gyants, and my Witches too,
Which are vast *Constancy*, and *Secretnesse*,
But these I neyther looke for, nor professe;   20
Kill mee as Woman, let mee die
As a meere man; doe you but try
Your passive valor, and you shall finde than,
In that you'have odds enough of any man.

The Dissolution

Shee'is dead; And all which die
To their first Elements resolve;
And wee were mutuall Elements to us,
    And made of one another.
My body then doth hers involve,   5
And those things whereof I consist, hereby
In me abundant grow, and burdenous,
    And nourish not, but smother.
My fire of Passion, sighes of ayre,
Water of teares, and earthly sad despaire,   10
     Which my materialls bee,
But neere worne out by loves securitie,
Shee, to my losse, doth by her death repaire,
    And I might live long wretched so
But that my fire doth with my fuell grow.   15
     Now as those Active Kings
    Whose foraine conquest treasure brings,
Receive more, and spend more, and soonest breake:
This (which I am amaz'd that I can speake)
     This death, hath with my store   20
     My use encreas'd.
And so my soule more earnestly releas'd,
Will outstrip hers; As bullets flowen before
A latter bullet may o'rtake, the pouder being more.

A Jeat Ring sent

Thou art not so black, as my heart,
Nor halfe so brittle, as her heart, thou art;
What would'st thou say? shall both our properties by thee
     bee spoke,
Nothing more endlesse, nothing sooner broke?   5

Marriage rings are not of this stuffe;
Oh, why should ought lesse precious, or lesse tough
Figure our loves? Except in thy name thou have bid it say,
I'am cheap, and nought but fashion, fling me'away.

Yet stay with mee since thou art come,   10
  Circle this fingers top, which did'st her thombe.
Be justly proud, and gladly safe, that thou dost dwell with
      me,
  She that, Oh, broke her faith, would soon breake thee.

Negative love

I never stoop'd so low, as they
Which on an eye, cheeke, lip, can prey,
  Seldome to them, which soare no higher
  Then vertue or the minde to'admire,
For sense, and understanding may   5
  Know, what gives fuell to their fire:
My love, though silly, is more brave,
For may I misse, when ere I crave,
If I know yet, what I would have.

If that be simply perfectest   10
Which can by no way be exprest
  But *Negatives*, my love is so.
  To All, which all love, I say no.
If any who deciphers best,
  What we know not, our selves, can know,   15
Let him teach mee that nothing; This
As yet my ease, and comfort is,
Though I speed not, I cannot misse.

The Prohibition

Take heed of loving mee,
At least remember, I forbade it thee;
Not that I shall repaire my'unthrifty wast
Of Breath and Blood, upon thy sighes, and teares,
By being to thee then what to me thou wast;   5
But, so great Joy, our life at once outweares,
Then, least thy love, by my death, frustrate bee,
If thou love mee, take heed of loving mee.

Take heed of hating mee,
Or too much triumph in the Victorie.   10
Not that I shall be mine owne officer,
And hate with hate againe retaliate;
But thou wilt lose the stile of conquerour,
If I, thy conquest, perish by thy hate.
Then, least my being nothing lessen thee,   15
If thou hate mee, take heed of hating mee.

Yet, love and hate mee too,
So, these extreames shall neithers office doe;
Love mee, that I may die the gentler way;
Hate mee, because thy love'is too great for mee;   20
Or let these two, themselves, not me decay;
So shall I, live, thy Stage, not triumph bee;
Lest thou thy love and hate and mee undoe,
To let mee live, O love and hate mee too.

The Expiration

So, so, breake off this last lamenting kisse,
    Which sucks two soules, and vapors Both away,
Turne thou ghost that way, and let mee turne this,
    And let our selves benight our happiest day,
We ask'd none leave to love; nor will we owe   5
    Any, so cheape a death, as saying, Goe;

Goe; and if that word have not quite kil'd thee,
    Ease mee with death, by bidding mee goe too.
Or, if it have, let my word worke on mee,
    And a just office on a murderer doe.   10
Except it be too late, to kill me so,
    Being double dead, going, and bidding, goe.

The Computation

For the first twenty yeares, since yesterday,
    I scarce beleev'd, thou could'st be gone away,
For forty more, I fed on favours past,
    And forty'on hopes, that thou would'st, they might last.

Teares drown'd one hundred, and sighes blew out two,   5
  A thousand, I did neither thinke, nor doe,
  Or not divide, all being one thought of you;
  Or in a thousand more, forgot that too.
Yet call not this long life; But thinke that I
Am, by being dead, Immortall; Can ghosts die?   10

The Paradox

  No Lover saith, I love, nor any other
      Can judge a perfect Lover;
  Hee thinkes that else none can, nor will agree
      That any loves but hee:
  I cannot say I lov'd, for who can say   5
      Hee was kill'd yesterday?
  Love with excesse of heat, more yong then old,
      Death kills with too much cold;
  Wee dye but once, and who lov'd last did die,
      Hee that saith twice, doth lye: 10
  For though hee seeme to move, and stirre a while,
      It doth the sense beguile.
  Such life is like the light which bideth yet
      When the lights life is set,
  Or like the heat, which fire in solid matter   15
      Leaves behinde, two houres after.
  Once I lov'd and dy'd; and am now become
      Mine Epitaph and Tombe.
  Here dead men speake their last, and so do I;
      Love-slaine, loe, here I lye.   20

Farewell to love

      Whilst yet to prove,
  I thought there was some Deitie in love
    So did I reverence, and gave
  Worship, as Atheists at their dying houre
  Call, what they cannot name, an unknowne power,   5
    As ignorantly did I crave:

Thus when
Things not yet knowne are coveted by men,
  Our desires give them fashion, and so
As they waxe lesser, fall, as they sise, grow.   10

        But, from late faire
His highnesse sitting in a golden Chaire,
  Is not lesse cared for after three dayes
By children, then the thing which lovers so
Blindly admire, and with such worship wooe;   15
    Being had, enjoying it decayes:
        And thence,
What before pleas'd them all, takes but one sense,
  And that so lamely, as it leaves behinde
A kinde of sorrowing dulnesse to the minde.   20

        Ah cannot wee,
As well as Cocks and Lyons jocund be,
  After such pleasures? Unlesse wise
Nature decreed (since each such Act, they say,
Diminisheth the length of life a day)   25
    This, as shee would man should despise
        The sport;
Because that other curse of being short,
  And onely for a minute made to be,
<Eagers desire> to raise posterity.   30

        Since so, my minde
Shall not desire what no man else can finde,
  I'll no more dote and runne
To pursue things which had indammag'd me.
And when I come where moving beauties be,   35
    As men doe when the summers Sunne
        Growes great,
Though I admire their greatnesse, shun their heat;
  Each place can afford shadowes. If all faile,
'Tis but applying worme-seed to the Taile.   40

A Lecture upon the Shadow

Stand still, and I will read to thee
A Lecture, Love, in loves philosophy.
    These three houres that we have spent,
    Walking here, Two shadowes went
Along with us, which we our selves produc'd;   5
But, now the Sunne is just above our head,
    We doe those shadowes tread;
    And to brave clearnesse all things are reduc'd.
  So whilst our infant loves did grow,
  Disguises did, and shadowes, flow,   10
  From us, and our cares; but, now 'tis not so.

That love hath not attain'd the high'st degree,
Which is still diligent lest others see.

Except our loves at this noone stay,
We shall new shadowes make the other way.   15
    As the first were made to blinde
    Others; these which come behinde
Will worke upon our selves, and blind our eyes.
If our loves faint, and westwardly decline;
    To me thou, falsly, thine,   20
    And I to thee mine actions shall disguise.
  The morning shadowes weare away,
  But these grow longer all the day,
  But oh, loves day is short, if love decay.

Love is a growing, or full constant light;   25
And his first minute, after noone, is night.

Sonnet. The Token

Send me some token, that my hope may live,
  Or that my easelesse thoughts may sleep and rest;
Send me some honey to make sweet my hive,
  That in my passion I may hope the best.
I beg noe ribbond wrought with thine owne hands,   5
  To knit our loves in the fantastick straine
Of new-toucht youth; nor Ring to shew the stands
  Of our affection, that as that's round and plaine,

So should our loves meet in simplicity;
   No, nor the Coralls which thy wrist infold,   10
Lac'd up together in congruity,
   To shew our thoughts should rest in the same hold;
No, nor thy picture, though most gracious,
   And most desir'd, because best like the best;
Nor witty Lines, which are most copious,   15
   Within the Writings which thou hast addrest.

Send me nor this, nor that, t'increase my store,
But swear thou thinkst I love thee, and no more.

\<Selfe Love\>

He that cannot chuse but love,
And strives against it still,
Never shall my fancy move;
For he loves 'gaynst his will;
Nor he which is all his own,   5
And can att pleasure chuse,
When I am caught he can be gone,
And when he list refuse.
Nor he that loves none but faire,
For such by all are sought;   10
Nor he that can for foul ones care,
For his Judgement then is nought:
Nor he that hath wit, for he
Will make me his jest or slave;
Nor a fool, for when others . . . .,   15
He can neither . . . . . .
Nor he that still his Mistresse payes,
For she is thrall'd therefore:
Nor he that payes not, for he sayes
Within, shee's worth no more.   20
Is there then no kinde of men
Whom I may freely prove?
I will vent that humour then
In mine owne selfe love.

EPIGRAMS

Hero and Leander

Both rob'd of aire, we both lye in one ground,
Both whom one fire had burnt, one water drownd.

Pyramus and Thisbe

Two, by themselves, each other, love and feare
Slaine, cruell friends, by parting have joyn'd here.

Niobe

By childrens births, and death, I am become
So dry, that I am now mine owne sad tombe.

A burnt ship

Out of a fired ship, which, by no way
But drowning, could be rescued from the flame,
Some men leap'd forth, and ever as they came
Neere the foes ships, did by their shot decay;
So all were lost, which in the ship were found,
   They in the sea being burnt, they in the burnt ship
     drown'd.

Fall of a wall

Vnder an undermin'd, and shot-bruis'd wall
A too-bold Captaine perish'd by the fall,
Whose brave misfortune, happiest men envi'd,
That had a towne for tombe, his bones to hide.

A lame begger

I am unable, yonder begger cries,
To stand, or move; if he say true, hee *lies*.

Cales and Guyana

If you from spoyle of th'old worlds farthest end
To the new world your kindled valors bend,
What brave examples then do prove it trew
That one things end doth still beginne a new.

Sir John Wingefield

Beyond th'old Pillers many have travailed
Towards the Suns cradle, and his throne, and bed:
A fitter Piller our Earle did bestow
In that late Island; for he well did know
Farther then Wingefield no man dares to goe.

A selfe accuser

Your mistris, that you follow whores, still taxeth you:
'Tis strange that she should thus confesse it, though'it
be true.

A licentious person

Thy sinnes and haires may no man equall call,
For, as thy sinnes increase, thy haires doe fall.

Antiquary

If in his Studie he hath so much care
To'hang all old strange things, let his wife beware.

Disinherited

Thy father all from thee, by his last Will,
Gave to the poore; Thou hast good title still.

Phryne

Thy flattering picture, *Phryne*, is like thee,
Onely in this, that you both painted be.

An obscure writer

Philo, with twelve yeares study, hath beene griev'd
To be understood; when will hee be beleev'd?

Klockius

Klockius so deeply hath sworne, ne'r more to come
In bawdie house, that hee dares not goe home.

Raderus

Why this man gelded *Martiall* I muse,
Except himselfe alone his tricks would use,
As *Katherine*, for the Courts sake, put downe Stewes.

Mercurius Gallo-Belgicus

Like *Esops* fellow-slaves, O *Mercury*,
Which could do all things, thy faith is; and I

Like *Esops* selfe, which nothing; I confesse
I should have had more faith, if thou hadst lesse;
Thy credit lost thy credit: 'Tis sinne to doe,
In this case, as thou wouldst be done unto,
To beleeve all: Change thy name: thou art like
Mercury in stealing, but lyest like a *Greeke*.

Ralphius

Compassion in the world againe is bred:
Ralphius is sick, the broker keeps his bed.

The Lier

Thou in the fields walkst out thy supping howers,
  And yet thou swear'st thou hast supp'd like a king:
Like Nebuchadnezar perchance with grass and flowers,
  A sallet worse then Spanish dieting.

ELEGIES

Elegie 1

Jealosie

Fond woman, which would'st have thy husband die,
And yet complain'st of his great jealousie;
If swolne with poyson, hee lay in'his last bed,
His body with a sere-barke covered,
Drawing his breath, as thick and short, as can   5
The nimblest crocheting Musitian,
Ready with loathsome vomiting to spue
His Soule out of one hell, into a new,
Made deafe with his poore kindreds howling cries,
Begging with few feign'd teares, great legacies,   10
Thou would'st not weepe, but jolly,'and frolicke bee,
As a slave, which to morrow should be free;
Yet weep'st thou, when thou seest him hungerly
Swallow his owne death, hearts-bane jealousie.
O give him many thanks, he'is courteous,   15
That in suspecting kindly warneth us.
Wee must not, as wee us'd, flout openly,
In scoffing ridles, his deformitie;
Nor at his boord together being satt,
With words, nor touch, scarce lookes adulterate.   20
Nor when he swolne, and pamper'd with great fare,
Sits downe, and snorts, cag'd in his basket chaire,
Must wee usurpe his owne bed any more,
Nor kisse and play in his house, as before.
Now I see many dangers; for that is   25
His realme, his castle, and his diocesse.
But if, as envious men, which would revile
Their Prince, or coyne his gold, themselves exile

93

Into another countrie,'and doe it there,
Wee play'in another house, what should we feare?   30
There we will scorne his houshold policies,
His seely plots, and pensionary spies,
As the inhabitants of Thames right side
Do Londons Major; or Germans, the Popes pride.

Elegie II

The Anagram

Marry, and love thy *Flavia*, for, shee
Hath all things, whereby others beautious bee,
For, though her eyes be small, her mouth is great,
Though they be Ivory, yet her teeth be jeat,
Though they be dimme, yet she is light enough,   5
And though her harsh haire fall, her skinne is rough;
What though her cheeks be yellow, her haire's red,
Give her thine, and she hath a maydenhead.
These things are beauties elements, where these
Meet in one, that one must, as perfect, please.   10
If red and white and each good quality
Be in thy wench, ne'r aske where it doth lye.
In buying things perfum'd, we aske; if there
Be muske and amber in it, but not where.
Though all her parts be not in th'usuall place,   15
She'hath yet an Anagram of a good face.
If we might put the letters but one way,
In the leane dearth of words, what could wee say?
When by the Gamut some Musitions make
A perfect song, others will undertake,   20
By the same Gamut chang'd, to equall it.
Things simply good, can never be unfit.
She's faire as any, if all be like her,
And if none bee, then she is singular.
All love is wonder; if wee justly doe   25
Account her wonderfull, why not lovely too?
Love built on beauty, soone as beauty, dies,
Chuse this face, chang'd by no deformities.
Women are all like Angels; the faire be
Like those which fell to worse; but such as shee,   30

Like to good Angels, nothing can impaire:
'Tis lesse griefe to be foule, then to'have beene faire.
For one nights revels, silke and gold we chuse,
But, in long journeyes, cloth, and leather use.
Beauty is barren oft; best husbands say,   35
There is best land, where there is foulest way.
Oh what a soveraigne Plaister will shee bee,
If thy past sinnes have taught thee jealousie!
Here needs no spies, nor eunuches; her commit
Safe to thy foes; yea, to a Marmosit.   40
When Belgiaes citties, the round countries drowne,
That durty foulenesse guards, and armes the towne:
So doth her face guard her; and so, for thee,
Which, forc'd by businesse, absent oft must bee,
Shee, whose face, like clouds, turnes the day to night,   45
Who, mightier then the sea, makes Moores seem white,
Who, though seaven yeares, she in the Stews had laid,
A Nunnery durst receive, and thinke a maid,
And though in childbeds labour she did lie,
Midwifes would sweare,'twere but a tympanie,   50
Whom, if shee accuse her selfe, I credit lesse
Then witches, which impossibles confesse,
Whom Dildoes, Bedstaves, and her Velvet Glasse
Would be as loath to touch as Joseph was:
One like none, and lik'd of none, fittest were,   55
For, things in fashion every man will weare.

Elegie III

Change

Although thy hand and faith, and good workes too,
Have seal'd thy love which nothing should undoe,
Yea though thou fall backe, that apostasie
Confirme thy love; yet much, much I feare thee.
Women are like the Arts, forc'd unto none,   5
Open to'all searchers, unpriz'd, if unknowne.
If I have caught a bird, and let him flie,
Another fouler using these meanes, as I,

May catch the same bird; and, as these things bee,
Women are made for men, not him, nor mee.   10
Foxes and goats; all beasts change when they please,
Shall women, more hot, wily, wild then these,
Be bound to one man, and did Nature then
Idly make them apter to'endure then men?
They'are our clogges, not their owne; if a man bee   15
Chain'd to a galley, yet the galley'is free;
Who hath a plow-land, casts all his seed corne there,
And yet allowes his ground more corne should beare;
Though Danuby into the sea must flow,
The sea receives the Rhene, Volga, and Po.   20
By nature, which gave it, this liberty
Thou lov'st, but Oh! canst thou love it and mee?
Likenesse glues love: and if that thou so doe,
To make us like and love, must I change too?
More then thy hate, I hate'it, rather let mee   25
Allow her change, then change as oft as shee,
And soe not teach, but force my'opinion
To love not any one, nor every one.
To live in one land, is captivitie,
To runne all countries, a wild roguery;   30
Waters stincke soone, if in one place they bide,
And in the vast sea are more putrifi'd:
But when they kisse one banke, and leaving this
Never looke backe, but the next banke doe kisse,
Then are they purest; Change'is the nursery   35
Of musicke, joy, life, and eternity.

Elegie IV

The Perfume

Once, and but once found in thy company,
All thy suppos'd escapes are laid on mee;
And as a thiefe at barre, is question'd there
By all the men, that have beene rob'd that yeare,
So am I, (by this traiterous meanes surpriz'd)   5
By thy Hydroptique father catechiz'd.
Though he had wont to search with glazed eyes,
As though he came to kill a Cockatrice,

Though hee hath oft sworne, that hee would remove
Thy beauties beautie, and food of our love,   10
Hope of his goods, if I with thee were seene,
Yet close and secret, as our soules, we'have beene.
Though thy immortall mother which doth lye
Still buried in her bed, yet will not dye,
Takes this advantage to sleepe out day-light,   15
And watch thy entries, and returnes all night,
And, when she takes thy hand, and would seeme kind,
Doth search what rings, and armelets she can finde,
And kissing notes the colour of thy face,
And fearing least thou'art swolne, doth thee embrace;   20
To trie if thou long, doth name strange meates,
And notes thy palenesse, blushing, sighs, and sweats;
And politiquely will to thee confesse
The sinnes of her owne youths ranke lustinesse;
Yet love these Sorceries did remove, and move   25
Thee to gull thine owne mother for my love.
Thy little brethren, which like Faiery Sprights
Oft skipt into our chamber, those sweet nights,
And kist, and ingled on thy fathers knee,
Were brib'd next day, to tell what they did see: 30
The grim eight-foot-high iron-bound serving-man,
That oft names God in oathes, and onely than,
He that to barre the first gate, doth as wide
As the great Rhodian Colossus stride,
Which, if in hell no other paines there were,   35
Makes mee feare hell, because he must be there:
Though by thy father he were hir'd to this,
Could never witnesse any touch or kisse.
But Oh, too common ill, I brought with mee
That, which betray'd mee to my enemie: 40
A loud perfume, which at my entrance cryed
Even at thy fathers nose, so were wee spied.
When, like a tyran King, that in his bed
Smelt gunpowder, the pale wretch shivered.
Had it beene some bad smell, he would have thought   45
That his owne feet, or breath, that smell had wrought.
But as wee in our Ile emprisoned,
Where cattell onely,'and diverse dogs are bred,

The pretious Vnicornes, strange monsters call,
So thought he good, strange, that had none at all.   50
I taught my silkes, their whistling to forbeare,
Even my opprest shoes, dumbe and speechlesse were,
Onely, thou bitter sweet, whom I had laid
Next mee, mee traiterously hast betraid,
And unsuspected hast invisibly   55
At once fled unto him, and staid with mee.
Base excrement of earth, which dost confound
Sense, from distinguishing the sicke from sound;
By thee the seely Amorous sucks his death
By drawing in a leprous harlots breath;   60
By thee, the greatest staine to mans estate
Falls on us, to be call'd effeminate;
Though you be much lov'd in the Princes hall,
There, things that seeme, exceed substantiall;
Gods, when yee fum'd on altars, were pleas'd well,   65
Because you'were burnt, not that they lik'd your smell;
You'are loathsome all, being taken simply alone,
Shall wee love ill things joyn'd, and hate each one?
If you were good, your good doth soone decay;
And you are rare, that takes the good away.   70
All my perfumes, I give most willingly
To'embalme thy fathers corse; What? will hee die?

Elegie v

His Picture

Here take my Picture; though I bid farewell,
Thine, in my heart, where my soule dwels, shall dwell.
'Tis like me now, but I dead, 'twill be more
When wee are shadowes both, then 'twas before.
When weather-beaten I come backe; my hand,   5
Perhaps with rude oares torne, or Sun beams tann'd,
My face and brest of hairecloth, and my head
With cares rash sodaine stormes, being o'rspread,
My body'a sack of bones, broken within,
And powders blew staines scatter'd on my skinne;   10

If rivall fooles taxe thee to'have lov'd a man,
So foule, and course, as, Oh, I may seeme than,
This shall say what I was: and thou shalt say,
Doe his hurts reach mee? doth my worth decay?
Or doe they reach his judging minde, that hee   15
Should now love lesse, what hee did love to see?
That which in him was faire and delicate,
Was but the milke, which in loves childish state
Did nurse it: who now is growne strong enough
To feed on that, which to disused tasts seemes tough.   20

Elegie VI

Oh, let mee not serve so, as those men serve
Whom honours smoakes at once fatten and sterve;
Poorely enrich't with great mens words or lookes;
Nor so write my name in thy loving bookes
As those Idolatrous flatterers, which still   5
Their Princes stiles, with many Realmes fulfill
Whence they no tribute have, and where no sway.
Such services I offer as shall pay
Themselves, I hate dead names: Oh then let mee
Favorite in Ordinary, or no favorite bee.   10
When my Soule was in her owne body sheath'd,
Nor yet by oathes betroth'd, nor kisses breath'd
Into my Purgatory, faithlesse thee,
Thy heart seem'd waxe, and steele thy constancie:
So carelesse flowers strow'd on the waters face,   15
The curled whirlepooles suck, smack, and embrace,
Yet drowne them; so, the tapers beamie eye
Amorously twinkling, beckens the giddie flie,
Yet burnes his wings; and such the devill is,
Scarce visiting them, who are intirely his.   20
When I behold a streame, which, from the spring,
Doth with doubtfull melodious murmuring,
Or in a speechlesse slumber, calmely ride
Her wedded channels bosome, and then chide
And bend her browes, and swell if any bough   25
Do but stoop downe, or kisse her upmost brow;
Yet, if her often gnawing kisses winne
The traiterous banke to gape, and let her in,

She rusheth violently, and doth divorce
Her from her native, and her long-kept course,   30
And rores, and braves it, and in gallant scorne,
In flattering eddies promising retorne,
She flouts the channell, who thenceforth is drie;
Then say I; that is shee, and this am I.
Yet let not thy deepe bitternesse beget   35
Carelesse despaire in mee, for that will whet
My minde to scorne; and Oh, love dull'd with paine
Was ne'r so wise, nor well arm'd as disdaine.
Then with new eyes I shall survay thee,'and spie
Death in thy cheekes, and darknesse in thine eye.   40
Though hope bred faith and love; thus taught, I shall
As nations do from Rome, from thy love fall.
My hate shall outgrow thine, and utterly
I will renounce thy dalliance: and when I
Am the Recusant, in that resolute state,   45
What hurts it mee to be'excommunicate?

Elegie VII

Natures lay Ideot, I taught thee to love,
And in that sophistrie, Oh, thou dost prove
Too subtile: Foole, thou didst not understand
The mystique language of the eye nor hand:
Nor couldst thou judge the difference of the aire   5
Of sighes, and say, this lies, this sounds despaire:
Nor by the'eyes water call a maladie
Desperately hot, or changing feaverously.
I had not taught thee then, the Alphabet
Of flowers, how they devisefully being set   10
And bound up, might with speechlesse secrecie
Deliver arrands mutely, and mutually.
Remember since all thy words us'd to bee
To every suitor; *I, if my friends agree;*
Since, household charmes, thy husbands name to teach,   15
Were all the love trickes, that thy wit could reach;
And since, an houres discourse could scarce have made
One answer in thee, and that ill arraid

In broken proverbs, and torne sentences.
Thou art not by so many duties his,   20
That from the worlds Common having sever'd thee,
Inlaid thee, neither to be seene, nor see,
As mine: who have with amorous delicacies
Refin'd thee'into a blis-full Paradise.
Thy graces and good words my creatures bee;   25
I planted knowledge and lifes tree in thee,
Which Oh, shall strangers taste? Must I alas
Frame and enamell Plate, and drinke in Glasse?
Chafe waxe for others seales? breake a colts force
And leave him then, beeing made a ready horse?   30

Elegie VIII

The Comparison

As the sweet sweat of Roses in a Still,
As that which from chaf'd muskats pores doth trill,
As the Almighty Balme of th'early East,
Such are the sweat drops of my Mistris breast,
And on her <brow> her skin such lustre sets,   5
They seeme no sweat drops, but pearle coronets.
Ranke sweaty froth thy Mistresse's brow defiles,
Like spermatique issue of ripe menstruous boiles,
Or like the skumme, which, by needs lawlesse law
Enforc'd, Sanserra's starved men did draw   10
From parboild shooes, and bootes, and all the rest
Which were with any soveraigne fatnes blest,
And like vile lying stones in saffrond tinne,
Or warts, or wheales, they hang upon her skinne.
Round as the world's her head, on every side,   15
Like to the fatall Ball which fell on Ide,
Or that whereof God had such jealousie,
As, for the ravishing thereof we die.
Thy *head* is like a rough-hewne statue of jeat,
Where marks for eyes, nose, mouth, are yet scarce set;   20
Like the first Chaos, or flat seeming face
Of Cynthia, when th'earths shadowes her embrace.

Like Proserpines white beauty-keeping chest,
Or Joves best fortunes urne, is her faire brest.
Thine's like worme eaten trunkes, cloth'd in seals skin,　25
Or grave, that's dust without, and stinke within.
And like that slender stalke, at whose end stands
The wood-bine quivering, are her armes and hands.
Like rough bark'd elmboughes, or the russet skin
Of men late scurg'd for madnes, or for sinne,　30
Like Sun-parch'd quarters on the citie gate,
Such is thy tann'd skins lamentable state.
And like a bunch of ragged carrets stand
The short swolne fingers of thy gouty hand.
Then like the Chymicks masculine equall fire,　35
Which in the Lymbecks warme wombe doth inspire
Into th'earths worthlesse durt a soule of gold,
Such cherishing heat her best lov'd part doth hold.
Thine's like the dread mouth of a fired gunne,
Or like hot liquid metalls newly runne　40
Into clay moulds, or like to that Ætna
Where round about the grasse is burnt away.
Are not your kisses then as filthy, and more,
As a worme sucking an invenom'd sore?
Doth not thy fearefull hand in feeling quake,　45
As one which gath'ring flowers, still feares a snake?
Is not your last act harsh, and violent,
As when a Plough a stony ground doth rent?
So kisse good Turtles, so devoutly nice
Are Priests in handling reverent sacrifice,　50
And such in searching wounds the Surgeon is
As wee, when wee embrace, or touch, or kisse.
Leave her, and I will leave comparing thus,
She, and comparisons are odious.

Elegie IX

The Autumnall

No *Spring*, nor *Summer* Beauty hath such grace,
　　As I have seen in one *Autumnall* face.
Yong *Beauties* force our love, and that's a *Rape*,
　　This doth but *counsaile*, yet you cannot scape.

If t'were a *shame* to love, here t'were no *shame*, 5
  Affection here takes *Reverences* name.
Were her first yeares the *Golden Age*; That's true,
  But now shee's *gold* oft tried, and ever new.
That was her torrid and inflaming time,
  This is her tolerable *Tropique clyme*. 10
Faire eyes, who askes more heate then comes from hence,
  He in a fever wishes pestilence.
Call not these wrinkles, *graves*; If *graves* they were,
  They were *Loves graves*; for else he is no where.
Yet lies not Love *dead* here, but here doth sit 15
  Vow'd to this trench, like an *Anachorit*.
And here, till hers, which must be his *death*, come,
  He doth not digge a *Grave*, but build a *Tombe*.
Here dwells he, though he sojourne ev'ry where,
  In *Progresse*, yet his standing house is here. 20
Here, where still *Evening* is; not *noone*, nor *night*;
  Where no *voluptuousnesse*, yet all *delight*.
In all her words, unto all hearers fit,
  You may at *Revels*, you at *Counsaile*, sit.
This is loves timber, youth his under-wood; 25
  There he, as wine in *June*, enrages blood,
Which then comes seasonabliest, when our tast
  And appetite to other things, is past.
Xerxes strange *Lydian* love, the *Platane* tree,
  Was lov'd for age, none being so large as shee, 30
Or else because, being yong, nature did blesse
  Her youth with ages glory, *Barrennesse*.
If we love things long sought, *Age* is a thing
  Which we are fifty yeares in compassing.
If transitory things, which soone decay, 35
  Age must be lovelyest at the latest day.
But name not *Winter-faces*, whose skin's slacke;
  Lanke, as an unthrifts purse; but a soules sacke;
Whose *Eyes* seeke light within, for all here's shade;
  Whose *mouthes* are holes, rather worne out, then made; 40
Whose every tooth to a severall place is gone,
  To vexe their soules at *Resurrection*;
Name not these living *Deaths-heads* unto mee,
  For these, not *Ancient*, but *Antique* be.

I hate extreames; yet I had rather stay 45
    With *Tombs*, then *Cradles*, to weare out a day.
Since such loves naturall lation is, may still
    My love descend, and journey downe the hill,
Not panting after growing beauties, so,
    I shall ebbe out with them, who home-ward goe. 50

Elegie x

The Dreame

Image of her whom I love, more then she,
    Whose faire impression in my faithfull heart,
Makes mee her *Medall*, and makes her love mee,
    As Kings do coynes, to which their stamps impart
The value: goe, and take my heart from hence, 5
    Which now is growne too great and good for me:
Honours oppresse weake spirits, and our sense
    Strong objects dull; the more, the lesse wee see.
When you are gone, and *Reason* gone with you,
    Then *Fantasie* is Queene and Soule, and all; 10
She can present joyes meaner then you do;
    Convenient, and more proportionall.
So, if I dreame I have you, I have you,
    For, all our joyes are but fantasticall.
And so I scape the paine, for paine is true; 15
    And sleepe which locks up sense, doth lock out all.
After a such fruition I shall wake,
    And, but the waking, nothing shall repent;
And shall to love more thankfull Sonnets make,
    Then if more *honour*, *teares*, and *paines* were spent. 20
But dearest heart, and dearer image stay;
    Alas, true joyes at best are *dreame* enough;
Though you stay here you passe too fast away:
    For even at first lifes *Taper* is a snuffe.
Fill'd with her love, may I be rather grown 25
Mad with much *heart*, then *ideott* with none.

Elegie xi

The Bracelet

Vpon the losse of his Mistresses Chaine, for which
he made satisfaction

Not that in colour it was like thy haire,
For Armelets of that thou maist let me weare:
Nor that thy hand it oft embrac'd and kist,
For so it had that good, which oft I mist:
Nor for that silly old moralitie,   5
That as these linkes were knit, our love should bee:
Mourne I that I thy seavenfold chaine have lost;
Nor for the luck sake; but the bitter cost.
O, shall twelve righteous Angels, which as yet
No leaven of vile soder did admit;   10
Nor yet by any way have straid or gone
From the first state of their Creation;
Angels, which heaven commanded to provide
All things to me, and be my faithfull guide;
To gaine new friends, t'appease great enemies;   15
To comfort my soule, when I lie or rise;
Shall these twelve innocents, by thy severe
Sentence (dread judge) my sins great burden beare?
Shall they be damn'd, and in the furnace throwne,
And punisht for offences not their owne?   20
They save not me, they doe not ease my paines,
When in that hell they'are burnt and tyed in chains.
Were they but Crownes of France, I cared not,
For, most of these, their naturall Countreys rot
I think possesseth, they come here to us,   25
So pale, so lame, so leane, so ruinous;
And howsoe'r French Kings most Christian be,
Their Crownes are circumcis'd most Jewishly.
Or were they Spanish Stamps, still travelling,
That are become as Catholique as their King,   30
Those unlickt beare-whelps, unfil'd pistolets
That (more than Canon shot) availes or lets;
Which negligently left unrounded, looke
Like many angled figures, in the booke

Of some great Conjurer that would enforce 35
Nature, as these doe justice, from her course;
Which, as the soule quickens head, feet and heart,
As streames, like veines, run through th'earth's every part,
Visit all Countries, and have slily made
Gorgeous *France*, ruin'd, ragged and decay'd; 40
Scotland, which knew no State, proud in one day:
And mangled seventeen-headed *Belgia.*
Or were it such gold as that wherewithall
Almighty *Chymiques* from each minerall,
Having by subtle fire a soule out-pull'd; 45
Are dirtely and desperately gull'd:
I would not spit to quench the fire they'are in,
For, they are guilty of much hainous Sin.
But, shall my harmlesse angels perish? Shall
I lose my guard, my ease, my food, my all? 50
Much hope which they should nourish will be dead,
Much of my able youth, and lustyhead
Will vanish; if thou love let them alone,
For thou will love me lesse when they are gone;
And be content that some lowd squeaking Cryer 55
Well-pleas'd with one leane thred-bare groat, for hire,
May like a devill roare through every street;
And gall the finders conscience, if they meet.
Or let mee creepe to some dread Conjurer,
That with phantastique scheames fils full much paper; 60
Which hath divided heaven in tenements,
And with whores, theeves, and murderers stuft his rents,
So full, that though hee passe them all in sinne,
He leaves himselfe no roome to enter in.
But if, when all his art and time is spent, 65
Hee say 'twill ne'r be found; yet be content;
Receive from him that doome ungrudgingly,
Because he is the mouth of destiny.
    Thou say'st (alas) the gold doth still remaine,
Though it be chang'd, and put into a chaine; 70
So in the first falne angels, resteth still
Wisdome and knowledge; but,'tis turn'd to ill:
As these should doe good works; and should provide
Necessities; but now must nurse thy pride.

And they are still bad angels; Mine are none; 75
For, forme gives being, and their forme is gone:
Pitty these Angels; yet their dignities
Passe Vertues, Powers, and Principalities.
  But, thou art resolute; Thy will be done!
Yet with such anguish, as her onely sonne 80
The Mother in the hungry grave doth lay,
Vnto the fire these Martyrs I betray.
Good soules, (for you give life to every thing)
Good Angels, (for good messages you bring)
Destin'd you might have beene to such an one, 85
As would have lov'd and worship'd you alone:
One that would suffer hunger, nakednesse,
Yea death, ere he would make your number lesse.
But, I am guilty of your sad decay;
May your few fellowes longer with me stay. 90
  But ô thou wretched finder whom I hate
So, that I almost pitty thy estate:
Gold being the heaviest metal amongst all,
May my most heavy curse upon thee fall:
Here fetter'd, manacled, and hang'd in chains, 95
First mayst thou bee; then chaind to hellish paines;
Or be with forraine gold brib'd to betray
Thy Countrey, and faile both of that and thy pay.
May the next thing thou stoop'st to reach, containe
Poyson, whose nimble fume rot thy moist braine; 100
Or libels, or some interdicted thing,
Which negligently kept, thy ruine bring.
Lust-bred diseases rot thee; and dwell with thee
Itching desire, and no abilitie.
May all the evils that gold ever wrought; 105
All mischiefes that all devils ever thought;
Want after plenty; poore and gouty age;
The plagues of travellers; love; marriage
Afflict thee, and at thy lives last moment,
May thy swolne sinnes themselves to thee present. 110
  But, I forgive; repent thee honest man:
Gold is Restorative, restore it then:
But if from it thou beest loath to depart,
Because 'tis cordiall, would twere at thy heart.

Elegie XII

His parting from her

Since she must go, and I must mourn, come Night,
Environ me with darkness, whilst I write:
Shadow that hell unto me, which alone
I am to suffer when my Love is gone.
Alas the darkest Magick cannot do it,   5
Thou and greate Hell to boot are shadows to it.
Should *Cinthia* quit thee, *Venus*, and each starre,
It would not forme one thought dark as mine are.
I could lend thee obscureness now, and say,
Out of my self, There should be no more Day,   10
Such is already my felt want of sight,
Did not the fires within me force a light.
Oh Love, that fire and darkness should be mixt,
Or to thy Triumphs soe strange torments fixt?
Is't because thou thy self art blind, that wee   15
Thy Martyrs must no more each other see?
Or tak'st thou pride to break us on the wheel,
And view old Chaos in the Pains we feel?
Or have we left undone some mutual Right,
Through holy fear, that merits thy despight?   20
No, no. The falt was mine, impute it to me,
Or rather to conspiring destinie,
Which (since I lov'd for forme before) decreed,
That I should suffer when I lov'd indeed:
And therefore now, sooner then I can say,   25
I saw the golden fruit, 'tis rapt away.
Or as I had watcht one drop in a vast stream,
And I left wealthy only in a dream.
Yet Love, thou'rt blinder then thy self in this,
To vex my Dove-like friend for my amiss: 30
And, where my own sad truth may expiate
Thy wrath, to make her fortune run my fate:
So blinded Justice doth, when Favorites fall,
Strike them, their house, their friends, their followers all.
Was't not enough that thou didst dart thy fires   35
Into our blouds, inflaming our desires,

And made'st us sigh and glow, and pant, and burn,
And then thy self into our flame did'st turn?
Was't not enough, that thou didst hazard us
To paths in love so dark, so dangerous: 40
And those so ambush'd round with houshold spies,
And over all, thy husbands towring eyes
That flam'd with oylie sweat of jealousie:
Yet went we not still on with Constancie?
Have we not kept our guards, like spie on spie?   45
Had correspondence whilst the foe stood by?
Stoln (more to sweeten them) our many blisses
Of meetings, conference, embracements, kisses?
Shadow'd with negligence our most respects?
Varied our language through all dialects,   50
Of becks, winks, looks, and often under-boards
Spoak dialogues with our feet far from our words?
Have we prov'd all these secrets of our Art,
Yea, thy pale inwards, and thy panting heart?
And, after all this passed Purgatory,   55
Must sad divorce make us the vulgar story?
First let our eyes be rivited quite through
Our turning brains, and both our lips grow to:
Let our armes clasp like Ivy, and our fear
Freese us together, that we may stick here,   60
Till Fortune, that would rive us, with the deed
Strain her eyes open, and it make them bleed:
For Love it cannot be, whom hitherto
I have accus'd, should such a mischief doe.
Oh Fortune, thou'rt not worth my least exclame,   65
And plague enough thou hast in thy own shame.
Do thy great worst, my friend and I have armes,
Though not against thy strokes, against thy harmes.
Rend us in sunder, thou canst not divide
Our bodies so, but that our souls are ty'd,   70
And we can love by letters still and gifts,
And thoughts and dreams; Love never wanteth shifts.
I will not look upon the quickning Sun,
But straight her beauty to my sense shall run;
The ayre shall note her soft, the fire most pure;   75
Water suggest her clear, and the earth sure.

Time shall not lose our passages; the Spring
How fresh our love was in the beginning;
The Summer how it ripened in the eare;
And Autumn, what our golden harvests were.   80
The Winter I'll not think on to spite thee,
But count it a lost season, so shall shee.
And dearest Friend, since we must part, drown night
With hope of Day, burthens well born are light.
Though cold and darkness longer hang somewhere,   85
Yet *Phoebus* equally lights all the Sphere.
And what he cannot in like Portions pay,
The world enjoyes in Mass, and so we may.
Be then ever your self, and let no woe
Win on your health, your youth, your beauty: so   90
Declare your self base fortunes Enemy,
No less by your contempt then constancy:
That I may grow enamoured on your mind,
When my own thoughts I there reflected find.
For this to th'comfort of my Dear I vow,   95
My Deeds shall still be what my words are now;
The Poles shall move to teach me ere I start;
And when I change my Love, I'll change my heart;
Nay, if I wax but cold in my desire,
Think, heaven hath motion lost, and the world, fire: 100
Much more I could, but many words have made
That, oft, suspected which men would perswade;
Take therefore all in this: I love so true,
As I will never look for less in you.

Elegie XIII

Julia

Harke newes, ô envy, thou shalt heare descry'd
My *Julia*; who as yet was ne'r envy'd.
To vomit gall in slander, swell her vaines
With calumny, that hell it selfe disdaines,
Is her continuall practice; does her best,   5
To teare opinion even out of the brest

Of dearest friends, and (which is worse than vilde)
Sticks jealousie in wedlock; her owne childe
Scapes not the showres of envie, To repeate
The monstrous fashions, how, were, alive, to eate   10
Deare reputation. Would to God she were
But halfe so loath to act vice, as to heare
My milde reproofe. Liv'd *Mantuan* now againe,
That fœmall Mastix, to limme with his penne
This she *Chymera*, that hath eyes of fire,   15
Burning with anger, anger feeds desire,
Tongued like the night-crow, whose ill boding cries
Give out for nothing but new injuries,
Her breath like to the juice in *Tenarus*
That blasts the springs, though ne'r so prosperous,   20
Her hands, I know not how, us'd more to spill
The food of others, then her selfe to fill.
But oh her minde, that *Orcus*, which includes
Legions of mischiefs, countlesse multitudes
Of formlesse curses, projects unmade up,   25
Abuses yet unfashion'd, thoughts corrupt,
Mishapen Cavils, palpable untroths,
Inevitable errours, self-accusing oaths:
These, like those Atoms swarming in the Sunne,
Throng in her bosome for creation.   30
I blush to give her halfe her due; yet say,
No poyson's halfe so bad as *Julia*.

Elegie XIV

A Tale of a Citizen and his Wife

I sing no harme good sooth to any wight,
To Lord or foole, Cuckold, begger or knight,
To peace-teaching Lawyer, Proctor, or brave
Reformed or reduced Captaine, Knave,
Officer, Jugler, or Justice of peace,   5
Juror or Judge; I touch no fat sowes grease,
I am no Libeller, nor will be any,
But (like a true man) say there are too many.
I feare not *ore tenus*; for my tale,
Nor Count nor Counsellour will redd or pale.   10

A Citizen and his wife the other day
Both riding on one horse, upon the way
I overtooke, the wench a pretty peate,
And (by her eye) well fitting for the feate.
I saw the lecherous Citizen turne backe   15
His head, and on his wifes lip steale a smacke,
Whence apprehending that the man was kinde,
Riding before, to kisse his wife behinde,
To get acquaintance with him I began
To sort discourse fit for so fine a man: 20
I ask'd the number of the Plaguy Bill,
Ask'd if the Custome Farmers held out still,
Of the Virginian plot, and whether Ward
The traffique of the Iland seas had marr'd,
Whether the Brittaine *Burse* did fill apace,   25
And likely were to give th'Exchange disgrace;
Of new-built *Algate*, and the *More-field* crosses,
Of store of Bankerouts, and poore Merchants losses
I urged him to speake; But he (as mute
As an old Courtier worne to his last suite)   30
Replies with onely yeas and nayes; At last
(To fit his element) my theame I cast
On Tradesmens gaines; that set his tongue agoing:
Alas, good sir (quoth he) *There is no doing
In Court nor City now*; she smil'd and I,   35
And (in my conscience) both gave him the lie
In one met thought: but he went on apace,
And at the present time with such a face
He rail'd, as fray'd me; for he gave no praise,
To any but my Lord of *Essex* dayes;   40
Call'd those the age of action; true (quoth Hee)
There's now as great an itch of bravery,
And heat of taking up, but cold lay downe,
For, put to push of pay, away they runne;
Our onely City trades of hope now are   45
Bawd, Tavern-keeper, Whore and Scrivener;
The much of Privileg'd kingsmen, and the store
Of fresh protections make the rest all poore;
In the first state of their Creation,
Though many stoutly stand, yet proves not one   50
A righteous pay-master. Thus ranne he on

In a continued rage: so void of reason
Seem'd his harsh talke, I sweat for feare of treason.
And (troth) how could I lesse? when in the prayer
For the protection of the wise Lord Major,   55
And his wise brethrens worships, when one prayeth,
He swore that none could say Amen with faith.
To get him off from what I glowed to heare,
(In happy time) an Angel did appeare,
The bright Signe of a lov'd and wel-try'd Inne,   60
Where many Citizens with their wives have bin
Well us'd and often; here I pray'd him stay,
To take some due refreshment by the way.
Looke how hee look'd that hid the gold (his hope)
And at's returne found nothing but a Rope,   65
So he on me, refus'd and made away,
Though willing she pleaded a weary day:
I found my misse, struck hands, and praid him tell
(To hold acquaintance still) where he did dwell;
He barely nam'd the street, promis'd the Wine,   70
But his kinde wife gave me the very Signe.

Elegie xv

The Expostulation

To make the doubt cleare, that no woman's true,
    Was it my fate to prove it strong in you?
Thought I, but one had breathed purest aire,
    And must she needs be false because she's faire?
Is it your beauties marke, or of your youth,   5
    Or your perfection, not to study truth?
Or thinke you heaven is deafe, or hath no eyes?
    Or those it hath, smile at your perjuries?
Are vowes so cheape with women, or the matter
    Whereof they are made, that they are writ in water,   10
And blowne away with winde? Or doth their breath
    (Both hot and cold at once) make life and death?
Who could have thought so many accents sweet
    Form'd into words, so many sighs should meete

As from our hearts, so many oathes, and teares   15
    Sprinkled among, (all sweeter by our feares
And the divine impression of stolne kisses,
    That seal'd the rest) should now prove empty blisses?
Did you draw bonds to forfet? signe to breake?
    Or must we reade you quite from what you speake,   20
And finde the truth out the wrong way? or must
    Hee first desire you false, would wish you just?
O I prophane, though most of women be
    This kinde of beast, my thought shall except thee;
My dearest love, though froward jealousie,   25
    With circumstance might urge thy'inconstancie,
Sooner I'll thinke the Sunne will cease to cheare
    The teeming earth, and *that* forget to beare,
Sooner that rivers will runne back, or Thames
    With ribs of Ice in June would bind his streames,   30
Or Nature, by whose strength the world endures,
    Would change her course, before you alter yours.
But O that treacherous breast to whom weake you
    Did trust our Counsells, and wee both may rue,
Having his falshood found too late, 'twas hee   35
    That made me *cast* you guilty, and you me,
Whilst he, black wretch, betray'd each simple word
    Wee spake, unto the cunning of a third.
Curst may hee be, that so our love hath slaine,
    And wander on the earth, wretched as *Cain*,   40
Wretched as hee, and not deserve least pitty;
    In plaguing him, let misery be witty;
Let all eyes shunne him, and hee shunne each eye,
    Till hee be noysome as his infamie;
May he without remorse deny God thrice,   45
    And not be trusted more on his Soules price;
And after all selfe torment, when hee dyes,
    May Wolves teare out his heart, Vultures his eyes,
Swine eate his bowels, and his falser tongue
    That utter'd all, be to some Raven flung,   50
And let his carrion coarse be a longer feast
    To the Kings dogges, then any other beast.
Now have I curst, let us our love revive;
    In mee the flame was never more alive;

I could beginne againe to court and praise,   55
   And in that pleasure lengthen the short dayes
Of my lifes lease; like Painters that do take
   Delight, not in made worke, but whiles they make;
I could renew those times, when first I saw
   Love in your eyes, that gave my tongue the law   60
To like what you lik'd; and at maskes and playes
   Commend the selfe same Actors, the same wayes;
Aske how you did, and often with intent
   Of being officious, be impertinent;
All which were such soft pastimes, as in these   65
   Love was as subtilly catch'd, as a disease;
But being got it is a treasure sweet,
   Which to defend is harder then to get:
And ought not be prophan'd on either part,
   For though 'tis got by *chance*, 'tis kept by *art*.   70

Elegie XVI

On his Mistris

By our first strange and fatall interview,
By all desires which thereof did ensue,
By our long starving hopes, by that remorse
Which my words masculine perswasive force
Begot in thee, and by the memory   5
Of hurts, which spies and rivals threatned me,
I calmly beg: But by thy fathers wrath,
By all paines, which want and divorcement hath,
I conjure thee, and all the oathes which I
And thou have sworne to seale joynt constancy,   10
Here I unsweare, and overswear them thus,
Thou shalt not love by wayes so dangerous.
Temper, ô faire Love, loves impetuous rage,
Be my true Mistris still, not my faign'd Page;
I'll goe, and, by thy kinde leave, leave behinde   15
Thee, onely worthy to nurse in my minde,

Thirst to come backe; ô if thou die before,
My soule from other lands to thee shall soare.
Thy (else Almighty) beautie cannot move
Rage from the Seas, nor thy love teach them love,   20
Nor tame wilde Boreas harshnesse; Thou hast reade
How roughly hee in peeces shivered
Faire Orithea, whom he swore he lov'd.
Fall ill or good, 'tis madnesse to have prov'd
Dangers unurg'd; Feed on this flattery,   25
That absent Lovers one in th'other be.
Dissemble nothing, not a boy, nor change
Thy bodies habite, nor mindes; bee not strange
To thy selfe onely; All will spie in thy face
A blushing womanly discovering grace;   30
Richly cloath'd Apes, are call'd Apes, and as soone
Ecclips'd as bright we call the Moone the Moone.
Men of France, changeable Camelions,
Spittles of diseases, shops of fashions,
Loves fuellers, and the rightest company   35
Of Players, which upon the worlds stage be,
Will quickly know thee, and no lesse, alas!
Th'indifferent Italian, as we passe
His warme land, well content to thinke thee Page,
Will hunt thee with such lust, and hideous rage,   40
As *Lots* faire guests were vext. But none of these
Nor spungy hydroptique Dutch shall thee displease,
If thou stay here. O stay here, for, for thee
England is onely a worthy Gallerie,
To walke in expectation, till from thence   45
Our greatest King call thee to his presence.
When I am gone, dreame me some happinesse,
Nor let thy lookes our long hid love confesse,
Nor praise, nor dispraise me, nor blesse nor curse
Openly loves force, nor in bed fright thy Nurse   50
With midnights startings, crying out, oh, oh
Nurse, ô my love is slaine, I saw him goe
O'r the white Alpes alone; I saw him I,
Assail'd, fight, taken, stabb'd, bleed, fall, and die.
Augure me better chance, except dread *Jove*   55
Thinke it enough for me to'have had thy love.

Elegie XVII

<*Variety*>

The heavens rejoyce in motion, why should I
Abjure my so much lov'd variety,
And not with many youth and love divide?
Pleasure is none, if not diversifi'd:
The sun that sitting in the chaire of light   5
Sheds flame into what else so ever doth seem bright,
Is not contented at one Signe to Inne,
But ends his year and with a new beginnes.
All things doe willingly in change delight,
The fruitfull mother of our appetite: 10
Rivers the clearer and more pleasing are,
Where their fair spreading streames run wide and farr;
And a dead lake that no strange bark doth greet,
Corrupts it self and what doth live in it.
Let no man tell me such a one is faire,   15
And worthy all alone my love to share.
Nature in her hath done the liberall part
Of a kinde Mistresse, and imploy'd her art
To make her loveable, and I aver
Him not humane that would turn back from her: 20
I love her well, and would, if need were, dye
To doe her service. But followes it that I
Must serve her onely, when I may have choice
Of other beauties, and in change rejoice?
The law is hard, and shall not have my voice.   25
The last I saw in all extreames is faire,
And holds me in the Sun-beames of her haire;
Her nymph-like features such agreements have
That I could venture with her to the grave:
Another's brown, I like her not the worse,   30
Her tongue is soft and takes me with discourse.
Others, for that they well descended are,
Do in my love obtain as large a share;
And though they be not fair, 'tis much with mee
To win their love onely for their degree.   35

And though I faile of my required ends,
The attempt is glorious and it self commends.
How happy were our Syres in ancient times,
Who held plurality of loves no crime!
With them it was accounted charity   40
To stirre up race of all indifferently;
Kindreds were not exempted from the bands:
Which with the Persian still in usage stands.
Women were then no sooner asked then won,
And what they did was honest and well done.   45
But since this title honour hath been us'd,
Our weake credulity hath been abus'd;
The golden laws of nature are repeald,
Which our first Fathers in such reverence held;
Our liberty's revers'd, our Charter's gone,   50
And we're made servants to opinion,
A monster in no certain shape attir'd,
And whose originall is much desir'd,
Formlesse at first, but growing on it fashions,
And doth prescribe manners and laws to nations.   55
Here love receiv'd immedicable harmes,
And was dispoiled of his daring armes.
A greater want then is his daring eyes,
He lost those awfull wings with which he flies;
His sinewy bow, and those immortall darts   60
Wherewith he'is wont to bruise resisting hearts.
Onely some few strong in themselves and free
Retain the seeds of antient liberty,
Following that part of Love although deprest,
And make a throne for him within their brest,   65
In spight of modern censures him avowing
Their Soveraigne, all service him allowing.
Amongst which troop although I am the least,
Yet equall in perfection with the best,
I glory in subjection of his hand,   70
Nor ever did decline his least command:
For in whatever forme the message came
My heart did open and receive the same.
But time will in his course a point discry
When I this loved service must deny,   75

For our allegiance temporary is,
With firmer age returnes our liberties.
What time in years and judgement we repos'd,
Shall not so easily be to change dispos'd,
Nor to the art of severall eyes obeying;   80
But beauty with true worth securely weighing,
Which being found assembled in some one,
Wee'l love her ever, and love her alone.

Elegie XVIII

Loves Progress

Who ever loves, if he do not propose
The right true end of love, he's one that goes
To sea for nothing but to make him sick:
Love is a bear-whelp born, if we o're lick
Our love, and force it new strange shapes to take,   5
We erre, and of a lump a monster make.
Were not a Calf a monster that were grown
Face'd like a man, though better then his own?
Perfection is in unitie: preferr
One woman first, and then one thing in her.   10
I, when I value gold, may think upon
The ductilness, the application,
The wholsomness, the ingenuitie,
From rust, from soil, from fire ever free:
But if I love it, 'tis because 'tis made   15
By our new nature (Use) the soul of trade.
    All these in women we might think upon
(If women had them) and yet love but one.
Can men more injure women then to say
They love them for that, by which they're not they?   20
Makes virtue woman? must I cool my bloud
Till I both be, and find one wise and good?
May barren Angels love so. But if we
Make love to woman; virtue is not she:
As beauty'is not nor wealth: He that strayes thus   25
From her to hers, is more adulterous,

Then if he took her maid. Search every spheare
And firmament, our *Cupid* is not there:
He's an infernal god and under ground,
With *Pluto* dwells, where gold and fire abound: 30
Men to such Gods, their sacrificing Coles
Did not in Altars lay, but pits and holes.
Although we see Celestial bodies move
Above the earth, the earth we Till and love:
So we her ayres contemplate, words and heart,   35
And virtues; but we love the Centrique part.
    Nor is the soul more worthy, or more fit
For love, then this, as infinite as it.
But in attaining this desired place
How much they erre; that set out at the face?   40
The hair a Forest is of Ambushes,
Of springes, snares, fetters and manacles:
The brow becalms us when 'tis smooth and plain,
And when 'tis wrinckled, shipwracks us again.
Smooth, 'tis a Paradice, where we would have   45
Immortal stay, and wrinkled 'tis our grave.
The Nose (like to the first Meridian) runs
Not 'twixt an East and West, but 'twixt two suns;
It leaves a Cheek, a rosie Hemisphere
On either side, and then directs us where   50
Upon the Islands fortunate we fall,
(Not faynte *Canaries,* but *Ambrosiall*)
Her swelling lips; To which when wee are come,
We anchor there, and think our selves at home,
For they seem all: there Syrens songs, and there   55
Wise Delphick Oracles do fill the ear;
There in a Creek where chosen pearls do swell,
The Remora, her cleaving tongue doth dwell.
These, and the glorious Promontory, her Chin
Ore past; and the streight *Hellespont* betweene   60
The *Sestos* and *Abydos* of her breasts,
(Not of two Lovers, but two Loves the neasts)
Succeeds a boundless sea, but yet thine eye
Some Island moles may scattered there descry;
And Sailing towards her *India,* in that way   65
Shall at her fair Atlantick Navell stay;

Though thence the Current be thy Pilot made,
Yet ere thou be where thou wouldst be embay'd,
Thou shalt upon another Forest set,
Where many Shipwrack, and no further get.   70
When thou art there, consider what this chace
Mispent by thy beginning at the face.
   Rather set out below; practice my Art,
Some Symetry the foot hath with that part
Which thou dost seek, and is thy Map for that   75
Lovely enough to stop, but not stay at:
Least subject to disguise and change it is;
Men say the Devil never can change his.
It is the Emblem that hath figured
Firmness; 'tis the first part that comes to bed.   80
Civilitie we see refin'd: the kiss
Which at the face began, transplanted is,
Since to the hand, since to the Imperial knee,
Now at the Papal foot delights to be:
If Kings think that the nearer way, and do   85
Rise from the foot, Lovers may do so too;
For as free Spheres move faster far then can
Birds, whom the air resists, so may that man
Which goes this empty and Ætherial way,
Then if at beauties elements he stay.   90
Rich Nature hath in women wisely made
Two purses, and their mouths aversely laid:
They then, which to the lower tribute owe,
That way which that Exchequer looks, must go:
He which doth not, his error is as great,   95
As who by Clyster gave the Stomack meat.

Elegie xix

Going to Bed

Come, Madam, come, all rest my powers defie,
Until I labour, I in labour lie.
The foe oft-times having the foe in sight,
Is tir'd with standing though he never fight.

Off with that girdle, like heavens Zone glittering,   5
But a far fairer world incompassing.
Unpin that spangled breastplate which you wear,
That th'eyes of busie fooles may be stopt there.
Unlace your self, for that harmonious chyme,
Tells me from you, that now it is bed time.   10
Off with that happy busk, which I envie,
That still can be, and still can stand so nigh.
Your gown going off, such beautious state reveals,
As when from flowry meads th'hills shadow steales.
Off with that wyerie Coronet and shew   15
The haiery Diademe which on you doth grow:
Now off with those shooes, and then safely tread
In this loves hallow'd temple, this soft bed.
In such white robes, heaven's Angels us'd to be
Receavd by men; Thou Angel bringst with thee   20
A heaven like Mahomets Paradise; and though
Ill spirits walk in white, we easly know,
By this these Angels from an evil sprite,
Those set our hairs, but these our flesh upright.

    Licence my roaving hands, and let them go,   25
Before, behind, between, above, below.
O my America! my new-found-land,
My kingdome, safeliest when with one man man'd,
My Myne of precious stones, My Emperie,
How blest am I in this discovering thee!   30
To enter in these bonds, is to be free;
Then where my hand is set, my seal shall be.

    Full nakedness! All joyes are due to thee,
As souls unbodied, bodies uncloth'd must be,
To taste whole joyes. Gems which you women use   35
Are like Atlanta's balls, cast in mens views,
That when a fools eye lighteth on a Gem,
His earthly soul may covet theirs, not them.
Like pictures, or like books gay coverings made
For lay-men, are all women thus array'd;   40
Themselves are mystick books, which only wee
(Whom their imputed grace will dignifie)
Must see reveal'd. Then since that I may know;
As liberally, as to a Midwife, shew

Thy self: cast all, yea, this white lynnen hence,   45
There is no pennance due to innocence.
    To teach thee, I am naked first; why than
What needst thou have more covering then a man.

Elegie xx

Loves Warre

Till I have peace with thee, warr other men,
And when I have peace, can I leave thee then?
All other Warrs are scrupulous; Only thou
O fayr free Citty, maist thyselfe allowe
To any one: In Flanders, who can tell   5
Whether the Master presse; or men rebell?
Only we know, that which all Ideots say,
They beare most blows which come to part the fray.
France in her lunatique giddiness did hate
Ever our men, yea and our God of late;   10
Yet she relyes upon our Angels well,
Which nere returne; no more then they which fell.
Sick Ireland is with a strange warr possest
Like to an Ague; now raging, now at rest;
Which time will cure: yet it must doe her good   15
If she were purg'd, and her head vayne let blood.
And Midas joyes our Spanish journeys give,
We touch all gold, but find no food to live.
And I should be in the hott parching clyme,
To dust and ashes turn'd before my time.   20
To mew me in a Ship, is to inthrall
Mee in a prison, that weare like to fall;
Or in a Cloyster; save that there men dwell
In a calme heaven, here in a swaggering hell.
Long voyages are long consumptions,   25
And ships are carts for executions.
Yea they are Deaths; Is't not all one to flye
Into an other World, as t'is to dye?
Here let mee warr; in these armes lett mee lye;
Here lett mee parlee, batter, bleede, and dye.   30
Thyne armes imprison me, and myne armes thee;
Thy hart thy ransome is; take myne for mee.

Other men war that they their rest may gayne;
But wee will rest that wee may fight agayne.
Those warrs the ignorant, these th'experienc'd love,   35
There wee are alwayes under, here above.
There Engins farr off breed a just true feare,
Neere thrusts, pikes, stabs, yea bullets hurt not here.
There lyes are wrongs; here safe uprightly lye;
There men kill men, we'will make one by and by.   40
Thou nothing; I not halfe so much shall do
In these Warrs, as they may which from us two
Shall spring. Thousands wee see which travaile not
To warrs; But stay swords, armes, and shott
To make at home; And shall not I do then   45
More glorious service, staying to make men?

Heroicall Epistle

Sapho to *Philaenis*

Where is that holy fire, which *Verse* is said
    To have? is that inchanting force decai'd?
Verse that drawes *Natures* workes, from *Natures* law,
    Thee, her best worke, to her worke cannot draw.
Have my teares quench'd my old *Poetique* fire;   5
    Why quench'd they not as well, that of *desire?*
Thoughts, my mindes creatures, often are with thee,
    But I, their maker, want their libertie.
Onely thine image, in my heart, doth sit,
    But that is waxe, and fires environ it.   10
My fires have driven, thine have drawne it hence;
    And I am rob'd of *Picture*, *Heart*, and *Sense*.
Dwells with me still mine irksome *Memory*,
    Which, both to keepe, and lose, grieves equally.
That tells me'how faire thou art: Thou art so faire,   15
    As, *gods*, when *gods* to thee I doe compare,
Are grac'd thereby; And to make blinde men see,
    What things *gods* are, I say they'are like to thee.

For, if we justly call each silly *man*
   A *litle world,* What shall we call thee than?   20
Thou art not soft, and cleare, and strait, and faire,
   As *Down,* as *Stars, Cedars,* and *Lillies* are,
But thy right hand, and cheek, and eye, only
   Are like thy other hand, and cheek, and eye.
Such was my *Phao* awhile, but shall be never,   25
   As thou, wast, art, and, oh, maist be ever.
Here lovers sweare in their *Idolatrie,*
   That I am such; but *Griefe* discolors me.
And yet I grieve the lesse, least *Griefe* remove
   My beauty, and make me'unworthy of thy love.   30
Plaies some soft boy with thee, oh there wants yet
   A mutuall feeling which should sweeten it.
His chinne, a thorny hairy unevennesse
   Doth threaten, and some daily change possesse.
Thy body is a naturall *Paradise,*   35
   In whose selfe, unmanur'd, all pleasure lies,
Nor needs *perfection*; why shouldst thou than
   Admit the tillage of a harsh rough man?
Men leave behinde them that which their sin showes,
   And are as theeves trac'd, which rob when it snowes.   40
But of our dallyance no more signes there are,
   Then *fishes* leave in streames, or *Birds* in aire.
And betweene us all sweetnesse may be had;
   All, all that *Nature* yields, or *Art* can adde.
My two lips, eyes, thighs, differ from thy two,   45
   But so, as thine from one another doe;
And, oh, no more; the likenesse being such,
   Why should they not alike in all parts touch?
Hand to strange hand, lippe to lippe none denies;
   Why should they brest to brest, or thighs to thighs?   50
Likenesse begets such strange selfe flatterie,
   That touching my selfe, all seemes done to thee.
My selfe I embrace, and mine owne hands I kisse,
   And amorously thanke my selfe for this.
Me, in my glasse, I call thee; But, alas,   55
   When I would kisse, teares dimme mine *eyes,* and *glasse.*
O cure this loving madnesse, and restore
   Me to mee; thee, my *halfe,* my *all,* my *more.*
So may thy cheekes red outweare scarlet dye,

And their white, whitenesse of the *Galaxy*,   60
So may thy mighty, amazing beauty move
     Envy'in all *women*, and in all *men, love*,
And so be *change*, and *sicknesse*, farre from thee,
     As thou by comming neere, keep'st them from me.

EPITHALAMIONS,

OR

MARRIAGE SONGS

*An Epithalamion, Or mariage Song on the
Lady* Elizabeth, *and* Count Palatine
being married on St. Valentines *day.*

Haile Bishop Valentine, whose day this is,
  All the Aire is thy Diocis,
  And all the chirping Choristers
And other birds are thy Parishioners,
   Thou marryest every yeare   5
The Lirique Larke, and the grave whispering Dove,
The Sparrow that neglects his life for love,
The household Bird, with the red stomacher,
  Thou mak'st the black bird speed as soone,
As doth the Goldfinch, or the Halcyon;   10
The husband cocke lookes out, and straight is sped,
And meets his wife, which brings her feather-bed.
This day more cheerfully then ever shine,
This day, which might enflame thy self, Old Valentine.

Till now, Thou warmd'st with multiplying loves   15
  Two larkes, two sparrowes, or two Doves,
   All that is nothing unto this,
For thou this day couplest two Phœnixes;
   Thou mak'st a Taper see
What the sunne never saw, and what the Arke   20
(Which was of foules, and beasts, the cage, and park,)
Did not containe, one bed containes, through Thee,
  Two Phœnixes, whose joyned breasts
Are unto one another mutuall nests,

127

Where motion kindles such fires, as shall give   25
Yong Phœnixes, and yet the old shall live.
Whose love and courage never shall decline,
But make the whole year through, thy day, O Valentine.

Up then faire Phœnix Bride, frustrate the Sunne,
        Thy selfe from thine affection   30
        Takest warmth enough, and from thine eye
All lesser birds will take their Jollitie.
        Up, up, faire Bride, and call,
Thy starres, from out their severall boxes, take
Thy Rubies, Pearles, and Diamonds forth, and make   35
Thy selfe a constellation, of them All,
        And by their blazing, signifie,
That a Great Princess falls, but doth not die;
Bee thou a new starre, that to us portends
Ends of much wonder; And be Thou those ends.   40
Since thou dost this day in new glory shine,
May all men date Records, from this thy Valentine.

Come forth, come forth, and as one glorious flame
        Meeting Another, growes the same,
        So meet thy Fredericke, and so   45
To an unseparable union growe.
        Since separation
Falls not on such things as are infinite,
Nor things which are but one, can disunite,
You'are twice inseparable, great, and one;   50
        Goe then to where the Bishop staies,
To make you one, his way, which divers waies
Must be effected; and when all is past,
And that you'are one, by hearts and hands made fast,
You two have one way left, your selves to'entwine,   55
Besides this Bishops knot, or Bishop Valentine.

But oh, what ailes the Sunne, that here he staies,
        Longer to day, then other daies?
        Staies he new light from these to get?
And finding here such store, is loth to set?   60

And why doe you two walke,
So slowly pac'd in this procession?
Is all your care but to be look'd upon,
And be to others spectacle, and talke?
    The feast, with gluttonous delaies,   65
Is eaten, and too long their meat they praise,
The masquers come too late, and'I thinke, will stay,
Like Fairies, till the Cock crow them away.
Alas, did not Antiquity assigne
A night, as well as day, to thee, O Valentine?   70

They did, and night is come; and yet wee see
    Formalities retarding thee.
    What meane these Ladies, which (as though
They were to take a clock in peeces,) goe
    So nicely about the Bride;   75
A Bride, before a good night could be said,
Should vanish from her cloathes, into her bed,
As Soules from bodies steale, and are not spy'd.
    But now she is laid; What though shee bee?
Yet there are more delayes, For, where is he?   80
He comes, and passes through Spheare after Spheare,
First her sheetes, then her Armes, then any where.
Let not this day, then, but this night be thine,
Thy day was but the eve to this, O Valentine.

Here lyes a shee Sunne, and a hee Moone here,   85
    She gives the best light to his Spheare,
    Or each is both, and all, and so
They unto one another nothing owe,
    And yet they doe, but are
So just and rich in that coyne which they pay,   90
That neither would, nor needs forbeare, nor stay;
Neither desires to be spar'd, nor to spare,
    They quickly pay their debt, and then
Take no acquittances, but pay again;
They pay, they give, they lend, and so let fall   95
No such occasion to be liberall.
More truth, more courage in these two do shine,
Then all thy turtles have, and sparrows, Valentine.

And by this act of these two Phenixes
    Nature againe restored is,   100
    For since these two are two no more,
Ther's but one Phenix still, as was before.
    Rest now at last, and wee
As Satyres watch the Sunnes uprise, will stay
Waiting, when your eyes opened, let out day,   105
Onely desir'd, because your face wee see;
    Others neare you shall whispering speake,
And wagers lay, at which side day will breake,
And win by'observing, then, whose hand it is
That opens first a curtaine, hers or his;   110
This will be tryed to morrow after nine,
Till which houre, wee thy day enlarge, O Valentine.

Ecclogve
1613. *December* 26

Allophanes *finding* Idios *in the country in Christmas time,*
   reprehends his absence from court, at the mariage Of
   the Earle of Sommerset; Idios *gives an account of his*
   purpose therein, and of his absence thence.

Allophanes.
Vnseasonable man, statue of ice,
    What could to countries solitude entice
Thee, in this yeares cold and decrepit time?
    Natures instinct drawes to the warmer clime   5
Even small birds, who by that courage dare,
    In numerous fleets, saile through their Sea, the aire.
What delicacie can in fields appeare,
    Whil'st Flora'herselfe doth a freeze jerkin weare?
Whil'st windes do all the trees and hedges strip   10
    Of leafes, to furnish roddes enough to whip
Thy madnesse from thee; and all springs by frost
    Have taken cold, and their sweet murmures lost;
If thou thy faults or fortunes would'st lament
    With just solemnity, do it in Lent;   15

At Court the spring already advanced is,
    The Sunne stayes longer up; and yet not his
The glory is, farre other, other fires.
    First, zeale to Prince and State; then loves desires
Burne in one brest, and like heavens two great lights,   20
    The first doth governe dayes, the other nights.
And then that early light, which did appeare
    Before the Sunne and Moone created were,
The Princes favour is defus'd o'r all,
    From which all Fortunes, Names, and Natures fall;   25
Then from those wombes of starres, the Brides bright eyes,
    At every glance, a constellation flyes,
And sowes the Court with starres, and doth prevent
    In light and power, the all-ey'd firmament;
First her eyes kindle other Ladies eyes,   30
    Then from their beames their jewels lusters rise,
And from their jewels torches do take fire,
    And all is warmth, and light, and good desire;
Most other Courts, alas, are like to hell,
    Where in darke plotts, fire without light doth dwell: 35
Or but like Stoves, for lust and envy get
    Continuall, but artificiall heat;
Here zeale and love growne one, all clouds disgest,
    And make our Court an everlasting East.
And can'st thou be from thence?   40

Idios.

                No, I am there.
    As heaven, to men dispos'd, is every where,
So are those Courts, whose Princes animate,
    Not onely all their house, but all their State.   45
Let no man thinke, because he is full, he hath all,
    Kings (as their patterne, God) are liberall
Not onely in fulnesse, but capacitie,
    Enlarging narrow men, to feele and see,
And comprehend the blessings they bestow.   50
    So, reclus'd hermits often times do know
More of heavens glory, then a worldling can.
    As man is of the world, the heart of man,

Is an epitome of Gods great booke
    Of creatures, and man need no farther looke;   55
So is the Country of Courts, where sweet peace doth,
    As their one common soule, give life to both,
I am not then from Court.

Allophanes.
                        Dreamer, thou art.   60
    Think'st thou fantastique that thou hast a part
In the East-Indian fleet, because thou hast
    A little spice, or Amber in thy taste?
Because thou art not frozen, art thou warme?
    Seest thou all good because thou seest no harme?   65
The earth doth in her inward bowels hold
    Stuffe well dispos'd, and which would faine be gold,
But never shall, except it chance to lye,
    So upward, that heaven gild it with his eye;
As, for divine things, faith comes from above,   70
    So, for best civil use, all tinctures move
From higher powers; From God religion springs,
    Wisdome, and honour from the use of Kings.
Then unbeguile thy selfe, and know with mee,
    That Angels, though on earth employd they bee,   75
Are still in heav'n, so is hee still at home
    That doth, abroad, to honest actions come.
Chide thy selfe then, O foole, which yesterday
    Might'st have read more then all thy books bewray;
Hast thou a history, which doth present   80
    A Court, where all affections do assent
Unto the Kings, and that, that Kings are just?
    And where it is no levity to trust?
Where there is no ambition, but to'obey,
    Where men need whisper nothing, and yet may;   85
Where the Kings favours are so plac'd, that all
    Finde that the King therein is liberall
To them, in him, because his favours bend
    To vertue, to the which they all pretend?
Thou hast no such; yet here was this, and more,   90
    An earnest lover, wise then, and before.
Our little Cupid hath sued Livery,
    And is no more in his minority,

Hee is admitted now into that brest
　　Where the Kings Counsells and his secrets rest.　　95
What hast thou lost, O ignorant man?

Idios.

　　　　　　　　I knew
　　All this, and onely therefore I withdrew.
To know and feele all this, and not to have　　100
　　Words to expresse it, makes a man a grave
Of his owne thoughts; I would not therefore stay
　　At a great feast, having no Grace to say.
And yet I scap'd not here; for being come
　　Full of the common joy, I utter'd some;　　105
Reade then this nuptiall song, which was not made
　　Either the Court or mens hearts to invade,
But since I'am dead, and buried, I could frame
　　No Epitaph, which might advance my fame
So much as this poore song, which testifies　　110
　　I did unto that day some sacrifice.

Epithalamion

The time of the Mariage

Thou art repriv'd old yeare, thou shalt not die,
　　Though thou upon thy death bed lye,
　　And should'st within five dayes expire,
Yet thou art rescu'd by a mightier fire,
　　Then thy old Soule, the Sunne,　　5
When he doth in his largest circle runne.
The passage of the West or East would thaw,
And open wide their easie liquid jawe
To all our ships, could a Promethean art
Either unto the Northerne Pole impart　　10
The fire of these inflaming eyes, or of this loving heart.

Equality of persons

But undiscerning Muse, which heart, which eyes,
　　In this new couple, dost thou prize,

When his eye as inflaming is
As hers, and her heart loves as well as his?
   Be tryed by beauty, and than   5
The bridegroome is a maid, and not a man.
If by that manly courage they be tryed,
Which scornes unjust opinion; then the bride
Becomes a man. Should chance or envies Art
Divide these two, whom nature scarce did part?   10
Since both have both th'enflaming eyes, and both the
     loving heart.

Raysing of the Bridegroome

Though it be some divorce to thinke of you
   Singly, so much one are you two,
   Yet let me here contemplate thee,
First, cheerfull Bridegroome, and first let mee see,
   How thou prevent'st the Sunne,   5
And his red foming horses dost outrunne,
How, having laid downe in thy Soveraignes brest
All businesses, from thence to reinvest
Them, when these triumphs cease, thou forward art
To shew to her, who doth the like impart,   10
The fire of thy inflaming eyes, and of thy loving heart.

Raising of the Bride

But now, to Thee, faire Bride, it is some wrong,
   To thinke thou wert in Bed so long,
   Since Soone thou lyest downe first, tis fit
Thou in first rising should'st allow for it.
   Pouder thy Radiant haire,   5
Which if without such ashes thou would'st weare,
Thou, which to all which come to looke upon,
Art meant for Phœbus, would'st be Phaëton.
For our ease, give thine eyes th'unusual part
Of joy, a Teare; so quencht, thou maist impart,   10
To us that come, thy inflaming eyes, to him, thy loving heart.

Her Apparrelling

Thus thou descend'st to our infirmitie,
    Who can the Sun in water see.
    Soe dost thou, when in silke and gold,
Thou cloudst thy selfe; since wee which doe behold,
      Are dust, and wormes, 'tis just   5
Our objects be the fruits of wormes and dust;
Let every Jewell be a glorious starre,
Yet starres are not so pure, as their spheares are.
And though thou stoope, to'appeare to us in part,
Still in that Picture thou intirely art,   10
Which thy inflaming eyes have made within his loving heart.

Going to the Chappell

Now from your Easts you issue forth, and wee,
    As men which through a Cipres see
    The rising sun, doe thinke it two,
Soe, as you goe to Church, doe thinke of you,
      But that vaile being gone,   5
By the Church rites you are from thenceforth one.
The Church Triumphant made this match before,
And now the Militant doth strive no more;
Then, reverend Priest, who Gods Recorder art,
Doe, from his Dictates, to these two impart   10
All blessings, which are seene, or thought, by Angels eye
    or heart.

The Benediction

Blest payre of Swans, Oh may you interbring
    Daily new joyes, and never sing,
    Live, till all grounds of wishes faile,
Till honor, yea till wisedome grow so stale,
      That, new great heights to trie,   5
It must serve your ambition, to die;
Raise heires, and may here, to the worlds end, live
Heires from this King, to take thankes, you, to give,

Nature and grace doe all, and nothing Art.
May never age, or error overthwart   10
With any West, these radiant eyes, with any North, this
    heart.

Feasts and Revells

But you are over-blest. Plenty this day
        Injures; it causeth time to stay;
        The tables groane, as though this feast
Would, as the flood, destroy all fowle and beast.
            And were the doctrine new   5
That the earth mov'd, this day would make it true;
For every part to dance and revell goes.
They tread the ayre, and fal not where they rose.
Though six houres since, the Sunne to bed did part,
The masks and banquets will not yet impart   10
A sunset to these weary eyes, A Center to this heart.

The Brides going to bed

What mean'st thou Bride, this companie to keep?
        To sit up, till thou faine wouldst sleep?
        Thou maist not, when thou art laid, doe so.
Thy selfe must to him a new banquet grow,
            And you must entertaine   5
And doe all this daies dances o'r againe.
Know that if Sun and Moone together doe
Rise in one point, they doe not set so too;
Therefore thou maist, faire Bride, to bed depart,
Thou art not gone, being gone; where e'r thou art,   10
Thou leav'st in him thy watchfull eyes, in him thy loving
    heart.

The Bridegroomes comming

As he that sees a starre fall, runs apace,
        And findes a gellie in the place,

So doth the Bridegroome hast as much,
Being told this starre is falne, and findes her such.
    And as friends may looke strange,   5
By a new fashion, or apparrells change,
Their soules, though long acquainted they had beene,
These clothes, their bodies, never yet had seene;
Therefore at first shee modestly might start,
But must forthwith surrender every part,   10
As freely, as each to each before, gave either eye or heart.

The good-night

Now, as in Tullias tombe, one lampe burnt cleare,
    Unchang'd for fifteene hundred yeare,
    May these love-lamps we here enshrine,
In warmth, light, lasting, equall the divine.
    Fire ever doth aspire,   5
And makes all like it selfe, turnes all to fire,
But ends in ashes, which these cannot doe,
For none of these is fuell, but fire too.
This is joyes bonfire, then, where loves strong Arts
Make of so noble individuall parts   10
One fire of foure inflaming eyes, and of two loving hearts.

Idios.
As I have brought this song, that I may doe
    A perfect sacrifice, I'll burne it too.

Allophanes.   15
No Sr. This paper I have justly got,
    For, in burnt incense, the perfume is not
His only that presents it, but of all;
    What ever celebrates this Festivall
Is common, since the joy thereof is so.   20
    Nor may your selfe be Priest: But let me goe,
Backe to the Court, and I will lay'it upon
    Such Altars, as prize your devotion.

Epithalamion made at Lincolnes Inne

    The Sun-beames in the East are spred,
    Leave, leave, faire Bride, your solitary bed,

No more shall you returne to it alone,
It nourseth sadnesse, and your bodies print,
Like to a grave, the yielding downe doth dint;   5
      You and your other you meet there anon;
        Put forth, put forth that warme balme-breathing thigh,
Which when next time you in these sheets wil smother,
      There it must meet another,
        Which never was, but must be, oft, more nigh;   10
Come glad from thence, goe gladder then you came,
To day put on perfection, and a womans name.

Daughters of London, you which bee
Our Golden Mines, and furnish'd Treasurie,
      You which are Angels, yet still bring with you   15
Thousands of Angels on your mariage daies,
Help with your presence and devise to praise
      These rites, which also unto you grow due;
        Conceitedly dresse her, and be assign'd,
By you, fit place for every flower and jewell,   20
      Make her for love fit fewell
        As gay as Flora, and as rich as Inde;
So may shee faire, rich, glad, and in nothing lame,
To day put on perfection, and a womans name.

And you frolique Patricians,   25
Sonnes of these Senators, wealths deep oceans,
      Ye painted courtiers, barrels of others wits,
Yee country men, who but your beasts love none,
Yee of those fellowships whereof hee's one,
      Of study and play made strange Hermaphrodits,   30
        Here shine; This Bridegroom to the Temple bring.
Loe, in yon path which store of straw'd flowers graceth,
      The sober virgin paceth;
        Except my sight faile, 'tis no other thing;
Weep not nor blush, here is no griefe nor shame,   35
To day put on perfection, and a womans name.

Thy two-leav'd gates faire Temple unfold,
And these two in thy sacred bosome hold,
      Till, mystically joyn'd, but one they bee;

Then may thy leane and hunger-starved wombe   40
Long time expect their bodies and their tombe,
   Long after their owne parents fatten thee.
   All elder claimes, and all cold barrennesse,
All yeelding to new loves bee far for ever,
     Which might these two dissever,   45
       All wayes all th'other may each one possesse;
For, the best Bride, best worthy of praise and fame,
To day puts on perfection, and a womans name.

Oh winter dayes bring much delight,
Not for themselves, but for they soon bring night;   50
   Other sweets wait thee then these diverse meats,
Other disports then dancing jollities,
Other love tricks then glancing with the eyes,
     But that the Sun still in our halfe Spheare sweates;
       Hee flies in winter, but he now stands still.   55
Yet shadowes turne; Noone point he hath attain'd,
   His steeds nill bee restrain'd,
     But gallop lively downe the Westerne hill;
Thou shalt, when he hath runne the worlds half frame,
To night put on perfection, and a womans name.   60

The amorous evening starre is rose,
Why then should not our amorous starre inclose
   Her selfe in her wish'd bed? Release your strings
Musicians, and dancers take some truce
With these your pleasing labours, for great use   65
     As much wearinesse as perfection brings;
       You, and not only you, but all toyl'd beasts
Rest duly; at night all their toyles are dispensed;
   But in their beds commenced
     Are other labours, and more dainty feasts;   70
She goes a maid, who, least she turne the same,
To night puts on perfection, and a womans name.

Thy virgins girdle now untie,
And in thy nuptiall bed (loves altar) lye
   A pleasing sacrifice; now dispossesse   75
Thee of these chaines and robes which were put on
T'adorne the day, not thee; for thou, alone,
     Like vertue'and truth, art best in nakednesse;

This bed is onely to virginitie
A grave, but, to a better state, a cradle;   80
Till now thou wast but able
    To be what now thou art; then that by thee
No more be said, *I may bee*, but, *I am*,
To night put on perfection, and a womans name.

Even like a faithfull man content,   85
That this life for a better should be spent,
    So, shee a mothers rich stile doth preferre,
And at the Bridegroomes wish'd approach doth lye,
Like an appointed lambe, when tenderly
    The priest comes on his knees t'embowell her;   90
        Now sleep or watch with more joy; and O light
Of heaven, to morrow rise thou hot, and early;
This Sun will love so dearely
        Her rest, that long, long we shall want her sight;
Wonders are wrought, for shee which had no maime,   95
To night puts on perfection, and a womans name.

SATYRES

Satyre I

Away thou fondling motley humorist,
Leave mee, and in this standing woodden chest,
Consorted with these few bookes, let me lye
In prison, and here be coffin'd, when I dye;
Here are Gods conduits, grave Divines; and here   5
Natures Secretary, the Philosopher;
And jolly Statesmen, which teach how to tie
The sinewes of a cities mistique bodie;
Here gathering Chroniclers, and by them stand
Giddie fantastique Poëts of each land.   10
Shall I leave all this constant company,
And follow headlong, wild uncertaine thee?
First sweare by thy best love in earnest
(If thou which lov'st all, canst love any best)
Thou wilt not leave mee in the middle street,   15
Though some more spruce companion thou dost meet,
Not though a Captaine do come in thy way
Bright parcell gilt, with forty dead mens pay,
Not though a briske perfum'd piert Courtier
Deigne with a nod, thy courtesie to answer.   20
Nor come a velvet Justice with a long
Great traine of blew coats, twelve, or fourteen strong,
Wilt thou grin or fawne on him, or prepare
A speech to Court his beautious sonne and heire!
For better or worse take mee, or leave mee: 25
To take, and leave mee is adultery.
Oh monstrous, superstitious puritan,
Of refin'd manners, yet ceremoniall man,
That when thou meet'st one, with enquiring eyes
Dost search, and like a needy broker prize   30

The silke, and gold he weares, and to that rate
So high or low, dost raise thy formall hat:
That wilt consort none, untill thou have knowne
What lands hee hath in hope, or of his owne,
As though all thy companions should make thee   35
Jointures, and marry thy deare company.
Why should'st thou (that dost not onely approve,
But in ranke itchie lust, desire, and love
The nakednesse and barenesse to enjoy,
Of thy plumpe muddy whore, or prostitute boy)   40
Hate vertue, though shee be naked, and bare?
At birth, and death, our bodies naked are;
And till our Soules be unapparrelled
Of bodies, they from blisse are banished.
Mans first blest state was naked, when by sinne   45
Hee lost that, yet hee was cloath'd but in beasts skin,
And in this course attire, which I now weare,
With God, and with the Muses I conferre.
But since thou like a contrite penitent,
Charitably warn'd of thy sinnes, dost repent   50
These vanities, and giddinesses, loe
I shut my chamber doore, and come, lets goe.
But sooner may a cheape whore, who hath beene
Worne by as many severall men in sinne,
As are black feathers, or musk-colour hose,   55
Name her childs right true father, 'mongst all those:
Sooner may one guesse, who shall beare away
The Infanta of London, Heire to an India;
And sooner may a gulling weather Spie
By drawing forth heavens Scheme tell certainly   60
What fashioned hats, or ruffes, or suits next yeare
Our subtile-witted antique youths will weare;
Then thou, when thou depart'st from mee, canst show
Whither, why, when, or with whom thou wouldst go.
But how shall I be pardon'd my offence   65
That thus have sinn'd against my conscience?
Now we are in the street; He first of all
Improvidently proud, creepes to the wall,
And so imprisoned, and hem'd in by mee
Sells for a little state his libertie;   70

Yet though he cannot skip forth now to greet
Every fine silken painted foole we meet,
He them to him with amorous smiles allures,
And grins, smacks, shrugs, and such an itch endures,
As prentises, or schoole-boyes which doe know   75
Of some gay sport abroad, yet dare not goe.
And as fidlers stop lowest, at highest sound,
So to the most brave, stoops hee nigh'st the ground.
But to a grave man, he doth move no more
Then the wise politique horse would heretofore,   80
Or thou O Elephant or Ape wilt doe,
When any names the King of Spaine to you.
Now leaps he upright, Joggs me, & cryes, Do you see
Yonder well favoured youth? Which? Oh, 'tis hee
That dances so divinely; Oh, said I,   85
Stand still, must you dance here for company?
Hee droopt, wee went, till one (which did excell
Th'Indians, in drinking his Tobacco well)
Met us; they talk'd; I whispered, let'us goe,
'T may be you smell him not, truely I doe;   90
He heares not mee, but, on the other side
A many-coloured Peacock having spide,
Leaves him and mee; I for my lost sheep stay;
He followes, overtakes, goes on the way,
Saying, him whom I last left, all repute   95
For his device, in hansoming a sute,
To judge of lace, pinke, panes, print, cut, and pleite,
Of all the Court, to have the best conceit;
Our dull Comedians want him, let him goe;
But Oh, God strengthen thee, why stoop'st thou so?   100
Why? he hath travayld; Long? No; but to me
(Which understand none,) he doth seeme to be
Perfect French, and Italian; I replyed,
So is the Poxe; He answered not, but spy'd
More men of sort, of parts, and qualities;   105
At last his Love he in a windowe spies,
And like light dew exhal'd, he flings from mee
Violently ravish'd to his lechery.
Many were there, he could command no more;
Hee quarrell'd, fought, bled; and turn'd out of dore 110

Directly came to mee hanging the head,
And constantly a while must keepe his bed.

Satyre ii

Sir; though (I thanke God for it) I do hate
Perfectly all this towne, yet there's one state
In all ill things so excellently best,
That hate, toward them, breeds pitty towards the rest.
Though Poëtry indeed be such a sinne   5
As I thinke That brings dearths, and Spaniards in,
Though like the Pestilence and old fashion'd love,
Ridlingly it catch men; and doth remove
Never, till it be sterv'd out; yet their state
Is poore, disarm'd, like Papists, not worth hate.   10
One, (like a wretch, which at Barre judg'd as dead,
Yet prompts him which stands next, and cannot reade,
And saves his life) gives ideot actors meanes
(Starving himselfe) to live by his labor'd sceanes;
As in some Organ, Puppits dance above   15
And bellows pant below, which them do move.
One would move Love by rithmes; but witchcrafts charms
Bring not now their old feares, nor their old harmes:
Rammes, and slings now are seely battery,
Pistolets are the best Artillerie.   20
And they who write to Lords, rewards to get,
Are they not like singers at doores for meat?
And they who write, because all write, have still
That excuse for writing, and for writing ill;
But hee is worst, who (beggarly) doth chaw   25
Others wits fruits, and in his ravenous maw
Rankly digested, doth those things out-spue,
As his owne things; and they are his owne, 'tis true,
For if one eate my meate, though it be knowne
The meate was mine, th'excrement is his owne: 30
But these do mee no harme, nor they which use
To out-doe Dildoes, and out-usure Jewes;
To out-drinke the sea, to out-sweare the Letanie;
Who with sinnes all kindes as familiar bee
As Confessors; and for whose sinfull sake,   35
Schoolemen new tenements in hell must make:

Whose strange sinnes, Canonists could hardly tell
In which Commandements large receit they dwell.
But these punish themselves; the insolence
Of Coscus onely breeds my just offence,   40
Whom time (which rots all, and makes botches poxe,
And plodding on, must make a calfe an oxe)
Hath made a Lawyer, which was (alas) of late
But a scarce Poët; jollier of this state,
Then are new benefic'd ministers, he throwes   45
Like nets, or lime-twigs, wheresoever he goes,
His title of Barrister, on every wench,
And wooes in language of the Pleas, and Bench:
A motion, Lady; Speake Coscus; I have beene
In love, ever since *tricesimo* of the Queene,   50
Continuall claimes I have made, injunctions got
To stay my rivals suit, that hee should not
Proceed; spare mee; In Hillary terme I went,
You said, If I return'd next size in Lent,
I should be in remitter of your grace;   55
In th'interim my letters should take place
Of affidavits: words, words, which would teare
The tender labyrinth of a soft maids eare,
More, more, then ten Sclavonians scolding, more
Then when winds in our ruin'd Abbeyes rore.   60
When sicke with Poëtrie, and possest with muse
Thou wast, and mad, I hop'd; but men which chuse
Law practise for meere gaine, bold soule, repute
Worse then imbrothel'd strumpets prostitute.
Now like an owelike watchman, hee must walke   65
His hand still at a bill, now he must talke
Idly, like prisoners, which whole months will sweare
That onely suretiship hath brought them there,
And to every suitor lye in every thing,
Like a Kings favourite, yea like a King;   70
Like a wedge in a blocke, wring to the barre,
Bearing-like Asses; and more shamelesse farre
Then carted whores, lye, to the grave Judge; for
Bastardy abounds not in Kings titles, nor
Symonie and Sodomy in Churchmens lives,   75
As these things do in him; by these he thrives.

Shortly (as the sea) hee will compasse all our land;
From Scots, to Wight; from Mount, to Dover strand.
And spying heires melting with luxurie,
Satan will not joy at their sinnes, as hee.　　　　　　80
For as a thrifty wench scrapes kitching-stuffe,
And barrelling the droppings, and the snuffe,
Of wasting candles, which in thirty yeare
(Relique-like kept) perchance buyes wedding geare;
Peecemeale he gets lands, and spends as much time　　85
Wringing each Acre, as men pulling prime.
In parchments then, large as his fields, hee drawes
Assurances, bigge, as gloss'd civill lawes,
So huge, that men (in our times forwardnesse)
Are Fathers of the Church for writing lesse.　　　　　90
These hee writes not; nor for these written payes,
Therefore spares no length; as in those first dayes
When Luther was profest, He did desire
Short *Pater nosters*, saying as a Fryer
Each day his beads, but having left those lawes,　　95
Addes to Christs prayer, the Power and glory clause.
But when he sells or changes land, he'impaires
His writings, and (unwatch'd) leaves out, *ses heires*,
As slily as any Commenter goes by
Hard words, or sense; or in Divinity　　　　　　　　100
As controverters, in vouch'd Texts, leave out
Shrewd words, which might against them cleare the doubt.
Where are those spred woods which cloth'd hertofore
Those bought lands? not built, nor burnt within dore.
Where's th'old landlords troops, and almes? In great hals　105
Carthusian fasts, and fulsome Bachanalls
Equally I hate; meanes blesse; in rich mens homes
I bid kill some beasts, but no Hecatombs,
None starve, none surfet so; But (Oh) we allow,
Good workes as good, but out of fashion now,　　　110
Like old rich wardrops; but my words none drawes
Within the vast reach of th'huge statute lawes.

Satyre III

Kinde pitty chokes my spleene; brave scorn forbids
Those teares to issue which swell my eye-lids;
I must not laugh, nor weepe sinnes, and be wise,
Can railing then cure these worne maladies?
Is not our Mistresse faire Religion,   5
As worthy of all our Soules devotion,
As vertue was to the first blinded age?
Are not heavens joyes as valiant to asswage
Lusts, as earths honour was to them? Alas,
As wee do them in meanes, shall they surpasse   10
Us in the end, and shall thy fathers spirit
Meete blinde Philosophers in heaven, whose merit
Of strict life may be imputed faith, and heare
Thee, whom hee taught so easie wayes and neare
To follow, damn'd? O if thou dar'st, feare this;   15
This feare great courage, and high valour is.
Dar'st thou ayd mutinous Dutch, and dar'st thou lay
Thee in ships woodden Sepulchers, a prey
To leaders rage, to stormes, to shot, to dearth?
Dar'st thou dive seas, and dungeons of the earth?   20
Hast thou couragious fire to thaw the ice
Of frozen North discoveries? and thrise
Colder then Salamanders, like divine
Children in th'oven, fires of Spaine, and the line,
Whose countries limbecks to our bodies bee,   25
Canst thou for gaine beare? and must every hee
Which cryes not, Goddesse, to thy Mistresse, draw,
Or eate thy poysonous words? courage of straw!
O desperate coward, wilt thou seeme bold, and
To thy foes and his (who made thee to stand   30
Sentinell in his worlds garrison) thus yeeld,
And for forbidden warres, leave th'appointed field?
Know thy foes: The foule Devill (whom thou
Strivest to please,) for hate, not love, would allow
Thee faine, his whole Realme to be quit; and as   35
The worlds all parts wither away and passe,
So the worlds selfe, thy other lov'd foe, is
In her decrepit wayne, and thou loving this,

Dost love a withered and worne strumpet; last,
Flesh (it selfes death) and joyes which flesh can taste, 40
Thou lovest; and thy faire goodly soule, which doth
Give this flesh power to taste joy, thou dost loath.
Seeke true religion. O where? Mirreus
Thinking her unhous'd here, and fled from us,
Seekes her at Rome, there, because hee doth know 45
That shee was there a thousand yeares agoe,
He loves her ragges so, as wee here obey
The statecloth where the Prince sate yesterday.
Crantz to such brave Loves will not be inthrall'd,
But loves her onely, who at Geneva is call'd 50
Religion, plaine, simple, sullen, yong,
Contemptuous, yet unhansome; As among
Lecherous humors, there is one that judges
No wenches wholsome, but course country drudges.
Graius stayes still at home here, and because 55
Some Preachers, vile ambitious bauds, and lawes
Still new like fashions, bid him thinke that shee
Which dwels with us, is onely perfect, hee
Imbraceth her, whom his Godfathers will
Tender to him, being tender, as Wards still 60
Take such wives as their Guardians offer, or
Pay valewes. Carelesse Phrygius doth abhorre
All, because all cannot be good, as one
Knowing some women whores, dares marry none.
Graccus loves all as one, and thinkes that so 65
As women do in divers countries goe
In divers habits, yet are still one kinde,
So doth, so is Religion; and this blind-
nesse too much light breeds; but unmoved thou
Of force must one, and forc'd but one allow; 70
And the right; aske thy father which is shee,
Let him aske his; though truth and falshood bee
Neare twins, yet truth a little elder is;
Be busie to seeke her, beleeve mee this,
Hee's not of none, nor worst, that seekes the best. 75
To adore, or scorne an image, or protest,
May all be bad; doubt wisely; in strange way
To stand inquiring right, is not to stray;

To sleepe, or runne wrong, is. On a huge hill,
Cragged, and steep, Truth stands, and hee that will   80
Reach her, about must, and about must goe;
And what the hills suddennes resists, winne so;
Yet strive so, that before age, deaths twilight,
Thy Soule rest, for none can worke in that night.
To will, implyes delay, therefore now doe: 85
Hard deeds, the bodies paines; hard knowledge too
The mindes indeavours reach, and mysteries
Are like the Sunne, dazling, yet plaine to all eyes.
Keepe the truth which thou hast found; men do not stand
In so ill case here, that God hath with his hand   90
Sign'd Kings blanck-charters to kill whom they hate,
Nor are they Vicars, but hangmen to Fate.
Foole and wretch, wilt thou let thy Soule be tyed
To mans lawes, by which she shall not be tryed
At the last day? Oh, will it then boot thee   95
To say a Philip, or a Gregory,
A Harry, or a Martin taught thee this?
Is not this excuse for mere contraries,
Equally strong? cannot both sides say so?
That thou mayest rightly obey power, her bounds know; 100
Those past, her nature, and name is chang'd; to be
Then humble to her is idolatrie.
As streames are, Power is; those blest flowers that dwell
At the rough streames calme head, thrive and do well,
But having left their roots, and themselves given   105
To the streames tyrannous rage, alas, are driven
Through mills, and rockes, and woods, and at last, almost
Consum'd in going, in the sea are lost:
So perish Soules, which more chuse mens unjust
Power from God claym'd, then God himselfe to trust.   110

Satyre IIII

Well; I may now receive, and die; My sinne
Indeed is great, but I have beene in
A Purgatorie, such as fear'd hell is
A recreation to, and scarse map of this.

My minde, neither with prides itch nor yet hath been 5
Poyson'd with love to see, or to bee seene,
I had no suit there, nor new suite to shew,
Yet went to Court; But as Glaze which did goe
To'a Masse in jest, catch'd, was faine to disburse
The hundred markes, which is the Statutes curse; 10
Before he scapt, So'it pleas'd my destinie
(Guilty of my sin of going,) to thinke me
As prone to all ill, and of good as forget-
full, as proud, as lustfull, and as much in debt,
As vaine, as witlesse, and as false as they 15
Which dwell at Court, for once going that way.
Therefore I suffered this; Towards me did runne
A thing more strange, then on Niles slime, the Sunne
E'r bred; or all which into Noahs Arke came;
A thing, which would have pos'd Adam to name; 20
Stranger then seaven Antiquaries studies,
Then Africks Monsters, Guianaes rarities.
Stranger then strangers; One, who for a Dane,
In the Danes Massacre had sure beene slaine,
If he had liv'd then; And without helpe dies, 25
When next the Prentises 'gainst Strangers rise.
One, whom the watch at noone lets scarce goe by,
One, to whom, the examining Justice sure would cry,
Sir, by your priesthood tell me what you are.
His cloths were strange, though coarse; and black, though 30
    bare;
Sleevelesse his jerkin was, and it had beene
Velvet, but 'twas now (so much ground was seene)
Become Tufftaffatie; and our children shall
See it plaine Rashe awhile, then nought at all. 35
This thing hath travail'd, and saith, speakes all tongues
And only knoweth what to all States belongs.
Made of th'Accents, and best phrase of all these,
He speakes no language; If strange meats displease,
Art can deceive, or hunger force my tast, 40
But Pedants motley tongue, souldiers bumbast,
Mountebankes drugtongue, nor the termes of law
Are strong enough preparatives, to draw
Me to beare this: yet I must be content
With his tongue, in his tongue call'd complement: 45

In which he can win widdowes, and pay scores,
Make men speake treason, cosen subtlest whores,
Out-flatter favorites, or outlie either
Jovius, or Surius, or both together.
He names mee, and comes to mee; I whisper, God!   50
How have I sinn'd, that thy wraths furious rod,
This fellow chuseth me? He saith, Sir,
I love your judgement; Whom doe you prefer,
For the best linguist? And I seelily
Said, that I thought Calepines Dictionarie;   55
Nay, but of men, most sweet Sir; Beza then,
Some other Jesuites, and two reverend men
Of our two Academies, I named; There
He stopt mee, and said; Nay, your Apostles were
Good pretty linguists, and so Panurge was;   60
Yet a poore gentleman, all these may passe
By travaile. Then, as if he would have sold
His tongue, he prais'd it, and such wonders told
That I was faine to say, If you'had liv'd, Sir,
Time enough to have beene Interpreter   65
To Babells bricklayers, sure the Tower had stood.
He adds, If of court life you knew the good,
You would leave lonenesse. I said, not alone
My lonenesse is, but Spartanes fashion,
To teach by painting drunkards, doth not last   70
Now; Aretines pictures have made few chast;
No more can Princes courts, though there be few
Better pictures of vice, teach me vertue;
He, like to a high stretcht lute string squeakt, O Sir,
'Tis sweet to talke of Kings. At Westminster,   75
Said I, The man that keepes the Abbey tombes,
And for his price doth with who ever comes,
Of all our Harries, and our Edwards talke,
From King to King and all their kin can walke:
Your eares shall heare nought, but Kings; your eyes meet   80
Kings only; The way to it, is Kingstreet.
He smack'd, and cry'd, He's base, Mechanique, coarse,
So are all your Englishmen in their discourse.
Are not your Frenchmen neate? Mine? as you see,
I have but one Frenchman, looke, hee followes mee.   85

Certes they are neatly cloth'd; I, of this minde am,
Your only wearing is your Grogaram.
Not so Sir, I have more. Under this pitch
He would not flie; I chaff'd him; But as Itch
Scratch'd into smart, and as blunt iron ground   90
Into an edge, hurts worse: So, I (foole) found,
Crossing hurt mee; To fit my sullennesse,
He to another key, his stile doth addresse,
And askes, what newes? I tell him of new playes.
He takes my hand, and as a Still, which staies   95
A Sembriefe, 'twixt each drop, he nigardly,
As loth to enrich mee, so tells many a lye.
More then ten Hollensheads, or Halls, or Stowes,
Of triviall houshold trash he knowes; He knowes
When the Queene frown'd, or smil'd, and he knowes what
A subtle States-man may gather of that;   [100
He knowes who loves; whom; and who by poyson
Hasts to an Offices reversion;
He knowes who'hath sold his land, and now doth beg
A licence, old iron, bootes, shooes, and egge-   105
shels to transport; Shortly boyes shall not play
At span-counter, or blow-point, but they pay
Toll to some Courtier; And wiser then all us,
He knowes what Ladie is not painted; Thus
He with home-meats tries me; I belch, spue, spit,   110
Looke pale, and sickly, like a Patient; Yet
He thrusts on more; And as if he'd undertooke
To say Gallo-Belgicus without booke
Speakes of all States, and deeds, that have been since
The Spaniards came, to the losse of Amyens.   115
Like a bigge wife, at sight of loathed meat,
Readie to travaile: So I sigh, and sweat
To heare this Makeron talke: In vaine; for yet,
Either my humour, or his owne to fit,
He like a priviledg'd spie, whom nothing can   120
Discredit, Libells now 'gainst each great man.
He names a price for every office paid;
He saith, our warres thrive ill, because delai'd;
That offices are entail'd, and that there are
Perpetuities of them, lasting as farre   125

As the last day; And that great officers,
Doe with the Pirates share, and Dunkirkers.
Who wasts in meat, in clothes, in horse, he notes;
Who loves whores, who boyes, and who goats.
I more amas'd then Circes prisoners, when   130
They felt themselves turne beasts, felt my selfe then
Becomming Traytor, and mee thought I saw
One of our Giant Statutes ope his jaw
To sucke me in, for hearing him. I found
That as burnt venome Leachers do grow sound   135
By giving others their soares, I might growe
Guilty, and he free: Therefore I did shew
All signes of loathing; But since I am in,
I must pay mine, and my forefathers sinne
To the last farthing; Therefore to my power   140
Toughly and stubbornly I beare this crosse; But the'houre
Of mercy now was come; He tries to bring
Me to pay a fine to scape his torturing,
And saies, Sir, can you spare me; I said, willingly;
Nay, Sir, can you spare me a crowne? Thankfully I   145
Gave it, as Ransome; But as fidlers, still,
Though they be paid to be gone, yet needs will
Thrust one more jigge upon you; so did hee
With his long complementall thankes vexe me.
But he is gone, thankes to his needy want,   150
And the prerogative of my Crowne: Scant
His thankes were ended, when I, (which did see
All the court fill'd with more strange things then hee)
Ran from thence with such or more hast, then one
Who feares more actions, doth make from prison.   155
At home in wholesome solitarinesse
My precious soule began, the wretchednesse
Of suiters at court to mourne, and a trance
Like his, who dreamt he saw hell, did advance
It selfe on mee; Such men as he saw there,   160
I saw at court, and worse, and more; Low feare
Becomes the guiltie, not the accuser; Then,
Shall I, nones slave, of high borne, or rais'd men
Feare frownes? And, my Mistresse Truth, betray thee
To th'huffing braggart, puft Nobility?   165

No, no, Thou which since yesterday hast beene
Almost about the whole world, hast thou seene,
O Sunne, in all thy journey, Vanitie,
Such as swells the bladder of our court? I
Thinke he which made your waxen garden, and   170
Transported it from Italy to stand
With us, at London, flouts our Presence, for
Just such gay painted things, which no sappe, nor
Tast have in them, ours are; And naturall
Some of the stocks are, their fruits, bastard all.   175
'Tis ten a clock and past; All whom the Mues,
Baloune, Tennis, Dyet, or the stewes,
Had all the morning held, now the second
Time made ready, that day, in flocks, are found
In the Presence, and I, (God pardon mee.)   180
As fresh, and sweet their Apparrells be, as bee
The fields they sold to buy them; For a King
Those hose are, cry the flatterers; And bring
Them next weeke to the Theatre to sell;
Wants reach all states; Me seemes they doe as well   185
At stage, as court; All are players; who e'r lookes
(For themselves dare not goe) o'r Cheapside books,
Shall finde their wardrops Inventory. Now,
The Ladies come; As Pirats, which doe know
That there came weak ships fraught with Cutchannel,   190
The men board them; and praise, as they thinke, well,
Their beauties; they the mens wits; Both are bought.
Why good wits ne'r weare scarlet gownes, I thought
This cause, These men, mens wits for speeches buy,
And women buy all reds which scarlets die.   195
He call'd her beauty limetwigs, her haire net;
She feares her drugs ill laid, her haire loose set.
Would not Heraclitus laugh to see Macrine,
From hat to shooe, himselfe at doore refine,
As if the Presence were a Moschite, and lift   200
His skirts and hose, and call his clothes to shrift,
Making them confesse not only mortall
Great staines and holes in them; but veniall
Feathers and dust, wherewith they fornicate:
And then by *Durers* rules survay the state   205

Of his each limbe, and with strings the odds trye
Of his neck to his legge, and wast to thighe.
So in immaculate clothes, and Symetrie
Perfect as circles, with such nicetie
As a young Preacher at his first time goes   210
To preach, he enters, and a Lady which owes
Him not so much as good will, he arrests,
And unto her protests protests protests,
So much as at Rome would serve to have throwne
Ten Cardinalls into the Inquisition;   215
And whispered by Jesu, so often, that A
Pursevant would have ravish'd him away
For saying of our Ladies psalter; But'tis fit
That they each other plague, they merit it.
But here comes Glorius that will plague them both,   220
Who, in the other extreme, only doth
Call a rough carelessenesse, good fashion;
Whose cloak his spurres teare; whom he spits on
He cares not, His ill words doe no harme
To him; he rusheth in, as if arme, arme,   225
He meant to crie; And though his face be as ill
As theirs which in old hangings whip Christ, still
He strives to looke worse, he keepes all in awe;
Jeasts like a licenc'd foole, commands like law.
Tyr'd, now I leave this place, and but pleas'd so   230
As men which from gaoles to'execution goe,
Goe through the great chamber (why is it hung
With the seaven deadly sinnes?). Being among
Those Askaparts, men big enough to throw
Charing Crosse for a barre, men that doe know   235
No token of worth, but Queenes man, and fine
Living, barrells of beefe, flaggons of wine;
I shooke like a spyed Spie. Preachers which are
Seas of Wit and Arts, you can, then dare,
Drowne the sinnes of this place, for, for mee   240
Which am but a scarce brooke, it enough shall bee
To wash the staines away; Although I yet
With *Macchabees* modestie, the knowne merit
Of my worke lessen: yet some wise man shall,
I hope, esteeme my writs Canonicall.   245

Satyre v

Thou shalt not laugh in this leafe, Muse, nor they
Whom any pitty warmes; He which did lay
Rules to make Courtiers, (hee being understood
May make good Courtiers, but who Courtiers good?)
Frees from the sting of jests all who in extreme   5
Are wreched or wicked: of these two a theame
Charity and liberty give me. What is hee
Who Officers rage, and Suiters misery
Can write, and jest? If all things be in all,
As I thinke, since all, which were, are, and shall   10
Bee, be made of the same elements:
Each thing, each thing implyes or represents.
Then man is a world; in which, Officers
Are the vast ravishing seas; and Suiters,
Springs; now full, now shallow, now drye; which, to   15
That which drownes them, run: These selfe reasons do
Prove the world a man, in which, officers
Are the devouring stomacke, and Suiters
The excrements, which they voyd. All men are dust;
How much worse are Suiters, who to mens lust   20
Are made preyes? O worse then dust, or wormes meat,
For they do eate you now, whose selves wormes shall eate.
They are the mills which grinde you, yet you are
The winde which drives them; and a wastfull warre
Is fought against you, and you fight it; they   25
Adulterate lawe, and you prepare their way
Like wittals; th'issue your owne ruine is.
Greatest and fairest Empresse, know you this?
Alas, no more then Thames calme head doth know
Whose meades her armes drowne, or whose corne o'rflow: 30
You Sir, whose righteousnes she loves, whom I
By having leave to serve, am most richly
For service paid, authoriz'd, now beginne
To know and weed out this enormous sinne.
O Age of rusty iron! Some better wit   35
Call it some worse name, if ought equall it;
The iron Age *that* was, when justice was sold; now
Injustice is sold dearer farre. Allow

All demands, fees, and duties, gamsters, anon
The mony which you sweat, and sweare for, is gon   40
Into other hands: So controverted lands
Scape, like Angelica, the strivers hands.
If Law be in the Judges heart, and hee
Have no heart to resist letter, or fee,
Where wilt thou appeale? powre of the Courts below   45
Flow from the first maine head, and these can throw
Thee, if they sucke thee in, to misery,
To fetters, halters; But if the injury
Steele thee to dare complaine, Alas, thou go'st
Against the stream, when upwards: when thou art most   50
Heavy and most faint; and in these labours they,
'Gainst whom thou should'st complaine, will in the way
Become great seas, o'r which, when thou shalt bee
Forc'd to make golden bridges, thou shalt see
That all thy gold was drown'd in them before;   55
All things follow their like, only who have may have more.
Judges are Gods; he who made and said them so,
Meant not that men should be forc'd to them to goe,
By meanes of Angels; When supplications
We send to God, to Dominations,   60
Powers, Cherubins, and all heavens Courts, if wee
Should pay fees as here, Daily bread would be
Scarce to Kings; so 'tis. Would it not anger
A Stoicke, a coward, yea a Martyr,
To see a Pursivant come in, and call   65
All his cloathes, Copes; Bookes, Primers; and all
His Plate, Challices; and mistake them away,
And aske a fee for comming? Oh, ne'r may
Faire lawes white reverend name be strumpeted,
To warrant thefts: she is established   70
Recorder to Destiny, on earth, and shee
Speakes Fates words, and but tells us who must bee
Rich, who poore, who in chaires, who in jayles:
Shee is all faire, but yet hath foule long nailes,
With which she scracheth Suiters; In bodies   75
Of men, so in law, nailes are th'extremities,
So Officers stretch to more then Law can doe,
As our nailes reach what no else part comes to.

Why barest thou to yon Officer? Foole, Hath hee
Got those goods, for which erst men bar'd to thee?   80
Foole, twice, thrice, thou hast bought wrong, and now
     hungerly
Beg'st right; But that dole comes not till these dye.
Thou had'st much, and lawes Urim and Thummim trie
Thou wouldst for more; and for all hast paper   85
Enough to cloath all the great Carricks Pepper.
Sell that, and by that thou much more shalt leese,
Then Haman, when he sold his Antiquities.
O wretch that thy fortunes should moralize
Esops fables, and make tales, prophesies.   90
Thou'art the swimming dog whom shadows cosened,
And div'st, neare drowning, for what's vanished.

Vpon Mr. Thomas Coryats Crudities

Oh to what height will love of greatnesse drive
Thy leavened spirit, *Sesqui-superlative*?
Venice vast lake thou hadst seen, and would seek than
Some vaster thing, and found'st a Curtizan.
That inland Sea having discovered well,   5
A Cellar gulfe, where one might saile to hell
From Heydelberg, thou longdst to see: And thou
This Booke, greater then all, producest now.
Infinite worke, which doth so far extend,
That none can study it to any end.   10
'Tis no one thing, it is not fruit nor roote;
Nor poorely limited with head or foot.
If man be therefore man, because he can
Reason, and laugh, thy booke doth halfe make man.
One halfe being made, thy modestie was such,   15
That thou on th'other half wouldst never touch.
When wilt thou be at full, great Lunatique?
Not till thou exceed the world? Canst thou be like
A prosperous nose-borne wenne, which sometimes growes
To be farre greater then the Mother-nose?   20
Goe then; and as to thee, when thou didst go,
Munster did Townes, and *Gesner* Authors show,

Mount now to *Gallo-belgicus;* appear
As deepe a States-man, as a Gazettier.
Homely and familiarly, when thou com'st back,   25
Talke of *Will. Conquerour*, and *Prester Jack.*
Go bashfull man, lest here thou blush to looke
Vpon the progresse of thy glorious booke,
To which both Indies sacrifices send;
The West sent gold, which thou didst freely spend,   30
(Meaning to see't no more) upon the presse.
The East sends hither her deliciousnesse;
And thy leaves must imbrace what comes from thence,
The Myrrhe, the Pepper, and the Frankincense.
This magnifies thy leaves; but if they stoope   35
To neighbour wares, when Merchants do unhoope
Voluminous barrels; if thy leaves do then
Convey these wares in parcels unto men;
If for vast Tons of Currans, and of Figs,
Of Medicinall and Aromatique twigs,   40
Thy leaves a better method to provide,
Divide to pounds, and ounces sub-divide;
If they stoope lower yet, and vent our wares,
Home-*manufactures*, to thick popular Faires,
If *omni-praegnant* there, upon warme stalls,   45
They hatch all wares for which the buyer calls;
Then thus thy leaves we justly may commend,
That they all kinde of matter comprehend.
Thus thou, by means which th'Ancients never took,
A Pandect makest, and Vniversall Booke.   50
The bravest Heroes, for publike good,
Scattered in divers Lands their limbs and blood.
Worst malefactors, to whom men are prize,
Do publike good, cut in Anatomies;
So will thy booke in peeces; for a Lord   55
Which casts at Portescues, and all the board,
Provide whole books; each leafe enough will be
For friends to passe time, and keep company.
Can all carouse up thee? no, thou must fit
Measures; and fill out for the half-pint wit: 60
Some shall wrap pils, and save a friends life so,
Some shall stop muskets, and so kill a foe.

Thou shalt not ease the Criticks of next age
So much, at once their hunger to asswage:
Nor shall wit-pirats hope to finde thee lye   65
All in one bottome, in one Librarie.
Some Leaves may paste strings there in other books,
And so one may, which on another looks,
Pilfer, alas, a little wit from you;
But hardly much; and yet I think this true;   70
As *Sibyls* was, your booke is mysticall,
For every peece is as much worth as all.
Therefore mine impotency I confesse,
The healths which my braine bears must be far lesse:
Thy Gyant-wit'orethrowes me, I am gone;   75
And rather then read all, I would reade none.

LETTERS

TO SEVERALL PERSONAGES

The Storme

To Mr. *Christopher Brooke*

Thou which art I, ('tis nothing to be soe)
Thou which art still thy selfe, by these shalt know
Part of our passage; And, a hand, or eye
By *Hilliard* drawne, is worth an history,
By a worse painter made; and (without pride)   5
When by thy judgment they are dignifi'd,
My lines are such: 'Tis the preheminence
Of friendship onely to'impute excellence.
England to whom we'owe, what we be, and have,
Sad that her sonnes did seeke a forraine grave   10
(For, Fates, or Fortunes drifts none can soothsay,
Honour and misery have one face and way.)
From out her pregnant intrailes sigh'd a winde
Which at th'ayres middle marble roome did finde
Such strong resistance, that it selfe it threw   15
Downeward againe; and so when it did view
How in the port, our fleet deare time did leese,
Withering like prisoners, which lye but for fees,
Mildly it kist our sailes, and, fresh and sweet,
As to a stomack sterv'd, whose insides meete,   20
Meate comes, it came; and swole our sailes, when wee
So joyd, as *Sara*'her swelling joy'd to see.
But 'twas but so kinde, as our countrimen,
Which bring friends one dayes way, and leave them then.
Then like two mighty Kings, which dwelling farre   25
Asunder, meet against a third to warre,

The South and West winds joyn'd, and, as they blew,
Waves like a rowling trench before them threw.
Sooner then you read this line, did the gale,
Like shot, not fear'd till felt, our sailes assaile;   30
And what at first was call'd a gust, the same
Hath now a stormes, anon a tempests name.
Jonas, I pitty thee, and curse those men,
Who when the storm rag'd most, did wake thee then;
Sleepe is paines easiest salve, and doth fullfill   35
All offices of death, except to kill.
But when I wakt, I saw, that I saw not;
I, and the Sunne, which should teach mee'had forgot
East, West, Day, Night, and I could onely say,
If'the world had lasted, now it had beene day.   40
Thousands our noyses were, yet wee'mongst all
Could none by his right name, but thunder call:
Lightning was all our light, and it rain'd more
Then if the Sunne had drunke the sea before.
Some coffin'd in their cabbins lye,'equally   45
Griev'd that they are not dead, and yet must dye;
And as sin-burd'ned soules from graves will creepe,
At the last day, some forth their cabbins peepe:
And tremblingly'aske what newes, and doe heare so,
Like jealous husbands, what they would not know.   50
Some sitting on the hatches, would seeme there,
With hideous gazing to feare away feare.
Then note they the ships sicknesses, the Mast
Shak'd with this ague, and the Hold and Wast
With a salt dropsie clog'd, and all our tacklings   55
Snapping, like too-high-stretched treble strings.
And from our totterd sailes, ragges drop downe so,
As from one hang'd in chaines, a yeare agoe.
Even our Ordinance plac'd for our defence,
Strive to breake loose, and scape away from thence.   60
Pumping hath tir'd our men, and what's the gaine?
Seas into seas throwne, we suck in againe;
Hearing hath deaf'd our saylers; and if they
Knew how to heare, there's none knowes what to say.
Compar'd to these stormes, death is but a qualme,   65
Hell somewhat lightsome, and the'Bermuda calme.

Darknesse, lights elder brother, his birth-right
Claims o'r this world, and to heaven hath chas'd light.
All things are one, and that one none can be,
Since all formes, uniforme deformity 70
Doth cover, so that wee, except God say
Another *Fiat*, shall have no more day.
So violent, yet long these furies bee,
That though thine absence sterve me, I wish not thee.

The Calme

Our storme is past, and that storms tyrannous rage,
A stupid calme, but nothing it, doth swage.
The fable is inverted, and farre more
A blocke afflicts, now, then a storke before.
Stormes chafe, and soone weare out themselves, or us; 5
In calmes, Heaven laughs to see us languish thus.
As steady'as I can wish, that my thoughts were,
Smooth as thy mistresse glasse, or what shines there,
The sea is now. And, as the Iles which wee
Seeke, when wee can move, our ships rooted bee. 10
As water did in stormes, now pitch runs out:
As lead, when a fir'd Church becomes one spout.
And all our beauty, and our trimme, decayes,
Like courts removing, or like ended playes.
The fighting place now seamens ragges supply; 15
And all the tackling is a frippery.
No use of lanthornes; and in one place lay
Feathers and dust, to day and yesterday.
Earths hollownesses, which the worlds lungs are,
Have no more winde then the upper valt of aire. 20
We can nor lost friends, nor sought foes recover,
But meteorlike, save that wee move not, hover.
Onely the Calenture together drawes
Deare friends, which meet dead in great fishes jawes:
And on the hatches as on Altars lyes 25
Each one, his owne Priest, and owne Sacrifice.
Who live, that miracle do multiply
Where walkers in hot Ovens, doe not dye.

If in despite of these, wee swimme, that hath
No more refreshing, then our brimstone Bath,   30
But from the sea, into the ship we turne,
Like parboyl'd wretches, on the coales to burne.
Like *Bajazet* encag'd, the shepheards scoffe,
Or like slacke sinew'd *Sampson*, his haire off,
Languish our ships. Now, as a Miriade   35
Of Ants, durst th'Emperours lov'd snake invade,
The crawling Gallies, Sea-goales, finny chips,
Might brave our Pinnaces, now bed-ridde ships.
Whether a rotten state, and hope of gaine,
Or to disuse mee from the queasie paine   40
Of being belov'd, and loving, or the thirst
Of honour, or faire death, out pusht mee first,
I lose my end: for here as well as I
A desperate may live, and a coward die.
Stagge, dogge, and all which from, or towards flies,   45
Is paid with life, or pray, or doing dyes.
Fate grudges us all, and doth subtly lay
A scourge,'gainst which wee all forget to pray,
He that at sea prayes for more winde, as well
Under the poles may begge cold, heat in hell.   50
What are wee then? How little more alas
Is man now, then before he was? he was
Nothing; for us, wee are for nothing fit;
Chance, or our selves still disproportion it.
Wee have no power, no will, no sense; I lye,   55
I should not then thus feele this miserie.

To Sr *Henry Wotton*

Sir, more then kisses, letters mingle Soules;
For, thus friends absent speake. This ease controules
The tediousnesse of my life: But for these
I could ideate nothing, which could please,
But I should wither in one day, and passe   5
To'a bottle'of Hay, that am a locke of Grasse.
Life is a voyage, and in our lifes wayes
Countries, Courts, Towns are Rockes, or Remoraes;

They breake or stop all ships, yet our state's such,
That though then pitch they staine worse, wee must touch.
If in the furnace of the even line,   [10
Or under th'adverse icy poles thou pine,
Thou know'st two temperate Regions girded in,
Dwell there: But Oh, what refuge canst thou winne
Parch'd in the Court, and in the country frozen?   15
Shall cities, built of both extremes, be chosen?
Can dung and garlike be'a perfume? or can
A Scorpion and Torpedo cure a man?
Cities are worst of all three; of all three
(O knottie riddle) each is worst equally.   20
Cities are Sepulchers; they who dwell there
Are carcases, as if no such there were.
And Courts are Theaters, where some men play
Princes, some slaves, all to one end, and of one clay.
The Country is a desert, where no good,   25
Gain'd (as habits, not borne,) is understood.
There men become beasts, and prone to more evils;
In cities blockes, and in a lewd court, devills.
As in the first Chaos confusedly
Each elements qualities were in the'other three;   30
So pride, lust, covetize, being severall
To these three places, yet all are in all,
And mingled thus, their issue incestuous.
Falshood is denizon'd. Virtue is barbarous.
Let no man say there, Virtues flintie wall   35
Shall locke vice in mee, I'll do none, but know all.
Men are spunges, which to poure out, receive.
Who know false play, rather then lose, deceive.
For in best understandings, sinne beganne,
Angels sinn'd first, then Devills, and then man.   40
Onely perchance beasts sinne not; wretched wee
Are beasts in all, but white integritie.
I thinke if men, which in these places live
Durst looke for themselves, and themselves retrive,
They would like strangers greet themselves, seeing than   45
Utopian youth, growne old Italian.
    Be thou thine owne home, and in thy selfe dwell;
Inne any where, continuance maketh hell.

And seeing the snaile, which every where doth rome,
Carrying his owne house still, still is at home,　　　50
Follow (for he is easie pac'd) this snaile,
Bee thine owne Palace, or the world's thy gaile.
And in the worlds sea, do not like corke sleepe
Upon the waters face; nor in the deepe
Sinke like a lead without a line: but as　　　55
Fishes glide, leaving no print where they passe,
Nor making sound; so closely thy course goe,
Let men dispute, whether thou breathe, or no.
Onely'in this one thing, be no Galenist: To make
Courts hot ambitions wholesome, do not take　　　60
A dramme of Countries dulnesse; do not adde
Correctives, but as chymiques, purge the bad.
But, Sir, I advise not you, I rather doe
Say o'er those lessons, which I learn'd of you:
Whom, free from German schismes, and lightnesse　　　65
Of France, and faire Italies faithlesnesse,
Having from these suck'd all they had of worth,
And brought home that faith, which you carried forth,
I throughly love. But if my selfe, I'have wonne
To know my rules, I have, and you have　　　70

DONNE:

To Sr *Henry Goodyere*

Who makes the Past, a patterne for next yeare,
　　Turnes no new leafe, but still the same things reads,
Seene things, he sees againe, heard things doth heare,
　　And makes his life, but like a paire of beads.

A Palace, when 'tis that, which it should be,　　　5
　　Leaves growing, and stands such, or else decayes:
But hee which dwels there, is not so; for hee
　　Strives to urge upward, and his fortune raise;

So had your body'her morning, hath her noone,
　　And shall not better; her next change is night:　　　10
But her faire larger guest, to'whom Sun and Moone
　　Are sparkes, and short liv'd, claimes another right.

The noble Soule by age growes lustier,
   Her appetite, and her digestion mend,
Wee must not sterve, nor hope to pamper her   15
   With womens milke, and pappe unto the end.

Provide you manlyer dyet; you have seene
   All libraries, which are Schools, Camps, and Courts;
But aske your Garners if you have not beene
   In harvests, too indulgent to your sports.   20

Would you redeeme it? then your selfe transplant
   A while from hence. Perchance outlandish ground
Beares no more wit, then ours, but yet more scant
   Are those diversions there, which here abound.

To be a stranger hath that benefit,   25
   Wee can beginnings, but not habits choke.
Goe; whither? Hence; you get, if you forget;
   New faults, till they prescribe in us, are smoake.

Our soule, whose country'is heaven, and God her father,
   Into this world, corruptions sinke, is sent,   30
Yet, so much in her travaile she doth gather,
   That she returnes home, wiser then she went;

It payes you well, if it teach you to spare,
   And make you,'asham'd, to make your hawks praise,
      yours,   35
Which when herselfe she lessens in the aire,
   You then first say, that high enough she toures.

However, keepe the lively tast you hold
   Of God, love him as now, but feare him more,
And in your afternoones thinke what you told   40
   And promis'd him, at morning prayer before.

Let falshood like a discord anger you,
   Else be not froward. But why doe I touch
Things, of which none is in your practise new,
   And Tables, or fruit-trenchers teach as much;   45

But thus I make you keepe your promise Sir,
   Riding I had you, though you still staid there,
And in these thoughts, although you never stirre,
   You came with mee to Micham, and are here.

To Mr *Rowland Woodward*

Like one who'in her third widdowhood doth professe
Her selfe a Nunne, tyed to retirednesse,
So'affects my muse now, a chast fallownesse;

Since shee to few, yet to too many'hath showne
How love-song weeds, and Satyrique thornes are growne   5
Where seeds of better Arts, were early sown.

Though to use, and love Poëtrie, to mee,
Betroth'd to no'one Art, be no'adulterie;
Omissions of good, ill, as ill deeds bee.

For though to us it seeme,'and be light and thinne,   10
Yet in those faithfull scales, where God throwes in
Mens workes, vanity weighs as much as sinne.

If our Soules have stain'd their first white, yet wee
May cloth them with faith, and deare honestie,
Which God imputes, as native puritie.   15

There is no Vertue, but Religion:
Wise, valiant, sober, just, are names, which none
Want, which want not Vice-covering discretion.

Seeke wee then our selves in our selves; for as
Men force the Sunne with much more force to passe,   20
By gathering his beames with a christall glasse;

So wee, If wee into our selves will turne,
Blowing our sparkes of vertue, may outburne
The straw, which doth about our hearts sojourne.

You know, Physitians, when they would infuse   25
Into any'oyle, the Soules of Simples, use
Places, where they may lie still warme, to chuse.

So workes retirednesse in us; To rome
Giddily, and be every where, but at home,
Such freedome doth a banishment become.   30

Wee are but farmers of our selves, yet may,
If we can stocke our selves, and thrive, uplay
Much, much deare treasure for the great rent day.

Manure thy selfe then, to thy selfe be'approv'd,
And with vaine outward things be no more mov'd,   35
But to know, that I love thee'and would be lov'd.

To Sʳ *Henry Wootton*

Here's no more newes, then vertue,'I may as well
Tell you *Cales*, or Sᵗ *Michaels* tale for newes, as tell
That vice doth here habitually dwell.

Yet, as to'get stomachs, we walke up and downe,
And toyle to sweeten rest, so, may God frowne,   5
If, but to loth both, I haunt Court, or Towne.

For here no one is from the'extremitie
Of vice, by any other reason free,
But that the next to'him, still, is worse then hee.

In this worlds warfare, they whom rugged Fate,   10
(Gods Commissary,) doth so throughly hate,
As in'the Courts Squadron to marshall their state:

If they stand arm'd with seely honesty,
With wishing prayers, and neat integritie,
Like Indians 'gainst Spanish hosts they bee.   15

Suspitious boldnesse to this place belongs,
And to'have as many eares as all have tongues;
Tender to know, tough to acknowledge wrongs.

Beleeve mee Sir, in my youths giddiest dayes,
When to be like the Court, was a playes praise,   20
Playes were not so like Courts, as Courts'are like playes.

Then let us at these mimicke antiques jeast,
Whose deepest projects, and egregious gests
Are but dull Moralls of a game at Chests.

But now 'tis incongruity to smile,   25
Therefore I end; and bid farewell a while,
At Court; though *From Court*, were the better stile.

H: W: in Hiber: belligeranti

Went you to conquer? and have so much lost
Yourself, that what in you was best and most,
Respective friendship, should so quickly dye?
In publique gaine my share'is not such that I
Would lose your love for Ireland: better cheap   5
I pardon death (who though he do not reap
Yet gleanes hee many of our frends away)
Then that your waking mind should bee a prey
To lethargies. Lett shott, and boggs, and skeines
With bodies deale, as fate bids and restreynes;   10
Ere sicknesses attack, yong death is best,
Who payes before his death doth scape arrest.
Lett not your soule (at first with graces fill'd,
And since, and thorough crooked lymbecks, still'd
In many schools and courts, which quicken it,)   15
It self unto the Irish negligence submit.
I aske not labored letters which should weare
Long papers out: nor letters which should feare
Dishonest carriage: or a seers art:
Nor such as from the brayne come, but the hart.   20

To the Countesse of Bedford

Madame,
Reason is our Soules left hand, Faith her right,
By these wee reach divinity, that's you;
Their loves, who have the blessings of your light,
Grew from their reason, mine from faire faith grew. 5

But as, although a squint lefthandednesse
Be'ungracious, yet we cannot want that hand,
So would I, not to encrease, but to expresse
My faith, as I beleeve, so understand.

Therefore I study you first in your Saints, 10
Those friends, whom your election glorifies,
Then in your deeds, accesses, and restraints,
And what you reade, and what your selfe devize.

But soone, the reasons why you'are lov'd by all,
Grow infinite, and so passe reasons reach, 15
Then backe againe to'implicite faith I fall,
And rest on what the Catholique voice doth teach;

That you are good: and not one Heretique
Denies it: if he did, yet you are so.
For, rockes, which high top'd and deep rooted sticke, 20
Waves wash, not undermine, nor overthrow.

In every thing there naturally growes
A *Balsamum* to keepe it fresh, and new,
If'twere not injur'd by extrinsique blowes;
Your birth and beauty are this Balme in you. 25

But you of learning and religion,
And vertue,'and such ingredients, have made
A methridate, whose operation
Keepes off, or cures what can be done or said.

Yet, this is not your physicke, but your food,   30
A dyet fit for you; for you are here
The first good Angell, since the worlds frame stood,
That ever did in womans shape appeare.

Since you are then Gods masterpeece, and so
His Factor for our loves; do as you doe,   35
Make your returne home gracious; and bestow
This life on that; so make one life of two.
     For so God helpe mee,'I would not misse you there
     For all the good which you can do me here.

To the Countesse of Bedford

MADAME,
You have refin'd mee, and to worthyest things
(Vertue, Art, Beauty, Fortune,) now I see
Rarenesse, or use, not nature value brings;
And such, as they are circumstanc'd, they bee.   5
     Two ills can ne're perplexe us, sinne to'excuse;
     But of two good things, we may leave and chuse.

Therefore at Court, which is not vertues clime,
(Where a transcendent height, (as, lownesse mee)
Makes her not be, or not show) all my rime   10
Your vertues challenge, which there rarest bee;
     For, as darke texts need notes: there some must bee
     To usher vertue, and say, *This is shee.*

So in the country'is beauty; to this place
You are the season (Madame) you the day,   15
'Tis but a grave of spices, till your face
Exhale them, and a thick close bud display.
     Widow'd and reclus'd else, her sweets she'enshrines;
     As China, when the Sunne at Brasill dines.

Out from your chariot, morning breaks at night,   20
And falsifies both computations so;
Since a new world doth rise here from your light,

We your new creatures, by new recknings goe.
   This showes that you from nature lothly stray,
   That suffer not an artificiall day.   25

In this you'have made the Court the Antipodes,
And will'd your Delegate, the vulgar Sunne,
To doe profane autumnall offices,
Whilst here to you, wee sacrificers runne;
   And whether Priests, or Organs, you wee'obey,   30
   We sound your influence, and your Dictates say.

Yet to that Deity which dwels in you,
Your vertuous Soule, I now not sacrifice;
These are *Petitions*, and not *Hymnes*; they sue
But that I may survay the edifice.   35
   In all Religions as much care hath bin
   Of Temples frames, and beauty,'as Rites within.

As all which goe to Rome, doe not thereby
Esteeme religions, and hold fast the best,
But serve discourse, and curiosity,   40
With that which doth religion but invest,
   And shunne th'entangling laborinths of Schooles,
   And make it wit, to thinke the wiser fooles:

So in this pilgrimage I would behold
You as you'are vertues temple, not as shee,   45
What walls of tender christall her enfold,
What eyes, hands, bosome, her pure Altars bee;
   And after this survay, oppose to all
   Bablers of Chappels, you th'Escuriall.

Yet not as consecrate, but merely'as faire,   50
On these I cast a lay and country eye.
Of past and future stories, which are rare,
I finde you all record, and prophecie.
   Purge but the booke of Fate, that it admit
   No sad nor guilty legends, you are it.   55

If good and lovely were not one, of both
You were the transcript, and originall,
The Elements, the Parent, and the Growth,
And every peece of you, is both their All:
    So'intire are all your deeds, and you, that you   60
    Must do the same thinge still; you cannot two.

But these (as nice thinne Schoole divinity
Serves heresie to furder or represse)
Tast of Poëtique rage, or flattery,
And need not, where all hearts one truth professe;   65
    Oft from new proofes, and new phrase, new doubts grow,
    As strange attire aliens the men wee know.

Leaving then busie praise, and all appeale
To higher Courts, senses decree is true,
The Mine, the Magazine, the Commonweale,   70
The story of beauty,'in Twicknam is, and you.
    Who hath seene one, would both; As, who had bin
    In Paradise, would seeke the Cherubin.

To Sʳ *Edward Herbert*. at *Julyers*

Man is a lumpe, where all beasts kneaded bee,
    Wisdome makes him an Arke where all agree;
The foole, in whom these beasts do live at jarre,
    Is sport to others, and a Theater,
Nor scapes hee so, but is himselfe their prey;   5
    All which was man in him, is eate away,
And now his beasts on one another feed,
    Yet couple'in anger, and new monsters breed.
How happy'is hee, which hath due place assign'd
    To'his beasts, and disaforested his minde!   10
Empail'd himselfe to keepe them out, not in;
    Can sow, and dares trust corne, where they have bin;
Can use his horse, goate, wolfe, and every beast,
    And is not Asse himselfe to all the rest.
Else, man not onely is the heard of swine,   15
    But he's those devills too, which did incline

Them to a headlong rage, and made them worse:
   For man can adde weight to heavens heaviest curse.
As Soules (they say) by our first touch, take in
   The poysonous tincture of Originall sinne,   20
So, to the punishments which God doth fling,
   Our apprehension contributes the sting.
To us, as to his chickins, he doth cast
   Hemlocke, and wee as men, his hemlocke taste;
We do infuse to what he meant for meat,   25
   Corrosivenesse, or intense cold or heat.
For, God no such specifique poyson hath
   As kills we know not how; his fiercest wrath
Hath no antipathy, but may be good
   At least for physicke, if not for our food.   30
Thus man, that might be'his pleasure, is his rod,
   And is his devill, that might be his God.
Since then our businesse is, to rectifie
   Nature, to what she was, wee'are led awry
By them, who man to us in little show;   35
   Greater then due, no forme we can bestow
On him; for Man into himselfe can draw
   All; All his faith can swallow,'or reason chaw.
All that is fill'd, and all that which doth fill,
   All the round world, to man is but a pill,   40
In all it workes not, but it is in all
   Poysonous, or purgative, or cordiall,
For, knowledge kindles Calentures in some,
   And is to others icy *Opium*.
As brave as true, is that profession than   45
   Which you doe use to make; that you know man.
This makes it credible; you have dwelt upon
   All worthy bookes, and now are such an one.
Actions are authors, and of those in you
   Your friends finde every day a mart of new.   50

To the Countesse of Bedford

T'have written then, when you writ, seem'd to mee
   Worst of spirituall vices, Simony,

And not t'have written then, seemes little lesse
    Then worst of civill vices, thanklessenesse.
In this, my debt I seem'd loath to confesse,   5
    In that, I seem'd to shunne beholdingnesse.
But 'tis not soe; *nothings*, as I am, may
    Pay all they have, and yet have all to pay.
Such borrow in their payments, and owe more
    By having leave to write so, then before.   10
Yet since rich mines in barren grounds are showne,
    May not I yeeld (not gold) but coale or stone?
Temples were not demolish'd, though prophane:
    Here *Peter Joves*, there *Paul* hath *Dian's* Fane.
So whether my hymnes you admit or chuse,   15
    In me you'have hallowed a Pagan Muse,
And denizend a stranger, who mistaught
    By blamers of the times they mard, hath sought
Vertues in corners, which now bravely doe
    Shine in the worlds best part, or all It; You.   20
I have beene told, that vertue in Courtiers hearts
    Suffers an Ostracisme, and departs.
Profit, ease, fitnesse, plenty, bid it goe,
    But whither, only knowing you, I know;
Your (or you) vertue two vast uses serves,   25
    It ransomes one sex, and one Court preserves.
There's nothing but your worth, which being true,
    Is knowne to any other, not to you:
And you can never know it; To admit
    No knowledge of your worth, is some of it.   30
But since to you, your praises discords bee,
    Stoop, others ills to meditate with mee.
Oh! to confesse wee know not what we should,
    Is halfe excuse; wee know not what we would:
Lightnesse depresseth us, emptinesse fills,   35
    We sweat and faint, yet still goe downe the hills.
As new Philosophy arrests the Sunne,
    And bids the passive earth about it runne,
So wee have dull'd our minde, it hath no ends;
    Onely the bodie's busie, and pretends;   40
As dead low earth ecclipses and controules
    The quick high Moone: so doth the body, Soules.

In none but us, are such mixt engines found,
    As hands of double office: For, the ground
We till with them; and them to heav'n wee raise;   45
    Who prayer-lesse labours, or, without this, prayes,
Doth but one halfe, that's none; He which said, *Plough*
    And looke not back, to looke up doth allow.
Good seed degenerates, and oft obeyes
    The soyles disease, and into cockle strayes;   50
Let the minds thoughts be but transplanted so,
    Into the body,'and bastardly they grow.
What hate could hurt our bodies like our love?
    Wee (but no forraine tyrants could) remove
These not ingrav'd, but inborne dignities,   55
    Caskets of soules; Temples, and Palaces:
For, bodies shall from death redeemed bee,
    Soules but preserv'd, not naturally free.
As men to'our prisons, new soules to us are sent,
    Which learne vice there, and come in innocent.   60
First seeds of every creature are in us,
    What ere the world hath bad, or pretious,
Mans body can produce, hence hath it beene
    That stones, wormes, frogges, and snakes in man are
        seene: 65
But who ere saw, though nature can worke soe,
    That pearle, or gold, or corne in man did grow?
We'have added to the world Virginia,'and sent
    Two new starres lately to the firmament;
Why grudge wee us (not heaven) the dignity   70
    T'increase with ours, those faire soules company.
But I must end this letter, though it doe
    Stand on two truths, neither is true to you.
Vertue hath some perversenesse; For she will
    Neither beleeve her good, nor others ill.   75
Even in you, vertues best paradise,
    Vertue hath some, but wise degrees of vice.
Too many vertues, or too much of one
    Begets in you unjust suspition;
And ignorance of vice, makes vertue lesse,   80
    Quenching compassion of our wrechednesse.

But these are riddles; Some aspersion
    Of vice becomes well some complexion.
Statesmen purge vice with vice, and may corrode
    The bad with bad, a spider with a toad: 85
For so, ill thralls not them, but they tame ill
    And make her do much good against her will,
But in your Commonwealth, or world in you,
    Vice hath no office, or good worke to doe.
Take then no vitious purge, but be content   90
    With cordiall vertue, your knowne nourishment.

To the Countesse of Bedford

On New-yeares day

This twilight of two yeares, not past nor next,
    Some embleme is of mee, or I of this,
Who Meteor-like, of stuffe and forme perplext,
    Whose *what*, and *where*, in disputation is,
    If I should call mee *any thing*, should misse.   5

I summe the yeares, and mee, and finde mee not
    Debtor to th'old, nor Creditor to th'new,
That cannot say, My thankes I have forgot,
    Nor trust I this with hopes, and yet scarce true
    This bravery is, since these times shew'd mee you.   10

In recompence I would show future times
    What you were, and teach them to'urge towards such.
Verse embalmes vertue;'and Tombs, or Thrones of rimes,
    Preserve fraile transitory fame, as much
    As spice doth bodies from corrupt aires touch.   15

Mine are short-liv'd; the tincture of your name
    Creates in them, but dissipates as fast,
New spirits: for, strong agents with the same
    Force that doth warme and cherish, us doe wast;
    Kept hot with strong extracts, no bodies last: 20

So, my verse built of your just praise, might want
   Reason and likelihood, the firmest Base,
And made of miracle, now faith is scant,
   Will vanish soone, and so possesse no place,
    And you, and it, too much grace might disgrace.   25

When all (as truth commands assent) confesse
   All truth of you, yet they will doubt how I,
One corne of one low anthills dust, and lesse,
   Should name, know, or expresse a thing so high,
    And not an inch, measure infinity.   30

I cannot tell them, nor my selfe, nor you,
   But leave, lest truth b'endanger'd by my praise,
And turne to God, who knowes I thinke this true,
   And useth oft, when such a heart mis-sayes,
    To make it good, for, such a praiser prayes.   35

Hee will best teach you, how you should lay out
   His stock of *beauty, learning, favour, blood*;
He will perplex security with doubt,
   And cleare those doubts; hide from you,'and shew you
     good,   40
    And so increase your appetite and food;

Hee will teach you, that good and bad have not
   One latitude in cloysters, and in Court;
Indifferent there the greatest space hath got;
   Some pitty'is not good there, some vaine disport,   45
    On this side sinne, with that place may comport.

Yet he, as hee bounds seas, will fixe your houres,
   Which pleasure, and delight may not ingresse,
And though what none else lost, be truliest yours,
   Hee will make you, what you did not, possesse,   50
    By using others, not vice, but weakenesse.

He will make you speake truths, and credibly,
   And make you doubt, that others doe not so:
Hee will provide you keyes, and locks, to spie,

And scape spies, to good ends, and hee will show   55
  What you may not acknowledge, what not know.

For your owne conscience, he gives innocence,
    But for your fame, a discreet warinesse,
And though to scape, then to revenge offence
    Be better, he showes both, and to represse   60
    Joy, when your state swells, *sadnesse* when'tis lesse.

From need of teares he will defend your soule,
    Or make a rebaptizing of one teare;
Hee cannot, (that's, he will not) dis-inroule
    Your name; and when with active joy we heare   65
    This private Ghospell, then'tis our New Yeare.

To the Countesse of Huntingdon

Madame,
Man to Gods image; *Eve*, to mans was made,
    Nor finde wee that God breath'd a soule in her.
Canons will not Church functions you invade,
    Nor lawes to civill office you preferre.   5

Who vagrant transitory Comets sees,
    Wonders, because they'are rare; But a new starre
Whose motion with the firmament agrees,
    Is miracle; for, there no new things are;

In woman so perchance milde innocence   10
    A seldome comet is, but active good
A miracle, which reason scapes, and sense;
    For, Art and Nature this in them withstood.

As such a starre, the *Magi* led to view
    The manger-cradled infant, God below: 15
By vertues beames by fame deriv'd from you,
    May apt soules, and the worst may, vertue know.

If the worlds age, and death be argued well
    By the Sunnes fall, which now towards earth doth bend,
Then we might feare that vertue, since she fell   20
    So low as woman, should be neare her end.

But she's not stoop'd, but rais'd; exil'd by men
    She fled to heaven, that's heavenly things, that's you;
She was in all men, thinly scatter'd then,
    But now amass'd, contracted in a few.   25

She guilded us: But you are gold, and Shee;
    Us she inform'd, but transubstantiates you;
Soft dispositions which ductile bee,
    Elixarlike, she makes not cleane, but new.

Though you a wifes and mothers name retaine,   30
    'Tis not as woman, for all are not soe,
But vertue having made you vertue,'is faine
    T'adhere in these names, her and you to show,

Else, being alike pure, wee should neither see;
    As, water being into ayre rarify'd,   35
Neither appeare, till in one cloud they bee,
    So, for our sakes you do low names abide;

Taught by great constellations, which being fram'd,
    Of the most starres, take low names, *Crab*, and *Bull*,
When single planets by the *Gods* are nam'd,   40
    You covet not great names, of great things full.

So you, as woman, one doth comprehend,
    And in the vaile of kindred others see;
To some ye are reveal'd, as in a friend,
    And as a vertuous Prince farre off, to mee.   45

To whom, because from you all vertues flow,
    And 'tis not none, to dare contemplate you,
I, which doe so, as your true subject owe
    Some tribute for that, so these lines are due.

If you can thinke these flatteries, they are,   50
   For then your judgement is below my praise,
If they were so, oft, flatteries worke as farre,
   As Counsels, and as farre th'endeavour raise.

So my ill reaching you might there grow good,
   But I remaine a poyson'd fountaine still;   55
But not your beauty, vertue, knowledge, blood
   Are more above all flattery, then my will.

And if I flatter any,'tis not you
   But my owne judgement, who did long agoe
Pronounce, that all these praises should be true,   60
   And vertue should your beauty,'and birth outgrow.

Now that my prophesies are all fulfill'd,
   Rather then God should not be honour'd too,
And all these gifts confess'd, which hee instill'd,
   Your selfe were bound to say that which I doe.   65

So I, but your Recorder am in this,
   Or mouth, or Speaker of the universe,
A ministeriall Notary, for 'tis
   Not I, but you and fame, that make this verse;

I was your Prophet in your yonger dayes,   70
And now your Chaplaine, God in you to praise.

To Mʳ *T. W.*

All haile sweet Poët, more full of more strong fire,
   Then hath or shall enkindle any spirit,
   I lov'd what nature gave thee, but this merit
Of wit and Art I love not but admire;
   Who have before or shall write after thee,   5
Their workes, though toughly laboured, will bee
   Like infancie or age to mans firme stay,
   Or earely and late twilights to mid-day.

Men say, and truly, that they better be
    Which be envyed then pittied: therefore I,   10
    Because I wish thee best, doe thee envie:
O wouldst thou, by like reason, pitty mee!
But care not for mee: I, that ever was
In Natures, and in Fortunes gifts, (alas,
    Before thy grace got in the Muses Schoole)   15
    A monster and a begger, am now a foole.

Oh how I grieve, that late borne modesty
    Hath got such root in easie waxen hearts,
    That men may not themselves, their owne good parts
Extoll, without suspect of surquedrie,   20
For, but thy selfe, no subject can be found
Worthy thy quill, nor any quill resound
    Thy worth but thine: how good it were to see
    A Poëm in thy praise, and writ by thee.

Now if this song be too'harsh for rime, yet, as   25
    The Painters bad god made a good devill,
    'Twill be good prose, although the verse be evill,
If thou forget the rime as thou dost passe.
Then write, that I may follow, and so bee
Thy debter, thy'eccho, thy foyle, thy zanee.   30
    I shall be thought, if mine like thine I shape,
    All the worlds Lyon, though I be thy Ape.

To Mr *T. W.*

Hast thee harsh verse, as fast as thy lame measure
    Will give thee leave, to him, my pain and pleasure.
I have given thee, and yet thou art too weake,
    Feete, and a reasoning soule and tongue to speake.
Plead for me, and so by thine and my labour   5
    I am thy Creator, thou my Saviour.
Tell him, all questions, which men have defended
    Both of the place and paines of hell, are ended;
And 'tis decreed our hell is but privation
    Of him, at least in this earths habitation: 10

And 'tis where I am, where in every street
  Infections follow, overtake, and meete:
Live I or die, by you my love is sent,
    And you'are my pawnes, or else my Testament.

To Mr *T. W.*

Pregnant again with th'old twins Hope, and Feare,
Oft have I askt for thee, both how and where
Thou wert, and what my hopes of letters were;

As in our streets sly beggers narrowly
Watch motions of the givers hand and eye,   5
And evermore conceive some hope thereby.

And now thy Almes is given, thy letter'is read,
The body risen againe, the which was dead,
And thy poore starveling bountifully fed.

After this banquet my Soule doth say grace,   10
And praise thee for'it, and zealously imbrace
Thy love; though I thinke thy love in this case
    To be as gluttons, which say 'midst their meat,
    They love that best of which they most do eat.

To Mr *T. W.*

At once, from hence, my lines and I depart,
I to my soft still walks, they to my Heart;
I to the Nurse, they to the child of Art;

Yet as a firme house, though the Carpenter
Perish, doth stand: As an Embassadour   5
Lyes safe, how e'r his king be in danger:

So, though I languish, prest with Melancholy,
My verse, the strict Map of my misery,
Shall live to see that, for whose want I dye.

Therefore I envie them, and doe repent,   10
That from unhappy mee, things happy'are sent;
Yet as a Picture, or bare Sacrament,
   Accept these lines, and if in them there be
   Merit of love, bestow that love on mee.

To Mr *R. W.*

Zealously my Muse doth salute all thee,
Enquiring of that mistique trinitee
Whereof thou,'and all to whom heavens do infuse
Like fyer, are made; thy body, mind, and Muse.
Dost thou recover sicknes, or prevent?   5
Or is thy Mind travail'd with discontent?
Or art thou parted from the world and mee,
In a good skorn of the worlds vanitee?
Or is thy devout Muse retyr'd to sing
Vpon her tender Elegiaque string?   10
Our Minds part not, joyne then thy Muse with myne,
For myne is barren thus devorc'd from thyne.

To Mr *R. W.*

Mvse not that by thy mind thy body is led:
For by thy mind, my mind's distempered.
So thy Care lives long, for I bearing part
It eates not only thyne, but my swolne heart.
And when it gives us intermission   5
We take new harts for it to feede upon.
But as a Lay Mans Genius doth controule
Body and mind; the Muse beeing the Soules Soule
Of Poets, that methinks should ease our anguish,
Although our bodyes wither and minds languish.   10
Write then, that my griefes which thine got may bee
Cur'd by thy charming soveraigne melodee.

To Mr *C. B.*

Thy friend, whom thy deserts to thee enchaine,
    Urg'd by this unexcusable occasion,
    Thee and the Saint of his affection
Leaving behinde, doth of both wants complaine;
And let the love I beare to both sustaine   5
    No blott nor maime by this division,
    Strong is this love which ties our hearts in one,
And strong that love pursu'd with amorous paine;
But though besides thy selfe I leave behind
    Heavens liberall, and earths thrice-fairer Sunne,   10
    Going to where sterne winter aye doth wonne,
Yet, loves hot fires, which martyr my sad minde,
    Doe send forth scalding sighes, which have the Art
    To melt all Ice, but that which walls her heart.

To Mr *E. G.*

Even as lame things thirst their perfection, so
The slimy rimes bred in our vale below,
Bearing with them much of my love and hart,
Fly unto that Parnassus, where thou art.
There thou oreseest London: Here I have beene,   5
By staying in London, too much overseene.
Now pleasures dearth our City doth posses,
Our Theaters are fill'd with emptines;
As lancke and thin is every street and way
As a woman deliver'd yesterday.   10
Nothing whereat to laugh my spleen espyes
But bearbaitings or Law exercise.
Therefore I'le leave it, and in the Country strive
Pleasure, now fled from London, to retrive.
Do thou so too: and fill not like a Bee   15
Thy thighs with hony, but as plenteously
As Russian Marchants, thy selfes whole vessell load,
And then at Winter retaile it here abroad.
Blesse us with Suffolks sweets; and as it is
Thy garden, make thy hive and warehouse this.   20

To Mʳ R. W.

If, as mine is, thy life a slumber be,
   Seeme, when thou read'st these lines, to dreame of me,
Never did Morpheus nor his brother weare
   Shapes soe like those Shapes, whom they would appeare,
As this my letter is like me, for it   5
   Hath my name, words, hand, feet, heart, minde and wit;
It is my deed of gift of mee to thee,
   It is my Will, my selfe the Legacie.
So thy retyrings I love, yea envie,
   Bred in thee by a wise melancholy,   10
That I rejoyce, that unto where thou art,
   Though I stay here, I can thus send my heart,
As kindly'as any enamored Patient
   His Picture to his absent Love hath sent.

All newes I thinke sooner reach thee then mee;   15
   Havens are Heavens, and Ships wing'd Angels be,
The which both Gospell, and sterne threatnings bring;
   Guyanaes harvest is nip'd in the spring,
I feare; And with us (me thinkes) Fate deales so
   As with the Jewes guide God did; he did show   20
Him the rich land, but bar'd his entry in:
   Oh, slownes is our punishment and sinne.
Perchance, these Spanish businesse being done,
   Which as the Earth betweene the Moone and Sun
Eclipse the light which Guyana would give,   25
   Our discontinued hopes we shall retrive:
But if (as all th'All must) hopes smoake away,
   Is not Almightie Vertue'an India?

If men be worlds, there is in every one
   Some thing to answere in some proportion   30
All the worlds riches: And in good men, this,
   Vertue, our formes forme and our soules soule, is.

To Mʳ R. W.

Kindly I envy thy songs perfection
   Built of all th'elements as our bodyes are:
   That Litle of earth that is in it, is a faire
Delicious garden where all sweetes are sowne.
In it is cherishing fyer which dryes in mee   5
   Griefe which did drowne me: and halfe quench'd by it
   Are satirique fyres which urg'd me to have writt
In skorne of all: for now I admyre thee.
   And as Ayre doth fulfill the hollownes
   Of rotten walls; so it myne emptines,   10
Where tost and mov'd it did beget this sound
Which as a lame Eccho of thyne doth rebound.
   Oh, I was dead; but since thy song new Life did give,
   I recreated, even by thy creature, live.

To Mʳ S. B.

O Thou which to search out the secret parts
   Of the India, or rather Paradise
   Of knowledge, hast with courage and advise
Lately launch'd into the vast Sea of Arts,
Disdaine not in thy constant travailing   5
   To doe as other Voyagers, and make
   Some turnes into lesse Creekes, and wisely take
Fresh water at the Heliconian spring;
I sing not, Siren like, to tempt; for I
   Am harsh; nor as those Scismatiques with you,   10
   Which draw all wits of good hope to their crew;
But seeing in you bright sparkes of Poetry,
   I, though I brought no fuell, had desire
   With these Articulate blasts to blow the fire.

To Mʳ I. L.

Of that short Roll of friends writ in my heart
   Which with thy name begins, since their depart,

Whether in the English Provinces they be,
  Or drinke of Po, Sequan, or Danubie,
There's none that sometimes greets us not, and yet   5
  Your Trent is Lethe; that past, us you forget.
You doe not duties of Societies,
  If from the'embrace of a lov'd wife you rise,
View your fat Beasts, stretch'd Barnes, and labour'd fields,
  Eate, play, ryde, take all joyes which all day yeelds,   10
And then againe to your embracements goe:
  Some houres on us your frends, and some bestow
Upon your Muse, else both wee shall repent,
  I that my love, she that her guifts on you are spent.

To Mr *B. B.*

Is not thy sacred hunger of science
  Yet satisfy'd? Is not thy braines rich hive
  Fulfil'd with hony which thou dost derive
From the Arts spirits and their Quintessence?
Then weane thy selfe at last, and thee withdraw   5
  From Cambridge thy old nurse, and, as the rest,
  Here toughly chew, and sturdily digest
Th'immense vast volumes of our common law;
And begin soone, lest my griefe grieve thee too,
  Which is, that that which I should have begun   10
  In my youthes morning, now late must be done;
And I as Giddy Travellers must doe,
  Which stray or sleepe all day, and having lost
  Light and strength, darke and tir'd must then ride post.

If thou unto thy Muse be marryed,   15
  Embrace her ever, ever multiply,
  Be far from me that strange Adulterie
To tempt thee and procure her widowhed.
My Muse, (for I had one,) because I'am cold,
  Divorc'd her selfe: the cause being in me,   20
  That I can take no new in Bigamye,
Not my will only but power doth withhold.

Hence comes it, that these Rymes which never had
   Mother, want matter, and they only have
   A little forme, the which their Father gave;   25
They are prophane, imperfect, oh, too bad
   To be counted Children of Poetry
   Except confirm'd and Bishoped by thee.

To Mr *I. L.*

Blest are your North parts, for all this long time
   My Sun is with you, cold and darke'is our Clime;
Heavens Sun, which staid so long from us this yeare,
   Staid in your North (I thinke) for she was there,
And hether by kinde nature drawne from thence,   5
   Here rages, chafes, and threatens pestilence;
Yet I, as long as shee from hence doth staie,
   Thinke this no South, no Sommer, nor no day.
With thee my kinde and unkinde heart is run,
   There sacrifice it to that beauteous Sun: 10
And since thou art in Paradise and need'st crave
   No joyes addition, helpe thy friend to save.
So may thy pastures with their flowery feasts,
   As suddenly as Lard, fat thy leane beasts;
So may thy woods oft poll'd, yet ever weare   15
   A greene, and when thee list, a golden haire;
So may all thy sheepe bring forth Twins; and so
   In chace and race may thy horse all out goe;
So may thy love and courage ne'r be cold;
   Thy Sonne ne'r Ward; Thy lov'd wife ne'r seem old; 20
But maist thou wish great things, and them attaine,
   As thou telst her, and none but her, my paine.

To Sir *H. W.* at his going Ambassador to *Venice*

After those reverend papers, whose soule is
   Our good and great Kings lov'd hand and fear'd name,
By which to you he derives much of his,
   And (how he may) makes you almost the same,

A Taper of his Torch, a copie writ   5
   From his Originall, and a faire beame
Of the same warme, and dazeling Sun, though it
   Must in another Sphere his vertue streame:

After those learned papers which your hand
   Hath stor'd with notes of use and pleasure too,   10
From which rich treasury you may command
   Fit matter whether you will write or doe:

After those loving papers, where friends send
   With glad griefe, to your Sea-ward steps, farewel,
Which thicken on you now, as prayers ascend   15
   To heaven in troupes at'a good mans passing bell:

Admit this honest paper, and allow
   It such an audience as your selfe would aske;
What you must say at Venice this meanes now,
   And hath for nature, what you have for taske: 20

To sweare much love, not to be chang'd before
   Honour alone will to your fortune fit;
Nor shall I then honour your fortune, more
   Then I have done your honour wanting it.

But 'tis an easier load (though both oppresse)   25
   To want, then governe greatnesse, for wee are
In that, our owne and onely businesse,
   In this, wee must for others vices care;

'Tis therefore well your spirits now are plac'd
   In their last Furnace, in activity;   30
Which fits them (Schooles and Courts and Warres o'rpast)
   To touch and test in any best degree.

For mee, (if there be such a thing as I)
   Fortune (if there be such a thing as shee)
Spies that I beare so well her tyranny,   35
   That she thinks nothing else so fit for mee;

But though she part us, to heare my oft prayers
   For your increase, God is as neere mee here;
And to send you what I shall begge, his staires
   In length and ease are alike every where.   40

To Mrs *M. H.*

Mad paper stay, and grudge not here to burne
   With all those sonnes whom my braine did create,
At lest lye hid with mee, till thou returne
   To rags againe, which is thy native state.

What though thou have enough unworthinesse   5
   To come unto great place as others doe,
That's much; emboldens, pulls, thrusts I confesse,
   But 'tis not all; Thou should'st be wicked too.

And, that thou canst not learne, or not of mee;
   Yet thou wilt goe? Goe, since thou goest to her   10
Who lacks but faults to be a Prince, for shee,
   Truth, whom they dare not pardon, dares preferre.

But when thou com'st to that perplexing eye
   Which equally claimes *love* and *reverence*,
Thou wilt not long dispute it, thou wilt die;   15
   And, having little now, have then no sense.

Yet when her warme redeeming hand, which is
   A miracle; and made such to worke more,
Doth touch thee (saples leafe) thou grow'st by this
   Her creature; glorify'd more then before.   20

Then as a mother which delights to heare
   Her early child mis-speake halfe uttered words,
Or, because majesty doth never feare
   Ill or bold speech, she Audience affords.

And then, cold speechlesse wretch, thou diest againe, 25
 And wisely; what discourse is left for thee?
For, speech of ill, and her, thou must abstaine,
 And is there any good which is not shee?
Yet maist thou praise her servants, though not her,
 And wit, and vertue,'and honour her attend, 30
And since they'are but her cloathes, thou shalt not erre,
 If thou her shape and beauty'and grace commend.

Who knowes thy destiny? when thou hast done,
 Perchance her Cabinet may harbour thee,
Whither all noble ambitious wits doe runne, 35
 A nest almost as full of Good as shee.

When thou art there, if any, whom wee know,
 Were sav'd before, and did that heaven partake,
When she revolves his papers, marke what show
 Of favour, she alone, to them doth make. 40

Marke, if to get them, she o'r skip the rest,
 Marke, if shee read them twice, or kisse the name;
Marke, if she doe the same that they protest,
 Marke, if she marke whether her woman came.

Marke, if slight things be'objected, and o'r blowne, 45
 Marke, if her oathes against him be not still
Reserv'd, and that shee grieves she's not her owne,
 And chides the doctrine that denies Freewill.

I bid thee not doe this to be my spie;
 Nor to make my selfe her familiar; 50
But so much I doe love her choyce, that I
 Would faine love him that shall be lov'd of her.

To the Countesse of Bedford

Honour is so sublime perfection,
And so refinde; that when God was alone
And creaturelesse at first, himselfe had none;

But as of the elements, these which wee tread,
Produce all things with which wee'are joy'd or fed,   5
And, those are barren both above our head:

So from low persons doth all honour flow;
Kings, whom they would have honoured, to us show,
And but *direct* our honour, not *bestow*.

For when from herbs the pure part must be wonne   10
From grosse, by Stilling, this is better done
By despis'd dung, then by the fire or Sunne.

Care not then, Madame,'how low your praysers lye;
In labourers balads oft more piety
God findes, then in *Te Deums* melodie.   15

And, ordinance rais'd on Towers, so many mile
Send not their voice, nor last so long a while
As fires from th'earths low vaults in *Sicil* Isle.

Should I say I liv'd darker then were true,
Your radiation can all clouds subdue;   20
But one,'tis best light to contemplate you.

You, for whose body God made better clay,
Or tooke Soules stuffe such as shall late decay,
Or such as needs small change at the last day.

This, as an Amber drop enwraps a Bee,   25
Covering discovers your quicke Soule; that we
May in your through-shine front your hearts thoughts see.

You teach (though wee learne not) a thing unknowne
To our late times, the use of specular stone,
Through which all things within without were shown.   30

Of such were Temples; so and of such you are;
Beeing and *seeming* is your equall care,
And *vertues* whole *summe* is but *know* and *dare*.

But as our Soules of growth and Soules of sense
Have birthright of our reasons Soule, yet hence   35
They fly not from that, nor seeke presidence:

Natures first lesson, so, discretion,
Must not grudge zeale a place, nor yet keepe none,
Not banish it selfe, nor religion.   .

Discretion is a wisemans Soule, and so   40
Religion is a Christians, and you know
How these are one; her *yea*, is not her *no*.

Nor may we hope to sodder still and knit
These two, and dare to breake them; nor must wit
Be colleague to religion, but be it.   45

In those poor types of God (round circles) so
Religions tipes, the peecelesse centers flow,
And are in all the lines which all wayes goe.

If either ever wrought in you alone
Or principally, then religion   50
Wrought your ends, and your wayes discretion.

Goe thither still, goe the same way you went,
Who so would change, do covet or repent;
Neither can reach you, great and innocent.

To the Countesse of Huntington

That unripe side of earth, that heavy clime
That gives us man up now, like *Adams* time
Before he ate; mans shape, that would yet bee
(Knew they not it, and fear'd beasts companie)
So naked at this day, as though man there   5
From Paradise so great a distance were,
As yet the newes could not arrived bee
Of *Adams* tasting the forbidden tree;

Depriv'd of that free state which they were in,
And wanting the reward, yet beare the sinne.   10
　　But, as from extreme hights who downward looks,
Sees men at childrens shapes, Rivers at brookes,
And loseth younger formes; so, to your eye,
These (Madame) that without your distance lie,
Must either mist, or nothing seeme to be,   15
Who are at home but wits mere *Atomi*.
But, I who can behold them move, and stay,
Have found my selfe to you, just their midway;
And now must pitty them; for, as they doe
Seeme sick to me, just so must I to you.   20
Yet neither will I vexe your eyes to see
A sighing Ode, nor crosse-arm'd Elegie.
I come not to call pitty from your heart,
Like some white-liver'd dotard that would part
Else from his slipperie soule with a faint groane,   25
And faithfully, (without you smil'd) were gone.
I cannot feele the tempest of a frowne,
I may be rais'd by love, but not throwne down.
Though I can pittie those sigh twice a day,
I hate that thing whispers it selfe away.   30
Yet since all love is fever, who to trees
Doth talke, doth yet in loves cold ague freeze.
'Tis love, but, with such fatall weaknesse made,
That it destroyes it selfe with its owne shade.
Who first look'd sad, griev'd, pin'd, and shew'd his paine, 35
Was he that first taught women, to disdaine.
　　As all things were one nothing, dull and weake,
Vntill this raw disordered heape did breake,
And severall desires led parts away,
Water declin'd with earth, the ayre did stay,   40
Fire rose, and each from other but unty'd,
Themselves unprison'd were and purify'd:
So was love, first in vast confusion hid,
An unripe willingnesse which nothing did,
A thirst, an Appetite which had no ease,   45
That found a want, but knew not what would please.
What pretty innocence in those dayes mov'd?
Man ignorantly walk'd by her he lov'd;

Both sigh'd and enterchang'd a speaking eye,
Both trembled and were sick, both knew not why. 50
That naturall fearefulnesse that struck man dumbe,
Might well (those times consider'd) man become.
As all discoverers whose first assay
Findes but the place, after, the nearest way:
So passion is to womans love, about, 55
Nay, farther off, than when we first set out.
It is not love that sueth, or doth contend;
Love either conquers, or but meets a friend.
Man's better part consists of purer fire,
And findes it selfe allow'd, ere it desire. 60
Love is wise here, keepes home, gives reason sway,
And journeys not till it finde summer-way.
A weather-beaten Lover but once knowne,
Is sport for every girle to practise on.
Who strives through womans scornes, women to know, 65
Is lost, and seekes his shadow to outgoe;
It must bee sicknesse, after one disdaine,
Though he be call'd aloud, to looke againe.
Let others sigh, and grieve; one cunning sleight
Shall freeze my Love to Christall in a night. 70
I can love first, and (if I winne) love still;
And cannot be remov'd, unlesse she will.
It is her fault if I unsure remaine,
Shee onely can untie, and binde againe.
The honesties of love with ease I doe, 75
But am no porter for a tedious woo.
   But (madame) I now thinke on you; and here
Where we are at our hights, you but appeare,
We are but clouds you rise from, our noone-ray
But a foule shadow, not your breake of day. 80
You are at first hand all that's faire and right,
And others good reflects but backe your light.
You are a perfectnesse, so curious hit,
That youngest flatteries doe scandall it.
For, what is more doth what you are restraine, 85
And though beyond, is downe the hill againe.
We'have no next way to you, we crosse to it:
You are the straight line, thing prais'd, attribute;

Each good in you's a light; so many a shade
You make, and in them are your motions made. 90
These are your pictures to the life. From farre
We see you move, and here your *Zani's* are:
So that no fountaine good there is, doth grow
In you, but our dimme actions faintly shew.
 Then finde I, if mans noblest part be love, 95
Your purest luster must that shadow move.
The soule with body, is a heaven combin'd
With earth, and for mans ease, but nearer joyn'd.
Where thoughts the starres of soule we understand,
We guesse not their large natures, but command. 100
And love in you, that bountie is of light,
That gives to all, and yet hath infinite.
Whose heat doth force us thither to intend,
But soule we finde too earthly to ascend,
'Till slow accesse hath made it wholy pure, 105
Able immortall clearnesse to endure.
Who dare aspire this journey with a staine,
Hath waight will force him headlong backe againe.
No more can impure man retaine and move
In that pure region of a worthy love: 110
Then earthly substance can unforc'd aspire,
And leave his nature to converse with fire:
Such may have eye, and hand; may sigh, may speak;
But like swoln bubles, when they are high'st they break.
 Though far removed Northerne fleets scarce finde 115
The Sunnes comfort; others thinke him too kinde.
There is an equall distance from her eye,
Men perish too farre off, and burne too nigh.
But as ayre takes the Sunne-beames equall bright
From the first Rayes, to his last opposite: 120
So able men, blest with a vertuous Love,
Remote or neare, or howsoe'r they move;
Their vertue breakes all clouds that might annoy,
There is no Emptinesse, but all is Ioy.
He much profanes whom violent heats do move 125
To stile his wandring rage of passion, *Love*:
Love that imparts in every thing delight,
Is fain'd, which only tempts mans appetite.

Why love among the vertues is not knowne
Is, that love is them all contract in one.   130

To the Countesse of Bedford

Begun in France but never perfected

Though I be *dead*, and buried, yet I have
  (Living in you,) Court enough in my grave,
As oft as there I thinke my selfe to bee,
  So many resurrections waken mee.
That thankfullnesse your favours have begot   5
  In mee, embalmes mee, that I doe not rot.
This season as 'tis Easter, as 'tis spring,
  Must both to growth and to confession bring
My thoughts dispos'd unto your influence; so,
  These verses bud, so these confessions grow.   10
First I confesse I have to others lent
  Your stock, and over prodigally spent
Your treasure, for since I had never knowne
  Vertue or beautie, but as they are growne
In you, I should not thinke or say they shine,   15
  (So as I have) in any other Mine.
Next I confesse this my confession,
  For, 'tis some fault thus much to touch upon
Your praise to you, where half rights seeme too much,
  And make your minds sincere complexion blush.   20
Next I confesse my'impenitence, for I
  Can scarce repent my first fault, since thereby
Remote low Spirits, which shall ne'r read you,
  May in lesse lessons finde enough to doe,
By studying copies, not Originals,   25
      Desunt cætera.

A Letter to the Lady Carey, *and* M*rs* Essex Riche, *From* Amyens

Madame,
Here where by All All Saints invoked are,
'Twere too much schisme to be singular,
And 'gainst a practise generall to warre.

Yet turning to Saincts, should my'humility   5
To other Sainct then you directed bee,
That were to make my schisme, heresie.

Nor would I be a Convertite so cold,
As not to tell it; If this be too bold,
Pardons are in this market cheaply sold.   10

Where, because Faith is in too low degree,
I thought it some Apostleship in mee
To speake things which by faith alone I see.

That is, of you, who are a firmament
Of virtues, where no one is growne, or spent,   15
They'are your materials, not your ornament.

Others whom wee call vertuous, are not so
In their whole substance, but, their vertues grow
But in their humours, and at seasons show.

For when through tastlesse flat humilitie   20
In dow bak'd men some harmelessenes we see,
'Tis but his *flegme* that's *Vertuous*, and not Hee:

Soe is the Blood sometimes; who ever ran
To danger unimportun'd, he was than
No better then a *sanguine* Vertuous man.   25

So cloysterall men, who, in pretence of feare
All contributions to this life forbeare,
Have Vertue in *Melancholy*, and only there.

Spirituall *Cholerique* Crytiques, which in all
Religions find faults, and forgive no fall,   30
Have, through this zeale, Vertue but in their Gall.

We'are thus but parcel guilt; to Gold we'are growne
When Vertue is our Soules complexion;
Who knowes his Vertues name or place, hath none.

Vertue'is but aguish, when 'tis severall,   35
By occasion wak'd, and circumstantiall.
True vertue is *Soule*, Alwaies in all deeds *All*.

This Vertue thinking to give dignitie
To your soule, found there no infirmitie,
For, your soule was as good Vertue, as shee;   40

Shee therefore wrought upon that part of you
Which is scarce lesse then soule, as she could do,
And so hath made your beauty, Vertue too.

Hence comes it, that your Beauty wounds not hearts,
As Others, with prophane and sensuall Darts,   45
But as an influence, vertuous thoughts imparts.

But if such friends by the honor of your sight
Grow capable of this so great a light,
As to partake your vertues, and their might,

What must I thinke that influence must doe,   50
Where it findes sympathie and matter too,
Vertue, and beauty of the same stuffe, as you?

Which is, your noble worthie sister, shee
Of whom, if what in this my Extasie
And revelation of you both I see,   55

I should write here, as in short Galleries
The Master at the end large glasses ties,
So to present the roome twice to our eyes,

So I should give this letter length, and say
That which I said of you; there is no way   60
From either, but by the other, not to stray.

May therefore this be enough to testifie
My true devotion, free from flattery;
He that beleeves himselfe, doth never lie.

To the Countesse of Salisbury

August. 1614

Faire, great, and good, since seeing you, wee see
What Heaven can doe, and what any Earth can be:
Since now your beauty shines, now when the Sunne
Growne stale, is to so low a value runne,
That his disshevel'd beames and scattered fires   5
Serve but for Ladies Periwigs and Tyres
In lovers Sonnets: you come to repaire
Gods booke of creatures, teaching what is faire.
Since now, when all is withered, shrunke, and dri'd,
All Vertues ebb'd out to a dead low tyde,   10
All the worlds frame being crumbled into sand,
Where every man thinks by himselfe to stand,
Integritie, friendship, and confidence,
(Ciments of greatnes) being vapor'd hence,
And narrow man being fill'd with little shares,   15
Court, Citie, Church, are all shops of small-wares,
All having blowne to sparkes their noble fire,
And drawne their sound gold-ingot into wyre;
All trying by a love of littlenesse
To make abridgments, and to draw to lesse,   20
Even that nothing, which at first we were;
Since in these times, your greatnesse doth appeare,
And that we learne by it, that man to get
Towards him that's infinite, must first be great.
Since in an age so ill, as none is fit   25
So much as to accuse, must lesse mend it,
(For who can judge, or witnesse of those times
Where all alike are guiltie of the crimes?)
Where he that would be good, is thought by all
A monster, or at best fantasticall;   30
Since now you durst be good, and that I doe
Discerne, by daring to contemplate you,
That there may be degrees of faire, great, good,
Through your light, largenesse, vertue understood;
If in this sacrifice of mine, be showne   35
Any small sparke of these, call it your owne.

And if things like these, have been said by mee
Of others; call not that Idolatrie.
For had God made man first, and man had seene
The third daies fruits, and flowers, and various greene,   40
He might have said the best that he could say
Of those faire creatures, which were made that day;
And when next day he had admir'd the birth
Of Sun, Moone, Stars, fairer then late-prais'd earth,
Hee might have said the best that he could say,   45
And not be chid for praising yesterday;
So though some things are not together true,
As, that another is worthiest, and, that you:
Yet, to say so, doth not condemne a man,
If when he spoke them, they were both true than.   50
How faire a proofe of this, in our soule growes?
Wee first have soules of growth, and sense, and those,
When our last soule, our soule immortall came,
Were swallowed into it, and have no name.
Nor doth he injure those soules, which doth cast   55
The power and praise of both them, on the last;
No more doe I wrong any; I adore
The same things now, which I ador'd before,
The subject chang'd, and measure; the same thing
In a low constable, and in the King   60
I reverence; His power to work on mee:
So did I humbly reverence each degree
Of faire, great, good; but more, now I am come
From having found their *walkes*, to find their *home*.
And as I owe my first soules thankes, that they   65
For my last soule did fit and mould my clay,
So am I debtor unto them, whose worth,
Enabled me to profit, and take forth
This new great lesson, thus to study you;
Which none, not reading others, first, could doe.   70
Nor lacke I light to read this booke, though I
In a darke Cave, yea in a Grave doe lie;
For as your fellow Angells, so you doe
Illustrate them who come to study you.
The first whom we in Histories doe finde   75
To have profest all Arts, was one borne blinde:

He lackt those eyes beasts have as well as wee,
Not those, by which Angels are seene and see;
So, though I'am borne without those eyes to live,
Which fortune, who hath none her selfe, doth give,   80
Which are, fit meanes to see bright courts and you,
Yet may I see you thus, as now I doe;
I shall by that, all goodnesse have discern'd,
And though I burne my librarie, be learn'd.

To the Lady Bedford

You that are she and you, that's double shee,
　　In her dead face, halfe of your selfe shall see;
Shee was the other part, for so they doe
　　Which build them friendships, become one of two;
So two, that but themselves no third can fit,   5
　　Which were to be so, when they were not yet;
Twinnes, though their birth *Cusco*, and *Musco* take,
　　As divers starres one Constellation make;
Pair'd like two eyes, have equall motion, so
　　Both but one meanes to see, one way to goe.   10
Had you dy'd first, a carcasse shee had beene;
　　And wee your rich Tombe in her face had seene;
She like the Soule is gone, and you here stay,
　　Not a live friend; but th'other halfe of clay.
And since you act that part, As men say, here   15
　　Lies such a Prince, when but one part is there,
And do all honour and devotion due
　　Unto the whole, so wee all reverence you;
For, such a friendship who would not adore
　　In you, who are all what both were before,   20
Not all, as if some perished by this,
　　But so, as all in you contracted is.
As of this all, though many parts decay,
　　The pure which elemented them shall stay;
And though diffus'd, and spread in infinite,   25
　　Shall recollect, and in one All unite:
So madame, as her Soule to heaven is fled,
　　Her flesh rests in the earth, as in the bed;

Her vertues do, as to their proper spheare,
   Returne to dwell with you, of whom they were: 30
As perfect motions are all circular,
   So they to you, their sea, whence lesse streames are.
Shee was all spices, you all metalls; so
   In you two wee did both rich Indies know.
And as no fire, nor rust can spend or waste   35
   One dramme of gold, but what was first shall last,
Though it bee forc'd in water, earth, salt, aire,
   Expans'd in infinite, none will impaire;
So, to your selfe you may additions take,
   But nothing can you lesse, or changed make.   40
Seeke not in seeking new, to seeme to doubt,
   That you can match her, or not be without;
But let some faithfull booke in her roome be,
   Yet but of *Judith* no such booke as shee.

AN
ANATOMIE
OF THE WORLD

WHEREIN,
BY OCCASION OF THE
UNTIMELY DEATH OF
MISTRIS ELIZABETH DRVRY,
THE FRAILTY AND THE DECAY
OF THIS WHOLE WORLD
IS REPRESENTED

To the praise of the dead,
and the ANATOMIE

Well dy'd the World, that we might live to see
This world of wit, in his Anatomie:
No evill wants his good; so wilder heires
Bedew their Fathers Tombes, with forced teares,
Whose state requites their losse: whiles thus we gain,   5
Well may wee walke in blacks, but not complaine.
Yet how can I consent the world is dead
While this Muse lives? which in his spirits stead
Seemes to informe a World; and bids it bee,
In spight of losse or fraile mortalitie?   10
And thou the subject of this welborne thought,
Thrice noble maid, couldst not have found nor sought
A fitter time to yeeld to thy sad Fate,
Then whiles this spirit lives, that can relate
Thy worth so well to our last Nephews eyne,   15
That they shall wonder both at his and thine:

Admired match! where strives in mutuall grace
The cunning pencill, and the comely face:
A taske which thy faire goodnesse made too much
For the bold pride of vulgar pens to touch;   20
Enough is us to praise them that praise thee,
And say, that but enough those prayses bee,
Which hadst thou liv'd, had hid their fearfull head
From th'angry checkings of thy modest red:
Death barres reward and shame: when envy's gone,   25
And gaine, 'tis safe to give the dead their owne.
As then the wise Egyptians wont to lay
More on their Tombes, then houses: these of clay,
But those of brasse, or marble were: so wee
Give more unto thy Ghost, then unto thee.   30
Yet what wee give to thee, thou gav'st to us,
And may'st but thanke thy selfe, for being thus:
Yet what thou gav'st, and wert, O happy maid,
Thy grace profest all due, where 'tis repayd.
So these high songs that to thee suited bin   35
Serve but to sound thy Makers praise, in thine,
Which thy deare soule as sweetly sings to him
Amid the Quire of Saints, and Seraphim,
As any Angels tongue can sing of thee;
The subjects differ, though the skill agree: 40
For as by infant-yeares men judge of age,
Thy early love, thy vertues, did presage
What an high part thou bear'st in those best songs,
Whereto no burden, nor no end belongs.
Sing on thou virgin Soule, whose lossfull gaine   45
Thy lovesick parents have bewail'd in vaine;
Never may thy Name be in our songs forgot,
Till wee shall sing thy ditty and thy note.

The first Anniversary

When that rich Soule which to her heaven is gone,
Whom all do celebrate, who know they have one,
(For who is sure he hath a Soule, unlesse
It see, and judge, and follow worthinesse,

And by Deedes praise it? hee who doth not this,   5
May lodge an In-mate soule, but 'tis not his.)
When that Queene ended here her progresse time,
And, as t'her standing house to heaven did climbe,
Where loath to make the Saints attend her long,
She's now a part both of the Quire, and Song,   10
This World, in that great earthquake languished;
For in a common bath of teares it bled,
Which drew the strongest vitall spirits out:
But succour'd then with a perplexed doubt,
Whether the world did lose, or gaine in this,   15
(Because since now no other way there is,
But goodnesse, to see her, whom all would see,
All must endeavour to be good as shee,)
This great consumption to a fever turn'd,
And so the world had fits; it joy'd, it mourn'd;   20
And, as men thinke, that Agues physick are,
And th'Ague being spent, give over care,
So thou sicke World, mistak'st thy selfe to bee
Well, when alas, thou'rt in a Lethargie.
Her death did wound and tame thee than, and than   25
Thou might'st have better spar'd the Sunne, or Man.
That wound was deep, but 'tis more misery,
That thou hast lost thy sense and memory.
'Twas heavy then to heare thy voyce of mone,
But this is worse, that thou art speechlesse growne.   30
Thou hast forgot thy name, thou hadst; thou wast
Nothing but shee, and her thou hast o'rpast.
For as a child kept from the Font, untill
A prince, expected long, come to fulfill
The ceremonies, thou unnam'd had'st laid,   35
Had not her comming, thee her Palace made:
Her name defin'd thee, gave thee forme, and frame,
And thou forgett'st to celebrate thy name.
Some moneths she hath beene dead (but being dead,
Measures of times are all determined)   40
But long she'ath beene away, long, long, yet none
Offers to tell us who it is that's gone.
But as in states doubtfull of future heires,
When sicknesse without remedie empaires

The present Prince, they're loth it should be said,   45
The Prince doth languish, or the Prince is dead:
So mankinde feeling now a generall thaw,
A strong example gone, equall to law,
The Cyment which did faithfully compact,
And glue all vertues, now resolv'd, and slack'd,   50
Thought it some blasphemy to say sh'was dead,
Or that our weakenesse was discovered
In that confession; therefore spoke no more
Then tongues, the Soule being gone, the losse deplore.
But though it be too late to succour thee,   55
Sicke World, yea, dead, yea putrified, since shee
Thy'intrinsique balme, and thy preservative,
Can never be renew'd, thou never live,
I (since no man can make thee live) will try,
What wee may gaine by thy Anatomy.   60
Her death hath taught us dearely, that thou art
Corrupt and mortall in thy purest part.
Let no man say, the world it selfe being dead,
'Tis labour lost to have discovered
The worlds infirmities, since there is none   65
Alive to study this dissection;
For there's a kinde of World remaining still,
Though shee which did inanimate and fill
The world, be gone, yet in this last long night,
Her Ghost doth walke; that is, a glimmering light,   70
A faint weake love of vertue, and of good,
Reflects from her, on them which understood
Her worth; and though she have shut in all day,
The twilight of her memory doth stay;
Which, from the carcasse of the old world, free,   75
Creates a new world, and new creatures bee
Produc'd: the matter and the stuffe of this,
Her vertue, and the forme our practice is:
And though to be thus elemented, arme
These creatures, from home-borne intrinsique harme,   80
(For all assum'd unto this dignitie,
So many weedlesse Paradises bee,
Which of themselves produce no venemous sinne,
Except some forraine Serpent bring it in)

Yet, because outward stormes the strongest breake,   85
And strength it selfe by confidence growes weake,
This new world may be safer, being told
The dangers and diseases of the old:
For with due temper men doe then forgoe,
Or covet things, when they their true worth know.   90
There is no health; Physitians say that wee,
At best, enjoy but a neutralitie.
And can there bee worse sicknesse, then to know
That we are never well, nor can be so?
Wee are borne ruinous: poore mothers cry,   95
That children come not right, nor orderly;
Except they headlong come and fall upon
An ominous precipitation.
How witty's ruine! how importunate
Upon mankinde! it labour'd to frustrate   100
Even Gods purpose; and made woman, sent
For mans reliefe, cause of his languishment.
They were to good ends, and they are so still,
But accessory, and principall in ill;
For that first marriage was our funerall: 105
One woman at one blow, then kill'd us all,
And singly, one by one, they kill us now.
We doe delightfully our selves allow
To that consumption; and profusely blinde,
Wee kill our selves to propagate our kinde.   110
And yet we do not that; we are not men:
There is not now that mankinde, which was then,
When as the Sunne and man did seeme to strive,
(Joynt tenants of the world) who should survive;
When, Stagge, and Raven, and the long-liv'd tree,   115
Compar'd with man, dy'd in minoritie;
When, if a slow pac'd starre had stolne away
From the observers marking, he might stay
Two or three hundred yeares to see't againe,
And then make up his observation plaine;   120
When, as the age was long, the sise was great;
Mans growth confess'd, and recompenc'd the meat;
So spacious and large, that every Soule
Did a faire Kingdome, and large Realme controule:

And when the very stature, thus erect, 125
Did that soule a good way towards heaven direct.
Where is this mankinde now? who lives to age,
Fit to be made *Methusalem* his page?
Alas, we scarce live long enough to try
Whether a true made clocke run right, or lie. 130
Old Grandsires talke of yesterday with sorrow,
And for our children wee reserve to morrow.
So short is life, that every peasant strives,
In a torne house, or field, to have three lives.
And as in lasting, so in length is man 135
Contracted to an inch, who was a spanne;
For had a man at first in forrests stray'd,
Or shipwrack'd in the Sea, one would have laid
A wager, that an Elephant, or Whale,
That met him, would not hastily assaile 140
A thing so equall to him: now alas,
The Fairies, and the Pigmies well may passe
As credible; mankinde decayes so soone,
We'are scarce our Fathers shadowes cast at noone:
Onely death addes t'our length: nor are wee growne 145
In stature to be men, till we are none.
But this were light, did our lesse volume hold
All the old Text; or had wee chang'd to gold
Their silver; or dispos'd into lesse glasse
Spirits of vertue, which then scatter'd was. 150
But 'tis not so: w'are not retir'd, but dampt;
And as our bodies, so our mindes are crampt:
'Tis shrinking, not close weaving that hath thus,
In minde, and body both bedwarfed us.
Wee seeme ambitious, Gods whole worke t'undoe; 155
Of nothing hee made us, and we strive too,
To bring our selves to nothing backe; and wee
Doe what wee can, to do't so soone as hee.
With new diseases on our selves we warre,
And with new Physicke, a worse Engin farre. 160
Thus man, this worlds Vice-Emperour, in whom
All faculties, all graces are at home;
And if in other creatures they appeare,
They're but mans Ministers, and Legats there,

To worke on their rebellions, and reduce   165
Them to Civility, and to mans use:
This man, whom God did wooe, and loth t'attend
Till man came up, did downe to man descend,
This man, so great, that all that is, is his,
Oh what a trifle, and poore thing he is!   170
If man were any thing, he's nothing now:
Helpe, or at least some time to wast, allow
T'his other wants, yet when he did depart
With her whom we lament, hee lost his heart.
She, of whom th'Ancients seem'd to prophesie,   175
When they call'd vertues by the name of *shee*;
Shee in whom vertue was so much refin'd,
That for Allay unto so pure a minde
Shee tooke the weaker Sex; shee that could drive
The poysonous tincture, and the staine of *Eve*,   180
Out of her thoughts, and deeds; and purifie
All, by a true religious Alchymie;
Shee, shee is dead; shee's dead: when thou knowest this,
Thou knowest how poore a trifling thing man is.
And learn'st thus much by our Anatomie,   185
The heart being perish'd, no part can be free.
And that except thou feed (not banquet) on
The supernaturall food, Religion,
Thy better Growth growes withered, and scant;
Be more then man, or thou'rt lesse then an Ant.   190
Then, as mankinde, so is the worlds whole frame
Quite out of joynt, almost created lame:
For, before God had made up all the rest,
Corruption entred, and deprav'd the best:
It seis'd the Angels, and then first of all   195
The world did in her cradle take a fall,
And turn'd her braines, and tooke a generall maime,
Wronging each joynt of th'universall frame.
The noblest part, man, felt it first; and than
Both beasts and plants, curst in the curse of man.   200
So did the world from the first houre decay,
That evening was beginning of the day,
And now the Springs and Sommers which we see,
Like sonnes of women after fiftie bee.

And new Philosophy calls all in doubt,   205
The Element of fire is quite put out;
The Sun is lost, and th'earth, and no mans wit
Can well direct him where to looke for it.
And freely men confesse that this world's spent,
When in the Planets, and the Firmament   210
They seeke so many new; they see that this
Is crumbled out againe to his Atomies.
'Tis all in peeces, all cohaerence gone;
All just supply, and all Relation:
Prince, Subject, Father, Sonne, are things forgot,   215
For every man alone thinkes he hath got
To be a Phœnix, and that then can bee
None of that kinde, of which he is, but hee.
This is the worlds condition now, and now
She that should all parts to reunion bow,   220
She that had all Magnetique force alone,
To draw, and fasten sundred parts in one;
She whom wise nature had invented then
When she observ'd that every sort of men
Did in their voyage in this worlds Sea stray,   225
And needed a new compasse for their way;
She that was best, and first originall
Of all faire copies, and the generall
Steward to Fate; she whose rich eyes, and brest
Guilt the West Indies, and perfum'd the East;   230
Whose having breath'd in this world, did bestow
Spice on those Iles, and bad them still smell so,
And that rich Indie which doth gold interre,
Is but as single money, coyn'd from her:
She to whom this world must it selfe refer,   235
As Suburbs, or the Microcosme of her,
Shee, shee is dead; shee's dead: when thou knowst this,
Thou knowst how lame a cripple this world is.
And learn'st thus much by our Anatomy,
That this worlds generall sickenesse doth not lie   240
In any humour, or one certaine part;
Thou seest a Hectique feaver hath got hold
Of the whole substance, not to be contrould,
And that thou hast but one way, not t'admit
The worlds infection, to be none of it.   245

For the worlds subtilst immateriall parts
Feele this consuming wound, and ages darts.
For the worlds beauty is decai'd, or gone,
Beauty, that's colour, and proportion.
We thinke the heavens enjoy their Sphericall,   250
Their round proportion embracing all.
But yet their various and perplexed course,
Observ'd in divers ages, doth enforce
Men to finde out so many Eccentrique parts,
Such divers downe-right lines, such overthwarts,   255
As disproportion that pure forme: It teares
The Firmament in eight and forty sheires,
And in these Constellations then arise
New starres, and old doe vanish from our eyes:
As though heav'n suffered earthquakes, peace or war,   260
When new Towers rise, and old demolish't are.
They have impal'd within a Zodiake
The free-borne Sun, and keepe twelve Signes awake
To watch his steps; the Goat and Crab controule,
And fright him backe, who else to either Pole   265
(Did not these Tropiques fetter him) might runne:
For his course is not round; nor can the Sunne
Perfit a Circle, or maintaine his way
One inch direct; but where he rose to-day
He comes no more, but with a couzening line,   270
Steales by that point, and so is Serpentine:
And seeming weary with his reeling thus,
He meanes to sleepe, being now falne nearer us.
So, of the Starres which boast that they doe runne
In Circle still, none ends where he begun.   275
All their proportion's lame, it sinkes, it swels.
For of Meridians, and Parallels,
Man hath weav'd out a net, and this net throwne
Upon the Heavens, and now they are his owne.
Loth to goe up the hill, or labour thus   280
To goe to heaven, we make heaven come to us.
We spur, we reine the starres, and in their race
They're diversly content t'obey our pace.
But keepes the earth her round proportion still?
Doth not a Tenarif, or higher Hill   285

Rise so high like a Rocke, that one might thinke
The floating Moone would shipwracke there, and sinke?
Seas are so deepe, that Whales being strooke to day,
Perchance to morrow, scarce at middle way
Of their wish'd journies end, the bottome, die.   290
And men, to sound depths, so much line untie,
As one might justly thinke, that there would rise
At end thereof, one of th'Antipodies:
If under all, a Vault infernall bee,
(Which sure is spacious, except that we   295
Invent another torment, that there must
Millions into a strait hot roome be thrust)
Then solidnesse, and roundnesse have no place.
Are these but warts, and pock-holes in the face
Of th'earth? Thinke so: but yet confesse, in this   300
The worlds proportion disfigured is;
That those two legges whereon it doth rely,
Reward and punishment are bent awry.
And, Oh, it can no more be questioned,
That beauties best, proportion, is dead,   305
Since even griefe it selfe, which now alone
Is left us, is without proportion.
Shee by whose lines proportion should bee
Examin'd, measure of all Symmetree,
Whom had that Ancient seen, who thought soules made 310
Of Harmony, he would at next have said
That Harmony was shee, and thence infer,
That soules were but Resultances from her,
And did from her into our bodies goe,
As to our eyes, the formes from objects flow: 315
Shee, who if those great Doctors truly said
That the Arke to mans proportions was made,
Had been a type for that, as that might be
A type of her in this, that contrary
Both Elements, and Passions liv'd at peace   320
In her, who caus'd all Civill war to cease.
Shee, after whom, what former <fo'er> we see,
Is discord, and rude incongruitie;
Shee, shee is dead, shee's dead; when thou knowst this
Thou knowst how ugly a monster this world is: 325

And learn'st thus much by our Anatomie,
That here is nothing to enamour thee:
And that, not only faults in inward parts,
Corruptions in our braines, or in our hearts,
Poysoning the fountaines, whence our actions spring,   330
Endanger us: but that if every thing
Be not done fitly'and in proportion,
To satisfie wise, and good lookers on,
(Since most men be such as most thinke they bee)
They're lothsome too, by this Deformitee.   335
For good, and well, must in our actions meete;
Wicked is not much worse than indiscreet.
But beauties other second Element,
Colour, and lustre now, is as neere spent.
And had the world his just proportion,   340
Were it a ring still, yet the stone is gone.
As a compassionate Turcoyse which doth tell
By looking pale, the wearer is not well,
As gold falls sicke being stung with Mercury,
All the worlds parts of such complexion bee.   345
When nature was most busie, the first weeke,
Swadling the new borne earth, God seem'd to like
That she should sport her selfe sometimes, and play,
To mingle, and vary colours every day:
And then, as though shee could not make inow,   350
Himselfe his various Rainbow did allow.
Sight is the noblest sense of any one,
Yet sight hath only colour to feed on,
And colour is decai'd: summers robe growes
Duskie, and like an oft dyed garment showes.   355
Our blushing red, which us'd in cheekes to spred,
Is inward sunke, and only our soules are red.
Perchance the world might have recovered,
If she whom we lament had not beene dead:
But shee, in whom all white, and red, and blew   360
(Beauties ingredients) voluntary grew,
As in an unvext Paradise; from whom
Did all things verdure, and their lustre come,
Whose composition was miraculous,
Being all colour, all Diaphanous,   365

(For Ayre, and Fire but thick grosse bodies were,
And liveliest stones but drowsie, and pale to her,)
Shee, shee, is dead: shee's dead: when thou know'st this,
Thou knowst how wan a Ghost this our world is:
And learn'st thus much by our Anatomie,   370
That it should more affright, then pleasure thee.
And that, since all faire colour then did sinke,
'Tis now but wicked vanitie, to thinke
To colour vicious deeds with good pretence,
Or with bought colors to illude mens sense.   375
Nor in ought more this worlds decay appeares,
Then that her influence the heav'n forbeares,
Or that the Elements doe not feele this,
The father, or the mother barren is.
The cloudes conceive not raine, or doe not powre,   380
In the due birth time, downe the balmy showre;
Th'Ayre doth not motherly sit on the earth,
To hatch her seasons, and give all things birth;
Spring-times were common cradles, but are tombes;
And false-conceptions fill the generall wombes;   385
Th'Ayre showes such Meteors, as none can see,
Not only what they meane, but what they bee;
Earth such new wormes, as would have troubled much
Th'Ægyptian *Mages* to have made more such.
What Artist now dares boast that he can bring   390
Heaven hither, or constellate any thing,
So as the influence of those starres may bee
Imprison'd in an Hearbe, or Charme, or Tree,
And doe by touch, all which those stars could doe?
The art is lost, and correspondence too.   395
For heaven gives little, and the earth takes lesse,
And man least knowes their trade and purposes.
If this commerce twixt heaven and earth were not
Embarr'd, and all this traffique quite forgot,
She, for whose losse we have lamented thus,   400
Would worke more fully, and pow'rfully on us:
Since herbes, and roots, by dying lose not all,
But they, yea Ashes too, are medicinall,
Death could not quench her vertue so, but that
It would be (if not follow'd) wondred at: 405

And all the world would be one dying Swan,
To sing her funerall praise, and vanish than.
But as some Serpents poyson hurteth not,
Except it be from the live Serpent shot,
So doth her vertue need her here, to fit   410
That unto us; shee working more then it.
But shee, in whom to such maturity
Vertue was growne, past growth, that it must die;
She, from whose influence all Impressions came,
But, by Receivers impotencies, lame,   415
Who, though she could not transubstantiate
All states to gold, yet guilded every state,
So that some Princes have some temperance;
Some Counsellers some purpose to advance
The common profit; and some people have   420
Some stay, no more then Kings should give, to crave;
Some women have some taciturnity,
Some nunneries some graines of chastitie.
She that did thus much, and much more could doe,
But that our age was Iron, and rustie too,   425
Shee, shee is dead; shee's dead; when thou knowst this,
Thou knowst how drie a Cinder this world is.
And learn'st thus much by our Anatomy,
That 'tis in vaine to dew, or mollifie
It with thy teares, or sweat, or blood: nothing   430
Is worth our travaile, griefe, or perishing,
But those rich joyes, which did possesse her heart,
Of which she's now partaker, and a part.
But as in cutting up a man that's dead,
The body will not last out, to have read   435
On every part, and therefore men direct
Their speech to parts, that are of most effect;
So the worlds carcasse would not last, if I
Were punctuall in this Anatomy;
Nor smels it well to hearers, if one tell   440
Them their disease, who faine would think they're well.
Here therefore be the end: And, blessed maid,
Of whom is meant what ever hath been said,
Or shall be spoken well by any tongue,
Whose name refines course lines, and makes prose song, 445

Accept this tribute, and his first yeares rent,
Who till his darke short tapers end be spent,
As oft as thy feast sees this widowed earth,
Will yearely celebrate thy second birth,
That is, thy death; for though the soule of man   450
Be got when man is made, 'tis borne but than
When man doth die; our body's as the wombe,
And, as a Mid-wife, death directs it home.
And you her creatures, whom she workes upon,
And have your last, and best concoction   455
From her example, and her vertue, if you
In reverence to her, do thinke it due,
That no one should her praises thus rehearse,
As matter fit for Chronicle, not verse;
Vouchsafe to call to minde that God did make   460
A last, and lasting'st peece, a song. He spake
To *Moses* to deliver unto all,
That song, because hee knew they would let fall
The Law, the Prophets, and the History,
But keepe the song still in their memory: 465
Such an opinion (in due measure) made
Me this great Office boldly to invade:
Nor could incomprehensiblenesse deterre
Mee, from thus trying to emprison her,
Which when I saw that a strict grave could doe,   470
I saw not why verse might not do so too.
Verse hath a middle nature: heaven keepes Soules,
The Grave keepes bodies, Verse the Fame enroules.

A *Funerall* ELEGIE

'Tis lost, to trust a Tombe with such a guest,
Or to confine her in a marble chest.
Alas, what's Marble, Jeat, or Porphyrie,
Priz'd with the Chrysolite of either eye,
Or with those Pearles, and Rubies, which she was?   5
Joyne the two Indies in one Tombe, 'tis glasse;
And so is all to her materials,
Though every inch were ten Escurials,

Yet she's demolish'd: can wee keepe her then
In works of hands, or of the wits of men?   10
Can these memorials, ragges of paper, give
Life to that name, by which name they must live?
Sickly, alas, short-liv'd, aborted bee
Those carcasse verses, whose soule is not shee.
And can shee, who no longer would be shee,   15
Being such a Tabernacle, stoop to be
In paper wrapt; or, when shee would not lie
In such a house, dwell in an Elegie?
But 'tis no matter; wee may well allow
Verse to live so long as the world will now,   20
For her death wounded it. The world containes
Princes for armes, and Counsellors for braines,
Lawyers for tongues, Divines for hearts, and more,
The Rich for stomackes, and for backes, the Poore;
The Officers for hands, Merchants for feet,   25
By which, remote and distant Countries meet.
But those fine spirits which do tune, and set
This Organ, are those peeces which beget
Wonder and love; and these were shee; and shee
Being spent, the world must needs decrepit bee;   30
For since death will proceed to triumph still,
He can finde nothing, after her, to kill,
Except the world it selfe, so great as shee.
Thus brave and confident may Nature bee,
Death cannot give her such another blow,   35
Because shee cannot such another show.
But must wee say she's dead? may't not be said
That as a sundred clocke is peecemeale laid,
Not to be lost, but by the makers hand
Repollish'd, without errour then to stand,   40
Or as the Affrique Niger streame enwombs
It selfe into the earth, and after comes
(Having first made a naturall bridge, to passe
For many leagues) farre greater then it was,
May't not be said, that her grave shall restore   45
Her, greater, purer, firmer, then before?
Heaven may say this, and joy in't, but can wee
Who live, and lacke her, here this vantage see?

What is't to us, alas, if there have beene
An Angell made a Throne, or Cherubin?   50
Wee lose by't: and as aged men are glad
Being tastlesse growne, to joy in joyes they had,
So now the sick starv'd world must feed upon
This joy, that we had her, who now is gone.
Rejoyce then Nature, and this World, that you,   55
Fearing the last fires hastning to subdue
Your force and vigour, ere it were neere gone,
Wisely bestow'd and laid it all on one.
One, whose cleare body was so pure and thinne,
Because it need disguise no thought within.   60
'Twas but a through-light scarfe, her minde t'inroule;
Or exhalation breath'd out from her Soule.
One, whom all men who durst no more, admir'd:
And whom, who ere had worth enough, desir'd;
As when a Temple's built, Saints emulate   65
To which of them, it shall be consecrate.
But, as when heaven lookes on us with new eyes,
Those new starres every Artist exercise,
What place they should assigne to them they doubt,
Argue,'and agree not, till those starres goe out: 70
So the world studied whose this peece should be,
Till shee can be no bodies else, nor shee:
But like a Lampe of Balsamum, desir'd
Rather t'adorne, then last, she soone expir'd,
Cloath'd in her virgin white integritie,   75
For marriage, though it doe not staine, doth dye.
To scape th'infirmities which wait upon
Woman, she went away, before sh'was one;
And the worlds busie noyse to overcome,
Tooke so much death, as serv'd for *opium*;   80
For though she could not, nor could chuse to dye,
She'ath yeelded to too long an extasie:
Hee which not knowing her said History,
Should come to reade the booke of destiny,
How faire, and chast, humble, and high she'ad been,   85
Much promis'd, much perform'd, at not fifteene,
And measuring future things, by things before,
Should turne the leafe to reade, and reade no more,

Would thinke that either destiny mistooke,
Or that some leaves were torne out of the booke.   90
But 'tis not so; Fate did but usher her
To yeares of reasons use, and then inferre
Her destiny to her selfe, which liberty
She tooke but for thus much, thus much to die.
Her modestie not suffering her to bee   95
Fellow-Commissioner with Destinie,
She did no more but die; if after her
Any shall live, which dare true good prefer,
Every such person is her deligate,
T'accomplish that which should have beene her Fate.   100
They shall make up that Booke and shall have thanks
Of Fate, and her, for filling up their blankes.
For future vertuous deeds are Legacies,
Which from the gift of her example rise;
And 'tis in heav'n part of spirituall mirth,   105
To see how well the good play her, on earth.

OF THE
PROGRESSE
OF THE SOULE

WHEREIN,
BY OCCASION OF THE RELIGIOUS
DEATH OF
MISTRIS ELIZABETH DRVRY,
THE INCOMMODITIES OF THE
SOULE IN THIS LIFE, AND HER
EXALTATION IN THE NEXT,
ARE CONTEMPLATED

The Harbinger to the
Progresse

Two soules move here, and mine (a third) must move
Paces of admiration, and of love;
Thy Soule (deare virgin) whose this tribute is,
Mov'd from this mortall Spheare to lively blisse;
And yet moves still, and still aspires to see   5
The worlds last day, thy glories full degree:
Like as those starres which thou o'r-lookest farre,
Are in their place, and yet still moved are:
No soule (whiles with the luggage of this clay
It clogged is) can follow thee halfe way;   10
Or see thy flight, which doth our thoughts outgoe
So fast, that now the lightning moves but slow:

But now thou art as high in heaven flowne
As heaven's from us; what soule besides thine owne
Can tell thy joyes, or say he can relate   15
Thy glorious Journals in that blessed state?
I envie thee (Rich soule) I envy thee,
Although I cannot yet thy glory see:
And thou (great spirit) which hers follow'd hast
So fast, as none can follow thine so fast;   20
So far, as none can follow thine so farre,
(And if this flesh did not the passage barre
Hadst caught her) let me wonder at thy flight
Which long agone hadst lost the vulgar sight,
And now mak'st proud the better eyes, that they   25
Can see thee less'ned in thine ayery way;
So while thou mak'st her soule by progresse knowne
Thou mak'st a noble progresse of thine owne,
From this worlds carkasse having mounted high
To that pure life of immortalitie.   30
Since thine aspiring thoughts themselves so raise
That more may not beseeme a creatures praise,
Yet still thou vow'st her more; and every yeare
Mak'st a new progresse, while thou wandrest here;
Still upward mount; and let thy Makers praise   35
Honor thy Laura, and adorne thy laies.
And since thy Muse her head in heaven shrouds,
Oh let her never stoope below the clouds:
And if those glorious sainted soules may know
Or what wee doe, or what wee sing below,   40
Those acts, those songs shall still content them best
Which praise those awfull Powers that make them blest.

The second Anniversarie.

Nothing could make me sooner to confesse
That this world had an everlastingnesse,
Then to consider, that a yeare is runne,
Since both this lower world's, and the Sunnes Sunne,
The Lustre, and the vigor of this All,   5
Did set; 'twere blasphemie to say, did fall.

But as a ship which hath strooke saile, doth runne
By force of that force which before, it wonne:
Or as sometimes in a beheaded man,
Though at those two Red seas, which freely ranne,   10
One from the Trunke, another from the Head,
His soule be sail'd, to her eternall bed,
His eyes will twinckle, and his tongue will roll,
As though he beckned, and cal'd backe his soule,
He graspes his hands, and he pulls up his feet,   15
And seemes to reach, and to step forth to meet
His soule; when all these motions which we saw,
Are but as Ice, which crackles at a thaw:
Or as a Lute, which in moist weather, rings
Her knell alone, by cracking of her strings: 20
So struggles this dead world, now shee is gone;
For there is motion in corruption.
As some daies are at the Creation nam'd,
Before the Sunne, the which fram'd daies, was fram'd,
So after this Sunne's set, some shew appeares,   25
And orderly vicissitude of yeares.
Yet a new Deluge, and of *Lethe* flood,
Hath drown'd us all, All have forgot all good,
Forgetting her, the maine reserve of all.
Yet in this deluge, grosse and generall,   30
Thou seest me strive for life; my life shall bee,
To be hereafter prais'd, for praysing thee;
Immortall Maid, who though thou would'st refuse
The name of Mother, be unto my Muse
A Father, since her chast Ambition is,   35
Yearely to bring forth such a child as this.
These Hymnes may worke on future wits, and so
May great Grand children of thy prayses grow.
And so, though not revive, embalme and spice
The world, which else would putrifie with vice.   40
For thus, Man may extend thy progeny,
Untill man doe but vanish, and not die.
These Hymnes thy issue, may encrease so long,
As till Gods great *Venite* change the song.
Thirst for that time, O my insatiate soule,   45
And serve thy thirst, with Gods safe-sealing Bowle.

Be thirstie still, and drinke still till thou goe
To th'only Health, to be Hydroptique so.
Forget this rotten world; And unto thee
Let thine owne times as an old storie bee.   50
Be not concern'd: studie not why, nor when;
Doe not so much as not beleeve a man.
For though to erre, be worst, to try truths forth,
Is far more businesse, then this world is worth.
The world is but a carkasse; thou art fed   55
By it, but as a worme, that carkasse bred;
And why should'st thou, poore worme, consider more,
When this world will grow better then before,
Then those thy fellow wormes doe thinke upon
That carkasses last resurrection.   60
Forget this world, and scarce thinke of it so,
As of old clothes, cast off a yeare agoe.
To be thus stupid is Alacritie;
Men thus Lethargique have best Memory.
Look upward; that's towards her, whose happy state   65
We now lament not, but congratulate.
Shee, to whom all this world was but a stage,
Where all sat harkning how her youthfull age
Should be emploi'd, because in all shee did,
Some Figure of the Golden times was hid.   70
Who could not lacke, what e'r this world could give,
Because shee was the forme, that made it live;
Nor could complaine, that this world was unfit
To be staid in, then when shee was in it;
Shee that first tried indifferent desires   75
By vertue, and vertue by religious fires,
Shee to whose person Paradise adher'd,
As Courts to Princes, shee whose eyes ensphear'd
Star-light enough, t'have made the South controule,
(Had shee beene there) the Star-full Northerne Pole,   80
Shee, shee is gone; she is gone; when thou knowest this,
What fragmentary rubbidge this world is
Thou knowest, and that it is not worth a thought;
He honors it too much that thinkes it nought.
Thinke then, my soule, that death is but a Groome,   85
Which brings a Taper to the outward roome,

Whence thou spiest first a little glimmering light,
And after brings it nearer to thy sight:
For such approaches doth heaven make in death.
Thinke thy selfe labouring now with broken breath,   90
And thinke those broken and soft Notes to bee
Division, and thy happyest Harmonie.
Thinke thee laid on thy death-bed, loose and slacke;
And thinke that, but unbinding of a packe,
To take one precious thing, thy soule from thence.   95
Thinke thy selfe parch'd with fevers violence,
Anger thine ague more, by calling it
Thy Physicke; chide the slacknesse of the fit.
Thinke that thou hear'st thy knell, and think no more,
But that, as Bels cal'd thee to Church before,   100
So this, to the Triumphant Church, calls thee.
Thinke Satans Sergeants round about thee bee,
And thinke that but for Legacies they thrust;
Give one thy Pride, to'another give thy Lust:
Give them those sinnes which they gave thee before,   105
And trust th'immaculate blood to wash thy score.
Thinke thy friends weeping round, and thinke that they
Weepe but because they goe not yet thy way.
Thinke that they close thine eyes, and thinke in this,
That they confesse much in the world, amisse,   110
Who dare not trust a dead mans eye with that,
Which they from God, and Angels cover not.
Thinke that they shroud thee up, and think from thence
They reinvest thee in white innocence.
Thinke that thy body rots, and (if so low,   115
Thy soule exalted so, thy thoughts can goe,)
Think thee a Prince, who of themselves create
Wormes which insensibly devoure their State.
Thinke that they bury thee, and thinke that right
Laies thee to sleepe but a Saint Lucies night.   120
Thinke these things cheerefully: and if thou bee
Drowsie or slacke, remember then that shee,
Shee whose Complexion was so even made,
That which of her Ingredients should invade
The other three, no Feare, no Art could guesse: 125
So far were all remov'd from more or lesse.

But as in Mithridate, or just perfumes,
Where all good things being met, no one presumes
To governe, or to triumph on the rest,
Only because all were, no part was best.   130
And as, though all doe know, that quantities
Are made of lines, and lines from Points arise,
None can these lines or quantities unjoynt,
And say this is a line, or this a point,
So though the Elements and Humors were   135
In her, one could not say, this governes there.
Whose even constitution might have wonne
Any disease to venter on the Sunne,
Rather then her: and make a spirit feare,
That hee to disuniting subject were.   140
To whose proportions if we would compare
Cubes, th'are unstable; Circles, Angular;
She who was such a chaine as Fate employes
To bring mankinde all Fortunes it enjoyes;
So fast, so even wrought, as one would thinke,   145
No Accident could threaten any linke;
Shee, shee embrac'd a sicknesse, gave it meat,
The purest blood, and breath, that e'r it eate;
And hath taught us, that though a good man hath
Title to heaven, and plead it by his Faith,   150
And though he may pretend a conquest, since
Heaven was content to suffer violence,
Yea though hee plead a long possession too,
(For they're in heaven on earth who heavens workes do)
Though hee had right and power and place, before,   155
Yet Death must usher, and unlocke the doore.
Thinke further on thy selfe, my Soule, and thinke
How thou at first wast made but in a sinke;
Thinke that it argued some infirmitie,
That those two soules, which then thou foundst in me,   160
Thou fedst upon, and drewst into thee, both
My second soule of sense, and first of growth.
Thinke but how poore thou wast, how obnoxious;
Whom a small lumpe of flesh could poyson thus.
This curded milke, this poore unlittered whelpe   165
My body, could, beyond escape or helpe,

Infect thee with Originall sinne, and thou
Couldst neither then refuse, nor leave it now.
Thinke that no stubborne sullen Anchorit,
Which fixt to a pillar, or a grave, doth sit   170
Bedded, and bath'd in all his ordures, dwels
So fowly as our Soules in their first-built Cels.
Thinke in how poore a prison thou didst lie
After, enabled but to suck, and crie.
Thinke, when'twas growne to most,'twas a poore Inne,   175
A Province pack'd up in two yards of skinne,
And that usurp'd or threatned with the rage
Of sicknesses, or their true mother, Age.
But thinke that Death hath now enfranchis'd thee,
Thou hast thy'expansion now, and libertie;   180
Thinke that a rustie Peece, discharg'd, is flowne
In peeces, and the bullet is his owne,
And freely flies: This to thy Soule allow,
Thinke thy shell broke, thinke thy Soule hatch'd but now.
And think this slow-pac'd soule, which late did cleave   185
To'a body, and went but by the bodies leave,
Twenty, perchance, or thirty mile a day,
Dispatches in a minute all the way
Twixt heaven, and earth; she stayes not in the ayre,
To looke what Meteors there themselves prepare;   190
She carries no desire to know, nor sense,
Whether th'ayres middle region be intense;
For th'Element of fire, she doth not know,
Whether she past by such a place or no;
She baits not at the Moone, nor cares to trie   195
Whether in that new world, men live, and die.
Venus retards her not, to'enquire, how shee
Can, (being one starre) *Hesper*, and *Vesper* bee;
Hee that charm'd *Argus* eyes, sweet *Mercury*,
Workes not on her, who now is growne all eye;   200
Who, if she meet the body of the Sunne,
Goes through, not staying till his course be runne;
Who findes in *Mars* his Campe no corps of Guard;
Nor is by *Jove*, nor by his father barr'd;
But ere she can consider how she went,   205
At once is at, and through the Firmament.

And as these starres were but so many beads
Strung on one string, speed undistinguish'd leads
Her through those Spheares, as through the beads, a string,
Whose quick succession makes it still one thing: 210
As doth the pith, which, lest our bodies slacke,
Strings fast the little bones of necke, and backe;
So by the Soule doth death string Heaven and Earth;
For when our Soule enjoyes this her third birth,
(Creation gave her one, a second, grace,)   215
Heaven is as neare, and present to her face,
As colours are, and objects, in a roome
Where darknesse was before, when Tapers come.
This must, my Soule, thy long-short Progresse bee;
To'advance these thoughts, remember then, that shee,   220
Shee, whose faire body no such prison was,
But that a Soule might well be pleas'd to passe
An age in her; she whose rich beauty lent
Mintage to other beauties, for they went
But for so much as they were like to her;   225
Shee, in whose body (if we dare preferre
This low world, to so high a marke as shee,)
The Westerne treasure, Easterne spicerie,
Europe, and Afrique, and the unknowne rest
Were easily found, or what in them was best;   230
And when w'have made this large discoverie
Of all, in her some one part then will bee
Twenty such parts, whose plenty and riches is
Enough to make twenty such worlds as this;
Shee, whom had they knowne who did first betroth   235
The Tutelar Angels, and assign'd one, both
To Nations, Cities, and to Companies,
To Functions, Offices, and Dignities,
And to each severall man, to him, and him,
They would have given her one for every limbe;   240
She, of whose soule, if wee may say, 'twas Gold,
Her body was th'Electrum, and did hold
Many degrees of that; wee understood
Her by her sight; her pure, and eloquent blood
Spoke in her cheekes, and so distinctly wrought,   245
That one might almost say, her body thought;

Shee, shee, thus richly and largely hous'd, is gone:
And chides us slow-pac'd snailes who crawle upon
Our prisons prison, earth, nor thinke us well,
Longer, then whil'st wee beare our brittle shell.   250
But 'twere but little to have chang'd our roome,
If, as we were in this our living Tombe
Oppress'd with ignorance, wee still were so.
Poore soule, in this thy flesh what dost thou know?
Thou know'st thy selfe so little, as thou know'st not,   255
How thou didst die, nor how thou wast begot.
Thou neither know'st, how thou at first cam'st in,
Nor how thou took'st the poyson of mans sinne.
Nor dost thou, (though thou know'st, that thou art so)
By what way thou art made immortall, know.   260
Thou art too narrow, wretch, to comprehend
Even thy selfe: yea though thou wouldst but bend
To know thy body. Have not all soules thought
For many ages, that our body'is wrought
Of Ayre, and Fire, and other Elements?   265
And now they thinke of new ingredients,
And one Soule thinkes one, and another way
Another thinkes, and 'tis an even lay.
Knowst thou but how the stone doth enter in
The bladders cave, and never breake the skinne?   270
Know'st thou how blood, which to the heart doth flow,
Doth from one ventricle to th'other goe?
And for the putrid stuffe, which thou dost spit,
Know'st thou how thy lungs have attracted it?
There are no passages, so that there is   275
(For ought thou know'st) piercing of substances.
And of those many opinions which men raise
Of Nailes and Haires, dost thou know which to praise?
What hope have wee to know our selves, when wee
Know not the least things, which for our use be?   280
Wee see in Authors, too stiffe to recant,
A hundred controversies of an Ant;
And yet one watches, starves, freeses, and sweats,
To know but Catechismes and Alphabets
Of unconcerning things, matters of fact;   285
How others on our stage their parts did Act;

What *Cæsar* did, yea, and what *Cicero* said.
Why grasse is greene, or why our blood is red,
Are mysteries which none have reach'd unto.
In this low forme, poore soule, what wilt thou doe?   290
When wilt thou shake off this Pedantery,
Of being taught by sense, and Fantasie?
Thou look'st through spectacles; small things seeme great
Below; But up unto the watch-towre get,
And see all things despoyl'd of fallacies: 295
Thou shalt not peepe through lattices of eyes,
Nor heare through Labyrinths of eares, nor learne
By circuit, or collections to discerne.
In heaven thou straight know'st all, concerning it,
And what concernes it not, shalt straight forget.   300
There thou (but in no other schoole) maist bee
Perchance, as learned, and as full, as shee,
Shee who all libraries had throughly read
At home in her owne thoughts, and practised
So much good as would make as many more: 305
Shee whose example they must all implore,
Who would or doe, or thinke well, and confesse
That all the vertuous Actions they expresse,
Are but a new, and worse edition
Of her some one thought, or one action: 310
She who in th'art of knowing Heaven, was growne
Here upon earth, to such perfection,
That she hath, ever since to Heaven she came,
(In a far fairer print,) but read the same:
Shee, shee not satisfied with all this waight,   315
(For so much knowledge, as would over-fraight
Another, did but ballast her) is gone
As well t'enjoy, as get perfection.
And cals us after her, in that shee tooke,
(Taking her selfe) our best, and worthiest booke.   320
Returne not, my Soule, from this extasie,
And meditation of what thou shalt bee,
To earthly thoughts, till it to thee appeare,
With whom thy conversation must be there.
With whom wilt thou converse? what station   325
Canst thou choose out, free from infection,

That will not give thee theirs, nor drinke in thine?
Shalt thou not finde a spungie slacke Divine
Drinke and sucke in th'instructions of Great men,
And for the word of God, vent them agen?   330
Are there not some Courts (and then, no things bee
So like as Courts) which, in this let us see,
That wits and tongues of Libellers are weake,
Because they do more ill, then these can speake?
The poyson's gone through all, poysons affect   335
Chiefly the chiefest parts, but some effect
In nailes, and haires, yea excrements, will show;
So lyes the poyson of sinne in the most low.
Up, up, my drowsie Soule, where thy new eare
Shall in the Angels songs no discord heare;   340
Where thou shalt see the blessed Mother-maid
Joy in not being that, which men have said.
Where she is exalted more for being good,
Then for her interest of Mother-hood.
Up to those Patriarchs, which did longer sit   345
Expecting Christ, then they'have enjoy'd him yet.
Up to those Prophets, which now gladly see
Their Prophesies growne to be Historie.
Up to th'Apostles, who did bravely runne
All the Suns course, with more light then the Sunne.   350
Up to those Martyrs, who did calmly bleed
Oyle to th'Apostles Lamps, dew to their seed.
Up to those Virgins, who thought, that almost
They made joyntenants with the Holy Ghost,
If they to any should his Temple give.   355
Up, up, for in that squadron there doth live
She, who hath carried thither new degrees
(As to their number) to their dignities.
Shee, who being to her selfe a State, injoy'd
All royalties which any State employ'd;   360
For shee made warres, and triumph'd; reason still
Did not o'rthrow, but rectifie her will:
And she made peace, for no peace is like this,
That beauty, and chastity together kisse:
She did high justice, for she crucified   365
Every first motion of rebellious pride:

And she gave pardons, and was liberall,
For, onely her selfe except, she pardon'd all:
Shee coy'nd, in this, that her impressions gave
To all our actions all the worth they have: 370
She gave protections; the thoughts of her brest
Satans rude Officers could ne'r arrest.
As these prerogatives being met in one,
Made her a soveraigne State; religion
Made her a Church; and these two made her all.   375
She who was all this All, and could not fall
To worse, by company, (for she was still
More Antidote, then all the world was ill,)
Shee, shee doth leave it, and by Death, survive
All this, in Heaven; whither who doth not strive   380
The more, because shees there, he doth not know
That accidentall joyes in Heaven doe grow.
But pause, my soule; And study, ere thou fall
On accidentall joyes, th'essentiall.
Still before Accessories doe abide   385
A triall, must the principall be tride.
And what essentiall joy can'st thou expect
Here upon earth? what permanent effect
Of transitory causes? Dost thou love
Beauty? (And beauty worthy'st is to move)   390
Poore cousened cousenor, *that* she, and *that* thou,
Which did begin to love, are neither now;
You are both fluid, chang'd since yesterday;
Next day repaires, (but ill) last dayes decay.
Nor are, (although the river keepe the name)   395
Yesterdaies waters, and to daies the same.
So flowes her face, and thine eyes, neither now
That Saint, nor Pilgrime, which your loving vow
Concern'd, remaines; but whil'st you thinke you bee
Constant, you'are hourely in inconstancie.   400
Honour may have pretence unto our love,
Because that God did live so long above
Without this Honour, and then lov'd it so,
That he at last made Creatures to bestow
Honour on him; not that he needed it,   405
But that, to his hands, man might grow more fit.
But since all Honours from inferiours flow,
(For they doe give it; Princes doe but shew

Whom they would have so honor'd) and that this
On such opinions, and capacities   410
Is built, as rise and fall, to more and lesse:
Alas, 'tis but a casuall happinesse.
Hath ever any man to'himselfe assign'd
This or that happinesse to'arrest his minde,
But that another man which takes a worse,   415
Thinks him a foole for having tane that course?
They who did labour Babels tower to'erect,
Might have considered, that for that effect,
All this whole solid Earth could not allow
Nor furnish forth materialls enow;   420
And that this Center, to raise such a place,
Was farre too little, to have beene the Base;
No more affords this world, foundation
To erect true joy, were all the meanes in one.
But as the Heathen made them severall gods,   425
Of all Gods Benefits, and all his Rods,
(For as the Wine, and Corne, and Onions are
Gods unto them, so Agues bee, and Warre)
And as by changing that whole precious Gold
To such small Copper coynes, they lost the old,   430
And lost their only God, who ever must
Be sought alone, and not in such a thrust:
So much mankinde true happinesse mistakes;
No Joy enjoyes that man, that many makes.
Then, Soule, to thy first pitch worke up againe;   435
Know that all lines which circles doe containe,
For once that they the Center touch, doe touch
Twice the circumference; and be thou such;
Double on heaven thy thoughts on earth emploid;
All will not serve; Only who have enjoy'd   440
The sight of God, in fulnesse, can thinke it;
For it is both the object, and the wit.
This is essentiall joy, where neither hee
Can suffer diminution, nor wee;
'Tis such a full, and such a filling good,   445
Had th'Angels once look'd on him, they had stood.
To fill the place of one of them, or more,
Shee whom wee celebrate, is gone before.
She, who had Here so much essentiall joy,
As no chance could distract, much lesse destroy;   450

Who with Gods presence was acquainted so,
(Hearing, and speaking to him) as to know
His face in any naturall Stone, or Tree,
Better then when in Images they bee:
Who kept by diligent devotion,   455
Gods Image, in such reparation,
Within her heart, that what decay was growne,
Was her first Parents fault, and not her owne:
Who being solicited to any act,
Still heard God pleading his safe precontract;   460
Who by a faithfull confidence, was here
Betroth'd to God, and now is married there;
Whose twilights were more cleare, then our mid-day;
Who dreamt devoutlier, then most use to pray;
Who being here fil'd with grace, yet strove to bee,   465
Both where more grace, and more capacitie
At once is given: she to Heaven is gone,
Who made this world in some proportion
A heaven, and here, became unto us all,
Joy, (as our joyes admit) essentiall.   470
But could this low world joyes essentiall touch,
Heavens accidentall joyes would passe them much.
How poore and lame, must then our casuall bee?
If thy Prince will his subjects to call thee
My Lord, and this doe swell thee, thou art than,   475
By being greater, growne to bee lesse Man.
When no Physitian of redresse can speake,
A joyfull casuall violence may breake
A dangerous Apostem in thy breast;
And whil'st thou joyest in this, the dangerous rest,   480
The bag may rise up, and so strangle thee.
What e'r was casuall, may ever bee.
What should the nature change? Or make the same
Certaine, which was but casuall, when it came?
All casuall joy doth loud and plainly say,   485
Only by comming, that it can away.
Only in Heaven joyes strength is never spent;
And accidentall things are permanent.
Joy of a soules arrivall ne'r decaies;
For that soule ever joyes and ever staies.   490

Joy that their last great Consummation
Approaches in the resurrection;
When earthly bodies more celestiall
Shall be, then Angels were, for they could fall;
This kinde of joy doth every day admit   495
Degrees of growth, but none of losing it.
In this fresh joy, 'tis no small part, that shee,
Shee, in whose goodnesse, he that names degree,
Doth injure her; ('Tis losse to be cal'd best,
There where the stuffe is not such as the rest) 500
Shee, who left such a bodie, as even shee
Only in Heaven could learne, how it can bee
Made better; for shee rather was two soules,
Or like to full on both sides written Rols,
Where eyes might reade upon the outward skin,   505
As strong Records for God, as mindes within;
Shee, who by making full perfection grow,
Peeces a Circle, and still keepes it so,
Long'd for, and longing for it, to heaven is gone,
Where shee receives, and gives addition.   510
Here in a place, where mis-devotion frames
A thousand Prayers to Saints, whose very names
The ancient Church knew not, Heaven knows not yet:
And where, what lawes of Poetry admit,
Lawes of Religion have at least the same,   515
Immortall Maide, I might invoke thy name.
Could any Saint provoke that appetite,
Thou here should'st make me a French convertite.
But thou would'st not; nor would'st thou be content,
To take this, for my second yeares true Rent,   520
Did this Coine beare any other stampe, then his,
That gave thee power to doe, me, to say this.
Since his will is, that to posteritie,
Thou should'st for life, and death, a patterne bee,
And that the world should notice have of this,   525
The purpose, and th'Authoritie is his;
Thou art the Proclamation; and I am
The Trumpet, at whose voyce the people came.

EPICEDES AND OBSEQVIES

VPON
THE DEATHS OF SUNDRY
PERSONAGES

Elegie upon the untimely death of the incomparable
Prince Henry

Looke to mee faith, and looke to my faith, God;
For both my centers feele this period.
Of waight one center, one of greatnesse is;
And Reason is that center, Faith is this;
For into'our reason flow, and there do end   5
All, that this naturall world doth comprehend:
Quotidian things, and equidistant hence,
Shut in, for man, in one circumference.
But for th'enormous greatnesses, which are
So disproportion'd, and so angulare,   10
As is Gods essence, place and providence,
Where, how, when, what soules do, departed hence,
These things (eccentrique else) on faith do strike;
Yet neither all, nor upon all, alike.
For reason, put to'her best extension,   15
Almost meetes faith, and makes both centers one.
And nothing ever came so neare to this,
As contemplation of that Prince, wee misse.
For all that faith might credit mankinde could,
Reason still seconded, that this prince would.   20
If then least moving of the center, make
More, then if whole hell belch'd, the world to shake,

238

What must this do, centers distracted so,
That wee see not what to beleeve or know?
Was it not well beleev'd till now, that hee,   25
Whose reputation was an extasie
On neighbour States, which knew not why to wake,
Till hee discover'd what wayes he would take;
For whom, what Princes angled, when they tryed,
Met a *Torpedo*, and were stupified;   30
And others studies, how he would be bent;
Was his great fathers greatest instrument,
And activ'st spirit, to convey and tie
This soule of peace, through Christianity?
Was it not well beleev'd, that hee would make   35
This generall peace, th'Eternall overtake,
And that his times might have stretch'd out so farre,
As to touch those, of which they emblems are?
For to confirme this just beleefe, that now
The last dayes came, wee saw heav'n did allow,   40
That, but from his aspect and exercise,
In peacefull times, Rumors of war did rise.
But now this faith is heresie: we must
Still stay, and vexe our great-grand-mother, Dust.
Oh, is God prodigall? hath he spent his store   45
Of plagues, on us; and onely now, when more
Would ease us much, doth he grudge misery;
And will not let's enjoy our curse; to dy?
As, for the earth throwne lowest downe of all,
T'were an ambition to desire to fall,   50
So God, in our desire to dye, doth know
Our plot for ease, in being wretched so.
Therefore we live; though such a life wee have,
As but so many mandrakes on his grave.
What had his growth, and generation done,   55
When, what we are, his putrefaction
Sustaines in us; Earth, which griefes animate?
Nor hath our world now, other Soule then that.
And could griefe get so high as heav'n, that Quire,
Forgetting this their new joy, would desire   60
(With griefe to see him) hee had staid below,
To rectifie our errours, They foreknow.

Is th'other center, Reason, faster then?
Where should we looke for that, now we'are not men?
For if our Reason be'our connexion   65
Of causes, now to us there can be none.
For, as, if all the substances were spent,
'Twere madnesse, to enquire of accident,
So is't to looke for reason, hee being gone,
The onely subject reason wrought upon.   70
If Fate have such a chaine, whose divers links
Industrious man discerneth, as hee thinks;
When miracle doth come, and so steale in
A new linke, man knowes not, where to begin:
At a much deader fault must reason bee,   75
Death having broke off such a linke as hee.
But now, for us, with busie proofe to come,
That we'have no reason, would prove wee had some.
So would just lamentations: Therefore wee
May safelyer say, that we are dead, then hee.   80
So, if our griefs wee do not well declare,
We'have double excuse; he'is not dead; and we are.
Yet I would not dy yet; for though I bee
Too narrow, to thinke him, as hee is hee,
(Our Soules best baiting, and midd-period,   85
In her long journey, of considering God)
Yet, (no dishonour) I can reach him thus,
As he embrac'd the fires of love, with us.
Oh may I, (since I live) but see, or heare,
That she-Intelligence which mov'd this spheare,   90
I pardon Fate, my life: Who ere thou bee,
Which hast the noble conscience, thou art shee,
I conjure thee by all the charmes he spoke,
By th'oathes, which onely you two never broke,
By all the soules yee sigh'd, that if you see   95
These lines, you wish, I knew your history.
So much, as you two mutuall heav'ns were here,
I were an Angell, singing what you were.

Obsequies to the Lord Harrington, brother to the Lady Lucy, Countesse of Bedford

Faire soule, which wast, not onely, as all soules bee,
Then when thou wast infused, harmony,
But did'st continue so; and now dost beare
A part in Gods great organ, this whole Spheare:
If looking up to God; or downe to us,   5
Thou finde that any way is pervious,
Twixt heav'n and earth, and that mans actions doe
Come to your knowledge, and affections too,
See, and with joy, mee to that good degree
Of goodnesse growne, that I can studie thee,   10
And, by these meditations refin'd,
Can unapparell and enlarge my minde,
And so can make by this soft extasie,
This place a map of heav'n, my selfe of thee.
Thou seest mee here at midnight, now all rest;   15
Times dead-low water; when all mindes devest
To morrows businesse, when the labourers have
Such rest in bed, that their last Church-yard grave,
Subject to change, will scarce be'a type of this,
Now when the clyent, whose last hearing is   20
To morrow, sleeps, when the condemned man,
(Who when hee opes his eyes, must shut them than
Againe by death,) although sad watch hee keepe,
Doth practice dying by a little sleepe,
Thou at this midnight seest mee, and as soone   25
As that Sunne rises to mee, midnight's noone,
All the world growes transparent, and I see
Through all, both Church and State, in seeing thee;
And I discerne by favour of this light,
My selfe, the hardest object of the sight.   30
God is the glasse; as thou when thou dost see
Him who sees all, seest all concerning thee,
So, yet unglorified, I comprehend
All, in these mirrors of thy wayes, and end.
Though God be our true glasse, through which we see   35
All, since the beeing of all things is hee,
Yet are the trunkes which doe to us derive
Things, in proportion fit, by perspective,

Deeds of good men; for by their living here,
Vertues, indeed remote, seeme to be neare.   40
But where can I affirme, or where arrest
My thoughts on his deeds? which shall I call best?
For fluid vertue cannot be look'd on,
Nor can endure a contemplation.
As bodies change, and as I do not weare   45
Those Spirits, humors, blood I did last yeare,
And, as if on a streame I fixe mine eye,
That drop, which I looked on, is presently
Pusht with more waters from my sight, and gone,
So in this sea of vertues, can no one   50
Bee'insisted on; vertues, as rivers, passe,
Yet still remaines that vertuous man there was.
And as if man feed on mans flesh, and so
Part of his body to another owe,
Yet at the last two perfect bodies rise,   55
Because God knowes where every Atome lyes;
So, if one knowledge were made of all those,
Who knew his minutes well, hee might dispose
His vertues into names, and ranks; but I
Should injure Nature, Vertue, and Destinie,   60
Should I divide and discontinue so,
Vertue, which did in one intirenesse grow.
For as, hee that would say, spirits are fram'd
Of all the purest parts that can be nam'd,
Honours not spirits halfe so much, as hee   65
Which sayes, they have no parts, but simple bee;
So is't of vertue; for a point and one
Are much entirer then a million.
And had Fate meant to have his vertues told,
It would have let him live to have beene old;   70
So, then that vertue in season, and then this,
We might have seene, and said, that now he is
Witty, now wise, now temperate, now just:
In good short lives, vertues are faine to thrust,
And to be sure betimes to get a place,   75
When they would exercise, lacke time, and space.
So was it in this person, forc'd to bee
For lack of time, his owne epitome:

So to exhibit in few yeares as much,
As all the long breath'd Chronicles can touch.   80
As when an Angell down from heav'n doth flye,
Our quick thought cannot keepe him company,
Wee cannot thinke, now hee is at the Sunne,
Now through the Moon, now he through th'aire doth run,
Yet when he's come, we know he did repaire   85
To all twixt Heav'n and Earth, Sunne, Moon, and Aire;
And as this Angell in an instant knowes,
And yet wee know, this sodaine knowledge growes
By quick amassing severall formes of things,
Which he successively to order brings;   90
When they, whose slow-pac'd lame thoughts cannot goe
So fast as hee, thinke that he doth not so;
Just as a perfect reader doth not dwell,
On every syllable, nor stay to spell,
Yet without doubt, hee doth distinctly see   95
And lay together every A, and B;
So, in short liv'd good men, is'not understood
Each severall vertue, but the compound good;
For, they all vertues paths in that pace tread,
As Angells goe, and know, and as men read.   100
O why should then these men, these lumps of Balme
Sent hither, this worlds tempests to becalme,
Before by deeds they are diffus'd and spred,
And so make us alive, themselves be dead?
O Soule, O circle, why so quickly bee   105
Thy ends, thy birth and death, clos'd up in thee?
Since one foot of thy compasse still was plac'd
In heav'n, the other might securely'have pac'd
In the most large extent, through every path,
Which the whole world, or man the abridgment hath.   110
Thou knowst, that though the tropique circles have
(Yea and those small ones which the Poles engrave,)
All the same roundnesse, evennesse, and all
The endlesnesse of the equinoctiall;
Yet, when we come to measure distances,   115
How here, how there, the Sunne affected is,
When he doth faintly worke, and when prevaile,
Onely great circles, then can be our scale:

So, though thy circle to thy selfe expresse
All, tending to thy endlesse happinesse,   120
And wee, by our good use of it may trye,
Both how to live well young, and how to die,
Yet, since we must be old, and age endures
His Torrid Zone at Court, and calentures
Of hot ambitions, irreligions ice,   125
Zeales agues, and hydroptique avarice,
Infirmities which need the scale of truth,
As well as lust, and ignorance of youth;
Why did'st thou not for these give medicines too,
And by thy doing tell us what to doe?   130
Though as small pocket-clocks, whose every wheele
Doth each mismotion and distemper feele,
Whose *hand* gets shaking palsies, and whose *string*
(His sinewes) slackens, and whose *Soule*, the spring,
Expires, or languishes, whose pulse, the *flye*,   135
Either beates not, or beates unevenly,
Whose voice, the *Bell*, doth rattle, or grow dumbe,
Or idle,'as men, which to their last houres come,
If these clockes be not wound, or be wound still,
Or be not set, or set at every will;   140
So, youth is easiest to destruction,
If then wee follow all, or follow none.
Yet, as in great clocks, which in steeples chime,
Plac'd to informe whole towns, to'imploy their time,
An error doth more harme, being generall,   145
When, small clocks faults, only'on the wearer fall;
So worke the faults of age, on which the eye
Of children, servants, or the State relie.
Why wouldst not thou then, which hadst such a soule,
A clock so true, as might the Sunne controule,   150
And daily hadst from him, who gave it thee,
Instructions, such as it could never be
Disordered, stay here, as a generall
And great Sun-dyall, to have set us All?
O why wouldst thou be any instrument   155
To this unnaturall course, or why consent
To this, not miracle, but Prodigie,
That when the ebbs, longer then flowings be,

Vertue, whose flood did with thy youth begin,
Should so much faster ebb out, then flow in? 160
Though her flood was blowne in, by thy first breath,
All is at once sunke in the whirle-poole death.
Which word I would not name, but that I see
Death, else a desert, growne a Court by thee.
Now I grow sure, that if a man would have 165
Good companie, his entry is a grave.
Mee thinkes all Cities, now, but Anthills bee,
Where, when the severall labourers I see,
For children, house, Provision, taking paine,
They'are all but Ants, carrying eggs, straw, and grain; 170
And Church-yards are our cities, unto which
The most repaire, that are in goodnesse rich.
There is the best concourse, and confluence,
There are the holy suburbs, and from thence
Begins Gods City, New Jerusalem, 175
Which doth extend her utmost gates to them.
At that gate then Triumphant soule, dost thou
Begin thy Triumph; But since lawes allow
That at the Triumph day, the people may,
All that they will, 'gainst the Triumpher say, 180
Let me here use that freedome, and expresse
My griefe, though not to make thy Triumph lesse.
By law, to Triumphs none admitted bee,
Till they as Magistrates get victorie;
Though then to thy force, all youthes foes did yield, 185
Yet till fit time had brought thee to that field,
To which thy ranke in this state destin'd thee,
That there thy counsailes might get victorie,
And so in that capacitie remove
All jealousies 'twixt Prince and subjects love, 190
Thou could'st no title, to this triumph have,
Thou didst intrude on death, usurp'dst a grave.
Then (though victoriously) thou hadst fought as yet
But with thine owne affections, with the heate
Of youths desires, and colds of ignorance, 195
But till thou should'st successefully advance
Thine armes 'gainst forraine enemies, which are
Both Envy, and acclamations popular,

(For, both these engines equally defeate,
Though by a divers Mine, those which are great,)   200
Till then thy War was but a civill War,
For which to Triumph, none admitted are.
No more are they, who though with good successe,
In a defensive war, their power expresse;
Before men triumph, the dominion   205
Must be *enlarg'd*, and not *preserv'd* alone;
Why should'st thou then, whose battailes were to win
Thy selfe, from those straits nature put thee in,
And to deliver up to God that state,
Of which he gave thee the vicariate,   210
(Which is thy soule and body) as intire
As he, who takes endeavours, doth require,
But didst not stay, t'enlarge his kingdome too,
By making others, what thou didst, to doe;
Why shouldst thou Triumph now, when Heav'n no more 215
Hath got, by getting thee, then't had before?
For, Heav'n and thou, even when thou livedst here,
Of one another in possession were.
But this from Triumph most disables thee,
That, that place which is conquered, must bee   220
Left safe from present warre, and likely doubt
Of imminent commotions to breake out:
And hath he left us so? or can it bee
His territory was no more then Hee?
No, we were all his charge, the Diocis   225
Of ev'ry exemplar man, the whole world is,
And he was joyned in commission
With Tutelar Angels, sent to every one.
But though this freedome to upbraid, and chide
Him who Triumph'd, were lawfull, it was ty'd   230
With this, that it might never reference have
Unto the Senate, who this triumph gave;
Men might at Pompey jeast, but they might not
At that authoritie, by which he got
Leave to Triumph, before, by age, he might;   235
So, though, triumphant soule, I dare to write,
Mov'd with a reverentiall anger, thus,
That thou so earely wouldst abandon us;

Yet I am farre from daring to dispute
With that great soveraigntie, whose absolute   240
Prerogative hath thus dispens'd with thee,
'Gainst natures lawes, which just impugners bee
Of early triumphs; And I (though with paine)
Lessen our losse, to magnifie thy gaine
Of triumph, when I say, It was more fit,   245
That all men should lacke thee, then thou lack it.
Though then in our time, be not suffered
That testimonie of love, unto the dead,
To die with them, and in their graves be hid,
As Saxon wives, and French soldurii did;   250
And though in no degree I can expresse
Griefe in great Alexanders great excesse,
Who at his friends death, made whole townes devest
Their walls and bullwarks which became them best:
Doe not, faire soule, this sacrifice refuse,   255
That in thy grave I doe interre my Muse,
Who, by my griefe, great as thy worth, being cast
Behind hand, yet hath spoke, and spoke her last.

Elegie on the Lady Marckham

Man is the World, and death th'Ocean,
   To which God gives the lower parts of man.
This Sea invirons all, and though as yet
   God hath set markes, and bounds, twixt us and it,
Yet doth it rore, and gnaw, and still pretend,   5
   And breaks our bankes, when ere it takes a friend.
Then our land waters (teares of passion) vent;
   Our waters, then, above our firmament,
(Teares which our Soule doth for her sins let fall)
   Take all a brackish tast, and Funerall,   10
And even these teares, which should wash sin, are sin.
   We, after Gods *Noe*, drowne our world againe.
Nothing but man of all invenom'd things
   Doth worke upon itselfe, with inborne stings.
Teares are false Spectacles, we cannot see   15
   Through passions mist, what wee are, or what shee.

In her this sea of death hath made no breach,
   But as the tide doth wash the slimie beach,
And leaves embroder'd workes upon the sand,
   So is her flesh refin'd by deaths cold hand.   20
As men of China,'after an ages stay,
   Do take up Porcelane, where they buried Clay;
So at this grave, her limbecke, which refines
   The Diamonds, Rubies, Saphires, Pearles, and Mines,
Of which this flesh was, her soule shall inspire   25
   Flesh of such stuffe, as God, when his last fire
Annuls this world, to recompence it, shall,
   Make and name then, th'Elixar of this All.
They say, the sea, when it gaines, loseth too;
   If carnall Death (the younger brother) doe   30
Usurpe the body,'our soule, which subject is
   To th'elder death, by sinne, is freed by this;
They perish both, when they attempt the just;
   For, graves our trophies are, and both deaths dust.
So, unobnoxious now, she'hath buried both;   35
   For, none to death sinnes, that to sinne is loth,
Nor doe they die, which are not loth to die;
   So hath she this, and that virginity.
Grace was in her extremely diligent,
   That kept her from sinne, yet made her repent.   40
Of what small spots pure white complaines! Alas,
   How little poyson cracks a christall glasse!
She sinn'd, but just enough to let us see
   That God's word must be true, All, sinners be.
Soe much did zeale her conscience rarefie,   45
   That, extreme truth lack'd little of a lye,
Making omissions, acts; laying the touch
   Of sinne, on things that sometimes may be such.
As *Moses* Cherubines, whose natures doe
   Surpasse all speed, by him are winged too: 50
So would her soule, already'in heaven, seeme then,
   To clyme by teares, the common staires of men.
How fit she was for God, I am content
   To speake, that Death his vaine hast may repent.
How fit for us, how even and how sweet,   55
   How good in all her titles, and how meet,

To have reform'd this forward heresie,
   That women can no parts of friendship bee;
How Morall, how Divine shall not be told,
   Lest they that heare her vertues, thinke her old: 60
And lest we take Deaths part, and make him glad
   Of such a prey, and to his tryumph adde.

*Elegie on M*ris *Boulstred*

Death I recant, and say, unsaid by mee
   What ere hath slip'd, that might diminish thee.
Spirituall treason, atheisme 'tis, to say,
   That any can thy Summons disobey.
Th'earths face is but thy Table; there are set   5
   Plants, cattell, men, dishes for Death to eate.
In a rude hunger now hee millions drawes
   Into his bloody, or plaguy, or sterv'd jawes.
Now hee will seeme to spare, and doth more wast,
   Eating the best first, well preserv'd to last.   10
Now wantonly he spoiles, and eates us not,
   But breakes off friends, and lets us peecemeale rot.
Nor will this earth serve him; he sinkes the deepe
   Where harmelesse fish monastique silence keepe,
Who (were Death dead) by Roes of living sand,   15
   Might spunge that element, and make it land.
He rounds the aire, and breakes the hymnique notes
   In birds (Heavens choristers,) organique throats,
Which (if they did not dye) might seeme to bee
   A tenth ranke in the heavenly hierarchie.   20
O strong and long-liv'd death, how cam'st thou in?
   And how without Creation didst begin?
Thou hast, and shalt see dead, before thou dyest,
   All the foure Monarchies, and Antichrist.
How could I thinke thee nothing, that see now   25
   In all this All, nothing else is, but thou.
Our births and lives, vices, and vertues, bee
   Wastfull consumptions, and degrees of thee.
For, wee to live, our bellowes weare, and breath,
   Nor are wee mortall, dying, dead, but death.   30

And though thou beest, O mighty bird of prey,
    So much reclaim'd by God, that thou must lay
All that thou kill'st at his feet, yet doth hee
    Reserve but few, and leaves the most to thee.
And of those few, now thou hast overthrowne   35
    One whom thy blow makes, not ours, nor thine own.
She was more stories high: hopelesse to come
    To her Soule, thou'hast offer'd at her lower roome.
Her Soule and body was a King and Court:
    But thou hast both of Captaine mist and fort.   40
As houses fall not, though the King remove,
    Bodies of Saints rest for their soules above.
Death gets 'twixt soules and bodies such a place
    As sinne insinuates 'twixt just men and grace,
Both worke a separation, no divorce.   45
    Her Soule is gone to usher up her corse,
Which shall be'almost another soule, for there
    Bodies are purer, then best Soules are here.
Because in her, her virtues did outgoe
    Her yeares, would'st thou, O emulous death, do so?   50
And kill her young to thy losse? must the cost
    Of beauty,'and wit, apt to doe harme, be lost?
What though thou found'st her proofe 'gainst sins of youth?
    Oh, every age a diverse sinne pursueth.
Thou should'st have stay'd, and taken better hold,   55
    Shortly, ambitious; covetous, when old,
She might have prov'd: and such devotion
    Might once have stray'd to superstition.
If all her vertues must have growne, yet might
    Abundant virtue'have bred a proud delight.   60
Had she persever'd just, there would have bin
    Some that would sinne, mis-thinking she did sinne.
Such as would call her friendship, love, and faine
    To sociablenesse, a name profane;
Or sinne, by tempting, or, not daring that,   65
    By wishing, though they never told her what.
Thus might'st thou'have slain more soules, had'st thou not
    crost
    Thy selfe, and to triumph, thine army lost.
Yet though these wayes be lost, thou hast left one,   70
    Which is, immoderate griefe that she is gone.

But we may scape that sinne, yet weepe as much,
   Our teares are due, because we are not such.
Some teares, that knot of friends, her death must cost,
   Because the chaine is broke, though no linke lost.   75

Elegie

Death

Language thou art too narrow, and too weake
   To ease us now; great sorrow cannot speake;
If we could sigh out accents, and weepe words,
   Griefe weares, and lessens, that tears breath affords.
Sad hearts, the lesse they seeme the more they are,   5
   (So guiltiest men stand mutest at the barre)
Not that they know not, feele not their estate,
   But extreme sense hath made them desperate.
Sorrow, to whom we owe all that we bee;
   Tyrant, in the fift and greatest Monarchy,   10
Was't, that she did possesse all hearts before,
   Thou hast kil'd her, to make thy Empire more?
Knew'st thou some would, that knew her not, lament,
   As in a deluge perish th'innocent?
Was't not enough to have that palace wonne,   15
   But thou must raze it too, that was undone?
Had'st thou staid there, and look'd out at her eyes,
   All had ador'd thee that now from thee flies,
For they let out more light, then they tooke in,
   They told not when, but did the day beginne.   20
She was too Saphirine, and cleare for thee;
   Clay, flint, and jeat now thy fit dwellings be;
Alas, shee was too pure, but not too weake;
   Who e'r saw Christall Ordinance but would break?
And if wee be thy conquest, by her fall   25
   Th'hast lost thy end, for in her perish all;
Or if we live, we live but to rebell,
   They know her better now, that knew her well.
If we should vapour out, and pine, and die;
   Since, shee first went, that were not miserie.   30

Shee chang'd our world with hers; now she is gone,
   Mirth and prosperity is oppression;
For of all morall vertues she was all,
   The Ethicks speake of vertues Cardinall.
Her soule was Paradise; the Cherubin   35
   Set to keepe it was grace, that kept out sinne.
Shee had no more then let in death, for wee
   All reape consumption from one fruitfull tree.
God tooke her hence, lest some of us should love
   Her, like that plant, him and his lawes above,   40
And when wee teares, hee mercy shed in this,
   To raise our mindes to heaven where now she is;
Who if her vertues would have let her stay
   Wee'had had a Saint, have now a holiday.
Her heart was that strange bush, where, sacred fire,   45
   Religion, did not consume, but'inspire
Such piety, so chast use of Gods day,
   That what we turne to *feast,* she turn'd to *pray,*
And did prefigure here, in devout tast,
   The rest of her high Sabaoth, which shall last.   50
Angels did hand her up, who next God dwell,
   (For she was of that order whence most fell)
Her body left with us, lest some had said,
   Shee could not die, except they saw her dead;
For from lesse vertue, and lesse beautiousnesse,   55
   The Gentiles fram'd them Gods and Goddesses.
The ravenous earth that now wooes her to be
   Earth too, will be a *Lemnia*; and the tree
That wraps that christall in a wooden Tombe,
   Shall be tooke up spruce, fill'd with diamond;   60
And we her sad glad friends all beare a part
   Of griefe, for all would waste a Stoicks heart.

Elegie on the L. C.

Sorrow, who to this house scarce knew the way:
Is, Oh, heire of it, our All is his prey.
This strange chance claimes strange wonder, and to us
Nothing can be so strange, as to weepe thus.

'Tis well his lifes loud speaking workes deserve,   5
And give praise too, our cold tongues could not serve:
'Tis well, hee kept teares from our eyes before,
That to fit this deepe ill, we might have store.
Oh, if a sweet briar, climbe up by'a tree,
If to a paradise that transplanted bee,   10
Or fell'd, and burnt for holy sacrifice,
Yet, that must wither, which by it did rise,
As we for him dead: though no familie
Ere rigg'd a soule for heavens discoverie
With whom more Venturers more boldly dare   15
Venture their states, with him in joy to share.
Wee lose what all friends lov'd, him; he gaines now
But life by death, which worst foes would allow,
If hee could have foes, in whose practise grew
All vertues, whose names subtile Schoolmen knew.   20
What ease, can hope that wee shall see'him, beget,
When wee must die first, and cannot dye yet?
His children are his pictures, Oh they bee
Pictures of him dead, senselesse, cold as he.
Here needs no marble Tombe, since hee is gone,   25
He, and about him, his, are turn'd to stone.

An hymne to the Saints, and to Marquesse Hamylton.

To Sir Robert Carr

Whether that soule which now comes up to you
Fill any former ranke or make a new;
Whether it take a name nam'd there before,
Or be a name it selfe, and *order* more
Then was in heaven till now; (for may not hee   5
Bee so, if every severall Angell bee
A *kind* alone?) What ever order grow
Greater by him in heaven, wee doe not so.
One of your orders growes by his accesse;
But, by his losse grow all our *orders* lesse;   10
The name of *Father, Master, Friend,* the name
Of *Subject* and of *Prince,* in one are lame;

Faire mirth is dampt, and conversation black,
The *household* widdow'd, and the *garter* slack;
The *Chappell* wants an eare, *Councell* a tongue;   15
Story, a theame; and *Musicke* lacks a song;
Blest *order* that hath him! the losse of him
Gangreend all *Orders* here; all lost a limbe.
Never made body such hast to confesse
What a soule was; All former comelinesse   20
Fled, in a minute, when the soule was gone,
And, having lost that beauty, would have none;
So fell our *Monasteries*, in one instant growne
Not to lesse houses, but, to heapes of stone;
So sent this body that faire forme it wore,   25
Unto the spheare of formes, and doth (before
His soule shall fill up his sepulchrall stone,)
Anticipate a Resurrection;
For, as in his fame, now, his soule is here,
So, in the forme thereof his bodie's there.   30
And if, faire soule, not with first *Innocents*
Thy station be, but with the *Pænitents*,
(And, who shall dare to aske then when I am
Dy'd scarlet in the blood of that pure Lambe,
Whether that colour, which is scarlet then,   35
Were black or white before in eyes of men?)
When thou rememb'rest what sins thou didst finde
Amongst those many friends now left behinde,
And seest such sinners as they are, with thee
Got thither by repentance, Let it bee   40
Thy wish to wish all there, to wish them cleane;
Wish *him* a *David*, *her* a *Magdalen*.

EPITAPHS

Epitaph on Himselfe

To the Countesse of Bedford

MADAME,
That I might make your Cabinet my tombe,
  And for my fame which I love next my soule,
Next to my soule provide the happiest roome,
  Admit to that place this last funerall Scrowle.   5
    Others by Wills give Legacies, but I
    Dying, of you doe beg a Legacie.

My fortune and my will this custome breake,
When we are senselesse grown to make stones speak,
Though no stone tell thee what I was, yet thou   10
In my graves inside see what thou art now:
Yet th'art not yet so good; till us death lay
To ripe and mellow there, w'are stubborne clay,
Parents make us earth, and soules dignifie
Vs to be glasse, here to grow gold we lie;   15
Whilst in our soules sinne bred and pampered is,
Our soules become worme-eaten Carkasses.

Omnibus

My Fortune and my choice this custome break,
When we are speechlesse grown, to make stones speak,
Though no stone tell thee what I was, yet thou
In my graves inside seest what thou art now:
Yet thou'art not yet so good, till death us lay   5
To ripe and mellow here, we are stubborne Clay.

Parents make us earth, and soules dignifie
Vs to be glasse; heere to grow gold we lie.
Whilst in our soules sinne bred and pamper'd is,
Our soules become wormeaten carkases;   10
So we our selves miraculously destroy.
Here bodies with lesse miracle enjoy
Such priviledges, enabled here to scale
Heaven, when the Trumpets ayre shall them exhale.
Heare this, and mend thy selfe, and thou mendst me,   15
By making me being dead, doe good to thee,
     And thinke me well compos'd, that I could now
     A last-sicke houre to syllables allow.

INFINITATI SACRUM,
16. AUGUSTI 1601

METEMPSYCHOSIS

Poêma Satyricon

The
Progresse
of the Soule

EPISTLE

Others at the Porches and entries of their Buildings set their
Armes; I, my picture; if any colours can deliver a minde so
plaine, and flat, and through light as mine. Naturally at a new
Author, I doubt, and sticke, and doe not say quickly, good. I
censure much and taxe; And this liberty costs mee more then
others, by how much my owne things are worse then others.
Yet I would not be so rebellious against my selfe, as not to doe
it, since I love it; nor so unjust to others, to do it *sine talione*.
As long as I give them as good hold upon mee, they must
pardon mee my bitings. I forbid no reprehender, but him that
like the Trent Councell forbids not bookes, but Authors, damn-
ing what ever such a name hath or shall write. None writes so
ill, that he gives not some thing exemplary, to follow, or flie.
Now when I beginne this booke, I have no purpose to come
into any mans debt; how my stocke will hold out I know not;
perchance waste, perchance increase in use; if I doe borrow
any thing of Antiquitie, besides that I make account that I pay
it to posterity, with as much and as good: You shall still finde
mee to acknowledge it, and to thanke not him onely that hath
digg'd out treasure for mee, but that hath lighted mee a can-
dle to the place. All which I will bid you remember, (for I

257

will have no such Readers as I can teach) is, that the Pithagorian doctrine doth not onely carry one soule from man to man, nor man to beast, but indifferently to plants also: and therefore you must not grudge to finde the same soule in an Emperour, in a Posthorse, and in a Mucheron, since no unreadinesse in the soule, but an indisposition in the organs workes this. And therefore though this soule could not move when it was a Melon, yet it may remember, and now tell mee, at what lascivious banquet it was serv'd. And though it could not speake, when it was a spider, yet it can remember, and now tell me, who used it for poyson to attaine dignitie. How ever the bodies have dull'd her other faculties, her memory hath ever been her owne, which makes me so seriously deliver you by her relation all her passages from her first making when shee was that apple which Eve eate, to this time when shee is hee, whose life you shall finde in the end of this booke.

First Song

I sing the progresse of a deathlesse soule,
Whom Fate, which God made, but doth not controule,
Plac'd in most shapes; all times before the law
Yoak'd us, and when, and since, in this I sing.
And the great world to his aged evening;   5
From infant morne, through manly noone I draw.
What the gold Chaldee, or silver Persian saw,
Greeke brasse, or Roman iron, is in this one;
A worke t'outweare *Seths* pillars, bricke and stone,
    And (holy writt excepted) made to yeeld to none.   10

Thee, eye of heaven, this great Soule envies not,
By thy male force, is all wee have, begot.
In the first East, thou now beginst to shine,
Suck'st early balme, and Iland spices there,
And wilt anon in thy loose-rein'd careere   15
At Tagus, Po, Sene, Thames, and Danow dine,
And see at night thy Westerne land of Myne,
Yet hast thou not more nations seene then shee,
That before thee, one day beganne to bee,

And thy fraile light being quench'd, shall long, long out
    live thee.   [20

Nor, holy *Janus*, in whose soveraigne boate
The Church, and all the Monarchies did floate;
That swimming Colledge, and free Hospitall
Of all mankinde, that cage and vivarie   25
Of fowles, and beasts, in whose wombe, Destinie
Us, and our latest nephewes did install
(From thence are all deriv'd, that fill this All,)
Did'st thou in that great stewardship embarke
So diverse shapes into that floating parke,   30
    As have beene moved, and inform'd by this heavenly
      sparke.

Great Destiny the Commissary of God,
That hast mark'd out a path and period
For every thing; who, where wee of-spring tooke,   35
Our wayes and ends seest at one instant; Thou
Knot of all causes, thou whose changelesse brow
Ne'r smiles nor frownes, O vouch thou safe to looke
And shew my story, in thy eternall booke:
That (if my prayer be fit) I may'understand   40
So much my selfe, as to know with what hand,
    How scant, or liberall this my lifes race is spand.

To my sixe lustres almost now outwore,
Except thy booke owe mee so many more,
Except my legend be free from the letts   45
Of steepe ambition, sleepie povertie,
Spirit-quenching sicknesse, dull captivitie,
Distracting businesse, and from beauties nets,
And all that calls from this, and to others whets,
O let me not launch out, but let mee save   50
Th'expense of braine and spirit; that my grave
    His right and due, a whole unwasted man may have.

But if my dayes be long, and good enough,
In vaine this sea shall enlarge, or enrough
It selfe; for I will through the wave, and fome,   55

And shall, in sad lone wayes a lively spright,
Make my darke heavy Poëm light, and light.
For though through many streights, and lands I roame,
I launch at paradise, and I saile towards home;
The course I there began, shall here be staid,   60
Sailes hoised there, stroke here, and anchors laid
   In Thames, which were at Tigrys, and Euphrates waide.

For the great soule which here amongst us now
Doth dwell, and moves that hand, and tongue, and brow,
Which, as the Moone the sea, moves us; to heare   65
Whose story, with long patience you will long;
(For 'tis the crowne, and last straine of my song)
This soule to whom *Luther,* and *Mahomet* were
Prisons of flesh; this soule which oft did teare,
And mend the wracks of th'Empire, and late Rome,   70
And liv'd when every great change did come,
   Had first in paradise, a low, but fatall roome.

Yet no low roome, nor then the greatest, lesse,
If (as devout and sharpe men fitly guesse)
That Crosse, our joy, and griefe, where nailes did tye   75
That All, which alwayes was all, every where;
Which could not sinne, and yet all sinnes did beare;
Which could not die, yet could not chuse but die;
Stood in the selfe same roome in Calvarie,
Where first grew the forbidden learned tree,   80
For on that tree hung in security
   This Soule, made by the Makers will from pulling free.

Prince of the orchard, faire as dawning morne,
Fenc'd with the law, and ripe as soone as borne
That apple grew, which this Soule did enlive,   85
Till the then climing serpent, that now creeps
For that offence, for which all mankinde weepes,
Tooke it, and t'her whom the first man did wive
(Whom and her race, only forbiddings drive)
He gave it, she t'her husband, both did eate;   90
So perished the eaters, and the meate:
   And wee (for treason taints the blood) thence die and
     sweat.

Man all at once was there by woman slaine,
And one by one we'are here slaine o'er againe   95
By them. The mother poison'd the well-head,
The daughters here corrupt us, Rivolets;
No smalnesse scapes, no greatnesse breaks their nets;
She thrust us out, and by them we are led
Astray, from turning to whence we are fled.   100
Were prisoners Judges, 'twould seeme rigorous,
Shee sinn'd, we beare; part of our paine is, thus
    To love them, whose fault to this painfull love yoak'd us.

So fast in us doth this corruption grow,
That now wee dare aske why wee should be so.   105
Would God (disputes the curious Rebell) make
A law, and would not have it kept? Or can
His creatures will, crosse his? Of every man
For one, will God (and be just) vengeance take?
Who sinn'd? t'was not forbidden to the snake   110
Nor her, who was not then made; nor is't writ
That Adam cropt, or knew the apple; yet
    The worme and she, and he, and wee endure for it.

But snatch mee heavenly Spirit from this vaine
Reckoning their vanities, lesse is their gaine   115
Then hazard still, to meditate on ill,
Though with good minde; their reasons, like those toyes
Of glassie bubbles, which the gamesome boyes
Stretch to so nice a thinnes through a quill
That they themselves breake, doe themselves spill: 120
Arguing is heretiques game, and Exercise
As wrastlers, perfects them; Not liberties
    Of speech, but silence; hands, not tongues, end heresies.

Just in that instant when the serpents gripe,
Broke the slight veines, and tender conduit-pipe,   125
Through which this soule from the trees root did draw
Life, and growth to this apple, fled away
This loose soule, old, one and another day.
As lightning, which one scarce dares say, he saw,
'Tis so soone gone, (and better proofe the law   130

Of sense, then faith requires) swiftly she flew
To a darke and foggie Plot; Her, her fates threw
   There through th'earths pores, and in a Plant hous'd her
     anew.

The plant thus abled, to it selfe did force   135
A place, where no place was; by natures course
As aire from water, water fleets away
From thicker bodies, by this root throng'd so
His spungie confines gave him place to grow:
Just as in our streets, when the people stay   140
To see the Prince, and have so fill'd the way
That weesels scarce could passe, when she comes nere
They throng and cleave up, and a passage cleare,
   As if, for that time, their round bodies flatned were.

His right arme he thrust out towards the East,   145
West-ward his left; th'ends did themselves digest
Into ten lesser strings, these fingers were:
And as a slumberer stretching on his bed,
This way he this, and that way scattered
His other legge, which feet with toes upbeare.   150
Grew on his middle parts, the first day, haire,
To show, that in loves businesse hee should still
A dealer bee, and be us'd well, or ill:
   His apples kindle, his leaves, force of conception kill.

A mouth, but dumbe, he hath; blinde eyes, deafe eares,   155
And to his shoulders dangle subtile haires;
A young *Colossus* there hee stands upright,
And as that ground by him were conquered
A leafie garland weares he on his head
Enchas'd with little fruits, so red and bright   160
That for them you would call your Loves lips white;
So, of a lone unhaunted place possest,
Did this soules second Inne, built by the guest,
   This living buried man, this quiet mandrake, rest.

No lustfull woman came this plant to grieve,   165
But 'twas because there was none yet but Eve:
And she (with other purpose) kill'd it quite;

Her sinne had now brought in infirmities,
And so her cradled child, the moist red eyes
Had never shut, nor slept since it saw light;   170
Poppie she knew, she knew the mandrakes might,
And tore up both, and so coold her childs blood;
Unvirtuous weeds might long unvex'd have stood;
   But hee's short liv'd, that with his death can doe most
      good.   175

To an unfetterd soules quick nimble hast
Are falling stars, and hearts thoughts, but slow pac'd:
Thinner then burnt aire flies this soule, and she
Whom foure new comming, and foure parting Suns
Had found, and left the Mandrakes tenant, runnes   180
Thoughtlesse of change, when her firme destiny
Confin'd, and enjayld her, that seem'd so free,
Into a small blew shell, the which a poore
Warme bird orespread, and sat still evermore,
   Till her inclos'd child kickt, and pick'd it selfe a dore.   185

Outcrept a sparrow, this soules moving Inne,
On whose raw armes stiffe feathers now begin,
As childrens teeth through gummes, to breake with paine,
His flesh is jelly yet, and his bones threds,
All a new downy mantle overspreads,   190
A mouth he opes, which would as much containe
As his late house, and the first houre speaks plaine,
And chirps alowd for meat. Meat fit for men
His father steales for him, and so feeds then
   One, that within a moneth, will beate him from his hen. 195

In this worlds youth wise nature did make hast,
Things ripened sooner, and did longer last;
Already this hot cocke, in bush and tree,
In field and tent, oreflutters his next hen;
He asks her not, who did so last, nor when,   200
Nor if his sister, or his neece shee be;
Nor doth she pule for his inconstancie
If in her sight he change, nor doth refuse

The next that calls; both liberty doe use;
   Where store is of both kindes, both kindes may freely
      chuse.   [205

Men, till they tooke laws which made freedome lesse,
Their daughters, and their sisters did ingresse;
Till now unlawfull, therefore ill, 'twas not.
So jolly, that it can move, this soule is,   210
The body so free of his kindnesses,
That selfe-preserving it hath now forgot,
And slackneth so the soules, and bodies knot,
Which temperance streightens; freely on his she friends
He blood, and spirit, pith, and marrow spends,   215
   Ill steward of himself, himselfe in three yeares ends.

Else might he long have liv'd; man did not know
Of gummie blood, which doth in holly grow,
How to make bird-lime, nor how to deceive
With faind calls, hid nets, or enwrapping snare,   220
The free inhabitants of the Plyant aire.
Man to beget, and woman to conceive
Askt not of rootes, nor of cock-sparrowes, leave:
Yet chuseth hee, though none of these he feares,
Pleasantly three, then streightned twenty yeares   225
   To live; and to encrease his race, himselfe outweares.

This cole with overblowing quench'd and dead,
The Soule from her too active organs fled
T'a brooke. A female fishes sandie Roe
With the males jelly, newly lev'ned was,   230
For they had intertouch'd as they did passe,
And one of those small bodies, fitted so,
This soule inform'd, and abled it to rowe
It selfe with finnie oares, which she did fit:
Her scales seem'd yet of parchment, and as yet   235
   Perchance a fish, but by no name you could call it.

When goodly, like a ship in her full trim,
A swan, so white that you may unto him
Compare all whitenesse, but himselfe to none,
Glided along, and as he glided watch'd,   240
And with his arched necke this poore fish catch'd.

It mov'd with state, as if to looke upon
Low things it scorn'd, and yet before that one
Could thinke he sought it, he had swallow'd cleare
This, and much such, and unblam'd devour'd there   245
    All, but who too swift, too great, or well armed were.

Now swome a prison in a prison put,
And now this Soule in double walls was shut,
Till melted with the Swans digestive fire,
She left her house the fish, and vapour'd forth;   250
Fate not affording bodies of more worth
For her as yet, bids her againe retire
T'another fish, to any new desire
Made a new prey; For, he that can to none
Resistance make, nor complaint, sure is gone.   255
    Weaknesse invites, but silence feasts oppression.

Pace with her native streame, this fish doth keepe,
And journeyes with her, towards the glassie deepe,
But oft retarded, once with a hidden net
Though with greate windowes, for when Need first taught
These tricks to catch food, then they were not wrought   [260
As now, with curious greedinesse to let
None scape, but few, and fit for use, to get,
As, in this trap a ravenous pike was tane,
Who, though himselfe distrest, would faine have slain   265
    This wretch; So hardly are ill habits left again.

Here by her smallnesse shee two deaths orepast,
Once innocence scap'd, and left the oppressor fast.
The net through-swome, she keepes the liquid path,
And whether she leape up sometimes to breath   270
And suck in aire, or finde it underneath,
Or working parts like mills or limbecks hath
To make the water thinne, and airelike faith
Cares not; but safe the Place she's come unto
Where fresh, with salt waves meet, and what to doe   275
    She knowes not, but betweene both makes a boord or two.

So farre from hiding her guests, water is,
That she showes them in bigger quantities

Then they are. Thus doubtfull of her way,
For game and not for hunger a sea Pie　　　　280
Spied through this traiterous spectacle, from high,
The seely fish where it disputing lay,
And t'end her doubts and her, beares her away:
Exalted she'is, but to the exalters good,
As are by great ones, men which lowly stood.　　285
　　It's rais'd, to be the Raisers instrument and food.

Is any kinde subject to rape like fish?
Ill unto man, they neither doe, nor wish:
Fishers they kill not, nor with noise awake,
They doe not hunt, nor strive to make a prey　　290
Of beasts, nor their yong sonnes to beare away;
Foules they pursue not, nor do undertake
To spoile the nests industrious birds do make;
Yet them all these unkinde kinds feed upon,
To kill them is an occupation,　　　　295
　　And lawes make Fasts, and Lents for their destruction.

A sudden stiffe land-winde in that selfe houre
To sea-ward forc'd this bird, that did devour
The fish; he cares not, for with ease he flies,
Fat gluttonies best orator: at last　　　300
So long hee hath flowen, and hath flowen so fast
That many leagues at sea, now tir'd hee lyes,
And with his prey, that till then languisht, dies:
The soules no longer foes, two wayes did erre,
The fish I follow, and keepe no calender　　305
　　Of the other; he lives yet in some great officer.

Into an embrion fish, our Soule is throwne,
And in due time throwne out againe, and growne
To such vastnesse as, if unmanacled
From Greece, Morea were, and that by some　　310
Earthquake unrooted, loose Morea swome,
Or seas from Africks body had severed
And torne the hopefull Promontories head,
This fish would seeme these, and, when all hopes faile,

A great ship overset, or without saile   315
  Hulling, might (when this was a whelp) be like this
    whale.

At every stroake his brazen finnes do take,
More circles in the broken sea they make
Then cannons voices, when the aire they teare:
His ribs are pillars, and his high arch'd roofe   320
Of barke that blunts best steele, is thunder-proofe:
Swimme in him swallow'd Dolphins, without feare,
And feele no sides, as if his vast wombe were
Some Inland sea, and ever as hee went
Hee spouted rivers up, as if he ment   325
  To joyne our seas, with seas above the firmament.

He hunts not fish, but as an officer,
Stayes in his court, at his owne net, and there
All suitors of all sorts themselves enthrall;
So on his backe lyes this whale wantoning,   330
And in his gulfe-like throat, sucks every thing
That passeth neare. Fish chaseth fish, and all,
Flyer and follower, in this whirlepoole fall;
O might not states of more equality
Consist? and is it of necessity   335
  That thousand guiltlesse smals, to make one great, must
    die?

Now drinkes he up seas, and he eates up flocks,
He justles Ilands, and he shakes firme rockes.
Now in a roomefull house this Soule doth float,   340
And like a Prince she sends her faculties
To all her limbes, distant as Provinces.
The Sunne hath twenty times both crab and goate
Parched, since first lanch'd forth this living boate;
'Tis greatest now, and to destruction   345
Nearest; There's no pause at perfection;
  Greatnesse a period hath, but hath no station.

Two little fishes whom hee never harm'd,
Nor fed on their kinde, two not throughly arm'd
With hope that they could kill him, nor could doe   350

Good to themselves by his death (they did not eate
His flesh, nor suck those oyles, which thence outstreat)
Conspir'd against him, and it might undoe
The plot of all, that the plotters were two,
But that they fishes were, and could not speake.   355
How shall a Tyran wise strong projects breake,
    If wreches can on them the common anger wreake?

The flaile-finn'd Thresher, and steel-beak'd Sword-fish
Onely attempt to doe, what all doe wish.
The Thresher backs him, and to beate begins;   360
The sluggard Whale yeelds to oppression,
And t'hide himselfe from shame and danger, downe
Begins to sinke; the Swordfish upward spins,
And gores him with his beake; his staffe-like finnes,
So well the one, his sword the other plyes,   365
That now a scoffe, and prey, this tyran dyes,
    And (his owne dole) feeds with himselfe all companies.

Who will revenge his death? or who will call
Those to account, that thought, and wrought his fall?
The heires of slaine kings, wee see are often so   370
Transported with the joy of what they get,
That they, revenge and obsequies forget,
Nor will against such men the people goe,
Because h'is now dead, to whom they should show
Love in that act; Some kings by vice being growne   375
So needy of subjects love, that of their own
    They thinke they lose, if love be to the dead Prince
    shown.

This Soule, now free from prison, and passion,
Hath yet a little indignation   380
That so small hammers should so soone downe beat
So great a castle. And having for her house
Got the streight cloyster of a wreched mouse
(As basest men that have not what to eate,
Nor enjoy ought, doe farre more hate the great   385
Then they, who good repos'd estates possesse)
This Soule, late taught that great things might by lesse
    Be slain, to gallant mischiefe doth herselfe addresse.

Natures great master-peece, an Elephant,
The onely harmlesse great thing; the giant   390
Of beasts; who thought, no more had gone, to make one
    wise
But to be just, and thankfull, loth to offend,
(Yet nature hath given him no knees to bend)
Himselfe he up-props, on himselfe relies,   395
And foe to none, suspects no enemies,
Still sleeping stood; vex't not his fantasie
Blacke dreames; like an unbent bow, carelesly
    His sinewy Proboscis did remisly lie:

In which as in a gallery this mouse   400
Walk'd, and surveid the roomes of this vast house,
And to the braine, the soules bedchamber, went,
And gnaw'd the life cords there; Like a whole towne
Cleane undermin'd, the slaine beast tumbled downe;
With him the murtherer dies, whom envy sent   405
To kill, not scape, (for, only hee that ment
To die, did ever kill a man of better roome,)
And thus he made his foe, his prey, and tombe:
    Who cares not to turn back, may any whither come.

Next, hous'd this Soule a Wolves yet unborne whelp,   410
Till the best midwife, Nature, gave it helpe,
To issue. It could kill, as soone as goe.
Abel, as white, and milde as his sheepe were,
(Who, in that trade, of Church, and kingdomes, there
Was the first type) was still infested soe,   415
With this wolfe, that it bred his losse and woe;
And yet his bitch, his sentinell attends
The flocke so neere, so well warnes and defends,
    That the wolfe, (hopelesse else) to corrupt her, intends.

Hee tooke a course, which since, succesfully,   420
Great men have often taken, to espie
The counsels, or to breake the plots of foes.
To Abels tent he stealeth in the darke,
On whose skirts the bitch slept; ere she could barke,
Attach'd her with streight gripes, yet hee call'd those,   425
Embracements of love; to loves worke he goes,

Where deeds move more then words; nor doth she show,
Nor <make> resist, nor needs hee streighten so
   His prey, for, were shee loose, she would nor barke, nor
      goe.   430

Hee hath engag'd her; his, she wholy bides;
Who not her owne, none others secrets hides.
If to the flocke he come, and Abell there,
She faines hoarse barkings, but she biteth not,
Her faith is quite, but not her love forgot.   435
At last a trap, of which some every where
Abell had plac'd, ends all his losse, and feare,
By the Wolves death; and now just time it was
That a quicke soule should give life to that masse
   Of blood in Abels bitch, and thither this did passe.   440

Some have their wives, their sisters some begot,
But in the lives of Emperours you shall not
Reade of a lust the which may equall this;
This wolfe begot himselfe, and finished
What he began alive, when hee was dead;   445
Sonne to himselfe, and father too, hee is
A ridling lust, for which Schoolemen would misse
A proper name. The whelpe of both these lay
In Abels tent, and with soft Moaba,
   His sister, being yong, it us'd to sport and play.   450

Hee soone for her too harsh, and churlish grew,
And Abell (the dam dead) would use this new
For the field. Being of two kindes thus made,
He, as his dam, from sheepe drove wolves away,
And as his Sire, he made them his owne prey.   455
Five yeares he liv'd, and cosened with his trade,
Then hopelesse that his faults were hid, betraid
Himselfe by flight, and by all followed,
From dogges, a wolfe; from wolves, a dogge he fled;
   And, like a spie to both sides false, he perished.   460

It quickned next a toyfull Ape, and so
Gamesome it was, that it might freely goe
   From tent to tent, and with the children play.

His organs now so like theirs hee doth finde,
That why he cannot laugh, and speake his minde,   465
He wonders. Much with all, most he doth stay
With Adams fift daughter *Siphatecia*,
Doth gaze on her, and, where she passeth, passe,
Gathers her fruits, and tumbles on the grasse,
   And wisest of that kinde, the first true lover was.   470

He was the first that more desir'd to have
One then another; first that ere did crave
Love by mute signes, and had no power to speake;
First that could make love faces, or could doe
The valters sombersalts, or us'd to wooe   475
With hoiting gambolls, his owne bones to breake
To make his mistresse merry; or to wreake
Her anger on himselfe. Sinnes against kinde
They easily doe, that can let feed their minde
   With outward beauty; beauty they in boyes and beasts
    do find.   480

By this misled, too low things men have prov'd,
And too high; beasts and angels have beene lov'd.
This Ape, though else through-vaine, in this was wise,
He reach'd at things too high, but open way
There was, and he knew not she would say nay;   485
His toyes prevaile not, likelier meanes he tries,
He gazeth on her face with teare-shot eyes,
And up lifts subtly with his russet pawe
Her kidskinne apron without feare or awe
   Of nature; nature hath no gaole, though shee hath law.   490

First she was silly and knew not what he ment.
That vertue, by his touches, chaft and spent,
Succeeds an itchie warmth, that melts her quite;
She knew not first, nowe cares not what he doth,
And willing halfe and more, more then halfe loth,   495
She neither puls nor pushes, but outright
Now cries, and now repents; when *Tethlemite*
Her brother, entred, and a great stone threw
After the Ape, who, thus prevented, flew.   [500
   This house thus batter'd downe, the Soule possest a new.

And whether by this change she lose or win,
She comes out next, where the Ape would have gone in.
Adam and *Eve* had mingled bloods, and now
Like Chimiques equall fires, her temperate wombe
Had stew'd and form'd it: and part did become   505
A spungie liver, that did richly allow,
Like a free conduit, on a high hils brow,
Life-keeping moisture unto every part;
Part hardned it selfe to a thicker heart,
   Whose busie furnaces lifes spirits do impart.   510

Another part became the well of sense,
The tender well-arm'd feeling braine, from whence,
Those sinowie strings which do our bodies tie,
Are raveld out; and fast there by one end,
Did this Soule limbes, these limbes a soule attend;   515
And now they joyn'd: keeping some quality
Of every past shape, she knew treachery,
Rapine, deceit, and lust, and ills enow
To be a woman. *Themech* she is now,
   Sister and wife to *Caine*, *Caine* that first did plow.   520

Who ere thou beest that read'st this sullen Writ,
Which just so much courts thee, as thou dost it,
Let me arrest thy thoughts; wonder with mee,
Why plowing, building, ruling and the rest,
Or most of those arts, whence our lives are blest,   525
By cursed *Cains* race invented be,
And blest *Seth* vext us with Astronomie.
Ther's nothing simply good, nor ill alone,
Of every quality Comparison
   The onely measure is, and judge, Opinion.   530

DIVINE POEMS

To *E*. of *D*. with six holy Sonnets

See Sir, how as the Suns hot Masculine flame
   Begets strange creatures on Niles durty slime,
   In me, your fatherly yet lusty Ryme
(For, these songs are their fruits) have wrought the same;
But though the ingendring force from whence they came   5
   Bee strong enough, and nature doe admit
   Seaven to be borne at once, I send as yet
But six; they say, the seaventh hath still some maime.
   I choose your judgement, which the same degree
   Doth with her sister, your invention, hold,   10
As fire these drossie Rymes to purifie,
   Or as Elixar, to change them to gold;
You are that Alchimist which alwaies had
Wit, whose one spark could make good things of bad.

To the Lady Magdalen Herbert: of St. Mary
Magdalen

Her of your name, whose fair inheritance
   Bethina was, and jointure Magdalo:
An active faith so highly did advance,
   That she once knew, more than the Church did know,
The Resurrection; so much good there is   5
   Deliver'd of her, that some Fathers be
Loth to believe one Woman could do this;
   But, think these Magdalens were two or three.
Increase their number, Lady, and their fame:
   To their Devotion, add your Innocence;   10
Take so much of th'example, as of the name;

The latter half; and in some recompence
That they did harbour Christ himself, a Guest,
Harbour these Hymns, to his dear name addrest.

Holy Sonnets

La Corona

Deigne at my hands this crown of prayer and praise,
Weav'd in my low devout melancholie,
Thou which of good, hast, yea art treasury,
All changing unchang'd Antient of dayes;
But doe not, with a vile crowne of fraile bayes,   5
Reward my muses white sincerity,
But what thy thorny crowne gain'd, that give mee,
A crowne of Glory, which doth flower alwayes;
The ends crowne our workes, but thou crown'st our ends,
For, at our end begins our endlesse rest;   10
The first last end, now zealously possest,
With a strong sober thirst, my soule attends.
'Tis time that heart and voice be lifted high,
Salvation to all that will is nigh.

Annvnciation

Salvation to all that will is nigh;
That All, which alwayes is All every where,
Which cannot sinne, and yet all sinnes must beare,
Which cannot die, yet cannot chuse but die,
Loe, faithfull Virgin, yeelds himselfe to lye   5
In prison, in thy wombe; and though he there
Can take no sinne, nor thou give, yet he'will weare
Taken from thence, flesh, which deaths force may trie.
Ere by the spheares time was created, thou
Wast in his minde, who is thy Sonne, and Brother;   10
Whom thou conceiv'st, conceiv'd; yea thou art now
Thy Makers maker, and thy Fathers mother;

Thou'hast light in darke; and shutst in little roome,
Immensity cloysterd in thy deare wombe.

Nativitie

Immensitie cloysterd in thy deare wombe,
Now leaves his welbelov'd imprisonment,
There he hath made himselfe to his intent
Weake enough, now into our world to come;
But Oh, for thee, for him, hath th'Inne no roome?   5
Yet lay him in this stall, and from the Orient,
Starres, and wisemen will travell to prevent
Th'effect of *Herods* jealous generall doome.
Seest thou, my Soule, with thy faiths eyes, how he
Which fils all place, yet none holds him, doth lye?   10
Was not his pity towards thee wondrous high,
That would have need to be pittied by thee?
Kisse him, and with him into Egypt goe,
With his kinde mother, who partakes thy woe.

Temple

With his kinde mother who partakes thy woe,
Joseph turne backe; see where your child doth sit,
Blowing, yea blowing out those sparks of wit,
Which himselfe on the Doctors did bestow;
The Word but lately could not speake, and loe,   5
It sodenly speakes wonders, whence comes it,
That all which was, and all which should be writ,
A shallow seeming child, should deeply know?
His Godhead was not soule to his manhood,
Nor had time mellowed him to this ripenesse,   10
But as for one which hath a long taske, 'tis good,
With the Sunne to beginne his businesse,
He in his ages morning thus began
By miracles exceeding power of man.

Crvcifying

By miracles exceeding power of man,
Hee faith in some, envie in some begat,
For, what weake spirits admire, ambitious, hate;
In both affections many to him ran,
But Oh! the worst are most, they will and can,   5
Alas, and do, unto the immaculate,
Whose creature Fate is, now prescribe a Fate,
Measuring selfe-lifes infinity to'a span,
Nay to an inch. Loe, where condemned hee
Beares his owne crosse, with paine, yet by and by   10
When it beares him, he must beare more and die.
Now thou art lifted up, draw mee to thee,
And at thy death giving such liberall dole,
Moyst, with one drop of thy blood, my dry soule.

Resvrrection

Moyst with one drop of thy blood, my dry soule
Shall (though she now be in extreme degree
Too stony hard, and yet too fleshly,) bee
Freed by that drop, from being starv'd, hard, or foule,
And life, by this death abled, shall controule   5
Death, whom thy death slue; nor shall to mee
Feare of first or last death, bring miserie,
If in thy little booke my name thou enroule,
Flesh in that long sleep is not putrified,
But made that there, of which, and for which 'twas;   10
Nor can by other meanes be glorified.
May then sinnes sleep, and deaths soone from me passe,
That wak't from both, I againe risen may
Salute the last, and everlasting day.

Ascention

Salute the last and everlasting day,
Joy at the uprising of this Sunne, and Sonne,
Yee whose just teares, or tribulation

Have purely washt, or burnt your drossie clay;
Behold the Highest, parting hence away,   5
Lightens the darke clouds, which hee treads upon,
Nor doth hee by ascending, show alone,
But first hee, and hee first enters the way.
O strong Ramme, which hast batter'd heaven for mee,
Mild Lambe, which with thy blood, hast mark'd the path; 10
Bright Torch, which shin'st, that I the way may see,
Oh, with thy owne blood quench thy owne just wrath,
And if thy holy Spirit, my Muse did raise,
Deigne at my hands this crowne of prayer and praise.

Holy Sonnets

I

Thou hast made me, And shall thy worke decay?
Repaire me now, for now mine end doth haste,
I runne to death, and death meets me as fast,
And all my pleasures are like yesterday;
I dare not move my dimme eyes any way,   5
Despaire behind, and death before doth cast
Such terrour, and my feeble flesh doth waste
By sinne in it, which it t'wards hell doth weigh;
Onely thou art above, and when towards thee
By thy leave I can looke, I rise againe;   10
But our old subtle foe so tempteth me,
That not one houre my selfe I can sustaine;
Thy Grace may wing me to prevent his art,
And thou like Adamant draw mine iron heart.

II

As due by many titles I resigne
My selfe to thee, O God, first I was made
By thee, and for thee, and when I was decay'd
Thy blood bought that, the which before was thine;
I am thy sonne, made with thy selfe to shine,   5

Thy servant, whose paines thou hast still repaid,
Thy sheepe, thine Image, and, till I betray'd
My selfe, a temple of thy Spirit divine;
Why doth the devill then usurpe on mee?
Why doth he steale, nay ravish that's thy right?   10
Except thou rise and for thine owne worke fight,
Oh I shall soone despaire, when I doe see
That thou lov'st mankind well, yet wilt'not chuse me.
And Satan hates mee, yet is loth to lose mee.

III

O might those sighes and teares returne againe
Into my breast and eyes, which I have spent,
That I might in this holy discontent
Mourne with some fruit, as I have mourn'd in vaine;
In mine Idolatry what showres of raine   5
Mine eyes did waste? what griefs my heart did rent?
That sufferance was my sinne; now I repent;
'Cause I did suffer I must suffer paine.
Th'hydroptique drunkard, and night-scouting thiefe,
The itchy Lecher, and selfe tickling proud   10
Have the remembrance of past joyes, for reliefe
Of comming ills. To (poore) me is allow'd
No ease; for, long, yet vehement griefe hath beene
Th'effect and cause, the punishment and sinne.

IV

Oh my blacke Soule! now thou art summoned
By sicknesse, deaths herald, and champion;
Thou art like a pilgrim, which abroad hath done
Treason, and durst not turne to whence hee is fled,
Or like a thiefe, which till deaths doome be read,   5
Wisheth himselfe delivered from prison;
But damn'd and hal'd to execution,
Wisheth that still he might be imprisoned.
Yet grace, if thou repent, thou canst not lacke;
But who shall give thee that grace to beginne?   10
Oh make thy selfe with holy mourning blacke,

And red with blushing, as thou art with sinne;
Or wash thee in Christs blood, which hath this might
That being red, it dyes red soules to white.

V

I am a little world made cunningly
Of Elements, and an Angelike spright,
But black sinne hath betraid to endlesse night
My worlds both parts, and (oh) both parts must die.
You which beyond that heaven which was most high   5
Have found new sphears, and of new lands can write,
Powre new seas in mine eyes, that so I might
Drowne my world with my weeping earnestly,
Or wash it, if it must be drown'd no more:
But oh it must be burnt! alas the fire   10
Of lust and envie have burnt it heretofore,
And made it fouler; Let their flames retire,
And burne me ô Lord, with a fiery zeale
Of thee and thy house, which doth in eating heale.

VI

This is my playes last scene, here heavens appoint
My pilgrimages last mile; and my race
Idly, yet quickly runne, hath this last pace,
My spans last inch, my minutes latest point,
And gluttonous death, will instantly unjoynt   5
My body, and soule, and I shall sleepe a space,
But my'ever-waking part shall see that face,
Whose feare already shakes my every joynt:
Then, as my soule, to'heaven her first seate, takes flight,
And earth-borne body, in the earth shall dwell,   10
So, fall my sinnes, that all may have their right,
To where they'are bred, and would presse me, to hell.
Impute me righteous, thus purg'd of evill,
For thus I leave the world, the flesh, the devill.

VII

At the round earths imagin'd corners, blow
Your trumpets, Angells, and arise, arise
From death, you numberlesse infinities
Of soules, and to your scattred bodies goe,
All whom the flood did, and fire shall o'erthrow,   5
All whom warre, dearth, age, agues, tyrannies,
Despaire, law, chance, hath slaine, and you whose eyes,
Shall behold God, and never tast deaths woe.
But let them sleepe, Lord, and mee mourne a space,
For, if above all these, my sinnes abound,   10
'Tis late to aske abundance of thy grace,
When wee are there; here on this lowly ground,
Teach mee how to repent; for that's as good
As if thou'hadst seal'd my pardon, with thy blood.

VIII

If faithfull soules be alike glorifi'd
As Angels, then my fathers soule doth see,
And adds this even to full felicitie,
That valiantly I hels wide mouth o'rstride:
But if our mindes to these soules be descry'd   5
By circumstances, and by signes that be
Apparent in us, not immediately,
How shall my mindes white truth by them be try'd?
They see idolatrous lovers weepe and mourne,
And vile blasphemous Conjurers to call   10
On Jesus name, and Pharisaicall
Dissemblers feigne devotion. Then turne
O pensive soule, to God, for he knowes best
Thy true griefe, for he put it in my breast.

IX

If poysonous mineralls, and if that tree,
Whose fruit threw death on else immortall us,
If lecherous goats, if serpents envious
Cannot be damn'd; Alas; why should I bee?
Why should intent or reason, borne in mee,   5

Make sinnes, else equall, in mee more heinous?
And mercy being easie, and glorious
To God; in his sterne wrath, why threatens hee?
But who am I, that dare dispute with thee
O God? Oh! of thine onely worthy blood,   10
And my teares, make a heavenly Lethean flood,
And drowne in it my sinnes blacke memorie;
That thou remember them, some claime as debt,
I thinke it mercy, if thou wilt forget.

X

Death be not proud, though some have called thee
Mighty and dreadfull, for, thou art not soe,
For, those, whom thou think'st, thou dost overthrow,
Die not, poore death, nor yet canst thou kill mee.
From rest and sleepe, which but thy pictures bee,   5
Much pleasure, then from thee, much more must flow,
And soonest our best men with thee doe goe,
Rest of their bones, and soules deliverie.
Thou art slave to Fate, Chance, kings, and desperate men,
And dost with poyson, warre, and sicknesse dwell,   10
And poppie, or charmes can make us sleepe as well,
And better then thy stroake; why swell'st thou then?
One short sleepe past, wee wake eternally,
And death shall be no more; death, thou shalt die.

XI

Spit in my face you Jewes, and pierce my side,
Buffet, and scoffe, scourge, and crucifie mee,
For I have sinn'd, and sinn'd, and onely hee,
Who could do no iniquitie hath dyed:
But by my death can not be satisfied   5
My sinnes, which passe the Jewes impiety:
They kill'd once an inglorious man, but I
Crucifie him daily, being now glorified.
Oh let mee then, his strange love still admire:
Kings pardon, but he bore our punishment.   10
And *Jacob* came cloth'd in vile harsh attire
But to supplant, and with gainfull intent:

God cloth'd himselfe in vile mans flesh, that so
Hee might be weake enough to suffer woe.

XII

Why are wee by all creatures waited on?
Why doe the prodigall elements supply
Life and food to mee, being more pure then I,
Simple, and further from corruption?
Why brook'st thou, ignorant horse, subjection?   5
Why dost thou bull, and bore so seelily
Dissemble weaknesse, and by'one mans stroke die,
Whose whole kinde, you might swallow and feed upon?
Weaker I am, woe is mee, and worse then you,
You have not sinn'd, nor need be timorous.   10
But wonder at a greater wonder, for to us
Created nature doth these things subdue,
But their Creator, whom sin, nor nature tyed,
For us, his Creatures, and his foes, hath dyed.

XIII

What if this present were the worlds last night?
Marke in my heart, O Soule, where thou dost dwell,
The picture of Christ crucified, and tell
Whether that countenance can thee affright,
Teares in his eyes quench the amasing light,   5
Blood fills his frownes, which from his pierc'd head fell.
And can that tongue adjudge thee unto hell,
Which pray'd forgivenesse for his foes fierce spight?
No, no; but as in my idolatrie
I said to all my profane mistresses,   10
Beauty, of pitty, foulnesse onely is
A signe of rigour: so I say to thee,
To wicked spirits are horrid shapes assign'd,
This beauteous forme assures a pitious minde.

XIV

Batter my heart, three person'd God; for, you
As yet but knocke, breathe, shine, and seeke to mend;
That I may rise, and stand, o'erthrow mee,'and bend

Your force, to breake, blowe, burn and make me new.
I, like an usurpt towne, to'another due,   5
Labour to'admit you, but Oh, to no end,
Reason your viceroy in mee, mee should defend,
But is captiv'd, and proves weake or untrue.
Yet dearely'I love you,'and would be loved faine,
But am betroth'd unto your enemie: 10
Divorce mee,'untie, or breake that knot againe,
Take mee to you, imprison mee, for I
Except you'enthrall mee, never shall be free,
Nor ever chast, except you ravish mee.

XV

Wilt thou love God, as he thee! then digest,
My Soule, this wholsome meditation,
How God the Spirit, by Angels waited on
In heaven, doth make his Temple in thy brest.
The Father having begot a Sonne most blest,   5
And still begetting, (for he ne'r begonne)
Hath deign'd to chuse thee by adoption,
Coheire to'his glory,'and Sabbaths endlesse rest.
And as a robb'd man, which by search doth finde
His stolne stuffe sold, must lose or buy'it againe: 10
The Sonne of glory came downe, and was slaine,
Us whom he'had made, and Satan stolne, to unbinde.
'Twas much, that man was made like God before,
But, that God should be made like man, much more.

XVI

Father, part of his double interest
Unto thy kingdome, thy Sonne gives to mee,
His joynture in the knottie Trinitie
Hee keepes, and gives to me his deaths conquest.
This Lambe, whose death, with life the world hath blest,   5
Was from the worlds beginning slaine, and he
Hath made two Wills, which with the Legacie
Of his and thy kingdome, doe thy Sonnes invest.
Yet such are thy laws, that men argue yet
Whether a man those statutes can fulfill;   10

None doth; but all-healing grace and spirit
Revive againe what law and letter kill.
Thy lawes abridgement, and thy last command
Is all but love; Oh let this last Will stand!

XVII

Since she whom I lov'd hath payd her last debt
To Nature, and to hers, and my good is dead,
And her Soule early into heaven ravished,
Wholly on heavenly things my mind is sett.
Here the admyring her my mind did whett   5
To seeke thee God; so streames do shew their head;
But though I have found thee, and thou my thirst hast fed,
A holy thirsty dropsy melts mee yett.
But why should I begg more Love, when as thou
Dost wooe my soule for hers; offring all thine: 10
And dost not only feare least I allow
My Love to Saints and Angels, things divine,
But in thy tender jealosy dost doubt
Least the World, Fleshe, yea Devill putt thee out.

XVIII

Show me deare Christ, thy spouse, so bright and clear.
What! is it She, which on the other shore
Goes richly painted? or which rob'd and tore
Laments and mournes in Germany and here?
Sleepes she a thousand, then peepes up one yeare?   5
Is she selfe truth and errs? now new, now outwore?
Doth she, and did she, and shall she evermore
On one, on seaven, or on no hill appeare?
Dwells she with us, or like adventuring knights
First travaile we to seeke and then make Love?   10
Betray kind husband thy spouse to our sights,
And let myne amorous soule court thy mild Dove,
Who is most trew, and pleasing to thee, then
When she'is embrac'd and open to most men.

XIX

Oh, to vex me, contraryes meet in one:
Inconstancy unnaturally hath begott
A constant habit; that when I would not
I change in vowes, and in devotione.
As humorous is my contritione   5
As my prophane Love, and as soone forgott:
As ridlingly distemper'd, cold and hott,
As praying, as mute; as infinite, as none.
I durst not view heaven yesterday; and to day
In prayers, and flattering speaches I court God: 10
To morrow I quake with true feare of his rod.
So my devout fitts come and go away
Like a fantastique Ague: save that here
Those are my best dayes, when I shake with feare.

The Crosse

Since Christ embrac'd the Crosse it selfe, dare I
His image, th'image of his Crosse deny?
Would I have profit by the sacrifice,
And dare the chosen Altar to despise?
It bore all other sinnes, but is it fit   5
That it should beare the sinne of scorning it?
Who from the picture would avert his eye,
How would he flye his paines, who there did dye?
From mee, no Pulpit, nor misgrounded law,
Nor scandall taken, shall this Crosse withdraw,   10
It shall not, for it cannot; for, the losse
Of this Crosse, were to mee another Crosse;
Better were worse, for, no affliction,
No Crosse is so extreme, as to have none.
Who can blot out the Crosse, which th'instrument   15
Of God, dew'd on mee in the Sacrament?
Who can deny mee power, and liberty
To stretch mine armes, and mine owne Crosse to be?
Swimme, and at every stroake, thou art thy Crosse;
The Mast and yard make one, where seas do tosse;   20
Looke downe, thou spiest out Crosses in small things;
Looke up, thou seest birds rais'd on crossed wings;
All the Globes frame, and spheares, is nothing else

But the Meridians crossing Parallels.
Materiall Crosses then, good physicke bee,   25
But yet spirituall have chiefe dignity.
These for extracted chimique medicine serve,
And cure much better, and as well preserve;
Then are you your own physicke, or need none,
When Still'd, or purg'd by tribulation.   30
For when that Crosse ungrudg'd, unto you stickes,
Then are you to your selfe, a Crucifixe.
As perchance, Carvers do not faces make,
But that away, which hid them there, do take;
Let Crosses, soe, take what hid Christ in thee,   35
And be his image, or not his, but hee.
But, as oft Alchimists doe coyners prove,
So may a selfe-dispising, get selfe-love,
And then as worst surfets, of best meates bee,
Soe is pride, issued from humility,   40
For, 'tis no child, but monster; therefore Crosse
Your joy in crosses, else, 'tis double losse.
And crosse thy senses, else, both they, and thou
Must perish soone, and to destruction bowe.
For if the'eye seeke good objects, and will take   45
No crosse from bad, wee cannot scape a snake.
So with harsh, hard, sowre, stinking, crosse the rest,
Make them indifferent all; call nothing best.
But most the eye needs crossing, that can rome,
And move; To th'other th'objects must come home.   50
And crosse thy heart: for that in man alone
Points downewards, and hath palpitation.
Crosse those dejections, when it downeward tends,
And when it to forbidden heights pretends.
And as the braine through bony walls doth vent   55
By sutures, which a Crosses forme present,
So when thy braine workes, ere thou utter it,
Crosse and correct concupiscence of witt.
Be covetous of Crosses, let none fall.
Crosse no man else, but crosse thy selfe in all.   60
Then doth the Crosse of Christ worke fruitfully
Within our hearts, when wee love harmlessly
That Crosses pictures much, and with more care
That Crosses children, which our Crosses are.

Resurrection, imperfect

Sleep sleep old Sun, thou canst not have repast
As yet, the wound thou took'st on friday last;
Sleepe then, and rest; The world may beare thy stay,
A better Sun rose before thee to day,
Who, not content to'enlighten all that dwell   5
On the earths face, as thou, enlightned hell,
And made the darke fires languish in that vale,
As, at thy presence here, our fires grow pale.
Whose body having walk'd on earth, and now
Hasting to Heaven, would, that he might allow   10
Himselfe unto all stations, and fill all,
For these three daies become a minerall;
Hee was all gold when he lay downe, but rose
All tincture, and doth not alone dispose
Leaden and iron wills to good, but is   15
Of power to make even sinfull flesh like his.
Had one of those, whose credulous pietie
Thought, that a Soule one might discerne and see
Goe from a body,'at this sepulcher been,
And, issuing from the sheet, this body seen,   20
He would have justly thought this body a soule,
If not of any man, yet of the whole.
                    Desunt cætera.

The Annuntiation and Passion

Tamely, fraile body,'abstaine to day; to day
My soule eates twice, Christ hither and away.
Shee sees him man, so like God made in this,
That of them both a circle embleme is,
Whose first and last concurre; this doubtfull day   5
Of feast or fast, Christ came, and went away.
Shee sees him nothing twice at once, who'is all;
Shee sees a Cedar plant it selfe, and fall,
Her Maker put to making, and the head
Of life, at once, not yet alive, yet dead.   10
She sees at once the virgin mother stay
Reclus'd at home, Publique at Golgotha;

Sad and rejoyc'd shee's seen at once, and seen
At almost fiftie, and at scarce fifteene.
At once a Sonne is promis'd her, and gone,   15
Gabriell gives Christ to her, He her to John;
Not fully a mother, Shee's in Orbitie,
At once receiver and the legacie.
All this, and all betweene, this day hath showne,
Th'Abridgement of Christs story, which makes one   20
(As in plaine Maps, the furthest West is East)
Of the'Angels *Ave,'* and *Consummatum est.*
How well the Church, Gods Court of faculties
Deales, in some times, and seldome joyning these!
As by the selfe-fix'd Pole wee never doe   25
Direct our course, but the next starre thereto,
Which showes where the'other is, and which we say
(Because it strayes not farre) doth never stray;
So God by his Church, neerest to him, wee know,
And stand firme, if wee by her motion goe;   30
His Spirit, as his fiery Pillar doth
Leade, and his Church, as cloud; to one end both.
This Church, by letting these daies joyne, hath shown
Death and conception in mankinde is one;
Or 'twas in him the same humility,   35
That he would be a man, and leave to be:
Or as creation he hath made, as God,
With the last judgement, but one period,
His imitating Spouse would joyne in one
Manhoods extremes: He shall come, he is gone: 40
Or as though one blood drop, which thence did fall,
Accepted, would have serv'd, he yet shed all;
So though the least of his paines, deeds, or words,
Would busie a life, she all this day affords;
This treasure then, in grosse, my Soule uplay,   45
And in my life retaile it every day.

Goodfriday, 1613. *Riding Westward*

Let mans Soule be a Spheare, and then, in this,
The intelligence that moves, devotion is,

And as the other Spheares, by being growne
Subject to forraigne motions, lose their owne,
And being by others hurried every day,   5
Scarce in a yeare their naturall forme obey:
Pleasure or businesse, so, our Soules admit
For their first mover, and are whirld by it.
Hence is't, that I am carryed towards the West
This day, when my Soules forme bends toward the East. 10
There I should see a Sunne, by rising set,
And by that setting endlesse day beget;
But that Christ on this Crosse, did rise and fall,
Sinne had eternally benighted all.
Yet dare I'almost be glad, I do not see   15
That spectacle of too much weight for mee.
Who sees Gods face, that is selfe life, must dye;
What a death were it then to see God dye?
It made his owne Lieutenant Nature shrinke,
It made his footstoole crack, and the Sunne winke.   20
Could I behold those hands which span the Poles,
And turne all spheares at once, peirc'd with those holes?
Could I behold that endlesse height which is
Zenith to us, and our Antipodes,
Humbled below us? or that blood which is   25
The seat of all our Soules, if not of his,
Made durt of dust, or that flesh which was worne
By God, for his apparell, rag'd, and torne?
If on these things I durst not looke, durst I
Upon his miserable mother cast mine eye,   30
Who was Gods partner here, and furnish'd thus
Halfe of that Sacrifice, which ransom'd us?
Though these things, as I ride, be from mine eye,
They'are present yet unto my memory,
For that looks towards them; and thou look'st towards mee, 35
O Saviour, as thou hang'st upon the tree;
I turne my backe to thee, but to receive
Corrections, till thy mercies bid thee leave.
O thinke mee worth thine anger, punish mee,
Burne off my rusts, and my deformity,   40
Restore thine Image, so much, by thy grace,
That thou may'st know mee, and I'll turne my face.

The Litanie

The Father

Father of Heaven, and him, by whom
  It, and us for it, and all else, for us
  Thou madest, and govern'st ever, come
And re-create mee, now growne ruinous:
    My heart is by dejection, clay,   5
    And by selfe-murder, red.
From this red earth, O Father, purge away
All vicious tinctures, that new fashioned
I may rise up from death, before I'am dead.

The Sonne

O Sonne of God, who seeing two things,
Sinne, and death crept in, which were never made,
  By bearing one, tryed'st with what stings
The other could thine heritage invade;
    O be thou nail'd unto my heart,   5
    And crucified againe,
Part not from it, though it from thee would part,
But let it be, by applying so thy paine,
Drown'd in thy blood, and in thy passion slaine.

The Holy Ghost

O Holy Ghost, whose temple I
Am, but of mudde walls, and condensed dust,
  And being sacrilegiously
Halfe wasted with youths fires, of pride and lust,
    Must with new stormes be weatherbeat;   5
    Double in my heart thy flame,
Which let devout sad teares intend; and let
(Though this glasse lanthorne, flesh, do suffer maime)
Fire, Sacrifice, Priest, Altar be the same.

The Trinity

O Blessed glorious Trinity,
Bones to Philosophy, but milke to faith,
   Which, as wise serpents, diversly
Most slipperinesse, yet most entanglings hath,
      As you distinguish'd undistinct   5
      By power, love, knowledge bee,
Give mee a such selfe different instinct
Of these; let all mee elemented bee,
Of power, to love, to know, you unnumbered three.

The Virgin Mary

For that faire blessed Mother-maid,
Whose flesh redeem'd us; That she-Cherubin,
   Which unlock'd Paradise, and made
One claime for innocence, and disseiz'd sinne,
      Whose wombe was a strange heav'n, for there   5
      God cloath'd himselfe, and grew,
Our zealous thankes wee poure. As her deeds were
Our helpes, so are her prayers; nor can she sue
In vaine, who hath such titles unto you.

The Angels

And since this life our nonage is,
And wee in Wardship to thine Angels be,
   Native in heavens faire Palaces,
Where we shall be but denizen'd by thee,
      As th'earth conceiving by the Sunne,   5
      Yeelds faire diversitie,
Yet never knowes which course that light doth run,
So let mee study, that mine actions bee
Worthy their sight, though blinde in how they see.

The Patriarches

And let thy Patriarches Desire
(Those great Grandfathers of thy Church, which saw
   More in the cloud, then wee in fire,
Whom Nature clear'd more, then us Grace and Law,
     And now in Heaven still pray, that wee   5
     May use our new helpes right,)
Be satisfy'd, and fructifie in mee;
Let not my minde be blinder by more light
Nor Faith, by Reason added, lose her sight.

The Prophets

Thy Eagle-sighted Prophets too,
Which were thy Churches Organs, and did sound
   That harmony, which made of two
One law, and did unite, but not confound;
     Those heavenly Poëts which did see   5
     Thy will, and it expresse
In rythmique feet, in common pray for mee,
That I by them excuse not my excesse
In seeking secrets, or Poëtiquenesse.

The Apostles

And thy illustrious Zodiacke
Of twelve Apostles, which ingirt this All,
   (From whom whosoever do not take
Their light, to darke deep pits, throw downe, and fall,)
     As through their prayers, thou'hast let mee know   5
     That their bookes are divine;
May they pray still, and be heard, that I goe
Th'old broad way in applying; O decline
Mee, when my comment would make thy word mine.

The Martyrs

And since thou so desirously
Did'st long to die, that long before thou could'st,
   And long since thou no more couldst dye,
Thou in thy scatter'd mystique body wouldst
      Though they have not obtain'd of thee,   5
      In thine; let their blood come
To begge for us, a discreet patience
Of death, or of worse life: for Oh, to some
Not to be Martyrs, is a martyrdome.

The Confessors

Therefore with thee triumpheth there
A Virgin Squadron of white Confessors,
   Whose bloods betroth'd, not marryed were,
Tender'd, not taken by those Ravishers:
      In Abel dye, and ever since   5
      In every Christian
Hourly tempestuous persecutions grow;
Tentations martyr us alive; A man
Is to himselfe a Dioclesian.

The Virgins

The cold white snowie Nunnery,
Which, as thy mother, their high Abbesse, sent
   Their bodies backe againe to thee,
As thou hadst lent them, cleane and innocent,
      They know, and pray, that wee may know,   5
      That or thy Church, or I,
Should keep, as they, our first integrity;
Divorce thou sinne in us, or bid it die,
And call chast widowhead Virginitie.

The Doctors

Thy sacred Academie above
Of Doctors, whose paines have unclasp'd, and taught
   Both bookes of life to us (for love
To know thy Scriptures tells us, we are wrote
     In thy other booke) pray for us there   5
     That what they have misdone
Or mis-said, wee to that may not adhere;
Their zeale may be our sinne. Lord let us runne
Meane waies, and call them stars, but not the Sunne.

And whil'st this universall Quire,   10
That Church in triumph, this in warfare here,
   Warm'd with one all-partaking fire
Of love, that none be lost, which cost thee deare,
     Prayes ceaslesly,'and thou hearken too,
     (Since to be gratious   15
Our taske is treble, to pray, beare, and doe)
Heare this prayer Lord: O Lord deliver us
From trusting in those prayers, though powr'd out thus.

From being anxious, or secure,
Dead clods of sadnesse, or light squibs of mirth,   20
   From thinking, that great courts immure
All, or no happinesse, or that this earth
     Is only for our prison fram'd,
     Or that thou art covetous
To them whom thou lovest, or that they are maim'd   25
From reaching this worlds sweet, who seek thee thus,
With all their might, Good Lord deliver us.

From needing danger, to bee good,
From owing thee yesterdaies teares to day,
   From trusting so much to thy blood,   30
That in that hope, wee wound our soule away,
     From bribing thee with Almes, to excuse
     Some sinne more burdenous,
From light affecting, in religion, newes,
From thinking us all soule, neglecting thus   35
Our mutuall duties, Lord deliver us.

From tempting Satan to tempt us,
By our connivence, or slack companie,
   From measuring ill by vitious,
Neglecting to choake sins spawne, Vanitie,   40
      From indiscreet humilitie,
      Which might be scandalous,
And cast reproach on Christianitie,
From being spies, or to spies pervious,
From thirst, or scorne of fame, deliver us.   45

   Deliver us for thy descent
Into the Virgin, whose wombe was a place
   Of middle kind; and thou being sent
To'ungratious us, staid'st at her full of grace;
      And through thy poore birth, where first thou   50
      Glorifiedst Povertie,
And yet soone after riches didst allow,
By accepting Kings gifts in the Epiphanie,
Deliver, and make us, to both waies free.

   And through that bitter agonie,   55
Which is still the agonie of pious wits,
   Disputing what distorted thee,
And interrupted evennesse, with fits;
      And through thy free confession
      Though thereby they were then   60
Made blind, so that thou might'st from them have gone,
Good Lord deliver us, and teach us when
Wee may not, and we may blinde unjust men.

   Through thy submitting all, to blowes
Thy face, thy clothes to spoile; thy fame to scorne,   65
   All waies, which rage, or Justice knowes,
And by which thou could'st shew, that thou wast born;
      And through thy gallant humblenesse
      Which thou in death did'st shew,
Dying before thy soule they could expresse,   70
Deliver us from death, by dying so,
To this world, ere this world doe bid us goe.

When senses, which thy souldiers are,
Wee arme against thee, and they fight for sinne,
   When want, sent but to tame, doth warre   75
And worke despaire a breach to enter in,
      When plenty, Gods image, and seale
      Makes us Idolatrous,
And love it, not him, whom it should reveale,
When wee are mov'd to seeme religious   80
Only to vent wit, Lord deliver us.

In Churches, when the'infirmitie
Of him which speakes, diminishes the Word,
   When Magistrates doe mis-apply
To us, as we judge, lay or ghostly sword,   85
      When plague, which is thine Angell, raignes,
      Or wars, thy Champions, swaie,
When Heresie, thy second deluge, gaines;
In th'houre of death, the'Eve of last judgement day,
Deliver us from the sinister way.   90

Heare us, O heare us Lord; to thee
A sinner is more musique, when he prayes,
   Then spheares, or Angels praises bee,
In Panegyrique Allelujaes;
      Heare us, for till thou heare us, Lord   95
      We know not what to say;
Thine eare to'our sighes, teares, thoughts gives voice and
      word.
O Thou who Satan heard'st in Jobs sicke day,
Heare thy selfe now, for thou in us dost pray.   100

That wee may change to evennesse
This intermitting aguish Pietie;
   That snatching cramps of wickednesse
And Apoplexies of fast sin, may die;
      That musique of thy promises,   105
      Not threats in Thunder may
Awaken us to our just offices;
What in thy booke, thou dost, or creatures say,
That we may heare, Lord heare us, when wee pray.

That our eares sicknesse wee may cure,   110
And rectifie those Labyrinths aright;
  That wee, by harkning, not procure
Our praise, nor others dispraise so invite;
        That wee get not a slipperinesse
          And senslesly decline,   115
From hearing bold wits jeast at Kings excesse,
To'admit the like of majestie divine;
That we may locke our eares, Lord open thine.

That living law, the Magistrate,
Which to give us, and make us physicke, doth   120
  Our vices often aggravate,
That Preachers taxing sinne, before her growth,
        That Satan, and invenom'd men
          Which well, if we starve, dine,
When they doe most accuse us, may see then   125
Us, to amendment, heare them; thee decline:
That we may open our eares, Lord lock thine.

That learning, thine Ambassador,
From thine allegeance wee never tempt,
  That beauty, paradises flower   130
For physicke made, from poyson be exempt,
        That wit, borne apt high good to doe,
          By dwelling lazily
On Natures nothing, be not nothing too,
That our affections kill us not, nor dye,   135
Heare us, weake ecchoes, O thou eare, and cry.

Sonne of God heare us, and since thou
By taking our blood, owest it us againe,
  Gaine to thy self, or us allow;
And let not both us and thy selfe be slaine;   140
        O Lambe of God, which took'st our sinne
          Which could not stick to thee,
O let it not returne to us againe,
But Patient and Physition being free,
As sinne is nothing, let it no where be.   145

Vpon the translation of the Psalmes by Sir Philip Sydney, *and the Countesse of Pembroke his Sister*

Eternall God, (for whom who ever dare
Seeke new expressions, doe the Circle square,
And thrust into strait corners of poore wit
Thee, who art cornerlesse and infinite)
I would but blesse thy Name, not name thee now;   5
(And thy gifts are as infinite as thou:)
Fixe we our prayses therefore on this one,
That, as thy blessed Spirit fell upon
These Psalmes first Author in a cloven tongue;
(For 'twas a double power by which he sung   10
The highest matter in the noblest forme;)
So thou hast cleft that spirit, to performe
That worke againe, and shed it, here, upon
Two, by their bloods, and by thy Spirit one;
A Brother and a Sister, made by thee   15
The Organ, where thou art the Harmony.
Two that make one *John Baptists* holy voyce,
And who that Psalme, *Now let the Iles rejoyce,*
Have both translated, and apply'd it too,
Both told us what, and taught us how to doe.   20
They shew us Ilanders our joy, our King,
They tell us *why*, and teach us *how* to sing;
Make all this All, three Quires, heaven, earth, and sphears;
The first, Heaven, hath a song, but no man heares,
The Spheares have Musick, but they have no tongue,   25
Their harmony is rather danc'd than sung;
But our third Quire, to which the first gives eare,
(For, Angels learne by what the Church does here)
This Quire hath all. The Organist is hee
Who hath tun'd God and Man, the Organ we: 30
The songs are these, which heavens high holy Muse
Whisper'd to *David*, *David* to the Jewes:
And *Davids* Successors, in holy zeale,
In formes of joy and art doe re-reveale
To us so sweetly and sincerely too,   35
That I must not rejoyce as I would doe

When I behold that these Psalmes are become
So well attyr'd abroad, so ill at home,
So well in Chambers, in thy Church so ill,
As I can scarce call that reform'd untill   40
This be reform'd; Would a whole State present
A lesser gift than some one man hath sent?
And shall our Church, unto our Spouse and King
More hoarse, more harsh than any other, sing?
For *that* we pray, we praise thy name for *this*,   45
Which, by <this> *Moses* and this *Miriam*, is
Already done; and as those Psalmes we call
(Though some have other Authors) *Davids* all:
So though some have, some may some Psalmes translate,
We thy Sydnean Psalmes shall celebrate,   50
And, till we come th'Extemporall song to sing,
(Learn'd the first hower, that we see the King,
Who hath translated those translators) may
These their sweet learned labours, all the way
Be as our tuning; that, when hence we part,   55
We may fall in with them, and sing our part.

To Mr Tilman *after he had taken orders*

Thou, whose diviner soule hath caus'd thee now
To put thy hand unto the holy Plough,
Making Lay-scornings of the Ministry,
Not an impediment, but victory;
What bringst thou home with thee? how is thy mind   5
Affected since the vintage? Dost thou finde
New thoughts and stirrings in thee? and as Steele
Toucht with a Loadstone, dost new motions feele?
Or, as a Ship after much paine and care,
For Iron and Cloth brings home rich Indian ware,   10
Hast thou thus traffiqu'd, but with farre more gaine
Of noble goods, and with lesse time and paine?
Thou art the same materials, as before,
Onely the stampe is changed; but no more.
And as new crowned Kings alter the face,   15
But not the monies substance; so hath grace

Chang'd onely Gods old Image by Creation,
To Christs new stampe, at this thy Coronation;
Or, as we paint Angels with wings, because
They beare Gods message, and proclaime his lawes,   20
Since thou must doe the like, and so must move,
Art thou new feather'd with cœlestiall love?
Deare, tell me where thy purchase lies, and shew
What thy advantage is above, below.
But if thy gainings doe surmount expression,   25
Why doth the foolish world scorne that profession,
Whose joyes passe speech? Why do they think unfit
That Gentry should joyne families with it?
As if their day were onely to be spent
In dressing, Mistressing and complement;   30
Alas poore joyes, but poorer men, whose trust
Seemes richly placed in sublimed dust;
(For, such are cloathes and beauty, which though gay,
Are, at the best, but of sublimed clay.)
Let then the world thy calling disrespect,   35
But goe thou on, and pitty their neglect.
What function is so noble, as to bee
Embassadour to God and destinie?
To open life, to give kingdomes to more
Than Kings give dignities; to keepe heavens doore?   40
Maries prerogative was to beare Christ, so
'Tis preachers to convey him, for they doe
As Angels out of clouds, from Pulpits speake;
And blesse the poore beneath, the lame, the weake.
If then th'Astronomers, whereas they spie   45
A new-found Starre, their Opticks magnifie,
How brave are those, who with their Engine, can
Bring man to heaven, and heaven againe to man?
These are thy titles and preheminences,
In whom must meet Gods graces, mens offences,   50
And so the heavens which beget all things here,
And the earth our mother, which these things doth beare,
Both these in thee, are in thy Calling knit,
And make thee now a blest Hermaphrodite.

A Hymne to Christ, at the Authors last
going into Germany

In what torne ship soever I embarke,
That ship shall be my embleme of thy Arke;
What sea soever swallow mee, that flood
Shall be to mee an embleme of thy blood;
Though thou with clouds of anger do disguise   5
Thy face; yet through that maske I know those eyes,
   Which, though they turne away sometimes,
     They never will despise.

I sacrifice this Iland unto thee,
And all whom I lov'd there, and who lov'd mee;   10
When I have put our seas twixt them and mee,
Put thou thy sea betwixt my sinnes and thee.
As the trees sap doth seeke the root below
In winter, in my winter now I goe,
   Where none but thee, th'Eternall root   15
     Of true Love I may know.

Nor thou nor thy religion dost controule,
The amorousnesse of an harmonious Soule,
But thou would'st have that love thy selfe: As thou
Art jealous, Lord, so I am jealous now,   20
Thou lov'st not, till from loving more, thou free
My soule: Who ever gives, takes libertie:
   O, if thou car'st not whom I love
     Alas, thou lov'st not mee.

Seale then this bill of my Divorce to All,   25
On whom those fainter beames of love did fall;
Marry those loves, which in youth scattered bee
On Fame, Wit, Hopes (false mistresses) to thee.
Churches are best for Prayer, that have least light:
To see God only, I goe out of sight: 30
   And to scape stormy dayes, I chuse
     An Everlasting night.

The Lamentations of Jeremy, for the most part according to Tremelius

CHAP. I

How sits this citie, late most populous,
  Thus solitary, and like a widdow thus!
Amplest of Nations, Queene of Provinces
  She was, who now thus tributary is!

Still in the night shee weepes, and her teares fall   5
  Downe by her cheekes along, and none of all
Her lovers comfort her; Perfidiously
  Her friends have dealt, and now are enemie.

Unto great bondage, and afflictions
  Juda is captive led; Those nations   10
With whom shee dwells, no place of rest afford,
  In streights shee meets her Persecutors sword.

Emptie are the gates of Sion, and her waies
  Mourne, because none come to her solemne dayes.
Her Priests doe groane, her maides are comfortlesse,   15
  And shee's unto her selfe a bitternesse.

Her foes are growne her head, and live at Peace,
  Because when her transgressions did increase,
The Lord strooke her with sadnesse: Th'enemie
  Doth drive her children to captivitie.   20

From Sions daughter is all beauty gone,
  Like Harts, which seeke for Pasture, and find none,
Her Princes are, and now before the foe
  Which still pursues them, without strength they go.

Now in her daies of Teares, Jerusalem   25
  (Her men slaine by the foe, none succouring them)
Remembers what of old, shee esteemed most,
  Whilest her foes laugh at her, for what she hath lost.

Jerusalem hath sinn'd, therefore is shee
  Remov'd, as women in uncleannesse bee;   30
Who honor'd, scorne her, for her foulnesse they
    Have seene; her selfe doth groane, and turne away.

Her foulnesse in her skirts was seene, yet she
  Remembred not her end; Miraculously
Therefore shee fell, none comforting: Behold   35
    O Lord my affliction, for the Foe growes bold.

Upon all things where her delight hath beene,
  The foe hath stretch'd his hand, for shee hath seene
Heathen, whom thou command'st, should not doe so,
    Into her holy Sanctuary goe.   40

And all her people groane, and seeke for bread;
  And they have given, only to be fed,
All precious things, wherein their pleasure lay:
    How cheape I'am growne, O Lord, behold, and weigh.

All this concernes not you, who passe by mee,   45
  O see, and marke if any sorrow bee
Like to my sorrow, which Jehova hath
    Done to mee in the day of his fierce wrath?

That fire, which by himselfe is governed
  He hath cast from heaven on my bones, and spred   50
A net before my feet, and mee o'rthrowne,
    And made me languish all the day alone.

His hand hath of my sinnes framed a yoake
  Which wreath'd, and cast upon my neck, hath broke
My strength. The Lord unto those enemies   55
    Hath given mee, from whom I cannot rise.

He under foot hath troden in my sight
  My strong men; He did company invite
To breake my young men; he the winepresse hath
    Trod upon Juda's daughter in his wrath.   60

For these things doe I weepe, mine eye, mine eye
   Casts water out; For he which should be nigh
To comfort mee, is now departed farre;
   The foe prevailes, forlorne my children are.

There's none, though *Sion* do stretch out her hand,   65
   To comfort her, it is the Lords command
That *Jacobs* foes girt him. *Jerusalem*
   Is as an uncleane woman amongst them.

But yet the Lord is just, and righteous still,
   I have rebell'd against his holy will;   70
O heare all people, and my sorrow see,
   My maides, my young men in captivitie.

I called for my *lovers* then, but they
   Deceiv'd mee, and my Priests, and Elders lay
Dead in the citie; for they sought for meat   75
   Which should refresh their soules, they could not get.

Because I am in streights, *Jehova* see
   My heart o'rturn'd, my bowells muddy bee,
Because I have rebell'd so much, as fast
   The sword without, as death within, doth wast.   80

Of all which heare I mourne, none comforts mee,
   My foes have heard my griefe, and glad they be,
That thou hast done it; But thy promis'd day
   Will come, when, as I suffer, so shall they.

Let all their wickednesse appeare to thee,   85
   Doe unto them, as thou hast done to mee,
For all my sinnes: The sighs which I have had
   Are very many, and my heart is sad.

CHAP. II

How over Sions daughter hath God hung
His wraths thicke cloud! and from heaven hath flung
To earth the beauty of *Israel*, and hath
    Forgot his foot-stoole in the day of wrath!

The Lord unsparingly hath swallowed   5
All Jacobs dwellings, and demolished
To ground the strengths of *Juda,* and prophan'd
    The Princes of the Kingdome, and the land.

In heat of wrath, the horne of *Israel* hee
Hath cleane cut off, and lest the enemie   10
Be hindred, his right hand he doth retire,
    But is towards *Jacob,* All-devouring fire.

Like to an enemie he bent his bow,
His right hand was in posture of a foe,
To kill what *Sions* daughter did desire,   15
    'Gainst whom his wrath, he poured forth, like fire.

For like an enemie *Jehova* is,
Devouring *Israel,* and his Palaces,
Destroying holds, giving additions
    To *Juda's* daughters lamentations.   20

Like to a garden hedge he hath cast downe
The place where was his congregation,
And *Sions* feasts and sabbaths are forgot;
    Her King, her Priest, his wrath regardeth not.

The Lord forsakes his Altar, and detests   25
His Sanctuary, and in the foes hand rests
His Palace, and the walls, in which their cries
    Are heard, as in the true solemnities.

The Lord hath cast a line, so to confound
And levell *Sions* walls unto the ground;   30
He drawes not back his hand, which doth oreturne
    The wall, and Rampart, which together mourne.

Their gates are sunke into the ground, and hee
Hath broke the barres; their King and Princes bee
Amongst the heathen, without law, nor there   35
    Unto their Prophets doth the Lord appeare.

There *Sions Elders* on the ground are plac'd,
And silence keepe; Dust on their heads they cast,
In sackcloth have they girt themselves, and low
    The Virgins towards ground, their heads do throw.   40

My bowells are growne muddy, and mine eyes
Are faint with weeping: and my liver lies
Pour'd out upon the ground, for miserie
    That sucking children in the streets doe die.

When they had cryed unto their Mothers, where   45
Shall we have bread, and drinke? they fainted there,
And in the streets like wounded persons lay
    Till 'twixt their mothers breasts they went away.

Daughter Jerusalem, Oh what may bee
A witnesse, or comparison for thee?   50
Sion, to ease thee, what shall I name like thee?
    Thy breach is like the sea, what help can bee?

For thee vaine foolish things thy Prophets sought,
Thee, thine iniquities they have not taught,
Which might disturne thy bondage: but for thee   55
    False burthens, and false causes they would see.

The passengers doe clap their hands, and hisse,
And wag their head at thee, and say, Is this
That citie, which so many men did call
    Joy of the earth, and perfectest of all?   60

Thy foes doe gape upon thee, and they hisse,
And gnash their teeth, and say, Devoure wee this,
For this is certainly the day which wee
    Expected, and which now we finde, and see.

The Lord hath done that which he purposed,   65
   Fulfill'd his word of old determined;
He hath throwne downe, and not spar'd, and thy foe
   Made glad above thee, and advanc'd him so.

But now, their hearts against the Lord do call,
   Therefore, O walls of *Sion*, let teares fall   70
Downe like a river, day and night; take thee
   No rest, but let thine eye incessant be.

Arise, cry in the night, poure, for thy sinnes,
   Thy heart, like water, when the watch begins;
Lift up thy hands to God, lest children dye,   75
   Which, faint for hunger, in the streets doe lye.

Behold O Lord, consider unto whom
   Thou hast done this; what, shall the women come
To eate their children of a spanne? shall thy
   Prophet and Priest be slaine in Sanctuary?   80

On ground in streets, the yong and old do lye,
   My virgins and yong men by sword do dye;
Them in the day of thy wrath thou hast slaine,
   Nothing did thee from killing them containe.

As to a solemne feast, all whom I fear'd   85
   Thou call'st about mee; when thy wrath appear'd,
None did remaine or scape, for those which I
   Brought up, did perish by mine enemie.

CHAP. III

I am the man which have affliction seene,
   Under the rod of Gods wrath having beene,
He hath led mee to darknesse, not to light,
   And against mee all day, his hand doth fight.

Hee hath broke my bones, worne out my flesh and skinne,　5
　　Built up against mee; and hath girt mee in
With hemlocke, and with labour; and set mee
　　In darke, as they who dead for ever bee.

Hee hath hedg'd me lest I scape, and added more
　　To my steele fetters, heavier then before.　　　　10
When I crie out, he out shuts my prayer: And hath
　　Stop'd with hewn stone my way, and turn'd my path.

And like a Lion hid in secrecie,
　　Or Beare which lyes in wait, he was to mee.
He stops my way, teares me, made desolate,　　　15
　　And hee makes mee the marke he shooteth at.

Hee made the children of his quiver passe
　　Into my reines, I with my people was
All the day long, a song and mockery.
　　Hee hath fill'd mee with bitternesse, and he　　20

Hath made me drunke with wormewood. He hath burst
　　My teeth with stones, and covered mee with dust;
And thus my Soule farre off from peace was set,
　　And my prosperity I did forget.

My strength, my hope (unto my selfe I said)　　　25
　　Which from the Lord should come, is perished.
But when my mournings I do thinke upon,
　　My wormwood, hemlocke, and affliction,

My Soule is humbled in remembering this;
　　My heart considers, therefore, hope there is.　　30
'Tis Gods great mercy we'are not utterly
　　Consum'd, for his compassions do not die;

For every morning they renewed bee,
　　For great, O Lord, is thy fidelity.
The Lord is, saith my Soule, my portion,　　　　35
　　And therefore in him will I hope alone.

The Lord is good to them, who on him relie,
  And to the Soule that seeks him earnestly.
It is both good to trust, and to attend
  (The Lords salvation) unto the end: 40

'Tis good for one his yoake in youth to beare;
  He sits alone, and doth all speech forbeare,
Because he hath borne it. And his mouth he layes
  Deepe in the dust, yet then in hope he stayes.

He gives his cheekes to whosoever will   45
  Strike him, and so he is reproched still.
For, not for ever doth the Lord forsake,
  But when he'hath strucke with sadnes, hee doth take

Compassion, as his mercy'is infinite;
  Nor is it with his heart, that he doth smite;   50
That underfoot the prisoners stamped bee,
  That a mans right the Judge himselfe doth see

To be wrung from him, That he subverted is
  In his just cause; the Lord allowes not this.
Who then will say, that ought doth come to passe,   55
  But that which by the Lord commanded was?

Both good and evill from his mouth proceeds;
  Why then grieves any man for his misdeeds?
Turne wee to God, by trying out our wayes;
  To him in heaven, our hands with hearts upraise.   60

Wee have rebell'd, and falne away from thee,
  Thou pardon'st not; Usest no clemencie;
Pursuest us, kill'st us, coverest us with wrath,
  Cover'st thy selfe with clouds, that our prayer hath

No power to passe. And thou hast made us fall   65
  As refuse, and off-scouring to them all.
All our foes gape at us. Feare and a snare
  With ruine, and with waste, upon us are.

With watry rivers doth mine eye oreflow
    For ruine of my peoples daughter so;   70
Mine eye doth drop downe teares incessantly,
    Untill the Lord looke downe from heaven to see.

And for my citys daughters sake, mine eye
    Doth breake mine heart. Causles mine enemy,
Like a bird chac'd me. In a dungeon   75
    They have shut my life, and cast on me a stone.

Waters flow'd o'r my head, then thought I, I am
    Destroy'd; I called Lord, upon thy name
Out of the pit. And thou my voice didst heare;
    Oh from my sigh, and crye, stop not thine eare.   80

Then when I call'd upon thee, thou drew'st nere
    Unto mee, and said'st unto mee, do not feare.
Thou Lord my Soules cause handled hast, and thou
    Rescud'st my life. O Lord do thou judge now,

Thou heardst my wrong. Their vengeance all they have
        wrought;   [85
    How they reproach'd, thou hast heard, and what they
        thought,
What their lips uttered, which against me rose,
    And what was ever whisper'd by my foes.   90

I am their song, whether they rise or sit,
    Give them rewards Lord, for their working fit,
Sorrow of heart, thy curse. And with thy might
    Follow, and from under heaven destroy them quite.

CHAP. IV

How is the gold become so dimme? How is
Purest and finest gold thus chang'd to this?
The stones which were stones of the Sanctuary,
    Scattered in corners of each street do lye.

The pretious sonnes of Sion, which should bee 5
  Valued at purest gold, how do wee see
Low rated now, as earthen Pitchers, stand,
  Which are the worke of a poore Potters hand.

Even the Sea-calfes draw their brests, and give
  Sucke to their young; my peoples daughters live, 10
By reason of the foes great cruelnesse,
  As do the Owles in the vast Wildernesse.

And when the sucking child doth strive to draw,
  His tongue for thirst cleaves to his upper jaw.
And when for bread the little children crye, 15
  There is no man that doth them satisfie.

They which before were delicately fed,
  Now in the streets forlorne have perished,
And they which ever were in scarlet cloath'd,
  Sit and embrace the dunghills which they loath'd. 20

The daughters of my people have sinned more,
  Then did the towne of *Sodome* sinne before;
Which being at once destroy'd, there did remaine
  No hands amongst them, to vexe them againe.

But heretofore purer her Nazarite 25
  Was then the snow, and milke was not so white;
As carbuncles did their pure bodies shine,
  And all their polish'dnesse was Saphirine.

They are darker now then blacknes, none can know
  Them by the face, as through the streets they goe, 30
For now their skin doth cleave unto the bone,
  And withered, is like to dry wood growne.

Better by sword then famine 'tis to dye;
  And better through pierc'd, then through penury.
Women by nature pitifull, have eate 35
  Their children drest with their owne hands for meat.

Jehova here fully accomplish'd hath
His indignation, and powr'd forth his wrath,
Kindled a fire in *Sion*, which hath power
To eate, and her foundations to devour.   40

Nor would the Kings of the earth, nor all which live
In the inhabitable world beleeve,
That any adversary, any foe
Into *Jerusalem* should enter so.

For the Priests sins, and Prophets, which have shed   45
Blood in the streets, and the just murthered:
Which when those men, whom they made blinde, did stray
Thorough the streets, defiled by the way

With blood, the which impossible it was
Their garments should scape touching, as they passe,   50
Would cry aloud, depart defiled men,
Depart, depart, and touch us not; and then

They fled, and strayd, and with the *Gentiles* were,
Yet told their friends, they should not long dwell there;
For this they are scattered by Jehovahs face   55
Who never will regard them more; No grace

Unto their old men shall the foe afford,
Nor, that they are Priests, redeeme them from the
sword.
And wee as yet, for all these miseries   60
Desiring our vaine helpe, consume our eyes:

And such a nation as cannot save,
We in desire and speculation have.
They hunt our steps, that in the streets wee feare
To goe: our end is now approached neere,   65

Our dayes accomplish'd are, this the last day.
Eagles of heaven are not so swift as they
Which follow us, o'r mountaine tops they flye
At us, and for us in the desart lye.

The annointed Lord, breath of our nostrils, hee   70
   Of whom we said, under his shadow, wee
Shall with more ease under the Heathen dwell,
   Into the pit which these men digged, fell.

Rejoyce O *Edoms daughter*, joyfull bee
   Thou which inhabitst *Huz*, for unto thee   75
This cup shall passe, and thou with drunkennesse
   Shalt fill thy selfe, and shew thy nakednesse.

And then thy sinnes O *Sion*, shall be spent,
   The Lord will not leave thee in banishment.
Thy sinnes O *Edoms daughter*, hee will see,   80
   And for them, pay thee with captivitie.

CHAP. V

Remember, O Lord, what is fallen on us;
   See, and marke how we are reproached thus,
For unto strangers our possession
   Is turn'd, our houses unto Aliens gone,

Our mothers are become as widowes, wee   5
   As Orphans all, and without father be;
Waters which are our owne, wee drunke, and pay,
   And upon our owne wood a price they lay.

Our persecutors on our necks do sit,
   They make us travaile, and not intermit,   10
We stretch our hands unto th'*Egyptians*
   To get us bread; and to the *Assyrians*.

Our Fathers did these sinnes, and are no more,
   But wee do beare the sinnes they did before.
They are but servants, which do rule us thus,   15
   Yet from their hands none would deliver us.

With danger of our life our bread wee gat;
  For in the wildernesse, the sword did wait.
The tempests of this famine wee liv'd in,
  Black as an Oven colour'd had our skinne: 20

In *Judaes* cities they the maids abus'd
  By force, and so women in *Sion* us'd.
The Princes with their hands they hung; no grace
  Nor honour gave they to the Elders face.

Unto the mill our yong men carried are,   25
  And children fell under the wood they bare.
Elders, the gates; youth did their songs forbeare,
  Gone was our joy; our dancings, mournings were.

Now is the crowne falne from our head; and woe
  Be unto us, because we'have sinned so.   30
For this our hearts do languish, and for this
  Over our eyes a cloudy dimnesse is.

Because mount *Sion* desolate doth lye,
  And foxes there do goe at libertie:
But thou O Lord art ever, and thy throne   35
  From generation, to generation.

Why should'st thou forget us eternally?
  Or leave us thus long in this misery?
Restore us Lord to thee, that so we may
  Returne, and as of old, renew our day.   40

For oughtest thou, O Lord, despise us thus,
  And to be utterly enrag'd at us?

Hymne to God my God, in my sicknesse

Since I am comming to that Holy roome,
   Where, with thy Quire of Saints for evermore,
I shall be made thy Musique; As I come
   I tune the Instrument here at the dore,
   And what I must doe then, thinke here before.   5

Whilst my Physitians by their love are growne
   Cosmographers, and I their Mapp, who lie
Flat on this bed, that by them may be showne
   That this is my South-west discoverie
   Per fretum febris, by these streights to die,   10

I joy, that in these straits, I see my West;
   For, though theire currants yeeld returne to none,
What shall my West hurt me? As West and East
   In all flatt Maps (and I am one) are one,
   So death doth touch the Resurrection.   15

Is the Pacifique Sea my home? Or are
   The Easterne riches? Is *Jerusalem?*
Anyan, and *Magellan,* and *Gibraltare,*
   All streights, and none but streights, are wayes to them,
   Whether where *Japhet* dwelt, or *Cham,* or *Sem.*   20

We thinke that *Paradise* and *Calvarie,*
   Christs Crosse, and *Adams* tree, stood in one place;
Looke Lord, and finde both *Adams* met in me;
   As the first *Adams* sweat surrounds my face,
   May the last *Adams* blood my soule embrace.   25

So, in his purple wrapp'd receive mee Lord,
   By these his thornes give me his other Crowne;
And as to others soules I preach'd thy word,
   Be this my Text, my Sermon to mine owne,
   Therfore that he may raise the Lord throws down.   30

A *Hymne to God the Father*

Wilt thou forgive that sinne where I begunne,
  Which was my sin, though it were done before?
Wilt thou forgive that sinne; through which I runne,
  And do run still: though still I do deplore?
    When thou hast done, thou hast not done,   5
      For I have more.

Wilt thou forgive that sinne which I have wonne
  Others to sinne? and, made my sinne their doore?
Wilt thou forgive that sinne which I did shunne
  A yeare, or two: but wallowed in, a score?
    When thou hast done, thou hast not done,   10
      For I have more.

I have a sinne of feare, that when I have spunne
  My last thred, I shall perish on the shore;
But sweare by thy selfe, that at my death thy sonne
  Shall shine as he shines now, and heretofore;
    And, having done that, Thou hast done,   15
      I feare no more.

TRANSLATIONS
FROM LATIN POEMS

(TRANSLATED FROM DONNE'S OWN LATIN POEM, QUI PRIUS ASSUETUS SERPENTUM FASCE TABELLAS)

To Mr *George Herbert,* with one of my Seals, of the Anchor and Christ

A Sheafe of Snakes used heretofore to be
My Seal, The Crest of our poore Family.
Adopted in Gods Family, and so
Our old Coat lost, unto new armes I go.
The Crosse (my seal at Baptism) spred below,   5
Does, by that form, into an Anchor grow.
Crosses grow Anchors; Bear, as thou shouldst do
Thy Crosse, and that Crosse grows an Anchor too.
But he that makes our Crosses Anchors thus,
Is Christ, who there is crucifi'd for us.   10
Yet may I, with this, my first Serpents hold,
God gives new blessings, and yet leaves the old;
The Serpent, may, as wise, my pattern be;
My poison, as he feeds on dust, that's me.
And as he rounds the Earth to murder sure,   15
My death he is, but on the Crosse, my cure.
Crucifie nature then, and then implore
All Grace from him, crucified there before;
When all is Crosse, and that Crosse Anchor grown,
This Seal's a Catechism, not a Seal alone.   20

Under that little Seal great gifts I send,
<Wishes,> and prayers, pawns, and fruits of a friend.
And may that Saint which rides in our great Seal,
To you, who bear his name, great bounties deal.

(TRANSLATED OUT OF GAZAEUS, VOTA AMICO FACTA. FOL: 160)

God grant thee thine own wish, and grant thee mine,
Thou, who dost, best friend, in best things outshine;
May thy soul, ever chearfull, nere know cares,
Nor thy life, ever lively, know gray haires.
Nor thy hand, ever open, know base holds,   5
Nor thy purse, ever plump, know pleits, or folds.
Nor thy tongue, ever true, know a false thing,
Nor thy word, ever mild, know quarrelling.
Nor thy works, ever equall, know disguise,
Nor thy fame, ever pure, know contumelies.   10
Nor thy prayers, know low objects, still Divine;
God grant thee thine own wish, and grant thee mine.

George Herbert
1593-1633

George Herbert

GEORGE HERBERT is often idealized because his life was so quiet and his poetry is so gentle they both seem to be rewards for conscientious rusticity. To Aldous Huxley he is the poet of England's "inner weather"; to clergymen and historians, beginning with Izaak Walton who wrote his Life in 1670, he is the benevolent, saintly country parson at Bemerton, turning his back on the high life at court and the excitements of literary London to which his aristocratic birth and academic distinctions should have given him easy access. Yet his poetry, though enormously controlled, is anything but simple, showing a man engaged in a conflict between himself and his alter ego, the godhead. And his life, mild though it may have seemed to many, was full of desperate disappointments. These rose partly from ill health and partly from many unsuccessful attempts to enter a public career. Only in the last three years of his life did he marry, become a minister, and take up the post at Bemerton, in which role he has become legendary.

Born April 3, 1593, ostensibly in the family's Welsh border castle in Montgomery, George Herbert was the fifth son of Richard and Magdalen Herbert. The Herberts were a notable family and friendly to many poets, among them John Donne. It included George's mother, a woman of extraordinary sensibility, and his brother Lord Herbert of Cherbury, a poet and soldier of repute, who outlived his younger, more famous brother and wrote an interesting autobiography. The mother of seven sons and three daughters, Magdalen Herbert devoted herself to the education of her children, her husband having died when George was three; it was to her that George addressed his two early sonnets setting forth his desire to write of God and sacred things. He attended Westminster, then in 1609 went up to Trinity College, Cambridge. With many well-known poets of the time he contributed verse to the famous commemorative volume on the death of Prince Henry in 1612.

He became a fellow at Trinity and took a master's degree in 1616. This was the beginning of an academic career which lasted until 1627; during that period Herbert was Reader in Rhetoric and Orator of the University. All these years at Cambridge, Herbert was trying to get a position at Court in the public service. But these hopes failing, he resolved in 1625 to take religious orders. Ordained the following year, he went on to hold several minor posts in various churches until his marriage and subsequent acceptance of the rectorship at Bemerton in 1630. During the period before Bemerton, a contemporary, Barnabas Oley, wrote about him that he had "heard sober men censure him as a man that did not manage his brave parts to his best advantage and preferment, but lost himself *in an humble way*; that was the phrase, I well remember it."

His short period at Bemerton before his death in 1633 was quite fruitful. He was happy in his parishioners, zealous about his duties as parson, and wrote a treatise, *A Priest to the Temple, or The Country Parson*, which is still widely read. He also revised his early poems and wrote most of *The Temple*, thus preparing his poems for publication, which came posthumously the year of his death. The book was immediately popular and continued to be so for the next fifty years; like other metaphysicals, his reputation then went into eclipse. Herbert's reputation sprang up again mostly because of Coleridge's appreciative criticism, followed since by many new editions of *The Temple*.

THE TEMPLE

The Dedication

Lord, my first fruits present themselves to thee;
Yet not mine neither: for from thee they came,
And must return. Accept of them and me,
And make us strive, who shall sing best thy name.
 Turn their eyes hither, who shall make a gain: 5
 Theirs, who shall hurt themselves or me, refrain.

The Church-porch

Perirrhanterium

Thou, whose sweet youth and early hopes inhance
Thy rate and price, and mark thee for a treasure;
Hearken unto a Verser, who may chance
Ryme thee to good, and make a bait of pleasure.
 A verse may finde him, who a sermon flies, 5
 And turn delight into a sacrifice.

Beware of lust: it doth pollute and foul
Whom God in Baptisme washt with his own blood.
It blots thy lesson written in thy soul;
The holy lines cannot be understood. 10
 How dare those eyes upon a Bible look,
 Much lesse towards God, whose lust is all their book?

Abstain wholly, or wed. Thy bounteous Lord
Allows thee choise of paths: take no by-wayes;
But gladly welcome what he doth afford; 15

Not grudging, that thy lust hath bounds and staies.
   Continence hath his joy: weigh both; and so
   If rottennesse have more, let Heaven go.

If God had laid all common, certainly
Man would have been th' incloser: but since now   20
God hath impal'd us, on the contrarie
Man breaks the fence, and every ground will plough.
   O what were man, might he himself misplace!
   Sure to be crosse he would shift feet and face.

Drink not the third glasse, which thou canst not tame,   25
When once it is within thee; but before
Mayst rule it, as thou list; and poure the shame,
Which it would poure on thee, upon the floore.
   It is most just to throw that on the ground,
   Which would throw me there, if I keep the round.   30

He that is drunken, may his mother kill
Bigge with his sister: he hath lost the reins,
Is outlawd by himself: all kinde of ill
Did with his liquour slide into his veins.
   The drunkard forfets Man, and doth devest   35
   All worldly right, save what he hath by beast.

Shall I, to please anothers wine-sprung minde,
Lose all mine own? God hath giv'n me a measure
Short of his canne and bodie; must I finde
A pain in that, wherein he findes a pleasure?   40
   Stay at the third glasse: if thou lose thy hold,
   Then thou art modest, and the wine grows bold.

If reason move not Gallants, quit the room,
(All in a shipwrack shift their severall way)
Let not a common ruine thee intombe: 45
Be not a beast in courtesie; but stay,
   Stay at the third cup, or forgo the place.
   Wine above all things doth Gods stamp deface.

Yet, if thou sinne in wine or wantonnesse,
Boast not thereof; nor make thy shame thy glorie.   50
Frailtie gets pardon by submissivenesse;
But he that boasts, shuts that out of his storie.
  He makes flat warre with God, and doth defie
  With his poore clod of earth the spacious sky.

Take not his name, who made thy mouth, in vain: 55
It gets thee nothing, and hath no excuse.
Lust and wine plead a pleasure, avarice gain:
But the cheap swearer through his open sluce
  Lets his soul runne for nought, as little fearing.
  Were I an *Epicure*, I could bate swearing.   60

When thou dost tell anothers jest, therein
Omit the oathes, which true wit cannot need:
Pick out of tales the mirth, but not the sinne.
He pares his apple, that will cleanly feed.
  Play not away the vertue of that name,   65
  Which is thy best stake, when griefs make thee tame.

The cheapest sinnes most dearely punisht are;
Because to shun them also is so cheap:
For we have wit to mark them, and to spare.
O crumble not away thy souls fair heap.   70
  If thou wilt die, the gates of hell are broad:
  Pride and full sinnes have made the way a road.

Lie not; but let thy heart be true to God,
Thy mouth to it, thy actions to them both:
Cowards tell lies, and those that fear the rod;   75
The stormie working soul spits lies and froth.
  Dare to be true. Nothing can need a ly:
  A fault, which needs it most, grows two thereby.

Flie idlenesse, which yet thou canst not flie
By dressing, mistressing, and complement.   80
If those take up thy day, the sunne will crie
Against thee: for his light was onely lent.
  God gave thy soul brave wings; put not those feathers
  Into a bed, to sleep out all ill weathers.

Art thou a Magistrate? then be severe: 85
If studious, copie fair, what time hath blurr'd;
Redeem truth from his jawes: if souldier,
Chase brave employments with a naked sword
   Throughout the world. Fool not: for all may have,
    If they dare try, a glorious life, or grave. 90

O England! full of sinne, but most of sloth;
Spit out thy flegme, and fill thy brest with glorie:
Thy Gentrie bleats, as if thy native cloth
Transfus'd a sheepishnesse into thy storie:
   Not that they all are so; but that the most 95
    Are gone to grasse, and in the pasture lost.

This losse springs chiefly from our education.
Some till their ground, but let weeds choke their sonne:
Some mark a partridge, never their childes fashion:
Some ship them over, and the thing is done. 100
   Studie this art, make it thy great designe;
    And if Gods image move thee not, let thine.

Some great estates provide, but doe not breed
A mast'ring minde; so both are lost thereby:
Or els they breed them tender, make them need 105
All that they leave: this is flat povertie.
   For he, that needs five thousand pound to live,
    Is full as poore as he, that needs but five.

The way to make thy sonne rich is to fill
His minde with rest, before his trunk with riches: 110
For wealth without contentment climbes a hill
To feel those tempests, which fly over ditches.
   But if thy sonne can make ten pound his measure,
    Then all thou addest may be call'd his treasure.

When thou dost purpose ought within thy power, 115
Be sure to doe it, though it be but small:
Constancie knits the bones, and makes us stowre,
When wanton pleasures becken us to thrall.
   Who breaks his own bond, forfeiteth himself:
    What nature made a ship, he makes a shelf. 120

Doe all things like a man, not sneakingly:
Think the king sees thee still; for his King does.
Simpring is but a lay-hypocrisie:
Give it a corner, and the clue undoes.
    Who fears to do ill, sets himself to task: 125
    Who fears to do well, sure should wear a mask.

Look to thy mouth; diseases enter there.
Thou hast two sconces, if thy stomack call;
Carve, or discourse; do not a famine fear.
Who carves, is kind to two; who talks, to all.   130
    Look on meat, think it dirt, then eat a bit;
    And say withall, Earth to earth I commit.

Slight those who say amidst their sickly healths,
Thou liv'st by rule. What doth not so, but man?
Houses are built by rule, and common-wealths.   135
Entice the trusty sunne, if that thou can,
    From his Ecliptick line: becken the skie.
    Who lives by rule then, keeps good companie.

Who keeps no guard upon himself, is slack,
And rots to nothing at the next great thaw.   140
Man is a shop of rules, a well truss'd pack,
Whose every parcell under-writes a law.
    Lose not thy self, nor give thy humours way:
    God gave them to thee under lock and key.

By all means use sometimes to be alone.   145
Salute thy self: see what thy soul doth wear.
Dare to look in thy chest, for 'tis thine own:
And tumble up and down what thou find'st there.
    Who cannot rest till hee good-fellows finde,
    He breaks up house, turns out of doores his minde.   150

Be thriftie, but not covetous: therefore give
Thy need, thine honour, and thy friend his due.
Never was scraper brave man. Get to live;
Then live, and use it: els, it is not true
    That thou hast gotten. Surely use alone   155
    Makes money not a contemptible stone.

Never exceed thy income. Youth may make
Ev'n with the yeare: but age, if it will hit,
Shoots a bow short, and lessens still his stake,
As the day lessens, and his life with it.   160
    Thy children, kindred, friends upon thee call;
    Before thy journey fairly part with all.

Yet in thy thriving still misdoubt some evil;
Lest gaining gain on thee, and make thee dimme
To all things els. Wealth is the conjurers devil;   165
Whom when he thinks he hath, the devil hath him.
    Gold thou mayst safely touch; but if it stick
    Unto thy hands, it woundeth to the quick.

What skills it, if a bag of stones or gold
About thy neck do drown thee? raise thy head;   170
Take starres for money; starres not to be told
By any art, yet to be purchased.
    None is so wastefull as the scraping dame.
    She loseth three for one; her soul, rest, fame.

By no means runne in debt: take thine own measure.   175
Who cannot live on twentie pound a yeare,
Cannot on fourtie: he's a man of pleasure,
A kinde of thing that's for it self too deere.
    The curious unthrift makes his clothes too wide,
    And spares himself, but would his taylor chide.   180

Spend not on hopes. They that by pleading clothes
Do fortunes seek, when worth and service fail,
Would have their tale beleeved for their oathes,
And are like empty vessels under sail.
    Old courtiers know this; therefore set out so,   185
    As all the day thou mayst hold out to go.

In clothes, cheap handsomnesse doth bear the bell.
Wisedome's a trimmer thing then shop e're gave.
Say not then, This with that lace will do well;
But, This with my discretion will be brave.   190
    Much curiousnesse is a perpetuall wooing,
    Nothing with labour, folly long a-doing.

Play not for gain, but sport. Who playes for more
Then he can lose with pleasure, stakes his heart;
Perhaps his wives too, and whom she hath bore: 195
Servants and churches also play their part.
    Onely a herauld, who that way doth passe,
    Findes his crackt name at length in the church-glasse.

If yet thou love game at so deere a rate,
Learn this, that hath old gamesters deerely cost: 200
Dost lose? rise up: dost winne? rise in that state.
Who strive to sit out losing hands, are lost.
    Game is a civil gunpowder, in peace
    Blowing up houses with their whole increase.

In conversation boldnesse now bears sway.   205
But know, that nothing can so foolish be,
As empty boldnesse: therefore first assay
To stuffe thy minde with solid braverie;
    Then march on gallant: get substantiall worth.
    Boldnesse guilds finely, and will set it forth.   210

Be sweet to all. Is thy complexion sowre?
Then keep such companie; make them thy allay:
Get a sharp wife, a servant that will lowre.
A stumbler stumbles least in rugged way.
    Command thy self in chief. He lifes warre knows,   215
    Whom all his passions follow, as he goes.

Catch not at quarrels. He that dares not speak
Plainly and home, is coward of the two.
Think not thy fame at ev'ry twitch will break:
By great deeds shew, that thou canst little do;   220
    And do them not: that shall thy wisdome be;
    And change thy temperance into braverie.

If that thy fame with ev'ry toy be pos'd,
'Tis a thinne webbe, which poysonous fancies make:
But the great souldiers honour was compos'd   225
Of thicker stuffe, which would endure a shake.
    Wisdome picks friends; civilitie playes the rest.
    A toy shunn'd cleanly passeth with the best.

Laugh not too much: the wittie man laughs least:
For wit is newes onely to ignorance.   230
Lesse at thine own things laugh; lest in the jest
Thy person share, and the conceit advance.
    Make not thy sport, abuses: for the fly
    That feeds on dung, is coloured thereby.

Pick out of mirth, like stones out of thy ground,   235
Profanenesse, filthinesse, abusivenesse.
These are the scumme, with which course wits abound:
The fine may spare these well, yet not go lesse.
    All things are bigge with jest: nothing that's plain,
    But may be wittie, if thou hast the vein.   240

Wit's an unruly engine, wildly striking
Sometimes a friend, sometimes the engineer.
Hast thou the knack? pamper it not with liking:
But if thou want it, buy it not too deere.
    Many, affecting wit beyond their power,   245
    Have got to be a deare fool for an houre.

A sad wise valour is the brave complexion,
That leads the van, and swallows up the cities.
The gigler is a milk-maid, whom infection
Or a fir'd beacon frighteth from his ditties.   250
    Then he's the sport: the mirth then in him rests,
    And the sad man is cock of all his jests.

Towards great persons use respective boldnesse:
That temper gives them theirs, and yet doth take
Nothing from thine: in service, care or coldnesse   255
Doth ratably thy fortunes marre or make.
    Feed no man in his sinnes: for adulation
    Doth make thee parcell-devil in damnation.

Envie not greatnesse: for thou mak'st thereby
Thy self the worse, and so the distance greater.   260
Be not thine own worm: yet such jealousie,
As hurts not others, but may make thee better,
    Is a good spurre. Correct thy passions spite;
    Then may the beasts draw thee to happy light.

When basenesse is exalted, do not bate 265
The place its honour, for the persons sake.
The shrine is that which thou dost venerate,
And not the beast, that bears it on his back.
  I care not though the cloth of state should be
  Not of rich arras, but mean tapestrie. 270

Thy friend put in thy bosome: wear his eies
Still in thy heart, that he may see what's there.
If cause require, thou art his sacrifice;
Thy drops of bloud must pay down all his fear:
  But love is lost, the way of friendship's gone, 275
  Though *David* had his *Jonathan, Christ* his *John.*

Yet be not surety, if thou be a father.
Love is a personall debt. I cannot give
My childrens right, nor ought he take it: rather
Both friends should die, then hinder them to live. 280
  Fathers first enter bonds to natures ends;
  And are her sureties, ere they are a friends.

If thou be single, all thy goods and ground
Submit to love; but yet not more then all.
Give one estate, as one life. None is bound 285
To work for two, who brought himself to thrall.
  God made me one man; love makes me no more,
  Till labour come, and make my weaknesse score.

In thy discourse, if thou desire to please,
All such is courteous, usefull, new, or wittie. 290
Usefulnesse comes by labour, wit by ease;
Courtesie grows in court; news in the citie.
  Get a good stock of these, then draw the card
  That suites him best, of whom thy speech is heard.

Entice all neatly to what they know best; 295
For so thou dost thy self and him a pleasure:
(But a proud ignorance will lose his rest,
Rather then shew his cards.) Steal from his treasure
  What to ask further. Doubts well rais'd do lock
  The speaker to thee, and preserve thy stock. 300

If thou be Master-gunner, spend not all
That thou canst speak, at once; but husband it,
And give men turns of speech: do not forestall
By lavishnesse thine own, and others wit,
 As if thou mad'st thy will. A civil guest   305
 Will no more talk all, then eat all the feast.

Be calm in arguing: for fiercenesse makes
Errour a fault, and truth discourtesie.
Why should I feel another mans mistakes
More then his sicknesses or povertie?   310
 In love I should: but anger is not love,
 Nor wisdome neither: therefore gently move.

Calmnesse is great advantage: he that lets
Another chafe, may warm him at his fire,
Mark all his wandrings, and enjoy his frets;   315
As cunning fencers suffer heat to tire.
 Truth dwels not in the clouds: the bow that's there
 Doth often aim at, never hit the sphere.

Mark what another sayes: for many are
Full of themselves, and answer their own notion.   320
Take all into thee; then with equall care
Ballance each dramme of reason, like a potion.
 If truth be with thy friend, be with them both:
 Share in the conquest, and confesse a troth.

Be usefull where thou livest, that they may   325
Both want and wish thy pleasing presence still.
Kindnesse, good parts, great places are the way
To compasse this. Finde out mens wants and will,
 And meet them there. All worldly joyes go lesse
 To the one joy of doing kindnesses.   330

Pitch thy behaviour low, thy projects high;
So shalt thou humble and magnanimous be:
Sink not in spirit: who aimeth at the sky,
Shoots higher much then he that means a tree.
 A grain of glorie mixt with humblenesse   335
 Cures both a fever and lethargicknesse.

Let thy minde still be bent, still plotting where,
And when, and how the businesse may be done.
Slacknesse breeds worms; but the sure traveller,
Though he alight sometimes, still goeth on.   340
    Active and stirring spirits live alone.
    Write on the others, Here lies such a one.

Slight not the smallest losse, whether it be
In love or honour: take account of all;
Shine like the sunne in every corner: see   345
Whether thy stock of credit swell, or fall.
    Who say, I care not, those I give for lost;
    And to instruct them, will not quit the cost.

Scorn no mans love, though of a mean degree;
Love is a present for a mightie king.   350
Much lesse make any one thy enemie.
As gunnes destroy, so may a little sling.
    The cunning workman never doth refuse
    The meanest tool, that he may chance to use.

All forrain wisdome doth amount to this,   355
To take all that is given; whether wealth,
Or love, or language; nothing comes amisse:
A good digestion turneth all to health:
    And then as farre as fair behaviour may,
    Strike off all scores; none are so cleare as they. 360

Keep all thy native good, and naturalize
All forrain of that name; but scorn their ill:
Embrace their activenesse, not vanities.
Who follows all things, forfeiteth his will.
    If thou observest strangers in each fit,   365
    In time they'l runne thee out of all thy wit.

Affect in things about thee cleanlinesse,
That all may gladly board thee, as a flowre.
Slovens take up their stock of noisomnesse
Beforehand, and anticipate their last houre.   370
    Let thy mindes sweetnesse have his operation
    Upon thy body, clothes, and habitation.

In Almes regard thy means, and others merit.
Think heav'n a better bargain, then to give
Onely thy single market-money for it.   375
Joyn hands with God to make a man to live.
    Give to all something; to a good poore man,
    Till thou change names, and be where he began.

Man is Gods image; but a poore man is
Christs stamp to boot: both images regard.   380
God reckons for him, counts the favour his:
Write, So much giv'n to God; thou shalt be heard.
    Let thy almes go before, and keep heav'ns gate
    Open for thee; or both may come too late.

Restore to God his due in tithe and time: 385
A tithe purloin'd cankers the whole estate.
Sundaies observe: think when the bells do chime,
'Tis angels musick; therefore come not late.
    God then deals blessings: If a king did so,
    Who would not haste, nay give, to see the show?   390

Twice on the day his due is understood;
For all the week thy food so oft he gave thee.
Thy cheere is mended; bate not of the food,
Because 'tis better, and perhaps may save thee.
    Thwart not the Mighty God: O be not crosse.   395
    Fast when thou wilt but then, 'tis gain not losse.

Though private prayer be a brave designe,
Yet publick hath more promises, more love:
And love's a weight to hearts, to eies a signe.
We all are but cold suitours; let us move   400
    Where it is warmest. Leave thy six and seven;
    Pray with the most: for where most pray, is heaven.

When once thy foot enters the church, be bare.
God is more there, then thou: for thou art there
Onely by his permission. Then beware,   405
And make thy self all reverence and fear.
    Kneeling ne're spoil'd silk stocking: quit thy state.
    All equall are within the churches gate.

Resort to sermons, but to prayers most:
Praying 's the end of preaching. O be drest;   410
Stay not for th' other pin: why, thou hast lost
A joy for it worth worlds. Thus hell doth jest
    Away thy blessings, and extreamly flout thee,
      Thy clothes being fast, but thy soul loose about thee.

In time of service seal up both thine eies,   415
And send them to thine heart; that spying sinne,
They may weep out the stains by them did rise:
Those doores being shut, all by the eare comes in.
    Who marks in church-time others symmetrie,
      Makes all their beautie his deformitie.   420

Let vain or busie thoughts have there no part:
Bring not thy plough, thy plots, thy pleasures thither.
Christ purg'd his temple; so must thou thy heart.
All worldly thoughts are but theeves met together
    To couzin thee. Look to thy actions well: 425
      For churches are either our heav'n or hell.

Judge not the preacher; for he is thy Judge:
If thou mislike him, thou conceiv'st him not.
God calleth preaching folly. Do not grudge
To pick out treasures from an earthen pot.   430
    The worst speak something good: if all want sense,
      God takes a text, and preacheth patience.

He that gets patience, and the blessing which
Preachers conclude with, hath not lost his pains.
He that by being at church escapes the ditch,   435
Which he might fall in by companions, gains.
    He that loves Gods abode, and to combine
      With saints on earth, shall one day with them shine.

Jest not at preachers language, or expression:
How know'st thou, but thy sinnes made him miscarrie?   440
Then turn thy faults and his into confession:
God sent him, whatsoe're he be: O tarry,
    And love him for his Master: his condition,
      Though it be ill, makes him no ill Physician.

None shall in hell such bitter pangs endure,   445
As those, who mock at Gods way of salvation.
Whom oil and balsames kill, what salve can cure?
They drink with greedinesse a full damnation.
   The Jews refused thunder; and we, folly.
   Though God do hedge us in, yet who is holy?   450

Summe up at night, what thou hast done by day;
And in the morning, what thou hast to do.
Dresse and undresse thy soul: mark the decay
And growth of it: if with thy watch, that too
   Be down, then winde up both; since we shall be   455
   Most surely judg'd, make thy accounts agree.

In brief, acquit thee bravely; play the man.
Look not on pleasures as they come, but go.
Deferre not the least vertue: lifes poore span
Make not an ell, by trifling in thy wo.   460
   If thou do ill; the joy fades, not the pains:
   If well; the pain doth fade, the joy remains.

Superliminare

Thou, whom the former precepts have
Sprinkled and taught, how to behave
Thy self in church; approach, and taste
The churches mysticall repast.

Avoid, Profanenesse; come not here: 5
Nothing but holy, pure, and cleare,
Or that which groneth to be so,
May at his perill further go.

The Church

The Altar

A broken ALTAR, Lord, thy servant reares,
Made of a heart, and cemented with teares:
    Whose parts are as thy hand did frame;
    No workmans tool hath touch'd the same.
          A HEART alone   5
          Is such a stone ,
          As nothing but
          Thy pow'r doth cut.
          Wherefore each part
          Of my hard heart   10
          Meets in this frame,
          To praise thy Name:
    That, if I chance to hold my peace,
    These stones to praise thee may not cease.
O let thy blessed SACRIFICE be mine,   15
And sanctifie this ALTAR to be thine.

The Sacrifice

Oh all ye, who passe by, whose eyes and minde
To worldly things are sharp, but to me blinde;
To me, who took eyes that I might you finde:
                Was ever grief like mine?

The Princes of my people make a head   5
Against their Maker: they do wish me dead,
Who cannot wish, except I give them bread:
                Was ever grief like mine?

Without me each one, who doth now me brave,
Had to this day been an Egyptian slave.   10
They use that power against me, which I gave:
                Was ever grief like mine?

Mine own Apostle, who the bag did beare,
Though he had all I had, did not forbeare
To sell me also, and to put me there: 15
                Was ever grief, &c.

For thirtie pence he did my death devise,
Who at three hundred did the ointment prize,
Not half so sweet as my sweet sacrifice:
                Was ever grief, &c.   20

Therefore my soul melts, and my hearts deare treasure
Drops bloud (the onely beads) my words to measure:
O let this cup passe, if it be thy pleasure:
                Was ever grief, &c.

These drops being temper'd with a sinners tears   25
A Balsome are for both the Hemispheres:
Curing all wounds, but mine; all, but my fears:
                Was ever grief, &c.

Yet my Disciples sleep: I cannot gain
One houre of watching; but their drowsie brain   30
Comforts not me, and doth my doctrine stain:
                Was ever grief, &c.

Arise, arise, they come. Look how they runne!
Alas! what haste they make to be undone!
How with their lanterns do they seek the sunne!   35
                Was ever grief, &c.

With clubs and staves they seek me, as a thief,
Who am the Way and Truth, the true relief;
Most true to those, who are my greatest grief:
                Was ever grief, &c.   40

Judas, dost thou betray me with a kisse?
Canst thou finde hell about my lips? and misse
Of life, just at the gates of life and blisse?
                    Was ever grief like mine?

See, they lay hold on me, not with the hands   45
Of faith, but furie: yet at their commands
I suffer binding, who have loos'd their bands:
                    Was ever grief, &c.

All my Disciples flie; fear puts a barre
Betwixt my friends and me. They leave the starre,   50
That brought the wise men of the East from farre.
                    Was ever grief, &c.

Then from one ruler to another bound
They leade me; urging, that it was not sound
What I taught: Comments would the text confound.   55
                    Was ever grief, &c.

The Priest and rulers all false witnesse seek
'Gainst him, who seeks not life, but is the meek
And readie Paschal Lambe of this great week:
                    Was ever grief, &c.   60

Then they accuse me of great blasphemie,
That I did thrust into the Deitie,
Who never thought that any robberie:
                    Was ever grief, &c.

Some said, that I the Temple to the floore   65
In three dayes raz'd, and raised as before.
Why, he that built the world can do much more:
                    Was ever grief, &c.

Then they condemne me all with that same breath,
Which I do give them daily, unto death.   70
Thus *Adam* my first breathing rendereth:
                    Was ever grief, &c.

They binde, and leade me unto *Herod:* he
Sends me to *Pilate.* This makes them agree;
But yet their friendship is my enmitie: 75
                    Was ever grief like mine?

Herod and all his bands do set me light,
Who teach all hands to warre, fingers to fight,
And onely am the Lord of Hosts and might:
                    Was ever grief, &c.   80

Herod in judgement sits, while I do stand;
Examines me with a censorious hand:
I him obey, who all things else command:
                    Was ever grief, &c.

The *Jews* accuse me with despitefulnesse;   85
And vying malice with my gentlenesse,
Pick quarrels with their onely happinesse:
                    Was ever grief, &c.

I answer nothing, but with patience prove
If stonie hearts will melt with gentle love.   90
But who does hawk at eagles with a dove?
                    Was ever grief, &c.

My silence rather doth augment their crie;
My dove doth back into my bosome flie,
Because the raging waters still are high: 95
                    Was ever grief, &c.

Heark how they crie aloud still, *Crucifie:*
It is not fit he live a day, they crie,
Who cannot live lesse then eternally:
                    Was ever grief, &c.   100

Pilate, a stranger, holdeth off; but they,
Mine owne deare people, cry, *Away, away,*
With noises confused frighting the day:
                    Was ever grief, &c.

Yet still they shout, and crie, and stop their eares,   105
Putting my life among their sinnes and fears,
And therefore wish *my bloud on them and theirs*:
      Was ever grief like mine?

See how spite cankers things. These words aright
Used, and wished, are the whole worlds light: 110
But hony is their gall, brightnesse their night:
      Was ever grief, &c.

They choose a murderer, and all agree
In him to do themselves a courtesie:
For it was their own case who killed me: 115
      Was ever grief, &c.

And a seditious murderer he was:
But I the Prince of peace; peace that doth passe
All understanding, more then heav'n doth glasse:
      Was ever grief, &c.   120

Why, Cæsar is their onely King, not I:
He clave the stonie rock, when they were drie;
But surely not their hearts, as I well trie:
      Was ever grief, &c.

Ah! how they scourge me! yet my tendernesse   125
Doubles each lash: and yet their bitternesse
Windes up my grief to a mysteriousnesse:
      Was ever grief, &c.

They buffet him, and box him as they list,
Who grasps the earth and heaven with his fist,   130
And never yet, whom he would punish, miss'd:
      Was ever grief, &c.

Behold, they spit on me in scornfull wise,
Who by my spittle gave the blinde man eies,
Leaving his blindnesse to my enemies: 135
      Was ever grief like mine?

My face they cover, though it be divine.
As *Moses* face was vailed, so is mine,
Lest on their double-dark souls either shine:
                    Was ever grief, &c.   140

Servants and abjects flout me; they are wittie:
Now prophesie who strikes thee, is their dittie.
So they in me denie themselves all pitie:
                    Was ever grief, &c.

And now I am deliver'd unto death,   145
Which each one calls for so with utmost breath,
That he before me well nigh suffereth:
                    Was ever grief, &c.

Weep not, deare friends, since I for both have wept
When all my tears were bloud, the while you slept: 150
Your tears for your own fortunes should be kept:
                    Was ever grief, &c.

The souldiers lead me to the Common Hall;
There they deride me, they abuse me all:
Yet for twelve heav'nly legions I could call: 155
                    Was ever grief, &c.

Then with a scarlet robe they me aray;
Which shews my bloud to be the onely way
And cordiall left to repair mans decay:
                    Was ever grief, &c.   160

Then on my head a crown of thorns I wear:
For these are all the grapes *Sion* doth bear,
Though I my vine planted and watred there:
                    Was ever grief, &c.

So sits the earths great curse in *Adams* fall   165
Upon my head: so I remove it all
From th' earth unto my brows, and bear the thrall:
                    Was ever grief like mine?

Then with the reed they gave to me before,
They strike my head, the rock from whence all store 170
Of heav'nly blessings issue evermore:
    Was ever grief, &c.

They bow their knees to me, and cry, *Hail king:*
What ever scoffes & scornfulnesse can bring,
I am the floore, the sink, where they it fling: 175
    Was ever grief, &c.

Yet since mans scepters are as frail as reeds,
And thorny all their crowns, bloudie their weeds;
I, who am Truth, turn into truth their deeds:
    Was ever grief, &c. 180

The souldiers also spit upon that face,
Which Angels did desire to have the grace,
And Prophets, once to see, but found no place:
    Was ever grief, &c.

Thus trimmed, forth they bring me to the rout, 185
Who *Crucifie him,* crie with one strong shout.
God holds his peace at man, and man cries out:
    Was ever grief, &c.

They leade me in once more, and putting then
Mine own clothes on, they leade me out agen. 190
Whom devils flie, thus is he toss'd of men:
    Was ever grief, &c.

And now wearie of sport, glad to ingrosse
All spite in one, counting my life their losse,
They carrie me to my most bitter crosse: 195
    Was ever grief like mine?

My crosse I bear my self, untill I faint:
Then Simon bears it for me by constraint,
The decreed burden of each mortall Saint:
    Was ever grief, &c. 200

O all ye who passe by, behold and see;
Man stole the fruit, but I must climbe the tree;
The tree of life to all, but onely me:
    Was ever grief, &c.

Lo, here I hang, charg'd with a world of sinne, 205
The greater world o' th' two; for that came in
By words, but this by sorrow I must win:
    Was ever grief, &c.

Such sorrow as, if sinfull man could feel,
Or feel his part, he would not cease to kneel, 210
Till all were melted, though he were all steel:
    Was ever grief, &c.

But, *O my God, my God!* why leav'st thou me,
The sonne, in whom thou dost delight to be?
My God, my God——   215
    Never was grief like mine.

Shame tears my soul, my bodie many a wound;
Sharp nails pierce this, but sharper that confound;
Reproches, which are free, while I am bound.
    Was ever grief, &c. 220

Now heal thy self, Physician; now come down.
Alas! I did so, when I left my crown
And fathers smile for you, to feel his frown;
    Was ever grief like mine?

In healing not my self, there doth consist 225
All that salvation, which ye now resist;
Your safetie in my sicknesse doth subsist:
    Was ever grief, &c.

Betwixt two theeves I spend my utmost breath,
As he that for some robberie suffereth. 230
Alas! what have I stollen from you? Death.
    Was ever grief, &c.

A king my title is, prefixt on high;
Yet by my subjects am condemn'd to die
A servile death in servile companie: 235
               Was ever grief, &c.

They give me vineger mingled with gall,
But more with malice: yet, when they did call,
With Manna, Angels food, I fed them all:
               Was ever grief, &c.   240

They part my garments, and by lot dispose
My coat, the type of love, which once cur'd those
Who sought for help, never malicious foes:
               Was ever grief, &c.

Nay, after death their spite shall further go;   245
For they will pierce my side, I full well know;
That as sinne came, so Sacraments might flow:
               Was ever grief, &c.

But now I die; now all is finished.
My wo, mans weal: and now I bow my head.   250
Onely let others say, when I am dead,
               Never was grief like mine.

The Thanksgiving

Oh King of grief! (a title strange, yet true,
    To thee of all kings onely due)
Oh King of wounds! how shall I grieve for thee,
    Who in all grief preventest me?
Shall I weep bloud? why, thou hast wept such store   5
    That all thy body was one doore.
Shall I be scourged, flouted, boxed, sold?
    'Tis but to tell the tale is told.
My God, my God, why dost thou part from me?
    Was such a grief as cannot be.   10
Shall I then sing, skipping thy dolefull storie,
    And side with thy triumphant glorie?

Shall thy strokes be my stroking? thorns, my flower?
    Thy rod, my posie? crosse, my bower?
But how then shall I imitate thee, and   15
    Copie thy fair, though bloudie hand?
Surely I will revenge me on thy love,
    And trie who shall victorious prove.
If thou dost give me wealth, I will restore
    All back unto thee by the poore.   20
If thou dost give me honour, men shall see,
    The honour doth belong to thee.
I will not marry; or, if she be mine,
    She and her children shall be thine.
My bosome friend, if he blaspheme thy Name,   25
    I will tear thence his love and fame.
One half of me being gone, the rest I give
    Unto some Chappell, die or live.
As for thy passion—But of that anon,
    When with the other I have done.   30
For thy predestination I'le contrive,
    That three yeares hence, if I survive,
I'le build a spittle, or mend common wayes,
    But mend mine own without delayes.
Then I will use the works of thy creation,   35
    As if I us'd them but for fashion.
The world and I will quarrell; and the yeare
    Shall not perceive, that I am here.
My musick shall finde thee, and ev'ry string
    Shall have his attribute to sing;   40
That all together may accord in thee,
    And prove one God, one harmonie.
If thou shalt give me wit, it shall appeare,
    If thou hast giv'n it me, 'tis here.
Nay, I will reade thy book, and never move   45
    Till I have found therein thy love,
Thy art of love, which I'le turn back on thee:
    O my deare Saviour, Victorie!
Then for thy passion—I will do for that—
    Alas, my God, I know not what.   50

The Reprisall

I have consider'd it, and finde
There is no dealing with thy mighty passion:
For though I die for thee, I am behinde;
    My sinnes deserve the condemnation.

O make me innocent, that I   5
May give a disentangled state and free:
And yet thy wounds still my attempts defie,
    For by thy death I die for thee.

Ah! was it not enough that thou
By thy eternall glorie didst outgo me?   10
Couldst thou not griefs sad conquests me allow,
    But in all vict'ries overthrow me?

Yet by confession will I come
Into thy conquest: though I can do nought
Against thee, in thee I will overcome   15
    The man, who once against thee fought.

The Agonie

Philosophers have measur'd mountains,
Fathom'd the depths of seas, of states, and kings,
Walk'd with a staffe to heav'n, and traced fountains:
    But there are two vast, spacious things,
The which to measure it doth more behove: 5
Yet few there are that sound them; Sinne and Love.

Who would know Sinne, let him repair
Unto Mount Olivet; there shall he see
A man so wrung with pains, that all his hair,
    His skinne, his garments bloudie be.   10
Sinne is that presse and vice, which forceth pain
To hunt his cruell food through ev'ry vein.

Who knows not Love, let him assay
  And taste that juice, which on the crosse a pike
  Did set again abroach; then let him say   15
    If ever he did taste the like.
Love is that liquour sweet and most divine,
Which my God feels as bloud; but I, as wine.

The Sinner

Lord, how I am all ague, when I seek
  What I have treasur'd in my memorie!
  Since, if my soul make even with the week,
Each seventh note by right is due to thee.
I finde there quarries of pil'd vanities,   5
  But shreds of holinesse, that dare not venture
  To shew their face, since crosse to thy decrees:
There the circumference earth is, heav'n the centre.
In so much dregs the quintessence is small:
  The spirit and good extract of my heart   10
  Comes to about the many hundred part.
Yet Lord restore thine image, heare my call:
  And though my hard heart scarce to thee can grone,
  Remember that thou once didst write in stone.

Good Friday

   O my chief good,
How shall I measure out thy bloud?
How shall I count what thee befell,
   And each grief tell?

   Shall I thy woes   5
Number according to thy foes?
Or, since one starre show'd thy first breath,
   Shall all thy death?

       Or shall each leaf,
Which falls in Autumne, score a grief?   10
Or can not leaves, but fruit, be signe
       Of the true vine?

       Then let each houre
Of my whole life one grief devoure;
That thy distresse through all may runne,   15
       And be my sunne.

       Or rather let
My severall sinnes their sorrows get;
That as each beast his cure doth know,
       Each sinne may so.   20

Since bloud is fittest, Lord, to write
Thy sorrows in, and bloudie fight;
My heart hath store, write there, where in
One box doth lie both ink and sinne:

That when sinne spies so many foes,   25
Thy whips, thy nails, thy wounds, thy woes,
All come to lodge there, sinne may say,
No room for me, and flie away.

Sinne being gone, oh fill the place,
And keep possession with thy grace;   30
Lest sinne take courage and return,
And all the writings blot or burn.

Redemption

Having been tenant long to a rich Lord,
       Not thriving, I resolved to be bold,
       And make a suit unto him, to afford
A new small-rented lease, and cancell th' old.
In heaven at his manour I him sought: 5

They told me there, that he was lately gone
About some land, which he had dearly bought
Long since on earth, to take possession.
I straight return'd, and knowing his great birth,
    Sought him accordingly in great resorts;   10
    In cities, theatres, gardens, parks, and courts:
At length I heard a ragged noise and mirth
    Of theeves and murderers: there I him espied,
    Who straight, *Your suit is granted,* said, & died.

Sepulchre

O blessed bodie! Whither art thou thrown?
No lodging for thee, but a cold hard stone?
So many hearts on earth, and yet not one
    Receive thee?
Sure there is room within our hearts good store;   5
For they can lodge transgressions by the score:
Thousands of toyes dwell there, yet out of doore
    They leave thee.

But that which shews them large, shews them unfit.
What ever sinne did this pure rock commit,   10
Which holds thee now? Who hath indited it
    Of murder?
Where our hard hearts have took up stones to brain thee,
And missing this, most falsly did arraigne thee;
Onely these stones in quiet entertain thee,   15
    And order.

And as of old the Law by heav'nly art
Was writ in stone; so thou, which also art
The letter of the word, find'st no fit heart
    To hold thee.   20
Yet do we still persist as we began,
And so should perish, but that nothing can,
Though it be cold, hard, foul, from loving man
    Withhold thee.

Easter

Rise heart; thy Lord is risen. Sing his praise
        Without delayes,
Who takes thee by the hand, that thou likewise
        With him mayst rise:
That, as his death calcined thee to dust,   5
His life may make thee gold, and much more, just.

Awake, my lute, and struggle for thy part
        With all thy art.
The crosse taught all wood to resound his name,
        Who bore the same.   10
His stretched sinews taught all strings, what key
Is best to celebrate this most high day.

Consort both heart and lute, and twist a song
        Pleasant and long:
Or, since all musick is but three parts vied   15
        And multiplied,
O let thy blessed Spirit bear a part,
And make up our defects with his sweet art.

I got me flowers to straw thy way;
I got me boughs off many a tree: 20
But thou wast up by break of day,
And brought'st thy sweets along with thee.

The Sunne arising in the East,
Though he give light, & th' East perfume;
If they should offer to contest   25
With thy arising, they presume.

Can there be any day but this,
Though many sunnes to shine endeavour?
We count three hundred, but we misse:
There is but one, and that one ever.   30

Easter-wings

Lord, who createdst man in wealth and store,
 Though foolishly he lost the same,
  Decaying more and more,
   Till he became
    Most poore: 5
    With thee
   O let me rise
  As larks, harmoniously,
 And sing this day thy victories:
Then shall the fall further the flight in me.   10

My tender age in sorrow did beginne:
 And still with sicknesses and shame
  Thou didst so punish sinne,
   That I became
    Most thinne.   15
    With thee
   Let me combine
  And feel this day thy victorie:
 For, if I imp my wing on thine,
Affliction shall advance the flight in me.   20

H. Baptisme (1)

As he that sees a dark and shadie grove,
  Stayes not, but looks beyond it on the skie;
  So when I view my sinnes, mine eyes remove
More backward still, and to that water flie,
Which is above the heav'ns, whose spring and vent   5
  Is in my deare Redeemers pierced side.
  O blessed streams! either ye do prevent
And stop our sinnes from growing thick and wide,
Or else give tears to drown them, as they grow.
  In you Redemption measures all my time,   10
  And spreads the plaister equall to the crime.
You taught the Book of Life my name, that so
  What ever future sinnes should me miscall,
  Your first acquaintance might discredit all.

H. Baptisme (ii)

Since, Lord, to thee
A narrow way and little gate
Is all the passage, on my infancie
Thou didst lay hold, and antedate
My faith in me.   5

O let me still
Write thee great God, and me a childe:
Let me be soft and supple to thy will,
Small to my self, to others milde,
Behither ill.   10

Although by stealth
My flesh get on, yet let her sister
My soul bid nothing, but preserve her wealth:
The growth of flesh is but a blister;
Childhood is health.   15

Nature

Full of rebellion, I would die,
Or fight, or travell, or denie
That thou hast ought to do with me.
O tame my heart;
It is thy highest art   5
To captivate strong holds to thee.

If thou shalt let this venome lurk,
And in suggestions fume and work,
My soul will turn to bubbles straight,
And thence by kinde   10
Vanish into a winde,
Making thy workmanship deceit.

O smooth my rugged heart, and there
Engrave thy rev'rend Law and fear;
Or make a new one, since the old   15

Is saplesse grown,
And a much fitter stone
To hide my dust, then thee to hold.

Sinne (1)

Lord, with what care hast thou begirt us round!
    Parents first season us: then schoolmasters
    Deliver us to laws; they send us bound
To rules of reason, holy messengers,
Pulpits and Sundayes, sorrow dogging sinne,   5
    Afflictions sorted, anguish of all sizes,
    Fine nets and stratagems to catch us in,
Bibles laid open, millions of surprises,
Blessings beforehand, tyes of gratefulnesse,
    The sound of glorie ringing in our eares: 10
    Without, our shame; within, our consciences;
Angels and grace, eternall hopes and fears.
    Yet all these fences and their whole aray
    One cunning bosome-sinne blows quite away.

Affliction (1)

When first thou didst entice to thee my heart,
    I thought the service brave:
So many joyes I writ down for my part,
    Besides what I might have
Out of my stock of naturall delights,   5
Augmented with thy gracious benefits.

I looked on thy furniture so fine,
    And made it fine to me:
Thy glorious houshold-stuffe did me entwine,
    And 'tice me unto thee.   10
Such starres I counted mine: both heav'n and earth
Payd me my wages in a world of mirth.

What pleasures could I want, whose King I served,
    Where joyes my fellows were?

Thus argu'd into hopes, my thoughts reserved 15
    No place for grief or fear.
Therefore my sudden soul caught at the place,
And made her youth and fiercenesse seek thy face.

At first thou gav'st me milk and sweetnesses;
    I had my wish and way: 20
My dayes were straw'd with flow'rs and happinesse;
    There was no moneth but May.
But with my yeares sorrow did twist and grow,
And made a partie unawares for wo.

My flesh began unto my soul in pain, 25
    Sicknesses cleave my bones;
Consuming agues dwell in ev'ry vein,
    And tune my breath to grones.
Sorrow was all my soul; I scarce beleeved,
Till grief did tell me roundly, that I lived. 30

When I got health, thou took'st away my life,
    And more; for my friends die:
My mirth and edge was lost; a blunted knife
    Was of more use then I.
Thus thinne and lean without a fence or friend, 35
I was blown through with ev'ry storm and winde.

Whereas my birth and spirit rather took
    The way that takes the town;
Thou didst betray me to a lingring book,
    And wrap me in a gown. 40
I was entangled in the world of strife,
Before I had the power to change my life.

Yet, for I threatned oft the siege to raise,
    Not simpring all mine age,
Thou often didst with Academick praise 45
    Melt and dissolve my rage.
I took thy sweetned pill, till I came where
I could not go away, nor persevere.

Yet lest perchance I should too happie be
            In my unhappinesse,   50
Turning my purge to food, thou throwest me
            Into more sicknesses.
Thus doth thy power crosse-bias me, not making
Thine own gift good, yet me from my wayes taking.

Now I am here, what thou wilt do with me   55
            None of my books will show:
I reade, and sigh, and wish I were a tree;
            For sure then I should grow
To fruit or shade: at least some bird would trust
Her houshold to me, and I should be just.   60

Yet, though thou troublest me, I must be meek;
            In weaknesse must be stout.
Well, I will change the service, and go seek
            Some other master out.
Ah my deare God! though I am clean forgot,   65
Let me not love thee, if I love thee not.

Repentance

    Lord, I confesse my sinne is great;
    Great is my sinne. Oh! gently treat
With thy quick flow'r, thy momentarie bloom;
           Whose life still pressing
           Is one undressing,   5
    A steadie aiming at a tombe.

    Mans age is two houres work, or three:
    Each day doth round about us see.
Thus are we to delights: but we are all
           To sorrows old,   10
           If life be told
From what life feeleth, Adams fall.

    O let thy height of mercie then
    Compassionate short-breathed men.
Cut me not off for my most foul transgression: 15

I do confesse
My foolishnesse;
My God, accept of my confession.

Sweeten at length this bitter bowl,
Which thou hast pour'd into my soul;   20
Thy wormwood turn to health, windes to fair weather:
For if thou stay,
I and this day,
As we did rise, we die together.

When thou for sinne rebukest man,   25
Forthwith he waxeth wo and wan:
Bitternesse fills our bowels; all our hearts
Pine, and decay,
And drop away,
And carrie with them th' other parts.   30

But thou wilt sinne and grief destroy;
That so the broken bones may joy,
And tune together in a well-set song,
Full of his praises,
Who dead men raises.   35
Fractures well cur'd make us more strong.

Faith

Lord, how couldst thou so much appease
Thy wrath for sinne as, when man's sight was dimme,
And could see little, to regard his ease,
And bring by Faith all things to him?

Hungrie I was, and had no meat: 5
I did conceit a most delicious feast;
I had it straight, and did as truly eat,
As ever did a welcome guest.

There is a rare outlandish root,
Which when I could not get, I thought it here: 10
That apprehension cur'd so well my foot,
That I can walk to heav'n well neare.

I owed thousands and much more:
I did beleeve that I did nothing owe,
And liv'd accordingly; my creditor   15
    Beleeves so too, and lets me go.

    Faith makes me any thing, or all
That I beleeve is in the sacred storie:
And where sinne placeth me in Adams fall,
    Faith sets me higher in his glorie.   20

    If I go lower in the book,
What can be lower then the common manger?
Faith puts me there with him, who sweetly took
    Our flesh and frailtie, death and danger.

    If blisse had lien in art or strength,   25
None but the wise or strong had gained it:
Where now by Faith all arms are of a length;
    One size doth all conditions fit.

    A peasant may beleeve as much
As a great Clerk, and reach the highest stature.   30
Thus dost thou make proud knowledge bend & crouch,
    While grace fills up uneven nature.

    When creatures had no reall light
Inherent in them, thou didst make the sunne
Impute a lustre, and allow them bright;   35
    And in this shew, what Christ hath done.

    That which before was darkned clean
With bushie groves, pricking the lookers eie,
Vanisht away, when Faith did change the scene:
    And then appear'd a glorious skie.   40

    What though my bodie runne to dust?
Faith cleaves unto it, counting evr'y grain
With an exact and most particular trust,
    Reserving all for flesh again.

Prayer (1)

Prayer the Churches banquet, Angels age,
    Gods breath in man returning to his birth,
    The soul in paraphrase, heart in pilgrimage,
The Christian plummet sounding heav'n and earth;
Engine against th' Almightie, sinners towre,   5
    Reversed thunder, Christ-side-piercing spear,
    The six-daies world transposing in an houre,
A kinde of tune, which all things heare and fear;
Softnesse, and peace, and joy, and love, and blisse,
    Exalted Manna, gladnesse of the best,   10
    Heaven in ordinarie, man well drest,
The milkie way, the bird of Paradise,
    Church-bels beyond the starres heard, the souls bloud,
    The land of spices; something understood.

The H: Communion

    Not in rich furniture, or fine aray,
        Nor in a wedge of gold,
        Thou, who for me wast sold,
        To me dost now thy self convey;
    For so thou should'st without me still have been,   5
        Leaving within me sinne:

    But by the way of nourishment and strength
        Thou creep'st into my breast;
        Making thy way my rest,
        And thy small quantities my length;   10
    Which spread their forces into every part,
        Meeting sinnes force and art.

    Yet can these not get over to my soul,
        Leaping the wall that parts
        Our souls and fleshy hearts;   15
        But as th' outworks, they may controll
    My rebel-flesh, and carrying thy name,
        Affright both sinne and shame.

Onely thy grace, which with these elements comes,
    Knoweth the ready way,   20
    And hath the privie key,
    Op'ning the souls most subtile rooms;
While those to spirits refin'd, at doore attend
    Dispatches from their friend.

Give me my captive soul, or take   25
    My bodie also thither.
Another lift like this will make
    Them both to be together.

Before that sinne turn'd flesh to stone,
    And all our lump to leaven;   30
A fervent sigh might well have blown
    Our innocent earth to heaven.

For sure when Adam did not know
    To sinne, or sinne to smother;
He might to heav'n from Paradise go,   35
    As from one room t'another.

Thou hast restor'd us to this ease
    By this thy heav'nly bloud;
Which I can go to, when I please,
    And leave th' earth to their food.   40

Antiphon (1)

Cho. Let all the world in ev'ry corner sing,
        My God and King.

  Vers.   The heav'ns are not too high,
        His praise may thither flie:
        The earth is not too low,   5
        His praises there may grow.

Cho. Let all the world in ev'ry corner sing,
        My God and King.

Vers.   The church with psalms must shout,
No doore can keep them out: 10
But above all, the heart
Must bear the longest part.

Cho.   Let all the world in ev'ry corner sing,
My God and King.

Love

I

Immortall Love, authour of this great frame,
   Sprung from that beautie which can never fade;
   How hath man parcel'd out thy glorious name,
And thrown it on that dust which thou hast made,
While mortall love doth all the title gain!   5
   Which siding with invention, they together
   Bear all the sway, possessing heart and brain,
(Thy workmanship) and give thee share in neither.
Wit fancies beautie, beautie raiseth wit:
   The world is theirs; they two play out the game,   10
   Thou standing by: and though thy glorious name
Wrought our deliverance from th' infernall pit,
   Who sings thy praise? onely a skarf or glove
   Doth warm our hands, and make them write of love.

II

Immortall Heat, O let thy greater flame
   Attract the lesser to it: let those fires,
   Which shall consume the world, first make it tame;
And kindle in our hearts such true desires,
As may consume our lusts, and make thee way.   5
   Then shall our hearts pant thee; then shall our brain
   All her invention on thine Altar lay,
And there in hymnes send back thy fire again:
Our eies shall see thee, which before saw dust;

Dust blown by wit, till that they both were blinde: 10
Thou shalt recover all thy goods in kinde,
Who wert disseized by usurping lust:
All knees shall bow to thee; all wits shall rise,
And praise him who did make and mend our eies.

The Temper (1)

How should I praise thee, Lord! how should my rymes
    Gladly engrave thy love in steel,
        If what my soul doth feel sometimes,
            My soul might ever feel!

Although there were some fourtie heav'ns, or more, 5
    Sometimes I peere above them all;
        Sometimes I hardly reach a score,
            Sometimes to hell I fall.

O rack me not to such a vast extent;
    Those distances belong to thee: 10
        The world's too little for thy tent,
            A grave too big for me.

Wilt thou meet arms with man, that thou dost stretch
    A crumme of dust from heav'n to hell?
        Will great God measure with a wretch? 15
            Shall he thy stature spell?

O let me, when thy roof my soul hath hid,
    O let me roost and nestle there:
        Then of a sinner thou art rid,
            And I of hope and fear. 20

Yet take thy way; for sure thy way is best:
    Stretch or contract me, thy poore debter:
        This is but tuning of my breast,
            To make the musick better.

Whether I flie with angels, fall with dust,   25
   Thy hands made both, and I am there:
   Thy power and love, my love and trust
   Make one place ev'ry where.

The Temper (II)

It cannot be. Where is that mightie joy,
   Which just now took up all my heart?
   Lord, if thou must needs use thy dart,
Save that, and me; or sin for both destroy.

The grosser world stands to thy word and art;   5
   But thy diviner world of grace
   Thou suddenly dost raise and race,
And ev'ry day a new Creatour art.

O fix thy chair of grace, that all my powers
   May also fix their reverence: 10
   For when thou dost depart from hence,
They grow unruly, and sit in thy bowers.

Scatter, or binde them all to bend to thee:
   Though elements change, and heaven move,
   Let not thy higher Court remove,   15
But keep a standing Majestie in me.

Jordan (I)

Who sayes that fictions onely and false hair
Become a verse? Is there in truth no beautie?
Is all good structure in a winding stair?
May no lines passe, except they do their dutie
   Not to a true, but painted chair?   5

Is it no verse, except enchanted groves
And sudden arbours shadow course-spunne lines?
Must purling streams refresh a lovers loves?

Must all be vail'd, while he that reades, divines,
   Catching the sense at two removes?   10

Shepherds are honest people; let them sing:
Riddle who list, for me, and pull for Prime:
I envie no mans nightingale or spring;
Nor let them punish me with losse of rime,
   Who plainly say, *My God, My King*.   15

Employment (1)

If as a flowre doth spread and die,
   Thou wouldst extend me to some good,
Before I were by frosts extremitie
         Nipt in the bud;

The sweetnesse and the praise were thine;   5
   But the extension and the room,
Which in thy garland I should fill, were mine
         At thy great doom.

For as thou dost impart thy grace,
   The greater shall our glorie be.   10
The measure of our joyes is in this place,
         The stuffe with thee.

Let me not languish then, and spend
   A life as barren to thy praise,
As is the dust, to which that life doth tend,   15
         But with delaies.

All things are busie; onely I
   Neither bring hony with the bees,
Nor flowres to make that, nor the husbandrie
         To water these.   20

I am no link of thy great chain,
   But all my companie is a weed.
Lord place me in thy consort; give one strain
         To my poore reed.

The H. Scriptures

I

Oh Book! infinite sweetnesse! let my heart
    Suck ev'ry letter, and a hony gain,
    Precious for any grief in any part;
To cleare the breast, to mollifie all pain.
Thou art all health, health thriving till it make   5
    A full eternitie: thou art a masse
    Of strange delights, where we may wish & take.
Ladies, look here; this is the thankfull glasse,
That mends the lookers eyes: this is the well
    That washes what it shows. Who can indeare   10
    Thy praise too much? thou art heav'ns Lidger here,
Working against the states of death and hell.
    Thou art joyes handsell: heav'n lies flat in thee,
    Subject to ev'ry mounters bended knee.

II

Oh that I knew how all thy lights combine,
    And the configurations of their glorie!
    Seeing not onely how each verse doth shine,
But all the constellations of the storie.
This verse marks that, and both do make a motion   5
    Unto a third, that ten leaves off doth lie:
    Then as dispersed herbs do watch a potion,
These three make up some Christians destinie:
Such are thy secrets, which my life makes good,
    And comments on thee: for in ev'ry thing   10
    Thy words do finde me out, & parallels bring,
And in another make me understood.
    Starres are poore books, & oftentimes do misse:
    This book of starres lights to eternall blisse.

Whitsunday

Listen sweet Dove unto my song,
And spread thy golden wings in me;
Hatching my tender heart so long,
Till it get wing, and flie away with thee.

Where is that fire which once descended   5
On thy Apostles? thou didst then
Keep open house, richly attended,
Feasting all comers by twelve chosen men.

Such glorious gifts thou didst bestow,
That th' earth did like a heav'n appeare;   10
The starres were coming down to know
If they might mend their wages, and serve here.

The sunne, which once did shine alone,
Hung down his head, and wisht for night,
When he beheld twelve sunnes for one   15
Going about the world, and giving light.

But since those pipes of gold, which brought
That cordiall water to our ground,
Were cut and martyr'd by the fault
Of those, who did themselves through their side wound,   20

Thou shutt'st the doore, and keep'st within;
Scarce a good joy creeps through the chink:
And if the braves of conqu'ring sinne
Did not excite thee, we should wholly sink.

Lord, though we change, thou art the same;   25
The same sweet God of love and light:
Restore this day, for thy great name,
Unto his ancient and miraculous right.

Grace

My stock lies dead, and no increase
Doth my dull husbandrie improve:
O let thy graces without cease
                    Drop from above!

If still the sunne should hide his face,   5
Thy house would but a dungeon prove,
Thy works nights captives: O let grace
                    Drop from above!

The dew doth ev'ry morning fall;
And shall the dew out-strip thy Dove?   10
The dew, for which grasse cannot call,
                    Drop from above.

Death is still working like a mole,
And digs my grave at each remove:
Let grace work too, and on my soul   15
                    Drop from above.

Sinne is still hammering my heart
Unto a hardnesse, void of love:
Let suppling grace, to crosse his art,
                    Drop from above.   20

O come! for thou dost know the way:
Or if to me thou wilt not move,
Remove me, where I need not say,
                    Drop from above.

Praise (1)

To write a verse or two is all the praise,
                    That I can raise:
          Mend my estate in any wayes,
                    Thou shalt have more.

I go to Church; help me to wings, and I   5
        Will thither flie;
    Or, if I mount unto the skie,
        I will do more.

Man is all weaknesse; there is no such thing
        As Prince or King: 10
    His arm is short; yet with a sling
        He may do more.

An herb destill'd, and drunk, may dwell next doore,
        On the same floore,
    To a brave soul: exalt the poore,   15
        They can do more.

O raise me then! Poore bees, that work all day,
        Sting my delay,
    Who have a work, as well as they,
        And much, much more.   20

Affliction (II)

    Kill me not ev'ry day,
Thou Lord of life; since thy one death for me
    Is more then all my deaths can be,
        Though I in broken pay
Die over each houre of Methusalems stay.   5

        If all mens tears were let
Into one common sewer, sea, and brine;
    What were they all, compar'd to thine?
        Wherein if they were set,
They would discolour thy most bloudy sweat.   10

        Thou art my grief alone,
Thou Lord conceal it not: and as thou art
    All my delight, so all my smart:
        Thy crosse took up in one,
By way of imprest, all my future mone.   15

Mattens

I cannot ope mine eyes,
 But thou art ready there to catch
 My morning-soul and sacrifice:
Then we must needs for that day make a match.

My God, what is a heart? 5
 Silver, or gold, or precious stone,
 Or starre, or rainbow, or a part
Of all these things, or all of them in one?

My God, what is a heart,
 That thou shouldst it so eye, and wooe, 10
 Powring upon it all thy art,
As if that thou hadst nothing els to do?

Indeed mans whole estate
 Amounts (and richly) to serve thee:
 He did not heav'n and earth create, 15
Yet studies them, not him by whom they be.

Teach me thy love to know;
 That this new light, which now I see,
 May both the work and workman show:
Then by a sunne-beam I will climbe to thee. 20

Sinne (ii)

O that I could a sinne once see!
 We paint the devil foul, yet he
 Hath some good in him, all agree.
Sinne is flat opposite to th' Almighty, seeing
It wants the good of *vertue,* and of *being.* 5

But God more care of us hath had:
 If apparitions make us sad,
 By sight of sinne we should grow mad.
Yet as in sleep we see foul death, and live:
So devils are our sinnes in perspective. 10

Even-song

Blest be the God of love,
Who gave me eyes, and light, and power this day,
Both to be busie, and to play.
But much more blest be God above,
Who gave me sight alone,   5
Which to himself he did denie:
For when he sees my waies, I dy:
But I have got his sonne, and he hath none.

What have I brought thee home
For this thy love? have I discharg'd the debt,   10
Which this dayes favour did beget?
I ranne; but all I brought, was fome.
Thy diet, care, and cost
Do end in bubbles, balls of winde;
Of winde to thee whom I have crost,   15
But balls of wilde-fire to my troubled minde.

Yet still thou goest on,
And now with darknesse closest wearie eyes,
Saying to man, *It doth suffice:*
Henceforth repose; your work is done.   20
Thus in thy ebony box
Thou dost inclose us, till the day
Put our amendment in our way,
And give new wheels to our disorder'd clocks.

I muse, which shows more love,   25
The day or night: that is the gale, this th' harbour;
That is the walk, and this the arbour;
Or that the garden, this the grove.
My God, thou art all love.
Not one poore minute scapes thy breast,   30
But brings a favour from above;
And in this love, more then in bed, I rest.

Church-monuments

While that my soul repairs to her devotion,
Here I intombe my flesh, that it betimes
May take acquaintance of this heap of dust;
To which the blast of deaths incessant motion,
Fed with the exhalation of our crimes,   5
Drives all at last. Therefore I gladly trust

My bodie to this school, that it may learn
To spell his elements, and finde his birth
Written in dustie heraldrie and lines;
Which dissolution sure doth best discern,   10
Comparing dust with dust, and earth with earth.
These laugh at Jeat and Marble put for signes,

To sever the good fellowship of dust,
And spoil the meeting. What shall point out them,
When they shall bow, and kneel, and fall down flat   15
To kisse those heaps, which now they have in trust?
Deare flesh, while I do pray, learn here thy stemme
And true descent; that when thou shalt grow fat,

And wanton in thy cravings, thou mayst know,
That flesh is but the glasse, which holds the dust   20
That measures all our time; which also shall
Be crumbled into dust. Mark here below
How tame these ashes are, how free from lust,
That thou mayst fit thy self against thy fall.

Church-musick

Sweetest of sweets, I thank you: when displeasure
　　　　Did through my bodie wound my minde,
You took me thence, and in your house of pleasure
　　　　A daintie lodging me assign'd.

Now I in you without a bodie move,   5
　　　　Rising and falling with your wings:

We both together sweetly live and love,
        Yet say sometimes, *God help poore Kings.*

Comfort, I'le die; for if you poste from me,
        Sure I shall do so, and much more: 10
But if I travell in your companie,
        You know the way to heavens doore.

Church-lock and key

I know it is my sinne, which locks thine eares,
        And bindes thy hands,
Out-crying my requests, drowning my tears;
Or else the chilnesse of my faint demands.

But as cold hands are angrie with the fire,   5
        And mend it still;
So I do lay the want of my desire,
Not on my sinnes, or coldnesse, but thy will.

Yet heare, O God, onely for his blouds sake
        Which pleads for me: 10
For though sinnes plead too, yet like stones they make
His blouds sweet current much more loud to be.

The Church-floore

Mark you the floore? that square & speckled stone,
        Which looks so firm and strong,
            Is *Patience*:

And th' other black and grave, wherewith each one
        Is checker'd all along,   5
            Humilitie:

The gentle rising, which on either hand
        Leads to the Quire above,
            Is *Confidence*:

But the sweet cement, which in one sure band   10
      Ties the whole frame, is *Love*
        And *Charitie.*

     Hither sometimes Sinne steals, and stains
     The marbles neat and curious veins:
But all is cleansed when the marble weeps.   15
     Sometimes Death, puffing at the doore,
     Blows all the dust about the floore:
But while he thinks to spoil the room, he sweeps.
     Blest be the *Architect,* whose art
     Could build so strong in a weak heart.   20

The Windows

Lord, how can man preach thy eternall word?
     He is a brittle crazie glasse:
Yet in thy temple thou dost him afford
     This glorious and transcendent place,
     To be a window, through thy grace.   5

But when thou dost anneal in glasse thy storie,
     Making thy life to shine within
The holy Preachers; then the light and glorie
     More rev'rend grows, & more doth win:
     Which else shows watrish, bleak, & thin.   10

Doctrine and life, colours and light, in one
     When they combine and mingle, bring
A strong regard and aw: but speech alone
     Doth vanish like a flaring thing,
     And in the eare, not conscience ring.   15

Trinitie Sunday

Lord, who hast form'd me out of mud,
     And hast redeem'd me through thy bloud,
     And sanctifi'd me to do good;

Purge all my sinnes done heretofore:
     For I confesse my heavie score,   5
     And I will strive to sinne no more.

Enrich my heart, mouth, hands in me,
     With faith, with hope, with charitie;
     That I may runne, rise, rest with thee.

Content

Peace mutt'ring thoughts, and do not grudge to keep
     Within the walls of your own breast:
Who cannot on his own bed sweetly sleep,
     Can on anothers hardly rest.

Gad not abroad at ev'ry quest and call   5
     Of an untrained hope or passion.
To court each place or fortune that doth fall,
     Is wantonnesse in contemplation.

Mark how the fire in flints doth quiet lie,
     Content and warm t' it self alone: 10
But when it would appeare to others eye,
     Without a knock it never shone.

Give me the pliant minde, whose gentle measure
     Complies and suits with all estates;
Which can let loose to a crown, and yet with pleasure   15
     Take up within a cloisters gates.

This soul doth span the world, and hang content
     From either pole unto the centre:
Where in each room of the well-furnisht tent
     He lies warm, and without adventure.   20

The brags of life are but a nine dayes wonder;
     And after death the fumes that spring
From private bodies make as big a thunder,
     As those which rise from a huge King.

Onely thy Chronicle is lost; and yet   25
      Better by worms be all once spent,
Then to have hellish moths still gnaw and fret
      Thy name in books, which may not rent:

When all thy deeds, whose brunt thou feel'st alone,
      Are chaw'd by others pens and tongue;   30
And as their wit is, their digestion,
      Thy nourisht fame is weak or strong.

Then cease discoursing soul, till thine own ground,
      Do not thy self or friends importune.
He that by seeking hath himself once found,   35
      Hath ever found a happie fortune.

The Quidditie

   My God, a verse is not a crown,
   No point of honour, or gay suit,
   No hawk, or banquet, or renown,
   Nor a good sword, nor yet a lute:

   It cannot vault, or dance, or play;   5
   It never was in *France* or *Spain*;
   Nor can it entertain the day
   With my great stable or demain:

   It is no office, art, or news,
   Nor the Exchange, or busie Hall;   10
   But it is that which while I use
   I am with thee, and *most take all*.

Humilitie

I saw the Vertues sitting hand in hand
In sev'rall ranks upon an azure throne,
Where all the beasts and fowl by their command
Presented tokens of submission.
Humilitie, who sat the lowest there   5

To execute their call,
When by the beasts the presents tendred were,
Gave them about to all.

The angrie Lion did present his paw,
Which by consent was giv'n to Mansuetude.   10
The fearfull Hare her eares, which by their law
Humilitie did reach to Fortitude.
The jealous Turkie brought his corall-chain;
That went to Temperance.
On Justice was bestow'd the Foxes brain,   15
Kill'd in the way by chance.

At length the Crow bringing the Peacocks plume,
(For he would not) as they beheld the grace
Of that brave gift, each one began to fume,
And challenge it, as proper to his place,   20
Till they fell out: which when the beasts espied,
They leapt upon the throne;
And if the Fox had liv'd to rule their side,
They had depos'd each one.

Humilitie, who held the plume, at this   25
Did weep so fast, that the tears trickling down
Spoil'd all the train: then saying, *Here it is*
For which ye wrangle, made them turn their frown
Against the beasts: so joyntly bandying,
They drive them soon away;   30
And then amerc'd them, double gifts to bring
At the next Session-day.

Frailtie

Lord, in my silence how do I despise
What upon trust
Is styled *honour, riches,* or *fair eyes;*
But is *fair dust!*
I surname them *guilded clay,*   5
Deare earth, fine grasse or *hay;*

In all, I think my foot doth ever tread
        Upon their head.

But when I view abroad both Regiments;
        The worlds, and thine: 10
Thine clad with simplenesse, and sad events;
        The other fine,
    Full of glorie and gay weeds,
      Brave language, braver deeds:
That which was dust before, doth quickly rise,   15
        And prick mine eyes.

O brook not this, lest if what even now
        My foot did tread,
Affront those joyes, wherewith thou didst endow
        And long since wed   20
    My poore soul, ev'n sick of love:
      It may a Babel prove
Commodious to conquer heav'n and thee
        Planted in me.

Constancie

      Who is the honest man?
He that doth still and strongly good pursue,
To God, his neighbour, and himself most true:
      Whom neither force nor fawning can
Unpinne, or wrench from giving all their due.   5

      Whose honestie is not
So loose or easie, that a ruffling winde
Can blow away, or glittering look it blinde:
      Who rides his sure and even trot,
While the world now rides by, now lags behinde.   10

      Who, when great trials come,
Nor seeks, nor shunnes them; but doth calmly stay,
Till he the thing and the example weigh:

All being brought into a summe,
What place or person calls for, he doth pay.   15

Whom none can work or wooe
To use in any thing a trick or sleight;
For above all things he abhorres deceit:
    His words and works and fashion too
All of a piece, and all are cleare and straight.   20

Who never melts or thaws
At close tentations: when the day is done,
His goodnesse sets not, but in dark can runne:
    The sunne to others writeth laws,
And is their vertue; Vertue is his Sunne.   25

Who, when he is to treat
With sick folks, women, those whom passions sway,
Allows for that, and keeps his constant way:
    Whom others faults do not defeat;
But though men fail him, yet his part doth play.   30

Whom nothing can procure,
When the wide world runnes bias from his will,
To writhe his limbes, and share, not mend the ill.
    This is the Mark-man, safe and sure,
Who still is right, and prayes to be so still.   35

Affliction (III)

My heart did heave, and there came forth, *O God!*
By that I knew that thou wast in the grief,
To guide and govern it to my relief,
    Making a scepter of the rod:
      Hadst thou not had thy part,   5
Sure the unruly sigh had broke my heart.

But since thy breath gave me both life and shape,
Thou knowst my tallies; and when there's assign'd
So much breath to a sigh, what's then behinde?
    Or if some yeares with it escape,   10

The sigh then onely is
A gale to bring me sooner to my blisse.

Thy life on earth was grief, and thou art still
Constant unto it, making it to be
A point of honour, now to grieve in me,   15
    And in thy members suffer ill.
      They who lament one crosse,
Thou dying dayly, praise thee to thy losse.

The Starre

Bright spark, shot from a brighter place,
    Where beams surround my Saviours face,
      Canst thou be any where
      So well as there?

Yet, if thou wilt from thence depart,   5
    Take a bad lodging in my heart;
      For thou canst make a debter,
      And make it better.

First with thy fire-work burn to dust
    Folly, and worse then folly, lust: 10
      Then with thy light refine,
      And make it shine:

So disengag'd from sinne and sicknesse,
    Touch it with thy celestiall quicknesse,
      That it may hang and move   15
      After thy love.

Then with our trinitie of light,
    Motion, and heat, let's take our flight
      Unto the place where thou
      Before didst bow.   20

Get me a standing there, and place
    Among the beams, which crown the face
      Of him, who dy'd to part
      Sinne and my heart:

That so among the rest I may   25
    Glitter, and curle, and winde as they:
        That winding is their fashion
        Of adoration.

Sure thou wilt joy, by gaining me
    To flie home like a laden bee   30
        Unto that hive of beams
        And garland-streams.

Sunday

    O day most calm, most bright,
The fruit of this, the next worlds bud,
Th' indorsement of supreme delight,
Writ by a friend, and with his bloud;
The couch of time; cares balm and bay: 5
The week were dark, but for thy light:
    Thy torch doth show the way.

    The other dayes and thou
Make up one man; whose face thou art,
Knocking at heaven with thy brow: 10
The worky-daies are the back-part;
The burden of the week lies there,
Making the whole to stoup and bow,
    Till thy release appeare.

    Man had straight forward gone   15
To endlesse death: but thou dost pull
And turn us round to look on one,
Whom, if we were not very dull,
We could not choose but look on still;
Since there is no place so alone,   20
    The which he doth not fill.

    Sundaies the pillars are,
On which heav'ns palace arched lies:
The other dayes fill up the spare

And hollow room with vanities.   25
They are the fruitfull beds and borders
In Gods rich garden: that is bare,
                Which parts their ranks and orders.

                The Sundaies of mans life,
Thredded together on times string,   30
Make bracelets to adorn the wife
Of the eternall glorious King.
On Sunday heavens gate stands ope;
Blessings are plentifull and rife,
                More plentifull then hope.   35

                This day my Saviour rose,
And did inclose this light for his:
That, as each beast his manger knows,
Man might not of his fodder misse.
Christ hath took in this piece of ground,   40
And made a garden there for those
                Who want herbs for their wound.

                The rest of our Creation
Our great Redeemer did remove
With the same shake, which at his passion   45
Did th' earth and all things with it move.
As Sampson bore the doores away,
Christs hands, though nail'd, wrought our salvation,
                And did unhinge that day.

                The brightnesse of that day   50
We sullied by our foul offence:
Wherefore that robe we cast away,
Having a new at his expence,
Whose drops of bloud paid the full price,
That was requir'd to make us gay,   55
                And fit for Paradise.

                Thou art a day of mirth:
And where the week-dayes trail on ground,
Thy flight is higher, as thy birth.

O let me take thee at the bound,   60
Leaping with thee from sev'n to sev'n,
Till that we both, being toss'd from earth,
      Flie hand in hand to heav'n!

Avarice

Money, thou bane of blisse, & sourse of wo,
    When com'st thou, that thou art so fresh and fine?
    I know thy parentage is base and low:
Man found thee poore and dirtie in a mine.
Surely thou didst so little contribute   5
    To this great kingdome, which thou now hast got,
    That he was fain, when thou wert destitute,
To digge thee out of thy dark cave and grot:
Then forcing thee by fire he made thee bright:
    Nay, thou hast got the face of man; for we   10
    Have with our stamp and seal transferr'd our right:
Thou art the man, and man but drosse to thee.
    Man calleth thee his wealth, who made thee rich;
    And while he digs out thee, falls in the ditch.

Ana- $\left\{ \begin{array}{c} \text{M A R Y} \\ \text{A R M Y} \end{array} \right\}$ *gram*

How well her name an *Army* doth present,
In whom the *Lord of Hosts* did pitch his tent!

To all Angels and Saints

Oh glorious spirits, who after all your bands
See the smooth face of God without a frown
           Or strict commands;
Where ev'ry one is king, and hath his crown,
If not upon his head, yet in his hands: 5

Not out of envie or maliciousnesse
Do I forbear to crave your speciall aid:

I would addresse
My vows to thee most gladly, Blessed Maid,
And Mother of my God, in my distresse. 10

Thou art the holy mine, whence came the gold,
The great restorative for all decay
In young and old;
Thou art the cabinet where the jewell lay:
Chiefly to thee would I my soul unfold: 15

But now, alas, I dare not; for our King,
Whom we do all joyntly adore and praise,
Bids no such thing:
And where his pleasure no injunction layes,
('Tis your own case) ye never move a wing. 20

All worship is prerogative, and a flower
Of his rich crown, from whom lyes no appeal
At the last houre:
Therefore we dare not from his garland steal,
To make a posie for inferiour power. 25

Although then others court you, if ye know
What's done on earth, we shall not fare the worse,
Who do not so;
Since we are ever ready to disburse,
If any one our Masters hand can show. 30

Employment (II)

He that is weary, let him sit.
My soul would stirre
And trade in courtesies and wit,
Quitting the furre
To cold complexions needing it. 5

Man is no starre, but a quick coal
Of mortall fire:
Who blows it not, nor doth controll

A faint desire,
Lets his own ashes choke his soul.   10

When th' elements did for place contest
       With him, whose will
Ordain'd the highest to be best;
       The earth sat still,
And by the others is opprest.   15

Life is a businesse, not good cheer;
       Ever in warres.
The sunne still shineth there or here,
       Whereas the starres
Watch an advantage to appeare.   20

Oh that I were an Orenge-tree,
       That busie plant!
Then should I ever laden be,
       And never want
Some fruit for him that dressed me.   25

But we are still too young or old;
       The Man is gone,
Before we do our wares unfold:
       So we freeze on,
Untill the grave increase our cold.   30

Deniall

When my devotions could not pierce
       Thy silent eares;
Then was my heart broken, as was my verse:
       My breast was full of fears
             And disorder: 5

My bent thoughts, like a brittle bow,
       Did flie asunder:
Each took his way; some would to pleasures go,
       Some to the warres and thunder
             Of alarms.   10

As good go any where, they say,
        As to benumme
Both knees and heart, in crying night and day,
    Come, come, my God, O come,
           But no hearing.   15

O that thou shouldst give dust a tongue
        To crie to thee,
And then not heare it crying! all day long
      My heart was in my knee,
           But no hearing.   20

Therefore my soul lay out of sight,
        Untun'd, unstrung:
My feeble spirit, unable to look right,
      Like a nipt blossome, hung
           Discontented.   25

O cheer and tune my heartlesse breast,
        Deferre no time;
That so thy favours granting my request,
      They and my minde may chime,
           And mend my ryme.   30

Christmas

All after pleasures as I rid one day,
    My horse and I, both tir'd, bodie and minde,
    With full crie of affections, quite astray,
I took up in the next inne I could finde.
There when I came, whom found I but my deare,   5
    My dearest Lord, expecting till the grief
    Of pleasures brought me to him, readie there
To be all passengers most sweet relief?
O Thou, whose glorious, yet contracted light,
    Wrapt in nights mantle, stole into a manger;   10
    Since my dark soul and brutish is thy right,
To Man of all beasts be not thou a stranger:
    Furnish & deck my soul, that thou mayst have
    A better lodging then a rack or grave.

The shepherds sing; and shall I silent be? 15
        My God, no hymne for thee?
My soul's a shepherd too; a flock it feeds
        Of thoughts, and words, and deeds.
The pasture is thy word: the streams, thy grace
        Enriching all the place. 20
Shepherd and flock shall sing, and all my powers
        Out-sing the day-light houres.
Then we will chide the sunne for letting night
        Take up his place and right:
We sing one common Lord; wherefore he should 25
        Himself the candle hold.
I will go searching, till I finde a sunne
        Shall stay, till we have done;
A willing shiner, that shall shine as gladly,
        As frost-nipt sunnes look sadly. 30
Then we will sing, and shine all our own day,
        And one another pay:
His beams shall cheer my breast, and both so twine,
Till ev'n his beams sing, and my musick shine.

Ungratefulnesse

Lord, with what bountie and rare clemencie
        Hast thou redeem'd us from the grave!
        If thou hadst let us runne,
        Gladly had man ador'd the sunne,
        And thought his god most brave; 5
Where now we shall be better gods then he.

Thou hast but two rare cabinets full of treasure,
        The *Trinitie,* and *Incarnation:*
        Thou hast unlockt them both,
        And made them jewels to betroth 10
        The work of thy creation
Unto thy self in everlasting pleasure.

The statelier cabinet is the *Trinitie,*
        Whose sparkling light accesse denies:

Therefore thou dost not show 15
This fully to us, till death blow
The dust into our eyes:
For by that powder thou wilt make us see.

But all thy sweets are packt up in the other;
Thy mercies thither flock and flow: 20
That as the first affrights,
This may allure us with delights;
Because this box we know;
For we have all of us just such another.

But man is close, reserv'd, and dark to thee: 25
When thou demandest but a heart,
He cavils instantly.
In his poore cabinet of bone
Sinnes have their box apart,
Defrauding thee, who gavest two for one. 30

Sighs and Grones

O do not use me
After my sinnes! look not on my desert,
But on thy glorie! then thou wilt reform
And not refuse me: for thou onely art
The mightie God, but I a sillie worm; 5
O do not bruise me!

O do not urge me!
For what account can thy ill steward make?
I have abus'd thy stock, destroy'd thy woods,
Suckt all thy magazens: my head did ake, 10
Till it found out how to consume thy goods:
O do not scourge me!

O do not blinde me!
I have deserv'd that an Egyptian night
Should thicken all my powers; because my lust 15

Hath still sow'd fig-leaves to exclude thy light:
But I am frailtie, and already dust;
           O do not grinde me!

           O do not fill me
With the turn'd viall of thy bitter wrath!   20
For thou hast other vessels full of bloud,
A part whereof my Saviour empti'd hath,
Ev'n unto death: since he di'd for my good,
           O do not kill me!

           But O reprieve me!   25
For thou hast life and death at thy command;
Thou art both *Judge* and *Saviour, feast* and *rod,*
Cordiall and *Corrosive:* put not thy hand
Into the bitter box; but O my God,
           My God, relieve me!   30

The World

Love built a stately house; where *Fortune* came,
And spinning phansies, she was heard to say,
That her fine cobwebs did support the frame,
Whereas they were supported by the same:
But *Wisdome* quickly swept them all away.   5

Then *Pleasure* came, who, liking not the fashion,
Began to make *Balcones, Terraces,*
Till she had weakned all by alteration:
But rev'rend *laws,* and many a *proclamation*
Reformed all at length with menaces.   10

Then enter'd *Sinne,* and with that Sycomore,
Whose leaves first sheltred man from drought & dew,
Working and winding slily evermore,
The inward walls and sommers cleft and tore:
But *Grace* shor'd these, and cut that as it grew.   15

Then *Sinne* combin'd with *Death* in a firm band
To raze the building to the very floore:

Which they effected, none could them withstand.
But *Love* and *Grace* took *Glorie* by the hand,
And built a braver Palace then before.   20

Coloss. 3. 3

Our life is hid with Christ in God

My words & thoughts do both expresse this notion,
That *Life* hath with the sun a double motion.
The first *Is* straight and our diurnall friend,
The other *Hid* and doth obliquely bend.
One life is wrapt *In* flesh, and tends to earth: 5
The other winds towards *Him,* whose happie birth
Taught me to live here so, *That* still one eye
Should aim and shoot at that which *Is* on high:
Quitting with daily labour all *My* pleasure,
To gain at harvest an eternall *Treasure.* 10

Vanitie (1)

The fleet Astronomer can bore,
And thred the spheres with his quick-piercing minde:
He views their stations, walks from doore to doore,
Surveys, as if he had design'd
To make a purchase there: he sees their dances,   5
And knoweth long before
Both their full-ey'd aspects, and secret glances.

The nimble Diver with his side
Cuts through the working waves, that he may fetch
His dearely-earned pearl, which God did hide   10
On purpose from the ventrous wretch;
That he might save his life, and also hers,
Who with excessive pride
Her own destruction and his danger wears.

        The subtil Chymick can devest   15
And strip the creature naked, till he finde
The callow principles within their nest:
        There he imparts to them his minde,
Admitted to their bed-chamber, before
            They appeare trim and drest   20
To ordinarie suitours at the doore.

        What hath not man sought out and found,
But his deare God? who yet his glorious law
Embosomes in us, mellowing the ground
        With showres and frosts, with love & aw,   25
So that we need not say, Where 's this command?
           Poore man, thou searchest round
To finde out *death*, but missest *life* at hand.

Lent

Welcome deare feast of Lent: who loves not thee,
He loves not Temperance, or Authoritie,
          But is compos'd of passion.
The Scriptures bid us *fast*; the Church sayes, *now*:
Give to thy Mother, what thou wouldst allow   5
          To ev'ry Corporation.

The humble soul compos'd of love and fear
Begins at home, and layes the burden there,
          When doctrines disagree.
He sayes, in things which use hath justly got,   10
I am a scandall to the Church, and not
          The Church is so to me.

True Christians should be glad of an occasion
To use their temperance, seeking no evasion,
          When good is seasonable;   15
Unlesse Authoritie, which should increase
The obligation in us, make it lesse,
          And Power it self disable.

Besides the cleannesse of sweet abstinence,
Quick thoughts and motions at a small expense,   20
        A face not fearing light:
Whereas in fulnesse there are sluttish fumes,
Sowre exhalations, and dishonest rheumes,
        Revenging the delight.

Then those same pendant profits, which the spring   25
And Easter intimate, enlarge the thing,
        And goodnesse of the deed.
Neither ought other mens abuse of Lent
Spoil the good use; lest by that argument
        We forfeit all our Creed.   30

It 's true, we cannot reach Christs forti'th day;
Yet to go part of that religious way,
        Is better then to rest:
We cannot reach our Saviours puritie;
Yet are we bid, *Be holy ev'n as he.*   35
        In both let 's do our best.

Who goeth in the way which Christ hath gone,
Is much more sure to meet with him, then one
        That travelleth by-wayes:
Perhaps my God, though he be farre before,   40
May turn, and take me by the hand, and more
        May strengthen my decayes.

Yet Lord instruct us to improve our fast
By starving sinne and taking such repast
        As may our faults controll: 45
That ev'ry man may revell at his doore,
Not in his parlour; banquetting the poore,
        And among those his soul.

Vertue

Sweet day, so cool, so calm, so bright,
    The bridall of the earth and skie:
The dew shall weep thy fall to night;
        For thou must die.

Sweet rose, whose hue angrie and brave   5
Bids the rash gazer wipe his eye:
Thy root is ever in its grave,
          And thou must die.

Sweet spring, full of sweet dayes and roses,
A box where sweets compacted lie;   10
My musick shows ye have your closes,
          And all must die.

Onely a sweet and vertuous soul,
Like season'd timber, never gives;
But though the whole world turn to coal,   15
          Then chiefly lives.

The Pearl. Matth. 13. 45

I know the wayes of Learning; both the head
And pipes that feed the presse, and make it runne;
What reason hath from nature borrowed,
Or of it self, like a good huswife, spunne
In laws and policie; what the starres conspire,   5
What willing nature speaks, what forc'd by fire;
Both th' old discoveries, and the new-found seas,
The stock and surplus, cause and historie:
All these stand open, or I have the keyes:
          Yet I love thee.   10

I know the wayes of Honour, what maintains
The quick returns of courtesie and wit:
In vies of favours whether partie gains,
When glorie swells the heart, and moldeth it
To all expressions both of hand and eye,   15
Which on the world a true-love-knot may tie,
And bear the bundle, wheresoe're it goes:
How many drammes of spirit there must be
To sell my life unto my friends or foes:
          Yet I love thee.   20

I know the wayes of Pleasure, the sweet strains,
    The lullings and the relishes of it;
    The propositions of hot bloud and brains;
What mirth and musick mean; what love and wit
Have done these twentie hundred yeares, and more: 25
    I know the projects of unbridled store:
My stuffe is flesh, not brasse; my senses live,
    And grumble oft, that they have more in me
Then he that curbs them, being but one to five:
                Yet I love thee.   30

I know all these, and have them in my hand:
    Therefore not sealed, but with open eyes
    I flie to thee, and fully understand
Both the main sale, and the commodities;
And at what rate and price I have thy love;   35
    With all the circumstances that may move:
Yet through these labyrinths, not my groveling wit,
    But thy silk twist let down from heav'n to me,
Did both conduct and teach me, how by it
                To climbe to thee.   40

Affliction (IV)

Broken in pieces all asunder,
            Lord, hunt me not,
            A thing forgot,
Once a poore creature, now a wonder,
            A wonder tortur'd in the space   5
            Betwixt this world and that of grace.

My thoughts are all a case of knives,
            Wounding my heart
            With scatter'd smart,
As watring pots give flowers their lives.   10
            Nothing their furie can controll,
            While they do wound and pink my soul.

All my attendants are at strife,
             Quitting their place
             Unto my face: 15
Nothing performs the task of life:
             The elements are let loose to fight,
             And while I live, trie out their right.

Oh help, my God! let not their plot
             Kill them and me,   20
             And also thee,
Who art my life: dissolve the knot,
             As the sunne scatters by his light
             All the rebellions of the night.

Then shall those powers, which work for grief,   25
             Enter thy pay,
             And day by day
Labour thy praise, and my relief;
             With care and courage building me,
             Till I reach heav'n, and much more, thee.   30

Man

My God, I heard this day,
That none doth build a stately habitation,
             But he that means to dwell therein.
             What house more stately hath there been,
Or can be, then is Man? to whose creation   5
             All things are in decay.

For Man is ev'ry thing,
And more: He is a tree, yet bears more fruit;
             A beast, yet is, or should be more:
             Reason and speech we onely bring.   10
Parrats may thank us, if they are not mute,
             They go upon the score.

Man is all symmetrie,
Full of proportions, one limbe to another,

And all to all the world besides: 15
Each part may call the furthest, brother:
For head with foot hath private amitie,
And both with moons and tides.

Nothing hath got so farre,
But Man hath caught and kept it, as his prey. 20
His eyes dismount the highest starre:
He is in little all the sphere.
Herbs gladly cure our flesh; because that they
Finde their acquaintance there.

For us the windes do blow, 25
The earth doth rest, heav'n move, and fountains flow.
Nothing we see, but means our good,
As our delight, or as our treasure:
The whole is, either our cupboard of food,
Or cabinet of pleasure. 30

The starres have us to bed;
Night draws the curtain, which the sunne withdraws;
Musick and light attend our head.
All things unto our flesh are kinde
In their descent and being; to our minde 35
In their ascent and cause.

Each thing is full of dutie:
Waters united are our navigation;
Distinguished, our habitation;
Below, our drink; above, our meat;
Both are our cleanlinesse. Hath one such beautie? 40
Then how are all things neat?

More servants wait on Man,
Then he'l take notice of: in ev'ry path
He treads down that which doth befriend him, 45
When sicknesse makes him pale and wan.
Oh mightie love! Man is one world, and hath
Another to attend him.

> Since then, my God, thou hast
> So brave a Palace built; O dwell in it,   50
> That it may dwell with thee at last!
> Till then, afford us so much wit;
> That, as the world serves us, we may serve thee,
> And both thy servants be.

Antiphon (II)

Chor.   Praised be the God of love,
         Men.   Here below,
         Angels.   And here above:
Cho.   Who hath dealt his mercies so,
         Ang.   To his friend,   5
         Men.   And to his foe;

Cho.   That both grace and glorie tend
         Ang.   Us of old,
         Men.   And us in th'end.
Cho.   The great shepherd of the fold   10
         Ang.   Us did make,
         Men.   For us was sold.

Cho.   He our foes in pieces brake;
         Ang.   Him we touch;
         Men.   And him we take.   15
Cho.   Wherefore since that he is such,
         Ang.   We adore,
         Men.   And we do crouch.

Cho.   Lord, thy praises should be more.
         Men.   We have none,   20
         Ang.   And we no store.
Cho.   Praised be the God alone,
     Who hath made of two folds one.

Unkindnesse

Lord, make me coy and tender to offend:
In friendship, first I think, if that agree,
                    Which I intend,
              Unto my friends intent and end.
I would not use a friend, as I use Thee.   5

If any touch my friend, or his good name,
It is my honour and my love to free
                    His blasted fame
              From the least spot or thought of blame.
I could not use a friend, as I use Thee.   10

My friend may spit upon my curious floore:
Would he have gold? I lend it instantly;
                    But let the poore,
              And thou within them, starve at doore.
I cannot use a friend, as I use Thee.   15

When that my friend pretendeth to a place,
I quit my interest, and leave it free:
                    But when thy grace
              Sues for my heart, I thee displace,
Nor would I use a friend, as I use Thee.   20

Yet can a friend what thou hast done fulfill?
O write in brasse, *My God upon a tree*
                    His bloud did spill
              Onely to purchase my good-will.
Yet use I not my foes, as I use Thee.   25

Life

I made a posie, while the day ran by:
Here will I smell my remnant out, and tie
                    My life within this band.
But Time did becken to the flowers, and they
By noon most cunningly did steal away,   5
                    And wither'd in my hand.

My hand was next to them, and then my heart:
I took, without more thinking, in good part
           Times gentle admonition:
Who did so sweetly deaths sad taste convey,   10
Making my minde to smell my fatall day;
           Yet sugring the suspicion.

Farewell deare flowers, sweetly your time ye spent,
Fit, while ye liv'd, for smell or ornament,
           And after death for cures.   15
I follow straight without complaints or grief,
Since if my sent be good, I care not if
           It be as short as yours.

Submission

But that thou art my wisdome, Lord,
      And both mine eyes are thine,
My minde would be extreamly stirr'd
      For missing my designe.

Were it not better to bestow   5
      Some place and power on me?
Then should thy praises with me grow,
      And share in my degree.

But when I thus dispute and grieve,
      I do resume my sight,   10
And pilfring what I once did give,
      Disseize thee of thy right.

How know I, if thou shouldst me raise,
      That I should then raise thee?
Perhaps great places and thy praise   15
      Do not so well agree.

Wherefore unto my gift I stand;
      I will no more advise:
Onely do thou lend me a hand,
      Since thou hast both mine eyes.   20

Justice (1)

I cannot skill of these thy wayes.
Lord, thou didst make me, yet thou woundest me;
Lord, thou dost wound me, yet thou dost relieve me:
Lord, thou relievest, yet I die by thee:
Lord, thou dost kill me, yet thou dost reprieve me.   5
But when I mark my life and praise,
Thy justice me most fitly payes:
For, *I do praise thee, yet I praise thee not:*
My prayers mean thee, yet my prayers stray:
I would do well, yet sinne the hand hath got: 10
My soul doth love thee, yet it loves delay.
I cannot skill of these my wayes.

Charms and Knots

Who reade a chapter when they rise,
Shall ne're be troubled with ill eyes.

A poore mans rod, when thou dost ride,
Is both a weapon and a guide.

Who shuts his hand, hath lost his gold: 5
Who opens it, hath it twice told.

Who goes to bed and does not pray,
Maketh two nights to ev'ry day.

Who by aspersions throw a stone
At th' head of others, hit their own.   10

Who looks on ground with humble eyes,
Findes himself there, and seeks to rise.

When th' hair is sweet through pride or lust,
The powder doth forget the dust.

Take one from ten, and what remains?   15
Ten still, if sermons go for gains.

In shallow waters heav'n doth show;
But who drinks on, to hell may go.

Affliction (v)

My God, I read this day,
That planted Paradise was not so firm,
As was and is thy floting Ark; whose stay
And anchor thou art onely, to confirm
     And strengthen it in ev'ry age,   5
     When waves do rise, and tempests rage.

At first we liv'd in pleasure;
Thine own delights thou didst to us impart:
When we grew wanton, thou didst use displeasure
To make us thine: yet that we might not part,   10
     As we at first did board with thee,
     Now thou wouldst taste our miserie.

There is but joy and grief;
If either will convert us, we are thine:
Some Angels us'd the first; if our relief   15
Take up the second, then thy double line
     And sev'rall baits in either kinde
     Furnish thy table to thy minde.

Affliction then is ours;
We are the trees, whom shaking fastens more,   20
While blustring windes destroy the wanton bowres,
And ruffle all their curious knots and store.
     My God, so temper joy and wo,
     That thy bright beams may tame thy bow.

Mortification

How soon doth man decay!
When clothes are taken from a chest of sweets
   To swaddle infants, whose young breath
      Scarce knows the way;
   Those clouts are little winding sheets,   5
Which do consigne and send them unto death.

   When boyes go first to bed,
They step into their voluntarie graves,
   Sleep bindes them fast; onely their breath
      Makes them not dead: 10
   Successive nights, like rolling waves,
Convey them quickly, who are bound for death.

   When youth is frank and free,
And calls for musick, while his veins do swell,
   All day exchanging mirth and breath   15
      In companie;
   That musick summons to the knell,
Which shall befriend him at the houre of death.

   When man grows staid and wise,
Getting a house and home, where he may move   20
   Within the circle of his breath,
      Schooling his eyes;
   That dumbe inclosure maketh love
Unto the coffin, that attends his death.

   When age grows low and weak,   25
Marking his grave, and thawing ev'ry yeare,
   Till all do melt, and drown his breath
      When he would speak;
   A chair or litter shows the biere,
Which shall convey him to the house of death.   30

   Man, ere he is aware,
Hath put together a solemnitie,
   And drest his herse, while he has breath

As yet to spare:
Yet Lord, instruct us so to die,   35
That all these dyings may be life in death.

Decay

Sweet were the dayes, when thou didst lodge with Lot,
Struggle with Jacob, sit with Gideon,
Advise with Abraham, when thy power could not
Encounter Moses strong complaints and mone:
    Thy words were then, *Let me alone.*   5

One might have sought and found thee presently
At some fair oak, or bush, or cave, or well:
Is my God this way? No, they would reply:
He is to Sinai gone, as we heard tell:
    List, ye may heare great Aarons bell.   10

But now thou dost thy self immure and close
In some one corner of a feeble heart:
Where yet both Sinne and Satan, thy old foes,
Do pinch and straiten thee, and use much art
    To gain thy thirds and little part.   15

I see the world grows old, when as the heat
Of thy great love, once spread, as in an urn
Doth closet up it self, and still retreat,
Cold Sinne still forcing it, till it return,
    And calling *Justice,* all things burn.   20

Miserie

    Lord, let the Angels praise thy name.
Man is a foolish thing, a foolish thing,
    Folly and Sinne play all his game.
His house still burns, and yet he still doth sing,
    Man is but grasse,   5
    He knows it, fill the glasse.

How canst thou brook his foolishnesse?
Why, he'l not lose a cup of drink for thee:
   Bid him but temper his excesse;
Not he: he knows where he can better be,   10
         As he will swear,
         Then to serve thee in fear.

What strange pollutions doth he wed,
And make his own? as if none knew but he.
   No man shall beat into his head,   15
That thou within his curtains drawn canst see:
         They are of cloth,
         Where never yet came moth.

The best of men, turn but thy hand
For one poore minute, stumble at a pinne:
   They would not have their actions scann'd,   20
Nor any sorrow tell them that they sinne,
         Though it be small,
         And measure not their fall.

They quarrell thee, and would give over   25
The bargain made to serve thee: but thy love
   Holds them unto it, and doth cover
Their follies with the wing of thy milde Dove,
         Not suff'ring those
         Who would, to be thy foes.   30

My God, Man cannot praise thy name:
Thou art all brightnesse, perfect puritie;
   The sunne holds down his head for shame,
Dead with eclipses, when we speak of thee:
         How shall infection   35
         Presume on thy perfection?

As dirtie hands foul all they touch,
And those things most, which are most pure and fine:
   So our clay hearts, ev'n when we crouch
To sing thy praises, make them lesse divine.   40
         Yet either this,
         Or none, thy portion is.

Man cannot serve thee; let him go,
And serve the swine: there, there is his delight:
   He doth not like this vertue, no;   45
Give him his dirt to wallow in all night:
       These Preachers make
       His head to shoot and ake.

Oh foolish man! where are thine eyes?
How hast thou lost them in a croud of cares?   50
   Thou pull'st the rug, and wilt not rise,
No, not to purchase the whole pack of starres;
       There let them shine,
       Thou must go sleep, or dine.

The bird that sees a daintie bowre   55
Made in the tree, where she was wont to sit,
   Wonders and sings, but not his power
Who made the arbour: this exceeds her wit.
       But Man doth know
       The spring, whence all things flow: 60

And yet, as though he knew it not,
His knowledge winks, and lets his humours reigne;
   They make his life a constant blot,
And all the bloud of God to run in vain.
       Ah wretch! what verse   65
       Can thy strange wayes rehearse?

Indeed at first Man was a treasure,
A box of jewels, shop of rarities,
   A ring, whose posie was, *My pleasure:*
He was a garden in a Paradise: 70
       Glorie and grace
       Did crown his heart and face.

But sinne hath fool'd him. Now he is
A lump of flesh, without a foot or wing
   To raise him to a glimpse of blisse: 75
A sick toss'd vessel, dashing on each thing;

Nay, his own shelf:
My God, I mean my self.

Jordan (ii)

When first my lines of heav'nly joyes made mention,
Such was their lustre, they did so excell,
That I sought out quaint words, and trim invention;
My thoughts began to burnish, sprout, and swell,
Curling with metaphors a plain intention,   5
Decking the sense, as if it were to sell.

Thousands of notions in my brain did runne,
Off'ring their service, if I were not sped:
I often blotted what I had begunne;
This was not quick enough, and that was dead.   10
Nothing could seem too rich to clothe the sunne,
Much lesse those joyes which trample on his head.

As flames do work and winde, when they ascend,
So did I weave my self into the sense.
But while I bustled, I might heare a friend   15
Whisper, *How wide is all this long pretence!*
There is in love a sweetnesse readie penn'd:
Copie out onely that, and save expense.

Prayer (ii)

Of what an easie quick accesse,
My blessed Lord, art thou! how suddenly
May our requests thine eare invade!
To shew that state dislikes not easinesse,
If I but lift mine eyes, my suit is made: 5
Thou canst no more not heare, then thou canst die.

Of what supreme almightie power
Is thy great arm, which spans the east and west,
And tacks the centre to the sphere!

By it do all things live their measur'd houre:　　10
We cannot ask the thing, which is not there,
Blaming the shallownesse of our request.

　　Of what unmeasurable love
Art thou possest, who, when thou couldst not die,
　　Wert fain to take our flesh and curse,　　15
And for our sakes in person sinne reprove,
That by destroying that which ty'd thy purse,
Thou mightst make way for liberalitie!

　　Since then these three wait on thy throne,
Ease, Power, and *Love*; I value prayer so,　　20
　　That were I to leave all but one,
Wealth, fame, endowments, vertues, all should go;
I and deare prayer would together dwell,
And quickly gain, for each inch lost, an ell.

Obedience

　　My God, if writings may
　　Convey a Lordship any way
Whither the buyer and the seller please;
　　Let it not thee displease,
If this poore paper do as much as they.　　5

　　On it my heart doth bleed
　　As many lines, as there doth need
To passe it self and all it hath to thee.
　　To which I do agree,
And here present it as my speciall Deed.　　10

　　If that hereafter Pleasure
　　Cavill, and claim her part and measure,
As if this passed with a reservation,
　　Or some such words in fashion;
I here exclude the wrangler from thy treasure.　　15

O let thy sacred will
All thy delight in me fulfill!
Let me not think an action mine own way,
But as thy love shall sway,
Resigning up the rudder to thy skill.   20

Lord, what is man to thee,
That thou shouldst minde a rotten tree?
Yet since thou canst not choose but see my actions;
So great are thy perfections,
Thou mayst as well my actions guide, as see.   25

Besides, thy death and bloud
Show'd a strange love to all our good:
Thy sorrows were in earnest; no faint proffer,
Or superficiall offer
Of what we might not take, or be withstood.   30

Wherefore I all forgo:
To one word onely I say, No:
Where in the Deed there was an intimation
Of a gift or donation,
Lord, let it now by way of purchase go.   35

He that will passe his land,
As I have mine, may set his hand
And heart unto this Deed, when he hath read;
And make the purchase spread
To both our goods, if he to it will stand.   40

How happie were my part,
If some kinde man would thrust his heart
Into these lines; till in heav'ns Court of Rolls
They were by winged souls
Entred for both, farre above their desert!   45

Conscience

Peace pratler, do not lowre:
Not a fair look, but thou dost call it foul:
Not a sweet dish, but thou dost call it sowre:

Musick to thee doth howl.
By listning to thy chatting fears 5
I have both lost mine eyes and eares.

Pratler, no more, I say:
My thoughts must work, but like a noiselesse sphere;
Harmonious peace must rock them all the day:
No room for pratlers there. 10
If thou persistest, I will tell thee,
That I have physick to expell thee.

And the receit shall be
My Saviours bloud: when ever at his board
I do but taste it, straight it cleanseth me, 15
And leaves thee not a word;
No, not a tooth or nail to scratch,
And at my actions carp, or catch.

Yet if thou talkest still,
Besides my physick, know there's some for thee: 20
Some wood and nails to make a staffe or bill
For those that trouble me:
The bloudie crosse of my deare Lord
Is both my physick and my sword.

Sion

Lord, with what glorie wast thou serv'd of old,
When Solomons temple stood and flourished!
Where most things were of purest gold;
The wood was all embellished
With flowers and carvings, mysticall and rare: 5
All show'd the builders, crav'd the seeers care.

Yet all this glorie, all this pomp and state
Did not affect thee much, was not thy aim;
Something there was, that sow'd debate:
Wherefore thou quitt'st thy ancient claim: 10

And now thy Architecture meets with sinne;
For all thy frame and fabrick is within.

There thou art struggling with a peevish heart,
Which sometimes crosseth thee, thou sometimes it:
  The fight is hard on either part.   15
  Great God doth fight, he doth submit.
All Solomons sea of brasse and world of stone
Is not so deare to thee as one good grone.

And truly brasse and stones are heavie things,
Tombes for the dead, not temples fit for thee: 20
  But grones are quick, and full of wings,
  And all their motions upward be;
And ever as they mount, like larks they sing;
The note is sad, yet musick for a King.

Home

Come Lord, my head doth burn, my heart is sick,
  While thou dost ever, ever stay:
Thy long deferrings wound me to the quick,
  My spirit gaspeth night and day.
    O show thy self to me,   5
    Or take me up to thee!

How canst thou stay, considering the pace
  The bloud did make, which thou didst waste?
When I behold it trickling down thy face,
  I never saw thing make such haste.   10
    O show thy, &c.

When man was lost, thy pitie lookt about
  To see what help in th' earth or skie:
But there was none; at least no help without:
  The help did in thy bosome lie.   15
    O show thy, &c.

There lay thy sonne: and must he leave that nest,
    That hive of sweetnesse, to remove
Thraldome from those, who would not at a feast
    Leave one poore apple for thy love?   20
        O show thy self to me,
        Or take me up to thee!

He did, he came: O my Redeemer deare,
    After all this canst thou be strange?
So many yeares baptiz'd, and not appeare?   25
    As if thy love could fail or change.
        O show thy, &c.

Yet if thou stayest still, why must I stay?
    My God, what is this world to me,
This world of wo? hence all ye clouds, away,   30
    Away; I must get up and see.
        O show thy, &c.

What is this weary world; this meat and drink,
    That chains us by the teeth so fast?
What is this woman-kinde, which I can wink   35
    Into a blacknesse and distaste?
        O show thy, &c.

With one small sigh thou gav'st me th' other day
    I blasted all the joyes about me:
And scouling on them as they pin'd away,   40
    Now come again, said I, and flout me.
        O show thy, &c.

Nothing but drought and dearth, but bush and brake,
    Which way so-e're I look, I see.
Some may dream merrily, but when they wake,   45
    They dresse themselves and come to thee.
        O show thy, &c.

We talk of harvests; there are no such things,
    But when we leave our corn and hay:
There is no fruitfull yeare, but that which brings   50

The last and lov'd, though dreadfull day.
     O show thy self to me,
     Or take me up to thee!

Oh loose this frame, this knot of man untie!
     That my free soul may use her wing,   55
Which now is pinion'd with mortalitie,
     As an intangled, hamper'd thing.
     O show thy, &c.

What have I left, that I should stay and grone?
     The most of me to heav'n is fled: 60
My thoughts and joyes are all packt up and gone,
     And for their old acquaintance plead.
     O show thy, &c.

Come dearest Lord, passe not this holy season,
     My flesh and bones and joynts do pray: 65
And ev'n my verse, when by the ryme and reason
     The word is, *Stay*, sayes ever, *Come*.
     O show thy, &c.

The British Church

I joy, deare Mother, when I view
Thy perfect lineaments and hue
         Both sweet and bright.
Beautie in thee takes up her place,
And dates her letters from thy face,   5
         When she doth write.

A fine aspect in fit aray,
Neither too mean, nor yet too gay,
         Shows who is best.
Outlandish looks may not compare: 10
For all they either painted are,
         Or else undrest.

She on the hills, which wantonly
Allureth all in hope to be

By her preferr'd,   15
Hath kiss'd so long her painted shrines,
That ev'n her face by kissing shines,
For her reward.

She in the valley is so shie
Of dressing, that her hair doth lie   20
About her eares:
While she avoids her neighbours pride,
She wholly goes on th' other side,
And nothing wears.

But, dearest Mother, what those misse,   25
The mean, thy praise and glorie is,
And long may be.
Blessed be God, whose love it was
To double-moat thee with his grace,
And none but thee.   30

The Quip

The merrie world did on a day
With his train-bands and mates agree
To meet together, where I lay,
And all in sport to geere at me.

First, Beautie crept into a rose,   5
Which when I pluckt not, Sir, said she,
Tell me, I pray, Whose hands are those?
But thou shalt answer, Lord, for me.

Then Money came, and chinking still,
What tune is this, poore man? said he: 10
I heard in Musick you had skill.
But thou shalt answer, Lord, for me.

Then came brave Glorie puffing by
In silks that whistled, who but he?
He scarce allow'd me half an eie.   15
But thou shalt answer, Lord, for me.

Then came quick Wit and Conversation,
And he would needs a comfort be,
And, to be short, make an Oration.
But thou shalt answer, Lord, for me.   20

Yet when the houre of thy designe
To answer these fine things shall come;
Speak not at large; say, I am thine:
And then they have their answer home.

Vanitie (II)

Poore silly soul, whose hope and head lies low;
Whose flat delights on earth do creep and grow;
To whom the starres shine not so fair, as eyes;
Nor solid work, as false embroyderies;
Heark and beware, lest what you now do measure   5
And write for sweet, prove a most sowre displeasure.

O heare betimes, lest thy relenting
            May come too late!
To purchase heaven for repenting
            Is no hard rate.   10
If souls be made of earthly mold,
            Let them love gold;
            If born on high,
Let them unto their kindred flie:
For they can never be at rest,   15
Till they regain their ancient nest.
Then silly soul take heed; for earthly joy
Is but a bubble, and makes thee a boy.

The Dawning

Awake sad heart, whom sorrow ever drowns;
        Take up thine eyes, which feed on earth;
    Unfold thy forehead gather'd into frowns:

Thy Saviour comes, and with him mirth:
    Awake, awake;   5
And with a thankfull heart his comforts take.
  But thou dost still lament, and pine, and crie;
  And feel his death, but not his victorie.

Arise sad heart; if thou doe not withstand,
  Christs resurrection thine may be: 10
Do not by hanging down break from the hand,
  Which as it riseth, raiseth thee:
       Arise, arise;
And with his buriall-linen drie thine eyes:
  Christ left his grave-clothes, that we might, when grief
  Draws tears, or bloud, not want a handkerchief. [15

Jesu

JESU is in my heart, his sacred name
Is deeply carved there: but th'other week
A great affliction broke the little frame,
Ev'n all to pieces: which I went to seek:
And first I found the corner, where was J,   5
After, where *E S*, and next where *U* was graved.
When I had got these parcels, instantly
I sat me down to spell them, and perceived
That to my broken heart he was *I ease you*,
    And to my whole is J*E SU*.   10

Businesse

Canst be idle? canst thou play,
Foolish soul who sinn'd to day?

Rivers run, and springs each one
Know their home, and get them gone:
Hast thou tears, or hast thou none?   5

If, poore soul, thou hast no tears,
Would thou hadst no faults or fears!
Who hath these, those ill forbears.

Windes still work: it is their plot,
Be the season cold, or hot:
Hast thou sighs, or hast thou not?   10

If thou hast no sighs or grones,
Would thou hadst no flesh and bones!
Lesser pains scape greater ones.

      But if yet thou idle be,   15
      Foolish soul, Who di'd for thee?

Who did leave his Fathers throne,
To assume thy flesh and bone;
Had he life, or had he none?

If he had not liv'd for thee,   20
Thou hadst di'd most wretchedly;
And two deaths had been thy fee.

He so farre thy good did plot,
That his own self he forgot.
Did he die, or did he not?   25

If he had not di'd for thee,
Thou hadst liv'd in miserie.
Two lives worse then ten deaths be.

      And hath any space of breath
      'Twixt his sinnes and Saviours death?   30

He that loseth gold, though drosse,
Tells to all he meets, his crosse:
He that sinnes, hath he no losse?

He that findes a silver vein,
Thinks on it, and thinks again: 35
Brings thy Saviours death no gain?

      Who in heart not ever kneels,
      Neither sinne nor Saviour feels.

Dialogue

Sweetest Saviour, if my soul
    Were but worth the having,
Quickly should I then controll
    Any thought of waving.
But when all my care and pains   5
Cannot give the name of gains
To thy wretch so full of stains,
What delight or hope remains?

What, Child, is the ballance thine,
    Thine the poise and measure?   10
If I say, Thou shalt be mine;
    Finger not my treasure.
What the gains in having thee
Do amount to, onely he,
Who for man was sold, can see;   15
That transferr'd th' accounts to me.

But as I can see no merit,
    Leading to this favour:
So the way to fit me for it
    Is beyond my savour.   20
As the reason then is thine;
So the way is none of mine:
I disclaim the whole designe:
Sinne disclaims and I resigne.

That is all, if that I could   25
    Get without repining;
And my clay, my creature, would
    Follow my resigning:
That as I did freely part
With my glorie and desert,   30
Left all joyes to feel all smart——
    Ah! no more: thou break'st my heart.

Dulnesse

Why do I languish thus, drooping and dull,
      As if I were all earth?
O give me quicknesse, that I may with mirth
      Praise thee brim-full!

The wanton lover in a curious strain
      Can praise his fairest fair;
And with quaint metaphors her curled hair
      Curl o're again.

Thou art my lovelinesse, my life, my light,
      Beautie alone to me:
Thy bloudy death and undeserv'd, makes thee
      Pure red and white.

When all perfections as but one appeare,
      That those thy form doth show,
The very dust, where thou dost tread and go,
      Makes beauties here.

Where are my lines then? my approaches? views?
      Where are my window-songs?
Lovers are still pretending, & ev'n wrongs
      Sharpen their Muse:

But I am lost in flesh, whose sugred lyes
      Still mock me, and grow bold:
Sure thou didst put a minde there, if I could
      Finde where it lies.

Lord, cleare thy gift, that with a constant wit
      I may but look towards thee:
Look onely; for to *love* thee, who can be,
      What angel fit?

Love-joy

As on a window late I cast mine eye,
I saw a vine drop grapes with *J* and *C*
Anneal'd on every bunch. One standing by
Ask'd what it meant. I, who am never loth
To spend my judgement, said, It seem'd to me   5
To be the bodie and the letters both
Of *Joy* and *Charitie*. Sir, you have not miss'd,
The man reply'd; It figures *JESUS CHRIST*.

Providence

O Sacred Providence, who from end to end
Strongly and sweetly movest, shall I write,
And not of thee, through whom my fingers bend
To hold my quill? shall they not do thee right?

Of all the creatures both in sea and land   5
Onely to Man thou hast made known thy wayes,
And put the penne alone into his hand,
And made him Secretarie of thy praise.

Beasts fain would sing; birds dittie to their notes;
Trees would be tuning on their native lute   10
To thy renown: but all their hands and throats
Are brought to Man, while they are lame and mute.

Man is the worlds high Priest: he doth present
The sacrifice for all; while they below
Unto the service mutter an assent,   15
Such as springs use that fall, and windes that blow.

He that to praise and laud thee doth refrain,
Doth not refrain unto himself alone,
But robs a thousand who would praise thee fain,
And doth commit a world of sinne in one.   20

The beasts say, Eat me: but, if beasts must teach,
The tongue is yours to eat, but mine to praise.
The trees say, Pull me: but the hand you stretch,
Is mine to write, as it is yours to raise.

Wherefore, most sacred Spirit, I here present   25
For me and all my fellows praise to thee:
And just it is that I should pay the rent,
Because the benefit accrues to me.

We all acknowledge both thy power and love
To be exact, transcendent, and divine;   30
Who dost so strongly and so sweetly move,
While all things have their will, yet none but thine.

For either thy command or thy permission
Lay hands on all: they are thy right and left.
The first puts on with speed and expedition;   35
The other curbs sinnes stealing pace and theft.

Nothing escapes them both; all must appeare,
And be dispos'd, and dress'd, and tun'd by thee,
Who sweetly temper'st all. If we could heare
Thy skill and art, what musick would it be!   40

Thou art in small things great, not small in any:
Thy even praise can neither rise, nor fall.
Thou art in all things one, in each thing many:
For thou art infinite in one and all.

Tempests are calm to thee; they know thy hand,   45
And hold it fast, as children do their fathers,
Which crie and follow. Thou hast made poore sand
Check the proud sea, ev'n when it swells and gathers.

Thy cupboard serves the world: the meat is set,
Where all may reach: no beast but knows his feed.   50
Birds teach us hawking; fishes have their net:
The great prey on the lesse, they on some weed.

Nothing ingendred doth prevent his meat:
Flies have their table spread, ere they appeare.
Some creatures have in winter what to eat;   55
Others do sleep, and envie not their cheer.

How finely dost thou times and seasons spin,
And make a twist checker'd with night and day!
Which as it lengthens windes, and windes us in,
As bouls go on, but turning all the way.   60

Each creature hath a wisdome for his good.
The pigeons feed their tender off-spring, crying,
When they are callow; but withdraw their food
When they are fledge, that need may teach them flying.

Bees work for man; and yet they never bruise   65
Their masters flower, but leave it, having done,
As fair as ever, and as fit to use;
So both the flower doth stay, and hony run.

Sheep eat the grasse, and dung the ground for more:
Trees after bearing drop their leaves for soil: 70
Springs vent their streams, and by expense get store:
Clouds cool by heat, and baths by cooling boil.

Who hath the vertue to expresse the rare
And curious vertues both of herbs and stones?
Is there an herb for that? O that thy care   75
Would show a root, that gives expressions!

And if an herb hath power, what have the starres?
A rose, besides his beautie, is a cure.
Doubtlesse our plagues and plentie, peace and warres
Are there much surer then our art is sure.   80

Thou hast hid metals: man may take them thence;
But at his perill: when he digs the place,
He makes a grave; as if the thing had sense,
And threatned man, that he should fill the space.

Ev'n poysons praise thee. Should a thing be lost? 85
Should creatures want for want of heed their due?
Since where are poysons, antidotes are most:
The help stands close, and keeps the fear in view.

The sea, which seems to stop the traveller,
Is by a ship the speedier passage made. 90
The windes, who think they rule the mariner,
Are rul'd by him, and taught to serve his trade.

And as thy house is full, so I adore
Thy curious art in marshalling thy goods.
The hills with health abound; the vales with store; 95
The South with marble; North with furres & woods.

Hard things are glorious; easie things good cheap.
The common all men have; that which is rare
Men therefore seek to have, and care to keep.
The healthy frosts with summer-fruits compare. 100

Light without winde is glasse: warm without weight
Is wooll and furre: cool without closenesse, shade:
Speed without pains, a horse: tall without height,
A servile hawk: low without losse, a spade.

All countreys have enough to serve their need: 105
If they seek fine things, thou dost make them run
For their offence; and then dost turn their speed
To be commerce and trade from sunne to sunne.

Nothing wears clothes, but Man; nothing doth need
But he to wear them. Nothing useth fire, 110
But Man alone, to show his heav'nly breed:
And onely he hath fuell in desire.

When th' earth was dry, thou mad'st a sea of wet:
When that lay gather'd, thou didst broach the mountains:
When yet some places could no moisture get, 115
The windes grew gard'ners, and the clouds good fountains.

Rain, do not hurt my flowers; but gently spend
Your hony drops: presse not to smell them here:
When they are ripe, their odour will ascend,
And at your lodging with their thanks appeare.   120

How harsh are thorns to pears! and yet they make
A better hedge, and need lesse reparation.
How smooth are silks compared with a stake,
Or with a stone! yet make no good foundation.

Sometimes thou dost divide thy gifts to man,   125
Sometimes unite. The Indian nut alone
Is clothing, meat and trencher, drink and can,
Boat, cable, sail and needle, all in one.

Most herbs that grow in brooks, are hot and dry.
Cold fruits warm kernells help against the winde.   130
The lemmons juice and rinde cure mutually.
The whey of milk doth loose, the milk doth binde.

Thy creatures leap not, but expresse a feast,
Where all the guests sit close, and nothing wants.
Frogs marry fish and flesh; bats, bird and beast;   135
Sponges, non-sense and sense; mines, th' earth & plants.

To show thou art not bound, as if thy lot
Were worse then ours, sometimes thou shiftest hands.
Most things move th' under-jaw; the Crocodile not.
Most things sleep lying; th' Elephant leans or stands.   140

But who hath praise enough? nay, who hath any?
None can expresse thy works, but he that knows them:
And none can know thy works, which are so many,
And so complete, but onely he that owes them.

All things that are, though they have sev'rall wayes,   145
Yet in their being joyn with one advise
To honour thee: and so I give thee praise
In all my other hymnes, but in this twice.

Each thing that is, although in use and name
It go for one, hath many wayes in store   150
To honour thee; and so each hymne thy fame
Extolleth many wayes, yet this one more.

Hope

I gave to Hope a watch of mine: but he
                    An anchor gave to me.
Then an old prayer-book I did present:
                    And he an optick sent.
With that I gave a viall full of tears: 5
                    But he a few green eares.
Ah Loyterer! I'le no more, no more I'le bring:
                    I did expect a ring.

Sinnes round

Sorrie I am, my God, sorrie I am,
That my offences course it in a ring.
My thoughts are working like a busie flame,
Untill their cockatrice they hatch and bring:
And when they once have perfected their draughts,   5
My words take fire from my inflamed thoughts.

My words take fire from my inflamed thoughts,
Which spit it forth like the Sicilian Hill.
They vent the wares, and passe them with their faults,
And by their breathing ventilate the ill.   10
But words suffice not, where are lewd intentions:
My hands do joyn to finish the inventions.

My hands do joyn to finish the inventions:
And so my sinnes ascend three stories high,
As Babel grew, before there were dissensions.   15
Yet ill deeds loyter not: for they supplie
New thoughts of sinning: wherefore, to my shame,
Sorrie I am, my God, sorrie I am.

Time

Meeting with Time, Slack thing, said I,
Thy sithe is dull; whet it for shame.
No marvell Sir, he did replie,
If it at length deserve some blame:
    But where one man would have me grinde it,   5
    Twentie for one too sharp do finde it.

Perhaps some such of old did passe,
Who above all things lov'd this life;
To whom thy sithe a hatchet was,
Which now is but a pruning-knife.   10
    Christs coming hath made man thy debter,
    Since by thy cutting he grows better.

And in his blessing thou art blest:
For where thou onely wert before
An executioner at best;   15
Thou art a gard'ner now, and more,
    An usher to convey our souls
    Beyond the utmost starres and poles.

And this is that makes life so long,
While it detains us from our God.   20
Ev'n pleasures here increase the wrong,
And length of dayes lengthen the rod.
    Who wants the place, where God doth dwell,
    Partakes already half of hell.

Of what strange length must that needs be,   25
Which ev'n eternitie excludes!
Thus farre Time heard me patiently:
Then chafing said, This man deludes:
    What do I here before his doore?
    He doth not crave lesse time, but more.   30

Gratefulnesse

Thou that hast giv'n so much to me,
Give one thing more, a gratefull heart.
See how thy beggar works on thee
        By art.

He makes thy gifts occasion more,   5
And sayes, If he in this be crost,
All thou hast giv'n him heretofore
        Is lost.

But thou didst reckon, when at first
Thy word our hearts and hands did crave,   10
What it would come to at the worst
        To save.

Perpetuall knockings at thy doore,
Tears sullying thy transparent rooms,
Gift upon gift, much would have more,   15
        And comes.

This notwithstanding, thou wentst on,
And didst allow us all our noise:
Nay, thou hast made a sigh and grone
        Thy joyes.   20

Not that thou hast not still above
Much better tunes, then grones can make;
But that these countrey-aires thy love
        Did take.

Wherefore I crie, and crie again;   25
And in no quiet canst thou be,
Till I a thankfull heart obtain
        Of thee:

Not thankfull, when it pleaseth me;
As if thy blessings had spare dayes: 30
But such a heart, whose pulse may be
        Thy praise.

Peace

Sweet Peace, where dost thou dwell? I humbly crave,
          Let me once know.
    I sought thee in a secret cave,
        And ask'd, if Peace were there.
A hollow winde did seem to answer, No: 5
        Go seek elsewhere.

I did; and going did a rainbow note:
          Surely, thought I,
    This is the lace of Peaces coat:
        I will search out the matter.   10
But while I lookt, the clouds immediately
        Did break and scatter.

Then went I to a garden, and did spy
          A gallant flower,
    The Crown Imperiall: Sure, said I,   15
        Peace at the root must dwell.
But when I digg'd, I saw a worm devoure
        What show'd so well.

At length I met a rev'rend good old man,
          Whom when for Peace   20
    I did demand, he thus began:
        There was a Prince of old
At Salem dwelt, who liv'd with good increase
        Of flock and fold.

He sweetly liv'd; yet sweetnesse did not save   25
          His life from foes.
    But after death out of his grave
        There sprang twelve stalks of wheat:
Which many wondring at, got some of those
        To plant and set.   30

It prosper'd strangely, and did soon disperse
          Through all the earth:
    For they that taste it do rehearse,

That vertue lies therein,
A secret vertue bringing peace and mirth　　　　35
　　　　By flight of sinne.

Take of this grain, which in my garden grows,
　　　　And grows for you;
　　Make bread of it: and that repose
　　　　And peace, which ev'ry where　　　　40
With so much earnestnesse you do pursue,
　　　　Is onely there.

Confession

　　　O what a cunning guest
Is this same grief! within my heart I made
　　Closets; and in them many a chest;
　　And, like a master in my trade,
In those chests, boxes; in each box, a till:　　　5
Yet grief knows all, and enters when he will.

　　　No scrue, no piercer can
Into a piece of timber work and winde,
　　As Gods afflictions into man,
　　When he a torture hath design'd.
They are too subtill for the subt'llest hearts;　　10
And fall, like rheumes, upon the tendrest parts.

　　　We are the earth; and they,
Like moles within us, heave, and cast about:
　　And till they foot and clutch their prey,
　　They never cool, much lesse give out.　　15
No smith can make such locks but they have keyes:
Closets are halls to them; and hearts, high-wayes.

　　　Onely an open breast
Doth shut them out, so that they cannot enter;
　　Or, if they enter, cannot rest,
　　But quickly seek some new adventure.　　20
Smooth open hearts no fastning have; but fiction
Doth give a hold and handle to affliction.

Wherefore my faults and sinnes,   25
Lord, I acknowledge; take thy plagues away:
For since confession pardon winnes,
I challenge here the brightest day,
The clearest diamond: let them do their best,
They shall be thick and cloudie to my breast.   30

Giddinesse

Oh, what a thing is man! how farre from power,
    From setled peace and rest!
He is some twentie sev'rall men at least
    Each sev'rall houre.

One while he counts of heav'n, as of his treasure: 5
    But then a thought creeps in,
And calls him coward, who for fear of sinne
    Will lose a pleasure.

Now he will fight it out, and to the warres;
    Now eat his bread in peace,   10
And snudge in quiet: now he scorns increase;
    Now all day spares.

He builds a house, which quickly down must go,
    As if a whirlwinde blew
And crusht the building: and it's partly true,   15
    His minde is so.

O what a sight were Man, if his attires
    Did alter with his minde;
And like a Dolphins skinne, his clothes combin'd
    With his desires!   20

Surely if each one saw anothers heart,
    There would be no commerce,
No sale or bargain passe: all would disperse,
    And live apart.

Lord, mend or rather make us: one creation 25
Will not suffice our turn:
Except thou make us dayly, we shall spurn
Our own salvation.

The Bunch of Grapes

Joy, I did lock thee up: but some bad man
Hath let thee out again:
And now, me thinks, I am where I began
Sev'n yeares ago: one vogue and vein,
One aire of thoughts usurps my brain. 5
I did towards Canaan draw; but now I am
Brought back to the Red sea, the sea of shame.

For as the Jews of old by Gods command
Travell'd, and saw no town;
So now each Christian hath his journeys spann'd: 10
Their storie pennes and sets us down.
A single deed is small renown.
Gods works are wide, and let in future times;
His ancient justice overflows our crimes.

Then have we too our guardian fires and clouds; 15
Our Scripture-dew drops fast:
We have our sands and serpents, tents and shrowds;
Alas! our murmurings come not last.
But where's the cluster? where's the taste
Of mine inheritance? Lord, if I must borrow, 20
Let me as well take up their joy, as sorrow.

But can he want the grape, who hath the wine?
I have their fruit and more.
Blessed be God, who prosper'd *Noahs* vine,
And made it bring forth grapes good store. 25
But much more him I must adore,
Who of the Laws sowre juice sweet wine did make,
Ev'n God himself being pressed for my sake.

Love unknown

Deare Friend, sit down, the tale is long and sad:
And in my faintings I presume your love
Will more complie then help. A Lord I had,
And have, of whom some grounds, which may improve,
I hold for two lives, and both lives in me.   5
To him I brought a dish of fruit one day,
And in the middle plac'd my heart. But he
                              (I sigh to say)
Lookt on a servant, who did know his eye
Better then you know me, or (which is one)   10
Then I my self. The servant instantly
Quitting the fruit, seiz'd on my heart alone,
And threw it in a font, wherein did fall
A stream of bloud, which issu'd from the side
Of a great rock: I well remember all,   15
And have good cause: there it was dipt and dy'd,
And washt, and wrung: the very wringing yet
Enforceth tears. *Your heart was foul, I fear.*
Indeed 'tis true. I did and do commit
Many a fault more then my lease will bear;   20
Yet still askt pardon, and was not deni'd.
But you shall heare. After my heart was well,
And clean and fair, as I one even-tide
                              (I sigh to tell)
Walkt by my self abroad, I saw a large   25
And spacious fornace flaming, and thereon
A boyling caldron, round about whose verge
Was in great letters set *AFFLICTION.*
The greatnesse shew'd the owner. So I went
To fetch a sacrifice out of my fold,   30
Thinking with that, which I did thus present,
To warm his love, which I did fear grew cold.
But as my heart did tender it, the man,
Who was to take it from me, slipt his hand,
And threw my heart into the scalding pan;   35
My heart, that brought it (do you understand?)
The offerers heart. *Your heart was hard, I fear.*
Indeed it's true. I found a callous matter

Began to spread and to expatiate there:
But with a richer drug then scalding water   40
I bath'd it often, ev'n with holy bloud,
Which at a board, while many drunk bare wine,
A friend did steal into my cup for good,
Ev'n taken inwardly, and most divine
To supple hardnesses. But at the length   45
Out of the caldron getting, soon I fled
Unto my house, where to repair the strength
Which I had lost, I hasted to my bed.
But when I thought to sleep out all these faults
                    (I sigh to speak)   50
I found that some had stuff'd the bed with thoughts,
I would say *thorns*. Deare, could my heart not break,
When with my pleasures ev'n my rest was gone?
Full well I understood, who had been there:
For I had giv'n the key to none, but one: 55
It must be he. *Your heart was dull, I fear.*
Indeed a slack and sleepie state of minde
Did oft possesse me, so that when I pray'd,
Though my lips went, my heart did stay behinde.
But all my scores were by another paid,   60
Who took the debt upon him. *Truly, Friend,*
For ought I heare, your Master shows to you
More favour then you wot of. Mark the end.
The Font did onely, what was old, renew:
The Caldron suppled, what was grown too hard: 65
The Thorns did quicken, what was grown too dull:
All did but strive to mend, what you had marr'd.
Wherefore be cheer'd, and praise him to the full
Each day, each houre, each moment of the week,
Who fain would have you be new, tender, quick.   70

Mans medley

Heark, how the birds do sing,
            And woods do ring.
All creatures have their joy: and man hath his.

Yet if we rightly measure,
   Mans joy and pleasure   5
Rather hereafter, then in present, is.

To this life things of sense
   Make their pretence:
In th' other Angels have a right by birth:
   Man ties them both alone,   10
   And makes them one,
With th' one hand touching heav'n, with th' other earth.

In soul he mounts and flies,
   In flesh he dies.
He wears a stuffe whose thread is course and round,   15
   But trimm'd with curious lace,
   And should take place
After the trimming, not the stuffe and ground.

Not that he may not here
   Taste of the cheer,   20
But as birds drink, and straight lift up their head,
   So he must sip and think
   Of better drink
He may attain to, after he is dead.

But as his joyes are double;   25
   So is his trouble.
He hath two winters, other things but one:
   Both frosts and thoughts do nip,
   And bite his lip;
And he of all things fears two deaths alone.   30

Yet ev'n the greatest griefs
   May be reliefs,
Could he but take them right, and in their wayes.
   Happie is he, whose heart
   Hath found the art   35
To turn his double pains to double praise.

The Storm

If as the windes and waters here below
        Do flie and flow,
My sighs and tears as busie were above;
        Sure they would move
And much affect thee, as tempestuous times   5
Amaze poore mortals, and object their crimes.

Starres have their storms, ev'n in a high degree,
        As well as we.
A throbbing conscience spurred by remorse
        Hath a strange force: 10
It quits the earth, and mounting more and more
Dares to assault thee, and besiege thy doore.

There it stands knocking, to thy musicks wrong,
        And drowns the song.
Glorie and honour are set by, till it   15
        An answer get.
Poets have wrong'd poore storms: such dayes are best;
They purge the aire without, within the breast.

Paradise

I blesse thee, Lord, because I GROW
Among thy trees, which in a ROW
To thee both fruit and order OW.

What open force, or hidden CHARM
Can blast my fruit, or bring me HARM,   5
While the inclosure is thine ARM?

Inclose me still for fear I START.
Be to me rather sharp and TART,
Then let me want thy hand & ART.

When thou dost greater judgements SPARE,   10
And with thy knife but prune and PARE,
Ev'n fruitfull trees more fruitfull ARE.

Such sharpnes shows the sweetest FREND:
Such cuttings rather heal then REND:
And such beginnings touch their END.   15

The Method

Poore heart, lament.
For since thy God refuseth still,
There is some rub, some discontent,
Which cools his will.

Thy Father could   5
Quickly effect, what thou dost move;
For he is *Power*: and sure he would;
For he is *Love*.

Go search this thing,
Tumble thy breast, and turn thy book.   10
If thou hadst lost a glove or ring,
Wouldst thou not look?

What do I see
Written above there? *Yesterday*
I did behave me carelesly,   15
When I did pray.

And should Gods eare
To such indifferents chained be,
Who do not their own motions heare?
Is God lesse free?   20

But stay! what's there?
Late when I would have something done,
I had a motion to forbear,
Yet I went on.

And should Gods eare,   25
Which needs not man, be ty'd to those
Who heare not him, but quickly heare
His utter foes?

Then once more pray:
Down with thy knees, up with thy voice.   30
Seek pardon first, and God will say,
Glad heart rejoyce.

Divinitie

As men, for fear the starres should sleep and nod,
And trip at night, have spheres suppli'd;
As if a starre were duller then a clod,
Which knows his way without a guide:

Just so the other heav'n they also serve,   5
Divinities transcendent skie:
Which with the edge of wit they cut and carve.
Reason triumphs, and faith lies by.

Could not that Wisdome, which first broacht the wine,
Have thicken'd it with definitions?   10
And jagg'd his seamlesse coat, had that been fine,
With curious questions and divisions?

But all the doctrine, which he taught and gave,
Was cleare as heav'n, from whence it came.
At least those beams of truth, which onely save,   15
Surpasse in brightnesse any flame.

Love God, and love your neighbour. Watch and pray.
Do as ye would be done unto.
O dark instructions; ev'n as dark as day!
Who can these Gordian knots undo?   20

But he doth bid us take his bloud for wine.
Bid what he please; yet I am sure,
To take and taste what he doth there designe,
Is all that saves, and not obscure.

Then burn thy Epicycles, foolish man;   25
      Break all thy spheres, and save thy head.
Faith needs no staffe of flesh, but stoutly can
      To heav'n alone both go, and leade.

Ephes. 4. 30

Grieve not the Holy Spirit, &c

And art thou grieved, sweet and sacred Dove,
      When I am sowre,
      And crosse thy love?
Grieved for me? the God of strength and power
      Griev'd for a worm, which when I tread,   5
      I passe away and leave it dead?

Then weep mine eyes, the God of love doth grieve:
      Weep foolish heart,
      And weeping live:
For death is drie as dust. Yet if ye part,   10
      End as the night, whose sable hue
      Your sinnes expresse; melt into dew.

When sawcie mirth shall knock or call at doore,
      Cry out, Get hence,
      Or cry no more.   15
Almightie God doth grieve, he puts on sense:
      I sinne not to my grief alone,
      But to my Gods too; he doth grone.

Oh take thy lute, and tune it to a strain,
      Which may with thee   20
      All day complain.
There can no discord but in ceasing be.
      Marbles can weep; and surely strings
      More bowels have, then such hard things.

Lord, I adjudge my self to tears and grief,   25
      Ev'n endlesse tears
      Without relief.

If a cleare spring for me no time forbears,
    But runnes, although I be not drie;
    I am no Crystall, what shall I?   30

Yet if I wail not still, since still to wail
    Nature denies;
    And flesh would fail,
If my deserts were masters of mine eyes:
    Lord, pardon, for thy Sonne makes good   35
    My want of tears with store of bloud.

The Familie

What doth this noise of thoughts within my heart,
    As if they had a part?
What do these loud complaints and puling fears,
    As if there were no rule or eares?

But, Lord, the house and familie are thine,   5
    Though some of them repine.
Turn out these wranglers, which defile thy seat:
    For where thou dwellest all is neat.

First Peace and Silence all disputes controll,
    Then Order plaies the soul;   10
And giving all things their set forms and houres,
    Makes of wilde woods sweet walks and bowres.

Humble Obedience neare the doore doth stand,
    Expecting a command:
Then whom in waiting nothing seems more slow,   15
    Nothing more quick when she doth go.

Joyes oft are there, and griefs as oft as joyes;
    But griefs without a noise:
Yet speak they louder then distemper'd fears.
    What is so shrill as silent tears?   20

This is thy house, with these it doth abound:
    And where these are not found,

Perhaps thou com'st sometimes, and for a day;
But not to make a constant stay.

The Size

Content thee, greedie heart.
Modest and moderate joyes to those, that have
Title to more hereafter when they part,
   Are passing brave.
  Let th' upper springs into the low   5
  Descend and fall, and thou dost flow.

What though some have a fraught
Of cloves and nutmegs, and in cinamon sail;
If thou hast wherewithall to spice a draught,
   When griefs prevail;   10
  And for the future time art heir
  To th' Isle of spices, is 't not fair?

To be in both worlds full
Is more then God was, who was hungrie here.
Wouldst thou his laws of fasting disanull?   15
   Enact good cheer?
  Lay out thy joy, yet hope to save it?
  Wouldst thou both eat thy cake, and have it?

Great joyes are all at once;
But little do reserve themselves for more: 20
Those have their hopes; these what they have renounce,
   And live on score:
  Those are at home; these journey still,
  And meet the rest on Sions hill.

Thy Saviour sentenc'd joy,   25
And in the flesh condemn'd it as unfit,
At least in lump: for such doth oft destroy;
   Whereas a bit
  Doth tice us on to hopes of more,
  And for the present health restore.   30

A Christians state and case
Is not a corpulent, but a thinne and spare,
Yet active strength: whose long and bonie face
    Content and care
  Do seem to equally divide,   35
  Like a pretender, not a bride.

    Wherefore sit down, good heart;
Grasp not at much, for fear thou losest all.
If comforts fell according to desert,
    They would great frosts and snows destroy: 40
  For we should count, Since the last joy.

    Then close again the seam,
Which thou hast open'd: do not spread thy robe
In hope of great things. Call to minde thy dream,
    An earthly globe,   45
  On whose meridian was engraven,
  These seas are tears, and heav'n the haven.

Artillerie

As I one ev'ning sat before my cell,
Me thoughts a starre did shoot into my lap.
I rose, and shook my clothes, as knowing well,
That from small fires comes oft no small mishap.
    When suddenly I heard one say,   5
    Do as thou usest, disobey,
    Expell good motions from thy breast,
Which have the face of fire, but end in rest.

I, who had heard of musick in the spheres,
But not of speech in starres, began to muse: 10
But turning to my God, whose ministers
The starres and all things are; If I refuse,
    Dread Lord, said I, so oft my good;
    Then I refuse not ev'n with bloud
    To wash away my stubborn thought: 15
For I will do or suffer what I ought.

But I have also starres and shooters too,
Born where thy servants both artilleries use.
My tears and prayers night and day do wooe,
And work up to thee; yet thou dost refuse.   20
     Not but I am (I must say still)
     Much more oblig'd to do thy will,
     Then thou to grant mine: but because
Thy promise now hath ev'n set thee thy laws.

Then we are shooters both, and thou dost deigne   25
To enter combate with us, and contest
With thine own clay. But I would parley fain:
Shunne not my arrows, and behold my breast.
     Yet if thou shunnest, I am thine:
     I must be so, if I am mine.   30
     There is no articling with thee:
I am but finite, yet thine infinitely.

Church-rents and schismes

Brave rose, (alas!) where art thou? in the chair
Where thou didst lately so triumph and shine
A worm doth sit, whose many feet and hair
Are the more foul, the more thou wert divine.
This, this hath done it, this did bite the root   5
And bottome of the leaves: which when the winde
Did once perceive, it blew them under foot,
Where rude unhallow'd steps do crush and grinde
     Their beauteous glories. Onely shreds of thee,
     And those all bitten, in thy chair I see.   10

Why doth my Mother blush? is she the rose,
And shows it so? Indeed Christs precious bloud
Gave you a colour once; which when your foes
Thought to let out, the bleeding did you good,
And made you look much fresher then before.   15
But when debates and fretting jealousies
Did worm and work within you more and more,
Your colour vaded, and calamities
     Turned your ruddie into pale and bleak:
     Your health and beautie both began to break.   20

Then did your sev'rall parts unloose and start:
Which when your neighbours saw, like a north-winde
They rushed in, and cast them in the dirt
Where Pagans tread. O Mother deare and kinde,
Where shall I get me eyes enough to weep,   25
As many eyes as starres? since it is night,
And much of Asia and Europe fast asleep,
And ev'n all Africk; would at least I might
      With these two poore ones lick up all the dew,
      Which falls by night, and poure it out for you!   30

Justice (II)

O Dreadfull Justice, what a fright and terrour
           Wast thou of old,
           When sinne and errour
      Did show and shape thy looks to me,
        And through their glasse discolour thee!   5
He that did but look up, was proud and bold.

The dishes of thy ballance seem'd to gape,
           Like two great pits;
           The beam and scape
      Did like some torturing engine show;   10
      Thy hand above did burn and glow,
Danting the stoutest hearts, the proudest wits.

But now that Christs pure vail presents the sight,
           I see no fears:
           Thy hand is white,   15
      Thy scales like buckets, which attend
      And interchangeably descend,
Lifting to heaven from this well of tears.

For where before thou still didst call on me,
           Now I still touch   20
           And harp on thee.
      Gods promises have made thee mine;
      Why should I justice now decline?
Against me there is none, but for me much.

The Pilgrimage

I travell'd on, seeing the hill, where lay
           My expectation.
    A long it was and weary way.
    The gloomy cave of Desperation
I left on th' one, and on the other side   5
           The rock of Pride.

And so I came to Fancies medow strow'd
           With many a flower:
    Fain would I here have made abode,
    But I was quicken'd by my houre.   10
So to Cares cops I came, and there got through
           With much ado.

That led me to the wilde of Passion, which
           Some call the wold;
    A wasted place, but sometimes rich.   15
    Here I was robb'd of all my gold,
Save one good Angell, which a friend had ti'd
           Close to my side.

At length I got unto the gladsome hill,
           Where lay my hope,   20
    Where lay my heart; and climbing still,
    When I had gain'd the brow and top,
A lake of brackish waters on the ground
           Was all I found.

With that abash'd and struck with many a sting   25
           Of swarming fears,
    I fell, and cry'd, Alas my King!
    Can both the way and end be tears?
Yet taking heart I rose, and then perceiv'd
           I was deceiv'd: 30

My hill was further: so I flung away,
           Yet heard a crie
    Just as I went, *None goes that way*

And lives: If that be all, said I,
After so foul a journey death is fair,   35
            And but a chair.

The Holdfast

I threatned to observe the strict decree
    Of my deare God with all my power & might.
    But I was told by one, it could not be;
Yet I might trust in God to be my light.
Then will I trust, said I, in him alone.   5
    Nay, ev'n to trust in him, was also his:
    We must confesse that nothing is our own.
Then I confesse that he my succour is:
But to have nought is ours, not to confesse
    That we have nought. I stood amaz'd at this,   10
    Much troubled, till I heard a friend expresse,
That all things were more ours by being his.
    What Adam had, and forfeited for all,
    Christ keepeth now, who cannot fail or fall.

Complaining

        Do not beguile my heart,
            Because thou art
    My power and wisdome. Put me not to shame,
            Because I am
        Thy clay that weeps, thy dust that calls.   5

        Thou art the Lord of glorie;
            The deed and storie
    Are both thy due: but I a silly flie,
            That live or die
        According as the weather falls.   10

        Art thou all justice, Lord?
            Shows not thy word

More attributes? Am I all throat or eye,
To weep or crie?
Have I no parts but those of grief?   15

Let not thy wrathfull power
Afflict my houre,
My inch of life: or let thy gracious power
Contract my houre,
That I may climbe and finde relief.   20

The Discharge

Busie enquiring heart, what wouldst thou know?
Why dost thou prie,
And turn, and leer, and with a licorous eye
Look high and low;
And in thy lookings stretch and grow?   5

Hast thou not made thy counts, and summ'd up all?
Did not thy heart
Give up the whole, and with the whole depart?
Let what will fall:
That which is past who can recall?   10

Thy life is Gods, thy time to come is gone,
And is his right.
He is thy night at noon: he is at night
Thy noon alone.
The crop is his, for he hath sown.   15

And well it was for thee, when this befell,
That God did make
Thy businesse his, and in thy life partake:
For thou canst tell,
If it be his once, all is well.   20

Onely the present is thy part and fee.
And happy thou,
If, though thou didst not beat thy future brow,

Thou couldst well see
What present things requir'd of thee. 25

They ask enough; why shouldst thou further go?
Raise not the mudde
Of future depths, but drink the cleare and good.
Dig not for wo
In times to come; for it will grow. 30

Man and the present fit: if he provide,
He breaks the square.
This houre is mine: if for the next I care,
I grow too wide,
And do encroach upon deaths side. 35

For death each houre environs and surrounds.
He that would know
And care for future chances, cannot go
Unto those grounds, [40
But through a Church-yard which them bounds.

Things present shrink and die: but they that spend
Their thoughts and sense
On future grief, do not remove it thence,
But it extend,
And draw the bottome out an end. 45

God chains the dog till night: wilt loose the chain,
And wake thy sorrow?
Wilt thou forestall it, and now grieve to morrow,
And then again
Grieve over freshly all thy pain? 50

Either grief will not come: or if it must,
Do not forecast.
And while it cometh, it is almost past.
Away distrust:
My God hath promis'd; he is just. 55

Praise (II)

King of Glorie, King of Peace,
    I will love thee:
And that love may never cease,
    I will move thee.

Thou hast granted my request,   5
    Thou hast heard me:
Thou didst note my working breast,
    Thou hast spar'd me.

Wherefore with my utmost art
    I will sing thee,   10
And the cream of all my heart
    I will bring thee.

Though my sinnes against me cried,
    Thou didst cleare me;
And alone, when they replied,   15
    Thou didst heare me.

Sev'n whole dayes, not one in seven,
    I will praise thee.
In my heart, though not in heaven,
    I can raise thee.   20

Thou grew'st soft and moist with tears,
    Thou relentedst:
And when Justice call'd for fears,
    Thou dissentedst.

Small it is, in this poore sort   25
    To enroll thee:
Ev'n eternitie is too short
    To extoll thee.

An Offering

Come, bring thy gift. If blessings were as slow
As mens returns, what would become of fools?
What hast thou there? a heart? but is it pure?
Search well and see; for hearts have many holes.
Yet one pure heart is nothing to bestow: 5
In Christ two natures met to be thy cure.

O that within us hearts had propagation,
Since many gifts do challenge many hearts!
Yet one, if good, may title to a number;
And single things grow fruitfull by deserts.   10
In publick judgements one may be a nation,
And fence a plague, while others sleep and slumber.

But all I fear is lest thy heart displease,
As neither good, nor one: so oft divisions
Thy lusts have made, and not thy lusts alone;   15
Thy passions also have their set partitions.
These parcell out thy heart: recover these,
And thou mayst offer many gifts in one.

There is a balsome, or indeed a bloud,
Dropping from heav'n, which doth both cleanse and close
All sorts of wounds; of such strange force it is.   [20
Seek out this All-heal, and seek no repose,
Untill thou finde and use it to thy good:
Then bring thy gift, and let thy hymne be this;

       Since my sadnesse   25
       Into gladnesse
Lord thou dost convert,
        O accept
       What thou hast kept,
As thy due desert.   30

Had I many,
Had I any,
(For this heart is none)
All were thine
And none of mine: 35
Surely thine alone.

Yet thy favour
May give savour
To this poore oblation;
And it raise   40
To be thy praise,
And be my salvation.

Longing

With sick and famisht eyes,
With doubling knees and weary bones,
To thee my cries,
To thee my grones,
To thee my sighs, my tears ascend: 5
No end?

My throat, my soul is hoarse;
My heart is wither'd like a ground
Which thou dost curse.
My thoughts turn round,   10
And make me giddie; Lord, I fall,
Yet call.

From thee all pitie flows.
Mothers are kinde, because thou art,
And dost dispose   15
To them a part:
Their infants, them; and they suck thee
More free.

Bowels of pitie, heare!
Lord of my soul, love of my minde,   20
Bow down thine eare!

Let not the winde
Scatter my words, and in the same
Thy name!

Look on my sorrows round!   25
Mark well my furnace! O what flames,
What heats abound!
What griefs, what shames!
Consider, Lord; Lord, bow thine eare,
And heare!   30

Lord Jesu, thou didst bow
Thy dying head upon the tree:
O be not now
More dead to me!
Lord heare! *Shall he that made the eare,*   35
Not heare?

Behold, thy dust doth stirre,
It moves, it creeps, it aims at thee:
Wilt thou deferre
To succour me,   40
Thy pile of dust, wherein each crumme
Sayes, Come?

To thee help appertains.
Hast thou left all things to their course,
And laid the reins   45
Upon the horse?
Is all lockt? hath a sinners plea
No key?

Indeed the world's thy book,
Where all things have their leafe assign'd: 50
Yet a meek look
Hath interlin'd.
Thy board is full, yet humble guests
Finde nests.

Thou tarriest, while I die,　　　　　　55
And fall to nothing: thou dost reigne,
　　　　　And rule on high,
　　　　　While I remain
In bitter grief: yet am I stil'd
　　　　　　Thy childe.　　　　　60

　　　Lord, didst thou leave thy throne,
Not to relieve? how can it be,
　　　　　That thou art grown
　　　　　Thus hard to me?
Were sinne alive, good cause there were　　65
　　　　　　To bear.

　　　But now both sinne is dead,
And all thy promises live and bide.
　　　　　That wants his head;
　　　　　These speak and chide,　　70
And in thy bosome poure my tears,
　　　　　As theirs.

　　　Lord JESU, heare my heart,
Which hath been broken now so long,
　　　　　That ev'ry part　　　75
　　　　　Hath got a tongue!
Thy beggars grow; rid them away
　　　　　To day.

　　　My love, my sweetnesse, heare!
By these thy feet, at which my heart　　80
　　　　　Lies all the yeare,
　　　　　Pluck out thy dart,
And heal my troubled breast which cryes,
　　　　　Which dyes.

The Bag

Away despair! my gracious Lord doth heare.
　　　Though windes and waves assault my keel,

He doth preserve it: he doth steer,
　　Ev'n when the boat seems most to reel.
　　Storms are the triumph of his art:　　5
Well may he close his eyes, but not his heart.

Hast thou not heard, that my Lord Jesus di'd?
　　Then let me tell thee a strange storie.
　　The God of power, as he did ride
　　In his majestick robes of glorie,　　10
　　Resolv'd to light; and so one day
He did descend, undressing all the way.

The starres his tire of light and rings obtain'd,
　　The cloud his bow, the fire his spear,
　　The sky his azure mantle gain'd.　　15
　　And when they ask'd, what he would wear;
　　He smil'd and said as he did go,
He had new clothes a making here below.

When he was come, as travellers are wont,
　　He did repair unto an inne.　　20
　　Both then, and after, many a brunt
　　He did endure to cancell sinne:
　　And having giv'n the rest before,
Here he gave up his life to pay our score.

But as he was returning, there came one　　25
　　That ran upon him with a spear.
　　He, who came hither all alone,
　　Bringing nor man, nor arms, nor fear,
　　Receiv'd the blow upon his side,
And straight he turn'd, and to his brethren cry'd,　　30

If ye have any thing to send or write,
　　I have no bag, but here is room:
　　Unto my Fathers hands and sight,
　　Beleeve me, it shall safely come.
　　That I shall minde, what you impart,　　35
Look, you may put it very neare my heart.

Or if hereafter any of my friends
    Will use me in this kinde, the doore
    Shall still be open; what he sends
    I will present, and somewhat more,   40
    Not to his hurt. Sighs will convey
Any thing to me. Harke, Despair away.

The Jews

    Poore nation, whose sweet sap and juice
Our cyens have purloin'd, and left you drie:
Whose streams we got by the Apostles sluce,
And use in baptisme, while ye pine and die:
Who by not keeping once, became a debter;   5
    And now by keeping lose the letter:

    Oh that my prayers! mine, alas!
Oh that some Angel might a trumpet sound;
At which the Church falling upon her face
Should crie so loud, untill the trump were drown'd,   10
And by that crie of her deare Lord obtain,
    That your sweet sap might come again!

The Collar

    I struck the board, and cry'd, No more.
        I will abroad.
    What? shall I ever sigh and pine?
My lines and life are free; free as the rode,
    Loose as the winde, as large as store.   5
        Shall I be still in suit?
    Have I no harvest but a thorn
    To let me bloud, and not restore
    What I have lost with cordiall fruit?
        Sure there was wine   10
Before my sighs did drie it: there was corn
        Before my tears did drown it.
    Is the yeare onely lost to me?

Have I no bayes to crown it?
No flowers, no garlands gay? all blasted?   15
All wasted?
Not so, my heart: but there is fruit,
And thou hast hands.
Recover all thy sigh-blown age
On double pleasures: leave thy cold dispute   20
Of what is fit, and not. Forsake thy cage,
Thy rope of sands,
Which pettie thoughts have made, and made to thee
Good cable, to enforce and draw,
And be thy law,   25
While thou didst wink and wouldst not see.
Away; take heed:
I will abroad.
Call in thy deaths head there: tie up thy fears.
He that forbears   30
To suit and serve his need,
Deserves his load.
But as I rav'd and grew more fierce and wilde
At every word,
Me thoughts I heard one calling, *Child!*   35
And I reply'd, *My Lord.*

The Glimpse

Whither away delight?
Thou cam'st but now; wilt thou so soon depart,
And give me up to night?
For many weeks of lingering pain and smart
But one half houre of comfort to my heart?   5

Me thinks delight should have
More skill in musick, and keep better time.
Wert thou a winde or wave,
They quickly go and come with lesser crime:
Flowers look about, and die not in their prime.   10

Thy short abode and stay
Feeds not, but addes to the desire of meat.

Lime begg'd of old, they say,
A neighbour spring to cool his inward heat;
Which by the springs accesse grew much more great.   15

In hope of thee my heart
Pickt here and there a crumme, and would not die;
But constant to his part,
When as my fears foretold this, did replie,
A slender thread a gentle guest will tie.   20

Yet if the heart that wept
Must let thee go, return when it doth knock.
Although thy heap be kept
For future times, the droppings of the stock
May oft break forth, and never break the lock.   25

If I have more to spinne,
The wheel shall go, so that thy stay be short.
Thou knowst how grief and sinne
Disturb the work. O make me not their sport,
Who by thy coming may be made a court!   30

Assurance

O spitefull bitter thought!
Bitterly spitefull thought! Couldst thou invent
So high a torture? Is such poyson bought?
Doubtlesse, but in the way of punishment.
When wit contrives to meet with thee,   5
No such rank poyson can there be.

Thou said'st but even now,
That all was not so fair, as I conceiv'd,
Betwixt my God and me; that I allow
And coin large hopes, but that I was deceiv'd: 10
Either the league was broke, or neare it;
And, that I had great cause to fear it.

And what to this? what more
Could poyson, if it had a tongue, expresse?
What is thy aim? wouldst thou unlock the doore   15
To cold despairs, and gnawing pensivenesse?
    Wouldst thou raise devils? I see, I know,
    I writ thy purpose long ago.

    But I will to my Father,
Who heard thee say it. O most gracious Lord,   20
If all the hope and comfort that I gather,
Were from my self, I had not half a word,
    Not half a letter to oppose
    What is objected by my foes.

    But thou art my desert: 25
And in this league, which now my foes invade,
Thou art not onely to perform thy part,
But also mine; as when the league was made
    Thou didst at once thy self indite,
    And hold my hand, while I did write.   30

    Wherefore if thou canst fail,
Then can thy truth and I: but while rocks stand,
And rivers stirre, thou canst not shrink or quail:
Yea, when both rocks and all things shall disband,
    Then shalt thou be my rock and tower,   35
    And make their ruine praise thy power.

    Now foolish thought go on,
Spin out thy thread, and make thereof a coat
To hide thy shame: for thou hast cast a bone
Which bounds on thee, and will not down thy throat: 40
    What for it self love once began,
    Now love and truth will end in man.

The Call

    Come, my Way, my Truth, my Life:
    Such a Way, as gives us breath:

Such a Truth, as ends all strife:
Such a Life, as killeth death.

Come, my Light, my Feast, my Strength: 5
Such a Light, as shows a feast:
Such a Feast, as mends in length:
Such a Strength, as makes his guest.

Come, my Joy, my Love, my Heart:
Such a Joy, as none can move: 10
Such a Love, as none can part:
Such a Heart, as joyes in love.

Clasping of hands

Lord, thou art mine, and I am thine,
If mine I am: and thine much more,
Then I or ought, or can be mine.
Yet to be thine, doth me restore;
So that again I now am mine,   5
And with advantage mine the more,
Since this being mine, brings with it thine,
And thou with me dost thee restore.
  If I without thee would be mine,
  I neither should be mine nor thine.   10

Lord, I am thine, and thou art mine:
So mine thou art, that something more
I may presume thee mine, then thine.
For thou didst suffer to restore
Not thee, but me, and to be mine,   15
And with advantage mine the more,
Since thou in death wast none of thine,
Yet then as mine didst me restore.
  O be mine still! still make me thine!
  Or rather make no Thine and Mine!   20

Praise (III)

Lord, I will mean and speak thy praise,
    Thy praise alone.
My busie heart shall spin it all my dayes:
    And when it stops for want of store,
Then will I wring it with a sigh or grone,   5
    That thou mayst yet have more.

When thou dost favour any action,
    It runnes, it flies:
All things concurre to give it a perfection.
    That which had but two legs before,   10
When thou dost blesse, hath twelve: one wheel doth rise
    To twentie then, or more.

But when thou dost on businesse blow,
    It hangs, it clogs:
Not all the teams of Albion in a row   15
    Can hale or draw it out of doore.
Legs are but stumps, and Pharaohs wheels but logs,
    And struggling hinders more.

Thousands of things do thee employ
    In ruling all   20
This spacious globe: Angels must have their joy,
    Devils their rod, the sea his shore,
The windes their stint: and yet when I did call,
    Thou heardst my call, and more.

I have not lost one single tear: 25
    But when mine eyes
Did weep to heav'n, they found a bottle there
    (As we have boxes for the poore)
Readie to take them in; yet of a size
    That would contain much more.   30

But after thou hadst slipt a drop
    From thy right eye,
(Which there did hang like streamers neare the top

Of some fair church, to show the sore
And bloudie battell which thou once didst trie)   35
    The glasse was full and more.

Wherefore I sing. Yet since my heart,
       Though press'd, runnes thin;
O that I might some other hearts convert,
    And so take up at use good store: 40
That to thy chest there might be coming in
    Both all my praise, and more!

Josephs coat

Wounded I sing, tormented I indite,
Thrown down I fall into a bed, and rest:
Sorrow hath chang'd its note: such is his will,
Who changeth all things, as him pleaseth best.
    For well he knows, if but one grief and smart   5
Among my many had his full career,
Sure it would carrie with it ev'n my heart,
And both would runne untill they found a biere
    To fetch the bodie; both being due to grief.
But he hath spoil'd the race; and giv'n to anguish   10
One of Joyes coats, ticing it with relief
To linger in me, and together languish.
    I live to shew his power, who once did bring
    My *joyes* to *weep*, and now my *griefs* to *sing*.

The Pulley

When God at first made man,
Having a glasse of blessings standing by;
Let us (said he) poure on him all we can:
Let the worlds riches, which dispersed lie,
    Contract into a span.   5

So strength first made a way;
Then beautie flow'd, then wisdome, honour, pleasure:

When almost all was out, God made a stay,
Perceiving that alone of all his treasure
      Rest in the bottome lay.   10

For if I should (said he)
Bestow this jewell also on my creature,
He would adore my gifts in stead of me,
And rest in Nature, not the God of Nature:
      So both should losers be.   15

Yet let him keep the rest,
But keep them with repining restlesnesse:
Let him be rich and wearie, that at least,
If goodnesse leade him not, yet wearinesse
      May tosse him to my breast.   20

The Priesthood

Blest Order, which in power dost so excell,
That with th' one hand thou liftest to the sky,
And with the other throwest down to hell
In thy just censures; fain would I draw nigh,
Fain put thee on, exchanging my lay-sword   5
      For that of th' holy Word.

But thou art fire, sacred and hallow'd fire;
And I but earth and clay: should I presume
To wear thy habit, the severe attire
My slender compositions might consume.   10
I am both foul and brittle; much unfit
      To deal in holy Writ.

Yet have I often seen, by cunning hand
And force of fire, what curious things are made
Of wretched earth. Where once I scorn'd to stand,   15
That earth is fitted by the fire and trade
Of skilfull artists, for the boards of those
      Who make the bravest shows.

But since those great ones, be they ne're so great,
Come from the earth, from whence those vessels come;   20
So that at once both feeder, dish, and meat
Have one beginning and one finall summe:
I do not greatly wonder at the sight,
            If earth in earth delight.

But th' holy men of God such vessels are,   25
As serve him up, who all the world commands:
When God vouchsafeth to become our fare,
Their hands convey him, who conveys their hands.
O what pure things, most pure must those things be,
            Who bring my God to me!   30

Wherefore I dare not, I, put forth my hand
To hold the Ark, although it seem to shake
Through th' old sinnes and new doctrines of our land.
Onely, since God doth often vessels make
Of lowly matter for high uses meet,   35
            I throw me at his feet.

There will I lie, untill my Maker seek
For some mean stuffe whereon to show his skill:
Then is my time. The distance of the meek
Doth flatter power. Lest good come short of ill   40
In praising might, the poore do by submission
            What pride by opposition.

The Search

Whither, O, whither art thou fled,
          My Lord, my Love?
My searches are my daily bread;
          Yet never prove.

My knees pierce th' earth, mine eies the skie;   5
          And yet the sphere
And centre both to me denie
          That thou art there.

Yet can I mark how herbs below
        Grow green and gay,   10
As if to meet thee they did know,
        While I decay.

Yet can I mark how starres above
        Simper and shine,
As having keyes unto thy love,   15
        While poore I pine.

I sent a sigh to seek thee out,
        Deep drawn in pain,
Wing'd like an arrow: but my scout
        Returns in vain.   20

I tun'd another (having store)
        Into a grone;
Because the search was dumbe before:
        But all was one.

Lord, dost thou some new fabrick mould,   25
        Which favour winnes,
And keeps thee present, leaving th' old
        Unto their sinnes?

Where is my God? what hidden place
        Conceals thee still?
What covert dare eclipse thy face?   30
        Is it thy will?

O let not that of any thing;
        Let rather brasse,
Or steel, or mountains be thy ring,   35
        And I will passe.

Thy will such an intrenching is,
        As passeth thought:
To it all strength, all subtilties
        Are things of nought.   40

Thy will such a strange distance is,
     As that to it
East and West touch, the poles do kisse,
     And parallels meet.

Since then my grief must be as large,   45
     As is thy space,
Thy distance from me; see my charge,
     Lord, see my case.

O take these barres, these lengths away;
     Turn, and restore me: 50
Be not Almightie, let me say,
     Against, but for me.

When thou dost turn, and wilt be neare;
     What edge so keen,
What point so piercing can appeare   55
     To come between?

For as thy absence doth excell
     All distance known:
So doth thy nearenesse bear the bell,
     Making two one.   60

Grief

O who will give me tears? Come all ye springs,
Dwell in my head & eyes: come clouds, & rain:
My grief hath need of all the watry things,
That nature hath produc'd. Let ev'ry vein
Suck up a river to supply mine eyes,   5
My weary weeping eyes, too drie for me,
Unlesse they get new conduits, new supplies
To bear them out, and with my state agree.
What are two shallow foords, two little spouts
Of a lesse world? the greater is but small,   10
A narrow cupboard for my griefs and doubts,
Which want provision in the midst of all.

Verses, ye are too fine a thing, too wise
For my rough sorrows: cease, be dumbe and mute,
Give up your feet and running to mine eyes,   15
And keep your measures for some lovers lute,
Whose grief allows him musick and a ryme:
For mine excludes both measure, tune, and time.
                Alas, my God!

The Crosse

      What is this strange and uncouth thing?
To make me sigh, and seek, and faint, and die,
Untill I had some place, where I might sing,
      And serve thee; and not onely I,
But all my wealth and familie might combine   5
To set thy honour up, as our designe.

      And then when after much delay,
Much wrastling, many a combate, this deare end,
So much desir'd, is giv'n, to take away
      My power to serve thee; to unbend   10
All my abilities, my designes confound,
And lay my threatnings bleeding on the ground.

      One ague dwelleth in my bones,
Another in my soul (the memorie
What I would do for thee, if once my grones   15
      Could be allow'd for harmonie):
I am in all a weak disabled thing,
Save in the sight thereof, where strength doth sting.

      Besides, things sort not to my will,
Ev'n when my will doth studie thy renown: 20
Thou turnest th' edge of all things on me still,
      Taking me up to throw me down:
So that, ev'n when my hopes seem to be sped,
I am to grief alive, to them as dead.

To have my aim, and yet to be 25
Further from it then when I bent my bow;
To make my hopes my torture, and the fee
  Of all my woes another wo,
Is in the midst of delicates to need,
And ev'n in Paradise to be a weed. 30

Ah my deare Father, ease my smart!
These contrarieties crush me: these crosse actions
Doe winde a rope about, and cut my heart:
  And yet since these thy contradictions
Are properly a crosse felt by thy Sonne, 35
With but foure words, my words, *Thy will be done*.

The Flower

How fresh, O Lord, how sweet and clean
Are thy returns! ev'n as the flowers in spring;
  To which, besides their own demean,
The late-past frosts tributes of pleasure bring.
    Grief melts away 5
    Like snow in May,
As if there were no such cold thing.

Who would have thought my shrivel'd heart
Could have recover'd greennesse? It was gone
  Quite under ground; as flowers depart 10
To see their mother-root, when they have blown;
    Where they together
    All the hard weather,
Dead to the world, keep house unknown.

These are thy wonders, Lord of power, 15
Killing and quickning, bringing down to hell
  And up to heaven in an houre;
Making a chiming of a passing-bell.
    We say amisse,
    This or that is: 20
Thy word is all, if we could spell.

O that I once past changing were,
Fast in thy Paradise, where no flower can wither!
Many a spring I shoot up fair,
Offring at heav'n, growing and groning thither: 25
            Nor doth my flower
            Want a spring-showre,
My sinnes and I joining together.

But while I grow in a straight line,
Still upwards bent, as if heav'n were mine own,   30
        Thy anger comes, and I decline:
What frost to that? what pole is not the zone,
            Where all things burn,
            When thou dost turn,
And the least frown of thine is shown?   35

And now in age I bud again,
After so many deaths I live and write;
I once more smell the dew and rain,
And relish versing: O my onely light,
            It cannot be   40
            That I am he
On whom thy tempests fell all night.

These are thy wonders, Lord of love,
To make us see we are but flowers that glide:
        Which when we once can finde and prove,   45
Thou hast a garden for us, where to bide.
            Who would be more,
            Swelling through store,
Forfeit their Paradise by their pride.

Dotage

False glozing pleasures, casks of happinesse,
Foolish night-fires, womens and childrens wishes,
Chases in Arras, guilded emptinesse,
Shadows well mounted, dreams in a career,
Embroider'd lyes, nothing between two dishes;   5
            These are the pleasures here.

True earnest sorrows, rooted miseries,
Anguish in grain, vexations ripe and blown,
Sure-footed griefs, solid calamities,
Plain demonstrations, evident and cleare,   10
Fetching their proofs ev'n from the very bone;
        These are the sorrows here.

But oh the folly of distracted men,
Who griefs in earnest, joyes in jest pursue;
Preferring, like brute beasts, a lothsome den   15
Before a court, ev'n that above so cleare,
Where are no sorrows, but delights more true
        Then miseries are here!

The Sonne

Let forrain nations of their language boast,
What fine varietie each tongue affords:
I like our language, as our men and coast:
Who cannot dresse it well, want wit, not words.
How neatly doe we give one onely name   5
To parents issue and the sunnes bright starre!
A sonne is light and fruit; a fruitfull flame
Chasing the fathers dimnesse, carri'd farre
From the first man in th' East, to fresh and new
Western discov'ries of posteritie.   10
So in one word our Lords humilitie
We turn upon him in a sense most true:
      For what Christ once in humblenesse began,
      We him in glorie call, *The Sonne of Man.*

A *true Hymne*

      My joy, my life, my crown!
      My heart was meaning all the day,
        Somewhat it fain would say:
And still it runneth mutt'ring up and down
With onely this, *My joy, my life, my crown.*   5

Yet slight not these few words:
If truly said, they may take part
Among the best in art.
The finenesse which a hymne or psalme affords,
Is, when the soul unto the lines accords.   10

He who craves all the minde,
And all the soul, and strength, and time,
If the words onely ryme,
Justly complains, that somewhat is behinde
To make his verse, or write a hymne in kinde.   15

Whereas if th' heart be moved,
Although the verse be somewhat scant,
God doth supplie the want.
As when th' heart sayes (sighing to be approved)
O, could I love! and stops: God writeth, Loved.   20

The Answer

My comforts drop and melt away like snow:
I shake my head, and all the thoughts and ends,
Which my fierce youth did bandie, fall and flow
Like leaves about me: or like summer friends,
Flyes of estates and sunne-shine. But to all,   5
Who think me eager, hot, and undertaking,
But in my prosecutions slack and small;
As a young exhalation, newly waking,
Scorns his first bed of dirt, and means the sky;
But cooling by the way, grows pursie and slow,   10
And setling to a cloud, doth live and die
In that dark state of tears: to all, that so
    Show me, and set me, I have one reply,
    Which they that know the rest, know more then I.

A Dialogue-Antheme

CHRISTIAN DEATH

Chr. Alas, poore Death, where is thy glorie?
    Where is thy famous force, thy ancient sting?
Dea. *Alas poore mortall, void of storie,*
    Go spell and reade how I have kill'd thy King.
Chr. Poore Death! and who was hurt thereby?   5
    Thy curse being laid on him, makes thee accurst.
Dea. *Let losers talk: yet thou shalt die;*
    These arms shall crush thee.
Chr.   Spare not, do thy worst.
    I shall be one day better then before: 10
    Thou so much worse, that thou shalt be no more.

The Water-course

Thou who dost dwell and linger here below,
Since the condition of this world is frail,
Where of all plants afflictions soonest grow;
If troubles overtake thee, do not wail:

   For who can look for lesse, that loveth $\begin{cases} \text{Life?} \\ \text{Strife?} \end{cases}$ 5

But rather turn the pipe and waters course
To serve thy sinnes, and furnish thee with store
Of sov'raigne tears, springing from true remorse:
That so in purenesse thou mayst him adore,

   Who gives to man, as he sees fit, $\begin{cases} \text{Salvation.} \\ \text{Damnation.} \end{cases}$ 10

Self-condemnation

Thou who condemnest Jewish hate,
For choosing Barrabas a murderer
       Before the Lord of glorie;
Look back upon thine own estate,

Call home thine eye (that busie wanderer): 5
    That choice may be thy storie.

  He that doth love, and love amisse,
This worlds delights before true Christian joy,
    Hath made a Jewish choice:
  The world an ancient murderer is; 10
Thousands of souls it hath and doth destroy
    With her enchanting voice.

  He that hath made a sorrie wedding
Between his soul and gold, and hath preferr'd
    False gain before the true, 15
  Hath done what he condemnes in reading:
For he hath sold for money his deare Lord,
    And is a Judas-Jew.

  Thus we prevent the last great day,
And judge our selves. That light, which sin & passion 20
    Did before dimme and choke,
  When once those snuffes are ta'ne away,
Shines bright and cleare, ev'n unto condemnation,
    Without excuse or cloke.

Bitter-sweet

    Ah my deare angrie Lord,
    Since thou dost love, yet strike;
    Cast down, yet help afford;
    Sure I will do the like.

    I will complain, yet praise; 5
    I will bewail, approve:
    And all my sowre-sweet dayes
    I will lament, and love.

The Glance

When first thy sweet and gracious eye
Vouchsaf'd ev'n in the midst of youth and night
To look upon me, who before did lie
        Weltring in sinne;
I felt a sugred strange delight,   5
Passing all cordials made by any art,
Bedew, embalme, and overrunne my heart,
        And take it in.

Since that time many a bitter storm
My soul hath felt, ev'n able to destroy,   10
Had the malicious and ill-meaning harm
        His swing and sway:
But still thy sweet originall joy,
Sprung from thine eye, did work within my soul,
And surging griefs, when they grew bold, controll,   15
        And got the day.

If thy first glance so powerfull be,
A mirth but open'd and seal'd up again;
What wonders shall we feel, when we shall see
        Thy full-ey'd love!   20
When thou shalt look us out of pain,
And one aspect of thine spend in delight
More than a thousand sunnes disburse in light,
        In heav'n above.

The 23d Psalme

The God of love my shepherd is,
        And he that doth me feed:
While he is mine, and I am his,
        What can I want or need?

He leads me to the tender grasse,   5
        Where I both feed and rest;

Then to the streams that gently passe:
    In both I have the best.

Or if I stray, he doth convert
    And bring my minde in frame: 10
And all this not for my desert,
    But for his holy name.

Yea, in deaths shadie black abode
    Well may I walk, not fear:
For thou art with me; and thy rod   15
    To guide, thy staffe to bear.

Nay, thou dost make me sit and dine,
    Ev'n in my enemies sight:
My head with oyl, my cup with wine
    Runnes over day and night.   20

Surely thy sweet and wondrous love
    Shall measure all my dayes;
And as it never shall remove,
    So neither shall my praise.

Marie Magdalene

When blessed Marie wip'd her Saviours feet,
(Whose precepts she had trampled on before)
And wore them for a jewell on her head,
    Shewing his steps should be the street,
    Wherein she thenceforth evermore   5
With pensive humblenesse would live and tread:

She being stain'd her self, why did she strive
To make him clean, who could not be defil'd?
Why kept she not her tears for her own faults,
    And not his feet? Though we could dive   10
    In tears like seas, our sinnes are pil'd
Deeper then they, in words, and works, and thoughts.

Deare soul, she knew who did vouchsafe and deigne
To bear her filth; and that her sinnes did dash
Ev'n God himself: wherefore she was not loth,   15
    As she had brought wherewith to stain,
    So to bring in wherewith to wash:
And yet in washing one, she washed both.

Aaron

    Holinesse on the head,
    Light and perfections on the breast,
Harmonious bells below, raising the dead
    To leade them unto life and rest:
        Thus are true Aarons drest.   5

    Profanenesse in my head,
    Defects and darknesse in my breast,
A noise of passions ringing me for dead
    Unto a place where is no rest:
        Poore priest thus am I drest.   10

    Onely another head
    I have, another heart and breast,
Another musick, making live not dead,
    Without whom I could have no rest:
        In him I am well drest.   15

    Christ is my onely head,
    My alone onely heart and breast,
My onely musick, striking me ev'n dead;
    That to the old man I may rest,
        And be in him new drest.   20

    So holy in my head,
    Perfect and light in my deare breast,
My doctrine tun'd by Christ, (who is not dead,
    But lives in me while I do rest)
        Come people; Aaron's drest.   25

The Odour. 2. Cor. 2. 15

How sweetly doth *My Master* sound! *My Master!*
  As Amber-greese leaves a rich sent
    Unto the taster:
  So do these words a sweet content,
An orientall fragrancie, *My Master.*   5

With these all day I do perfume my minde,
  My minde ev'n thrust into them both:
    That I might finde
  What cordials make this curious broth,
This broth of smells, that feeds and fats my minde. 10

My Master, shall I speak? O that to thee
  My servant were a little so,
    As flesh may be;
  That these two words might creep & grow
To some degree of spicinesse to thee!   15

Then should the Pomander, which was before
  A speaking sweet, mend by reflection,
    And tell me more:
  For pardon of my imperfection
Would warm and work it sweeter then before. 20

For when *My Master,* which alone is sweet,
  And ev'n in my unworthinesse pleasing,
    Shall call and meet,
  My servant, as thee not displeasing,
That call is but the breathing of the sweet. 25

This breathing would with gains by sweetning me
  (As sweet things traffick when they meet)
    Return to thee.
  And so this new commerce and sweet
Should all my life employ and busie me.   30

The Foil

> If we could see below
> The sphere of vertue, and each shining grace
> As plainly as that above doth show;
> This were the better skie, the brighter place.
>
> God hath made starres the foil   5
> To set off vertues; griefs to set off sinning:
> Yet in this wretched world we toil,
> As if grief were not foul, nor vertue winning.

The Forerunners

> The harbingers are come. See, see their mark;
> White is their colour, and behold my head.
> But must they have my brain? must they dispark
> Those sparkling notions, which therein were bred?
> Must dulnesse turn me to a clod?   5
> Yet have they left me, *Thou art still my God.*
>
> Good men ye be, to leave me my best room,
> Ev'n all my heart, and what is lodged there:
> I passe not, I, what of the rest become,
> So *Thou art still my God,* be out of fear.   10
> He will be pleased with that dittie;
> And if I please him, I write fine and wittie.
>
> Farewell sweet phrases, lovely metaphors.
> But will ye leave me thus? when ye before
> Of stews and brothels onely knew the doores,   15
> Then did I wash you with my tears, and more,
> Brought you to Church well drest and clad:
> My God must have my best, ev'n all I had.
>
> Lovely enchanting language, sugar-cane,
> Hony of roses, whither wilt thou flie?   20
> Hath some fond lover tic'd thee to thy bane?
> And wilt thou leave the Church, and love a stie?

Fie, thou wilt soil thy broider'd coat,
And hurt thy self, and him that sings the note.

Let foolish lovers, if they will love dung,   25
With canvas, not with arras, clothe their shame:
Let follie speak in her own native tongue.
True beautie dwells on high: ours is a flame
        But borrow'd thence to light us thither.
Beautie and beauteous words should go together.   30

Yet if you go, I passe not; take your way:
For, *Thou art still my God,* is all that ye
Perhaps with more embellishment can say.
Go birds of spring: let winter have his fee;
        Let a bleak palenesse chalk the doore,   35
So all within be livelier then before.

The Rose

Presse me not to take more pleasure
        In this world of sugred lies,
And to use a larger measure
        Then my strict, yet welcome size.

First, there is no pleasure here: 5
        Colour'd griefs indeed there are,
Blushing woes, that look as cleare
        As if they could beautie spare.

Or if such deceits there be,
        Such delights I meant to say;   10
There are no such things to me,
        Who have pass'd my right away.

But I will not much oppose
        Unto what you now advise:
Onely take this gentle rose,   15
        And therein my answer lies.

What is fairer then a rose?
        What is sweeter? yet it purgeth.
Purgings enmitie disclose,
        Enmitie forbearance urgeth.   20

If then all that worldlings prize
        Be contracted to a rose;
Sweetly there indeed it lies,
        But it biteth in the close.

So this flower doth judge and sentence   25
        Worldly joyes to be a scourge:
For they all produce repentance,
        And repentance is a purge.

But I health, not physick choose:
        Onely though I you oppose,   30
Say that fairly I refuse,
        For my answer is a rose.

Discipline

Throw away thy rod,
Throw away thy wrath:
        O my God,
Take the gentle path.

For my hearts desire   5
Unto thine is bent:
        I aspire
To a full consent.

Not a word or look
I affect to own,   10
        But by book,
And thy book alone.

Though I fail, I weep:
Though I halt in pace,

                    Yet I creep   15
To the throne of grace.

Then let wrath remove;
Love will do the deed:
                    For with love
Stonie hearts will bleed.   20

Love is swift of foot;
Love's a man of warre,
                    And can shoot,
And can hit from farre.

Who can scape his bow?   25
That which wrought on thee,
                    Brought thee low,
Needs must work on me.

Throw away thy rod;
Though man frailties hath,   30
                    Thou art God:
Throw away thy wrath.

The Invitation

Come ye hither All, whose taste
                    Is your waste;
Save your cost, and mend your fare.
God is here prepar'd and drest,
                    And the feast,   5
God, in whom all dainties are.

Come ye hither All, whom wine
                    Doth define,
Naming you not to your good:
Weep what ye have drunk amisse,   10
                    And drink this,
Which before ye drink is bloud.

Come ye hither All, whom pain
      Doth arraigne,
Bringing all your sinnes to sight: 15
Taste and fear not: God is here
      In this cheer,
And on sinne doth cast the fright.

Come ye hither All, whom joy
      Doth destroy,   20
While ye graze without your bounds:
Here is joy that drowneth quite
      Your delight,
As a floud the lower grounds.

Come ye hither All, whose love   25
      Is your dove,
And exalts you to the skie:
Here is love, which having breath
      Ev'n in death,
After death can never die.   30

Lord I have invited all,
      And I shall
Still invite, still call to thee:
For it seems but just and right
      In my sight,   35
Where is All, there All should be.

The Banquet

Welcome sweet and sacred cheer,
      Welcome deare;
With me, in me, live and dwell:
For thy neatnesse passeth sight,
      Thy delight   5
Passeth tongue to taste or tell.

O what sweetnesse from the bowl
      Fills my soul,

Such as is, and makes divine!
Is some starre (fled from the sphere) 10
  Melted there,
As we sugar melt in wine?

Or hath sweetnesse in the bread
  Made a head
To subdue the smell of sinne; 15
Flowers, and gummes, and powders giving
  All their living,
Lest the Enemy should winne?

Doubtlesse, neither starre nor flower
  Hath the power 20
Such a sweetnesse to impart:
Onely God, who gives perfumes,
  Flesh assumes,
And with it perfumes my heart.

But as Pomanders and wood 25
  Still are good,
Yet being bruis'd are better sented:
God, to show how farre his love
  Could improve,
Here, as broken, is presented. 30

When I had forgot my birth,
  And on earth
In delights of earth was drown'd;
God took bloud, and needs would be
  Spilt with me, 35
And so found me on the ground.

Having rais'd me to look up,
  In a cup
Sweetly he doth meet my taste.
But I still being low and short, 40
  Farre from court,
Wine becomes a wing at last.

For with it alone I flie
　　　　　To the skie:
Where I wipe mine eyes, and see　　　　45
What I seek, for what I sue;
　　　　　Him I view,
Who hath done so much for me.

Let the wonder of his pitie
　　　　　Be my dittie,　　　　50
And take up my lines and life:
Hearken under pain of death,
　　　　　Hands and breath;
Strive in this, and love the strife.

The Posie

Let wits contest,
And with their words and posies windows fill:
　　Lesse then the least
Of all thy mercies, is my posie still.

This on my ring,　　　　5
This by my picture, in my book I write:
　　Whether I sing,
Or say, or dictate, this is my delight.

Invention rest,
Comparisons go play, wit use thy will:　　　　10
　　Lesse then the least
Of all Gods mercies, is my posie still.

A Parodie

Souls joy, when thou art gone,
　　　　And I alone,
　　　　　Which cannot be,
Because thou dost abide with me,
　　And I depend on thee;　　　　5

Yet when thou dost suppresse
          The cheerfulnesse
          Of thy abode,
And in my powers not stirre abroad,
          But leave me to my load: 10

O what a damp and shade
          Doth me invade!
          No stormie night
Can so afflict or so affright,
          As thy eclipsed light.   15

Ah Lord! do not withdraw,
          Lest want of aw
          Make Sinne appeare;
And when thou dost but shine lesse cleare,
          Say, that thou art not here.   20

And then what life I have,
          While Sinne doth rave,
          And falsly boast,
That I may seek, but thou art lost;
          Thou and alone thou know'st.   25

O what a deadly cold
          Doth me infold!
          I half beleeve,
That Sinne sayes true: but while I grieve,
          Thou com'st and dost relieve.   30

The Elixir

Teach me, my God and King,
          In all things thee to see,
And what I do in any thing,
          To do it as for thee:

Not rudely, as a beast,   5
          To runne into an action;

But still to make thee prepossest,
   And give it his perfection.

A man that looks on glasse,
   On it may stay his eye;   10
Or if he pleaseth, through it passe,
   And then the heav'n espie.

All may of thee partake:
   Nothing can be so mean,
Which with his tincture (for thy sake)   15
   Will not grow bright and clean.

A servant with this clause
   Makes drudgerie divine:
Who sweeps a room, as for thy laws,
   Makes that and th' action fine.   20

This is the famous stone
   That turneth all to gold:
For that which God doth touch and own
   Cannot for lesse be told.

A Wreath

A wreathed garland of deserved praise,
Of praise deserved, unto thee I give,
I give to thee, who knowest all my wayes,
My crooked winding wayes, wherein I live,
Wherein I die, not live: for life is straight,   5
Straight as a line, and ever tends to thee,
To thee, who art more farre above deceit,
Then deceit seems above simplicitie.
Give me simplicitie, that I may live,
So live and like, that I may know, thy wayes,   10
Know them and practise them: then shall I give
For this poore wreath, give thee a crown of praise.

Death

Death, thou wast once an uncouth hideous thing,
    Nothing but bones,
   The sad effect of sadder grones:
Thy mouth was open, but thou couldst not sing.

For we consider'd thee as at some six   5
    Or ten yeares hence,
   After the losse of life and sense,
Flesh being turn'd to dust, and bones to sticks.

We lookt on this side of thee, shooting short;
    Where we did finde   10
   The shells of fledge souls left behinde,
Dry dust, which sheds no tears, but may extort.

But since our Saviours death did put some bloud
    Into thy face;
   Thou art grown fair and full of grace, 15
Much in request, much sought for as a good.

For we do now behold thee gay and glad,
    As at dooms-day;
   When souls shall wear their new aray,
And all thy bones with beautie shall be clad. 20

Therefore we can go die as sleep, and trust
    Half that we have
   Unto an honest faithfull grave;
Making our pillows either down, or dust.

Dooms-day

   Come away,
  Make no delay.
Summon all the dust to rise,
Till it stirre, and rubbe the eyes;

While this member jogs the other,   5
Each one whispring, *Live you brother?*

        Come away,
        Make this the day.
Dust, alas, no musick feels,
But thy trumpet: then it kneels,   10
As peculiar notes and strains
Cure Tarantulas raging pains.

        Come away,
        O make no stay!
Let the graves make their confession,   15
Lest at length they plead possession:
Fleshes stubbornnesse may have
Read that lesson to the grave.

        Come away,
        Thy flock doth stray.   20
Some to windes their bodie lend,
And in them may drown a friend:
Some in noisome vapours grow
To a plague and publick wo.

        Come away,   25
        Help our decay.
Man is out of order hurl'd,
Parcel'd out to all the world.
Lord, thy broken consort raise,
And the musick shall be praise.   30

Judgement

Almightie Judge, how shall poore wretches brook
        Thy dreadfull look,
Able a heart of iron to appall,
        When thou shalt call
For ev'ry mans peculiar book?   5

What others mean to do, I know not well;
           Yet I heare tell,
That some will turn thee to some leaves therein
           So void of sinne,
    That they in merit shall excell.   10

But I resolve, when thou shalt call for mine,
           That to decline,
And thrust a Testament into thy hand:
           Let that be scann'd.
    There thou shalt finde my faults are thine.   15

Heaven

O who will show me those delights on high?
        Echo.   I.
Thou Echo, thou art mortall, all men know.
        Echo.   No.
Wert thou not born among the trees and leaves?   5
        Echo.   Leaves.
And are there any leaves, that still abide?
        Echo.   Bide.
What leaves are they? impart the matter wholly.
        Echo.   Holy.   10
Are holy leaves the Echo then of blisse?
        Echo.   Yes.
Then tell me, what is that supreme delight?
        Echo.   Light.
Light to the minde: what shall the will enjoy?   15
        Echo.   Joy.
But are there cares and businesse with the pleasure?
        Echo.   Leisure.
Light, joy, and leisure; but shall they persever?
        Echo.   Ever.   20

Love (III)

Love bade me welcome: yet my soul drew back,
    Guiltie of dust and sinne.

But quick-ey'd Love, observing me grow slack
        From my first entrance in,
Drew nearer to me, sweetly questioning,   5
        If I lack'd any thing.

A guest, I answer'd, worthy to be here:
        Love said, You shall be he.
I the unkinde, ungratefull? Ah my deare,
        I cannot look on thee.   10
Love took my hand, and smiling did reply,
        Who made the eyes but I?

Truth Lord, but I have marr'd them: let my shame
        Go where it doth deserve.
And know you not, sayes Love, who bore the blame?   15
        My deare, then I will serve.
You must sit down, sayes Love, and taste my meat:
        So I did sit and eat.

FINIS.

Glory be to God *on high*
And on earth peace
     Good will towards men.

The Church Militant

Almightie Lord, who from thy glorious throne
Seest and rulest all things ev'n as one:
The smallest ant or atome knows thy power,
Known also to each minute of an houre:
Much more do Common-weals acknowledge thee,   5
And wrap their policies in thy decree,
Complying with thy counsels, doing nought
Which doth not meet with an eternall thought.
But above all, thy Church and Spouse doth prove
Not the decrees of power, but bands of love.   10
Early didst thou arise to plant this vine,

Which might the more indeare it to be thine.
Spices come from the East; so did thy Spouse,
Trimme as the light, sweet as the laden boughs
Of *Noahs* shadie vine, chaste as the dove;   15
Prepar'd and fitted to receive thy love.
The course was westward, that the sunne might light
As well our understanding as our sight.
Where th' Ark did rest, there *Abraham* began
To bring the other Ark from *Canaan.*   20
Moses pursu'd this: but King *Solomon*
Finish'd and fixt the old religion.
When it grew loose, the Jews did hope in vain
By nailing Christ to fasten it again.
But to the Gentiles he bore crosse and all,   25
Rending with earthquakes the partition-wall:
Onely whereas the Ark in glorie shone,
Now with the crosse, as with a staffe, alone,
Religion, like a pilgrime, westward bent,
Knocking at all doores, ever as she went.   30
Yet as the sunne, though forward be his flight,
Listens behinde him, and allows some light,
Till all depart: so went the Church her way,
Letting, while one foot stept, the other stay
Among the eastern nations for a time,   35
Till both removed to the western clime.
To *Egypt* first she came, where they did prove
Wonders of anger once, but now of love.
The ten Commandments there did flourish more
Then the ten bitter plagues had done before.   40
Holy *Macarius* and great *Anthonie*
Made *Pharaoh Moses,* changing th' historie.
Goshen was darknesse, *Egypt* full of lights,
Nilus for monsters brought forth Israelites.
Such power hath mightie Baptisme to produce   45
For things misshapen, things of highest use.
How deare to me, O God, thy counsels are!
                Who may with thee compare?
Religion thence fled into *Greece,* where arts
Gave her the highest place in all mens hearts.   50

Learning was pos'd, Philosophie was set,
Sophisters taken in a fishers net.
Plato and *Aristotle* were at a losse,
And wheel'd about again to spell *Christ-Crosse.*
Prayers chas'd syllogismes into their den,   55
And *Ergo* was transform'd into *Amen.*
Though *Greece* took horse as soon as *Egypt* did,
And *Rome* as both; yet *Egypt* faster rid,
And spent her period and prefixed time
Before the other. *Greece* being past her prime,   60
Religion went to *Rome,* subduing those,
Who, that they might subdue, made all their foes.
The Warrier his deere skarres no more resounds,
But seems to yeeld Christ hath the greater wounds,
Wounds willingly endur'd to work his blisse,   65
Who by an ambush lost his Paradise.
The great heart stoops, and taketh from the dust
A sad repentance, not the spoils of lust:
Quitting his spear, lest it should pierce again
Him in his members, who for him was slain.   70
The Shepherds hook grew to a scepter here,
Giving new names and numbers to the yeare.
But th' Empire dwelt in *Greece,* to comfort them
Who were cut short in *Alexanders* stemme.
In both of these Prowesse and Arts did tame   75
And tune mens hearts against the Gospel came:
Which using, and not fearing skill in th' one,
Or strength in th' other, did erect her throne.
Many a rent and struggling th' Empire knew,
(As dying things are wont) untill it flew   80
At length to *Germanie,* still westward bending,
And there the Churches festivall attending:
That as before Empire and Arts made way,
(For no lesse Harbingers would serve then they)
So they might still, and point us out the place   85
Where first the Church should raise her down-cast face.
Strength levels grounds, Art makes a garden there;
Then showres Religion, and makes all to bear.
Spain in the Empire shar'd with *Germanie,*
But *England* in the higher victorie: 90

Giving the Church a crown to keep her state,
And not go lesse then she had done of late.
Constantines British line meant this of old,
And did this mysterie wrap up and fold
Within a sheet of paper, which was rent 95
From times great Chronicle, and hither sent.
Thus both the Church and Sunne together ran
Unto the farthest old meridian.
How deare to me, O God, thy counsels are!
          Who may with thee compare? 100
Much about one and the same time and place,
Both where and when the Church began her race,
Sinne did set out of Eastern *Babylon,*
And travell'd westward also: journeying on
He chid the Church away, where e're he came, 105
Breaking her peace, and tainting her good name.
At first he got to *Egypt,* and did sow
Gardens of gods, which ev'ry yeare did grow
Fresh and fine deities. They were at great cost,
Who for a god clearely a sallet lost. 110
Ah, what a thing is man devoid of grace,
Adoring garlick with an humble face,
Begging his food of that which he may eat,
Starving the while he worshippeth his meat!
Who makes a root his god, how low is he, 115
If God and man be sever'd infinitely!
What wretchednesse can give him any room,
Whose house is foul, while he adores his broom?
None will beleeve this now, though money be
In us the same transplanted foolerie. 120
Thus Sinne in *Egypt* sneaked for a while;
His highest was an ox or crocodile,
And such poore game. Thence he to *Greece* doth passe,
And being craftier much then Goodnesse was,
He left behinde him garrisons of sinnes 125
To make good that which ev'ry day he winnes.
Here Sinne took heart, and for a garden-bed
Rich shrines and oracles he purchased:
He grew a gallant, and would needs foretell
As well what should befall, as what befell. 130

Nay, he became a poet, and would serve
His pills of sublimate in that conserve.
The world came in with hands and purses full
To this great lotterie, and all would pull.
But all was glorious cheating, brave deceit,   135
Where some poore truths were shuffled for a bait
To credit him, and to discredit those
Who after him should braver truths disclose.
From *Greece* he went to *Rome:* and as before
He was a God, now he's an Emperour.   140
Nero and others lodg'd him bravely there,
Put him in trust to rule the Roman sphere.
Glorie was his chief instrument of old:
Pleasure succeeded straight, when that grew cold.
Which soon was blown to such a mightie flame,   145
That though our Saviour did destroy the game,
Disparking oracles, and all their treasure,
Setting affliction to encounter pleasure;
Yet did a rogue with hope of carnall joy
Cheat the most subtill nations. Who so coy,   150
So trimme, as *Greece* and *Egypt?* yet their hearts
Are given over, for their curious arts,
To such Mahometan stupidities,
As the old heathen would deem prodigies.
How deare to me, O God, thy counsels are!   155
                Who may with thee compare?
Onely the West and *Rome* do keep them free
From this contagious infidelitie.
And this is all the Rock, whereof they boast,
As *Rome* will one day finde unto her cost.   160
Sinne being not able to extirpate quite
The Churches here, bravely resolv'd one night
To be a Church-man too, and wear a Mitre:
The old debauched ruffian would turn writer.
I saw him in his studie, where he sate   165
Busie in controversies sprung of late.
A gown and pen became him wondrous well:
His grave aspect had more of heav'n then hell:
Onely there was a handsome picture by,
To which he lent a corner of his eye.   170

As Sinne in *Greece* a Prophet was before,
And in old *Rome* a mightie Emperour;
So now being Priest he plainly did professe
To make a jest of Christs three offices:
The rather since his scatter'd jugglings were   175
United now in one both time and sphere.
From *Egypt* he took pettie deities,
From *Greece* oracular infallibilities,
And from old *Rome* the libertie of pleasure
By free dispensings of the Churches treasure.   180
Then in memoriall of his ancient throne
He did surname his palace, *Babylon.*
Yet that he might the better gain all nations,
And make that name good by their transmigrations,
From all these places, but at divers times,   185
He took fine vizards to conceal his crimes:
From *Egypt* Anchorisme and retirednesse,
Learning from *Greece,* from old *Rome* statelinesse:
And blending these he carri'd all mens eyes,
While Truth sat by, counting his victories: 190
Whereby he grew apace and scorn'd to use
Such force as once did captivate the Jews;
But did bewitch, and finely work each nation
Into a voluntarie transmigration.
All poste to *Rome:* Princes submit their necks   195
Either t' his publick foot or private tricks.
It did not fit his gravitie to stirre,
Nor his long journey, nor his gout and furre.
Therefore he sent out able ministers,
Statesmen within, without doores cloisterers: 200
Who without spear, or sword, or other drumme
Then what was in their tongue, did overcome;
And having conquer'd, did so strangely rule,
That the whole world did seem but the Popes mule.
As new and old *Rome* did one Empire twist;   205
So both together are one Antichrist,
Yet with two faces, as their *Janus* was,
Being in this their old crackt looking-glasse.
How deare to me, O God, thy counsels are!
                    Who may with thee compare?   210

Thus Sinne triumphs in Western *Babylon;*
Yet not as Sinne, but as Religion.
Of his two thrones he made the latter best,
And to defray his journey from the east.
Old and new *Babylon* are to hell and night, 215
As is the moon and sunne to heav'n and light.
When th' one did set, the other did take place,
Confronting equally the Law and Grace.
They are hells land-marks, Satans double crest:
They are Sinnes nipples, feeding th' east and west. 220
But as in vice the copie still exceeds
The pattern, but not so in vertuous deeds;
So though Sinne made his latter seat the better,
The latter Church is to the first a debter.
The second Temple could not reach the first: 225
And the late reformation never durst
Compare with ancient times and purer yeares;
But in the Jews and us deserveth tears.
Nay, it shall ev'ry yeare decrease and fade;
Till such a darknesse do the world invade 230
At Christs last coming, as his first did finde:
Yet must there such proportion be assign'd
To these diminishings, as is between
The spacious world and *Jurie* to be seen.
Religion stands on tip-toe in our land, 235
Readie to passe to the *American* strand.
When height of malice, and prodigious lusts,
Impudent sinning, witchcrafts, and distrusts
(The marks of future bane) shall fill our cup
Unto the brimme, and make our measure up; 240
When *Sein* shall swallow *Tiber,* and the *Thames*
By letting in them both pollutes her streams:
When *Italie* of us shall have her will,
And all her calender of sinnes fulfill;
Whereby one may foretell, what sinnes next yeare 245
Shall both in *France* and *England* domineer:
Then shall Religion to *America* flee:
They have their times of Gospel, ev'n as we.
My God, thou dost prepare for them a way
By carrying first their gold from them away: 250

For gold and grace did never yet agree:
Religion alwaies sides with povertie.
We think we rob them, but we think amisse:
We are more poore, and they more rich by this.
Thou wilt revenge their quarrell, making grace   255
To pay our debts, and leave her ancient place
To go to them, while that which now their nation
But lends to us, shall be our desolation.
Yet as the Church shall thither westward flie,
So Sinne shall trace and dog her instantly: 260
They have their period also and set times
Both for their vertuous actions and their crimes.
And where of old the Empire and the Arts
Usher'd the Gospel ever in mens hearts,
Spain hath done one; when Arts perform the other,   265
The Church shall come, & Sinne the Church shall smother:
That when they have accomplished their round,
And met in th' east their first and ancient sound,
Judgement may meet them both & search them round.
Thus do both lights, as well in Church as Sunne,   270
Light one another, and together runne.
Thus also Sinne and Darknesse follow still
The Church and Sunne with all their power and skill.
But as the Sunne still goes both west and east;
So also did the Church by going west   275
Still eastward go; because it drew more neare
To time and place, where judgement shall appeare.
How deare to me, O God, thy counsels are!
            Who may with thee compare?

L'Envoy

> *King of Glorie, King of Peace,*
> With the one make warre to cease;
> With the other blesse thy sheep,
> Thee to love, in thee to sleep.
> Let not Sinne devoure thy fold,   5
> Bragging that thy bloud is cold,

That thy death is also dead,
While his conquests dayly spread;
That thy flesh hath lost his food,
And thy Crosse is common wood.   10
Choke him, let him say no more,
But reserve his breath in store,
Till thy conquests and his fall
Make his sighs to use it all,
And then bargain with the winde   15
To discharge what is behinde.

     Blessed be God *alone*,
     Thrice blessed Three in One.

FINIS.

ENGLISH POEMS
NOT INCLUDED IN
THE TEMPLE

The H. Communion

O gratious Lord, how shall I know
Whether in these gifts thou bee so
   As thou art evry-where;
Or rather so, as thou alone
Tak'st all the Lodging, leaving none   5
   ffor thy poore creature there?

ffirst I am sure, whether bread stay
Or whether Bread doe fly away
   Concerneth bread, not mee.
But that both thou and all thy traine   10
Bee there, to thy truth, & my gaine,
   Concerneth mee & Thee.

And if in comming to thy foes
Thou dost come first to them, that showes
   The hast of thy good will.
Or if that thou two stations makest   15
In Bread & mee, the way thou takest
   Is more, but for mee still.

Then of this also I am sure
That thou didst all those pains endure
   To' abolish Sinn, not Wheat.   20
Creatures are good, & have their place;
Sinn onely, which did all deface,
   Thou drivest from his seat.

I could beleeue an Impanation 25
At the rate of an Incarnation,
   If thou hadst dyde for Bread.
But that which made my soule to dye,
My flesh, & fleshly villany,
   That allso made thee dead. 30

That fflesh is there, mine eyes deny:
And what shold flesh but flesh discry,
   The noblest sence of five?
If glorious bodies pass the sight,
Shall they be food & strength & might 35
   Euen there, where they deceiue?

Into my soule this cannot pass;
fflesh (though exalted) keeps his grass
   And cannot turn to soule.
Bodyes & Minds are different Spheres, 40
Nor can they change their bounds & meres,
   But keep a constant Pole.

This gift of all gifts is the best,
Thy flesh the least that I request.
   Thou took'st that pledg from mee: 45
Give me not that I had before,
Or give mee that, so I have more;
   My God, give mee all Thee.

Love

Thou art too hard for me in Love:
There is no dealing with thee in that Art:
   That is thy Master-peece I see.
   When I contrive & plott to prove
Something that may be conquest on my part, 5
   Thou still, O Lord, outstrippest mee.

Sometimes, when as I wash, I say,
And shrodely, as I think, Lord wash my soule

More spotted then my flesh can bee.
But then there comes into my way   10
Thy ancient baptism, which when I was foule
    And knew it not, yet cleansed mee.

I took a time when thou didst sleep,
Great waves of trouble combating my brest:
    I thought it braue to praise thee then,   15
    Yet then I found, that thou didst creep
Into my hart with ioye, giving more rest
    Then flesh did lend thee back agen.

Let mee but once the conquest have
Vpon the matter, 'twill thy conquest prove: 20
    If thou subdue mortalitie,
    Thou do'st no more then doth the graue:
Whereas if I orecome thee & thy Love,
    Hell, Death & Divel come short of mee.

Trinity Sunday

He that is one,
Is none.
Two reacheth thee
In some degree.
Nature & Grace   5
With Glory may attaine thy Face.
    Steele & a flint strike fire,
      Witt & desire
    Never to thee aspire,
Except life catch & hold those fast.   10
    That which beleefe
Did not confess in the first Theefe
    His fall can tell,
    ffrom Heaven, through Earth, to Hell.
    Lett two of those alone   15
      To them that fall,
Who God & Saints and Angels loose at last.
    Hee that has one,
      Has all.

Euen-song

The Day is spent, & hath his will on mee:
   I and the Sunn haue runn our races,
   I went the slower, yet more paces,
     ffor I decay, not hee.

Lord make my Losses vp, & sett mee free: 5
   That I who cannot now by day
   Look on his daring brightnes, may
     Shine then more bright then hee.

If thou deferr this light, then shadow mee:
   Least that the Night, earths gloomy shade,   10
   ffouling her nest, my earth invade,
     As if shades knew not Thee.

But thou art Light & darknes both togeather:
   If that bee dark we can not see,
   The sunn is darker then a Tree,   15
     And thou more dark then either.

Yet Thou art not so dark, since I know this,
   But that my darknes may touch thine,
   And hope, that may teach it to shine,
     Since Light thy Darknes is.   20

O lett my Soule, whose keyes I must deliver
   Into the hands of senceles Dreames
   Which know not thee, suck in thy beames
     And wake with thee for ever.

The Knell

   The Bell doth tolle:
Lord help thy servant whose perplexed Soule
    Doth wishly look
    On either hand
And sometimes offers, sometimes makes a stand,   5
    Strugling on th' hook.

Now is the season,
Now the great combat of our flesh & reason:
O help, my God!
See, they breake in,   10
Disbanded humours, sorrows, troops of Sinn,
Each with his rodd.

Lord make thy Blood
Convert & colour all the other flood
And streams of grief,   15
That they may bee
Julips & Cordials when wee call on thee
ffor some relief.

Perseverance

My God, the poore expressions of my Love
Which warme these lines & serve them vp to thee
Are so, as for the present I did moue,
    Or rather as thou mouedst mee.

But what shall issue, whither these my words   5
Shal help another, but my iudgment bee,
As a burst fouling-peece doth saue the birds
    But kill the man, is seald with thee.

ffor who can tell, though thou hast dyde to winn
And wedd my soule in glorious paradise,   10
Whither my many crymes and vse of sinn
    May yet forbid the banes and bliss?

Onely my soule hangs on thy promisses
With face and hands clinging vnto thy brest,
Clinging and crying, crying without cease,   15
    Thou art my rock, thou art my rest.

POEMS FROM
WALTON'S *LIVES*

Sonnets

My God, where is that ancient heat towards thee,
    Wherewith whole showls of *Martyrs* once did burn,
    Besides their other flames? Doth Poetry
Wear *Venus* Livery? only serve her turn?
Why are not *Sonnets* made of thee? and layes   5
    Upon thine Altar burnt? Cannot thy love
    Heighten a spirit to sound out thy praise
As well as any she? Cannot thy *Dove*
Out-strip their *Cupid* easily in flight?
    Or, since thy wayes are deep, and still the same,   10
    Will not a verse run smooth that bears thy name?
Why doth that fire, which by thy power and might
    Each breast does feel, no braver fuel choose
    Than that, which one day Worms may chance refuse?

Sure, Lord, there is enough in thee to dry   15
    Oceans of *Ink*; for, as the Deluge did
    Cover the Earth, so doth thy Majesty:
Each Cloud distills thy praise, and doth forbid
Poets to turn it to another use.
    Roses and *Lillies* speak thee; and to make   20
    A pair of Cheeks of them, is thy abuse.
Why should I *Womens eyes* for Chrystal take?
Such poor invention burns in their low mind
    Whose fire is wild, and doth not upward go
    To praise, and on thee, Lord, some *Ink* bestow.   25
Open the bones, and you shall nothing find
    In the best *face* but *filth*, when, Lord, in thee
    The *beauty* lies in the *discovery*.

To my Successor

If thou chance for to find
A new House to thy mind,
And built without thy Cost:
Be good to the Poor,
As God gives thee store,   5
And then, my Labour's not lost.

Another version

If thou dost find an house built to thy mind
Without thy cost,
Serve thou the more God and the poore;
My labour is not lost.

Richard Crashaw
1612/3-1649

Richard Crashaw

Richard Crashaw was born in London in late 1612 or early 1613. Little is known of his mother, who died either in childbirth or when he was still an infant. His stepmother died in childbirth in 1620. His father was the Reverend William Crashaw, a Puritan preacher at Temple Church in London, an amateur poet, and well known for his virulent anti-Catholic pamphlets. When he died at Whitechapel in 1626, he left a will which is a model of excoriation against the "poperie" which his son later embraced:

> I accounte Poperie (as nowe it is) the heape and chaos of all heresies and the channell whereinto the fowlest impieties & heresies y^t have byne in the christian Worlde have runn and closelye emptied themselues. I beleeue the Popes seate and power to be the power of the greate Antechrist and the doctrine of the Pope (as nowe it is) to be the doctrine of Antechriste. yea that doctrine of Divells prophecied of by the Apostle and that the true and absolute Papist soe livinge and dyeinge debarrs himself of salvation for oughte that we knowe, . . .

Richard had a classical education in the Charterhouse before going up to Pembroke College, Cambridge, in 1632. There he distinguished himself as a linguist and a poet in Latin, and was elected to a resident fellowship at Peterhouse, the center of High Church activity at the time. About 1639 Crashaw was ordained, for in that year he is referred to as curate of Little St. Mary's. Like Donne and Herbert he was an impressive preacher, listened to and admired for his style. As a contemporary witness noted, "Those thronged Sermons on each Sunday and Holiday, that ravished more like Poems . . . scattering not so much Sentences [as] Extasies." One of his first tutees was Ferrar Collet, through whom he was introduced to the Anglican community at Little Gidding, and came to know Nicholas Ferrar, its founder, and Mary Collet, its "mother" or guiding spirit.

By 1643, because of his Royalist sympathies—and, no doubt also, increasingly Roman Catholic sympathies—Crashaw was compelled to leave Cambridge. It was in this period, during the civil wars in Britain, that he was known to have lived continuously abroad, although he might have returned briefly to stay in Oxford, where the King resided. He went first to Leyden, perhaps to join Mary Collet, then to Paris, to be near the exiled court of the British Queen Henrietta Maria. There is a likelihood that he became a Roman Catholic priest in 1646. His friend and admirer, the poet Abraham Cowley, who was a Royalist, enlisted the aid of the Queen, who wrote to the Pope about Crashaw. Partly because of such interventions, Crashaw went to Rome where he lived in poverty and ruined his health. In 1647 he was known to have gotten a post with a Cardinal Palotto, and subsequently a minor office in Loretto. There is the report of a contemporary, Dr. John Bargrave, that Crashaw "infinitely commended his Cardinal, but complained extremely of the wickedness of those of his retinue; of which he, having the Cardinal's ear, complained to him. Upon which the Italians fell so far out with him that the Cardinal, to secure his life, was fain to put him from his service, and procuring him some small imploy at the Lady's of Loretto; whither he went in pilgrimage in summer time, and, overheating himself died in four weeks after he came thither, and it was doubtful whether he were not poisoned." He died in Loretto on August 21, 1649.

His book of poems, including *Steps to the Temple*—a title suggestive of Herbert's—and *Delights of the Muses*, was published in London in 1646, and again, in an expanded and revised edition, in 1648. A third volume, *Carmen Deo Nostro*, which appeared posthumously in 1652, contained much of the same material, but also some fine new poems for which Crashaw is still widely known.

STEPS TO THE TEMPLE

Sacred Poems,
with other Delights of the
Muses

The Authors Motto

Live Jesus, Live, and let it bee
My life to dye, for love of thee.

The Weeper*

Haile *Sister Springs*,
Parents of Silver-forded rills!
Ever bubling things!
Thawing Christall! Snowy Hills!
Still spending, never spent; I meane   5
Thy faire Eyes sweet *Magdalene*.

Heavens thy faire Eyes bee,
Heavens of ever-falling stars,
Tis seed-time still with thee
And stars thou sow'st whose harvest dares   10
Promise the earth; to countershine
What ever makes Heavens fore-head fine.

But wee are deceived all,
Stars they are indeed too true,
For they but seeme to fall   15
As Heavens other spangles doe:

* See also p. 659 for a second version of this poem.

It is not for our Earth and us,
To shine in things so pretious.

    Vpwards thou dost weepe,
  Heavens bosome drinks the gentle streame.   20
    Where th' milky rivers meet,
  Thine Crawles above and is the Creame.
Heaven, of such faire floods as this,
Heaven the Christall Ocean is.

    Every morne from hence,   25
  A briske Cherub something sips
    Whose soft influence
  Adds sweetnesse to his sweetest lips.
Then to his Musicke, and his song
Tastes of this breakefast all day long.   30

    When some new bright guest
  Takes up among the stars a roome,
    And Heaven will make a feast,
  Angels with their Bottles come ;
And draw from these full Eyes of thine,   35
Their Masters water, their owne Wine.

    The dew no more will weepe,
  The Primroses pale cheeke to decke,
    The deaw no more will sleepe,
  Nuzzel'd in the Lillies necke.   40
Much rather would it tremble heere,
And leave them both to bee thy Teare.

    Not the soft Gold which
  Steales from the Amber-weeping Tree,
    Makes sorrow halfe so Rich,   45
  As the drops distil'd from thee.

Sorrowes best Iewels lye in these
Caskets, of which Heaven keeps the Keyes.

When sorrow would be seene
In her brightest Majesty,   50
(For shee is a Queen)
Then is shee drest by none but thee.
Then, and onely then shee weares
Her richest Pearles, I meane thy Teares.

Not in the Evenings Eyes   55
When they red with weeping are,
For the Sun that dyes,
Sits sorrow with a face so faire.
Nowhere but heere did ever meet
Sweetnesse so sad, sadnes so sweet.   60

Sadnesse all the while
Shee sits in such a Throne as this,
Can doe nought but smile,
Nor beleeves shee sadnesse is.
Gladnesse it selfe would bee more glad   65
To bee made so sweetly sad.

There is no need at all
That the Balsame-sweating bough
So coyly should let fall,
His med'cinable Teares; for now   70
Nature hath learn't t' extract a dew,
More soveraigne and sweet from you.

Yet let the poore drops weepe,
Weeping is the ease of woe,
Softly let them creepe   75
Sad that they are vanquish't so,
They, though to others no releife
May Balsame bee for their own grief.

Golden though hee bee,
Golden *Tagus* murmurs though,   80
Might hee flow from thee
Content and quiet would he goe,
Richer far does he esteeme
Thy silver, then his golden streame.

Well does the *May* that lyes   85
Smiling in thy cheekes, confesse,
The *April* in thine eyes,
Mutuall sweetnesse they expresse.
No *April* e're lent softer showres,
Nor *May* returned fairer flowers.   90

Thus dost thou melt the yeare
Into a weeping motion,
Each minute waiteth heere ;
Takes his teare and gets him gone ;
By thine eyes tinct enobled thus   95
Time layes him up : he 's pretious.

Time as by thee he passes,
Makes thy ever-watry eyes
His Hower-Glasses.
By them his steps he rectifies.   100
The sands he us'd no longer please,
For his owne sands hee'l use thy seas.

Does thy song lull the Ayre ?
Thy teares just Cadence still keeps time.
Does thy sweet breath'd *Prayer*   105
Vp in clouds of Incense climbe ?
Still at each sigh, that is each stop :
A bead, that is a teare doth drop.

Does the Night arise?
Still thy teares doe fall, and fall.   110
Does night loose her eyes?
Still the fountaine weeps for all.
Let night or day doe what they will
Thou hast thy taske, thou weepest still.

Not, so long she liv'd,   115
Will thy tombe report of thee
But *so long she greiv'd,*
Thus must we date thy memory.
Others by Dayes, by Monthes, by Yeares
Measure their Ages, Thou by Teares.   120

Say watry Brothers
Yee simpering sons of those faire eyes,
Your fertile Mothers.
What hath our world that can entice
You to be borne? what is't can borrow   125
You from her eyes swolne wombes of sorrow.

Whither away so fast?
O whither? for the sluttish Earth
Your sweetnesse cannot tast
Nor does the dust deserve your Birth.   130
Whither hast ye then? o say
Why yee trip so fast away?

We goe not to seeke
The darlings of *Aurora's* bed,
The Roses modest cheeke   135
Nor the Violets humble head.
No such thing; we goe to meet
A worthier object, *Our Lords* feet.

The Teare

  What bright soft thing is this?
 Sweet *Mary* thy faire Eyes expence?
  A moist sparke it is,
 A watry Diamond; from whence
The very Terme, I think, was found   5
The water of a *Diamond*.

  O 'tis not a Teare,
 'Tis a starre about to drop
  From thine eye its spheare;
 The Sunne will stoope and take it up. 10
Proud will his sister be to weare
This thine eyes Iewell in her Eare.

  O 'tis a Teare,
 Too true a Teare; for no sad eyne,
  How sad so e're   15
 Raine so true a Teare as thine;
Each Drop leaving a place so deare,
Weeps for it selfe, is its owne Teare.

  Such a Pearle as this is,
 (Slipt from *Aurora's* dewy Brest) 20
  The Rose buds sweet lip kisses;
 And such the Rose its selfe when vext
With ungentle flames, does shed,
Sweating in too warme a Bed.

  Such the Maiden Gemme   25
 By the wanton Spring put on,
  Peeps from her Parent stemme,
 And blushes on the manly Sun:
This watry Blossome of thy Eyne
Ripe, will make the richer Wine.   30

  Faire Drop, why quak'st thou so?
 'Cause thou streight must lay thy Head
  In the Dust? ô no;

The Dust shall never bee thy Bed :
A pillow for thee will I bring,   35
Stuft with Downe of Angels wing.

Thus carryed up on high,
(For to Heaven thou must goe)
Sweetly shalt thou lye,
And in soft slumbers bath thy woe ;   40
Till the singing Orbes awake thee,
And one of their bright *Chorus* make thee.

There thy selfe shalt bee
An eye, but not a weeping one,
Yet I doubt of thee,   45
Whither th'hadst rather there have shone
An eye of Heaven ; or still shine here
In th'Heaven of *Mary's* eye, a *Teare*.

Divine Epigrams

On the water of our Lords Baptisme

Each blest drop, on each blest limme,
Is washt it selfe, in washing him :
Tis a Gemme while it stayes here,
While it falls hence 'tis a Teare.

Act. 8

On the baptized Æthiopian

Let it no longer be a forlorne hope
            To wash an Æthiope :
He 's washt, His gloomy skin a peacefull shade
            For his white soule is made :
And now, I doubt not, the Eternall Dove,   5
            A black-fac'd house will love.

On the miracle of multiplyed loaves

See here an easie Feast that knowes no wound,
　　That under Hungers Teeth will needs be sound :
A subtle Harvest of unbounded bread,
　　What would ye more? Here food it selfe is fed.

Vpon the Sepulchre of our Lord*

Here, where our Lord once laid his Head,
Now the Grave lies buried.

The Widowes Mites

Two Mites, two drops, (yet all her house and land)
Falls from a steady Heart, though trembling hand :
The others wanton wealth foams high, and brave,
The other cast away, she onely gave.

Luk. 15

On the Prodigall

Tell me bright Boy, tell me my golden Lad,
Whither away so frolick? why so glad?
What all thy Wealth in counsaile? all thy state?
Are Husks so deare? troth 'tis a mighty rate.

* See also p. 638.

On the still surviving markes of
our Saviours wounds

What ever story of their crueltie,
Or Naile, or Thorne, or Speare have writ in Thee,
    Are in another sence
      Still legible ;
    Sweet is the difference :   5
      Once I did spell

    Every red letter
      A wound of thine,
    Now, (what is better)
      Balsome for mine.   10

Act. 5

The sicke implore St. Peter's shadow

Vnder thy shadow may I lurke a while,
    Death's busie search I'le easily beguile :
Thy shadow *Peter*, must shew me the Sun,
    My light's thy shadowes shadow, or 'tis done.

Mar. 7

The dumbe healed, and the people
enjoyned silence

Christ bids the dumbe tongue speake, it speakes, the sound
Hee charges to be quiet, it runs round,
If in the first he us'd his fingers Touch :
His hands whole strength here, could not be too much.

Mat. 28

Come see the place where the Lord lay

Show me himselfe, himselfe (bright Sir) O show
  Which way my poore Tears to himselfe may goe,
Were it enough to show the place, and say,
  Looke, *Mary*, here see, where thy Lord once lay,
Then could I show these armes of mine, and say   5
  Looke, *Mary*, here see, where thy Lord once lay.

To Pontius *washing his hands*

  Thy hands are washt, but ô the waters spilt,
    That labour'd to have washt thy guilt:
  The flood, if any can, that can suffice,
    Must have its Fountaine in thine Eyes.

To the Infant Martyrs

  Goe smiling soules, your new built Cages breake,
  In Heav'n you'l learne to sing ere here to speake,
  Nor let the milky fonts that bath your thirst,
                Bee your delay;
  The place that calls you hence, is at the worst   5
                Milke all the way.

On the Miracle of Loaves

  Now Lord, or never, they'l beleeve on thee,
  Thou to their Teeth hast prov'd thy Deity.

Marke 4

Why are yee afraid, O yee of little faith?

As if the storme meant him;
Or, 'cause Heavens face is dim,
    His needs a cloud.
    Was ever froward wind
    That could be so unkind,   5
    Or wave so proud?
The Wind had need be angry, and the Water black,
That to the mighty *Neptune's* self dare threaten wrack.

    There is no storme but this
    Of your owne Cowardise   10
       That braves you out;
    You are the storme that mocks
    Your selves; you are the Rocks
       Of your owne doubt:
Besides this feare of danger, there's no danger here   15
And he that here feares Danger, does deserve his Feare.

On the Blessed Virgins bashfulnesse

That on her lap she casts her humble Eye;
'Tis the sweet pride of her Humility.
The faire starre is well fixt, for where, ô where
Could she have fixt it on a fairer Spheare?
'Tis Heav'n 'tis Heaven she sees, Heavens God there lyes   5
She can see heaven, and ne're lift up her eyes:
This new Guest to her Eyes new Lawes hath given,
'Twas once *looke up,* 'tis now *looke downe* to Heaven.

Vpon Lazarus his Teares

Rich *Lazarus!* richer in those Gems, thy Teares,
    Then *Dives* in the Roabes he weares:
He scornes them now, but o they'l sute full well
    With th'Purple he must weare in Hell.

Two went up into the Temple to pray

Two went to pray? ô rather say
One went to brag, th'other to pray:
One stands up close and treads on high,
Where th'other dares not send his eye.
One neerer to Gods Altar trod,   5
The other to the Altars God.

Vpon the Asse that bore our Saviour

Hath onely Anger an Omnipotence
        In Eloquence?
Within the lips of Love and Ioy doth dwell
        No miracle?
Why else had *Baalams* Asse a tongue to chide   5
        His Masters pride?
And thou (Heaven-burthen'd Beast) hast ne're a word
        To praise thy Lord?
That he should find a Tongue and vocall Thunder,
        Was a great wonder.   10
But ô me thinkes 'tis a farre greater one
        That thou find'st none.

Matthew 8

I am not worthy that thou should'st
come under my roofe

Thy God was making hast into thy roofe,
    Thy humble faith and feare keepes him aloofe:
Hee'l be thy Guest, because he may not be,
    Hee'l come—into thy house? no, into thee.

I am the Doore

And now th'art set wide ope, The Speare's sad Art,
Lo! hath unlockt thee at the very Heart :
　　　Hee to himselfe (I feare the worst)
　　　　And his owne hope
　　　Hath *shut* these Doores of Heaven, that durst　　5
　　　　Thus set them *ope.*

Matthew 9

The blind cured by the word
of our Saviour

Thou speak'st the word (thy word's a Law)
Thou spak'st and streight the blind man saw.

To speake and make the blind man see,
Was never man Lord spake like Thee.

To speake thus, was to speake (say I)　　5
Not to his Eare, but to his Eye.

Matthew 27

And he answered them nothing

O Mighty *Nothing!* unto thee,
Nothing, wee owe all things that bee.
God spake once when hee all things made,
Hee sav'd all when hee *Nothing* said.
The world was made of *Nothing* then ;　　5
'Tis made by *Nothyng* now againe.

To our Lord, upon the Water made Wine

Thou water turn'st to Wine (faire friend of Life)
    Thy foe to crosse the sweet Arts of thy Reigne
Distills from thence the Teares of wrath and strife,
    And so turnes wine to Water backe againe.

Matthew 22

Neither durst any man from that Day aske him any more Questions

Midst all the darke and knotty Snares,
Blacke wit or malice can or dares,
Thy glorious wisdome breakes the Nets,
And treads with uncontrouled steps.
Thy quel'd foes are not onely now   5
Thy triumphes, but thy Trophies too :
They, both at once thy Conquests bee,
And thy Conquests memorye.
Stony amazement makes them stand
Waiting on thy victorious hand,   10
Like statues fixed to the fame
Of thy renoune, and their owne shame.
As if they onely meant to breath,
To bee the Life of their owne Death.
'Twas time to hold their Peace when they,   15
Had nere another word to say :
Yet is their silence unto thee,
The full sound of thy victory.
Their silence speakes aloud, and is
Thy well pronounc'd *Panegyris*.   20
While they speake nothing, they speake all
Their share, in thy Memoriall.
While they speake nothing, they proclaime
Thee, with the shrillest Trumpe of fame.
    To hold their peace is all the waies,   25
      These wretches have to speake thy praise.

Vpon our Saviours Tombe wherein never man was laid*

How Life and Death in Thee
   Agree?
Thou had'st a virgin Wombe
   And Tombe.
A *Joseph* did betroth   5
   Them both.

It is better to go into Heaven with one eye, &c.

One Eye? a thousand rather, and a Thousand more
 To fix those full-fac't Glories, ô he's poore
  Of Eyes that has but *Argus* store,
Yet if thou'lt fill one poore Eye, with thy Heaven and Thee,
 O grant (sweet Goodnesse) that one Eye may be   5
  All, and every whit of me.

Luk. 11

Vpon the dumbe Devill cast out, and the slanderous Jewes put to silence

Two Devills at one blow thou hast laid flat,
 A *speaking* Divell this, a *dumbe* one that.
Wa'st thy full victories fairer increase,
 That th'one spake, or that th'other held his peace?

* See also p. 640.

Luke 10

And a certaine Priest comming that way looked on him and passed by

Why dost Thou wound my wounds, ô Thou that passest by
Handling & turning them with an unwounded eye?
The calm that cools thine eye does shipwrack mine, for ô!
Vnmov'd to see one wretched, is to make him so.

Luke 11

Blessed be the paps which Thou hast sucked

Svppose he had been Tabled at thy Teates,
   Thy hunger feeles not what he eates:
Hee'l have his Teat e're long (a bloody one)
   The Mother then must suck the Son.

To Pontius washing his blood-stained hands

Is murther no sin? or a sin so cheape,
       That thou need'st heape
A Rape upon't? till thy Adult'rous touch
   Taught her these sullied cheeks this blubber'd face,
She was a Nimph, the meadowes knew none such,   5
   Of honest Parentage of unstain'd Race,
The Daughter of a faire and well-fam'd Fountaine
As ever Silver-tipt, the side of shady mountaine.

See how she weeps, and weeps, that she appeares
       Nothing but Teares;   10
Each drop 's a Teare that weeps for her own wast;
   Harke how at every Touch she does complaine her:
Harke how she bids her frighted Drops make hast,
   And with sad murmurs, chides the Hands that stain her.
Leave, leave, for shame, or else (Good judge) decree,   15
What water shal wash this, when this hath washed thee.

Matthew 23

Yee build the Sepulchres of the Prophets

Thou trim'st a Prophets Tombe, and dost bequeath
   The life thou took'st from him unto his *Death*.
Vaine man! the stones that on his Tombe doe lye,
   Keepe but the score of them that made him dye.

Vpon the Infant Martyrs

   To see both blended in one flood
   The Mothers Milke, the Childrens blood,
   Makes me doubt if Heaven will gather,
   Roses hence, or *Lillies* rather.

Joh. 16

Verily I say unto you, yee shall weep and lament

Welcome my Griefe, my Ioy; how deare 's
   To me my Legacy of Teares!
I'le weepe, and weepe, and will therefore
Weepe, 'cause I can weepe no more:
   Thou, thou (Deare Lord) even thou alone,   5
   Giv'st joy, even when thou givest none.

Joh. 15

Vpon our Lords last comfortable discourse with his Disciples

All *Hybla's* honey, all that sweetnesse can
Flowes in thy Song (ô faire, ô dying Swan!)
Yet is the joy I take in't small or none;
It is too sweet to be a long-liv'd one.

Luke 16

Dives *asking a drop*

A drop, one drop, how sweetly one faire drop
   Would tremble on my pearle-tipt fingers top?
My wealth is gone, ô goe it where it will,
   Spare this one Iewell; I'le be *Dives* still.

Marke 12

(*Give to Caesar*-------)
(*And to God*----------)

All we have is God's, and yet
Cæsar challenges a debt,
Nor hath God a thinner share,
What ever *Cæsar's* payments are;
All is God's; and yet 'tis true   5
All wee have is *Cæsar's* too;
All is *Cæsar's*; and what ods
So long as *Cæsar's* selfe is Gods?

But now they have seen, and hated

Seene? and yet hated thee? they did not see,
   They saw Thee not, that saw and hated thee:
No, no, they saw thee not, ô Life, ô Love,
   Who saw ought in thee, that their hate could move.

Vpon the Thornes taken downe from our Lords head bloody*

Know'st thou this, Souldier? 'tis a much chang'd plant,
   which yet

---

* See also p. 648.

Thy selfe did'st set,

'Tis chang'd indeed, did Autumn e're such beauties bring
To shame his Spring?   5

O! who so hard an husbandman could ever find
A soyle so kind?
Is not the soile a kind one (thinke ye) that returnes
Roses for *Thornes?*

Luc. 7

She began to wash his feet with teares and wipe them with the haires of her head

Her eyes flood lickes his feets faire staine,
Her haires flame lickes up that againe.
This flame thus quench't hath brighter beames:
This flood thus stained fairer streames.

On St. Peter *cutting of* Malchus *his eare*

Well *Peter* dost thou wield thy active sword,
    Well for thy selfe (I meane) not for thy Lord.
To strike at eares, is to take heed there bee
    No witnesse *Peter* of thy perjury.

Joh. 3

But men loved darknesse rather then Light

The worlds light shines, shine as it will,
The world will love its Darknesse still:
I doubt though when the World's in Hell,
It will not love its Darknesse halfe so well.

Act. 21

I am ready not onely to be bound but to dye

Come death, come bands, nor do you shrink, my eares,
At those hard words mans cowardise calls feares.
Save those of feare, no other bands feare I;
Nor other death then this; the feare to dye.

On St. Peter *casting away his Nets*
at our Saviours call

Thou hast the art on't *Peter*; and canst tell
To cast thy Nets on all occasions well.
When Christ calls, and thy Nets would have thee stay:
To cast them well's to cast them quite away.

Our Lord in his Circumcision
to his Father

To thee these first fruits of my growing death
(For what else is my life?) lo I bequeath.
Tast this, and as thou lik'st this lesser flood
Expect a Sea, my heart shall make it good.
Thy wrath that wades heere now, e're long shall swim   5
The flood-gate shall be set wide ope for him.
Then let him drinke, and drinke, and doe his worst,
To drowne the wantonnesse of his wild thirst.
Now's but the Nonage of my paines, my feares
Are yet but in their hopes, not come to yeares.   10
The day of my darke woes is yet but morne,
My teares but tender and my death new-borne.
Yet may these unfledg'd griefes give fate some guesse,
These Cradle-torments have their towardnesse.
These purple buds of blooming death may bee,   15
Erst the full stature of a fatall tree.
And till my riper woes to age are come,
This knife may be the speares *Præludium*.

On the wounds of our crucified Lord

O these wakefull wounds of thine!
   Are they Mouthes? or are they eyes?
Be they Mouthes, or be they eyne,
   Each bleeding part some one supplies.

Lo! a mouth, whose full-bloom'd lips   5
   At too deare a rate are roses.
Lo! a blood-shot eye! that weepes
   And many a cruell teare discloses.

O thou that on this foot hast laid
   Many a kisse, and many a Teare,   10
Now thou shal't have all repaid,
   Whatsoe're thy charges were.

This foot hath got a Mouth and lippes,
   To pay the sweet summe of thy kisses:
To pay thy Teares, an Eye that weeps   15
   In stead of Teares such Gems as this is.

The difference onely this appeares,
   (Nor can the change offend)
The debt is paid in *Ruby*-Teares,
   Which thou in Pearles did'st lend.   20

On our crucified Lord Naked, and bloody*

Th' have left thee naked Lord, O that they had;
This Garment too I would they had deny'd.
Thee with thy selfe they have too richly clad,
Opening the purple wardrobe of thy side.
   O never could bee found Garments too good   5
   For thee to weare, but these, of thine owne blood.

* See also p. 648.

Easter day

Rise, Heire of fresh Eternity,
   From thy Virgin Tombe :
Rise mighty man of wonders, and thy world with thee
   Thy Tombe, the universall East,
   Natures new wombe,   5
Thy Tombe, faire Immortalities perfumed Nest.

Of all the Gloryes Make Noone gay
   This is the Morne.
This rocke buds forth the fountaine of the streames of Day.
   In joyes white Annals live this houre,   10
   When life was borne,
No cloud scoule on his radiant lids no tempest lowre.

Life, by this light's Nativity
   All creatures have.
Death onely by this Dayes just Doome is forc't to Dye ;   15
   Nor is Death forc't ; for may hee ly
   Thron'd in thy Grave ;
Death will on this condition be content to Dy.

On the bleeding wounds of our
crucified Lord*

   Iesu, no more, it is full tide
      From thy hands and from thy feet,
   From thy head, and from thy side,
      All thy *Purple Rivers* meet.

   Thy restlesse feet they cannot goe,   5
      For us and our eternall good

* See also p. 646.

As they are wont; what though?
   They swim, alas! in their owne flood.

Thy hand to give thou canst not lift;
   Yet will thy hand still giving bee;   10
It gives, but ô it self's the Guift,
   It drops though bound, though bound 'tis free.

But ô thy side! thy deepe dig'd side
   That hath a double *Nilus* going,
Nor ever was the *Pharian* tide   15
   Halfe so fruitfull, halfe so flowing.

What need thy faire head beare a part
   In Teares? as if thine eyes had none?
What need they helpe to drowne thine heart,
   That strives in Torrents of its owne?   20

Water'd by the showres they bring,
   The thornes that thy blest browes encloses
(A cruell and a costly spring)
   Conceive proud hopes of proving Roses.

Not a haire but payes his River   25
   To this *Red Sea* of thy blood,
Their little channels can deliver
   Something to the generall flood.

But while I speake, whither are run
   All the Rivers nam'd before?   30
I counted wrong; there is but one,
   But ô that one is one all o're.

Raine-swolne Rivers may rise proud
   Threatning all to overflow,
But when indeed all's overflow'd   35
   They themselves are drowned too.

This thy Bloods deluge (a dire chance
   Deare Lord to thee) to us is found
A deluge of deliverance,
   A deluge least we should be drown'd.   40

Nere was't thou in a sence so sadly true,
The well of living Waters, Lord, till now.

Sampson *to his* Dalilah

Could not once blinding me, cruell, suffice?
When first I look't on thee, I lost mine eyes.

Psalme 23

Happy me! ô happy sheepe!
Whom my God vouchsafes to keepe
Ev'en my God, ev'en he it is,
That points me to these wayes of blisse;
On whose pastures cheerefull spring,   5
All the yeare doth sit and sing,
And rejoycing smiles to see
Their greene backs were his liverie:
Pleasure sings my soule to rest,
Plenty weares me at her brest,   10
Whose sweet temper teaches me
Nor wanton, nor in want to be.
At my feet the blubb'ring Mountaine
Weeping, melts into a Fountaine,
Whose soft silver-sweating streames   15
Make high Noone forget his beames:
When my waiward breath is flying,
Hee calls home my soule from dying,

Strokes and tames my rabid Griefe,
And does woe me into life :   20
When my simple weaknesse strayes,
(Tangled in forbidden wayes)
Hee (my Shepheard) is my Guide,
Hee's before me, on my side,
And behind me, he beguiles   25
Craft in all her knotty wiles :
Hee expounds the giddy wonder
Of my weary steps, and under
Spreads a Path cleare as the Day,
Where no churlish rub saies nay   30
To my joy-conducted Feet,
Whil'st they Gladly goe to meet
Grace and peace, to meet new laies
Tun'd to my great Shepheards praise.
Come now all yee terrors, sally   35
Muster forth into the valley,
Where triumphant darknesse hovers
With a sable wing, that covers
Brooding Horror. Come thou Death,
Let the damps of thy dull Breath   40
Overshadow even the shade,
And make darknesse selfe afraid ;
There my feet, even there shall find
Way for a resolved mind.
Still my Shepheard, still my God   45
Thou art with me, Still thy rod,
And thy staffe, whose influence
Gives direction, gives defence.
At the whisper of thy Word
Crown'd abundance spreads my Bord :   50
While I feast, my foes doe feed
Their rank malice not their need,
So that with the self-same bread
They are starv'd, and I am fed.
How my head in ointment swims !   55
How my cup orelooks her Brims !
So, even so still may I move
By the Line of thy deare Love ;

Still may thy sweet mercy spread
A shady Arme above my head,   60
About my Paths, so shall I find
The faire Center of my mind
Thy Temple, and those lovely walls
Bright ever with a beame that falls
Fresh from the pure glance of thine eye,   65
Lighting to Eternity.
There I'le dwell for ever, there
Will I find a purer aire
To feed my Life with, there I'le sup
Balme and Nectar in my Cup,   70
And thence my ripe soule will I breath
Warme into the Armes of Death.

Psalme 137

On the proud bankes of great Euphrates flood,
      There we sate, and there we wept :
Our Harpes that now no Musicke understood,
      Nodding on the Willowes slept,
            While unhappy captiv'd wee   5
            Lovely Sion thought on thee.

They, they that snatcht us from our Countries brest
      Would have a Song carv'd to their Eares
In Hebrew numbers, then (ô cruell jest!)
      When Harpes and hearts were drown'd in Teares : 10
            Come, they cry'd, come sing and play
            One of Sions songs to day.

Sing? play? to whom (ah) shall we sing or play,
      If not *Jerusalem* to thee?
Ah thee *Jerusalem*! ah sooner may   15
      This hand forget the mastery
            Of Musicks dainty touch, then I
            The Musicke of thy memory.

Which when I lose, ô may at once my Tongue
   Lose this same busie speaking art   20
Vnpearcht, her vocall Arteries unstrung,
   No more acquainted with my Heart,
      On my dry pallats roofe to rest
      A wither'd Leafe, an idle Guest.

No, no, thy good, Sion, alone must crowne   25
   The head of all my hope-nurst joyes.
But *Edom* cruell thou! thou cryd'st downe, downe
   Sinke Sion, downe and never rise,
      Her falling thou did'st urge and thrust,
      And haste to dash her into dust.   30

Dost laugh? proud *Babels* Daughter! do, laugh on,
   Till thy ruine teach thee Teares,
Even such as these, laugh, till a venging throng
   Of woes, too late doe rouze thy feares.
      Laugh, till thy childrens bleeding bones   35
      Weepe pretious Teares upon the stones.

A *Hymne of the Nativity, sung by*
*the Shepheards**

Chorus.   Come wee Shepheards who have seene
           Dayes King deposed by Nights Queene.
           Come lift we up our lofty song,
           To wake the Sun that sleeps too long.

           Hee in this our generall joy,   5
              Slept, and dreampt of no such thing
           While we found out the fair-ey'd Boy,
              And kist the Cradle of our King;
           Tell him hee rises now too late,
           To shew us ought worth looking at.   10

           Tell him wee now can shew him more
              Then hee e're shewd to mortall sight,

* See also p. 619.

Then hee himselfe e're saw before,
    Which to be seene needs not his light:
Tell him *Tityrus* where th'hast been,   15
Tell him *Thyrsis* what th'hast seen.

Tityrus. Gloomy Night embrac't the place
        Where the noble Infant lay:
    The Babe lookt up, and shew'd his face,
        In spight of Darknesse it was Day.   20
    It was thy Day, Sweet, and did rise,
    Not from the East, but from thy eyes.

Thyrsis. Winter chid the world, and sent
        The angry North to wage his warres:
    The North forgot his fierce intent,   25
        And left perfumes, in stead of scarres:
    By those sweet Eyes persuasive Powers,
    Where he meant frosts, he scattered Flowers.

Both.   We saw thee in thy Balmy Nest,
        Bright Dawne of our *Eternall Day*;   30
    Wee saw thine Eyes break from the East,
        And chase the trembling shades away:
    Wee saw thee (and wee blest the sight)
    Wee saw thee by thine owne sweet Light.

Tityrus. I saw the curl'd drops, soft and slow   35
        Come hovering o're the places head,
    Offring their whitest sheets of snow,
        To furnish the faire Infants Bed.
    Forbeare (said I) be not too bold,
    Your fleece is white, but 'tis too cold.   40

Thyrsis. I saw th'officious Angels bring,
        The downe that their soft brests did strow,
    For well they now can spare their wings,
        When Heaven it selfe lyes here below.
    Faire Youth (said I) be not too rough,   45
    Thy Downe though soft's not soft enough.

Tityrus.   The Babe no sooner 'gan to seeke,
  Where to lay his lovely head,
 But streight his eyes advis'd his Cheeke,
  'Twixt Mothers Brests to goe to bed. 50
 Sweet choise (said I) no way but so,
 Not to lye cold, yet sleepe in snow.

All. Welcome to our wondring sight
  Eternity shut in a span!
 Summer in Winter! Day in Night! 55
Chorus. Heaven in Earth! and God in Man!
 Great litle one, whose glorious Birth,
 Lifts Earth to Heaven, stoops heaven to earth.

 Welcome, though not to Gold, nor Silke,
  To more then *Cæsars* Birthright is. 60
 Two sister-Seas of virgins Milke,
  With many a rarely-temper'd kisse,
 That breathes at once both Maid and Mother,
 Warmes in the one, cooles in the other.

 Shee sings thy Teares asleepe, and dips 65
  Her Kisses in thy weeping Eye,
 Shee spreads the red leaves of thy Lips,
  That in their Buds yet blushing lye.
 Shee 'gainst those Mother-Diamonds tryes
 The points of her young Eagles Eyes. 70

 Welcome, (though not to those gay flyes
  Guilded i'th' Beames of Earthly Kings
 Slippery soules in smiling eyes)
  But to poore Shepheards, simple things,
 That use no varnish, no oyl'd Arts, 75
 But lift clean hands full of cleare hearts.

 Yet when young *Aprils* husband showres,
  Shall blesse the fruitfull *Maia's* Bed,
 Wee'l bring the first-borne of her flowers,
  To kisse thy feet, and crowne thy head. 80

To thee (Dread Lambe) whose Love must keepe
The Shepheards, while they feed their sheepe.

To thee meeke Majesty, soft King
   Of simple Graces, and sweet Loves,
Each of us his Lamb will bring,   85
   Each his payre of silver Doves.
At last, in fire of thy faire Eyes,
Wee'l burne, our owne best sacrifice.

Sospetto d' Herode

Libro Primo

Argomento

Casting the times with their strong signes,
Death's Master his owne death divines.
Strugling for helpe, his best hope is
Herod's suspition may heale his.
Therefore he sends a fiend to wake   5
The sleeping Tyrant's fond mistake;
Who feares (in vaine) that he whose Birth
Meanes Heav'n, should meddle with his Earth.

Mvse, now the servant of soft Loves no more,
Hate is thy Theame, and *Herod*, whose unblest   10
Hand (ô what dares not jealous Greatnesse?) tore
A thousand sweet Babes from their Mothers Brest:
The Bloomes of Martyrdome. O be a Dore
Of language to my infant Lips, yee best
   Of Confessours: whose Throates answering his swords, 15
   Gave forth your Blood for breath, spoke soules for words.

Great *Anthony*! *Spains* well-beseeming pride,
Thou mighty branch of Emperours and Kings.
The Beauties of whose dawne what eye may bide,
Which with the Sun himselfe weigh's equall wings.   **20**
Mappe of Heroick worth! whom farre and wide
To the beleeving world Fame boldly sings:

Deigne thou to weare this humble Wreath that bowes,
To be the sacred Honour of thy Browes.

Nor needs my Muse a blush, or these bright Flowers   25
Other then what their owne blest beauties bring.
They were the smiling sons of those sweet Bowers,
That drinke the deaw of Life, whose deathlesse spring,
Nor *Sirian* flame, nor *Borean* frost deflowers:
From whence Heav'n-labouring Bees with busie wing,   30
    Suck hidden sweets, which well digested proves
    Immortall Hony for the Hive of Loves.

Thou, whose strong hand with so transcendent worth,
Holds high the reine of faire *Parthenope*,
That neither *Rome*, nor *Athens* can bring forth   35
A Name in noble deedes Rivall to thee!
Thy Fames full noise, makes proud the patient Earth,
Farre more then matter for my Muse and mee.
    The *Tyrrhene* Seas, and shores sound all the same,
    And in their murmures keepe thy mighty Name.   40

Below the Botome of the great Abysse,
There where one Center reconciles all things;
The worlds profound Heart pants; There placed is
Mischifes old Master, close about him clings
A curl'd knot of embracing Snakes, that kisse   45
His correspondent cheekes: these loathsome strings
    Hold the perverse Prince in eternall Ties
    Fast bound, since first he forfeited the skies,

The Iudge of Torments, and the King of Teares:
Hee fills a burnisht Throne of quenchlesse fire: 50
And for his old faire Roabes of Light, hee weares
A gloomy Mantle of darke flames, the Tire
That crownes his hated head on high appeares;
Where seav'n tall Hornes (his Empires pride) aspire.
    And to make up Hells Majesty, each Horne   55
    Seav'n crested *Hydra's* horribly adorne.

His Eyes, the sullen dens of Death and Night,
Startle the dull Ayre with a dismall red:
Such his fell glances as the fatall Light
Of staring Comets, that looke Kingdomes dead.   60
From his black nostrills, and blew lips, in spight
Of Hells owne stinke, a worser stench is spread.
   His breath Hells lightning is: and each deepe grone
   Disdaines to thinke that Heav'n Thunders alone.

His flaming Eyes dire exhalation,   65
Vnto a dreadfull pile gives fiery Breath;
Whose unconsum'd consumption preys upon
The never-dying Life, of a long Death.
In this sad House of slow Destruction,
(His shop of flames) hee fryes himselfe, beneath   70
   A masse of woes, his Teeth for Torment gnash,
   While his steele sides sound with his Tayles strong lash.

Three Rigourous Virgins waiting still behind,
Assist the Throne of th' Iron-Sceptred King.
With whips of Thornes and knotty vipers twin'd   75
They rouse him, when his ranke Thoughts need a sting.
Their lockes are beds of uncomb'd snakes that wind
About their shady browes in wanton Rings.
   Thus reignes the wrathfull King, and while he reignes
   His Scepter and himselfe both he disdaines.   80

Disdainefull wretch! how hath one bold sinne cost
Thee all the Beauties of thy once bright Eyes?
How hath one blacke Eclipse cancell'd, and crost
The glories that did guild thee in thy Rise?
Proud Morning of a perverse Day! how lost   85
Art thou unto thy selfe, thou too selfe-wise
   Narcissus? foolish *Phaeton*? who for all
   Thy high-aym'd hopes, gaind'st but a flaming fall.

From Death's sad shades, to the Life-breathing Ayre,
This mortall Enemy to mankinds good,   90
Lifts his malignant Eyes, wasted with care,
To become beautifull in humane blood.

Where *Iordan* melts his Chrystall, to make faire
The fields of *Palestine*, with so pure a flood,
    There does he fixe his Eyes: and there detect   95
    New matter, to make good his great suspect.

He calls to mind th'old quarrell, and what sparke
Set the contending Sons of Heav'n on fire:
Oft in his deepe thought he revolves the darke
Sibills divining leaves: hee does enquire   100
Into th'old Prophesies, trembling to marke
How many present prodigies conspire,
    To crowne their past predictions, both hee layes
    Together, in his pondrous mind both weighes.

Heavens Golden-winged Herald, late hee saw   105
To a poore *Galilean* virgin sent:
How low the Bright Youth bow'd, and with what awe
Immortall flowers to her faire hand present.
Hee saw th'old *Hebrewes* wombe, neglect the Law
Of Age and Barennesse, and her Babe prevent   110
    His Birth, by his Devotion, who began
    Betimes to be a Saint, before a Man.

Hee saw rich Nectar thawes, release the rigour
Of th'Icy North, from frost-bcount *Atlas* hands
His Adamantine fetters fall: greene vigour   115
Gladding the *Scythian* Rocks, and *Libian* sands.
Hee saw a vernall smile, sweetly disfigure
Winters sad face, and through the flowry lands
    Of faire *Engaddi* hony-sweating Fountaines   [120
    With *Manna*, Milk, and Balm, new broach the Mountaines.

Hee saw how in that blest Day-bearing Night,
The Heav'n-rebuked shades made hast away;
How bright a Dawne of Angels with new Light
Amaz'd the midnight world, and made a Day
Of which the Morning knew not: Mad with spight   125
Hee markt how the poore Shepheards ran to pay
    Their simple Tribute to the Babe, whose Birth
    Was the great businesse both of Heav'n and Earth.

Hee saw a threefold Sun, with rich encrease,
Make proud the Ruby portalls of the East.　　　　130
Hee saw the Temple sacred to sweet Peace,
Adore her Princes Birth, flat on her Brest.
Hee saw the falling Idols, all confesse
A comming Deity. Hee saw the Nest
　　Of pois'nous and unnaturall loves, Earth-nurst;　　135
　　Toucht with the worlds true *Antidote* to burst.

He saw Heav'n blossome with a new-borne light,
On which, as on a glorious stranger gaz'd
The Golden eyes of Night: whose Beame made bright
The way to *Beth'lem*, and as boldly blaz'd,　　　　140
(Nor askt leave of the Sun) by Day as Night.
By whom (as Heav'ns illustrious Hand-maid) rais'd
　　Three Kings (or what is more) three Wise men went
　　Westward to find the worlds true *Orient*.

Strucke with these great concurrences of things,　　145
Symptomes so deadly, unto Death and him;
Faine would hee have forgot what fatall strings,
Eternally bind each rebellious limbe.
Hee shooke himselfe, and spread his spatious wings:
Which like two Bosom'd sailes embrace the dimme　　150
　　Aire, with a dismall shade, but all in vaine,
　　Of sturdy Adamant is his strong chaine.

While thus Heav'ns highest counsails, by the low
Footsteps of their Effects, hee trac'd too well,
Hee tost his troubled eyes, Embers that glow　　　155
Now with new Rage, and wax too hot for Hell.
With his foule clawes hee fenc'd his furrowed Brow,
And gave a gastly shreeke, whose horrid yell
　　Ran trembling through the hollow vaults of Night,
　　The while his twisted Tayle hee gnaw'd for spight.　　160

Yet on the other side, faine would he start
Above his feares, and thinke it cannot be.
Hee studies Scripture, strives to sound the heart,
And feele the pulse of every Prophecy.

Hee knowes (but knowes not how, or by what Art)   165
The Heav'n expecting Ages, hope to see
   A mighty Babe, whose pure, unspotted Birth,
   From a chast Virgin wombe, should blesse the Earth.

But these vast Mysteries his senses smother,
And Reason (for what's Faith to him?) devoure.   170
How she that is a maid should prove a Mother,
Yet keepe inviolate her virgin flower;
How Gods eternall Sonne should be mans Brother,
Poseth his proudest Intellectuall power.
   How a pure Spirit should incarnate bee,   175
   And life it selfe weare Deaths fraile Livery.

That the Great Angell-blinding light should shrinke
His blaze, to shine in a poore Shepheards eye.
That the unmeasur'd God so low should sinke,
As Pris'ner in a few poore Rags to lye.   180
That from his Mothers Brest hee milke should drinke,
Who feeds with Nectar Heav'ns faire family.
   That a vile Manger his low Bed should prove,
   Who in a Throne of stars Thunders above.

That hee whom the Sun serves, should faintly peepe   185
Through clouds of Infant flesh: that hee the old
Eternall Word should bee a Child, and weepe.
That hee who made the fire, should feare the cold;
That Heav'ns high Majesty his Court should keepe
In a clay-cottage, by each blast control'd.   190
   That Glories selfe should serve our Griefs, & feares:
   And free Eternity, submit to yeares.

And further, that the Lawes eternall Giver,
Should bleed in his owne lawes obedience:
And to the circumcising Knife deliver   195
Himselfe, the forfeit of his slaves offence.
That the unblemisht Lambe, blessed for ever,
Should take the marke of sin, and paine of sence.
   These are the knotty Riddles, whose darke doubt
   Intangles his lost Thoughts, past getting out.   200

While new Thoughts boyl'd in his enraged Brest,
His gloomy Bosomes darkest Character,
Was in his shady forehead seen exprest.
The forehead's shade in Griefes expression there,
Is what in signe of joy among the blest   205
The faces lightning, or a smile is here.
    Those stings of care that his strong Heart opprest,
    A desperate, *Oh mee*, drew from his deepe Brest.

Oh mee! (thus bellow'd hee) *oh mee*! what great
Portents before mine eyes their Powers advance?   210
And serves my purer sight, onely to beat
Downe my proud Thought, and leave it in a Trance?
Frowne I; and can great Nature keep her seat?
And the gay starrs lead on their Golden dance?
    Can his attempts above still prosp'rous be,   215
    Auspicious still, in spight of Hell and me?

Hee has my Heaven (what would he more?) whose bright
And radiant Scepter this bold hand should beare.
And for the never-fading fields of Light
My faire Inheritance, hee confines me here,   220
To this darke House of shades, horrour, and Night,
To draw a long-liv'd Death, where all my cheere
    Is the solemnity my sorrow weares,
    That Mankinds Torment waits upon my Teares.

Darke, dusty Man, he needs would single forth,   225
To make the partner of his owne pure ray:
And should we Powers of Heav'n, Spirits of worth
Bow our bright Heads, before a King of clay?
It shall not be, said I, and clombe the *North*,
Where never wing of *Angell* yet made way   230
    What though I mist my blow? yet I strooke high,
    And to dare something, is some victory.

Is hee not satisfied? meanes he to wrest
Hell from me too, and sack my Territories?
Vile humane Nature means he now t'invest   235
(O my despight!) with his divinest Glories?

And rising with rich spoiles upon his Brest,
With his faire Triumphs fill all future stories?
 Must the bright armes of Heav'n, rebuke these eyes?
 Mocke me, and dazle my darke Mysteries?   240

Art thou not *Lucifer?* hee to whom the droves
Of Stars, that guild the Morne in charge were given?
The nimblest of the lightning-winged Loves?
The fairest, and the first-borne smile of Heav'n?
Looke in what Pompe the Mistresse Planet moves   245
Rev'rently circled by the lesser seaven,
 Such, and so rich, the flames that from thine eyes,
 Oprest the common-people of the skyes.

Ah wretch! what bootes thee to cast back thy eyes,
Where dawning hope no beame of comfort showes?   250
While the reflection of thy forepast joyes,
Renders thee double to thy present woes.
Rather make up to thy new miseries,
And meet the mischiefe that upon thee growes.
 If Hell must mourne, Heav'n sure shall sympathize   255
 What force cannot effect, fraud shall devise.

And yet whose force feare I? have I so lost
My selfe? my strength too with my innocence?
Come try who dares, *Heav'n, Earth,* what ere dost boast,
A borrowed being, make thy bold defence.   260
Come thy Creator too, what though it cost
Mee yet a second fall? wee'd try our strengths.
 Heav'n saw us struggle once, as brave a fight
 Earth now should see, and tremble at the sight.

Thus spoke th'impatient Prince, and made a pause,   265
His foule Hags rais'd their heads, & clapt their hands.
And all the Powers of Hell in full applause
Flourisht their Snakes, and tost their flaming brands.
Wee (said the horrid sisters) wait thy lawes,
Th'obsequious handmaids of thy high commands.   270
 Be it thy part, Hells mighty Lord, to lay
 On us thy dread commands, ours to obey.

What thy *Alecto*, what these hands can doe,
Thou mad'st bold proofe upon the brow of Heav'n,
Nor should'st thou bate in pride, because that now,   275
To these thy sooty Kingdomes thou art driven.
Let Heav'ns Lord chide above lowder then thou
In language of his Thunder, thou art even
   With him below: here thou art Lord alone
   Boundlesse and absolute: Hell is thine owne.   280

If usuall wit, and strength will doe no good,
Vertues of stones, nor herbes: use stronger charmes,
Anger, and love, best hookes of humane blood.
If all faile wee'l put on our proudest Armes,
And pouring on Heav'ns face the Seas huge flood   285
Quench his curl'd fires, wee'l wake with our Alarmes
   Ruine, where e're she sleepes at Natures feet;
   And crush the world till his wide corners meet.

Reply'd the proud King, O my Crownes Defence?
Stay of my strong hopes, you of whose brave worth,   290
The frighted stars tooke faint experience,
When 'gainst the Thunders mouth wee marched forth:
Still you are prodigal of your Love's expence
In our great projects, both 'gainst Heav'n and Earth.
   I thanke you all, but one must single out,   295
   Cruelty, she alone shall cure my doubt.

Fourth of the cursed knot of Hags is shee,
Or rather all the other three in one;
Hells shop of slaughter shee do's oversee,
And still assist the Execution.   300
But chiefly there do's shee delight to be,
Where Hells capacious Cauldron is set on:
   And while the black soules boile in their owne gore,
   To hold them down, and looke that none seethe o're.

Thrice howl'd the Caves of Night, and thrice the sound, 305
Thundring upon the bankes of those black lakes
Rung, through the hollow vaults of Hell profound:
At last her listning Eares the noise o'retakes,

Shee lifts her sooty lampes, and looking round
A gen'rall hisse, from the whole Tire of snakes 310
    Rebounding, through Hells inmost Cavernes came,
    In answer to her formidable Name.

Mongst all the Palaces in Hells command,
No one so mercilesse as this of hers.
The Adamantine Doors, for ever stand 315
Impenetrable, both to prai'rs and Teares,
The walls inexorable steele, no hand
Of *Time*, or Teeth of hungry *Ruine* feares.
    Their ugly ornaments are the bloody staines,
    Of ragged limbs, torne sculls, & dasht out Braines. 320

There has the purple *Vengeance* a proud seat,
Whose ever-brandisht Sword is sheath'd in blood.
About her *Hate*, *Wrath*, *Warre*, and *slaughter* sweat;
Bathing their hot limbs in life's pretious flood.
There rude impetuous Rage do's storme, and fret: 325
And there, as Master of this murd'ring brood,
    Swinging a huge Sith stands impartiall *Death*,
    With endlesse businesse almost out of Breath.

For Hangings and for Curtaines, all along
The walls, (abominable ornaments!) 330
Are tooles of wrath, Anvills of Torments hung;
Fell Executioners of foule intents,
Nailes, hammers, hatchets sharpe, and halters strong,
Swords, Speares, with all the fatall Instruments
    Of sin, and Death, twice dipt in the dire staines 335
    Of Brothers mutuall blood, and Fathers braines.

The Tables furnisht with a cursed Feast,
Which *Harpyes*, with leane *Famine* feed upon,
Vnfill'd for ever. Here among the rest,
Inhumane *Erisi-cthon* too makes one; 340
Tantalus, *Atreus*, *Progne*, here are guests:
Wolvish *Lycaon* here a place hath won.
    The cup they drinke in is *Medusa's* scull,
    Which mixt with gall & blood they quaffe brim full.

The foule Queens most abhorred Maids of Honour 345
Medæa, Jezabell, many a meager Witch
With *Circe, Scylla,* stand to wait upon her.
But her best huswifes are the *Parcæ,* which
Still worke for her, and have their wages from her.
They prick a bleeding heart at every stitch. 350
   Her cruell cloathes of costly threds they weave,
   Which short-cut lives of murdred *Infants* leave.

The house is hers'd about with a black wood,
Which nods with many a heavy headed tree.
Each flowers a pregnant poyson, try'd and good, 355
Each herbe a Plague. The winds sighes timed-bee
By a black Fount, which weeps into a flood.
Through the thick shades obscurely might you see
   Minotaures, Cyclopses, with a darke drove
   Of *Dragons, Hydraes, Sphinxes,* fill the Grove. 360

Here *Diomed's* Horses, *Phereus* dogs appeare,
With the fierce Lyons of *Therodamas.*
Busiris ha's his bloody Altar here,
Here *Sylla* his severest prison has.
The *Lestrigonians* here their Table reare; 365
Here strong *Procrustes* plants his Bed of Brasse.
   Here cruell *Scyron* boasts his bloody rockes,
   And hatefull *Schinis* his so feared Oakes.

What ever Schemes of Blood, fantastick frames
Of Death *Mezentius,* or *Geryon* drew; 370
Phalaris, Ochus, Ezelinus, names
Mighty in mischiefe, with dread *Nero* too,
Here are they all, Here all the swords or flames
Assyrian Tyrants, or *Egyptian* knew.
   Such was the House, so furnisht was the Hall, 375
   Whence the fourth *Fury,* answer'd *Pluto's* call.

Scarce to this Monster could the shady King,
The horrid summe of his intentions tell;
But shee (swift as the momentary wing
Of lightning, or the words he spoke) left Hell. 380

Shee rose, and with her to our world did bring,
Pale proofe of her fell presence. Th'aire too well
    With a chang'd countenance witnest the sight,
    And poore fowles intercepted in their flight.

Heav'n saw her rise, and saw Hell in the sight.   385
The field's faire Eyes saw her, and saw no more,
But shut their flowry lids for ever. Night,
And Winter strow her way; yea, such a sore
Is shee to Nature, that a generall fright,
An universall palsie spreading o're   390
    The face of things, from her dire eyes had run,
    Had not her thick Snakes hid them from the Sun.

Now had the Night's companion from her den,
Where all the busie day shee close doth ly,
With her soft wing, wipt from the browes of men   395
Day's sweat, and by a gentle Tyranny,
And sweet oppression, kindly cheating them
Of all their cares, tam'd the rebellious eye
    Of sorrow, with a soft and downy hand,
    Sealing all brests in a *Lethæan* band.   400

When the *Erinnys* her black pineons spread,
And came to *Bethlem*, where the cruell King
Had now retyr'd himselfe, and borrowed
His Brest a while from care's unquiet sting.
Such as at *Thebes* dire feast shee shew'd her head,   405
Her sulphur-breathed Torches brandishing,
    Such to the frighted Palace now shee comes,
    And with soft feet searches the silent roomes.

By *Herod* leige to Cesar now was borne
The Scepter, which of old great *David* swaid.   410
Whose right by *David's* linage so long worne,
Himselfe a stranger to, his owne had made:
And from the head of *Iudahs* house quite torne
The Crowne, for which upon their necks he laid
    A sad yoake, under which they sigh'd in vaine,   415
    And looking on their lost state sigh'd againe.

Vp, through the spatious Pallace passed she,
To where the Kings proudly-reposed head
(If any can be soft to *Tyranny*
And selfe-tormenting sin) had a soft bed.   420
She thinkes not fit such he her face should see,
As it is seene by Hell; and seene with dread.
   To change her faces stile she doth devise,
   And in a pale Ghost's shape to spare his Eyes.

Her selfe a while she layes aside, and makes   425
Ready to personate a mortall part.
Ioseph the Kings dead Brothers shape she takes,
What he by Nature was, is she by Art.
She comes to th' King and with her cold hand slakes
His Spirits, the Sparkes of Life, and chills his heart,   430
   Lifes forge; fain'd is her voice, and false too, be
   Her words, sleep'st thou fond man? sleep'st thou?
     (said she)

So sleeps a Pilot, whose poore Barke is prest
With many a mercylesse o're mastring wave;   435
For whom (as dead) the wrathfull winds contest,
Which of them deep'st shall digge her watry Grave.
Why dost thou let thy brave soule lye supprest,
In Death-like slumbers; while thy dangers crave
   A waking eye and hand? looke up and see   440
   The fates ripe, in their great conspiracy.

Know'st thou not how of th' Hebrewes royall stemme
(That old dry stocke) a despair'd branch is sprung
A most strange Babe! who here conceal'd by them
In a neglected stable lies, among   445
Beasts and base straw: Already is the streame
Quite turn'd: th' ingratefull Rebells this their young
   Master (with voyce free as the Trumpe of *Fame*)
   Their new King, and thy Successour proclaime.

What busy motions, what wild Engines stand   450
On tiptoe in their giddy Braynes? th' have fire
Already in their Bosomes; and their hand

Already reaches at a sword: They hire
Poysons to speed thee; yet through all the Land
What one comes to reveale what they conspire? 455
    Goe now, make much of these; wage still their wars
    And bring home on thy Brest more thanklesse scarrs.

Why did I spend my life, and spill my Blood,
That thy firme hand for ever might sustaine
A well-pois'd Scepter? does it now seeme good 460
Thy Brothers blood be-spilt life spent in vaine?
'Gainst thy owne sons and Brothers thou hast stood
In Armes, when lesser cause was to complaine:
    And now crosse Fates a watch about thee keepe,
    Can'st thou be carelesse now? now can'st thou sleep? 465

Where art thou man? what cowardly mistake
Of thy great selfe, hath stolne King *Herod* from thee?
O call thy selfe home to thy selfe, wake, wake,
And fence the hanging sword Heav'n throws upon thee.
Redeeme a worthy wrath, rouse thee, and shake 470
Thy selfe into a shape that may become thee.
    Be *Herod*, and thou shalt not misse from mee
    Immortall stings to thy great thoughts, and thee.

So said, her richest snake, which to her wrist
For a beseeming bracelet shee had ty'd 475
(A speciall Worme it was as ever kist
The foamy lips of *Cerberus*) shee apply'd
To the Kings Heart, the Snake no sooner hist,
But vertue heard it, and away shee hy'd,
    Dire flames diffuse themselves through every veine, 480
    This done, Home to her Hell shee hy'd amaine.

Hee wakes, and with him (ne're to sleepe) new feares:
His Sweat-bedewed Bed had now betrai'd him,
To a vast field of thornes, ten thousand Speares
All pointed in his heart seem'd to invade him: 485
So mighty were th'amazing Characters
With which his feeling Dreame had thus dismay'd him,
    Hee his owne fancy-framed foes defies:
    In rage, *My armes, give me my armes,* hee cryes.

As when a Pile of food-preparing fire,   490
The breath of artificiall lungs embraves,
The Caldron-prison'd waters streight conspire,
And beat the hot Brasse with rebellious waves:
He murmures, and rebukes their bold desire;
Th'impatient liquor, frets, and foames, and raves;   495
    Till his o'reflowing pride suppresse the flame,
    Whence all his high spirits, and hot courage came.

So boyles the fired *Herods* blood-swolne brest,
Not to be slakt but by a Sea of blood.
His faithlesse Crowne he feeles loose on his Crest,   500
Which on false Tyrants head ne're firmly stood.
The worme of jealous envy and unrest,
To which his gnaw'd heart is the growing food
    Makes him impatient of the lingring light.
    Hate the sweet peace of all-composing Night.   505

A Thousand Prophecies that talke strange things,
Had sowne of old these doubts in his deepe brest.
And now of late came tributary Kings,
Bringing him nothing but new feares from th'East,
More deepe suspicions, and more deadly stings,   510
With which his feav'rous cares their cold increast.
    And now his dream (Hels firebrand) stil more bright,
    Shew'd him his feares, and kill'd him with the sight.

No sooner therefore shall the Morning see
(Night hangs yet heavy on the lids of Day)   515
But all his Counsellours must summon'd bee,
To meet their troubled Lord without delay.
Heralds and Messengers immediately
Are sent about, who poasting every way
    To th'heads and Officers of every band;   520
    Declare who sends, and what is his command.

Why art thou troubled *Herod?* what vaine feare
Thy blood-revolving Brest to rage doth move?
Heavens King, who doffs himselfe weake flesh to weare,
Comes not to rule in wrath, but serve in love.   525

Nor would he this thy fear'd Crown from three Teare,
But give thee a better with himselfe above.
    Poore jealousie! why should he wish to prey
    Vpon thy Crowne, who gives his owne away?

Make to thy reason man; and mocke thy doubts,   530
Looke how below thy feares their causes are;
Thou art a Souldier *Herod*; send thy Scouts
See how hee's furnish't for so fear'd a warre.
What armour does he weare? A few thin clouts.
His Trumpets? tender cryes, his men to dare   535
    So much? rude Shepheards. What his steeds? alas
    Poore Beasts! a slow Oxe, and a simple Asse.

Il fine del libro primo.

On a prayer booke sent
to Mrs. M. R.*

Loe here a little volume, but large booke,
    (Feare it not, sweet,
    It is no hipocrit)
Much larger in it selfe then in its looke.

    It is in one rich handfull, heaven and all   5
        Heavens royall Hoasts incampt, thus small;
        To prove that true, schooles use to tell,
    A thousand Angells in one point can dwell.

It is loves great Artillery,
Which here contracts it selfe and comes to lye   10
Close coucht in your white bosome, and from thence
As from a snowy fortresse of defence
Against the ghostly foe to take your part:
And fortifie the hold of your chast heart.

* See also p. 675.

It is the Armory of light,   15
Let constant use but keep it bright,
   Youl find it yeelds
To holy hands, and humble hearts,
   More swords and sheilds
Then sinne hath snares, or hell hath darts.   20

     Onely bee sure,
     The hands bee pure,
That hold these weapons and the eyes
Those of turtles, chast, and true,
    Wakefull, and wise   25
Here is a friend shall fight for you,
Hold but this booke before your heart,
Let prayer alone to play his part.

But o', the heart
That studyes this high art,   30
Must bee a sure house keeper,
And yet no sleeper.

Deare soule bee strong,
Mercy will come ere long,
And bring her bosome full of blessings,   35
Flowers of never fading graces;
To make immortall dressings
For worthy souls whose wise embraces
Store up themselves for him, who is alone
The spouse of Virgins, and the Virgins son.   40
But if the noble Bridegrome when hee comes
   Shall find the wandring heart from home,
     Leaving her chast abode,
      To gad abroad:

Amongst the gay mates of the god of flyes;   45
   To take her pleasures, and to play
    And keep the divells holy day.
To dance in the Sunneshine of some smiling
     but beguiling
Spheare of sweet, and sugred lies,   50

Some slippery paire,
Of false perhaps as faire
Flattering but forswearing eyes

Doubtles some other heart
    Will git the start,   55
    And stepping in before,
Will take possession of the sacred store
    Of hidden sweets, and holy joyes,
    Words which are not heard with eares,
(These tumultuous shops of noise)   60
    Effectuall whispers whose still voyce,
The soule it selfe more feeles then heares.

Amorous Languishments, Luminous trances,
    Sights which are not seen with eyes,
Spirituall and soule peircing glances.   65
    Whose pure and subtle lightning, flies
Home to the heart, and setts the house on fire;
And melts it downe in sweet desire:
    Yet doth not stay
To aske the windowes leave, to passe that way.   70
Delicious deaths, soft exhalations
Of soule; deare, and divine annihilations.
    A thousand unknowne rites
    Of joyes, and rarifyed delights.

An hundred thousand loves and graces,   75
    And many a misticke thing,
    Which the divine embraces
Of the deare spowse of spirits with them will bring.
    For which it is no shame,
That dull mortality must not know a name.   80

Of all this hidden store
Of blessings, and ten thousand more;
    If when hee come
Hee find the heart from home,
    Doubtless hee will unload   85
Himselfe some other where,

And powre abroad
His precious sweets,
On the faire soule whom first hee meets.

O faire! ô fortunate! ô rich! ô deare!   90
    O happy and thrice happy shee
    Deare silver breasted dove
        Who ere shee bee,
        Whose early Love
        With winged vowes,   95
Makes haste to meet her morning spowse:
And close with his immortall kisses.
    Happy soule who never misses,
    To improve that precious houre:
        And every day,   100
        Seize her sweet prey;
    All fresh and fragrant as hee rises,
    Dropping with a balmy showre
    A delicious dew of spices.

O let that happy soule hold fast   105
Her heavenly armefull, shee shall tast
At once, ten thousand paradises
        Shee shall have power,
        To rifle and deflower,
The rich and roseall spring of those rare sweets,   110
Which with a swelling bosome there shee meets,
Boundlesse and infinite————————————
——————————————bottomlesse treasures,
            Of pure inebriating pleasures,
Happy soule shee shall discover,   115
        What joy, what blisse,
    How many heavens at once it is,
To have a God become her lover.

On Mr. G. Herberts *booke intitu-*
led the Temple of Sacred Po-
ems, sent to a Gentle-
woman

Know you faire, on what you looke;
Divinest love lyes in this booke:
Expecting fire from your eyes,
To kindle this his sacrifice.
When your hands unty these strings,   5
Thinke you have an Angell by th' wings.
One that gladly will bee nigh,
To wait upon each morning sigh.
To flutter in the balmy aire,
Of your well perfumed prayer.   10
These white plumes of his heele lend you,
Which every day to heaven will send you:
To take acquaintance of the spheare,
And all the smooth faced kindred there.
And though *Herberts* name doe owe   15
These devotions, fairest; know
That while I lay them on the shrine
Of your white hand, they are mine.

In memory of the Vertuous and Lear-
ned Lady Madre de Teresa
that sought an early
*Martyrdome**

Love thou art absolute, sole Lord
Of life and death—To prove the word,
Wee need to goe to none of all
Those thy old souldiers, stout and tall
Ripe and full growne, that could reach downe,   5
With strong armes their triumphant crowne:
Such as could with lusty breath,
Speake lowd unto the face of death
Their great Lords glorious name, to none
Of those whose large breasts built a throne   10

* See also p. 665.

For love their Lord, glorious and great,
Weell see him take a private seat,
And make his mansion in the milde
And milky soule of a soft childe.

Scarce had shee learnt to lisp a name   15
Of Martyr, yet shee thinkes it shame
Life should so long play with that breath,
Which spent can buy so brave a death.

Shee never undertooke to know,
What death with love should have to doe   20
Nor hath shee ere yet understood
Why to show love shee should shed blood,
Yet though shee cannot tell you why,
Shee can love and shee can dye.

Scarce had shee blood enough, to make   25
A guilty sword blush for her sake;
Yet has shee a heart dares hope to prove,
How much lesse strong is death then love.

Bee love but there, let poore six yeares,
Bee posed with the maturest feares   30
Man trembles at, wee straight shall find
Love knowes no nonage, nor the mind.
Tis love, not yeares, or Limbes, that can
Make the martyr or the man.
Love toucht her heart, and loe it beats   35
High, and burnes with such brave heats:
Such thirst to dye, as dare drinke up,
A thousand cold deaths in one cup.
Good reason for shee breaths all fire,
Her weake breast heaves with strong desire,   40
Of what shee may with fruitlesse wishes
Seeke for, amongst her mothers kisses.

Since tis not to bee had at home,
Sheel travell to a martyrdome.
No home for her confesses shee,   45
But where shee may A martyr bee.
   Sheel to the Moores, and trade with them,
   For this unvalued Diadem,
   Shee offers them her dearest breath,
   With Christs name int in change for death.   50
Sheel bargain with them, and will give
Them God, and teach them how to live
In him, or if they this denye,
For him sheel teach them how to dye.
So shall shee leave amongst them sowne,   55
Her Lords blood, or at lest her owne.

Farewell then all the world, adieu,
Teresa is no more for you:
Farewell all pleasures, sports and joyes,
Never till now esteemed toyes.   60
Farewell what ever deare may bee,
Mothers armes, or fathers knee.
Farewell house, and farewell home:
Shees for the Moores and Martyrdome.

   Sweet not so fast, Loe thy faire spouse,   65
   Whom thou seek'st with so swift vowes
   Calls thee back, and bids thee come,
   T'embrace a milder Martyrdome.

Blest powers forbid thy tender life,
Should bleed upon a barbarous knife.   70
Or some base hand have power to race,
Thy Breasts chast cabinet; and uncase
A soule kept there so sweet. O no,
Wise heaven will never have it so.
Thou art Loves victim, and must dye   75
A death more misticall and high.
Into Loves hand thou shalt let fall,
A still surviving funerall.

His is the dart must make the death
Whose stroake shall taste thy hallowed breath;   80
A dart thrice dipt in that rich flame,
Which writes thy spowses radiant name
Vpon the roofe of heaven where ay
It shines, and with a soveraigne ray,
Beats bright upon the burning faces   85
Of soules, which in that names sweet graces,
Find everlasting smiles. So rare,
So spirituall, pure and faire,
Must be the immortall instrument,
Vpon whose choice point shall be spent,   90
A life so loved, and that there bee
Fit executioners for thee,
The fairest, and the first borne sons of fire,
Blest Seraphims shall leave their quire,
And turne Loves souldiers, upon thee,   95
To exercise their Archerie.

O how oft shalt thou complaine
Of a sweet and subtile paine?
Of intollerable joyes?
Of a death in which who dyes   100
Loves his death, and dyes againe,
And would for ever so be slaine!
And lives and dyes, and knowes not why
To live, but that he still may dy.

How kindly will thy gentle heart,   105
Kisse the sweetly—killing dart:
And close in his embraces keep,
Those delicious wounds that weep
Balsome, to heale themselves with————
—————————————————————————thus   110
When these thy deaths so numerous,
Shall all at last dye into one,
And melt thy soules sweet mansion:
Like a soft lumpe of Incense, hasted
By too hot a fire, and wasted,   115
Into perfuming cloudes. So fast
Shalt thou exhale to heaven at last,

In a disolving sigh, and then
   O what! aske not the tongues of men,
Angells cannot tell, suffice,   120
Thy selfe shalt feel thine owne full joyes.
And hold them fast for ever. There,
So soone as thou shalt first appeare,
The moone of maiden starres; thy white
Mistresse attended by such bright   125
Soules as thy shining selfe, shall come,
And in her first rankes make thee roome.
Where mongst her snowy family,
Immortall wellcomes wait on thee.
O what delight when shee shall stand,   130
And teach thy Lipps heaven, with her hand,
On which thou now maist to thy wishes,
Heap up thy consecrated kisses.
What joy shall seize thy soule when shee
Bending her blessed eyes on thee   135
Those second smiles of heaven shall dart,
Her mild rayes, through thy melting heart:

Angells thy old friends there shall greet thee,
Glad at their owne home now to meet thee.
All thy good workes which went before,   140
And waited for thee at the doore:
Shall owne thee there: and all in one
Weave a Constellation
Of Crownes, with which the King thy spouse,
Shall build up thy triumphant browes.   145

All thy old woes shall now smile on thee,
And thy pains set bright upon thee.
All thy sorrows here shall shine,
And thy sufferings bee devine.
Teares shall take comfort, and turne Gems.   150
And wrongs repent to diadems.
Even thy deaths shall live, and new
Dresse the soule, which late they slew.
Thy wounds shall blush to such bright scarres,
As keep account of the Lambes warres   155

Those rare workes, where thou shalt leave writ,
Loves noble history, with witt
Taught thee by none but him, while here
They feed our soules, shall cloath thine there.
Each heavenly word, by whose hid flame   160
Our hard hearts shall strike fire, the same
Shall flourish on thy browes; and bee
Both fire to us, and flame to thee:
Whose light shall live bright, in thy face
By glory, in our hearts by grace.   165

Thou shalt looke round about, and see
Thousands of crownd soules, throng to bee
Themselves thy crowne, sonnes of thy vowes:
The Virgin births with which thy spowse
Made fruitfull thy faire soule; Goe now   170
And with them all about thee, bow

To him, put on (heel say) put on
My Rosy Love, that thy rich Zone,
Sparkeling with the sacred flames,
Of thousand soules whose happy names,   175
Heaven keeps upon thy score (thy bright
Life, brought them first to kisse the light
That kindled them to starres,) and so
Thou with the Lambe thy Lord shall goe.
And where so e're hee sitts his white   180
Steps, walke with him those wayes of Light.
Which who in death would live to see,
Must learne in life to dye like thee.

An Apologie for the precedent Hymne[*]

Thus have I back againe to thy bright name
Faire sea of holy fires transfused the flame
I tooke from reading thee. 'Tis to thy wrong
I know that in my weak and worthlesse song

[*] See also p. 670.

Thou here art set to shine, where thy full day   5
Scarce dawnes, ô pardon, if I dare to say
Thine own deare books are guilty, for from thence
I learnt to know that Love is eloquence.
That heavenly maxim gave me heart to try
If what to other tongues is tun'd so high,   10
Thy praise might not speak English too, forbid
(by all thy mysteries that there lye hid;)
Forbid it mighty Love, let no fond hate
Of names and words so farre prejudicate;
Soules are not Spaniards too, one frendly flood   15
Of Baptisme, blends them all into one blood.
Christs Faith makes but one body of all soules,
And loves that bodies soule; no Law controules
Our free trafick for heaven, we may maintaine,
Peace sure with piety, though it dwell in *Spaine*.   20
What soule soever in any Language can
Speake heaven like hers, is my soules country-man.
O 'tis not Spanish, but 'tis heaven she speakes,
'Tis heaven that lies in ambush there, and breakes
From thence into the wondring readers breast,   25
Who finds his warme heart, hatcht into a nest
Of little Eagles, and young Loves, whose high
Flights scorne the lazie dust, and things that dye.
There are enow whose draughts as deep as hell
Drinke up all *Spaine* in Sack, let my soule swell   30
With thee strong wine of Love, let others swimme
In puddles, we will pledge this Seraphim
Bowles full of richer blood then blush of grape
Was ever guilty of, change wee our shape,
My soule, some drinke from men to beasts; ô then,   35
Drinke wee till we prove more, not lesse then men:
And turne not beasts, but Angels. Let the King,
Mee ever into these his Cellars bring;
Where flowes such Wine as we can have of none
But him, who trod the Wine-presse all alone: 40
Wine of youths Life, and the sweet deaths of Love,
Wine of immortall mixture, which can prove
Its tincture from the Rosie Nectar, wine
That can exalt weak earth, and so refine
Our dust, that in one draught, Mortality   45
May drinke it selfe up, and forget to dy.

On a Treatise of Charity

Rise then, immortall maid! *Religion* rise!
Put on thy selfe in thine own looks: t' our eyes
Be what thy beauties, not our blots, have made thee,
Such as (e're our dark sinnes to dust betray'd thee)
Heav'n set thee down new drest; when thy bright birth   5
Shot thee like lightning, to th'astonisht earth.
From th' dawn of thy faire eye-lids wipe away
Dull mists and melancholy clouds: take day
And thine owne beames about thee: bring the best
Of whatsoe're perfum'd thy *Eastern nest.*   10
Girt all thy glories to thee: then sit down,
Open this booke, faire Queen, *and take thy crown.*
These learned leaves shall vindicate to thee
Thy holyest, humblest, handmaid Charitie.
Sh'l dresse thee like thy selfe, set thee on high   15
Where thou shalt reach all hearts, command each eye.
Lo where I see thy offrings wake, and rise
From the pale dust of that strange sacrifice
Which they themselves were; each one putting on
A majestie that may beseem thy throne.   20
The holy youth of heav'n, whose golden rings
Girt round thy awfull Altars, with bright wings
Fanning thy faire locks (which the world beleeves
As much as sees) shall with these sacred leaves
Trick their tall plumes, and in that garb shall go   25
If not more glorious, more conspicuous tho.
———— Be it enacted then
By the faire lawes of thy firm-pointed pen,
Gods services no longer shall put on
A *sluttishnesse,* for *pure religion:*   30
No longer shall our Churches frighted stones
Lie scatter'd like the burnt and martyr'd bones
Of dead Devotion; nor faint marbles weep
In their sad ruines; nor Religion keep
A melancholy mansion in those cold   35
Vrns. Like Gods Sanctuaries they lookt of old:
Now seem they Temples consecrate to *none,*
Or to a *new* God *Desolation.*
No more the hypocrite shall th'*upright* be
Because he's stiffe, and will confesse no knee: 40

While others bend their knee, no more shalt thou
(Disdainfull dust and ashes) bend thy brow;
Nor on Gods Altar cast *two scorching eyes*
Bak't in hot scorn, for *a burnt sacrifice:*
But (for a *Lambe*) thy tame and tender *heart*   45
New struck by love, still trembling on his dart;
Or (for two *Turtle doves*) it shall suffice
To bring a paire of meek and humble *eyes.*
This shall from hence-forth be the masculine theme
Pulpits and pennes shall sweat in; to redeem   50
Vertue to action, that life-feeding flame
That keeps Religion warme: not swell *a name*
Of faith, *a mountaine word,* made up of aire,
With those deare spoiles that wont to dresse the faire
And fruitfull Charities full breasts (of old)   55
Turning her out to tremble in the cold.
What can the poore hope from us, when we be
Vncharitable ev'n to *Charitie.*

On the Assumption of the Virgin Marie*

Harke shee is called, the parting houre is come,
Take thy farewel poore world, heaven must go home.
A peece of heavenly Light purer and brighter
Then the chast stars, whose choice Lamps come to light her.
While through the christall orbs clearer then they   5
Shee climbes, and makes a farre more milky way;
Shee's call'd againe, harke how th'immortall Dove
Sighs to his silver mate: rise up my Love,
Rise up my faire, my spotlesse one,
The Winter's past, the raine is gone: 10
The Spring is come, the Flowers appeare,
No sweets since thou art wanting here.

> Come away my Love,
> Come away my Dove
>   cast off delay: 15
> The Court of Heav'n is come,
> To wait upon thee home;
>   Come away, come away.

* See also p. 657.

Shee's call'd againe, and will shee goe;
When heaven bids come, who can say no?   20
Heav'n calls her, and she must away,
Heaven will not, and she cannot stay.
Goe then, goe (glorious) on the golden wings
Of the bright youth of Heaven, that sings
Vnder so sweet a burden: goe,   25
Since thy great Sonne will have it so:
And while thou goest, our song and wee,
Will as wee may reach after thee.
Haile holy Queen of humble hearts,
Wee in thy praise will have our parts.   30
And though thy dearest looks must now be light
To none but the blest heavens, whose bright
Beholders lost in sweet delight
Feed for ever their faire sight
With those divinest eyes, which wee   35
And our darke world no more shall see.
Though, our poore joyes are parted so,
Yet shall our lips never let goe
Thy gracious name, but to the last,
Our Loving song shall hold it fast.   40

    Thy sacred Name shall bee
    Thy selfe to us, and wee
    With holy cares will keepe it by us,
      Wee to the last,
      Will hold it fast,   45
    And no Assumption shall deny us.
    All the sweetest showers,
    Of our fairest Flowers,
    Will wee strow upon it:
    Though our sweetnesse cannot make   50
    It sweeter, they may take
    Themselves new sweetnesse from it.

Mary, men and Angels sing,
Maria Mother of our King.
Live rarest Princesse, and may the bright   55
Crown of an incomparable Light
Embrace thy radiant browes, ô may the best
Of everlasting joyes bath thy white brest.

Live our chaste love, the holy mirth
Of heaven, and humble pride of Earth: 60
Live Crowne of Women, Queen of men:
Live Mistris of our Song, and when
Our weak desires have done their best;
Sweet Angels come, and sing the rest.

An Himne for the Circumcision day of our Lord*

Rise thou first and fairest morning,
    Rosie with a double red:
With thine owne blush thy cheekes adorning,
    And the deare drops this day were shed.

All the purple pride of Laces,   5
    The crimson curtaines of thy bed;
Guild thee not with so sweet graces;
    Nor sets thee in so rich a red.

Of all the faire cheekt flowers that fill thee,
    None so faire thy bosome strowes;   10
As this modest Maiden Lilly,
    Our sinnes have sham'd into a Rose.

Bid the golden god the Sunne,
    Burnisht in his glorious beames:
Put all his red eyed rubies on,   15
    These Rubies shall put out his eyes.

Let him make poore the purple East,
    Rob the rich store her Cabinets keep,
The pure birth of each sparkling nest,
    That flaming in their faire bed sleep.   20

Let him embrace his owne bright tresses,
    With a new morning made of gems;
And weare in them his wealthy dresses,
    Another day of Diadems.

* See also p. 623.

When he hath done all he may,   25
    To make himselfe rich in his rise,
All will be darknesse, to the day
    That breakes from one of these faire eyes.

And soone the sweet truth shall appeare,
    Deare Babe e're many dayes be done: 30
The Moone shall come to meet thee here,
    And leave the long adored Sunne.

Thy nobler beauty shall bereave him,
    Of all his Easterne Paramours:
His Persian Lovers all shall leave him,   35
    And sweare faith to thy sweeter powers.

Nor while they leave him shall they loose the Sunne,
    But in thy fairest eyes find two for one.

On Hope,

By way of Question and Answer, betweene
A. Cowley, and R. Crashaw*

Cowley.   Hope, whose weake being ruin'd is
    Alike, if it succeed, and if it misse.
    Whom Ill, and Good doth equally confound,
    And both the hornes of Fates dilemma wound.
      Vaine shadow! that doth vanish quite   5
      Both at full noone, and perfect night.
      The Fates have not a possibility
        Of blessing thee.
    If things then from their ends wee happy call,
    'Tis hope is the most hopelesse thing of all.   10

Crashaw. Deare Hope! Earths dowry, and Heavens debt,
    The entity of things that are not yet.
    Subt'lest, but surest being! Thou by whom
    Our Nothing hath a definition.

* See also pp. 688-691.

         Faire cloud of fire, both shade, and light,   15
         Our life in death, our day in night.
         Fates cannot find out a capacity
            Of hurting thee.
         From thee their thinne dilemma with blunt horne
         Shrinkes, like the sick Moone at the wholsome   20
            morne.

Cowley.   Hope, thou bold taster of delight,
         Who, in stead of doing so, devour'st it quite.
         Thou bring'st us an estate, yet leav'st us poore,
         By clogging it with Legacies before.   25
            The joyes, which wee intire should wed,
            Come deflour'd virgins to our bed.
            Good fortunes without gaine imported bee,
              So mighty Custome's paid to thee.
         For joy, like Wine kept close doth better taste: 30
         If it take ayre before, its spirits waste.

Crashaw.   Thou art Loves Legacie under lock
         Of Faith: the steward of our growing stocke.
         Our Crown-lands lye above, yet each meale
            brings   35
         A seemly portion for the Sons of Kings.
            Nor will the Virgin-joyes wee wed
            Come lesse unbroken to our bed,
            Because that from the bridall cheeke of Blisse,
             Thou thus steal'st downe a distant kisse,   40
         Hopes chaste kisse wrongs no more joyes
            maidenhead,
         Then Spousall rites prejudge the marriage-bed.

Cowley.   Hope, Fortunes cheating Lotterie,
         Where for one prize an hundred blankes there   45
            bee.
         Fond Archer Hope, who tak'st thine ayme so
            farre,
         That still, or short, or wide thine arrowes are.
            Thine empty cloud the eye, it selfe deceives   50
            With shapes that our owne fancie gives:

A cloud, which gilt, and painted now appeares,
    But must drop presently in teares.
When thy false beames o're Reasons light
        prevaile,   55
By *ignes fatui,* not North starres we sayle.

Crashaw.   Faire *Hope*! our earlier Heaven! by thee
Young *Time* is taster to Eternity.
The generous wine with age growes strong, not
        sower;   60
Nor need wee kill thy fruit to smell thy flower.
    Thy golden head never hangs downe,
    Till in the lap of Loves full noone
    It falls, and dyes: oh no, it melts away
      As doth the dawne into the day: 65
As lumpes of Sugar lose themselves, and twine
Their subtile essence with the soule of Wine.

Cowley.   Brother of Feare! more gaily clad
The merrier Foole o'th' two, yet quite as mad.
Sire of Repentance! Child of fond desire,   70
That blows the Chymicks, and the Lovers fire,
    Still leading them insensibly on,
    With the strange witchcraft of *Anon.*
    By thee the one doth changing Nature through
      Her endlesse Laborinths pursue,   75
And th' other chases woman, while she goes
More wayes, and turnes, then hunted Nature
        knowes.

Crashaw.   *Fortune* alas above the worlds law warres:
Hope kicks the curl'd heads of conspiring starres. 80
Her keele cuts not the waves, where our winds
        stirre,
And *Fates* whole Lottery is one blanke to her.
    Her shafts, and shee fly farre above,
    And forrage in the fields of light, and love.   85
    Sweet *Hope!* kind cheat! faire fallacy! by thee
      Wee are not where, or what wee bee,

But what, and where wee would bee: thus art
    thou
Our absent presence, and our future now.   90

Crashaw.   *Faith's* Sister! Nurse of faire desire!
Feares Antidote! a wise, and well stay'd fire
Temper'd 'twixt cold despaire, and torrid joy:
Queen Regent in young Loves minoritie.
    Though the vext Chymick vainly chases   95
    His fugitive gold through all her faces,
    And loves more fierce, more fruitlesse fires
        assay
    One face more fugitive then all they,
True *Hope's* a glorious Huntresse, and her chase
The God of Nature in the field of Grace.   [100

THE DELIGHTS
OF THE MUSES

Musicks Duell

Now Westward *Sol* had spent the richest Beames
Of Noons high Glory, when hard by the streams
Of *Tiber,* on the sceane of a greene plat,
Vnder protection of an Oake; there sate
A sweet Lutes-master: in whose gentle aires   5
Hee lost the Dayes heat, and his owne hot cares.
    Close in the covert of the leaves there stood
A Nightingale, come from the neighbouring wood:
(The sweet inhabitant of each glad Tree,
Their Muse, their *Syren.* harmlesse *Syren* shee)   10
There stood she listning, and did entertaine
The Musicks soft report: and mold the same
In her owne murmures, that what ever mood
His curious fingers lent, her voyce made good:
The man perceiv'd his Rivall, and her Art,   15
Dispos'd to give the light-foot Lady sport
Awakes his Lute, and 'gainst the fight to come
Informes it, in a sweet *Præludium*
Of closer straines, and ere the warre begin,
Hee lightly skirmishes on every string   20
Charg'd with a flying touch: and streightway shee
Carves out her dainty voyce as readily,
Into a thousand sweet distinguish'd Tones,
And reckons up in soft divisions,
Quicke volumes of wild Notes; to let him know   25
By that shrill taste, shee could doe something too.
    His nimble hands instinct then taught each string
A capring cheerefullnesse; and made them sing

To their owne dance; now negligently rash
Hee throwes his Arme, and with a long drawne dash   30
Blends all together; then distinctly tripps
From this to that; then quicke returning skipps
And snatches this againe, and pauses there.
Shee measures every measure, every where
Meets art with art; sometimes as if in doubt   35
Not perfect yet, and fearing to bee out
Trayles her playne Ditty in one long-spun note,
Through the sleeke passage of her open throat:
A cleare unwrinckled song, then doth shee point it
With tender accents, and severely joynt it   40
By short diminutives, that being rear'd
In controverting warbles evenly shar'd,
With her sweet selfe shee wrangles; Hee amazed
That from so small a channell should be rais'd
The torrent of a voyce, whose melody   45
Could melt into such sweet variety
Straines higher yet; that tickled with rare art
The tatling strings (each breathing in his part)
Most kindly doe fall out; the grumbling Base
In surly groanes disdaines the Trebles Grace.   50
The high-perch't treble chirps at this, and chides,
Vntill his finger (Moderatour) hides
And closes the sweet quarrell, rowsing all
Hoarce, shrill, at once; as when the Trumpets call
Hot Mars to th' Harvest of Deaths field, and woo   55
Mens hearts into their hands; this lesson too
Shee gives him backe; her supple Brest thrills out
Sharpe Aires, and staggers in a warbling doubt
Of dallying sweetnesse, hovers ore her skill,
And folds in wav'd notes with a trembling bill,   60
The plyant Series of her slippery song.
Then starts shee suddenly into a Throng
Of short thicke sobs, whose thundring volleyes float,
And roule themselves over her lubricke throat
In panting murmurs, still'd out of her Breast   65
That ever-bubling spring; the sugred Nest
Of her delicious soule, that there does lye
Bathing in streames of liquid Melodie;

Musicks best seed-plot, whence in ripened Aires
A Golden-headed Harvest fairely reares   70
His Honey-dropping tops, plow'd by her breath
Which there reciprocally laboureth
In that sweet soyle. It seemes a holy quire
Founded to th' Name of great *Apollo's* lyre.
Whose sylver-roofe rings with the sprightly notes   75
Of sweet-lipp'd Angell-Imps, that swill their throats
In creame of Morning *Helicon*, and then
Preferre soft Anthems to the Eares of men,
To woo them from their Beds, still murmuring
That men can sleepe while they their Mattens sing: 80
(Most divine service) whose so early lay,
Prevents the Eye-lidds of the blushing day.
There might you heare her kindle her soft voyce,
In the close murmur of a sparkling noyse.
And lay the ground-worke of her hopefull song,   85
Still keeping in the forward streame, so long
Till a sweet whirle-wind (striving to gett out)
Heaves her soft Bosome, wanders round about,
And makes a pretty Earthquake in her Breast,
Till the fledg'd Notes at length forsake their Nest;   90
Fluttering in wanton shoales, and to the Sky
Wing'd with their owne wild Eccho's pratling fly.
Shee opes the floodgate, and lets loose a Tide
Of streaming sweetnesse, which in state doth ride
On the wav'd backe of every swelling straine,   95
Rising and falling in a pompous traine.
And while shee thus discharges a shrill peale
Of flashing Aires; shee qualifies their zeale
With the coole Epode of a graver Noat,
Thus high, thus low, as if her silver throat   100
Would reach the brasen voyce of warr's hoarce Bird;
Her little soule is ravisht: and so pour'd
Into loose extasies, that shee is plac't
Above her selfe, Musicks *Enthusiast*.

    Shame now and anger mixt a double staine   105
In the Musitians face; yet once againe
(Mistresse) I come; now reach a straine my Lute
Above her mocke, or bee for ever mute.

Or tune a song of victory to mee,
Or to thy selfe, sing thine owne Obsequie;   110
So said, his hands sprightly as fire hee flings,
And with a quavering coynesse tasts the strings.
The sweet-lip't sisters musically frighted,
Singing their feares are fearfully delighted.
Trembling as when *Appollo's* golden haires   115
Are fan'd and frizled, in the wanton ayres
Of his owne breath: which marryed to his lyre
Doth tune the *Sphæares*, and make Heavens selfe looke
    higher.
From this to that, from that to this hee flyes   120
Feeles Musicks pulse in all her Arteryes,
Caught in a net which there *Appollo* spreads,
His fingers struggle with the vocall threads,
Following those little rills, hee sinkes into
A Sea of *Helicon;* his hand does goe   125
Those parts of sweetnesse which with *Nectar* drop,
Softer then that which pants in *Hebe's* cup.
The humourous strings expound his learned touch,
By various Glosses; now they seeme to grutch,
And murmur in a buzzing dinne, then gingle   130
In shrill tongu'd accents: striving to bee single.
Every smooth turne, every delicious stroake
Gives life to some new Grace; thus doth h'invoke
Sweetnesse by all her Names; thus, bravely thus
(Fraught with a fury so harmonious)   135
The Lutes light *Genius* now does proudly rise,
Heav'd on the surges of swolne Rapsodyes.
Whose flourish (Meteor-like) doth curle the aire
With flash of high-borne fancyes: here and there
Dancing in lofty measures, and anon   140
Creeps on the soft touch of a tender tone:
Whose trembling murmurs melting in wild aires
Runs to and fro, complaining his sweet cares
Because those pretious mysteryes that dwell,
In musick's ravish't soule hee dare not tell,   145
But whisper to the world: thus doe they vary
Each string his Note, as if they meant to carry

Their Masters blest soule (snatcht out at his Eares
By a strong Extasy) through all the sphæares
Of Musicks heaven; and seat it there on high 150
In th' *Empyræum* of pure Harmony.
At length (after so long, so loud a strife
Of all the strings, still breathing the best life
Of blest variety attending on
His fingers fairest revolution 155
In many a sweet rise, many as sweet a fall)
A full-mouth *Diapason* swallowes all.
    This done, hee lists what shee would say to this,
And shee although her Breath's late exercise
Had dealt too roughly with her tender throate, 160
Yet summons all her sweet powers for a Noate
Alas! in vaine! for while (sweet soule) shee tryes
To measure all those wild diversities
Of chatt'ring stringes, by the small size of one
Poore simple voyce, rais'd in a Naturall Tone; 165
Shee failes, and failing grieves, and grieving dyes.
Shee dyes; and leaves her life the Victors prise,
Falling upon his Lute; ô fit to have
(That liv'd so sweetly) dead, so sweet a Grave!

Out of Virgil,
In the praise of the Spring

All Trees, all leavy Groves confesse the Spring
Their gentlest friend, then, then the lands begin
To swell with forward pride, and seed desire
To generation; Heavens Almighty Sire
Melts on the Bosome of his Love, and powres 5
Himselfe into her lap in fruitfull showers.
And by a soft insinuation, mixt
With earths large Masse, doth cherish and assist
Her weake conceptions; No loane shade, but rings
With chatting Birds delicious murmurings. 10
Then *Venus* mild instinct (at set times) yeilds
The Herds to kindly meetings, then the fields
(Quick with warme *Zephires* lively breath) lay forth
Their pregnant Bosomes in a fragrant Birth.

Each body's plump and jucy, all things full   15
Of supple moisture: no coy twig but will
Trust his beloved bosome to the Sun
(Growne lusty now;) No Vine so weake and young
That feares the foule-mouth'd Auster, or those stormes
That the Southwest-wind hurries in his Armes,   20
But hasts her forward Blossomes, and layes out
Freely layes out her leaves: Nor doe I doubt
But when the world first out of *Chaos* sprang
So smil'd the Dayes, and so the tenor ran
Of their felicity. A spring was there,   25
An everlasting spring, the jolly yeare
Led round in his great circle; No winds Breath
As then did smell of Winter, or of Death.
When Lifes sweet Light first shone on Beasts, and when
From their hard Mother Earth, sprang hardy men,   30
When Beasts tooke up their lodging in the Wood,
Starres in their higher Chambers: never cou'd
The tender growth of things endure the sence
Of such a change, but that the Heav'ns Indulgence
Kindly supplies sick Nature, and doth mold   35
A sweetly temper'd meane, nor hot nor cold.

With a Picture sent to a Friend

I paint so ill, my peece had need to bee
    Painted againe by some good Poesie.
I write so ill, my slender Line is scarce
    So much as th' Picture of a well-lim'd verse:
Yet may the love I send be true, though I   5
    Send nor true Picture, nor true Poesie.
Both which away, I should not need to feare,
    My Love, or *Feign'd* or *painted* should appeare.

In praise of Lessius his rule of health*

Goe now with some dareing drugg,
    Baite thy disease, and while they tugg
* See also p. 687.

Thou to maintaine their cruell strife,
Spend the deare treasure of thy life:
Goe take phisicke, doat upon   5
Some bigg-named composition,
The oraculous doctors mistick bills,
Certain hard words made into pills;
And what at length shalt get by these?
Onely a costlyer disease.   10
Goe poore man thinke what shall bee,
Remedie against thy remedie.
That which makes us have no need
Of Phisick thats Phisick indeed.

    Harke hether, Reader, wouldst thou see   15
Nature her owne Physitian bee.
Wouldst see a man all, his owne wealth,
His owne Physick, his owne health?
A man whose sober soule can tell,
How to weare her garments well?   20
Her garments that upon her sit,
As garments should doe close and fit?
A well cloathed soule thats not opprest,
Nor choakt with what shee should bee drest?
A soule sheathed in a christall shrine,   25
Through which all her bright features shine?
As when a peece of wanton lawne,
A thinne aiereall vaile is drawne
O're beauties face, seeming to hide
More sweetly showes the blushing bride.   30
A soule whose intelectuall beames
No mistes doe maske no lazy steames?
A happy soule that all the way,
To heaven, hath a summers day?
Would'st thou see a man whose well warmed blood, 35
Bathes him in a genuine flood?
A man whose tuned humours bee,
A set of rarest harmony?
Wouldst see blith lookes, fresh cheeks beguile
Age, wouldst see *December* smile?   40
Wouldst see a nest of Roses grow
In a bed of reverend snow?

Warme thoughts free spirits, flattering
Winters selfe into a spring?
    In summe, wouldst see a man that can   45
    Live to bee old and still a man?

The beginning of Heliodorus

The smiling Morne had newly wak't the Day,
And tipt the mountaines in a tender ray:
When on a hill (whose high Imperious brow
Lookes downe, and sees the humble Nile below
Licke his proud feet, and hast into the seas   5
Through the great mouth thats nam'd from *Hercules*)
A band of men, rough as the Armes they wore
Look't round, first to the sea, then to the shore.
The shore that shewed them what the sea deny'd,
Hope of a prey. There to the maine land ty'd   10
A ship they saw, no men shee had; yet prest
Appear'd with other lading, for her brest
Deep in the groaning waters wallowed
Vp to the third Ring; o're the shore was spread
Death's purple triumph, on the blushing ground   15
Lifes late forsaken houses all lay drown'd
In their owne bloods deare deluge, some new dead,
Some panting in their yet warme ruines bled:
While their affrighted soules, now wing'd for flight
Lent them the last flash of her glimmering light.   20
Those yet fresh streames which crawled every where
Shew'd, that sterne warre had newly bath'd him there:
Nor did the face of this disaster show
Markes of a fight alone, but feasting too,
A miserable and a monstrous feast,   25
Where hungry warre had made himself a Guest:
And comming late had eat up Guests and all,
Who prov'd the feast to their owne funerall, &c.

Out of the Greeke
Cupid's *Cryer*

Love is lost, nor can his Mother
Her little fugitive discover:
Shee seekes, shee sighs, but no where spyes him;
Love is lost; and thus shee cryes him.
   O yes! if any happy eye,   5
This roaving wanton shall descry:
Let the finder surely know
Mine is the wagge; Tis I that owe
The winged wand'rer, and that none
May thinke his labour vainely gone,   10
The glad descryer shall not misse,
To tast the *Nectar* of a kisse
From *Venus* lipps. But as for him
That brings him to mee, hee shall swim
In riper joyes: more shall bee his   15
(*Venus* assures him) then a kisse;
But least your eye discerning slide
These markes may bee your judgements guide;
His skin as with a fiery blushing
High-colour'd is; His eyes still flushing   20
With nimble flames, and though his mind
Be ne're so curst, his Tongue is kind:
For never were his words in ought
Found the pure issue of his thought.
The working Bees soft melting Gold,   25
That which their waxen Mines enfold,
Flow not so sweet as doe the Tones
Of his tun'd accents; but if once
His anger kindle, presently
It boyles out into cruelty,   30
And fraud: Hee makes poore mortalls hurts,
The objects of his cruell sports.
With dainty curles his froward face
Is crown'd about; But ô what place,
What farthest nooke of lowest Hell   35
Feeles not the strength, the reaching spell

Of his small hand? Yet not so small
As 'tis powerfull therewithall.
Though bare his skin, his mind hee covers,
And like a saucy Bird he hovers   40
With wanton wing, now here, now there,
'Bout men and women, nor will spare
Till at length he perching rest,
In the closet of their brest.
His weapon is a little Bow,   45
Yet such a one as (*Jove* knowes how)
Ne're suffred, yet his little Arrow,
Of Heavens high'st Arches to fall narrow.
The Gold that on his Quiver smiles,
Deceives mens feares with flattering wiles.   50
But ô (too well my wounds can tell)
With bitter shafts 'tis sauc't too well.
Hee is all cruell, cruell all;
His Torch Imperious though but small
Makes the Sunne (of flames the sire)   55
Worse then Sun-burnt in his fire.
Wheresoe're you chance to find him
Cease him, bring him, (but first bind him)
Pitty not him, but feare thy selfe
Though thou see the crafty Elfe,   60
Tell down his Silver-drops unto thee,
They'r counterfeit, and will undoe thee.
With baited smiles if he display
His fawning cheeks, looke not that way
If hee offer sugred kisses,   65
Start, and say, The Serpent hisses.
Draw him, drag him, though hee pray
Wooe, intreat, and crying say
Prethee, sweet now let me goe,
Here's my Quiver Shafts and Bow,   70
I'le give thee all, take all, take heed
Lest his kindnesse make thee bleed.
     What e're it be Love offers, still presume
     That though it shines, 'tis fire and will consume.

On Nanus *mounted upon an Ant*

High mounted on an Ant *Nanus* the tall
Was throwne alas, and got a deadly fall.
Vnder th'unruly Beasts proud feet he lies
All torne; with much adoe yet ere he dyes,
Hee straines these words; Base Envy, doe, laugh on.   5
Thus did I fall, and thus fell *Phaethon.*

Vpon Venus *putting on* Mars
his Armes

What? *Mars* his sword? faire *Cytherea* say,
   Why art thou arm'd so desperately to day?
Mars thou hast beaten naked, and ô then
   What need'st thou put on armes against poore men?

Vpon the same

Pallas saw *Venus* arm'd, and streight she cry'd,
   Come if thou dar'st, thus, thus let us be try'd.
Why foole! saies *Venus*, thus provok'st thou mee,
   That being nak't, thou know'st could conquer thee?

Vpon Bishop Andrewes *his*
Picture before his
Sermons

This reverend shadow cast that setting Sun,
Whose glorious course through our Horrizon run,
Left the dimme face of this dull Hemisphæare,
All one great eye, all drown'd in one great Teare.
Whose faire illustrious soule, led his free thought   5
Through Learnings Vniverse, and (vainely) sought
Roome for her spatious selfe, untill at length
Shee found the way home, with an holy strength

Snatch't her self hence, to Heaven: fill'd a bright place,
Mongst those immortall fires, and on the face   10
Of her great maker fixt her flaming eye,
There still to read true pure divinity.
And now that grave aspect hath deign'd to shrinke
Into this lesse appearance; If you thinke,
Tis but a dead face, art doth here bequeath: 15
Looke on the following leaves, and see him breath.

Vpon the Death of a Gentleman

Faithlesse and fond Mortality,
Who will ever credit thee?
Fond and faithlesse thing! that thus,
In our best hopes beguilest us.
What a reckoning hast thou made,   5
Of the hopes in him we laid?
For Life by volumes lengthened,
A Line or two, to speake him dead.
For the Laurell in his verse,
The sullen Cypresse o're his Herse.   10
For a silver-crowned Head,
A durty pillow in Death's Bed.
For so deare, so deep a trust,
Sad requitall, thus much dust!
Now though the blow that snatcht him hence,   15
Stopt the Mouth of Eloquence,
Though shee be dumbe e're since his Death,
Not us'd to speake but in his Breath,
Yet if at least shee not denyes,
The sad language of our eyes,   20
Wee are contented: for then this
Language none more fluent is.
Nothing speakes our Griefe so well
As to speake Nothing, Come then tell
Thy mind in Teares who e're Thou be,   25
That ow'st a Name to misery.
Eyes are vocall, Teares have Tongues,
And there be words not made with lungs;
Sententious showers, ô let them fall,
Their cadence is Rhetoricall.   30

Here's a Theame will drinke th'expence,
Of all thy watry Eloquence,
Weepe then, onely be exprest
Thus much, *Hee's Dead,* and weepe the rest.

Vpon the Death of Mr. Herrys

A Plant of noble stemme, forward and faire,
As ever whisper'd to the Morning Aire
Thriv'd in these happy Grounds, the Earth's just pride,
Whose rising Glories made such haste to hide
His head in Cloudes, as if in him alone   5
Impatient Nature had taught motion
To start from Time, and cheerfully to fly
Before, and seize upon Maturity.
Thus grew this gratious plant, in whose sweet shade
The Sunne himselfe oft wisht to sit, and made   10
The Morning Muses perch like Birds, and sing
Among his Branches: yea, and vow'd to bring
His owne delicious Phœnix from the blest
Arabia, there to build her Virgin nest,
To hatch her selfe in, 'mongst his leaves the Day   15
Fresh from the Rosie East rejoyc't to play.
To them shee gave the first and fairest Beame
That waited on her Birth: she gave to them
The purest Pearles, that wept her Evening Death,
The balmy *Zephirus* got so sweet a Breath   20
By often kissing them, and now begun
Glad Time to ripen expectation.
The timourous Maiden-Blossomes on each Bough,
Peept forth from their first blushes: so that now
A Thousand ruddy hopes smil'd in each Bud,   25
And flatter'd every greedy eye that stood
Fixt in Delight, as if already there
Those rare fruits dangled, whence the Golden Yeare
His crowne expected, when (ô Fate, ô Time
That seldome lett'st a blushing youthfull Prime   30
Hide his hot Beames in shade of silver Age;
So rare is hoary vertue) the dire rage

Of a mad storme these bloomy joyes all tore,
Ravisht the Maiden Blossoms, and downe bore
The trunke. Yet in this Ground his pretious Root   35
Still lives, which when weake Time shall be pour'd out
Into Eternity, and circular joyes
Dance in an endlesse round, againe shall rise
The faire son of an ever-youthfull Spring,
To be a shade for Angels while they sing,   40
Meane while who e're thou art that passest here,
O doe thou water it with one kind Teare.

Vpon the Death of the most desired
Mr. Herrys

Death, what dost? ô hold thy Blow,
What thou dost, thou dost not know.
Death thou must not here be cruell,
This is Natures choycest Iewell.
This is hee in whose rare frame,   5
Nature labour'd for a Name,
And meant to leave his pretious feature,
The patterne of a perfect Creature.
Ioy of Goodnesse, Love of Art,
Vertue weares him next her heart.   10
Him the Muses love to follow,
Him they call their vice-*Apollo*.
Apollo golden though thou bee,
Th'art not fairer then is hee.
Nor more lovely lift'st thy head,   15
Blushing from thine Easterne Bed.
The Gloryes of thy Youth ne're knew,
Brighter hopes then he can shew.
Why then should it e're be seene,
That his should fade, while thine is Greene?   20
And wilt Thou, (ô cruell boast!)
Put poore Nature to such cost?
O 'twill undoe our common Mother,
To be at charge of such another.
What? thinke we to no other end,   25
Gracious Heavens do use to send

Earth her best perfection,
But to vanish and be gone?
Therefore onely give to day,
To morrow to be snatcht away?   30
I've seen indeed the hopefull bud,
Of a ruddy Rose that stood
Blushing, to behold the Ray
Of the new-saluted Day;
(His tender toppe not fully spread)   35
The sweet dash of a shower now shead,
Invited him no more to hide
Within himselfe the purple pride
Of his forward flower, when lo
While he sweetly 'gan to show   40
His swelling Gloryes, *Auster* spide him,
Cruell *Auster* thither hy'd him,
And with the rush of one rude blast,
Sham'd not spitefully to wast
All his leaves, so fresh, so sweet,   45
And lay them trembling at his feet.
I've seene the Mornings lovely Ray,
Hover o're the new-borne Day:
With rosie wings so richly Bright,
As if he scorn'd to thinke of Night,   50
When a ruddy storme whose scoule,
Made Heavens radiant face looke foule;
Call'd for an untimely Night,
To blot the newly blossom'd Light.
But were the Roses blush so rare,   55
Were the Mornings smile so faire
As is he, nor cloud, nor wind
But would be courteous, would be kind.
   Spare him Death, ô spare him then,
Spare the sweetest among men.   60
Let not pitty with her Teares,
Keepe such distance from thine Eares.
But ô thou wilt not, canst not spare,
Haste hath never time to heare.
Therefore if hee needs must go,   65
And the Fates will have it so,

Softly may he be possest,
Of his monumentall rest.
Safe, thou darke home of the dead,
Safe ô hide his loved head.   70
For Pitties sake ô hide him quite,
From his Mother Natures sight:
Lest for Griefe his losse may move,
All her Births abortive prove.

Another

If ever Pitty were acquainted
With sterne Death, if e're he fainted,
Or forgot the cruell vigour,
Of an Adamantine rigour,
Here, ô here we should have knowne it,   5
Here or no where hee'd have showne it.
For hee whose pretious memory,
Bathes in Teares of every eye:
Hee to whom our sorrow brings,
All the streames of all her springs: 10
Was so rich in Grace and Nature,
In all the gifts that blesse a Creature.
The fresh hopes of his lovely Youth,
Flourisht in so faire a grouth.
So sweet the Temple was, that shrin'd   15
The Sacred sweetnesse of his mind.
That could the Fates know to relent?
Could they know what mercy meant;
Or had ever learnt to beare,
The soft tincture of a Teare: 20
Teares would now have flow'd so deepe,
As might have taught Griefe how to weepe.
Now all their steely operation,
Would quite have lost the cruell fashion.
Sicknesse would have gladly been,   25
Sick himselfe to have sav'd him:
And his Feaver wish'd to prove
Burning, onely in his Love.

Him when wrath it selfe had seene,
Wrath its selfe had lost his spleene.   30
Grim Destruction here amaz'd,
In stead of striking would have gaz'd.
Even the Iron-pointed pen,
That notes the Tragicke Doomes of men
Wet with teares still'd from the eyes,   35
Of the flinty Destinyes;
Would have learn't a softer style,
And have been asham'd to spoyle
His lives sweet story, by the hast,
Of a cruell stop ill plac't.   40
In the darke volume of our fate,
Whence each leafe of Life hath date,
Where in sad particulars,
The totall summe of Man appeares,
And the short clause of mortall Breath,   45
Bound in the period of Death,
In all the Booke if any where
Such a tearme as this, *spare here*
Could have been found 'twould have been read,
Writ in white Letters o're his head: 50
Or close unto his name annext,
The faire glosse of a fairer Text.
In briefe, if any one were free,
Hee was that one, and onely he.
    But he, alas! even hee is dead   55
And our hopes faire harvest spread
In the dust. Pitty now spend
All the teares that griefe can lend.
Sad mortality may hide,
In his ashes all her pride;   60
With this inscription o're his head
All hope of never dying, here lyes dead.

His Epitaph

Passenger who e're thou art,
Stay a while, and let thy Heart

Take acquaintance of this stone,
Before thou passest further on.
This stone will tell thee that beneath,   5
Is entomb'd the Crime of Death;
The ripe endowments of whose mind,
Left his Yeares so much behind,
That numbring of his vertues praise,
Death lost the reckoning of his Dayes;   10
And believing what they told,
Imagin'd him exceeding old.
In him perfection did set forth,
The strength of her united worth.
Him his wisdomes pregnant growth   15
Made so reverend, even in Youth,
That in the Center of his Brest
(Sweet as is the Phœnix nest)
Every reconciled Grace,
Had their Generall meeting place.   20
In him Goodnesse joy'd to see
Learning, learne Humility.
The splendor of his Birth and Blood,
Was but the Glosse of his owne Good:
The flourish of his sober Youth,   25
Was the Pride of Naked Truth.
In composure of his face,
Liv'd a faire, but manly Grace.
His Mouth was Rhetoricks best mold,
His Tongue the Touchstone of her Gold.   30
What word so e're his Breath kept warme,
Was no word now but a charme.
For all persuasive Graces thence
Suck't their sweetest Influence.
His vertue that within had root,   35
Could not chuse but shine without.
And th'heart-bred lustre of his worth,
At each corner peeping forth,
Pointed him out in all his wayes,
Circled round in his owne Rayes: 40
That to his sweetnesse, all mens eyes
Were vow'd Loves flaming Sacrifice.

Him while fresh and fragrant Time
Cherisht in his Golden Prime;
E're *Hebe's* hand had overlaid   45
His smooth cheekes, with a downy shade:
The rush of Death's unruly wave,
Swept him off into his Grave.
    Enough, now (if thou canst) passe on,
For now (alas) not in this stone   50
(Passenger who e're thou art)
Is he entomb'd, but in thy Heart.

An Epitaph

**Vpon Husband and Wife, which died, and
were buried together***

To these, Whom Death again did wed,
This Grave's the second Marriage-Bed.
For though the hand of Fate could force,
'Twixt Soule and body a Divorce:
It could not sever Man and Wife,   5
Because they both liv'd but one Life.
Peace, good Reader, doe not weepe;
Peace, the Lovers are asleepe:
They (sweet Turtles) folded lye,
In the last knot that love could tye.   10
Let them sleepe, let them sleepe on,
Till this stormy night be gone.
And th' eternall morrow dawne,
Then the Curtaines will bee drawne,
And they waken with that Light,   15
Whose day shall never sleepe in Night.

* See also p. 685.

An Epitaph

Vpon Doctor Brooke

A *Brooke* whose streame so great, so good,
Was lov'd was honour'd as a flood:
Whose Bankes the Muses dwelt upon,
More then their owne Helicon;
Here at length, hath gladly found   5
A quiet passage under ground;
Meane while his loved bankes now dry,
The Muses with their teares supply.

Vpon Mr. Staninough's Death*

Deare reliques of a dislodg'd soule, whose lacke
Makes many a mourning Paper put on blacke;
O stay a while e're thou draw in thy Head,
And wind thy selfe up close in thy cold Bed:
Stay but a little while, untill I call   5
A summons, worthy of thy Funerall.
   Come then youth, Beauty, and Blood, all ye soft powers,
Whose silken flatteryes swell a few fond houres
Into a false Eternity, come man,
(Hyperbolized nothing!) know thy span.   10
Take thine owne measure here, downe, downe, and bow
Before thy selfe in thy Idæa, thou
Huge emptinesse contract thy bulke, and shrinke
All thy wild Circle to a point! ô sinke
Lower, and lower yet; till thy small size,   15
Call Heaven to looke on thee with narrow eyes;
Lesser and lesser yet, till thou begin
To show a face, fit to confesse thy kin
Thy neighbour-hood to nothing! here put on
Thy selfe in this unfeign'd reflection;   20
Here gallant Ladyes, this unpartiall glasse
(Through all your painting) showes you your own face.
These Death-seal'd Lipps are they dare give the lye,
To the proud hopes of poor Mortality.

* See also p. 686.

These curtain'd windowes, this selfe-prison'd eye,   25
Out-stares the Liddes of large-look't Tyranny.
This posture is the brave one: this that lyes
Thus low stands up (me thinkes) thus, and defyes
The world——All daring Dust and Ashes; onely you
Of all interpreters read nature true.   30

To the Queen

An Apologie for the length of the fol-
lowing Panegyrick

When you are Mistresse of the song,
Mighty Queen, to thinke it long,
Were treason 'gainst that Majesty
Your vertue wears. Your modesty
Yet thinks it so. But ev'n that too   5
(Infinite, since part of You)
New matter for our Muse supplies,
And so allowes what it denies.
Say then Dread Queen, how may we doe
To mediate 'twixt your self and You?   10
That so our sweetly temper'd song
Nor be to short, nor seeme to long.
   Needs must your Noble prayses strength
   That made it long excuse the length.

To the Queen

Vpon the Duke of Yorke his Birth
A Panegyricke

Brittaine, the mighty Oceans lovely Bride,
Now stretch thy self (faire Ile) and grow, spread wide
Thy bosome and make roome; Thou art opprest
With thine owne Gloryes: and art strangely blest

Beyond thy selfe: for lo! the Gods, the Gods   5
Come fast upon thee, and those glorious ods,
Swell thy full gloryes to a pitch so high,
As sits above thy best capacitye.
　Are they not ods? and glorious? that to thee
Those mighty *Genii* throng, which well might bee   10
Each one an Ages labour, that thy dayes
Are guilded with the Vnion of those Rayes,
Whose each divided Beame would be a Sun,
To glad the Spheare of any Nation.
O if for these thou mean'st to find a seat,   15
Th'ast need ô *Brittaine* to be truly Great.
And so thou art, their presence makes thee so,
They are thy Greatnesse; Gods where e're they go
Bring their Heaven with them, their great footsteps place
An everlasting smile upon the face,   20
Of the glad Earth they tread on. While with thee
Those Beames that ampliate Mortalitie,
And teach it to expatiate, and swell
To Majesty, and fulnesse, deigne to dwell;
Thou by thy selfe maist sit, (blest Isle) and see   25
How thy Great Mother Nature doats on thee:
Thee therefore from the rest apart she hurl'd,
And seem'd to make an Isle, but made a world.
　Great *Charles*! thou sweet Dawne of a glorious day,
Center of those thy Grandsires, shall I say   30
Henry and *James*, or *Mars* and *Phœbus* rather?
If this were Wisdomes God, that Wars sterne father,
'Tis but the same is said, *Henry* and *James*
Are *Mars* and *Phœbus* under divers Names.
O thou full mixture of those mighty soules,   35
Whose vast intelligences tun'd the Poles
Of Peace and Warre; Thou for whose manly brow
Both Lawrels twine into one wreath, and wooe
To be thy Garland: see (sweet Prince) ô see
Thou and the lovely hopes that smile in thee   40
Are ta'ne out and transcrib'd by thy Great Mother,
See, see thy reall shadow, see thy Brother,
Thy little selfe in lesse, read in these Eyne
The beames that dance in those full starres of thine.

From the same snowy Alablaster Rocke 45
These hands and thine were hew'n, these cherryes mocke
The Corall of thy lips. Thou art of all
This well-wrought Copy the faire Principall.

Iustly, Great Nature, may'st thou brag and tell
How even th'ast drawne this faithfull Paralell, 50
And matcht thy Master-Peece: ô then go on
Make such another sweet comparison.
See'st thou that *Mary* there? ô teach her Mother
To shew her to her selfe in such another:
Fellow this wonder too, nor let her shine 55
Alone, light such another starre, and twine
Their Rosie Beames, so that the Morne for one
Venus, may have a Constellation.

So have I seene (to dresse their Mistresse *May*)
Two silken sister flowers consult, and lay 60
Their bashfull cheekes together, newly they
Peep't from their buds, shew'd like the Gardens eyes
Scarce wakt: like was the Crimson of their joyes,
Like were the Pearles they wept, so like that one
Seem'd but the others kind reflection. 65

But stay, what glimpse was that? why blusht the day?
Why ran the started aire trembling away?
Who's this that comes circled in rayes, that scorne
Acquaintance with the Sunne? what second Morne
At mid-day opes a presence which Heavens eye 70
Stands off and points at? is't some Deity
Stept from her Throne of starres deignes to be seene?
Is it some Deity? or is't our Queene?
'Tis shee, 'tis shee: her awfull Beauties chase
The Dayes abashed Glories, and in face 75
Of Noone weare their owne Sunshine, ô thou bright
Mistresse of wonders! *Cynthia's* is the Night,
But thou at Noone dost shine, and art all Day,
(Nor does the Sunne deny't) our *Cynthia,*
Illustrious sweetnesse! In thy faithfull wombe, 80
That Nest of *Heroes,* all our hopes finde roome.

Thou art the Mother *Phœnix*, and thy Breast
Chast as that Virgin honour of the East,
But much more fruitfull is; nor does, as shee,
Deny to mighty Love a Deity.   85
Then let the Easterne world bragge and be proud
Of one coy *Phœnix*, while we have a brood
A brood of *Phœnixes;* while we have Brother
And Sister *Phœnixes*, and still the Mother;
And may we long; long may'st thou live, t'encrease   90
The house and family of *Phœnixes*.
Nor may the light that gives their Eye-lids light,
E're prove the dismall Morning of thy Night:
Ne're may a Birth of thine be bought so deare,
To make his costly cradle of thy Beere.   95
O mayst thou thus make all the yeare thine owne,
And see such Names of joy sit white upon
The brow of every Moneth; and when that's done
Mayest in a son of his find every son
Repeated, and that son still in another,   100
And so in each child often prove a Mother:
Long mayest thou laden with such clusters leane
Vpon thy Royall Elme (faire Vine) and when
The Heavens will stay no longer, may thy glory
And Name dwell sweet in some eternall story!   105
Pardon (bright excellence) an untun'd string,
That in thy Eares thus keeps a murmuring.
O speake a lowly Muses pardon; speake
Her pardon or her sentence; onely breake
Thy silence; speake; and she shall take from thence   110
Numbers, and sweetnesse, and an influence
Confessing thee: or (if too long I stay)
O speake thou and my Pipe hath nought to say:
For see *Appollo* all this while stands mute,
Expecting by thy voyce to tune his Lute.   115
But Gods are gratious: and their Altars, make
Pretious their offerings that their Altars take.
Give then this rurall wreath fire from thine eyes.
This rurall wreath dares be thy sacrifice.

Vpon Ford's two Tragedyes

Loves Sacrifice
and
The Broken Heart

Thou cheat'st us *Ford,* mak'st one seeme two by Art.
What is *Loves Sacrifice,* but *the broken Heart?*

On a foule Morning, being then to
take a journey

Where art thou Sol, while thus the blind-fold Day
Staggers out of the East, looses her way
Stumbling on Night? Rouze thee Illustrious Youth,
And let no dull mists choake the Lights faire growth.
Point here thy Beames; ô glance on yonder flockes,   5
And make their fleeces Golden as thy lockes.
Vnfold thy faire front, and there shall appeare
Full glory, flaming in her owne free spheare.
Gladnesse shall cloath the Earth, we will instile
The face of things, an universall smile.   10
Say to the Sullen Morne, thou com'st to court her;
And wilt command proud *Zephirus* to sport her
With wanton gales: his balmy breath shall licke
The tender drops which tremble on her cheeke;
Which rarifyed, and in a gentle raine   15
On these delicious bankes distill'd againe
Shall rise in a sweet Harvest; which discloses
Two euer blushing beds of new-borne Roses.
Hee'l fan her bright locks teaching them to flow,
And friske in curl'd *Mæanders*: Hee will throw   20
A fragrant Breath suckt from the spicy nest
O'th pretious *Phœnix,* warme upon her Breast.
Hee with a dainty and soft hand, will trim
And brush her Azure Mantle, which shall swim

In silken Volumes; wheresoe're shee'l tread, 25
Bright clouds like Golden fleeces shall be spread.
   Rise then (faire blew-ey'd Maid) rise and discover
Thy silver brow, and meet thy Golden lover.
See how hee runs, with what a hasty flight
Into thy Bosome, bath'd with liquid Light. 30
Fly, fly prophane fogs, farre hence fly away,
Taint not the pure streames of the springing Day,
With your dull influence, it is for you,
To sit and scoule upon Nights heavy brow;
Not on the fresh cheekes of the virgin Morne, 35
Where nought but smiles, and ruddy joyes are worne.
Fly then, and doe not thinke with her to stay;
Let it suffice, shee'l weare no maske to day.

Vpon the faire Ethiopian sent to a Gentlewoman

Lo here the faire *Chariclia*! in whom strove
   So false a Fortune, and so true a Love.
Now after all her toyles by Sea and Land,
   O may she but arrive at your white hand,
Her hopes are crown'd, onely she feares that than, 5
   Shee shall appeare true Ethiopian.

On Marriage

I would be married, but I'de have no Wife,
I would be married to a single Life.

To the Morning. Satisfaction for sleepe

What succour can I hope the Muse will send
Whose drowsinesse hath wrong'd the Muses friend?
What hope *Aurora* to propitiate thee,
Vnlesse the Muse sing my Apology?
   O in that morning of my shame! when I 5
Lay folded up in sleepes captivity;
How at the sight did'st Thou draw back thine Eyes,
Into thy modest veyle? how did'st thou rise

Twice di'd in thine owne blushes, and did'st run
To draw the Curtaines, and awake the Sun?   10
Who rowzing his illustrious tresses came,
And seeing the loath'd object, hid for shame
His head in thy faire Bosome, and still hides
Mee from his Patronage; I pray, he chides:
And pointing to dull *Morpheus*, bids me take   15
My owne *Apollo*, try if I can make
His *Lethe* be my *Helicon*: and see
If *Morpheus* have a Muse to wait on mee.
Hence 'tis my humble fancy finds no wings,
No nimble rapture starts to Heaven and brings   20
Enthusiasticke flames, such as can give
Marrow to my plumpe *Genius*, make it live
Drest in the glorious madnesse of a Muse,
Whose feet can walke the milky way, and chuse
Her starry Throne; whose holy heats can warme   25
The Grave, and hold up an exalted arme
To lift me from my lazy Vrne, to climbe
Vpon the stooped shoulders of old Time;
And trace Eternity—But all is dead,
All these delicious hopes are buried,   30
In the deepe wrinckles of his angry brow,
Where mercy cannot find them: but ô thou
Bright Lady of the Morne, pitty doth lye
So warme in thy soft Brest it cannot dye.
Have mercy then, and when he next shall rise   35
O meet the angry God, invade his Eyes,
And stroake his radiant Cheekes; one timely kisse
Will kill his anger, and revive my blisse.
So to the treasure of thy pearly deaw,
Thrice will I pay three Teares, to show how true   40
My griefe is; so my wakefull lay shall knocke
At th' Orientall Gates; and duly mocke
The early Larkes shrill Orizons to be
An Anthem at the Dayes Nativitie.
And the same rosie-fingerd hand of thine,   45
That shuts Nights dying eyes, shall open mine.
     But thou, faint God of sleepe, forget that I
Was ever knowne to be thy votery.

No more my pillow shall thine Altar be,
Nor will I offer any more to thee   5(
My selfe a melting sacrifice; I'me borne
Againe a fresh Child of the Buxome Morne,
Heire of the Suns first Beames; why threat'st thou so?
Why dost thou shake thy leaden Scepter? goe,
Bestow thy Poppy upon wakefull woe,   55
Sicknesse, and sorrow, whose pale lidds ne're know
Thy downy finger, dwell upon their Eyes,
Shut in their Teares; Shut out their miseryes.

Vpon the Powder Day

How fit our well-rank'd Feasts doe follow,
All mischiefe comes after *All Hallow*.

Loves Horoscope

Love, brave vertues younger Brother,
    Erst hath made my Heart a Mother,
    Shee consults the conscious Spheares,
    To calculate her young sons yeares.
    Shee askes if sad, or saving powers,   5
    Gave Omen to his infant howers,
    Shee asks each starre that then stood by,
    If poore Love shall live or dy.

Ah my Heart, is that the way?
    Are these the Beames that rule thy Day?   10
    Thou know'st a Face in whose each looke,
    Beauty layes ope loves Fortune-booke,
    On whose faire revolutions wait
    The obsequious motions of Loves fate,
    Ah my Heart, her eyes and shee,   15
    Have taught thee new Astrology.
    How e're Loves native houres were set,
    What ever starry Synod met,

'Tis in the mercy of her eye,
If poore Love shall live or dye.   20

If those sharpe Rayes putting on
   Points of Death bid Love be gone
   (Though the Heavens in counsell sate,
   To crowne an uncontrouled Fate,
   Though their best Aspects twin'd upon   25
   The kindest Constellation,
   Cast amorous glances on his Birth,
   And whisper'd the confederate Earth
   To pave his pathes with all the good
   That warmes the Bed of youth and blood)   30
   Love ha's no plea against her eye
   Beauty frownes, and Love must dye.

But if her milder influence move;
   And guild the hopes of humble Love:
   (Though heavens inauspicious eye   35
   Lay blacke on loves Nativitye;
   Though every Diamond in *Ioves* crowne
   Fixt his forehead to a frowne,)
   Her Eye a strong appeale can give,
   Beauty smiles and love shall live.   40

O if Love shall live, ô where
   But in her Eye, or in her Eare,
   In her Brest, or in her Breath,
   Shall I hide poore Love from Death?
   For in the life ought else can give,   45
   Love shall dye although he live.

Or if Love shall dye, ô where,
   But in her Eye, or in her Eare,
   In her Breath, or in her Breast,
   Shall I Build his funerall Nest?   50
   While Love shall thus entombed lye,
   Love shall live, although he dye.

Out of Martiall

Foure Teeth thou had'st that ranck'd in goodly state
　　　　　Kept thy Mouthes Gate.

The first blast of thy cough left two alone,
　　　　　The second, none.

This last cough *Ælia*, cought out all thy feare,　　　　5
Th'hast left the third cough now no businesse here.

Out of the Italian

A Song

　　　To thy Lover
　　　Deere, discover
That sweet blush of thine that shameth
　　　(When those Roses
　　　It discloses)　　　　5
All the flowers that Nature nameth.

　　　In free Ayre,
　　　Flow thy Haire;
That no more Summers best dresses,
　　　Bee beholden　　　　10
　　　For their Golden
Lockes, to Phœbus *flaming Tresses.*

　　　O deliver
　　　Love his Quiver,
From thy Eyes he shoots his Arrowes,　　　　15
　　　Where Apollo
　　　Cannot follow:
Featherd with his Mothers Sparrowes.

　　　O envy not
　　　(That we dye not)　　　　20

Those deere lips whose doore encloses
    All the Graces
    In their places,
Brother Pearles, and sister Roses.

    From these treasures   25
    Of ripe pleasures
One bright smile to cleere the weather.
    Earth and Heaven
    Thus made even,
Both will be good friends together.   30

    The aire does wooe thee,
    Winds cling to thee,
Might a word once flye from out thee;
    Storme and Thunder
    Would sit under,   35
And keepe silence round about Thee.

    But if Natures
    Common Creatures,
So deare Glories dare not borrow:
    Yet thy Beauty   40
    Owes a Duty,
To my loving, lingring sorrow.

    When to end mee
    Death shall send mee
All his Terrors to affright mee: 45
    Thine eyes Graces,
    Guild their faces,
And those Terrors shall delight mee.

    When my dying
    Life is flying;   50
Those sweet Aires that often slew mee;
    Shall revive mee,
    Or reprive mee,
And to many Deaths renew mee.

Out of the Italian

Love now no fire hath left him,
We two betwixt us have divided it.
  Your Eyes the Light hath reft him.
The heat commanding in my *Heart* doth sit,
  O! that poore Love be not for ever spoyled,   5
Let my *Heat* to your *Light* be reconciled.

  So shall these flames, whose worth
     Now all obscured lyes
  (Drest in those Beames) start forth
     And dance before your eyes.   10

  Or else partake my flames
     (I care not whither)
  And so in mutuall Names
     Of Love, burne both together.

Out of the Italian

Would any one the true cause find
How Love came nak't, a Boy, and blind?
'Tis this; listning one day too long,
To th' Syrens in my Mistresse Song,
The extasie of a delight   5
So much o're-mastring all his might,
To that one Sense, made all else thrall,
  And so he lost his Clothes, eyes, heart and all.

On the Frontispiece of Isaacsons
Chronologie explained

Let hoary *Time's* vast Bowels be the Grave
To what his Bowels birth and being gave;
Let Nature die, if (*Phœnix*-like) from death
Revived Nature take a second breath;
If on *Times* right hand, sit faire *Historie*;   5
If, from the seed of empty Ruine, she

Can raise so faire an *Harvest*: Let Her be
Ne're so farre distant, yet *Chronologie*
(Sharpe sighted as the *Eagles* eye, that can
Out-stare the broad-beam'd Dayes Meridian) 10
Will have a *Perspicill* to find her out,
And, through the *Night* of error and dark doubt,
Discerne the *Dawne* of Truth's eternall ray,
As when the rosie *Morne* budds into Day.

  Now that *Time's* Empire might be amply fill'd, 15
Babels bold *Artists* strive (below) to build
Ruine a Temple; on whose fruitfull fall
History reares her *Pyramids* more tall
Then were th' *Ægyptian* (by the life, these give,
Th' *Egyptian Pyramids* themselves must live:) 20
On these she lifts the *World*; and on their base
Shewes the two termes and limits of *Time's* race:
That, the *Creation* is; the *Judgement,* this;
That, the World's *Morning*, this her *Midnight* is.

An Epitaph

Vpon Mr. Ashton *a conformable Citizen*

The modest front of this small floore
Beleeve mee, Reader, can say more
Then many a braver Marble can;
Here lyes a truly honest man.
One whose Conscience was a thing, 5
That troubled neither Church nor King.
One of those few that in this Towne,
Honour all Preachers; heare their owne.
Sermons he heard, yet not so many,
As left no time to practise any. 10
Hee heard them reverendly, and then
His practice preach'd them o're agen.
His *Parlour-Sermons* rather were
Those to the Eye, then to the Eare.
His prayers tooke their price and strength 15
Not from the lowdnesse, nor the length.

Hee was a Protestant at home,
Not onely in despight of *Rome*.
Hee lov'd his *Father*; yet his zeale
Tore not off his Mothers veile.   20
To th'Church hee did allow her Dresse,
True *Beauty*, to true *Holinesse*.
Peace, which hee lov'd in Life, did lend
Her hand to bring him to his end;
When Age and Death call'd for the score,   25
No surfets were to reckon for.
Death tore not (therefore) but sans strife
Gently untwin'd his thread of Life.
What remaines then, but that Thou
Write these lines, Reader, in thy Brow,   30
And by his faire Examples light,
Burne in thy Imitation bright.
So while these Lines can but bequeath
A Life perhaps unto his Death.
His better Epitaph shall bee,   35
His Life still kept alive in Thee.

Out of Catullus

Come and let us live my Deare,
Let us love and never feare,
What the sowrest Fathers say:
Brightest *Sol* that dyes to day
Lives againe as blith to morrow,   5
But if we darke sons of sorrow
Set; ô then, how long a Night
Shuts the Eyes of our short light!
Then let amorous kisses dwell
On our lips, begin and tell   10
A Thousand, and a Hundred, score
An Hundred, and a Thousand more,
Till another Thousand smother
That, and that wipe of another.
Thus at last when we have numbred   15
Many a Thousand, many a Hundred;

Wee'l confound the reckoning quite,
And lose our selves in wild delight:
While our joyes so multiply,
As shall mocke the envious eye.   20

Wishes

To his (supposed) Mistresse

Who ere shee bee,
That not impossible shee
That shall command my heart and mee;

Where ere shee lye,
Lock't up from mortall Eye,   5
In shady leaves of Destiny:

Till that ripe Birth
Of studied fate stand forth,
And teach her faire steps to our Earth;

Till that Divine   10
Idæa, take a shrine
Of Chrystall flesh, through which to shine:

Meet you her my wishes,
Bespeake her to my blisses,
And bee yee call'd my absent kisses.   15

I wish her Beauty,
That owes not all his Duty
To gaudy Tire, or glistring shoo-ty.

Something more than
Taffata or Tissew can,   20
Or rampant feather, or rich fan.

More then the spoyle
Of shop, or silkewormes Toyle
Or a bought blush, or a set smile.

A face thats best   25
By its owne beauty drest,
And can alone commend the rest.

A face made up
Out of no other shop,
Then what natures white hand sets ope.   30

A cheeke where Youth,
And Blood, with Pen of Truth
Write, what the Reader sweetly ru'th.

A Cheeke where growes
More then a Morning Rose: 35
Which to no Boxe his being owes.

Lipps, where all Day
A lovers kisse may play,
Yet carry nothing thence away.

Lookes that oppresse   40
Their richest Tires but dresse
And cloath their simplest Nakednesse.

Eyes, that displaces
The Neighbour Diamond, and out faces
That Sunshine by their owne sweet Graces.   45

Tresses, that weare
Iewells, but to declare
How much themselves more pretious are.

Whose native Ray,
Can tame the wanton Day   50
Of Gems, that in their bright shades play.

Each Ruby there,
Or Pearle that dare appeare,
Bee its owne blush, bee its owne Teare.

A well tam'd Heart,   55
For whose more noble smart,
Love may bee long chusing a Dart.

Eyes, that bestow
Full quivers on loves Bow;
Yet pay lesse Arrowes then they owe.   60

Smiles, that can warme
The blood, yet teach a charme,
That Chastity shall take no harme.

Blushes, that bin
The burnish of no sin,   65
Nor flames of ought too hot within.

Ioyes, that confesse,
Vertue their Mistresse,
And have no other head to dresse.

Feares, fond and flight,   70
As the coy Brides, when Night
First does the longing lover right.

Teares, quickly fled,
And vaine, as those are shed
For a dying Maydenhead.   75

Dayes, that need borrow,
No part of their good Morrow,
From a fore spent night of sorrow.

Dayes, that in spight
Of Darkenesse, by the Light   80
Of a cleere mind are Day all Night.

Nights, sweet as they,
Made short by lovers play,
Yet long by th'absence of the Day.

Life, that dares send   85
A challenge to his end,
And when it comes say *Welcome Friend*.

Sydnæan showers
Of sweet discourse, whose powers
Can Crowne old Winters head with flowers,   90

Soft silken Houres,
Open sunnes; shady Bowers,
Bove all; Nothing within that lowres.

What ere Delight
Can make Dayes forehead bright;   95
Or give Downe to the Wings of Night.

In her whole frame,
Have Nature all the Name,
Art and ornament the shame.

Her flattery,   100
Picture and Poesy,
Her counsell her owne vertue bee.

I wish, her store
Of worth, may leave her poore
Of wishes; And I wish ——— No more.   105

Now if Time knowes
That her whose radiant Browes,
Weave them a Garland of my vowes;

Her whose just Bayes,
My future hopes can raise,   110
A trophie to her present praise;

Her that dares bee,
What these Lines wish to see:
I seeke no further, it is shee.

'Tis shee, and heere 115
Lo I uncloath and cleare,
My wishes cloudy Character.

May shee enjoy it,
Whose merit dare apply it,
But Modesty dares still deny it. 120

Such worth as this is,
Shall fixe my flying wishes,
And determine them to kisses.

Let her full Glory,
My fancyes, fly before yee, 125
Bee ye my fictions; But her story.

Vpon two greene Apricockes sent to Cowley *by Sir* Crashaw

Take these, times tardy truants, sent by me,
To be chastis'd (sweet friend) and chidd by thee.
Pale sons of our *Pomona*! whose wan cheekes
Have spent the patience of expecting weekes,
Yet are scarce ripe enough at best to show 5
The redd, but of the blush to thee they ow.
By thy comparrison they shall put on
More summer in their shames reflection,
Than ere the fruitfull *Phœbus* flaming kisses
Kindled on their cold lips. O had my wishes 10
And the deare merits of your Muse, their due,
The yeare had found some fruit early as you;
Ripe as those rich composures time computes'
Blossoms, but our blest tast confesses fruits.
How does thy April-Autumne mocke these cold 15
Progressions 'twixt whose termes poor time grows old?
With thee alone he weares no beard, thy braine
Gives him the morning worlds fresh gold againe.
'Twas only Paradice, 'tis onely thou,
Whose fruit and blossoms both blesse the same bough. 20

Proud in the patterne of thy pretious youth,
Nature (methinks) might easily mend her growth.
Could she in all her births but coppie thee,
Into the publick yeares proficiencie,
No fruit should have the face to smile on thee   25
(Young master of the worlds maturitie)
But such whose sun-borne beauties what they borrow
Of beames to day, pay back againe to morrow,
Nor need be double-gilt. How then must these,
Poore fruites looke pale at thy Hesperides!   30
Faine would I chide their slownesse, but in their
Defects I draw mine owne dull character.
Take them, and me in them acknowledging,
How much my summer waites upon thy spring.

CARMEN DEO NOSTRO

> 'Tis not the work of force but skill
> To find the way into man's will.
> 'Tis loue alone can hearts vnlock.
> Who knowes the WORD, he needs not knock.

To The
Noblest & best of Ladyes, the
Countesse of Denbigh

Perswading her to Resolution in Religion,
& to render her selfe without further
delay into the Communion of
*the Catholick Church** *

What heau'n-intreated HEART is This?
Stands trembling at the gate of blisse;
Holds fast the door, yet dares not venture
Fairly to open it, and enter.
Whose DEFINITION is a doubt   5
Twixt life & death, twixt in & out.
Say, lingring fair! why comes the birth
Of your braue soul so slowly forth?
Plead your pretences (o you strong
In weaknes! why you choose so long   10
In labor of your selfe to ly,
Nor daring quite to liue nor dy?

* See also p. 692.

Ah linger not, lou'd soul! a slow
And late consent was a long no,
Who grants at last, long time tryd   15
And did his best to haue deny'd.
What magick bolts, what mystick Barres
Maintain the will in these strange warres!
What fatall, yet fantastick, bands
Keep The free Heart from it's own hands!   20
So when the year takes cold, we see
Poor waters their owne prisoners be.
Fettr'd, & lockt vp fast they ly
In a sad selfe-captiuity.
The' astonisht nymphs their flood's strange fate deplore, 25
To see themselues their own seuerer shore.
Thou that alone canst thaw this cold,
And fetch the heart from it's strong Hold;
Allmighty Love! end this long warr,
And of a meteor make a starr.   30
O fix this fair INDEFINITE.
And 'mongst thy shafts of soueraign light
Choose out that sure decisiue dart
Which has the Key of this close heart,
Knowes all the corners of't, & can controul   35
The self-shutt cabinet of an vnsearcht soul.
O let it be at last, loue's houre.
Raise this tall Trophee of thy Powre;
Come once the conquering way; not to confute
But kill this rebell-word, IRRESOLVTE   40
That so, in spite of all this peeuish strength
Of weaknes, she may write RESOLV'D AT LENGTH,
Vnfold at length, vnfold fair flowre
And vse the season of loue's showre,
Meet his well-meaning Wounds, wise heart!   45
And hast to drink the wholsome dart.
That healing shaft, which heaun till now
Hath in loue's quiuer hid for you.
O Dart of loue! arrow of light!
O happy you, if it hitt right,   50
It must not fall in vain, it must
Not mark the dry regardles dust.

Fair one, it is your fate; and brings
Æternall worlds vpon it's wings.
Meet it with wide-spread armes; & see   55
It's seat your soul's iust center be.
Disband dull feares; giue faith the day.
To saue your life, kill your delay
It is loue's seege; and sure to be
Your triumph, though his victory.   60
'Tis cowardise that keeps this feild
And want of courage not to yeild.
Yeild then, ô yeild, that loue may win
The Fort at last, and let life in.
Yeild quickly. Lest perhaps you proue   65
Death's prey, before the prize of loue.
This Fort of your fair selfe, if't be not won,
He is repulst indeed; But you'are vndone.

To
The Name
Above Every Name,
The
Name of
Iesvs

A Hymn

I sing the NAME which None can say
But touch't with An interiour RAY:
The Name of our New PEACE; our Good:
Our Blisse: & Supernaturall Blood:
The Name of All our Liues & Loues.   5
Hearken, And Help, ye holy Doues!
The high-born Brood of Day; you bright
Candidates of blissefull Light,
The HEIRS Elect of Loue; whose Names belong
Vnto The euerlasting life of Song;   10
All ye wise SOVLES, who in the wealthy Brest
Of This vnbounded NAME build your warm Nest.

Awake, MY glory. SOVL, (if such thou be,
And That fair WORD at all referr to Thee)
        Awake & sing   15
        And be All Wing;
Bring hither thy whole SELF; & let me see
What of thy Parent HEAVN yet speakes in thee.
        O thou art Poore
        Of noble POWRES, I see,   20
And full of nothing else but empty ME,
Narrow, & low, & infinitely lesse
Then this GREAT mornings mighty Busynes.
        One little WORLD or two
        (Alas) will neuer doe.   25
        We must haue store.
Goe, SOVL, out of thy Self, & seek for More.
        Goe & request
Great NATVRE for the KEY of her huge Chest
Of Heauns, the self inuoluing Sett of Sphears   30
(Which dull mortality more Feeles then heares)
        Then rouse the nest
Of nimble ART, & trauerse round
The Aiery Shop of soul-appeasing Sound:
And beat a summons in the Same   35
        All-soueraign Name
To warn each seuerall kind
And shape of sweetnes, Be they such
        As sigh with supple wind
        Or answer Artfull Touch,   40
That they conuene & come away
To wait at the loue-crowned Doores of
        This Illustrious DAY.
Shall we dare This, my Soul? we'l doe't and bring
No Other note for't, but the Name we sing   45
        Wake LVTE & HARP
        And euery sweet-lipp't Thing
        That talkes with tunefull string;
Start into life, And leap with me
Into a hasty Fitt-tun'd Harmony.   50
        Nor must you think it much
        T'obey my bolder touch;

I haue Authority in LOVE's name to take you
And to the worke of Loue this morning wake you
        Wake; In the Name   55
Of HIM who neuer sleeps, All Things that Are,
        Or, what's the same,
        Are Musicall;
        Answer my Call
        And come along;   60
Help me to meditate mine Immortall Song.
Come, ye soft ministers of sweet sad mirth,
Bring All your houshold stuffe of Heaun on earth;
O you, my Soul's most certain Wings,
Complaining Pipes, & prattling Strings,   65
        Bring All the store
Of SWEETS you haue; And murmur that you haue no more.
        Come, nere to part,
        NATVRE & ART!
        Come; & come strong,   70
To the conspiracy of our Spatious song.
        Bring All the Powres of Praise
Your Prouinces of well-vnited WORLDS can raise;
Bring All your LVTES & HARPS of HEAVN & EARTH;
What e're cooperates to The common mirthe   75
        Vessells of vocall Ioyes,
Or You, more noble Architects of Intellectuall Noise,
Cymballs of Heau'n, or Humane sphears,
Solliciters of SOVLES or EARES;
        And when you'are come, with All   80
That you can bring or we can call;
        O may you fix
        For euer here, & mix
        Your selues into the long
And euerlasting series of a deathlesse SONG;   85
Mix All your many WORLDS, Aboue,
And loose them into ONE of Loue.
        Chear thee my HEART!
        For Thou too hast thy Part
        And Place in the Great Throng   90
Of This vnbounded All-imbracing SONG.

Powres of my Soul, be Proud!
And speake lowd
To All the dear-bought Nations This Redeeming Name,
And in the wealth of one Rich WORD proclaim   95
New Similes to Nature.
            May it be no wrong
Blest Heauns, to you, & your Superiour song,
That we, dark Sons of Dust & Sorrow,
            A while Dare borrow   100
The Name of Your Delights & our Desires,
And fitt it to so farr inferior LYRES.
Our Murmurs haue their Musick too,
Ye mighty ORBES, as well as you,
            Nor yeilds the noblest Nest   105
Of warbling SERAPHIM to the eares of Loue,
A choicer Lesson then the ioyfull BREST
            Of a poor panting Turtle-Doue.
And we, low Wormes haue leaue to doe
The Same bright Busynes (ye Third HEAVENS) with you.
Gentle SPIRITS, doe not complain.   [110
            We will haue care
            To keep it fair,
And send it back to you again.
Come, louely NAME! Appeare from forth the Bright   115
            Regions of peacefull Light
Look from thine own Illustrious Home,
Fair KING of NAMES, & come.
Leaue All thy natiue Glories in their Gorgeous Nest,
And giue thy Self a while The gracious Guest   120
Of humble Soules, that seek to find
            The hidden Sweets
            Which man's heart meets
When Thou art Master of the Mind.
Come, louely Name; life of our hope!   125
Lo we hold our HEARTS wide ope!
Vnlock thy Cabinet of DAY
Dearest Sweet, & come away.
            Lo how the thirsty Lands
Gasp for thy Golden Showres! with long stretch't Hands 130
            Lo how the laboring EARTH

That hopes to be
All Heauen by THEE,
Leapes at thy Birth.
The'attending WORLD, to wait thy Rise,   135
First turn'd to eyes;
And then, not knowing what to doe;
Turn'd Them to TEARES, & spent Them too.
Come ROYALL Name, & pay the expence
Of All this Pretious Patience.   140
O come away
And kill the DEATH of This Delay.
O see, so many WORLDS of barren yeares
Melted & measur'd out in Seas of TEARES.
O see, The WEARY liddes of wakefull Hope   145
(LOVE's Eastern windowes) All wide ope
With Curtains drawn,
To catch The Day-break of Thy DAWN.
O dawn, at last, long look't for Day!
Take thine own wings, & come away.   150
Lo, where Aloft it comes! It comes, Among
The Conduct of Adoring SPIRITS, that throng
Like diligent Bees, And swarm about it.
O they are wise;
And know what SWEETES are suck't from out it.   155
It is the Hiue,
By which they thriue,
Where All their Hoard of Hony lyes.
Lo where it comes, vpon The snowy DOVE's
Soft Back; And brings a Bosom big with Loues.   160
WELCOME to our dark world, Thou
Womb of Day!
Vnfold thy fair Conceptions; And display
The Birth of our Bright Ioyes.
O thou compacted   165
Body of Blessings: spirit of Soules extracted!
O dissipate thy spicy Powres
(Clowd of condensed sweets) & break vpon vs
In balmy showrs;
O fill our senses, And take from vs   170
All force of so Prophane a Fallacy

To think ought sweet but that which smells of Thee.
Fair, flowry Name; In none but Thee
And Thy Nectareall Fragrancy,
      Hourly there meetes   175
An vniuersall Synod of All sweets;
By whom it is defined Thus
      That no Perfume
      For euer shall presume
To passe for Odoriferous,   180
But such alone whose sacred Pedigree
Can proue it Self some kin (sweet name) to Thee.
Sweet Name, in Thy each Syllable
A Thousand Blest Arabias dwell;
A Thousand Hills of Frankincense;   185
Mountains of myrrh, & Beds of spices,
And ten Thousand Paradises
The soul that tasts thee takes from thence.
How many vnknown Worlds there are
Of Comforts, which Thou hast in keeping!   190
How many Thousand Mercyes there
In Pitty's soft lap ly a sleeping!
Happy he who has the art
      To awake them,
      And to take them   195
Home, & lodge them in his Heart.
O that it were as it was wont to be!
When thy old Freinds of Fire, All full of Thee,
Fought against Frowns with smiles; gaue Glorious chase
To Persecutions; And against the Face   200
Of Death & feircest Dangers, durst with Braue
And sober pace march on to meet A Grave.
On their Bold Brests about the world they bore thee
And to the Teeth of Hell stood vp to teach thee,
In Center of their inmost Soules they wore thee,   205
Where Rackes & Torments striu'd, in vain, to reach thee.
      Little, alas, thought They
Who tore the Fair Brests of thy Freinds,
      Their Fury but made way
For Thee; And seru'd therein Thy glorious ends.   210
What did Their weapons but with wider pores
Inlarge thy flaming-brested Louers

More freely to transpire
That impatient Fire
The Heart that hides Thee hardly couers. 215
What did their Weapons but sett wide the Doores
For Thee: Fair, purple Doores, of loue's deuising;
The Ruby windowes which inrich't the EAST
Of Thy so oft repeated Rising.
Each wound of Theirs was Thy new Morning; 220
And reinthron'd thee in thy Rosy Nest,
With blush of thine own Blood thy day adorning,
It was the witt of loue o'reflowd the Bounds
Of WRATH, & made thee way through All Those WOVNDS.
Wellcome dear, All-Adored Name! 225
For sure there is no Knee
That knowes not THEE.
Or if there be such sonns of shame,
Alas what will they doe
When stubborn Rocks shall bow 230
And Hills hang down their Heaun-saluting Heads
To seek for humble Beds
Of Dust, where in the Bashfull shades of night
Next to their own low NOTHING they may ly,
And couch before the dazeling light of thy dread majesty. 235
They that by Loue's mild Dictate now
Will not adore thee,
Shall Then with Iust Confusion, bow
And break before thee.

In the Holy Nativity of Ovr Lord God

*A Hymn Svng as by the Shepheards**

The Hymn

Chorus. Come we shepheards whose blest Sight
Hath mett loue's Noon in Nature's night;
Come lift we vp our loftyer Song
And wake the SVN that lyes too long.

* See also p. 534.

To all our world of well-stoln joy   5
   He slept; and dream't of no such thing.
While we found out Heaun's fairer ey
   And Kis't the Cradle of our KING.
Tell him He rises now, too late
To show vs ought worth looking at.   10

Tell him we now can show Him more
   Then He e're show'd to mortall Sight;
Then he Himselfe e're saw before;
   Which to be seen needes not His light.
Tell him, Tityrus, where th'hast been   15
Tell him, Thyrsis, what th'hast seen.

Tityrus. Gloomy night embrac't the Place
   Where The Noble Infant lay.
The BABE look't vp & shew'd his Face;
   In spite of Darknes, it was DAY.   20
It was THY day, SWEET! & did rise
Not from the EAST, but from thine EYES.

Chorus. It was THY day, Sweet

Thyrs. WINTER chidde aloud; & sent
   The angry North to wage his warres.   25
The North forgott his feirce Intent;
   And left perfumes in stead of scarres.
By those sweet eyes' persuasiue powrs
Where he mean't frost, he scatter'd flowrs.

Chorus. By those sweet eyes'   30

Both. We saw thee in thy baulmy Nest,
   Young dawn of our æternall DAY!
We saw thine eyes break from their EASTE
   And chase the trembling shades away.
We saw thee; & we blest the sight   35
We saw thee by thine own sweet light.

Tity. Poor WORLD (said I.) what wilt thou doe
　　　To entertain this starry STRANGER?
　　Is this the best thou canst bestow?
　　　A cold, and not too cleanly, manger?　　40
　　Contend, ye powres of heau'n & earth.
　　To fitt a bed for this huge birthe.

Cho. Contend ye powers

Thyr. Proud world, said I; cease your contest
　　　And let the MIGHTY BABE alone.　　45
　　The Phœnix builds the Phœnix' nest.
　　　Love's architecture is his own.
　　The BABE whose birth embraues this morn,
　　Made his own bed e're he was born.

Cho. The BABE whose.　　50

Tit. I saw the curl'd drops, soft & slow,
　　　Come houering o're the place's head;
　　Offring their whitest sheets of snow
　　　To furnish the fair INFANT's bed
　　Forbear, said I; be not too bold.　　55
　　Your fleece is white But t'is too cold.

Cho. Forbear, sayd I

Thyr. I saw the obsequious SERAPHIMS
　　　Their rosy fleece of fire bestow.
　　For well they now can spare their wings　　60
　　　Since HEAVN itself lyes here below.
　　Well done, said I: but are you sure
　　Your down so warm, will passe for pure?

Cho. Well done sayd I

Tit. No no. your KING's not yet to seeke　　65
　　　Where to repose his Royall HEAD
　　See see, how soon his new-bloom'd CHEEK
　　　Twixt's mother's brests is gone to bed.

Sweet choise, said we! no way but so
Not to ly cold, yet sleep in snow.   70

Cho.   Sweet choise, said we.

Both.   We saw thee in thy baulmy nest,
       Bright dawn of our æternall Day!
We saw thine eyes break from their EAST
       And chase the trembling shades away.   75
We saw thee: & we blest the sight.
We saw thee, by thine own sweet light.

Cho.   We saw thee, &c.

FVLL CHORVS

Welcome, all WONDERS in one sight!
    Æternity shutt in a span.
Sommer in Winter. Day in Night.
    Heauen in earth, & GOD in MAN.
Great little one! whose all-embracing birth   5
Lifts earth to heauen, stoopes heau'n to earth.

WELCOME. Though nor to gold nor silk.
    To more then Cæsar's birthright is;
Two sister-seas of Virgin-Milk,
    With many a rarely-temper'd kisse   10
That breathes at once both MAID & MOTHER,
Warmes in the one, cooles in the other.

WELCOME, though not to those gay flyes.
    Guilded ith' Beames of earthly kings;
Slippery soules in smiling eyes;   15
    But to poor Shepheards, home-spun things:
Whose Wealth's their flock; whose witt, to be
    Well read in their simplicity.
Yet when young April's husband showrs
    Shall blesse the fruitfull Maja's bed   20
We'l bring the First-born of her flowrs

To kisse thy FEET & crown thy HEAD.
To thee, dread lamb! whose loue must keep
   The shepheards, more then they the sheep.
To THEE, meek Majesty! soft KING   25
   Of simple GRACES & sweet LOVES.
Each of vs his lamb will bring
   Each his pair of sylver Doues;
Till burnt at last in fire of Thy fair eyes,
   Our selues become our own best SACRIFICE.   30

New Year's Day*

Rise, thou best & brightest morning!
   Rosy with a double Red;
With thine own blush thy cheeks adorning
   And the dear drops this day were shed.

All the purple pride that laces   5
   The crimson curtains of thy bed,
Guilds thee not with so sweet graces
   Nor setts thee in so rich a red.

Of all the fair-cheek't flowrs that fill thee
   None so fair thy bosom strowes,   10
As this modest maiden lilly
   Our sins haue sham'd into a rose.

Bid thy golden GOD, the Sun,
   Burnisht in his best beames rise,
Put all his red-ey'd Rubies on;   15
   These Rubies shall putt out their eyes.

Let him make poor the purple east,
   Search what the world's close cabinets keep,
Rob the rich births of each bright nest
   That flaming in their fair beds sleep,   20

* See also p. 566.

Let him embraue his own bright tresses
    With a new morning made of gemmes;
And wear, in those his wealthy dresses,
    Another Day of Diadems.

When he hath done all he may   25
    To make himselfe rich in his rise,
All will be darknes to the Day
    That breakes from one of these bright eyes.

And soon this sweet truth shall appear
    Dear BABE, ere many dayes be done,   30
The morn shall come to meet thee here,
    And leaue her own neglected Sun.

Here are Beautyes shall bereaue him
    Of all his eastern Paramours.
His Persian Louers all shall leaue him,   35
    And swear faith to thy sweeter Powres.

In the Gloriovs Epiphanie of
Ovr Lord God

A Hymn Svng as by the three Kings

1st King.   Bright BABE! Whose awfull beautyes make
            The morn incurr a sweet mistake;
2nd King.   For whom the'officious heauns deuise
            To disinheritt the sun's rise,
3rd King.   Delicately to displace   5
            The Day, & plant it fairer in thy face;
     1.   O thou born KING of loues,
     2.   Of lights,
     3.   Of ioyes!
   Cho.   Look vp, sweet BABE, look vp & see   10
            For loue of Thee
            Thus farr from home
            The EAST is come
         To seek her self in thy sweet Eyes

1. We, who strangely went astray,   15
       Lost in a bright
       Meridian night,
2. A Darkenes made of too much day,
3.   Becken'd from farr
       By thy fair starr,   20
   Lo at last haue found our way.

Cho. To THEE, thou DAY of night! thou east of west!
   Lo we at last haue found the way.
   To thee, the world's great vniuersal east.
   The Generall & indifferent DAY.   25

1. All-circling point. All centring sphear.
   The world's one, round, Æternall year.
2. Whose full & all-vnwrinkled face
   Nor sinks nor swells with time or place;
3. But euery where & euery while   30
   Is One Consistent solid smile;
1.   Not vext & tost
2.   'Twixt spring & frost,
3. Nor by alternate shredds of light
   Sordidly shifting hands with shades & night.   35

Cho. O little all! in thy embrace
   The world lyes warm, & likes his place.
   Nor does his full Globe fail to be
   Kist on Both his cheeks by Thee.
   Time is too narrow for thy YEAR   40
   Nor makes the whole WORLD thy half-sphear.

1.   To Thee, to Thee
       From him we flee
2. From HIM, whom by a more illustrious ly,
   The blindnes of the world did call the eye;   45
3. To HIM, who by These mortall clouds hast made
   Thy self our sun, though thine own shade.
1. Farewell, the world's false light.
       Farewell, the white
       Ægypt! a long farewell to thee   50
       Bright IDOL; black IDOLATRY.
   The dire face of inferior DARKNES, kis't
   And courted in the pompous mask of a more specious mist.
2.   Farewell, farewell
       The proud & misplac't gates of hell,   55

Pertch't, in the morning's way
And double-guilded as the doores of DAY.
The deep hypocrisy of DEATH & NIGHT
More desperately dark, Because more bright.

3.   Welcome, the world's sure Way!   60
HEAVN's wholsom ray.

Cho.   Welcome to vs; and we
(SWEET) to our selues, in THEE.

1. The deathles HEIR of all thy FATHER's day!
2.   Decently Born.   65
Embosom'd in a much more Rosy MORN,
The Blushes of thy All-vnblemish't mother.

3.   No more that other
Aurora shall sett ope
Her ruby casements, or hereafter hope   70
From mortall eyes
To meet Religious welcomes at her rise.

Cho. We (Pretious ones!) in you haue won
A gentler MORN, a iuster sun.

1. His superficiall Beames sun-burn't our skin;   75
2.   But left within
3. The night & winter still of death & sin.

Cho. Thy softer yet more certaine DARTS
Spare our eyes, but peirce our HARTS.

1. Therefore with His proud persian spoiles   80
2. We court thy more concerning smiles.
3.   Therfore with his Disgrace
We guild the humble cheek of this chast place;

Cho. And at thy FEET powr forth his FACE.

1. The doating nations now no more   85
Shall any day but THINE adore.
2. Nor (much lesse) shall they leaue these eyes
For cheap Ægyptian Deityes.
3. In whatsoe're more Sacred shape
Of Ram, He-goat, or reuerend ape,   90
Those beauteous rauishers opprest so sore
The too-hard-tempted nations.

1.   Neuer more
By wanton heyfer shall be worn
2. A Garland, or a guilded horn.   95

        The altar-stall'd ox, fatt OSYRIS now
           With his fair sister cow,
3. Shall kick the clouds no more; But lean & tame,
Cho. See his horn'd face, & dy for shame.
        And MITHRA now shall be no name.   100
1. No longer shall the immodest lust
        Of Adulterous GODLES dust
2. Fly in the face of heau'n; As if it were
        The poor world's Fault that he is fair.
3. Nor with peruerse loues & Religious RAPES   105
        Reuenge thy Bountyes in their beauteous shapes;
        And punish Best Things worst; Because they stood
        Guilty of being much for them too Good.
1. Proud sons of death! that durst compell
        Heau'n it self to find them hell;   110
2. And by strange witt of madnes wrest
        From this world's EAST the other's WEST.
3. All-Idolizing wormes! that thus could crowd
        And vrge Their sun into thy cloud;
        Forcing his sometimes eclips'd face to be   115
        A long deliquium to the light of thee.
Cho. Alas with how much heauyer shade
        The shamefac't lamp hung down his head
           For that one eclipse he made
           Then all those he suffered!   120
1. For this he look't so bigg; & euery morn
        With a red face confes't this scorn.
        Or hiding his vex't cheeks in a hir'd mist
        Kept them from being so vnkindly kis't.
2. It was for this the day did rise   125
           So oft with blubber'd eyes.
        For this the euening wept; and we ne're knew
           But call'd it deaw.
3.   This dayly wrong
        Silenc't the morning-sons, & damp't their song   130
Cho. Nor was't our deafnes, but our sins, that thus
        Long made th'Harmonious orbes all mute to vs
1.   Time has a day in store
          When this so proudly poor
        And self-oppressed spark, that has so long   135

By the loue-sick world bin made
Not so much their sun as SHADE,
Weary of this Glorious wrong
From them & from himself shall flee
For shelter to the shadow of thy TREE;   140

Cho. Proud to haue gain'd this pretious losse
And chang'd his false crown for thy CROSSE.

2. That dark Day's clear doom shall define
Whose is the Master FIRE, which sun should shine.
That sable Iudgment-seat shall by new lawes   145
Decide & settle the Great cause
Of controuerted light,

Cho. And natur's wrongs rejoyce to doe thee Right.

3. That forfeiture of noon to night shall pay
All the idolatrous thefts done by this night of day; 150
And the Great Penitent presse his own pale lipps
With an elaborate loue-eclipse
To which the low world's lawes
Shall lend no cause

Cho. Saue those domestick which he borrowes   155
From our sins & his own sorrowes.

1. Three sad hour's sackcloth then shall show to vs
His penance, as our fault, conspicuous.

2. And he more needfully & nobly proue
The nation's terror now then erst their loue.   160

3. Their hated loues changd into wholsom feares,

Cho. The shutting of his eye shall open Theirs.

1. As by a fair-ey'd fallacy of day
Miss-ledde before they lost their way,
So shall they, by the seasonable fright   165
Of an vnseasonable night,
Loosing it once again, stumble'on true LIGHT

2. And as before his too-bright eye
Was Their more blind idolatry,
So his officious blindnes now shall be   170
Their black, but faithfull perspectiue of thee;

3.   His new prodigious night,
Their new & admirable light;
The supernaturall DAWN of Thy pure day.
While wondring they   175

     (The happy conuerts now of him
     Whom they compell'd before to be their sin)
         Shall henceforth see
     To kisse him only as their rod
     Whom they so long courted as GOD,   180
Cho. And their best vse of him they worship't be
     To learn of Him at lest, to worship Thee.
   1. It was their Weaknes woo'd his beauty;
         But it shall be
     Their wisdome now, as well as duty,   185
     To'injoy his Blott; & as a large black letter
     Vse it to spell Thy beautyes better;
     And make the night it self their torch to thee.
   2. By the oblique ambush of this close night
         Couch't in that conscious shade   190
     The right-ey'd Areopagite
     Shall with a vigorous guesse inuade
     And catche thy quick reflex; and sharply see
         On this dark Ground
         To descant THEE.   195
   3. O prize of the rich SPIRIT! with what feirce chase
         Of his strong soul, shall he
         Leap at thy lofty FACE,
     And seize the swift Flash, in rebound
     From this obsequious cloud;   200
         Once call'd a sun;
         Till dearly thus vndone,
Cho. Till thus triumphantly tam'd (o ye two
     Twinne SVNNES!) & taught now to negotiate you.
   1. Thus shall that reuerend child of light,   205
   2. By being scholler first of that new night,
     Come forth Great master of the mystick day;
   3. And teach obscure MANKIND a more close way
     By the frugall negatiue light
     Of a most wise & well-abused Night   210
     To read more legible thine originall Ray,
Cho. And make our Darknes serue THY day;
     Maintaining t'wixt thy world & ours
     A commerce of contrary powres,

A mutuall trade   215
    'Twixt sun & SHADE,
By confederate BLACK & WHITE
Borrowing day & lending night.

1. Thus we, who when with all the noble powres
   That (at thy cost) are call'd, not vainly, ours   220
      We vow to make braue way
   Vpwards, & presse on for the pure intelligentiall Prey;

2.   At lest to play
      The amorous Spyes
   And peep & proffer at thy sparkling Throne;   225

3. In stead of bringing in the blissfull PRIZE
      And fastening on Thine eyes,
      Forfeit our own
      And nothing gain
   But more Ambitious losse, at lest of brain;   230

Cho. Now by abased liddes shall learn to be
   Eagles; and shutt our eyes that we may see.

The Close

Therfore to THEE & thine Auspitious ray
      (Dread sweet!) lo thus
      At lest by vs,
The delegated EYE of DAY
Does first his Scepter, then HIMSELF in solemne   5
   Tribute pay.
      Thus he vndresses
      His sacred vnshorn tresses;
At thy adored FEET, thus, he layes down

1.   His gorgeous tire   10
      Of flame & fire,

2. His glittering ROBE, [3.] his sparkling CROWN,

1. His GOLD, [2.] his MIRRH, [3.] his FRANKINCENCE,

Cho. To which He now has no pretence.
   For being show'd by this day's light, how farr   15
   He is from sun enough to make THY starr,
   His best ambition now, is but to be
   Somthing a brighter SHADOW [sweet] of thee.

Or on heaun's azure forhead high to stand
Thy golden index; with a duteous Hand   20
Pointing vs Home to our own sun
The world's & his HYPERION.

**To the
Qveen's
Maiesty**

Madame.
'Mongst those long rowes of crownes that guild your race,
These Royall sages sue for decent place.
The day-break of the nations; their first ray;
When the Dark WORLD dawn'd into Christian DAY   5
And smil'd i'th' BABE's bright face, the purpling Bud
And Rosy dawn of the right Royall blood;
Fair first-fruits of the LAMB. Sure KINGS in this;
They took a kingdom while they gaue a kisse.
But the world's Homage, scarse in These well blown,   10
We read in you (Rare Queen) ripe & full-grown.
For from this day's rich seed of Diadems
Does rise a radiant croppe of Royalle stemms,
A Golden haruest of crown'd heads, that meet
And crowd for kisses from the LAMB's white feet.   15
In this Illustrious throng, your lofty floud
Swells high, fair Confluence of all highborn Bloud!
With your bright head whole groues of scepters bend
Their wealthy tops; & for these feet contend.
So swore the LAMB's dread sire. And so we see't.   20
Crownes, & the HEADS they kisse, must court these FEET.
Fix here, fair Majesty! May your Heart ne're misse
To reap new CROWNES & KINGDOMS from that kisse.
Nor may we misse the ioy to meet in you
The aged honors of this day still new.   25
May the great time, in you, still greater be
While all the YEAR is your EPIPHANY,
While your each day's deuotion duly brings
Three KINGDOMES to supply this day's three KINGS.

The Office of the Holy Crosse[*]

The Howres
For the Hovr of Matines

THE VERSICLE

LORD, by thy Sweet & Sauing SIGN,

THE RESPONSORY

Defend us from our foes & Thine.
V. Thou shalt open my lippes, O LORD.
R. And my mouth shall shew forth thy Prayse.
V. A GOD make speed to saue me.
R. O LORD make hast to help me.   5
GLORY be to the FATHER,
            and to the SON,
            and to the H. GHOST.
    As it was in the beginning, is now, & euer shall be, world
without end.   Amen.   10

THE HYMN

The wakefull Matines hast to sing
The vnknown sorrows of our king,
The FATHER's word & wisdom, made
MAN, for man, by man's betraid;
The world's price sett to sale, & by the bold
Merchants of Death & sin, is bought & sold.
Of his Best Freinds (yea of himself) forsaken,
By his worst foes (because he would) beseig'd & taken.

* Repetitious versicles, responsories, prayers, etc. have been de
leted after their first appearance in the text.

THE ANTIPHONA

All hail, fair TREE.
Whose Fruit we be.
What song shall raise
Thy seemly praise.
Who broughtst to light
Life out of death, Day out of night.   5

THE VERSICLE

Lo, we adore thee,
Dread LAMB! And bow thus low before thee,

THE RESPONSOR

'Cause, by the couenant of thy CROSSE,
Thou'hast sau'd at once the whole world's losse.

THE PRAYER

O Lord IESV-CHRIST, son of the liuing GOD! interpose, I
pray thee, thine own pretious death, thy CROSSE & Passion,
betwixt my soul & thy judgment, now & in the hour of my
death. And vouchsafe to graunt vnto me thy grace & mercy;
vnto all quick & dead, remission & rest; to thy church peace
& concord; to vs sinners life & glory euerlasting. Who liuest
and reignest with the FATHER, in the vnity of the HOLY
GHOST, one GOD, world without end. Amen.

For the Hovr of
Prime

THE HYMN

The early PRIME blushes to say
She could not rise so soon, as they
Call'd Pilat vp; to try if He
Could lend them any cruelty.

Their hands with lashes arm'd, their toungs with lyes,   5
And loathsom spittle, blott those beauteous eyes,
The blissfull springs of ioy; from whose all-chearing Ray
The fair starrs fill their wakefull fires the sun himselfe drinks
  Day.

THE ANTIPHONA

Victorious SIGN
That now dost shine,
Transcrib'd aboue
Into the land of light & loue;
O let vs twine
Our rootes with thine,
That we may rise
Vpon thy wings, & reach the skyes.

The Third

THE HYMN

The Third hour's deafen'd with the cry
Of crucify him, crucify.
So goes the vote (nor ask them, Why?)
Liue Barabbas! & let GOD dy.
But there is witt in wrath, and they will try
A HAIL more cruell then their crucify.
For while in sport he weares a spitefull crown,
The serious showres along his decent
  Face run sadly down.

THE ANTIPHONA

CHRIST when he dy'd
Deceiud the CROSSE;
And on death's side
Threw all the losse.

The captiue world awak't, & found 5
The prisoners loose, the Iaylor bound.

The Sixt

THE HIMN

Now is The noon of sorrow's night;
High in his patience, as their spite.
Lo the faint LAMB, with weary limb
Beares that huge tree which must bear Him.
That fatall plant, so great of fame 5
For fruit of sorrow & of shame,
Shall swell with both for HIM; & mix
All woes into one CRVCIFIX.
Is tortur'd Thirst, it selfe, too sweet a cup?
GALL, & more bitter mocks, shall make it vp. 10
Are NAILES blunt pens of superficiall smart?
Contempt & scorn can send sure wounds to search the
    inmost Heart.

THE ANTIPHONA

O deare & sweet Dispute
'Twixt death's & Loue's farr different FRVIT!
Different as farr
As antidotes & poysons are
By that first fatall TREE 5
Both life & liberty
Were sold and slain;
By this they both look vp, & liue again.

The Ninth

THE HYMN

The ninth with awfull horror hearkened to those groanes
Which taught attention eu'n to rocks & stones.
Hear, FATHER, hear! thy LAMB (at last) complaines.
Of some more painfull thing then all his paines.
Then bowes his all-obedient head, & dyes   5
His own loue's, & our sin's GREAT SACRIFICE.
The sun saw That; And would haue seen no more;
The center shook. Her vselesse veil th'inglorious Temple
    tore.

THE ANTIPHONA

O strange mysterious strife
Of open DEATH & hidden LIFE!
When on the crosse my king did bleed,
LIFE seem'd to dy, DEATH dy'd indeed.

Evensong

THE HYMN

Bvt there were Rocks would not relent at This.
Lo, for their own hearts, they rend his.
Their deadly hate liues still; & hath
A wild reserue of wanton wrath;
Superfluous SPEAR! But there's a HEART stands by   5
Will look no wounds be lost, no deaths shall dy.
Gather now thy Greif's ripe FRVIT. Great mother-maid!
Then sitt thee down, & sing thine Eu'nsong in the sad
    TREE's shade.

THE ANTIPHONA

O sad, sweet TREE!
Wofull & ioyfull we
Both weep & sing in shade of thee.
When the dear NAILES did lock
And graft into thy gracious Stock   5
The hope; the health,
The worth, the wealth
Of all the ransom'd WORLD, thou hadst the power
(In that propitious Hour)
To poise each pretious limb,   10
And proue how light the World was, when it weighd with
    HIM.
Wide maist thou spred
Thine Armes; And with thy bright & blisfull head
O'relook all Libanus. Thy lofty crown   15
The king himself is; Thou his humble THRONE.
Where yeilding & yet conquering he
Prou'd a new path of patient Victory.
When wondring death by death was slain,
And our Captiuity his Captiue ta'ne.   20

Compline

THE HIMN

The Complin hour comes last, to call
Vs to our own LIVE's funerall.
Ah hartlesse task! yet hope takes head;
And liues in Him that here lyes dead.
Run, MARY, run! Bring hither all the BLEST   5
ARABIA, for thy Royall Phœnix' nest;
Pour on thy noblest sweets, Which, when they touch
This sweeter BODY, shall indeed be such.
But must thy bed, lord, be a borow'd graue
Who lend'st to all things All the LIFE they haue.   10
O rather vse this HEART, thus farr a fitter STONE,
'Cause, though a hard & cold one, yet it is thine owne. Amen.

THE ANTIPHONA

O saue vs then
Mercyfull KING of men!
Since thou wouldst needs be thus
A SAVIOVR, & at such a rate, for vs;
Saue vs, o saue vs, lord.   5
We now will own no shorter wish, nor name a narrower
word.
Thy blood bids vs be bold.
Thy Wounds giue vs fair hold.
Thy Sorrows chide our shame.   10
Thy Crosse, thy Nature, & thy name
Aduance our claim
And cry with one accord
Saue them, o saue them, lord.

The
Recommendation

These Houres, & that which houer's o're my E N D,
Into thy hands, and hart, lord, I commend.

Take Both to Thine Account, that I & mine
In that Hour, & in these, may be all thine.

That as I dedicate my deuoutest BREATH   5
To make a kind of LIFE for my lord's DEATH,

So from his liuing, & life-giuing DEATH,
My dying LIFE may draw a new, & neuer fleeting BREATH.

Vpon
The
H. Sepvlcher*

Here where our LORD once lay'd his Head,
Now the graue lyes Buryed.

* See also p. 515.

Vexilla Regis,
The
Hymn
of the Holy
Crosse

Look vp, languishing Soul! Lo where the fair
　　Badg of thy faith calls back thy care,
　　　　And biddes thee ne're forget
　　　　Thy life is one long Debt
Of loue to Him, who on this painfull Tree　　　　5
Paid back the flesh he took for thee.

　　Lo, how the streames of life, from that full nest
Of loues, thy lord's too liberall brest,
　　　　Flow in an amorous floud
　　　　Of Water wedding Blood.　　　　10
With these he wash't thy stain, transfer'd thy smart,
And took it home to his own heart.

　　But though great Love, greedy of such sad gain
Vsurp't the Portion of Thy pain,
　　　　And from the nailes & spear　　　　15
　　　　Turn'd the steel point of fear,
Their vse is chang'd, not lost; and now they moue
Not stings of wrath, but wounds of loue.

　　Tall Tree of life! thy truth makes good
What was till now ne're vnderstood,　　　　20
　　　　Though the prophetick king
　　　　Struck lowd his faithfull string,
It was thy wood he meant should make the Throne
For a more then Salomon.

　　Larg throne of loue! Royally spred　　　　25
With purple of too Rich a red.

Thy crime is too much duty;
Thy Burthen, too much beauty;
Glorious, or Greiuous more? thus to make good
Thy costly excellence with thy KING's own BLOOD. 30

Euen ballance of both worlds! our world of sin,
And that of grace heaun way'd in HIM,
Vs with our price thou weighed'st;
Our price for vs thou payed'st;
Soon as the right-hand scale reioyc't to proue 35
How much Death weigh'd more light then loue.

Hail, our alone hope! let thy fair head shoot
Aloft; and fill the nations with thy noble fruit.
The while our hearts & we
Thus graft our selues on thee; 40
Grow thou & they. And be thy fair increase
The sinner's pardon & the iust man's peace.

Liue, o for euer liue & reign
The LAMB whom his own loue hath slain!
And let thy lost sheep liue to'inherit 45
That KINGDOM which this CROSSE did merit.
A M E N.

To Ovr B. Lord
Vpon the Choise of His
Sepulcher*

How life & death in Thee
Agree!
Thou hadst a virgin womb,
And tomb.
A IOSEPH did betroth
Them both.

* See also p. 522.

Charitas
Nimia
or
The
Dear Bargain

Lord, what is man? why should he coste thee
So dear? what had his ruin lost thee?
Lord what is man? that thou hast ouerbought
     So much a thing of nought?

Loue is too kind, I see; & can   5
Make but a simple merchant man.
'Twas for such sorry merchandise
Bold Painters haue putt out his Eyes.

Alas, sweet lord, what wer't to thee
If there were no such wormes as we?   10
Heau'n ne're the lesse still heaun would be,
     Should Mankind dwell
     In the deep hell.
What haue his woes to doe with thee?

     Let him goe weep   15
     O're his own wounds;
     Seraphims will not sleep
Nor spheares let fall their faithfull rounds.

Still would The youthfull Spirits sing;
And still thy spatious Palace ring.   20
Still would those beauteous ministers of light
     Burn all as bright,

And bow their flaming heads before thee
Still thrones & Dominations would adore thee
Still would those euer-wakefull sons of fire   25
     Keep warm thy prayse
     Both nights & dayes,
And teach thy lou'd name to their noble lyre.

Let froward Dust then doe it's kind;
And giue it self for sport to the proud wind. 30
Why should a peice of peeuish clay plead shares
In the Æternity of thy old cares?
Why shouldst thou bow thy awfull Brest to see
What mine own madnesses haue done with me?

    Should not the king still keepe his throne 35
Because some desperate Fool's vndone?
Or will the world's Illustrious eyes
Weep for euery worm that dyes;

        Will the gallant sun
          E're the lesse glorious run? 40
Will he hang down his golden head
Or e're the sooner seek his western bed,
          Because some foolish fly
          Growes wanton, & will dy?

    If I were lost in misery, 45
What was it to thy heaun & thee?
What was it to thy pretious blood
If my foul Heart call'd for a floud?

    What if my faithlesse soul & I
          Would needs fall in 50
          With guilt & sin,
What did the Lamb, that he should dy?
What did the lamb, that he should need,
When the wolf sins, himself to bleed?

          If my base lust, 55
Bargain'd with Death & well-beseeming dust
          Why should the white
          Lamb's bosom write
          The purple name
          Of my sin's shame? 60

    Why should his vnstaind brest make good
My blushes with his own heart-blood?

O my SAVIOVR, make me see
How dearly thou hast payd for me

That lost again my LIFE may proue   65
As then in DEATH, so now in loue.

Sancta Maria
Dolorvm
or
The Mother
of
Sorrows

A
Patheticall descant vpon the
deuout Plainsong
of
Stabat Mater
Dolorosa

In shade of death's sad TREE
Stood Dolefull SHEE.
Ah SHE! now by none other
Name to be known, alas, but SORROW'S MOTHER.
Before her eyes   5
Her's, & the whole world's ioyes,
Hanging all torn she sees; and in his woes
And Paines, her Pangs & throes.
Each wound of His, from euery Part,
All, more at home in her owne heart.   10

What kind of marble than
Is that cold man
Who can look on & see,
Nor keep such noble sorrowes company?
Sure eu'en from you   15
(My Flints) some drops are due
To see so many vnkind swords contest
So fast for one soft Brest.

While with a faithfull, mutuall, floud
Her eyes bleed Teares, his wounds weep Blood.   20

    O costly intercourse
    Of deaths, & worse,
    Diuided loues. While son & mother
Discourse alternate wounds to one another;
    Quick Deaths that grow   25
    And gather, as they come & goe:
His Nailes write swords in her, which soon her heart
    Payes back, with more then their own smart
Her Swords, still growing with his pain,
Turn Speares, & straight come home again.   30

    She sees her son, her God,
    Bow with a load
    Of borrowd sins; And swimme
In woes that were not made for Him.
    Ah hard command   35
    Of loue! Here must she stand
Charg'd to look on, & with a stedfast ey
    See her life dy:
Leauing her only so much Breath
As serues to keep aliue her death.   40

    O Mother turtle-doue!
    Soft sourse of loue
    That these dry lidds might borrow
Somthing from thy full Seas of sorrow!
    O in that brest   45
    Of thine (the noblest nest
Both of loue's fires & flouds) might I recline
    This hard, cold, Heart of mine!
The chill lump would relent, & proue
Soft subject for the seige of loue.   50

    O teach those wounds to bleed
    In me; me, so to read
    This book of loues, thus writ
In lines of death, my life may coppy it

With loyall cares.   55
     O let me, here, claim shares;
Yeild somthing in thy sad prærogatiue
     (Great Queen of greifes) & giue
Me too my teares; who, though all stone,
Think much that thou shouldst mourn alone.   60

     Yea let my life & me
     Fix here with thee,
     And at the Humble foot
Of this fair TREE take our eternall root.
     That so we may   65
     At least be in loues way;
And in these chast warres while the wing'd wounds flee
     So fast 'twixt him & thee,
My brest may catch the kisse of some kind dart,
Though as at second hand, from either heart.   70

     O you, your own best Darts
     Dear, dolefull hearts!
     Hail; & strike home & make me see
That wounded bosomes their own weapons be.
     Come wounds! come darts!   75
     Nail'd hands! & peirced hearts!
Come your whole selues, sorrow's great son & mother!
     Nor grudge a yonger-Brother
Of greifes his portion, who (had all their due)
One single wound should not haue left for you.   80

     Shall I, sett there
     So deep a share
     (Dear wounds) & onely now
In sorrows draw no Diuidend with you?
     O be more wise   85
     If not more soft, mine eyes!
Flow, tardy founts! & into decent showres
     Dissolue my Dayes & Howres.
And if thou yet (faint soul!) deferr
To bleed with him, fail not to weep with her.   90

Rich Queen, lend some releife;
At least an almes of greif
To'a heart who by sad right of sin
Could proue the whole summe (too sure) due to him.
By all those stings   95
Of loue, sweet bitter things,
Which these torn hands transcrib'd on thy true heart
O teach mine too the art
To study him so, till we mix
Wounds; and become one crucifix.   100

O let me suck the wine
So long of this chast vine
Till drunk of the dear wounds, I be
A lost Thing to the world, as it to me.
O faithfull freind   105
Of me & of my end!
Fold vp my life in loue; and lay't beneath
My dear lord's vitall death.
Lo, heart, thy hope's whole Plea! Her pretious Breath
Powr'd out in prayrs for thee; thy lord's in death.   110

Vpon
The
Bleeding
Crvcifix

A
*Song**

Iesu, no more! It is full tide.
From thy head & from thy feet,
From thy hands & from thy side
All the purple Riuers meet.

What need thy fair head bear a part   5
In showres, as if thine eyes had none?
What need They help to drown thy heart,
That striues in torrents of it's own?

* See also p. 529

Thy restlesse feet now cannot goe
For vs & our eternall good,   10
As they were euer wont. What though?
They swimme. Alas, in their own floud.

Thy hands to giue, thou canst not lift;
Yet will thy hand still giuing be.
It giues but ô, it self's the gift.   15
It giues though bound; though bound 'tis free.

But ô thy side, thy deep-digg'd side!
That hath a double Nilus going.
Nor euer was the pharian tide
Half so fruitfull, half so flowing.   20

No hair so small, but payes his riuer
To this red sea of thy blood
Their little channells can deliuer
Somthing to the Generall floud.

But while I speak, whither are run   25
All the riuers nam'd before?
I counted wrong. There is but one;
But ô that one is one all ore.

Rain-swoln riuers may rise proud,
Bent all to drown & ouerflow.   30
But when indeed all 's ouerflow'd
They themselues are drowned too.

This thy blood's deluge, a dire chance
Dear LORD to thee, to vs is found
A deluge of Deliuerance;   35
A deluge least we should be drown'd.

N'ere wast thou in a sense so sadly true,
The WELL of liuing WATERS, Lord, till now.

Vpon
The Crowne of Thorns
Taken Downe
From the head of our Bl. Lord,
all Bloody*

Know'st thou This, Souldier? 'Tis a much-chang'd plant
which yet
Thy selfe didst sett.
O who so hard a Husbandman did euer find
A soile so kind?
Is not the soile a kind one, which returnes
Roses for Thornes?

5

Vpon
The Body of Ovr
Bl. Lord,
Naked
and
Bloody*

They 'haue left thee naked, LORD, O that they had!
This garment too I would they had deny'd.
Thee with thy self they haue too richly clad;
Opening the purple wardrobe in thy side.
O neuer could there be garment too good
For thee to wear, But this, of thine own Blood.

5

* See also p. 525.
* See also p. 528.

The
Hymn
of
Sainte Thomas
in
Adoration of
The
Blessed
Sacrament

Adoro Te

With all the powres my poor Heart hath
Of humble loue & loyall Faith,
Thus lowe (my hidden life!) I bow to thee
Whom too much loue hath bow'd more low for me.
Down down, proud sense! Discourses dy.   5
Keep close, my soul's inquiring ey!
Nor touch nor tast must look for more
But each sitt still in his own Dore.

Your ports are all superfluous here,
Saue That which lets in faith, the eare.   10
Faith is my skill. Faith can beleiue
As fast as loue new lawes can giue.
Faith is my force. Faith strength affords
To keep pace with those powrfull words.
And words more sure, more sweet, then they   15
Loue could not think, truth could not say.

O let thy wretch find that releife
Thou didst afford the faithfull theife.
Plead for me, loue! Alleage & show
That faith has farther, here, to goe   20
And lesse to lean on. Because than
Though hidd as GOD, wounds writt thee man,
Thomas might touch; None but might see
At least the suffring side of thee;
And that too was thy self which thee did couer,   25
But here eu'n That's hid too which hides the other.

Sweet, consider then, that I
Though allow'd nor hand nor eye
To reach at thy lou'd Face; nor can
Tast thee GOD, or touch thee MAN   30
Both yet beleiue; and wittnesse thee
My LORD too & my GOD, as lowd as He.

Help lord, my Faith, my Hope increase;
And fill my portion in thy peace.
Giue loue for life; nor let my dayes   35
Grow, but in new powres to thy name & praise.

O dear memoriall of that Death
Which liues still, & allowes vs breath!
Rich, Royall food! Bountyfull BREAD!
Whose vse denyes vs to the dead;   40
Whose vitall gust alone can giue
The same leaue both to eat & liue;
Liue euer Bread of loues, & be
My life, my soul, my surer selfe to mee.

O soft self-wounding Pelican!   45
Whose brest weepes Balm for wounded man.
Ah this way bend thy benign floud
To'a bleeding Heart that gaspes for blood.
That blood, whose least drops soueraign be
To wash my worlds of sins from me.   50
Come loue! Come LORD! & that long day
For which I languish, come away.
When this dry soul those eyes shall see,
And drink the vnseal'd sourse of thee.
When Glory's sun faith's shades shall chase,   55
And for thy veil giue me thy FACE.

A M E N.

Lavda Sion Salvatorem
The Hymn
for
The Bl.
Sacrament

Rise, Royall SION! rise & sing
Thy soul's kind shepheard, thy hart's KING.
Stretch all thy powres; call if you can
Harpes of heaun to hands of man.
This soueraign subject sitts aboue   5
The best ambition of thy loue.

Lo the BREAD of LIFE, this day's
Triumphant Text, prouokes thy prayse.
The liuing & life-giuing bread,
To the great twelue distributed   10
When LIFE, himself, at point to dy
Of loue, was his own LEGACY.

Come, loue! & let vs work a song
Lowd & pleasant, sweet & long;
Let lippes & Hearts lift high the noise   15
Of so iust & solemn ioyes,
Which on his white browes this bright day
Shall hence for euer bear away.

Lo the new LAW of a new LORD
With a new Lamb blesses the Board.   20
The aged Pascha pleads not yeares
But spyes loue's dawn, & disappeares.
Types yeild to TRVTHES; shades shrink away;
And their NIGHT dyes into our Day.

But lest THAT dy too, we are bid   25
Euer to doe what he once did.
And by a mindfull, mystick breath
That we may liue, reuiue his DEATH;
With a well-bles't bread & wine
Transsum'd, & taught to turn diuine.   30

The Heaun-instructed house of FAITH
Here a holy Dictate hath
That they but lend their Form & face,
Themselues with reuerence leaue their place
Nature, & name, to be made good   35
By' a nobler Bread, more needfull BLOOD.

Where nature's lawes no leaue will giue,
Bold FAITH takes heart, & dares beleiue.
In different species, names not things
Himself to me my SAVIOVR brings,   40
As meat in That, as Drink in this;
But still in Both one CHRIST he is.

The Receiuing Mouth here makes
Nor wound nor breach in what he takes.
Let one, or one THOVSAND be   45
Here Diuiders, single he
Beares home no lesse, all they no more,
Nor leaue they both lesse then before.

Though in it self this SOVERAIN FEAST
Be all the same to euery Guest,   50
Yet on the same (life-meaning) Bread
The child of Death eates himself Dead.
Nor is't loue's fault, but sin's dire skill
That thus from LIFE can DEATH distill.

When the blest signes thou broke shall see,   55
Hold but thy Faith intire as he
Who, howsoe're clad, cannot come
Lesse then whole CHRIST in euery crumme.
In broken formes a stable FAITH
Vntouch't her pretious TOTALL hath.   60

Lo the life-food of ANGELLS then
Bow'd to the lowly mouths of men!
The children's BREAD; the Bridegroom's WINE.
Not to be cast to dogges, or swine.

Lo, the full, finall, SACRIFICE   65
On which all figures fix't their eyes.
The ransom'd ISACK, & his ramme;
The MANNA, & the PASCHAL Lamb.

IESV MASTER, Iust & true!
Our FOOD, & faithfull SHEPHARD too!   70
O by thy self vouchsafe to keep,
As with thy selfe thou feed'st thy SHEEP.

O let that loue which thus makes thee
Mix with our low Mortality,
Lift our lean Soules, & sett vs vp   75
Convictors of thine own full cup,
Coheirs of SAINTS. That so all may
Drink the same wine; and the same WAY.
Nor change the PASTVRE, but the PLACE
To feed of THEE in thine own FACE.   80

A M E N.

Dies Irae Dies Illa

*The
Hymn
of the
Chvrch,
In Meditation of
The Day of
Ivdgment*

Hears't thou, my soul, what serious things
Both the Psalm and sybyll sings
Of a sure iudge, from whose sharp Ray
The world in flames shall fly away.

O that fire! before whose face   5
Heaun & earth shall find no place.
O those eyes! whose angry light
Must be the day of that dread Night.

O that trump! whose blast shall run
An euen round with the circling Sun.   10
And vrge the murmuring graues to bring
Pale mankind forth to meet his king.

Horror of nature, hell & Death!
When a deep Groan from beneath
Shall cry we come, we come & all   15
The caues of night answer one call.

O that Book! whose leaues so bright
Will sett the world in seuere light.
O that Iudge! whose hand, whose eye
None can indure; yet none can fly.   20

Ah then, poor soul, what wilt thou say?
And to what Patron chuse to pray?
When starres themselues shall stagger; and
The most firm foot no more then stand.

But thou giu'st leaue (dread Lord) that we   25
Take shelter from thy self, in thee;
And with the wings of thine own doue
Fly to thy scepter of soft loue.

Dear, remember in that Day
Who was the cause thou cams't this way.   30
Thy sheep was stray'd; And thou wouldst be
Euen lost thy self in seeking me.

Shall all that labour, all that cost
Of loue, and eu'n that losse, be lost?
And this lou'd soul, iudg'd worth no lesse   35
Then all that way, and werynesse?

Iust mercy then, thy Reckning be
With my price, & not with me
'Twas pay'd at first with too much pain,
To be pay'd twice; or once, in vain.   40

Mercy (my iudge) mercy I cry
With blushing Cheek & bleeding ey,
The conscious colors of my sin
Are red without & pale within.

O let thine own soft bowells pay   45
Thy self; And so discharge that day.
If sin can sigh, loue can forgiue.
O say the word my Soul shall liue.

Those mercyes which thy MARY found
Or who thy crosse confes't & crown'd,   50
Hope tells my heart, the same loues be
Still aliue; and still for me.

Though both my Prayres & teares combine,
Both worthlesse are; For they are mine.
But thou thy bounteous self still be;   55
And show thou art, by sauing me.

O when thy last Frown shall proclaim
The flocks of goates to folds of flame,
And all thy lost sheep found shall be,
Let come ye blessed then call me.   60

When the dread ITE shall diuide
Those Limbs of death from thy left side,
Let those life-speaking lipps command
That I inheritt thy right hand.

O hear a supliant heart; all crush't   65
And crumbled into contrite dust.
My hope, my fear! my Iudge, my Freind!
Take charge of me, & of my END.

The
Himn
O Gloriosa Domina

Hail, most high, most humble one!
Aboue the world; below thy Son
Whose blush the moon beauteously marres
And staines the timerous light of starres.
He that made all things, had not done   5
Till he had made Himself thy son
The whole world's host would be thy guest
And board himself at thy rich Brest.
O boundles Hospitality!
The Feast of all things feeds on the.   10
   The first Eue, mother of our Fall,
E're she bore any one, slew all.
Of Her vnkind gift might we haue
The inheritance of a hasty Grave;
Quick burye'd in the wanton Tomb   15
      Of one forbidden bitt;
Had not a Better Frvit forbidden it.
         Had not thy healthfull womb
   The world's new eastern window bin
And giuen vs heau'n again, in giuing Him.   20
Thine was the Rosy Dawn that sprung the Day
Which renders all the starres she stole away.
   Let then the Aged world be wise, & all
Proue nobly, here, vnnaturall.
'Tis gratitude to forgett that other   25
And call the maiden Eue their mother.
   Yee redeem'd Nations farr & near,
Applaud your happy selues in her,
(All you to whom this loue belongs)
And keep't aliue with lasting songs.   30
   Let hearts & lippes speak lowd; and say
Hail, door of life: & sourse of day!
The door was shutt, the fountain seal'd;
Yet Light was seen & Life reueald.
The door was shutt, yet let in day,   35
The fountain seald, yet life found way.

Glory to thee, great virgin's son
In bosom of thy FATHER's blisse.
The same to thee, sweet SPIRIT be done;
As euer shall be, was, & is. 40

A M E N.

In The
Gloriovs
Assvmption
of
Ovr Blessed
*Lady**

The Hymn

Hark! she is call'd, the parting houre is come.
Take thy Farewell, poor world! heaun must goe home.
A peice of heau'nly earth; Purer & brighter
Then the chast starres, whose choise lamps come to light her
While through the crystall orbes, clearer then they 5
She climbes; and makes a farre more milkey way.
She's calld. Hark, how the dear immortall doue
Sighes to his syluer mate rise vp, my loue!
Rise vp, my fair, my spottlesse one!
The winter's past, the rain is gone. 10
 The spring is come, the flowrs appear
No sweets, but thou, are wanting here.
  Come away, my loue!
  Come away, my doue! cast off delay,
  The court of heau'n is come 15
  To wait vpon thee home; Come come away!
  The flowrs appear.
Or quickly would, wert thou once here.
The spring is come, or if it stay,
'Tis to keep time with thy delay. 20

* See also p. 564.

The rain is gone, except so much as we
Detain in needfull teares to weep the want of thee.
        The winter's past.
        or if he make lesse hast,
His answer is, why she does so.   25
If sommer come not, how can winter goe.
        Come away, come away.
The shrill winds chide, the waters weep thy stay;
The fountains murmur; & each loftyest tree
Bowes low'st his heauy top, to look for thee.   30
        Come away, my loue.
        Come away, my doue &c.
She's call'd again. And will she goe?
When heaun bidds come, who can say no?
Heaun calls her, & she must away.   35
Heaun will not, & she cannot stay.
Goe then; goe Gloriovs.
        On the golden wings
Of the bright youth of heaun, that sings
Vnder so sweet a Burthen. Goe,   40
Since thy dread son will haue it so.
And while thou goest, our song & we
Will, as we may, reach after thee.
Hail, holy Queen of humble hearts!
We in thy prayse will haue our parts.   45
        Thy pretious name shall be
        Thy self to vs; & we
        With holy care will keep it by vs.
        We to the last
        Will hold it fast   50
        And no Assvmption shall deny vs.
        All the sweetest showres
        Of our fairest flowres
        Will we strow vpon it.
        Though our sweets cannot make   55
        It sweeter, they can take
        Themselues new sweetnes from it.
M A R I A, men & Angels sing
M A R I A, mother of our King.

LIVE, rosy princesse, LIVE. And may the bright   60
Crown of a most incomparable light
Embrace thy radiant browes. O may the best
Of euerlasting ioyes bath thy white brest.
LIVE, our chast loue, the holy mirth
Of heaun; the humble pride of earth.   65
Liue, crown of woemen; Queen of men.
Liue mistresse of our song. And when
Our weak desires haue done their best,
Sweet Angels come, and sing the rest.

Sainte
Mary
Magdalene
or
The Weeper*

Loe where a WOVNDED HEART *with Bleeding* EYES *conspire.*
Is she a FLAMING *Fountain, or a Weeping fire!*

Hail, sister springs!
Parents of syluer-footed rills!
Euer bubling things!   5
Thawing crystall! snowy hills,
Still spending, neuer spent! I mean
Thy fair eyes, sweet MAGDALENE!

Heauens thy fair eyes be;
Heauens of euer-falling starres.   10
'Tis seed-time still with thee
And starres thou sow'st, whose haruest dares
Promise the earth to counter shine
Whateuer makes heaun's forhead fine.

But we'are deceiued all.   15
Starres indeed they are too true;
For they but seem to fall,

* See also p. 508.

As Heaun's other spangles doe.
It is not for our earth & vs
To shine in Things so pretious.   20

Vpwards thou dost weep.
Heaun's bosome drinks the gentle stream.
Where th'milky riuers creep,
Thine floates aboue; & is the cream.
Waters aboue th' Heauns, what they be   25
We' are taught best by thy TEARES & thee.

Euery morn from hence
A brisk Cherub somthing sippes
Whose sacred influence
Addes sweetnes to his sweetest Lippes.   30
Then to his musick. And his song
Tasts of this Breakfast all day long.

Not in the euening's eyes
When they Red with weeping are
For the Sun that dyes,   35
Sitts sorrow with a face so fair,
No where but here did euer meet
Sweetnesse so sad, sadnesse so sweet.

When sorrow would be seen
In her brightest majesty   40
(For she is a Queen)
Then is she drest by none but thee.
Then, & only then, she weares
Her proudest pearles; I mean, thy TEARES.

The deaw no more will weep   45
The primrose's pale cheek to deck,
The deaw no more will sleep
Nuzzel'd in the lilly's neck;
Much reather would it be thy TEAR,
And leaue them Both to tremble here.   50

    There's no need at all
    That the balsom-sweating bough
    So coyly should let fall
    His med'cinable teares; for now
Nature hath learn't to'extract a deaw   55
More soueraign & sweet from you.

    Yet let the poore drops weep
    (Weeping is the ease of woe)
    Softly let them creep,
    Sad that they are vanquish't so.   60
They, though to others no releife,
Balsom maybe, for their own greife.

    Such the maiden gemme
    By the purpling vine put on,
    Peeps from her parent stemme   65
    And blushes at the bridegroome sun.
This watry Blossom of thy eyn,
Ripe, will make the richer wine.

    When some new bright Guest
    Takes vp among the starres a room,   70
    And Heaun will make a feast,
    Angels with crystall violls come
And draw from these full eyes of thine
Their master's Water: their own Wine.

    Golden though he be,   75
    Golden Tagus murmures tho;
    Were his way by thee,
    Content & quiet he would goe.
So much more rich would he esteem
Thy syluer, then his golden stream.   80

    Well does the May that lyes
    Smiling in thy cheeks, confesse
    The April in thine eyes.
    Mutuall sweetnesse they expresse.
No April ere lent kinder showres,   85
Nor May return'd more faithfull flowres.

O cheeks! Bedds of chast loues
By your own showres seasonably dash't
Eyes! nests of milky doues
In your own wells decently washt,   90
O wit of loue! that thus could place
Fountain & Garden in one face.

     O sweet Contest; of woes
With loues, of teares with smiles disputing!
O fair, & Freindly Foes,   95
Each other kissing & confuting!
While rain & sunshine, Cheekes & Eyes
Close in kind contrarietyes.

     But can these fair Flouds be
Freinds with the bosom fires that fill thee   100
Can so great flames agree
Æternall Teares should thus distill thee!
O flouds, o fires! o suns ô showres!
Mixt & made freinds by loue's sweet powres.

     Twas his well-pointed dart   105
That digg'd these wells, & drest this Vine;
And taught the wounded HEART
The way into these weeping Eyn.
Vain loues auant! bold hands forbear!
The lamb hath dipp't his white foot here.   110

     And now where're he strayes,
Among the Galilean mountaines,
Or more vnwellcome wayes,
He's follow'd by two faithfull fountaines;
Two walking baths; two weeping motions;   115
Portable, & compendious oceans.

     O Thou, thy lord's fair store!
In thy so rich & rare expenses,
Euen when he show'd most poor,
He might prouoke the wealth of Princes.   120
What Prince's wanton'st pride e're could
Wash with Syluer, wipe with Gold.

Who is that King, but he
Who calls't his Crown to be call'd thine,
That thus can boast to be   125
Waited on by a wandring mine,
A voluntary mint, that strowes
Warm syluer shoures where're he goes!

O pretious Prodigall!
Fair spend-thrift of thy self! thy measure   130
(Mercilesse loue!) is all.
Euen to the last Pearle in thy treasure.
All places, Times, & obiects be
Thy teare's sweet opportunity.

Does the day-starre rise?   135
Still thy starres doe fall & fall
Does day close his eyes?
Still the FOVNTAIN weeps for all.
Let night or day doe what they will,
Thou hast thy task; thou weepest still.   140

Does thy song lull the air?
Thy falling teares keep faith full time.
Does thy sweet-breath'd praire
Vp in clouds of incense climb?
Still at each sigh, that is, each stop,   145
A bead, that is, A TEAR, does drop.

At these thy weeping gates,
(Watching their watry motion)
Each winged moment waits,
Takes his TEAR, & gets him gone.   150
By thine Ey's tinct enobled thus
Time layes him vp; he's pretious.

Not, so long she liued,
Shall thy tomb report of thee;
But, so long she greiued,   155
Thus must we date thy memory.
Others by moments, months, & yeares
Measure their ages; thou, by TEARES.

So doe perfumes expire.
So sigh tormented sweets, opprest   160
With proud vnpittying fire.
Such Teares the suffring Rose that 's vext
With vngentle flames does shed,
Sweating in a too warm bed.

Say, ye bright brothers,   165
The fugitiue sons of those fair Eyes
Your fruitfull mothers!
What make you here? what hopes can tice
You to be born? what cause can borrow
You from Those nests of noble sorrow?   170

Whither away so fast?
For sure the sordid earth
Your Sweetnes cannot tast
Nor does the dust deserue your birth.
Sweet, whither hast you then? o say   175
Why you trip so fast away?

We goe not to seek,
The darlings of Auroras bed,
The rose's modest Cheek
Nor the violet's humble head.   180
Though the Feild's eyes too WEEPERS be
Becàuse they want such TEARES as we.

Much lesse mean we to trace
The Fortune of inferior gemmes,
Preferr'd to some proud face   185
Or pertch't vpon fear'd Diadems.
Crown'd Heads are toyes. We goe to meet
A worthy object, our lord's FEET.

A Hymn
To
The Name and Honor
of
The Admirable
Sainte
Teresa,

Fovndresse
of the Reformation of the Discalced
Carmelites, both
men & Women;
A
Woman
for Angelicall heigth of speculation, for
Masculine courage of performance,
more then a woman.
Who
Yet a child, out ran maturity, and
*durst plott a Martyrdome**

Loue, thou art Absolute sole lord
OF LIFE & DEATH. To proue the word,
Wee'l now appeal to none of all
Those thy old Souldiers, Great & tall,
Ripe Men of Martyrdom, that could reach down   5
With strong armes, their triumphant crown;
Such as could with lusty breath
Speak lowd into the face of death
Their Great LORD's glorious name, to none
Of those whose spatious Bosomes spread a throne   10
For LOVE at larg to fill: spare blood & sweat;
And see him take a priuate seat,
Making his mansion in the mild
And milky soul of a soft child.
 Scarse has she learn't to lisp the name   15
Of Martyr; yet she thinks it shame

* See also p. 556.

Life should so long play with that breath
Which spent can buy so braue a death.
She neuer vndertook to know
What death with loue should haue to doe;   20
Nor has she e're yet vnderstood
Why to show loue, she should shed blood
Yet though she cannot tell you why,
She can LOVE, & she can DY.

   Scarse has she Blood enough to make   25
A guilty sword blush for her sake;
Yet has she'a HEART dares hope to proue
How much lesse strong is DEATH then LOVE.

   Be loue but there; let poor six yeares
Be pos'd with the maturest Feares   30
Man trembles at, you straight shall find
LOVE knowes no nonage, nor the MIND.
'Tis LOVE, not YEARES or LIMBS that can
Make the Martyr, or the man.

   LOVE touch't her HEART, & lo it beates   35
High, & burnes with such braue heates;
Such thirsts to dy, as dares drink vp,
A thousand cold deaths in one cup.
Good reason. For she breathes All fire.
Her weake brest heaues with strong desire   40
Of what she may with fruitles wishes
Seek for amongst her MOTHER's kisses.

   Since 'tis not to be had at home
She'l trauail to a Martyrdom.
No home for hers confesses she   45
But where she may a Martyr be.

   Sh'el to the Moores; And trade with them,
For this vnualued Diadem.
She'l offer them her dearest Breath,
With CHRIST's Name in't, in change for death.   50
Sh'el bargain with them; & will giue
Them GOD; teach them how to liue
In him: or, if they this deny,
For him she'l teach them how to DY.
So shall she leaue amongst them sown   55
Her LORD's Blood; or at lest her own.

FAREWEL then, all the world! Adieu.
TERESA is no more for you.
Farewell, all pleasures, sports, & ioyes,
(Neuer till now esteemed toyes) 60
Farewell what euer deare may bee,
MOTHER's armes or FATHER's knee
Farewell house, & farewell home!
SHE's for the Moores, & MARTYRDOM.

SWEET, not so fast! lo thy fair Spouse 65
Whom thou seekst with so swift vowes,
Calls thee back, & bidds thee come
T'embrace a milder MARTYRDOM.

Blest powres forbid, Thy tender life
Should bleed vpon a barborous knife; 70
Or some base hand haue power to race
Thy Brest's chast cabinet, & vncase
A soul kept there so sweet, ô no;
Wise heaun will neuer haue it so
THOV art love's victime; & must dy 75
A death more mysticall & high.
Into loue's armes thou shalt let fall
A still-suruiuing funerall.
His is the DART must make the DEATH
Whose stroke shall tast thy hallow'd breath; 80
A Dart thrice dip't in that rich flame
Which writes thy spouse's radiant Name
Vpon the roof of Heau'n; where ay
It shines, & with a soueraign ray
Beates bright vpon the burning faces 85
Of soules which in that name's sweet graces
Find euerlasting smiles. So rare,
So spirituall, pure, & fair
Must be th'immortall instrument
Vpon whose choice point shall be sent 90
A life so lou'd; And that there be
Fitt executioners for Thee,
The fair'st & first-born sons of fire
Blest SERAPHIM, shall leaue their quire
And turn loue's souldiers, vpon THEE 95
To exercise their archerie.

O how oft shalt thou complain
Of a sweet & subtle PAIN.
Of intolerable IOYES;
Of a DEATH, in which who dyes   100
Loues his death, and dyes again.
And would for euer so be slain.
And liues, & dyes; and knowes not why
To liue, But that he thus may neuer leaue to DY.
   How kindly will thy gentle HEART   105
Kisse the sweetly-killing DART!
And close in his embraces keep
Those delicious Wounds, that weep
Balsom to heal themselues with. Thus
When These thy DEATHS, so numerous,   110
Shall all at last dy into one,
And melt thy Soul's sweet mansion;
Like a soft lump of incense, hasted
By too hott a fire, & wasted
Into perfuming clouds, so fast   115
Shalt thou exhale to Heaun at last
In a resoluing SIGH, and then
O what? Ask not the Tongues of men.
Angells cannot tell, suffice,
Thy selfe shall feel thine own full ioyes   120
And hold them fast for euer. There
So soon as thou shalt first appear,
The MOON of maiden starrs, thy white
MISTRESSE, attended by such bright
Soules as thy shining self, shall come   125
And in her first rankes make thee room;
Where 'mongst her snowy family
Immortall wellcomes wait for thee.
   O what delight, when reueal'd LIFE shall stand
And teach thy lipps heau'n with his hand;   130
On which thou now maist to thy wishes
Heap vp thy consecrated kisses.
What ioyes shall seize thy soul, when she
Bending her blessed eyes on thee
(Those second Smiles of Heau'n) shall dart   135
Her mild rayes through thy melting heart!

Angels, thy old freinds, there shall greet thee
Glad at their own home now to meet thee.
　All thy good WORKES which went before
And waited for thee, at the door,　　　　　140
Shall own thee there; and all in one
Weaue a constellation
Of CROWNS, with which the KING thy spouse
Shall build vp thy triumphant browes.
　All thy old woes shall now smile on thee　145
And thy paines sitt bright vpon thee
All thy sorrows here shall shine,
All thy SVFFERINGS be diuine.
TEARES shall take comfort, & turn gemms
And WRONGS repent to Diademms.　　　150
Eu'n thy DEATHS shall liue; & new
Dresse the soul that erst they slew.
Thy wounds shall blush to such bright scarres
As keep account of the LAMB's warres.
　Those rare WORKES where thou shalt leaue writt,　155
Loue's noble history, with witt
Taught thee by none but him, while here
They feed our soules, shall cloth THINE there.
Each heaunly word by whose hid flame
Our hard Hearts shall strike fire, the same　160
Shall flourish on thy browes. & be
Both fire to vs & flame to thee;
Whose light shall liue bright in thy FACE
By glory, in our hearts by grace.
　Thou shalt look round about, & see　165
Thousands of crown'd Soules throng to be
Themselues thy crown. Sons of thy vowes
The virgin-births with which thy soueraign spouse
Made fruitfull thy fair soul, goe now
And with them all about thee bow　　　170
To Him, put on (hee'l say) put on
(My rosy loue) That thy rich zone
Sparkling with the sacred flames
Of thousand soules, whose happy names
Heau'n keeps vpon thy score. (Thy bright　175
Life brought them first to kisse the light

That kindled them to starrs.) and so
Thou with the LAMB, thy lord, shalt goe;
And whereso'ere he setts his white
Stepps, walk with HIM those wayes of light   180
Which who in death would liue to see,
Must learn in life to dy like thee.

An
Apologie
For
The Fore-Going Hymne
as hauing been writt when the au-
thor was yet among the
*protestantes**

Thus haue I back again to thy bright name
(Fair floud of holy fires!) transfus'd the flame
I took from reading thee, tis to thy wrong
I know, that in my weak & worthlesse song
Thou here art sett to shine where thy full day   5
Scarse dawnes. O pardon if I dare to say
Thine own dear bookes are guilty. For from thence
I learn't to know that loue is eloquence.
That hopefull maxime gaue me hart to try
If, what to other tongues is tun'd so high,   10
Thy praise might not speak English too; forbid
(By all thy mysteryes that here ly hidde)
Forbid it, mighty Loue! let no fond Hate
Of names & wordes, so farr præiudicate.
Souls are not SPANIARDS too, one freindly floud   15
Of BAPTISM blends them all into a blood.
CHRIST's faith makes but one body of all soules
And loue's that body's soul, no law controwlls
Our free traffique for heau'n, we may maintaine
Peace, sure, with piety, though it come from SPAIN.   20
What soul so e're, in any language, can
Speak heau'n like her's is my souls country-man.

* See also p. 561.

O 'tis not spanish, but 'tis heau'n she speaks!
'Tis heau'n that lyes in ambush there, & breaks
From thence into the wondring reader's brest;   25
Who feels his warm HEART hatch'd into a nest
Of little EAGLES & young loues, whose high
Flights scorn the lazy dust, & things that dy.
   There are enow, whose draughts (as deep as hell)
Drink vp al SPAIN in sack. Let my soul swell   30
With thee, strong wine of loue! let others swimme
In puddles; we will pledge this SERAPHIM
Bowles full of richer blood then blush of grape
Was euer guilty of, Change we too 'our shape
(My soul,) Some drink from men to beasts, o then   35
Drink we till we proue more, not lesse, then men,
And turn not beasts, but Angels. Let the king
Me euer into these his cellars bring
Where flowes such wine as we can haue of none
But HIM who trod the wine-presse all alone   40
Wine of youth, life, & the sweet Deaths of loue;
Wine of immortall mixture; which can proue
It's Tincture from the rosy nectar; wine
That can exalt weak EARTH; & so refine
Our dust, that at one draught, mortality   45
May drink it self vp, and forget to dy.

The
Flaming Heart
Vpon the Book and
Picture of the seraphicall saint
Teresa,

(As She Is Vsvally Ex-
pressed with a Seraphim
biside her)

Well meaning readers! you that come as freinds
And catch the pretious name this peice pretends;
Make not too much hast to' admire
That fair-cheek't fallacy of fire.
That is a SERAPHIM, they say   5
And this the great TERESIA.

Readers, be rul'd by me; & make
Here a well-plac't & wise mistake
You must transpose the picture quite,
And spell it wrong to read it right;   10
Read HIM for her, & her for him;
And call the SAINT the SERAPHIM.
    Painter, what didst thou vnderstand
To put her dart into his hand!
See, euen the yeares & size of him   15
Showes this the mother SERAPHIM.
This is the mistresse flame; & duteous he
Her happy fire-works, here, comes down to see.
O most poor-spirited of men!
Had thy cold Pencil kist her PEN   20
Thou couldst not so vnkindly err
To show vs This faint shade for HER
Why man, this speakes pure mortall frame;
And mockes with female FROST loue's manly flame.
One would suspect thou meant'st to paint   25
Some weak, inferiour, woman saint.
But had thy pale-fac't purple took
Fire from the burning cheeks of that bright Booke
Thou wouldst on her haue heap't vp all
That could be found SERAPHICALL;   30
What e're this youth of fire weares fair,
Rosy fingers, radiant hair,
Glowing cheek, & glistering wings,
All those fair & flagrant things,
But before all, that fiery DART   35
Had fill'd the Hand of this great HEART.
    Doe then as equall right requires,
Since HIS the blushes be, & her's the fires,
Resume & rectify thy rude design;
Vndresse thy Seraphim into MINE.   40
Redeem this iniury of thy art;
Giue HIM the vail, giue her the dart.
    Giue Him the vail; that he may couer
The Red cheeks of a riuall'd louer.
Asham'd that our world, now, can show   45
Nests of new Seraphims here below.

Giue her the Dart for it is she
(Fair youth) shootes both thy shaft & Thee
Say, all ye wise & well-peirc't hearts
That liue & dy amidst her darts,   50
What is't your tastfull spirits doe proue
In that rare life of Her, and loue?
Say & bear wittnes. Sends she not
A Seraphim at euery shott?
What magazins of immortall Armes there shine!   55
Heaun's great artillery in each loue-spun line.
Giue then the dart to her who giues the flame;
Giue him the veil, who kindly takes the shame.
    But if it be the frequent fate
Of worst faults to be fortunate;   60
If all 's præscription; & proud wrong
Hearkens not to an humble song;
For all the gallantry of him,
Giue me the suffring Seraphim.
His be the brauery of all those Bright things,   65
The glowing cheekes, the glistering wings;
The Rosy hand, the radiant Dart;
Leaue Her alone The Flaming Heart.
    Leaue her that; & thou shalt leaue her
Not one loose shaft but loue's whole quiuer.   70
For in loue's feild was neuer found
A nobler weapon then a Wovnd.
Loue's passiues are his actiu'st part.
The wounded is the wounding heart.
O Heart! the æquall poise of lou'es both parts   75
Bigge alike with wounds & darts.
Liue in these conquering leaues; liue all the same;
And walk through all tongues one triumphant Flame
Liue here, great Heart; & loue and dy & kill;
And bleed & wound; and yeild & conquer still.   80
Let this immortall life wherere it comes
Walk in a crowd of loues & Martyrdomes.
Let mystick Deaths wait on't; & wise soules be
The loue-slain wittnesses of this life of thee.
O sweet incendiary! shew here thy art,   85
Vpon this carcasse of a hard, cold, hart,

Let all thy scatter'd shafts of light, that play
Among the leaues of thy larg Books of day,
Combin'd against this BREST at once break in
And take away from me my self & sin, 90
This gratious Robbery shall thy bounty be;
And my best fortunes such fair spoiles of me.
O thou vndanted daughter of desires!
By all thy dowr of LIGHTS & FIRES;
By all the eagle in thee, all the doue; 95
By all thy liues & deaths of loue;
By thy larg draughts of intellectuall day,
And by thy thirsts of loue more large then they;
By all thy brim-fill'd Bowles of feirce desire
By thy last Morning's draught of liquid fire; 100
By the full kingdome of that finall kisse
That seiz'd thy parting Soul, & seal'd thee his;
By all the heau'ns thou hast in him
(Fair sister of the SERAPHIM!
By all of HIM we haue in THEE; 105
Leaue nothing of my SELF in me.
Let me so read thy life, that I
Vnto all life of mine may dy.

A Song

Lord, when the sense of thy sweet grace
Sends vp my soul to seek thy face.
Thy blessed eyes breed such desire,
I dy in loue's delicious Fire.
O loue, I am thy SACRIFICE.
Be still triumphant, blessed eyes.
Still shine on me, fair suns! that I
Still may behold, though still I dy.

Second part.

Though still I dy, I liue again; 1
Still longing so to be still slain,
So gainfull is such losse of breath,
I dy euen in desire of death.

Still liue in me this louing strife
Of liuing DEATH & dying LIFE.   15
For while thou sweetly slayest me
Dead to my selfe, I liue in Thee.

Prayer

An Ode, Which Was
Præfixed to a little Prayer-book
giuen to a young
*Gentle-Woman**

Lo here a little volume, but great Book!
A nest of new-born sweets;
          Whose natiue fires disdaining
          To ly thus folded, & complaining
          Of these ignoble sheets,   5
          Affect more comly bands
          (Fair one) from thy kind hands
          And confidently look
          To find the rest
Of a rich binding in your BREST.   10
It is, in one choise handfull, heauenn; & all
Heaun's Royall host; incamp't thus small
To proue that true, schooles vse to tell,
Ten thousand Angels in one point can dwell.
It is loue's great artillery   15
Which here contracts it self, & comes to ly
Close couch't in your white bosom: & from thence
As from a snowy fortresse of defence,
Against your ghostly foes to take your part,
And fortify the hold of your chast heart.   20
It is an armory of light
Let constant vse but keep it bright,
          You'l find it yeilds
To holy hands & humble hearts
          More swords & sheilds   25
Then sin hath snares, or Hell hath darts.

---

* See also p. 552.

Only be sure
The hands be pure
That hold these weapons; & the eyes
Those of turtles, chast & true;   30
Wakefull & wise;
Here is a freind shall fight for you,
Hold but this book before your heart
Let prayer alone to play his part,
But ô the heart   35
That studyes this high ART
Must be a sure house-keeper;
And yet no sleeper.
Dear soul, be strong.
MERCY will come e're long   40
And bring his bosom fraught with blessings,
Flowers of neuer fading graces
To make immortall dressings
For worthy soules, whose wise embraces
Store vp themselues for HIM, who is alone   45
The SPOVSE of Virgins & the Virgin's son.
But if the noble BRIDEGROOM, when he come,
Shall find the loytering HEART from home;
Leauing her chast aboad
To gadde abroad   50
Among the gay mates of the god of flyes;
To take her pleasure & to play
And keep the deuill's holyday;
To dance ith' sunshine of some smiling
But beguiling   55
Spheares of sweet & sugred Lyes,
Some slippery Pair
Of false, perhaps as fair,
Flattering but forswearing eyes;
Doubtlesse some other heart   60
Will gett the start
Mean while, & stepping in before
Will take possession of that sacred store
Of hidden sweets & holy ioyes.
WORDS which are not heard with EARES   65
(Those tumultuous shops of noise)
Effectuall wispers, whose still voice

The soul it selfe more feeles then heares;
Amorous languishments; luminous trances;
SIGHTS which are not seen with eyes;   70
Spirituall & soul-peircing glances
Whose pure & subtil lightning flyes
Home to the heart, & setts the house on fire
And melts it down in sweet desire
                    Yet does not stay   75
To ask the windows leaue to passe that way;
Delicious DEATHS; soft exalations
Of soul; dear & diuine annihilations;
                    A thousand vnknown rites
Of ioyes & rarefy'd delights;   80
A hundred thousand goods, glories, & graces,
                    And many a mystick thing
                    Which the diuine embraces
Of the deare spouse of spirits with them will bring
                    For which it is no shame   85
That dull mortality must not know a name.
                    Of all this store
Of blessings & ten thousand more
                    (If when he come
                    He find the Heart from home)   90
                    Doubtlesse he will vnload
                    Himself some other where,
                    And poure abroad
                    His pretious sweets
On the fair soul whom first he meets.   95
O fair, ô fortunate! O riche, ô dear!
O happy & thrice happy she
                    Selected doue
                    Who ere she be,
                    Whose early loue
                    With winged vowes   100
Makes hast to meet her morning spouse
And close with his immortall kisses.
Happy indeed, who neuer misses
To improue that pretious hour,   105
                    And euery day
                    Seize her sweet prey

All fresh & fragrant as he rises
Dropping with a baulmy Showr
A delicious dew of spices;   110
O let the blissfull heart hold fast
Her heaunly arm-full, she shall tast
At once ten thousand paradises;
    She shall haue power
    To rifle & deflour   115
The rich & roseall spring of those rare sweets
Which with a swelling bosome there she meets
    Boundles & infinite
    Bottomles treasures
Of pure inebriating pleasures.   120
Happy proof! she shal discouer
    What ioy, what blisse,
How many Heau'ns at once it is
To haue her GOD become her LOVER.

To
The Same Party
Covncel
Concerning Her
Choise

Dear, heaun-designed SOVL!
    Amongst the rest
Of suters that beseige your Maiden brest,
    Why may not I
    My fortune try   5
And venture to speak one good word
Not for my self alas, but for my dearer LORD?
You'aue seen allready, in this lower sphear
Of froth & bubbles, what to look for here.
Say, gentle soul, what can you find   10
    But painted shapes,
    Peacocks & Apes,
    Illustrious flyes,
Guilded dunghills, glorious L Y E S,
    Goodly surmises   15
    And deep disguises,

Oathes of water, words of wind?
TRVTH biddes me say, 'tis time you cease to trust
Your soul to any son of dust.
'Tis time you listen to a brauer loue, 20
 Which from aboue
 Calls you vp higher
 And biddes you come
 And choose your roome
Among his own fair sonnes of fire, 25
 Where you among
 The golden throng
That watches at his palace doores
 May passe along
And follow those fair starres of yours; 30
Starrs much too fair & pure to wait vpon
The false smiles of a sublunary sun.
Sweet, let me prophesy that at last t'will proue
 Your wary loue
Layes vp his purer & more pretious vowes, 35
And meanes them for a farre more worthy SPOVSE
Then this world of Lyes can giue ye
'Eun for Him with whom nor cost,
Nor loue, nor labour can be lost;
Him who neuer will deceiue ye. 40
Let not my lord, the Mighty louer
Of soules, disdain that I discouer
 The hidden art
Of his high stratagem to win your heart,
 It was his heaunly art 45
 Kindly to crosse you
 In your mistaken loue,
 That, at the next remoue
 Thence he might tosse you
 And strike your troubled heart 50
Home to himself; to hide it in his brest
 The bright ambrosiall nest,
Of loue, of life, & euerlasting rest.
 Happy Mystake!
 That thus shall wake 55

Your wise soul, neuer to be wonne
Now with a loue below the sun.
Your first choyce failes, ô when you choose agen
May it not be amongst the sonnes of Men.

Alexias

The
Complaint
of
The Forsaken Wife
of Sainte Alexis

The First Elegie

I late the roman youth's lou'd prayse & pride,
Whom long none could obtain, though thousands try'd,
Lo here am left (alas), For my lost mate
T'embrace my teares, & kisse an vnkind FATE.
Sure in my early woes starres were at strife,   5
And try'd to make a WIDOW ere a WIFE.
Nor can I tell (and this new teares doth breed)
In what strange path my lord's fair footsteppes bleed.
O knew I where he wander'd, I should see
Some solace in my sorrow's certainty   10
I'd send my woes in words should weep for me.
(Who knowes how powrfull well-writt praires would be?)
Sending's too slow a word, my selfe would fly.
Who knowes my own heart's woes so well as I?
But how shall I steal hence? ALEXIS thou   15
Ah thou thy self, alas, hast taught me how.
Loue too, that leads the way, would lend the wings
To bear me harmlesse through the hardest things.
And where loue lends the wing, & leads the way,
What dangers can there be dare say me nay?   20
If I be shipwrack't, Loue shall teach to swimme.
If drown'd; sweet is the death indur'd for HIM,

The noted sea shall change his name with me;
I, 'mongst the blest STARRES a new name shall be.
And sure where louers make their watry graues   25
The weeping mariner will augment the waues.
For who so hard, but passing by that way
Will take acquaintance of my woes, & say
Here 't was the roman MAID found a hard fate
While through the world she sought her wandring mate.   30
Here perish't she, poor heart, heauns, be my vowes
As true to me, as she was to her spouse.
O liue, so rare a loue! liue! & in thee
The too frail life of femal constancy.
Farewell; & shine, fair soul, shine there aboue   35
Firm in thy crown, as here fast in thy loue.
There thy lost fugitiue thou'hast found at last.
Be happy; and for euer hold him fast.

The
Seconde Elegie

Though All the ioyes I had fleed hence with Thee
Vnkind; yet are my TEARES still true to me
I'am wedded ore again since thou art gone;
Nor couldst thou, cruell, leaue me quite alone.
ALEXIS' widdow now is sorrow's wife.   5
With him shall I weep out my weary life.
Wellcome, my sad sweet Mate! Now haue I gott
At last a constant loue that leaues me not.
Firm he, as thou art false, Nor need my cryes
Thus vex the earth & teare the beauteous skyes.   10
For him, alas, n'ere shall I need to be
Troublesom to the world, thus, as for thee.
For thee I talk to trees; with silent groues
Expostulate my woes & much-wrong'd loues.
Hills & relentlesse rockes, or if there be   15
Things that in hardnesse more allude to thee;
To these I talk in teares, & tell my pain;
And answer too for them in teares again.

How oft haue I wept out the weary sun!
My watry hour-glasse hath old times outrunne.   20
O I am learned grown, Poor loue & I
Haue study'd ouer all astrology.
I'am perfect in heaun's state, with euery starr
My skillfull greife is grown familiar.
Rise, fairest of those fires; whate're thou be   25
Whose rosy beam shall point my sun to me.
Such as the sacred light that erst did bring
The EASTERN princes to their infant king.
O rise, pure lamp! & lend thy golden ray
That weary loue at last may find his way.   30

The
Third Elegie

Rich, churlish LAND! that hid'st so long in thee,
My treasures, rich, alas, by robbing mee.
Needs must my miseryes owe that man a spite
Who e're he be was the first wandring knight.
O had he nere been at that cruell cost   5
NATVRE's virginity had nere been lost.
Seas had not bin rebuk't by sawcy oares
But ly'n lock't vp safe in their sacred shores.
Men had not spurn'd at mountaines; nor made warrs
With rocks; nor bold hands struck the world's strong barres. 10
Nor lost in too larg bounds, our little Rome
Full sweetly with it selfe had dwell't at home.
My poor ALEXIS, then in peacefull life,
Had vnder some low roofe lou'd his plain wife.
But now, ah me, from where he has no foes   15
He flyes; & into willfull exile goes.
Cruell return. Or tell the reason why
Thy dearest parents haue deseru'd to dy.
And I, what is my crime I cannot tell.
Vnlesse it be a crime to'haue lou'd too well.   20
If Heates of holyer loue & high desire
Make bigge thy fair brest with immortall fire,
What needes my virgin lord fly thus from me,
Who only wish his virgin wife to be?

Wittnesse, chast heauns! no happyer vowes I know   25
Then to a virgin GRAVE vntouch't to goe.
Loue's truest Knott by Venus is not ty'd;
Nor doe embraces onely make a bride.
The QVEEN of angels, (and men chast as You)
Was MAIDEN WIFE & MAIDEN MOTHER too.   30
CECILIA, Glory of her name & blood
With happy gain her maiden vowes made good.
The lusty bridegroom made approach: young man,
Take heed (said she) take heed, VALERIAN!
My bosome's guard, a SPIRIT great & strong,   35
Stands arm'd, to sheild me from all wanton wrong.
My Chastity is sacred; & my sleep
Wakefull, her dear vowes vndefil'd to keep.
PALLAS beares armes, forsooth, and should there be
No fortresse built for true VIRGINITY?   40
No gaping gorgon, this. None, like the rest
Of your learn'd lyes. Here you'l find no such iest.
I'am yours, O were my GOD, my CHRIST so too,
I'd know no name of loue on earth but you.
He yeilds, and straight Baptis'd, obtains the grace   45
To gaze on the fair souldier's glorious face.
Both mixt at last their blood in one rich bed
Of rosy MARTYRDOME, twice Married.
O burn our hymen bright in such high Flame.
Thy torch, terrestriall loue, haue here no name.   50
How sweet the mutuall yoke of man & wife,
When holy fires maintain loue's Heaunly life!
But I, (so help me heaun my hopes to see)
When thousands sought my loue, lou'd none but Thee.
Still, as their vain teares my firm vowes did try,   55
ALEXIS, he alone is mine (said I)
Half true, alas, half false, proues that poor line.
ALEXIS is alone; But is not mine.

Description
of
A Religiovs Hovse
and Condition
of Life

(Ovt of Barclay)

No roofes of gold o're riotous tables shining
Whole dayes & suns deuour'd with endlesse dining;
No sailes of tyrian sylk proud pauements sweeping;
Nor iuory couches costlyer slumbers keeping;
False lights of flairing gemmes; tumultuous ioyes;   5
Halls full of flattering men & frisking boyes;
Whate're false showes of short & slippery good
Mix the mad sons of men in mutuall blood.
But WALKES & vnshorn woods; and soules, iust so
Vnforc't & genuine; but not shady tho.   10
Our lodgings hard & homely as our fare.
That chast & cheap, as the few clothes we weare.
Those, course & negligent, As the naturall lockes
Of these loose groues, rough as th'vnpolish't rockes.
A hasty Portion of præscribed sleep;   15
Obedient slumbers? that can wake & weep,
And sing, & sigh, & work, and sleep again;
Still rowling a round sphear of still-returning pain.
Hands full of harty labours; Paines that pay
And prize themselves; doe much, that more they may,   20
And work for work, not wages; let to morrow's
New drops, wash off the sweat of this daye's sorrows.
A long & dayly-dying life, which breaths
A respiration of reuiuing deaths.
But neither are there those ignoble stings   25
That nip the bosome of the world's best things,
And lash Earth-laboring souls.
No cruell guard of diligent cares, that keep
Crown'd woes awake; as things too wise for sleep.
But reuerent discipline, & religious fear,   30
And soft obedience, find sweet biding here;

Silence, & sacred rest; peace, & pure ioyes;
Kind loues keep house, ly close, and make no noise,
And room enough for Monarchs, while none swells
Beyond the kingdomes of contentfull Cells.   35
The self-remembring SOVL sweetly recouers
Her kindred with the starrs; not basely houers
Below: But meditates her immortall way
Home to the originall sourse of LIGHT & intellectuall Day.

An
Epitaph
Vpon
A Yovng Married Covple
Dead and Bvryed
*Together**

To these, whom DEATH again did wed,
This GRAVE's their second Marriage-bed.
For though the hand of fate could force
'Twixt SOVL & BODY a Diuorce,
It could not sunder man & WIFE,   5
'Cause They Both liued but one life.
Peace, good Reader. Doe not weep.
Peace, The Louers are asleep.
They, sweet Turtles, folded ly
In the last knott loue could ty.   10
And though they ly as they were dead,
Their Pillow stone, their sheetes of lead,
(Pillow hard, & sheetes not warm)
Loue made the bed; They'l take no harm
Let them sleep; let them sleep on.   15
Till this stormy night be gone,
Till the' Æternall morrow dawn;
Then the curtaines will be drawn
And they wake into a light,
Whose day shall neuer dy in Night.   20

* See also p. 589.

Death's Lectvre
At the
Fvneral
of
A Yovng Gentleman*

Dear Reliques of a dislodg'd Sovl, whose lack
Makes many a mourning paper put on black!
O stay a while, ere thou draw in thy head
And wind thy self vp close in thy cold bed.
Stay but a little while, vntill I call   5
A summons worthy of thy funerall.
Come then, Yovth, Beavty, & blood!
       All ye soft powres,
Whose sylken flatteryes swell a few fond howres
Into a false æternity. Come man;   10
Hyperbolized Nothing! know thy span;
Take thine own measure here: down, down, & bow
Before thy self in thine idæa; thou
Huge emptynes! contract thy self; & shrinke
All thy Wild circle to a Point. O sink   15
Lower & lower yet; till thy leane size
Call heaun to look on thee with narrow eyes.
Lesser & lesser yet; till thou begin
To show a face, fitt to confesse thy Kin,
Thy neigbourhood to Nothing.   20
Proud lookes, & lofty eyliddes, here putt on
Your selues in your vnfaign'd reflexion,
Here, gallant ladyes! this vnpartiall glasse
(Though you be painted) showes you your true face.
These death-seal'd lippes are they dare giue the ly   25
To the lowd Boasts of poor Mortality
These curtain'd windows, this retired eye
Outstares the liddes of larg-look't tyranny.
This posture is the braue one this that lyes
Thus low, stands vp (me thinkes,) thus & defies   30
The world. All-daring dust & ashes! only you
Of all interpreters read Nature True.

* See also p. 590.

Temperance
Or the
Cheap Physitian

*Vpon the Translation of Lessivs**

Goe now; and with some daring drugg
Bait thy disease. And whilst they tugge,
Thou to maintain their pretious strife
Spend the dear treasures of thy life.
Goe, take physick Doat vpon   5
Some big-nam'd composition.
Th'Oraculous Doctor's mystick bills;
Certain hard Words made into pills,
And what at last shalt' gain by these?
Only a costlyer disease.   10
That which makes vs haue no need
Of physick, that's Physick indeed.
Hark hither, Reader! wilt thou see
Nature her own physitian be?
Wilt' see a man, all his own wealth,   15
His own musick, his own health;
A man whose sober soul can tell
How to wear her garments well.
Her garments, that vpon her sitt
As garments should doe, close & fitt;   20
A well-cloth'd soul; that's not opprest
Nor choak't with what she should be drest.
A soul sheath'd in a christall shrine;
Through which all her bright features shine;
As when a peice of wanton lawn   25
A thinne, aeriall veil, is drawn
Or'e beauty's face; seeming to hide
More sweetly showes the blushing bride.
A soul, whose intellectuall beames
No mists doe mask, no lazy steames.   30
A happy soul, that all the way
To Heavn rides in a summer's day.

* See also p. 576.

Wouldst' see a man, whose well-warm'd blood
Bathes him in a genuine flood!
A man, whose tuned humors be   35
A set of rarest harmony?
Wouldst' see blith lookes, fresh cheekes beguil
Age? wouldst see december smile?
Wouldst' see nests of new roses grow
In a bed of reuerend snow?   40
Warm thoughts, free spirits flattering
Winter's selfe into a SPRING.
In summe, wouldst see a man that can
Liue to be old, and still a man?
Whose latest & most leaden houres   45
Fall with soft wings, stuck with soft flowres;
And when life's sweet fable ends,
Soul & body part like freinds;
No quarrells, murmurs, no delay;
A KISSE, a SIGH, and so away.   50
This rare one, reader, wouldst thou see?
Hark hither; and thy self be HE.

Hope*

Hope whose weak beeing ruin'd is
Alike if it succeed or if it misse!
Whom ill or good does equally confound
And both the hornes of fate's dilemma wound.
       Vain shadow; that dost vanish quite   5
       Both at full noon & perfect night!
The starres haue not a possibility
       Of blessing Thee.
If thinges then from their end we happy call,
'Tis hope is the most hopelesse thing of all.   10
   Hope, thou bold Taster of delight!
Who instead of doing so, deuourst it quite.
Thou bringst vs an estate, yet leau'st vs poor
By clogging it with legacyes before.

* See also p. 567 for this and the following poem in dialogue
form.

The ioyes which we intire should wed   15
Come deflour'd-virgins to our bed.
Good fortunes without gain imported be
    Such mighty custom's paid to Thee.
For ioy like wine kep't close, does better tast;
If it take air before his spirits wast.   20
  Hope fortun's cheating lottery
Where for one prize, an hundred blankes there be.
Fond archer, hope. Who tak'st thine aime so farr
That still or short or wide thine arrowes are
    Thinne empty cloud which th'ey deceiues   25
    With shapes that our own fancy giues.
A cloud which gilt & painted now appeares
    But must drop presently in teares
When thy false beames o're reason's light prevail,
By Ignes Fatvi for north starres we sail.   30
  Brother of fear more gayly clad.
The merryer fool oth two, yet quite as mad.
Sire of repentance, child of fond desire
That blow'st the chymick & the louer's fire.
    Still leading them insensibly'on   35
    With the strong witchcraft of Anon.
By thee the one does changing nature through
    Her endlesse labyrinth's pursue,
And th'other chases woman; while she goes
More wayes & turnes then hunted nature knowes.   40

M. COWLEY.

M. Crashaws
Answer
For Hope

Dear hope! earth's dowry, & heaun's debt!
The entity of those that are not yet.
Subtlest, but surest beeing! Thou by whom

Our nothing has a definition!
        Substantiall shade! whose sweet allay   5
        Blends both the noones of night & day.
Fates cannot find out a capacity
        Of hurting thee.
From Thee their lean dilemma, with blunt horn,
Shrinkes, as the sick moon from the wholsome morn.   10
    Rich hope! loue's legacy, vnder lock
Of faith! still spending, & still growing stock!
Our crown-land lyes aboue yet each meal brings
A seemly portion for the sonnes of kings.
        Nor will the virgin ioyes we wed   15
        Come lesse vnbroken to our bed,
Because that from the bridall cheek of blisse
        Thou steal'st vs down a distant kisse.
Hope's chast stealth harmes no more ioye's maidenhead.
Then spousall rites preiudge the marriage bed.   20
    Fair hope! our earlyer heau'n by thee
Young time is taster to eternity
Thy generous wine with age growes strong, not sowre.
Nor does it kill thy fruit, to smell thy flowre.
        Thy golden, growing, head neuer hangs down   25
        Till in the lappe of loues full noone
It falls; and dyes! o no, it melts away
        As does the dawn into the day.
As lumpes of sugar loose themselues; and twine
Their supple essence with the soul of wine.   30
    Fortune? alas, aboue the world's low warres
Hope walks; & kickes the curld heads of conspiring starres.
Her keel cutts not the waues where These winds stirr
Fortune's whole lottery is one blank to her.
        Her shafts, and shee fly farre above,   35
        And forrage in the fields of light and love.
Sweet hope! kind cheat! fair fallacy by thee
We are not WHERE nor What we be,
But WHAT & WHERE we would be. Thus art thou
Our absent PRESENCE, and our future Now.   40
    Faith's sister! nurse of fair desire!
Fear's antidote! a wise & well-stay'd fire!
Temper twixt chill despair, & torrid ioy!
Queen Regent in yonge loue's minority!

Though the vext chymick vainly chases 45
His fugitiue gold through all her faces;
Though loue's more feirce, more fruitlesse, fires assay
One face more fugitiue then all they;
True hope's a glorious hunter & her chase,
The GOD of nature in the feilds of grace. 50

VIVE IESV.

A LETTER
FROM
MR. CRASHAW
TO THE
COUNTESS OF
DENBIGH

AGAINST IRRESOLUTION AND
DELAY IN MATTERS OF RELIGION*

What Heav'n-besieged Heart is this
Stands Trembling at the Gate of Blisse:
Holds fast the Door, yet dares not venture
Fairly to open and to enter?
Whose Definition is, A Doubt   5
'Twixt Life and Death, 'twixt In and Out.
Ah! linger not, lov'd Soul: A slow
And late Consent was a long No.
Who grants at last, a great while try'de,
And did his best to have Deny'de.   10
   What Magick-Bolts, what mystick Barrs
Maintain the Will in these strange Warrs?
What Fatall, yet fantastick, Bands
Keep the free Heart from his own Hands?
Say, lingring Fair, why comes the Birth   15
Of your brave Soul so slowly forth?
Plead your Pretences, (O you strong
In weaknesse) why you chuse so long
In Labour of your self to ly,
Not daring quite to Live nor Die.   20

* See also p. 611.

So when the Year takes cold we see
  Poor Waters their own Prisoners be:
  Fetter'd and lock'd up fast they lie
  In a cold self-captivity.
Th'astonish'd Nymphs their Floud's strange Fate deplore, 25
To find themselves their own severer Shoar.
      Love, that lends haste to heaviest things,
      In you alone hath lost his wings.
      Look round and reade the World's wide face,
      The field of Nature or of Grace;   30
      Where can you fix, to find Excuse
      Or Pattern for the Pace you use?
      Mark with what Faith Fruits answer Flowers,
      And know the Call of Heav'n's kind showers:
      Each mindfull Plant hasts to make good   35
      The hope and promise of his Bud.
Seed-time's not all; there should be Harvest too.
Alas! and has the Year no Spring for you?
      Both Winds and Waters urge their way,
      And murmure if they meet a stay.   40
      Mark how the curl'd Waves work and wind,
      All hating to be left behind.
      Each bigge with businesse thrusts the other,
      And seems to say, Make haste, my Brother.
      The aiery nation of neat Doves,   45
      That draw the Chariot of chast Loves,
      Chide your delay: yea those dull things,
      Whose wayes have least to doe with wings,
      Make wings at least of their own Weight,
      And by their Love controll their Fate.   50
      So lumpish Steel, untaught to move,
      Learn'd first his Lightnesse by his Love.
      What e're Love's matter be, he moves
      By th'even wings of his own Doves,
      Lives by his own Laws, and does hold   55
      In grossest Metalls his own Gold.
      All things swear friends to Fair and Good,
      Yea Suitours; Man alone is wo'ed,
      Tediously wo'ed, and hardly wone:
      Only not slow to be undone.   60

As if the Bargain had been driven
So hardly betwixt Earth and Heaven;
Our God would thrive too fast, and be
Too much a gainer by't, should we
Our purchas'd selves too soon bestow
On him, who has not lov'd us so.
When love of Us call'd Him to see
If wee'd vouchsafe his company,
He left his Father's Court, and came
Lightly as a Lambent Flame,
Leaping upon the Hills, to be
The Humble King of You and Me.
Nor can the cares of his whole Crown
(When one poor Sigh sends for him down)
Detain him, but he leaves behind
The late wings of the lazy Wind,
Spurns the tame Laws of Time and Place,
And breaks through all ten Heav'ns to our embrace.
 Yield to his Siege, wise Soul, and see
Your Triumph in his Victory.
Disband dull Feares, give Faith the day:
To save your Life, kill your Delay.
'Tis Cowardise that keeps this Field;
And want of Courage not to Yield.
 Yield then, O yield, that Love may win
The Fort at last, and let Life in.
Yield quickly, lest perhaps you prove
Death's Prey, before the Prize of Love.
This Fort of your Fair Self if't be not wone,
He is repuls'd indeed, but You'r undone.

POEMS FROM
MANUSCRIPTS

❦❦

Luke 2. *Quaerit Jesum suum Maria*

And is he gone, whom these armes held but now?
      Their hope, their vow?
Did ever greife, & joy in one poore heart
      Soe soone change part?
Hee's gone. the fair'st flower, that e're bosome drest,   5
      My soules sweet rest.
My wombes chast pride is gone, my heau'en-borne boy;
      And where is joy?
Hee's gone. & his lou'd steppes to wait upon,
      My joy is gone.   10
My joyes, & hee are gone; my greife, & I
      Alone must ly.
Hee's gone. not leaving with me, till he come,
      One smile at home.
Oh come then. bring thy mother her lost joy: 15
      Oh come, sweet boy.
Make hast, & come, or e're my greife, & I
      Make hast, & dy.
Peace, heart! the heauens are angry. all their sphæres
      Rivall thy teares.   20
I was mistaken. some faire sphære, or other
      Was thy blest mother.
What, but the fairest heauen, could owne the birth
      Of soe faire earth?
Yet sure thou did'st lodge heere. this wombe of mine 25
      Was once call'd thine.
Oft haue these armes thy cradle envied,
      Beguil'd thy bed.

Oft to thy easy eares hath this shrill tongue
        Trembled, & sung.   30
Oft haue I wrapt thy slumbers in soft aires,
        And stroak't thy cares.
Oft hath this hand those silken casements kept,
        While their sunnes slept.
Oft haue my hungry kisses made thine eyes   35
        Too early rise.
Oft haue I spoild my kisses daintiest diet,
        To spare thy quiet.
Oft from this breast to thine my loue-tost heart
        Hath leapt, to part.   40
Oft my lost soule haue I bin glad to seeke
        On thy soft cheeke.
Oft haue these armes (alas!) show'd to these eyes
        Their now lost joyes.
Dawne then to me, thou morne of mine owne day,   45
        And lett heauen stay.
Oh, would'st thou heere still fixe thy faire abode,
        My bosome God:
What hinders, but my bosome still might be
        Thy heauen to thee?   50

Math. 16. 25. Whosoeuer shall loose his life &c.

Soe I may gaine thy death, my life I'le giue.
(My life's thy death, & in thy death I liue.)
Or else, my life, I'le hide thee in his graue,
By three daies losse æternally to saue.

In cicatrices Domini Jesu

Come, braue soldjers, come, & see
Mighty loue's Artillery.
This was the conquering dart; & loe
There shines his quiuer, there his bow.
These the passiue weapons are,   5
That made great Loue a man of warre.

The quiver, that he bore, did bide
Soe neare, it prov'd his very side.
In it there sate but one sole dart;
A peircing one.   his peirced heart.   10
His weapons were nor steele, nor brasse:
The weapon, that he wore, he was.
For bow his vnbent hand did serue,
Well strung with many a broken nerue.
Strange the quiuer, bow, & dart!   15
A bloody side, & hand, & heart!
But now the feild is wonne: & they
(The dust of Warre cleane wip'd away)
The weapons now of triumph be,
That were before of Victorie.   20

In amorem divinum (Hermannus Hugo)

Æternall loue!   what 'tis to loue thee well,
None, but himselfe, who feeles it, none can tell.
But oh, what to be lou'd of thee as well,
None, not himselfe, who feeles it, none can tell.

Out of Petronius

Ales Phasiacis petita Colchis &c. R. Cr.

The bird, that's fetch't from Phasis floud,
Or choicest hennes of Africk-brood;
These please our palates.   & why these?
'Cause they can but seldome please.
Whil'st the goose soe goodly white,   5
And the drake yeeld noe delight,
Though his wings conceited hewe
Paint each feather, as if new.
These for vulgar stomacks be,
And rellish not of rarity.   10
But the dainty Scarus, sought
In farthest clime; what e're is bought

With shipwracks toile, Oh, that is sweet,
'Cause the quicksands hanselld it.
The pretious Barbill, now groune rife,   15
Is cloying meat. How stale is Wife?
Deare wife hath ne're a handsome letter,
Sweet mistris sounds a great deale better.
Rose quakes at name of Cinnamon.
Vnlesse't be rare, what's thought upon?   20

Out of Horace

Ille & nefasto te posuit die &c. R. Cr.

Shame of thy mother soyle!   ill-nurtur'd tree!
Sett to the mischeife of posteritie!
That hand, (what e're it were) that was thy nurse,
Was sacrilegious, (sure) or somewhat worse.
Black, as the day was dismall, in whose sight
Thy rising topp first staind the bashfull light.
That man (I thinke) wrested the feeble life
From his old father.   that mans barbarous knife
Conspir'd with darknes 'gainst the strangers throate;
(Whereof the blushing walles tooke bloody note)   10
Huge high-floune poysons, eu'n of Colchos breed,
And whatsoe're wild sinnes black thoughts doe feed,
His hands haue padled in; his hands, that found
Thy traiterous root a dwelling in my ground.
Perfidious totterer! longing for the staines   15
Of thy kind Master's well-deseruing braines.
Mans daintiest care, & caution cannot spy
The subtile point of his coy destiny,
W^ch way it threats. With feare the merchants mind
Is plough'd as deepe, as is the sea with wind,   20
(Rowz'd in an angry tempest); Oh the sea!
Oh! that's his feare; there flotes his destiny:
While from another (unseene) corner blowes
The storme of fate, to wch his life he owes.
By Parthians bow the soldjer lookes to die,   25
(Whose hands are fighting, while their feet doe flie.)
The Parthian starts at Rome's imperiall name,
Fledg'd with her Eagles wing; the very chaine

Of his captivity rings in his eares.
Thus, ô thus fondly doe wee pitch our feares   30
Farre distant from our fates. our fates, that mocke
Our giddy feares with an unlook't for shocke.
    A little more, & I had surely seene
Thy greisly Majesty, Hell's blackest Queene;
And Æacus on his Tribunall too,   35
Sifting the soules of guilt; & you, (oh you!)
You euer-blushing meads, where doe the Blest
Farre from darke horrors home appeale to rest.
There amorous Sappho plaines upon her Lute
Her loues crosse fortune, that the sad dispute   40
Runnes murmuring on the strings. Alcæus there
In high-built numbers wakes his golden lyre,
To tell the world, how hard the matter went,
How hard by sea, by warre, by banishment.
There these braue soules deale to each wondring eare 45
Such words, soe precious, as they may not weare
Without religious silence; aboue all
Warres ratling tumults, or some tyrants fall.
The thronging clotted multitude doth feast.
What wonder? when the hundred-headed beast   50
Hangs his black lugges, stroakt with those heavenly lines;
The Furies curl'd snakes meet in gentle twines,
And stretch their cold limbes in a pleasing fire.
Prometheus selfe, & Pelops sterved Sire
Are cheated of their paines; Orion thinkes   55
Of Lions now noe more, or spotted Linx.

Out of Barclay's Euphormion

O Dea syderei seu tu stirps alma Tonantis &c.

Bright Goddesse, (whether Joue thy father be;
Or Jove a father will be made by thee)
Oh crowne these praie'rs (mov'd in a happy hower)
But with one cordiall smile. for (loe) that power
Of Loues all-daring hand, that makes me burne,   5
Makes me confess't. Oh, doe not thou with scorne,

Great Nymph, o'relooke my lownesse. heau'n you know,
And all their fellow Deities will bow
Even to the naked'st vowes. thou art my fate;
To thee the Parcæ haue given up of late   10
My threds of life. if then I shall not live
By thee; by thee yet lett me die. this giue,
High beauties soveraigne, that my funerall flames
May draw their first breath from thy starry beames.
The Phœnix selfe shall not more proudly burne,   15
That fetcheth fresh life from her fruitfull urne.

An Elegy upon the death of Mr Stanninow fellow of Queenes Colledge

Hath aged winter, fledg'd with feathered raine,
To frozen Caucasus his flight now tane?
Doth hee in downy snow there closely shrowd
His bedrid limmes, wrapt in a fleecy clowd?
Is th' earth disrobed of her apron white,   5
Kind winter's guift, & in a greene one dight?
Doth she beginne to dandle in her lappe
Her painted infants, fedd with pleasant pappe,
W^ch their bright father in a pretious showre
From heavens sweet milky streame doth gently poure? 10
Doth blith Apollo cloath the heavens with joye,
And with a golden waue wash cleane away
Those durty smutches, wch their faire fronts wore,
And make them laugh, wch frown'd, & wept before?
If heaven hath now forgot to weepe; ô then   15
W^t meane these shoures of teares amongst us men?
These Cataracts of greife, that dare eu'n vie
With th' richest clowds their pearly treasurie?
If winter's gone, whence this vntimely cold,
That on these snowy limmes hath laid such hold?   20
What more than winter hath that dire art found,
These purple currents hedg'd with violets round
To corrallize, wch softly wont to slide
In crimson waueletts, & in scarlet tide?
If Flora's darlings now awake from sleepe,   25
And out of their greene mantletts dare to peepe:

O tell me then, what rude outragious blast
Forc't this prime flowre of youth to make such hast
To hide his blooming glories, & bequeath
His balmy treasure to the bedd of death? 30
'Twas not the frozen zone; One sparke of fire,
Shott from his flaming eye, had thaw'd it's ire,
And made it burne in loue: 'Twas not the rage,
And too vngentle nippe of frosty age:
'Twas not the chast, & purer snow, whose nest 35
Was in the modest Nunnery of his brest:
Noe. none of these ravish't those virgin roses,
The Muses, & the Graces fragrant posies.
W^ch, while they smiling sate upon his face,
They often kist, & in the sugred place 40
Left many a starry teare, to thinke how soone
The golden harvest of our joyes, the noone
Of all our glorious hopes should fade,
And be eclipsed with an envious shade.
Noe. 'twas old doting Death, who, stealing by, 45
Dragging his crooked burthen, look't awry,
And streight his amorous syth (greedy of blisse)
Murdred the earth's just pride with a rude kisse.
A winged Herald, gladd of soe sweet a prey,
Snatch't vpp the falling starre, soe richly gay, 50
And plants it in a precious perfum'd bedd,
Amongst those Lillies, wch his bosome bredd.
Where round about hovers with siluer wing
A golden summer, an æternall spring.
Now that his root such fruit againe may beare, 55
Let each eye water't with a courteous teare.

Two Dedicatory Poems

I

At th' Iuory Tribunall of your hand
(Faire one) these tender leaues doe trembling stand.
Knowing 'tis in the doome of your sweet Eye
Whether the Muse they cloth shall liue or die.

Liue shee, or dye to Fame; each Leafe you meet   5
Is her Lifes wing, or her death's winding-sheet.

II

Though now 'tis neither May nor June
And Nightingales are out of tune,
Yett in these leaues (Faire one) there lyes
(Sworne seruant to your sweetest Eyes)
A Nightingale, who may shee spread   5
In your white bosome her chast bed,
Spite of all the Maiden snow
Those pure untroden pathes can show,
You streight shall see her wake and rise
Taking fresh Life from your fayre Eyes.   10
And with clasp't winges proclayme a spring
Where Loue and shee shall sit and sing
For lodg'd so ne're your sweetest throte
What Nightingale can loose her noate?
Nor lett her kinred birds complayne   15
Because shee breakes the yeares old raigne
For lett them know shee's none of those
Hedge-Quiristers whose Musicke owes
Onely such straynes as serue to keepe
Sad shades and sing dull Night asleepe.   20
No shee's a Priestesse of that Groue
The holy chappell of chast Love
Your Virgin bosome.   Then what e're
Poore Lawes diuide the publicke yeare,
Whose reuolutions wait upon   25
The wild turnes of the wanton sun;
Bee you the Lady of Loues Yeere:
Where your Eyes shine his suns appeare:
There all the yeare is Loues long spring.
There all the yeare Loues Nightingales   30
        shall sitt and sing.

Out of Grotius his Tragedy of Christes sufferinges

O thou the span of whose Omnipotence
Doth graspe the fate of thinges, and share th' euents
Of future chance! the world's grand sire; and mine
Before the world. Obedient lo! I joyne
An æquall pace thus farre; thy word my deedes   5
Haue flow'd together. if ought further needes
I shrinke not. but thus ready stand to beare
(ffor else why came I?) eu'n what e're I feare.
Yett o what end? where does the period dwell
Of my sad labours? no day yett could tell   10
My soule shee was secure. Still haue I borne
A still increasing burden; worse hath torne
His way through bad, to my successiue hurt.
I left my glorious Fathers star-pau'd Court
E're borne was banish't: borne was glad t' embrace   15
A poore (yea scarce a) roofe. whose narrow place
Was not so much as cleane: a stable kind;
The best my cradle and my birth could find.
Then was I knowne; and knowne unluckily
A weake a wretched child; eu'n then was I   20
For Juryes king an enemy, euen worth
His feare; the circle of a yeares round growth
Was not yett full, (a time that to my age
Made litle, not a litle to his rage)
When a wild sword eu'n from their brests, did lop   25
The Mothers Joyes in an untimely crop.
The search of one child (cruell industry!)
Was losse of multitudes; and missing mee
A bloud drunke errour spilt the costly ayme
Of their mad sin; (how great! and yett how uayne!)   30
I cal'd a hundred miracles to tell
The world my father. then does enuy swell
And breake upon mee: my owne uirtues height
Hurtes mee far worse then Herods highest spite;
A riddle! (father) still acknowledg'd thine   35
Am still refus'd; before the Infant Shrine

Of my weake feet the Persian Magi lay
And left their Mithra for my star: this they.
But Isaacks issue the peculiar heyres,
Of thy old goodnesse, know thee not for theires,   40
Basely degenerous. Against mee flocke
The stiffe neck'd Pharisees that use to mocke
Sound goodnesse with her shadow which they weare,
And 'gainst religion her owne colours beare.
The bloud hound brood of Priests against mee draw   45
Those Lawlesse tyrant masters of the Law.
Profane Sadocus too does fiercely lead
His court-fed impes against this hated head.
What would they more? th' aue seene when at my nod
Great Natures selfe hath shrunke and spoke mee god.   50
Drinke fayling there where I a guest did shine
The Water blush'd, and started into Wine.
Full of high sparkeling uigour: taught by mee
A sweet inebriated extasy.
And streight of all this approbation gate   55
Good wine in all poynts. but the easy rate;
Other mens hunger with strange feasts I quell'd
Mine owne with stranger fastings, when I held
Twice twenty dayes pure abstinence, To feed
My minds deuotion in my bodyes need.   60
A subtle inundation of quicke food
Sprang in the spending fingers, and o'reflow'd
The peoples hunger, and when all were full
The broken meate was much more then the whole.
The Wind in all his roaring brags stood still   65
And listned to the whisper of my will;
The wild waues couch'd; the sea forgott to sweat
Vnder my feet, the waters to bee wett.
In death-full desperate ills where art and all
Was nothing, there my uoyce was med'cinall.   70
Old clouds of thickest blindnesse fled my sight
And to my touch darke Eyes did owe the light.
Hee that ne're heard now speakes, and finds a tongue
To chaunt my prayses in a new-strung song.
Euen hee that belches out a foaming flood   75
Of hot defiance 'gainst what e're is good

Father and Heyre of darkenesse, when I chide
Sinkes into Horrours bosome, glad to hide
Himselfe in his owne hell; and now lets loose
Mans brest (his tenement) and breakes up house.   80
Yett here's not all: nor was't enough for mee
To freind the liuing world euen death did see
Mee ranging in his quarters; and the land
Of deepest silence answered my command.
Heau'n, Earth, and Sea, my triumphs. what remain'd   85
Now but the Graue? the Graue it selfe I tam'd.

&c:.

Andrew Marvell
1628-1678

Andrew Marvell

Born at Winestead-in-Holderness, Yorkshire, on March 31, 1621, Andrew Marvell was the son of a Puritan country parson. He attended Hull Grammar School, then entered Trinity College, Cambridge, in 1633. There is a rumor that he was converted to Catholicism before taking his degree in 1639, but he stayed on in Cambridge until 1641 with no sign that any conversion had taken place. During the civil war he went abroad and lived in Spain, Italy, Holland, France, and Switzerland until 1646. His Royalist sympathies are reflected in his poems of the late sixteen-forties; in his "Horatian Ode" to Cromwell, written in 1650, these sympathies persist together with his apparent admiration for Cromwell as a force of destiny.

Marvell was tutor for two years in the house of Lord General Fairfax, Yorkshireman, anti-royalist leader, and amateur poet, who broke with Cromwell and retired to the country. While staying with the Fairfaxes, Marvell wrote one of his great poems, "Upon Appleton House." In 1653 he tutored William Dutton, Cromwell's ward and future son-in-law, with whom Marvell traveled to France. The same year Milton recommended him to be Cromwell's Assistant Latin Secretary, but Marvell did not get this post until 1657, a year before the Protector's death. In 1659 Marvell was elected to Parliament from Hull and held the position for two decades until his

709

death. In this period, aside from the time (1663–1665) spent on diplomatic missions in Sweden, Russia, and Denmark, he served as a conscientious though often silent Parliament member.

Against corruption in Court and Commonwealth, Marvell was disturbed by the open acceptance of favors and bribes from France. He supported religious toleration and was known almost exclusively as a writer of political pamphlets and verse satires. He was John Milton's faithful friend, and an admirer of Lord Rochester and Samuel Butler, but was opposed to John Dryden and all Dryden stood for. Marvell's own poetry was inadvertently rescued for posterity by his housekeeper, Mary Palmer. Her motives, though, are suspect since she claimed to be his widow when she certified the publication of his poems in 1681. According to the story, Marvell's unexpected death on August 16, 1678, made it impossible for a certain pair of declared bankrupts, who claimed they had left their money with him, to touch that money. His housekeeper was persuaded by them to say she was Marvell's widow so that she in turn might claim his money and reimburse them. Her claim was denied in a chancery suit, and the tombstone under which she was buried in 1687 read Mary Palmer and not Mary Marvell.

In an age of violent religious and political conflicts, when men lost their lives or were maimed for what they said in public, Marvell displayed unusual courage in his writing and in his frequent defense of liberal and humane ideas. He was a complex man of warm and emphatic loyalties. John Aubrey's vivid contemporary description of him remains: ". . . a great master of the Latin tongue; an excellent poet in Latin or English . . . of a middling stature, pretty strong sett, roundish faced, cherry-cheek'd, hazell eie, browne haire . . . loved wine . . . would never drinke harde in company, and was wont to say that, *he would not play the good-fellow in any man's company in whose hands he would not trust his life.* . . ."

POEMS

To his Noble Friend Mr. Richard Lovelace,
upon his Poems

Sir,
    Our times are much degenerate from those
    Which your sweet Muse which your fair Fortune chose,
    And as complexions alter with the Climes,
    Our wits have drawne th' infection of our times.   5
    That candid Age no other way could tell
    To be ingenious, but by speaking well.
    Who best could prayse, had then the greatest prayse,
    Twas more esteemd to give, then weare the Bayes:
    Modest ambition studi'd only then,   10
    To honour not her selfe, but worthy men.
    These vertues now are banisht out of Towne,
    Our Civill Wars have lost the Civicke crowne.
    He highest builds, who with most Art destroys,
    And against others Fame his owne employs.   15
    I see the envious Caterpillar sit
    On the faire blossome of each growing wit.
      The Ayre 's already tainted with the swarms
    Of Insects which against you rise in arms.
    Word-peckers, Paper-rats, Book-scorpions,   20
    Of wit corrupted, the unfashion'd Sons.
    The barbed Censurers begin to looke
    Like the grim consistory on thy Booke;
    And on each line cast a reforming eye,
    Severer then the yong Presbytery.   25
    Till when in vaine they have thee all perus'd,
    You shall for being faultlesse be accus'd.
    Some reading your *Lucasta*, will alledge
    You wrong'd in her the Houses Priviledge.

Some that you under sequestration are,   30
Because you write when going to the Warre,
And one the Book prohibits, because *Kent*
Their first Petition by the Authour sent.
   But when the beauteous Ladies came to know
That their deare *Lovelace* was endanger'd so: 35
Lovelace that thaw'd the most congealed brest,
He who lov'd best and them defended best.
Whose hand so rudely grasps the steely brand,
Whose hand so gently melts the Ladies hand.
They all in mutiny though yet undrest   40
Sally'd, and would in his defence contest.
And one the loveliest that was yet e're seen,
Thinking that I too of the rout had been,
Mine eyes invaded with a female spight,
(She knew what pain 'twould be to lose that sight.)   45
O no, mistake not, I reply'd, for I
In your defence, or in his cause would dy.
But he secure of glory and of time
Above their envy, or mine aid doth clime.
Him, valianst men, and fairest Nymphs approve,   50
His Booke in them finds Judgement, with you Love.

Upon the Death of the Lord Hastings

Go, intercept some Fountain in the Vein,
Whose Virgin-Source yet never steept the Plain.
Hastings is dead, and we must finde a Store
Of Tears untoucht, and never wept before.
Go, stand betwixt the *Morning* and the *Flowers*;   5
And, ere they fall, arrest the early *Showers*.
Hastings is dead; and we, disconsolate,
With early *Tears* must mourn his early *Fate*.
   Alas, his *Vertues* did his *Death* presage:
Needs must he die, that doth out-run his *Age*.   10
The Phlegmatick and Slowe prolongs his day,
And on Times Wheel sticks like a *Remora*.
What man is he, that hath not *Heaven* beguil'd,
And is not thence mistaken for a *Childe*?

While those of growth more sudden, and more bold,   15
Are hurried hence, as if already old.
For, there above, They number not as here,
But weigh to Man the *Geometrick* yeer.
    Had he but at this Measure still increast,
And on *the Tree of Life* once made a Feast,   20
As that of *Knowledge*; what Loves had he given
To Earth, and then what Jealousies to Heaven!
But 't is a *Maxime* of that State, That none,
Lest He become like Them, taste more then one.
Therefore the *Democratick* Stars did rise,   25
And all that Worth from hence did *Ostracize*.
    Yet as some *Prince*, that, for State-Jealousie,
Secures his neerest and most lov'd *Ally*;
His Thought with richest Triumphs entertains,
And in the choicest Pleasures charms his Pains: 30
So he, not banisht hence, but there confin'd,
There better recreates his active Minde.
    Before the *Chrystal Palace* where he dwells,
The armed *Angels* hold their *Carouzels*;
And underneath, he views the *Turnaments*   35
Of all these Sublunary *Elements*.
But most he doth th' *Eternal Book* behold,
On which the *happie Names* do stand enroll'd;
And gladly there can all his Kinred claim,
But most rejoyces at his *Mothers* name.   40
    The gods themselves cannot their Joy conceal,
But draw their Veils, and their pure Beams reveal:
Onely they drooping *Hymeneus* note,
Who for sad *Purple*, tears his *Saffron* coat;
And trails his Torches th'row the Starry Hall   45
Reversed, at his *Darlings* Funeral.
    And *Æsculapius*, who, asham'd and stern,
Himself at once condemneth, and *Mayern*;
Like some sad *Chymist*, who, prepar'd to reap
The *Golden Harvest*, sees his Glasses leap.   50
For, how Immortal must their race have stood,
Had *Mayern* once been mixt with *Hastings* blood!
How Sweet and Verdant would these *Lawrels* be,
Had they been planted on that *Balsam*-tree!

But what could he, good man, although he bruis'd   55
All Herbs, and them a thousand ways infus'd?
All he had try'd, but all in vain, he saw,
And wept, as we, without Redress or Law.
For *Man* (alas) is but the *Heavens* sport;
And *Art* indeed is Long, but *Life* is Short.   60

A
Dialogue
Between
The Resolved Soul, and Created Pleasure

Courage my Soul, now learn to wield
The weight of thine immortal Shield.
Close on thy Head thy Helmet bright.
Ballance thy Sword against the Fight.
See where an Army, strong as fair,   5
With silken Banners spreads the air.
Now, if thou bee'st that thing Divine,
In this day's Combat let it shine:
And shew that Nature wants an Art
To conquer one resolved Heart.   10

Pleasure. Welcome the Creations Guest,
Lord of Earth, and Heavens Heir.
Lay aside that Warlike Crest,
And of Nature's banquet share:
Where the Souls of fruits and flow'rs   15
Stand prepar'd to heighten yours.

Soul. I sup above, and cannot stay
To bait so long upon the way.

Pleasure. On these downy Pillows lye,
Whose soft Plumes will thither fly: 20
On these Roses strow'd so plain
Lest one Leaf thy Side should strain.

Soul. My gentler Rest is on a Thought,
Conscious of doing what I ought.

Pleasure. If thou bee'st with Perfumes pleas'd,   25
       Such as oft the Gods appeas'd,
       Thou in fragrant Clouds shalt show
       Like another God below.

Soul. A Soul that knowes not to presume
       Is Heaven's and its own perfume.   30

Pleasure. Every thing does seem to vie
       Which should first attract thine Eye:
       But since none deserves that grace,
       In this Crystal view *thy* face.

Soul. When the Creator's skill is priz'd,   35
       The rest is all but Earth disguis'd.

Pleasure. Heark how Musick then prepares
       For thy Stay these charming Aires;
       Which the posting Winds recall,
       And suspend the Rivers Fall.   40

Soul. Had I but any time to lose,
       On this I would it all dispose.
       Cease Tempter. None can chain a mind
       Whom this sweet Chordage cannot bind.

Chorus. *Earth cannot shew so brave a Sight*   45
       As when a single Soul does fence
       The Batteries of alluring Sense,
       And Heaven views it with delight.
          Then persevere: for still new Charges sound:
          And if thou overcom'st thou shalt be crown'd.
          [50

Pleasure. All this fair, and soft, and sweet,
         Which scatteringly doth shine,
       Shall within one Beauty meet,
         And she be only thine.

Soul. If things of Sight such Heavens be,   55
       What Heavens are those we cannot see?

Pleasure. Where so e're thy Foot shall go
        The minted Gold shall lie;
     Till thou purchase all below,
        And want new Worlds to buy.   60

Soul. Wer't not a price who'ld value Gold?
    And that's worth nought that can be sold.

Pleasure. Wilt thou all the Glory have
        That War or Peace commend?
     Half the World shall be thy Slave   65
        The other half thy Friend.

Soul. What Friends, if to my self untrue?
    What Slaves, unless I captive you?

Pleasure. Thou shalt know each hidden Cause;
        And see the future Time: 70
     Try what depth the Centre draws;
        And then to Heaven climb.

Soul. None thither mounts by the degree
    Of Knowledge, but Humility.

Chorus. *Triumph, triumph, victorious Soul;*   75
    The World has not one Pleasure more:
    The rest does lie beyond the Pole,
    And is thine everlasting Store.

On a Drop of Dew

See how the Orient Dew,
Shed from the Bosom of the Morn
   Into the blowing Roses,
Yet careless of its Mansion new;
For the clear Region where 'twas born   5
   Round in its self incloses:
   And in its little Globes Extent,
Frames as it can its native Element.
   How it the purple flow'r does slight,

Scarce touching where it lyes, 10
But gazing back upon the Skies,
Shines with a mournful Light;
Like its own Tear,
Because so long divided from the Sphear.
Restless it roules and unsecure, 15
Trembling lest it grow impure:
Till the warm Sun pitty it's Pain,
And to the Skies exhale it back again.
So the Soul, that Drop, that Ray
Of the clear Fountain of Eternal Day, 20
Could it within the humane flow'r be seen,
Remembring still its former height,
Shuns the sweat leaves and blossoms green;
And, recollecting its own Light,
Does, in its pure and circling thoughts, express 25
The greater Heaven in an Heaven less.
In how coy a Figure wound,
Every way it turns away:
So the World excluding round,
Yet receiving in the Day. 30
Dark beneath, but bright above:
Here disdaining, there in Love,
How loose and easie hence to go:
How girt and ready to ascend.
Moving but on a point below, 35
It all about does upwards bend.
Such did the Manna's sacred Dew destil;
White, and intire, though congeal'd and chill.
Congeal'd on Earth: but does, dissolving, run
Into the Glories of th' Almighty Sun. 40

The Coronet

When for the Thorns with which I long, too long,
With many a piercing wound,
My Saviours head have crown'd,
I seek with Garlands to redress that Wrong:
Through every Garden, every Mead, 5

I gather flow'rs (my fruits are only flow'rs)
 Dismantling all the fragrant Towers
That once adorn'd my Shepherdesses head.
And now when I have summ'd up all my store,
 Thinking (so I my self deceive)   10
 So rich a Chaplet thence to weave
As never yet the king of Glory wore:
 Alas I find the Serpent old
 That, twining in his speckled breast,
 About the flow'rs disguis'd does fold, 15
 With wreaths of Fame and Interest.
Ah, foolish Man, that would'st debase with them.
And mortal Glory, Heaven's Diadem!
But thou who only could'st the Serpent tame,
Either his slipp'ry knots at once untie, 20
And disintangle all his winding Snare:
Or shatter too with him my curious frame
And let these wither, so that he may die,
Though set with Skill and chosen out with Care.
That they, while Thou on both their Spoils dost tread, 25
May crown thy Feet, that could not crown thy Head.

Eyes and Tears

How wisely Nature did decree,
With the same Eyes to weep and see!
That, having view'd the object vain,
They might be ready to complain.

And, since the Self-deluding Sight, 5
In a false Angle takes each hight;
These Tears which better measure all,
Like wat'ry Lines and Plummets fall.

Two Tears, which Sorrow long did weigh
Within the Scales of either Eye, 10
And then paid out in equal Poise,
Are the true price of all my Joyes.

What in the World most fair appears,
Yea even Laughter, turns to Tears:
And all the Jewels which we prize, 15
Melt in these Pendants of the Eyes.

I have through every Garden been,
Amongst the Red, the White, the Green;
And yet, from all the flow'rs I saw,
No Hony, but these Tears could draw. 20

So the all-seeing Sun each day
Distills the World with Chymick Ray;
But finds the Essence only Showers,
Which straight in pity back he powers.

Yet happy they whom Grief doth bless, 25
That weep the more, and see the less:
And, to preserve their Sight more true,
Bath still their Eyes in their own Dew.

So *Magdalen*, in Tears more wise
Dissolv'd those captivating Eyes, 30
Whose liquid Chaines could flowing meet
To fetter her Redeemers feet.

Not full sailes hasting loaden home,
Nor the chast Ladies pregnant Womb,
Nor *Cynthia* Teeming show's so fair, 35
As two Eyes swoln with weeping are.

The sparkling Glance that shoots Desire,
Drench'd in these Waves, does lose it fire.
Yea oft the Thund'rer pitty takes
And here the hissing Lightning slakes. 40

The Incense was to Heaven dear,
Not as a Perfume, but a Tear.
And Stars shew lovely in the Night,
But as they seem the Tears of Light.

Ope then mine Eyes your double Sluice,   45
And practise so your noblest Use.
For others too can see, or sleep;
But only humane Eyes can weep.

Now like two Clouds dissolving, drop,
And at each Tear in distance stop: 50
Now like two Fountains trickle down:
Now like two floods o'return and drown.

Thus let your Streams o'reflow your Springs,
Till Eyes and Tears be the same things:
And each the other's difference bears;   55
These weeping Eyes, those seeing Tears.

Bermudas

Where the remote *Bermudas* ride
In th' Oceans bosome unespy'd,
From a small Boat, that row'd along,
The listning Winds receiv'd this Song.
    What should we do but sing his Praise   5
That led us through the watry Maze,
Unto an Isle so long unknown,
And yet far kinder than our own?
Where he the huge Sea-Monsters wracks,
That lift the Deep upon their Backs.   10
He lands us on a grassy Stage;
Safe from the Storms, and Prelat's rage.
He gave us this eternal Spring,
Which here enamells every thing;
And sends the Fowl's to us in care,   15
On daily Visits through the Air.
He hangs in shades the Orange bright,
Like golden Lamps in a green Night.
And does in the Pomgranates close,
Jewels more rich than *Ormus* show's.   20
He makes the Figs our mouths to meet;
And throws the Melons at our feet.

But Apples plants of such a price,
No Tree could ever bear them twice.
With Cedars, chosen by his hand,   25
From *Lebanon,* he stores the Land.
And makes the hollow Seas, that roar,
Proclaime the Ambergris on shoar.
He cast (of which we rather boast)
The Gospels Pearl upon our Coast.   30
And in these Rocks for us did frame
A Temple, where to sound his Name.
Oh let our Voice his Praise exalt,
Till it arrive at Heavens Vault:
Which thence (perhaps) rebounding, may   35
Eccho beyond the *Mexique Bay.*
Thus sung they, in the *English* boat,
An holy and a chearful Note,
And all the way, to guide their Chime,
With falling Oars they kept the time.   40

Clorinda and Damon

C. *Damon* come drive thy flocks this way.
D. No: 'tis too late they went astray.
C. I have a grassy Scutcheon spy'd,
Where *Flora* blazons all her pride.
The Grass I aim to feast thy Sheep: 5
The Flow'rs I for thy Temples keep.
D. Grass withers; and the Flow'rs too fade.
C. Seize the short Joyes then, ere they vade.
Seest thou that unfrequented Cave?
D. That den? *C.* Loves Shrine. *D.* But Virtue's Grave. 10
C. In whose cool bosome we may lye
Safe from the Sun. *D.* not Heaven's Eye.
C. Near this, a Fountaines liquid Bell
Tinkles within the concave Shell.
D. Might a Soul bath there and be clean,   15
Or slake its Drought? *C.* What is't you mean?
D. These once had been enticing things,
Clorinda, Pastures, Caves, and Springs.

C. And what late change? D. The other day
   Pan met me. C. What did great *Pan* say?   20
D. Words that transcend poor Shepherds skill,
   But He ere since my Songs does fill:
   And his Name swells my slender Oate.
C. Sweet must *Pan* sound in *Damons* Note.
D. *Clorinda's* voice might make it sweet.   25
C. Who would not in *Pan's* Praises meet?

Chorus.

Of Pan *the flowry Pastures sing,*
Caves eccho, and the Fountains ring.
Sing then while he doth us inspire;   30
For all the World is our Pan's *Quire.*

A *Dialogue between* Thyrsis *and* Dorinda

Dorinda. When Death, shall part us from these Kids,
         And shut up our divided Lids,
         Tell me *Thyrsis,* prethee do,
         Whither thou and I must go.

Thyrsis. To the Elizium: (*Dorinda*) oh where i'st?   5
Thyrsis. A Chast Soul, can never mis't.
Dorinda. I know no way, but one, our home;
         Is our cell Elizium?

Thyrsis. Turn thine Eye to yonder Skie,
         There the milky way doth lye;   10
         'Tis a sure but rugged way,
         That leads to Everlasting day.

Dorinda. There Birds may nest, but how can I,
         That have no wings and cannot fly?

Thyrsis. Do not sigh (fair Nimph) for fire   15
         Hath no wings, yet doth aspire
         Till it hit, against the pole,
         Heaven's the Center of the Soul.

Dorinda.   But in Elizium how do they
           Pass Eternity away?   20

Thyrsis.   Oh, ther's, neither hope nor fear
           Ther's no Wolf, no Fox, nor Bear.
           No need of Dog to fetch our stray,
           Our Lightfoot we may give away;
           No Oat-pipe's needfull, there thine Ears   25
           May feast with Musick of the Spheres.

Dorinda.   Oh sweet! oh sweet! How I my future state
           By silent thinking, Antidate:
           I prethee let us spend our time to come
           In talking of *Elizium*.   30

Thyrsis.   Then I'le go on: There, sheep are full
           Of sweetest grass, and softest wooll;
           There, birds sing Consorts, garlands grow,
           Cold winds do whisper, springs do flow.
           There, alwayes is, a rising Sun,   35
           And day is ever, but begun.
           Shepheards there, bear equal sway,
           And every Nimph's a Queen of *May*.

Dorinda.   Ah me, ah me. (*Thyrsis.*) *Dorinda*, why do 'st
              Cry?   40

Dorinda.   I'm sick, I'm sick, and fain would dye:
           Convince me now, that this is true;
           By bidding, with mee, all adieu.

Thyrsis.   I cannot live, without thee, I
           Will for thee, much more with thee dye.   45

Chorus.   Then let us give *Clorillo* charge o'th Sheep,
           And thou and I'le pick poppies and them steep
           In wine, and drink on't even till we weep,
           So shall we smoothly pass away in sleep.

A *Dialogue between the Soul and Body*

Soul.   O who shall, from this Dungeon, raise
        A Soul inslav'd so many wayes?
        With bolts of Bones, that fetter'd stands
        In Feet; and manacled in Hands.
        Here blinded with an Eye; and there   5
        Deaf with the drumming of an Ear.
        A Soul hung up, as 'twere, in Chains
        Of Nerves, and Arteries, and Veins.
        Tortur'd, besides each other part,
        In a vain Head, and double Heart.   10

Body.   O who shall me deliver whole,
        From bonds of this Tyrannic Soul?
        Which, stretcht upright, impales me so,
        That mine own Precipice I go;
        And warms and moves this needless Frame: 15
        (A Fever could but do the same.)
        And, wanting where its spight to try,
        Has made me live to let me dye.
        A Body that could never rest,
        Since this ill Spirit it possest.   20

Soul.   What Magick could me thus confine
        Within anothers Grief to pine?
        Where whatsoever it complain,
        I feel, that cannot feel, the pain.
        And all my Care its self employes,   25
        That to preserve, which me destroys
        Constrain'd not only to indure
        Diseases, but, whats worse, the Cure:
        And ready oft the Port to gain,
        Am Shipwrackt into Health again.   30

Body.   But Physick yet could never reach
        The Maladies Thou me dost teach;
        Whom first the Cramp of Hope does Tear:
        And then the Palsie Shakes of Fear.

The Pestilence of Love does heat: 35
Or Hatred's hidden Ulcer eat.
Joy's chearful Madness does perplex:
Or Sorrow's other Madness vex.
Which Knowledge forces me to know;
And Memory will not foregoe.   40
What but a Soul could have the wit
To build me up for Sin so fit?
So Architects do square and hew,
Green Trees that in the Forest grew.

The Nymph complaining for the death of her Faun

The wanton Troopers riding by
Have shot my Faun and it will dye.
Ungentle men! They cannot thrive
To kill thee. Thou neer didst alive
Them any harm: alas nor cou'd   5
Thy death yet do them any good.
I'me sure I never wisht them ill;
Nor do I for all this; nor will:
But, if my simple Pray'rs may yet
Prevail with Heaven to forget   10
Thy murder, I will Joyn my Tears
Rather then fail. But, O my fears!
It cannot dye so. Heavens King
Keeps register of every thing:
And nothing may we use in vain.   15
Ev'n Beasts must be with justice slain;
Else Men are made their *Deodands*.
Though they should wash their guilty hands
In this warm life-blood, which doth part
From thine, and wound me to the Heart,   20
Yet could they not be clean: their Stain
Is dy'd in such a Purple Grain.
There is not such another in
The World, to offer for their Sin.
   Unconstant *Sylvio*, when yet   25
I had not found him counterfeit,

One morning (I remember well)
Ty'd in this silver Chain and Bell,
Gave it to me: nay and I know
What he said then; I'me sure I do.   30
Said He, look how your Huntsman here
Hath taught a Faun to hunt his *Dear*.
But *Sylvio* soon had me beguil'd.
This waxed tame, while he grew wild,
And quite regardless of my Smart,   35
Left me his Faun, but took his Heart.

   Thenceforth I set my self to play
My solitary time away,
With this: and very well content,
Could so mine idle Life have spent.   40
For it was full of sport; and light
Of foot, and heart; and did invite,
Me to its game: it seem'd to bless
Its self in me. How could I less
Than love it? O I cannot be   45
Unkind, t' a Beast that loveth me.

   Had it liv'd long, I do not know
Whether it too might have done so
As *Sylvio* did: his Gifts might be
Perhaps as false or more than he.   50
But I am sure, for ought that I
Could in so short a time espie,
Thy Love was far more better then
The love of false and cruel men.

   With sweetest milk, and sugar, first   55
I it at mine own fingers nurst.
And as it grew, so every day
It wax'd more white and sweet than they.
It had so sweet a Breath! And oft
I blusht to see its foot more soft,   60
And white, (shall I say then my hand?)
NAY any Ladies of the Land.

   It is a wond'rous thing, how fleet
'Twas on those little silver feet.
With what a pretty skipping grace,   65
It oft would challenge me the Race:

And when 'thad left me far away,
'Twould stay, and run again, and stay.
For it was nimbler much than Hindes;
And trod, as on the four Winds. 70
    I have a Garden of my own,
But so with Roses over grown,
And Lillies, that you would it guess
To be a little Wilderness.
And all the Spring time of the year 75
It onely loved to be there.
Among the beds of Lillyes, I
Have sought it oft, where it should lye,
Yet could not, till it self would rise,
Find it, although before mine Eyes. 80
For, in the flaxen Lillies shade,
It like a bank of Lillies laid.
Upon the Roses it would feed,
Until its Lips ev'n seem'd to bleed:
And then to me 'twould boldly trip, 85
And print those Roses on my Lip.
But all its chief delight was still
On Roses thus its self to fill:
And its pure virgin Limbs to fold
In whitest sheets of Lillies cold. 90
Had it liv'd long, it would have been
Lillies without, Roses within.
    O help! O help! I see it faint:
And dye as calmely as a Saint.
See how it weeps. The Tears do come 95
Sad, slowly dropping like a Gumme.
So weeps the wounded Balsome: so
The holy Frankincense doth flow.
The brotherless *Heliades*
Melt in such Amber Tears as these. 100
    I in a golden Vial will
Keep these two crystal Tears; and fill
It till it do o'reflow with mine;
Then place it in *Diana's* Shrine.
    Now my Sweet Faun is vanish'd to 105

Whether the Swans and Turtles go:
In fair *Elizium* to endure,
With milk-white Lambs, and Ermins pure.
O do not run too fast: for I
Will but bespeak thy Grave, and dye.   110
   First my unhappy Statue shall
Be cut in Marble; and withal,
Let it be weeping too: but there
Th' Engraver sure his Art may spare;
For I so truly thee bemoane,   115
That I shall weep though I be Stone:
Until my Tears, still dropping, wear
My breast, themselves engraving there.
There at my feet shalt thou be laid,
Of purest Alabaster made: 120
For I would have thine Image be
White as I can, though not as Thee.

Young Love

Come little Infant, Love me now,
   While thine unsuspected years
Clear thine aged Fathers brow
   From cold Jealousie and Fears.

Pretty surely 'twere to see   5
   By young Love old Time beguil'd:
While our Sportings are as free
   As the Nurses with the Child.

Common Beauties stay fifteen;
   Such as yours should swifter move;   10
Whose fair Blossoms are too green
   Yet for Lust, but not for Love.

Love as much the snowy Lamb
   Or the wanton Kid does prize,
As the lusty Bull or Ram,   15
   For his morning Sacrifice.

Now then love me: time may take
    Thee before thy time away:
Of this Need wee'l Virtue make,
    And learn Love before we may.   20

So we win of doubtful Fate;
    And, if good she to us meant,
We that Good shall antedate,
    Or, if ill, that Ill prevent.

Thus as Kingdomes, frustrating   25
    Other Titles to their Crown,
In the craddle crown their King,
    So all Forraign Claims to drown,

So, to make all Rivals vain,
    Now I crown thee with my Love: 30
Crown me with thy Love again,
    And we both shall Monarchs prove.

To his Coy Mistress

Had we but World enough, and Time,
This coyness Lady were no crime.
We would sit down, and think which way
To walk, and pass our long Loves Day.
Thou by the *Indian Ganges* side   5
Should'st Rubies find: I by the Tide
Of *Humber* would complain. I would
Love you ten years before the Flood:
And you should if you please refuse
Till the Conversion of the *Jews*.   10
My vegetable Love should grow
Vaster then Empires, and more slow.
An hundred years should go to praise
Thine Eyes, and on thy Forehead Gaze.
Two hundred to adore each Breast: 15
But thirty thousand to the rest.
An Age at least to every part,
And the last Age should show your Heart.

For Lady you deserve this State;
Nor would I love at lower rate.   20
    But at my back I alwaies hear
Times winged Charriot hurrying near:
And yonder all before us lye
Desarts of vast Eternity.
Thy Beauty shall no more be found;   25
Nor, in thy marble Vault, shall sound
My ecchoing Song: then Worms shall try
That long preserv'd Virginity:
And your quaint Honour turn to dust;
And into ashes all my Lust.   30
The Grave's a fine and private place,
But none I think do there embrace.
    Now therefore, while the youthful hew
Sits on thy skin like morning dew,
And while thy willing Soul transpires   35
At every pore with instant Fires,
Now let us sport us while we may;
And now, like am'rous birds of prey,
Rather at once our Time devour,
Than languish in his slow-chapt pow'r.   40
Let us roll all our Strength, and all
Our sweetness, up into one Ball:
And tear our Pleasures with rough strife,
Thorough the Iron gates of Life.
Thus, though we cannot make our Sun   45
Stand still, yet we will make him run.

The unfortunate Lover

Alas, how pleasant are their dayes
With whom the Infant Love yet playes!
Sorted by pairs, they still are seen
By Fountains cool, and Shadows green.
But soon these Flames do lose their light,   5
Like Meteors of a Summers night:
Nor can they to that Region climb,
To make impression upon Time.

'Twas in a Shipwrack, when the Seas
Rul'd, and the Winds did what they please,   10
That my poor Lover floting lay,
And, e're brought forth, was cast away:
Till at the last the master-Wave
Upon the Rock his Mother drave;
And there she split against the Stone,   15
In a *Cesarian Section*.

The Sea him lent these bitter Tears
Which at his Eyes he alwaies bears.
And from the Winds the Sighs he bore,
Which through his surging Breast do roar.   20
No Day he saw but that which breaks,
Through frighted Clouds in forked streaks.
While round the ratling Thunder hurl'd,
As at the Fun'ral of the World.

While Nature to his Birth presents   25
This masque of quarrelling Elements;
A num'rous fleet of Corm'rants black,
That sail'd insulting o're the Wrack,
Receiv'd into their cruel Care,
Th' unfortunate and abject Heir: 30
Guardians most fit to entertain
The Orphan of the *Hurricane*.

They fed him up with Hopes and Air,
Which soon digested to Despair.
And as one Corm'rant fed him, still   35
Another on his Heart did bill.
Thus while they famish him, and feast,
He both consumed, and increast:
And languished with doubtful Breath,
Th' *Amphibium* of Life and Death.   40

And now, when angry Heaven wou'd
Behold a spectacle of Blood,
Fortune and He are call'd to play
At sharp before it all the day:

And Tyrant Love his brest does ply   45
With all his wing'd Artillery.
Whilst he, betwixt the Flames and Waves,
Like *Ajax*, the mad Tempest braves.

See how he nak'd and fierce does stand,
Cuffing the Thunder with one hand;   50
While with the other he does lock,
And grapple, with the stubborn Rock:
From which he with each Wave rebounds,
Torn into Flames, and ragg'd with Wounds.
And all he saies, a Lover drest   55
In his own Blood does relish best.

This is the only *Banneret*
That ever Love created yet:
Who though, by the Malignant Starrs,
Forced to live in Storms and Warrs: 60
Yet dying leaves a Perfume here,
And Musick within every Ear:
And he in Story only rules,
In a Field *Sable* a Lover *Gules*.

The Gallery

Clora come view my Soul, and tell
Whether I have contriv'd it well.
Now all its several lodgings lye
Compos'd into one Gallery;
And the great *Arras*-hangings, made   5
Of various Faces, by are laid;
That, for all furniture, you'l find
Only your Picture in my Mind.

Here Thou art painted in the Dress
Of an Inhumane Murtheress;   10
Examining upon our Hearts
Thy fertile Shop of cruel Arts:
Engines more keen than ever yet
Adorned Tyrants Cabinet;

Of which the most tormenting are 15
Black Eyes, red Lips, and curled Hair.

But, on the other side, th' art drawn
Like to *Aurora* in the Dawn;
When in the East she slumb'ring lyes,
And stretches out her milky Thighs; 20
While all the morning Quire does sing,
And *Manna* falls, and Roses spring;
And, at thy Feet, the wooing Doves
Sit perfecting their harmless Loves.

Like an Enchantress here thou show'st, 25
Vexing thy restless Lover's Ghost;
And, by a Light obscure, dost rave
Over his Entrails, in the Cave;
Divining thence, with horrid Care,
How long thou shalt continue fair; 30
And (when inform'd) them throw'st away,
To be the greedy Vultur's prey.

But, against that, thou sit'st a float
Like *Venus* in her pearly Boat.
The *Halcyons,* calming all that 's nigh, 35
Betwixt the Air and Water fly.
Or, if some rowling Wave appears,
A Mass of Ambergris it bears.
Nor blows more Wind than what may well
Convoy the Perfume to the Smell. 40

These Pictures and a thousand more,
Of Thee, my Gallery do store;
In all the Forms thou can'st invent
Either to please me, or torment:
For thou alone to people me, 45
Art grown a num'rous Colony;
And a Collection choicer far
Then or *White-hall's,* or *Mantua's* were.

But, of these Pictures and the rest,
That at the Entrance likes me best: 50

Where the same Posture, and the Look
Remains, with which I first was took.
A tender Shepherdess, whose Hair
Hangs loosely playing in the Air,
Transplanting Flow'rs from the green Hill,   55
To crown her Head, and Bosome fill.

The Fair Singer

To make a final conquest of all me,
Love did compose so sweet an Enemy,
In whom both Beauties to my death agree,
Joyning themselves in fatal Harmony;
That while she with her Eyes my Heart does bind,   5
She with her Voice might captivate my Mind.

I could have fled from One but singly fair:
My dis-intangled Soul it self might save,
Breaking the curled trammels of her hair.
But how should I avoid to be her Slave,   10
Whose subtile Art invisibly can wreath
My Fetters of the very Air I breath?

It had been easie fighting in some plain,
Where Victory might hang in equal choice,
But all resistance against her is vain,   15
Who has th' advantage both of Eyes and Voice,
And all my Forces needs must be undone,
She having gained both the Wind and Sun.

Mourning

You, that decipher out the Fate
Of humane Off-springs from the Skies,
What mean these Infants which of late
Spring from the Starrs of *Chlora's* Eyes?

Her Eyes confus'd, and doubled ore,   5
With Tears suspended ere they flow;
Seem bending upwards, to restore
To Heaven, whence it came, their Woe.

When, molding of the watry Sphears,
Slow drops unty themselves away;   10
As if she, with those precious Tears,
Would strow the ground where *Strephon* lay.

Yet some affirm, pretending Art,
Her Eyes have so her Bosome drown'd,
Only to soften near her Heart   15
A place to fix another Wound.

And, while vain Pomp does her restrain
Within her solitary Bowr,
She courts her self in am'rous Rain;
Her self both *Danae* and the Showr.   20

Nay others, bolder, hence esteem
Joy now so much her Master grown,
That whatsoever does but seem
Like Grief, is from her Windows thrown.

Nor that she payes, while she survives,   25
To her dead Love this Tribute due;
But casts abroad these Donatives,
At the installing of a new.

How wide they dream! The *Indian* Slaves
That sink for Pearl through Seas profound,   30
Would find her Tears yet deeper Waves
And not of one the bottom sound.

I yet my silent Judgment keep,
Disputing not what they believe;
But sure as oft as Women weep,   35
It is to be suppos'd they grieve.

Daphnis and *Chloe*

Daphnis must from *Chloe* part:
Now is come the dismal Hour
That must all his Hopes devour,
All his Labour, all his Art.

Nature her own Sexes foe,   5
Long had taught her to be coy:
But she neither knew t'enjoy,
Nor yet let her Lover go.

But, with this sad News surpriz'd,
Soon she let that Niceness fall;   10
And would gladly yield to all,
So it had his stay compriz'd.

Nature so her self does use
To lay by her wonted State,
Lest the World should separate;   15
Sudden Parting closer glews.

He, well read in all the wayes
By which men their Siege maintain,
Knew not that the Fort to gain
Better 'twas the Siege to raise.   20

But he came so full possest
With the Grief of Parting thence,
That he had not so much Sence
As to see he might be blest.

Till Love in her Language breath'd   25
Words she never spake before;
But then Legacies no more
To a dying Man bequeath'd.

For, Alas, the time was spent,
Now the latest minut's run 30
When poor *Daphnis* is undone,
Between Joy and Sorrow rent.

At that *Why,* that *Stay my Dear,*
His disorder'd Locks he tare;
And with rouling Eyes did glare, 35
And his cruel Fate forswear.

As the Soul of one scarce dead,
With the shrieks of Friends aghast,
Looks distracted back in hast,
And then streight again is fled. 40

So did wretched *Daphnis* look,
Frighting her he loved most.
At the last, this Lovers Ghost
Thus his Leave resolved took.

Are my Hell and Heaven Joyn'd 45
More to torture him that dies?
Could departure not suffice,
But that you must then grow kind?

Ah my *Chloe* how have I
Such a wretched minute found, 50
When thy Favours should me wound
More than all thy Cruelty?

So to the condemned Wight
The delicious Cup we fill;
And allow him all he will, 55
For his last and short Delight.

But I will not now begin
Such a Debt unto my Foe;
Nor to my Departure owe
What my Presence could not win. 60

Absence is too much alone:
Better 'tis to go in peace,
Than my Losses to increase
By a late Fruition.

Why should I enrich my Fate?   65
'Tis a Vanity to wear,
For my Executioner,
Jewels of so high a rate.

Rather I away will pine
In a manly stubborness   70
Than be fatted up express
For the *Canibal* to dine.

Whilst this grief does thee disarm,
All th' Enjoyment of our Love
But the ravishment would prove   75
Of a Body dead while warm.

And I parting should appear
Like the Gourmand *Hebrew* dead,
While with Quailes and *Manna* fed,
He does through the Desert err.   80

Or the Witch that midnight wakes
For the Fern, whose magick Weed
In one minute casts the Seed,
And invisible him makes.

Gentler times for Love are ment   85
Who for parting pleasure strain
Gather Roses in the rain,
Wet themselves and spoil their Sent.

Farewel therefore all the fruit
Which I could from Love receive:
Joy will not with Sorrow weave,   90
Nor will I this Grief pollute.

Fate I come, as dark, as sad,
As thy Malice could desire;
Yet bring with me all the Fire   95
That Love in his Torches had.

At these words away he broke;
As who long has praying ly'n,
To his Heads-man makes the Sign,
And receives the parting stroke.   100

But hence Virgins all beware.
Last night he with *Phlogis* slept;
This night for *Dorinda* kept;
And but rid to take the Air.

Yet he does himself excuse;   105
Nor indeed without a Cause.
For, according to the Lawes,
Why did *Chloe* once refuse?

The Definition of Love

My Love is of a birth as rare
As 'tis for object strange and high:
It was begotten by despair
Upon Impossibility.

Magnanimous Despair alone   5
Could show me so divine a thing,
Where feeble Hope could ne'r have flown
But vainly flapt its Tinsel Wing.

And yet I quickly might arrive
Where my extended Soul is fixt   10
But Fate does Iron wedges drive,
And alwaies crouds it self betwixt.

For Fate with jealous Eye does see
Two perfect Loves; nor lets them close:
Their union would her ruine be,   15
And her Tyrannick pow'r depose.

And therefore her Decrees of Steel
Us as the distant Poles have plac'd,
(Though Loves whole World on us doth wheel)
Not by themselves to be embrac'd.   20

Unless the giddy Heaven fall,
And Earth some new Convulsion tear;
And, us to joyn, the World should all
Be cramp'd into a *Planisphere*.

As Lines so Loves *oblique* may well   25
Themselves in every Angle greet:
But ours so truly *Paralel*,
Though infinite can never meet.

Therefore the Love which us doth bind,
But Fate so enviously debarrs,   30
Is the Conjunction of the Mind,
And Opposition of the Stars.

The Picture of little T. C. in a Prospect of Flowers

See with what simplicity
This Nimph begins her golden daies!
In the green Grass she loves to lie,
And there with her fair Aspect tames
The Wilder flow'rs, and gives them names: 5
But only with the Roses playes;
         And them does tell
What Colour best becomes them, and what Smell.

Who can foretel for what high cause
This Darling of the Gods was born!   10
Yet this is She whose chaster Laws

The wanton Love shall one day fear,
And, under her command severe,
See his Bow broke and Ensigns torn.
          Happy, who can   15
Appease this virtuous Enemy of Man!

O then let me in time compound,
And parly with those conquering Eyes;
Ere they have try'd their force to wound,
Ere, with their glancing wheels, they drive   20
In Triumph over Hearts that strive,
And them that yield but more despise.
          Let me be laid,
Where I may see thy Glories from some shade.

Mean time, whilst every verdant thing   25
It self does at thy Beauty charm,
Reform the errours of the Spring;
Make that the Tulips may have share
Of sweetness, seeing they are fair;
And Roses of their thorns disarm: 30
          But most procure
That Violets may a longer Age endure.

But O young beauty of the Woods,
Whom Nature courts with fruits and flow'rs,
Gather the Flow'rs, but spare the Buds;   35
Lest *Flora* angry at thy crime,
To kill her Infants in their prime,
Do quickly make th' Example Yours;
          And, ere we see,
Nip in the blossome all our hopes and Thee.   40

The Match

Nature had long a Treasure made
    Of all her choisest store;
Fearing, when She should be decay'd,
    To beg in vain for more.

Her *Orientest* Colours there,   5
   And Essences most pure,
With sweetest Perfumes hoarded were,
   All as she thought secure.

She seldom them unlock'd, or us'd,
   But with the nicest care;   10
For, with one grain of them diffus'd,
   She could the World repair.

But likeness soon together drew
   What she did separate lay;
Of which one perfect Beauty grew,   15
   And that was *Celia*.

Love wisely had of long fore-seen
   That he must once grow old;
And therefore stor'd a Magazine,
   To save him from the cold.   20

He kept the several Cells repleat
   With Nitre thrice refin'd;
The Naphta's and the Sulphurs heat,
   And all that burns the Mind.

He fortifi'd the double Gate,   25
   And rarely thither came;
For, with one Spark of these, he streight
   All Nature could inflame.

Till, by vicinity so long,
   A nearer Way they sought;   30
And, grown magnetically strong,
   Into each other wrought.

Thus all his fewel did unite
   To make one fire high:
None ever burn'd so hot, so bright;   35
   And *Celia* that am I.

So we alone the happy rest,
    Whilst all the World is poor,
And have within our Selves possest
    All Love's and Nature's store.   40

The Mower against Gardens

Luxurious Man, to bring his Vice in use,
    Did after him the World seduce:
And from the fields the Flow'rs and Plants allure,
    Where Nature was most plain and pure.
He first enclos'd within the Gardens square   5
    A dead and standing pool of Air:
And a more luscious Earth for them did knead,
    Which stupifi'd them while it fed.
The Pink grew then as double as his Mind;
    The nutriment did change the kind.   10
With strange perfumes he did the Roses taint.
    And Flow'rs themselves were taught to paint.
The Tulip, white, did for complexion seek;
    And learn'd to interline its cheek:
Its Onion root they then so high did hold,   15
    That one was for a Meadow sold.
Another World was search'd, through Oceans new,
    To find the *Marvel of Peru*.
And yet these Rarities might be allow'd,
    To Man, that sov'raign thing and proud;   20
Had he not dealt between the Bark and Tree,
    Forbidden mixtures there to see.
No Plant now knew the Stock from which it came;
    He grafts upon the Wild the Tame:
That the uncertain and adult'rate fruit   25
    Might put the Palate in dispute.
His green *Seraglio* has its Eunuchs too;
    Lest any Tyrant him out-doe.
And in the Cherry he does Nature vex,
    To procreate without a Sex.   30
'Tis all enforc'd; the Fountain and the Grot;
    While the sweet Fields do lye forgot:

Where willing Nature does to all dispence
    A wild and fragrant Innocence:
And *Fauns* and *Faryes* do the Meadows till,   35
    More by their presence then their skill.
Their Statues polish'd by some ancient hand,
    May to adorn the Gardens stand:
But howso'ere the Figures do excel,
    The *Gods* themselves with us do dwell.   40

Damon *the Mower*

Heark how the Mower *Damon* Sung,
With love of *Juliana* stung!
While ev'ry thing did seem to paint
The Scene more fit for his complaint.
Like her fair Eyes the day was fair;   5
But scorching like his am'rous Care.
Sharp like his Sythe his Sorrow was,
And wither'd like his Hopes the Grass.

Oh what unusual Heats are here,
Which thus our Sun-burn'd Meadows sear!   10
The Grass-hopper its pipe gives ore;
And hamstring'd Frogs can dance no more.
But in the brook the green Frog wades;
And Grass-hoppers seek out the shades.
Only the Snake, that kept within,   15
Now glitters in its second skin.

This heat the Sun could never raise,
Nor Dog-star so inflame's the dayes.
It from an higher Beauty grow'th,
Which burns the Fields and Mower both: 20
Which made the Dog, and makes the Sun
Hotter then his own *Phaeton.*
Not *July* causeth these Extremes,
But *Juliana's* scorching beams.

Tell me where I may pass the Fires   25
Of the hot day, or hot desires.

To what cool Cave shall I descend,
Or to what gelid Fountain bend?
Alas! I look for Ease in vain,
When Remedies themselves complain.   30
No moisture but my Tears do rest,
Nor Cold but in her Icy Breast.

How long wilt Thou, fair Shepheardess,
Esteem me, and my Presents less?
To Thee the harmless Snake I bring,   35
Disarmed of its teeth and sting.
To Thee *Chameleons* changing-hue,
And Oak leaves tipt with hony due.
Yet Thou ungrateful hast not sought
Nor what they are, nor who them brought.   40

I am the Mower *Damon,* known
Through all the Meadows I have mown.
On me the Morn her dew distills
Before her darling Daffadils.
And, if at Noon my toil me heat,   45
The Sun himself licks off my Sweat.
While, going home, the Ev'ning sweet
In cowslip-water bathes my feet.

What, though the piping Shepherd stock
The plains with an unnum'red Flock,   50
This Sithe of mine discovers wide
More ground then all his Sheep do hide.
With this the golden fleece I shear
Of all these Closes ev'ry Year.
And though in Wooll more poor then they,   55
Yet am I richer far in Hay.

Nor am I so deform'd to sight,
If in my Sithe I looked right;
In which I see my Picture done,
As in a crescent Moon the Sun.   60
The deathless Fairyes take me oft
To lead them in their Danses soft;

And, when I tune my self to sing,
About me they contract their Ring.

How happy might I still have mow'd,   6
Had not Love here his Thistles sow'd!
But now I all the day complain,
Joyning my Labour to my Pain;
And with my Sythe cut down the Grass,
Yet still my Grief is where it was: 7(
But, when the Iron blunter grows,
Sighing I whet my Sythe and Woes.

While thus he threw his Elbow round,
Depopulating all the Ground,
And, with his whistling Sythe, does cut   7(
Each stroke between the Earth and Root,
The edged Stele by careless chance
Did into his own Ankle glance;
And there among the Grass fell down,
By his own Sythe, the Mower mown.   80

Alas! said He, these hurts are slight
To those that dye by Loves despight.
With Shepherds-purse, and Clowns-all-heal,
The Blood I stanch, and Wound I seal.
Only for him no Cure is found,   85
Whom *Julianas* Eyes do wound.
'Tis death alone that this must do:
For Death thou art a Mower too.

The Mower to the Glo-Worms

Ye living Lamps, by whose dear light
The Nightingale does sit so late,
And studying all the Summer-night,
Her matchless Songs does meditate;

Ye Country Comets, that portend   5
No War, nor Princes funeral,
Shining unto no higher end
Then to presage the Grasses fall;

Ye Glo-worms, whose officious Flame
To wandring Mowers shows the way,   10
That in the Night have lost their aim,
And after foolish Fires do stray;

Your courteous Lights in vain you wast,
Since *Juliana* here is come,
For She my Mind hath so displac'd   15
That I shall never find my home.

The Mower's Song

My Mind was once the true survey
Of all these Medows fresh and gay;
And in the greenness of the Grass
Did see its Hopes as in a Glass;
When *Juliana* came, and She   5
What I do to the Grass, does to my Thoughts and Me.

But these, while I with Sorrow pine,
Grew more luxuriant still and fine;
That not one Blade of Grass you spy'd,
But had a Flower on either side;   10
When *Juliana* came, and She
What I do to the Grass, does to my Thoughts and Me.

Unthankful Medows, could you so
A fellowship so true forego,
And in your gawdy May-games meet,   15
While I lay trodden under feet?
When *Juliana* came, and She
What I do to the Grass, does to my Thoughts and Me.

But what you in Compassion ought,
Shall now by my Revenge be wrought: 20
And Flow'rs, and Grass, and I and all,
Will in one common Ruine fall.
For *Juliana* comes, and She
What I do to the Grass, does to my Thoughts and Me.

And thus, ye Meadows, which have been   25
Companions of my thoughts more green,
Shall now the Heraldry become
With which I shall adorn my Tomb;
For *Juliana* comes, and She
What I do to the Grass, does to my Thoughts and Me.   30

Ametas *and* Thestylis *making Hay-Ropes*

Ametas.   Think'st Thou that this Love can stand,
Whilst Thou still dost say me nay?
Love unpaid does soon disband:
Love binds Love as Hay binds Hay.

Thestylis. Think'st Thou that this Rope would twine   5
If we both should turn one way?
Where both parties so combine,
Neither Love will twist nor Hay.

Ametas.   Thus you vain Excuses find,
Which your selve and us delay: 10
And Love tyes a Womans Mind
Looser then with Ropes of Hay.

Thestylis. What you cannot constant hope
Must be taken as you may.

Ametas.   Then let's both lay by our Rope,   15
And go kiss within the Hay.

Musicks Empire

First was the World as one great Cymbal made,
Where Jarring Windes to infant Nature plaid.
All Musick was a solitary sound,
To hollow Rocks and murm'ring Fountains bound.

Jubal first made the wilder Notes agree; 5
And *Jubal* tuned Musicks *Jubilee*:
He call'd the *Ecchoes* from their sullen Cell,
And built the Organs City where they dwell.

Each sought a consort in that lovely place;
And Virgin Trebles wed the manly Base. 10
From whence the Progeny of numbers new
Into harmonious Colonies withdrew.

Some to the Lute, some to the Viol went,
And others chose the Cornet eloquent.
These practising the Wind, and those the Wire, 15
To sing Mens Triumphs, or in Heavens quire.

Then Musick, the Mosaique of the Air,
Did of all these a solemn noise prepare:
With which She gain'd the Empire of the Ear,
Including all between the Earth and Sphear. 20

Victorious sounds! yet here your Homage do
Unto a gentler Conqueror then you;
Who though He flies the Musick of his praise,
Would with you Heavens Hallelujahs raise.

The Garden

How vainly men themselves amaze
To win the Palm, the Oke, or Bayes;
And their uncessant Labours see
Crown'd from some single Herb or Tree.
Whose short and narrow verged Shade 5
Does prudently their Toyles upbraid;
While all Flow'rs and all Trees do close
To weave the Garlands of repose.

Fair quiet, have I found thee here,
And Innocence thy Sister dear! 10
Mistaken long, I sought you then
In busie Companies of Men.

Your sacred Plants, if here below,
Only among the Plants will grow.
Society is all but rude,
To this delicious Solitude.

No white nor red was ever seen
So am'rous as this lovely green.
Fond Lovers, cruel as their Flame,
Cut in these Trees their Mistress name.
Little, Alas, they know, or heed,
How far these Beauties Hers exceed!
Fair Trees! where s'eer your barkes I wound,
No Name shall but your own be found.

When we have run our Passions heat,
Love hither makes his best retreat.
The *Gods*, that mortal Beauty chase,
Still in a Tree did end their race.
Apollo hunted *Daphne* so,
Only that She might Laurel grow.
And *Pan* did after *Syrinx* speed,
Not as a Nymph, but for a Reed.

What wond'rous Life in this I lead!
Ripe Apples drop about my head;
The Luscious Clusters of the Vine
Upon my Mouth do crush their Wine;
The Nectaren, and curious Peach,
Into my hands themselves do reach;
Stumbling on Melons, as I pass,
Insnar'd with Flow'rs, I fall on Grass.

Mean while the Mind, from pleasure less,
Withdraws into its happiness:
The Mind, that Ocean where each kind
Does streight its own resemblance find;
Yet it creates, transcending these,
Far other Worlds, and other Seas;
Annihilating all that 's made
To a green Thought in a green Shade.

Here at the Fountains sliding foot,
Or at some Fruit-trees mossy root,   50
Casting the Bodies Vest aside,
My Soul into the boughs does glide:
There like a Bird it sits, and sings,
Then whets, and combs its silver Wings;
And, till prepar'd for longer flight,   55
Waves in its Plumes the various Light.

Such was that happy Garden-state,
While Man there walk'd without a Mate:
After a Place so pure, and sweet,
What other Help could yet be meet!   60
But 'twas beyond a Mortal's share
To wander solitary there:
Two Paradises 'twere in one
To live in Paradise alone.

How well the skilful Gardner drew   65
Of flow'rs and herbes this Dial new;
Where from above the milder Sun
Does through a fragrant Zodiack run;
And, as it works, th' industrious Bee
Computes its time as well as we.   70
How could such sweet and wholsome Hours
Be reckon'd but with herbs and flow'rs!

Senec. Traged. ex Thyeste Chor. 2

*Stet quicunque volet potens
Aulæ culmine lubrico* &c.

TRANSLATED

Climb at *Court* for me that will
Tottering favors Pinacle;
All I seek is to lye still.
Settled in some secret Nest
In calm Leisure let me rest;   5

And far of the publick Stage
Pass away my silent Age.
Thus when without noise, unknown,
I have liv'd out all my span,
I shall dye, without a groan,
An old honest Country man.
Who expos'd to others Ey's,
Into his own Heart ne'r pry's,
Death to him 's a Strange surprise.

An Epitaph upon ——

Enough: and leave the rest to Fame.
'Tis to commend her but to name.
Courtship, which living she declin'd,
When dead to offer were unkind.
Where never any could speak ill,
Who would officious Praises spill?
Nor can the truest Wit or Friend,
Without Detracting, her commend.
To say she liv'd a *Virgin* chast,
In this Age loose and all unlac't;
Nor was, when Vice is so allow'd,
Of *Virtue* or asham'd, or proud;
That her Soul was on *Heaven* so bent
No Minute but it came and went;
That ready her last Debt to pay
She summ'd her Life up ev'ry day;
Modest as Morn; as Mid-day bright;
Gentle as Ev'ning; cool as Night;
'Tis true: but all so weakly said;
'Twere more Significant, *She's Dead*.

Upon the Hill and Grove at Bill-borow
To the Lord Fairfax

See how the arched Earth does here
Rise in a perfect Hemisphere!

The stiffest Compass could not strike
A Line more circular and like;
Nor softest Pensel draw a Brow   5
So equal as this Hill does bow.
It seems as for a Model laid,
And that the World by it was made.

Here learn ye Mountains more unjust,
Which to abrupter greatness thrust,   10
That do with your hook-shoulder'd height
The Earth deform and Heaven fright,
For whose excrescence ill design'd,
Nature must a new Center find,
Learn here those humble steps to tread,   15
Which to securer Glory lead.

See what a soft access and wide
Lyes open to its grassy side;
Nor with the rugged path deterrs
The feet of breathless Travellers.   20
See then how courteous it ascends,
And all the way it rises bends;
Nor for it self the height does gain,
But only strives to raise the Plain.

Yet thus it all the field commands,   25
And in unenvy'd Greatness stands,
Discerning further then the Cliff
Of Heaven-daring *Teneriff*.
How glad the weary Seamen hast
When they salute it from the Mast!   30
By Night the Northern Star their way
Directs, and this no less by Day.

Upon its crest this Mountain grave
A Plump of aged Trees does wave.
No hostile hand durst ere invade   35
With impious Steel the sacred Shade.
For something alwaies did appear
Of the *great Masters* terrour there:

And Men could hear his Armour still
Ratling through all the Grove and Hill.   40

Fear of the *Master,* and respect
Of the great *Nymph* did it protect;
Vera the *Nymph* that him inspir'd,
To whom he often here retir'd,
And on these Okes ingrav'd her Name;   45
Such Wounds alone these Woods became:
But ere he well the Barks could part
'Twas writ already in their Heart.

For they ('tis credible) have sense,
As We, of Love and Reverence,   50
And underneath the Courser Rind
The *Genius* of the house do bind.
Hence they successes seem to know,
And in their *Lord's* advancement grow;
But in no Memory were seen   55
As under this so streight and green.

Yet now no further strive to shoot,
Contented if they fix their Root.
Nor to the winds uncertain gust,
Their prudent Heads too far intrust.   60
Onely sometimes a flutt'ring Breez
Discourses with the breathing Trees;
Which in their modest Whispers name
Those Acts that swell'd the Cheek of Fame.

Much other Groves, say they, then these   6
And other Hills him once did please.
Through Groves of Pikes he thunder'd then,
And Mountains rais'd of dying Men.
For all the *Civick Garlands* due
To him our Branches are but few;   7
Nor are our Trunks enow to bear
The *Trophees* of one fertile Year.

'Tis true, ye Trees nor ever spoke
More certain *Oracles* in Oak.

But Peace (if you his favour prize)   75
That Courage its own Praises flies.
Therefore to your obscurer Seats
From his own Brightness he retreats:
Nor he the Hills without the Groves,
Nor Height but with Retirement loves.   80

Upon Appleton House, to my Lord Fairfax

Within this sober Frame expect
Work of no Forrain *Architect*;
That unto Caves the Quarries drew,
And Forrests did to Pastures hew;
Who of his great Design in pain   5
Did for a Model vault his Brain,
Whose Columnes should so high be rais'd
To arch the Brows that on them gaz'd.

Why should of all things Man unrul'd
Such unproportion'd dwellings build?   10
The Beasts are by their Denns exprest:
And Birds contrive an equal Nest;
The low roof'd Tortoises do dwell
In cases fit of Tortoise-shell:
No Creature loves an empty space;   15
Their Bodies measure out their Place.

But He, superfluously spread,
Demands more room alive then dead.
And in his hollow Palace goes
Where Winds as he themselves may lose.   20
What need of all this Marble Crust
T'impark the wanton Mote of Dust,
That thinks by Breadth the World t'unite
Though the first Builders fail'd in Height?

But all things are composed here   25
Like Nature, orderly and near:
In which we the Dimensions find
Of that more sober Age and Mind,

When larger sized Men did stoop
To enter at a narrow loop;   30
As practising, in doors so strait,
To strain themselves through *Heavens Gate*.

And surely when the after Age
Shall hither come in *Pilgrimage*,
These sacred Places to adore,   35
By *Vere* and *Fairfax* trod before,
Men will dispute how their Extent
Within such dwarfish Confines went:
And some will smile at this, as well
As *Romulus* his Bee-like Cell.   40

Humility alone designs
Those short but admirable Lines,
By which, ungirt and unconstrain'd,
Things greater are in less contain'd.
Let others vainly strive t'immure   45
The *Circle* in the *Quadrature*!
These *holy Mathematicks* can
In ev'ry Figure equal Man.

Yet thus the laden House does sweat,
And scarce indures the *Master* great: 50
But where he comes the swelling Hall
Stirs, and the *Square* grows *Spherical*;
More by his *Magnitude* distrest,
Then he is by its straitness prest:
And too officiously it slights   55
That in it self which him delights.

So Honour better Lowness bears,
Then That unwonted Greatness wears.
Height with a certain Grace does bend,
But low Things clownishly ascend.   60
And yet what needs there here Excuse,
Where ev'ry Thing does answer Use?
Where neatness nothing can condemn,
Nor Pride invent what to contemn?

A Stately *Frontispice of Poor*   65
Adorns without the open Door:
Nor less the Rooms within commends
Daily new *Furniture of Friends*.
The House was built upon the Place
Only as for *a Mark of Grace*;   70
And for an *Inn* to entertain
Its *Lord* a while, but not remain.

Him *Bishops-Hill,* or *Denton* may,
Or *Bilbrough,* better hold then they:
But Nature here hath been so free   75
As if she said leave this to me.
Art would more neatly have defac'd
What she had laid so sweetly wast;
In fragrant Gardens, shaddy Woods,
Deep Meadows, and transparent Floods.   80

While with slow Eyes we these survey,
And on each pleasant footstep stay,
We opportunly may relate
The Progress of this Houses Fate.
A *Nunnery* first gave it birth.   85
For *Virgin Buildings* oft brought forth.
And all that Neighbour-Ruine shows
The Quarries whence this dwelling rose.

Near to this gloomy Cloysters Gates
There dwelt the blooming Virgin *Thwates*;   90
Fair beyond Measure, and an Heir
Which might Deformity make fair.
And oft She spent the Summer Suns
Discoursing with the *Suttle Nunns*.
Whence in these Words one to her weav'd,   95
(As 'twere by Chance) Thoughts long conceiv'd.

' Within this holy leisure we
' Live innocently as you see.
' These Walls restrain the World without,
' But hedge our Liberty about.   100

'These Bars inclose that wider Den
'Of those wild Creatures, called Men.
'The Cloyster outward shuts its Gates,
'And, from us, locks on them the Grates.

'Here we, in shining Armour white,   105
'Like *Virgin Amazons* do fight.
'And our chast *Lamps* we hourly trim,
'Lest the great *Bridegroom* find them dim.
'Our *Orient* Breaths perfumed are
'With insense of incessant Pray'r.   110
'And Holy-water of our Tears
'Most strangly our Complexion clears.

'Not Tears of Grief; but such as those
'With which calm Pleasure overflows;
'Or Pity, when we look on you   115
'That live without this happy Vow.
'How should we grieve that must be seen
'Each one a *Spouse*, and each a *Queen*;
'And can in *Heaven* hence behold
'Our brighter Robes and Crowns of Gold?   120

'When we have prayed all our Beads,
'Some One the holy *Legend* reads;
'While all the rest with Needles paint
'The Face and Graces of the *Saint*.
'But what the Linnen can't receive   125
'They in their Lives do interweave.
'This Work the *Saints* best represents;
'That serves for *Altar's Ornaments*.

'But much it to our work would add
'If here your hand, your Face we had: 130
'By it we would *our Lady* touch;
'Yet thus She you resembles much.
'Some of your Features, as we sow'd,
'Through ev'ry *Shrine* should be bestow'd.
'And in one Beauty we would take   135
'Enough a thousand *Saints* to make.

' And (for I dare not quench the Fire
' That me does for your good inspire)
' 'Twere Sacriledge a Man t'admit
' To holy things, for *Heaven* fit.   140
' I see the *Angels* in a Crown
' On you the Lillies show'ring down:
' And round about you Glory breaks,
' That something more then humane speaks.

' All Beauty, when at such a height,   145
' Is so already consecrate.
' *Fairfax* I know; and long ere this
' Have mark'd the Youth, and what he is.
' But can he such a *Rival* seem
' For whom you *Heav'n* should disesteem?   150
' Ah, no! and 'twould more Honour prove
' He your *Devoto* were, then *Love*.

' Here live beloved, and obey'd:
' Each one your Sister, each your Maid.
' And, if our Rule seem strictly pend,   155
' The Rule it self to you shall bend.
' Our *Abbess* too, now far in Age,
' Doth your succession near presage.
' How soft the yoke on us would lye,
' Might such fair Hands as yours it tye!   160

' Your voice, the sweetest of the Quire,
' Shall draw *Heav'n* nearer, raise us higher.
' And your Example, if our Head,
' Will soon us to perfection lead.
' Those Virtues to us all so dear,   165
' Will straight grow Sanctity when here:
' And that, once sprung, increase so fast
' Till Miracles it work at last.

' Nor is our *Order* yet so nice,
' Delight to banish as a Vice.   170
' Here Pleasure Piety doth meet;
' One perfecting the other Sweet.

' So through the mortal fruit we boyl
' The Sugars uncorrupting Oyl:
' And that which perisht while we pull,   175
' Is thus preserved clear and full.

' For such indeed are all our Arts;
' Still handling Natures finest Parts.
' Flow'rs dress the Altars; for the Clothes,
" The Sea-born Amber we compose;   180
' Balms for the griv'd we draw; and Pasts
' We mold, as Baits for curious tasts.
' What need is here of Man? unless
' These as sweet Sins we should confess.

' Each Night among us to your side   185
' Appoint a fresh and Virgin Bride;
' Whom if *our Lord* at midnight find,
' Yet Neither should be left behind.
' Where you may lye as chast in Bed,
' As Pearls together billeted.   190
' All Night embracing Arm in Arm,
' Like Chrystal pure with Cotton warm.

' But what is this to all the store
' Of Joys you see, and may make more!
' Try but a while, if you be wise: 195
' The Tryal neither Costs, nor Tyes.
Now *Fairfax* seek her promis'd faith:
Religion that dispensed hath;
Which She hence forward does begin;
The *Nuns* smooth Tongue has suckt her in.   200

Oft, though he knew it was in vain,
Yet would he valiantly complain.
' Is this that *Sanctity* so great,
' An Art by which you finly'r cheat?
' Hypocrite Witches, hence *avant*,   205
' Who though in prison yet inchant!
' Death only can such Theeves make fast,
' As rob though in the Dungeon cast.

' Were there but, when this House was made,
' One Stone that a just Hand had laid,   210
' It must have fall'n upon her Head
' Who first Thee from thy Faith misled.
' And yet, how well soever ment,
' With them 'twould soon grow fraudulent:
' For like themselves they alter all,   215
' And vice infects the very Wall.

' But sure those Buildings last not long,
' Founded by Folly, kept by Wrong.
' I know what Fruit their Gardens yield,
' When they it think by Night conceal'd.   220
' Fly from their Vices. 'Tis thy state,
' Not Thee, that they would consecrate.
' Fly from their Ruine. How I fear
' Though guiltless lest thou perish there.

What should he do? He would respect   225
Religion, but not Right neglect:
For first Religion taught him Right,
And dazled not but clear'd his sight.
Sometimes resolv'd his Sword he draws,
But reverenceth then the Laws: 230
For Justice still that Courage led;
First from a Judge, then Souldier bred.

Small Honour would be in the Storm.
The *Court* him grants the lawful Form;
Which licens'd either Peace or Force,   235
To hinder the unjust Divorce.
Yet still the *Nuns* his Right debar'd,
Standing upon their holy Guard.
Ill-counsell'd Women, do you know
Whom you resist, or what you do?   240

Is not this he whose Offspring fierce
Shall fight through all the *Universe*;
And with successive Valour try
France, Poland, either *Germany*;

Till one, as long since prophecy'd, 245
His Horse through conquer'd *Britain* ride?
Yet, against Fate, his Spouse they kept;
And the great Race would intercept.

Some to the Breach against their Foes
Their *Wooden Saints* in vain oppose. 250
Another bolder stands at push
With their old *Holy-Water Brush*.
While the disjointed *Abbess* threads
The gingling Chain-shot of her *Beads*.
But their lowd'st Cannon were their Lungs; 255
And sharpest Weapons were their Tongues.

But, waving these aside like Flyes,
Young *Fairfax* through the Wall does rise.
Then, th' unfrequented Vault appear'd,
And superstitions vainly fear'd. 260
The *Relicks false* were set to view;
Only the Jewels there were true.
But truly bright and holy *Thwaites*
That weeping at the *Altar* waites.

But the glad Youth away her bears, 265
And to the *Nuns* bequeaths her Tears:
Who guiltily their Prize bemoan,
Like Gipsies that a Child hath stoln.
Thenceforth (as when th'Inchantment ends
The Castle vanishes or rends) 270
The wasting Cloister with the rest
Was in one instant dispossest.

At the demolishing, this Seat
To *Fairfax* fell as by Escheat.
And what both *Nuns* and *Founders* will'd 275
'Tis likely better thus fulfill'd.
For if the *Virgin* prov'd not theirs,
The *Cloyster* yet remained hers.
Though many a *Nun* there made her Vow,
'Twas no *Religious House* till now. 280

From that blest Bed the *Heroe* came,
Whom *France* and *Poland* yet does fame:
Who, when retired here to Peace,
His warlike Studies could not cease;
But laid these Gardens out in sport   285
In the just Figure of a Fort;
And with five Bastions it did fence,
As aiming one for ev'ry Sense.

When in the *East* the Morning Ray
Hangs out the Colours of the Day,   290
The Bee through these known Allies hums,
Beating the *Dian* with its *Drumms*.
Then Flow'rs their drowsie Eylids raise,
Their Silken Ensigns each displayes,
And dries its Pan yet dank with Dew,   295
And fills its Flask with Odours new.

These, as their *Governour* goes by,
In fragrant Vollyes they let fly;
And to salute their *Governess*
Again as great a charge they press: 300
None for the *Virgin Nymph*; for She
Seems with the Flow'rs a Flow'r to be.
And think so still! though not compare
With Breath so sweet, or Cheek so faire.

Well shot ye Firemen! Oh how sweet,   305
And round your equal Fires do meet;
Whose shrill report no Ear can tell,
But Ecchoes to the Eye and smell.
See how the Flow'rs, as at *Parade*,
Under their *Colours* stand displaid: 310
Each *Regiment* in order grows,
That of the Tulip Pinke and Rose.

But when the vigilant *Patroul*
Of Stars walks round about the *Pole*,
Their Leaves, that to the stalks are curl'd,   315
Seem to their Staves the *Ensigns* furl'd.

Then in some Flow'rs beloved Hut
Each Bee as Sentinel is shut;
And sleeps so too: but, if once stir'd,
She runs you through, or askes *the Word*.   320

Oh Thou, that dear and happy Isle
The Garden of the World ere while,
Thou *Paradise* of four Seas,
Which *Heaven* planted us to please,
But, to exclude the World, did guard   325
With watry if not flaming Sword;
What luckless Apple did we tast,
To make us Mortal, and The Wast?

Unhappy! shall we never more
That sweet *Militia* restore,   330
When Gardens only had their Towrs,
And all the Garrisons were Flowrs,
When Roses only Arms might bear,
And Men did rosie Garlands wear?
Tulips, in several Colours barr'd,   335
Were then the *Switzers* of our *Guard*.

The *Gardiner* had the *Souldiers* place,
And his more gentle Forts did trace.
The Nursery of all things green
Was then the only *Magazeen*.   340
The *Winter Quarters* were the Stoves,
Where he the tender Plants removes.
But War all this doth overgrow:
We Ord'nance Plant and Powder sow.

And yet their walks one on the Sod   345
Who, had it pleased him and *God*,
Might once have made our Gardens spring
Fresh as his own and flourishing.
But he preferr'd to the *Cinque Ports*
These five imaginary Forts: 350
And, in those half-dry Trenches, spann'd
Pow'r which the Ocean might command.

For he did, with his utmost Skill,
Ambition weed, but *Conscience* till.
Conscience, that Heaven-nursed Plant,　　　355
Which most our Earthly Gardens want.
A prickling leaf it bears, and such
As that which shrinks at ev'ry touch;
But Flowrs eternal, and divine,
That in the Crowns of Saints do shine.　　　360

The sight does from these *Bastions* ply,
Th' invisible *Artilery*;
And at proud *Cawood Castle* seems
To point the *Battery* of its Beams.
As if it quarrell'd in the Seat　　　365
Th' Ambition of its *Prelate* great.
But ore the Meads below it plays,
Or innocently seems to gaze.

And now to the Abbyss I pass
Of that unfathomable Grass,　　　370
Where Men like Grashoppers appear,
But Grashoppers are Gyants there:
They, in there squeking Laugh, contemn
Us as we walk more low then them:
And, from the Precipices tall　　　375
Of the green spir's, to us do call.

To see Men through this Meadow Dive,
We wonder how they rise alive.
As, under Water, none does know
Whether he fall through it or go.　　　380
But, as the Marriners that sound,
And show upon their Lead the Ground,
They bring up Flow'rs so to be seen,
And prove they've at the Bottom been.

No Scene that turns with Engines strange　　　385
Does oftner then these Meadows change.
For when the Sun the Grass hath vext,
The tawny Mowers enter next;

Who seem like *Israalites* to be,
Walking on foot through a green Sea.   39
To them the Grassy Deeps divide,
And crowd a Lane to either Side.

With whistling Sithe, and Elbow strong,
These Massacre the Grass along:
While one, unknowing, carves the *Rail*,   39
Whose yet unfeather'd Quils her fail.
The Edge all bloody from its Breast
He draws, and does his stroke detest;
Fearing the Flesh untimely mow'd
To him a Fate as black forebode.   40

But bloody *Thestylis*, that waites
To bring the mowing Camp their Cates,
Greedy as Kites has trust it up,
And forthwith means on it to sup:
When on another quick She lights,   40
And cryes, he call'd us *Israelites*;
But now, to make his saying true,
Rails rain for Quails, for Manna Dew.

Unhappy Birds! what does it boot
To build below the Grasses Root;   41
When Lowness is unsafe as Hight,
And Chance o'retakes what scapeth spight?
And now your Orphan Parents Call
Sounds your untimely Funeral.
Death-Trumpets creak in such a Note,   41
And 'tis the *Sourdine* in their Throat.

Or sooner hatch or higher build:
The Mower now commands the Field;
In whose new Traverse seemeth wrought
A Camp of Battail newly fought: 42
Where, as the Meads with Hay, the Plain
Lyes quilted ore with Bodies slain:
The Women that with forks it fling,
Do represent the Pillaging.

And now the careless Victors play, 425
Dancing the Triumphs of the Hay;
Where every Mowers wholesome Heat
Smells like an *Alexanders sweat*.
Their Females fragrant as the Mead
Which they in *Fairy Circles* tread: 430
When at their Dances End they kiss,
Their new-made Hay not sweeter is.

When after this 'tis pil'd in Cocks,
Like a calm Sea it shews the Rocks:
We wondring in the River near 435
How Boats among them safely steer.
Or, like the *Desert Memphis Sand,*
Short *Pyramids* of Hay do stand.
And such the *Roman Camps* do rise
In Hills for Soldiers Obsequies. 440

This *Scene* again withdrawing brings
A new and empty Face of things;
A levell'd space, as smooth and plain,
As Clothes for *Lilly* strecht to stain.
The World when first created sure 445
Was such a Table rase and pure.
Or rather such is the *Toril*
Ere the Bulls enter at Madril.

For to this naked equal Flat,
Which *Levellers* take Pattern at, 450
The Villagers in common chase
Their Cattle, which it closer rase;
And what below the Sith increast
Is pincht yet nearer by the Beast.
Such, in the painted World, appear'd 455
Davenant with th' Universal Heard.

They seem within the polisht Grass
A Landskip drawen in Looking-Glass.
And shrunk in the huge Pasture show
As Spots, so shap'd, on Faces do. 460

Such Fleas, ere they approach the Eye,
In Multiplying Glasses lye.
They feed so wide, so slowly move,
As *Constellations* do above.

Then, to conclude these pleasant Acts,   465
Denton sets ope its *Cataracts*;
And makes the Meadow truly be
(What it but seem'd before) a Sea.
For, jealous of its *Lords* long stay,
It try's t'invite him thus away.   470
The River in it self is drown'd,
And Isl's th' astonish'd Cattle round.

Let others tell the *Paradox*,
How Eels now bellow in the Ox;
How Horses at their Tails do kick,   475
Turn'd as they hang to Leeches quick;
How Boats can over Bridges sail;
And Fishes do the Stables scale.
How *Salmons* trespassing are found;
And Pikes are taken in the Pound.   480

But I, retiring from the Flood,
Take Sanctuary in the Wood;
And, while it lasts, my self imbark
In this yet green, yet growing Ark;
Where the first Carpenter might best   485
Fit Timber for his Keel have Prest.
And where all Creatures might have shares,
Although in Armies, not in Paires.

The double Wood of ancient Stocks
Link'd in so thick, an Union locks,   490
It like two *Pedigrees* appears,
On one hand *Fairfax*, th' other *Veres*:
Of whom though many fell in War,
Yet more to Heaven shooting are:
And, as they Natures Cradle deckt,   495
Will in green Age her Hearse expect.

When first the Eye this Forrest sees
It seems indeed as *Wood* not *Trees*:
As if their Neighbourhood so old
To one great Trunk them all did mold. 500
There the huge Bulk takes place, as ment
To thrust up a *Fifth Element*;
And stretches still so closely wedg'd
As if the Night within were hedg'd.

Dark all without it knits; within 505
It opens passable and thin;
And in as loose an order grows,
As the *Corinthean Porticoes*.
The arching Boughs unite between
The Columnes of the Temple green; 510
And underneath the winged Quires
Echo about their tuned Fires.

The *Nightingale* does here make choice
To sing the Tryals of her Voice.
Low Shrubs she sits in, and adorns 515
With Musick high the squatted Thorns.
But highest Oakes stoop down to hear,
And listning Elders prick the Ear.
The Thorn, lest it should hurt her, draws
Within the Skin its shrunken claws. 520

But I have for my Musick found
A Sadder, yet more pleasing Sound:
The *Stock-doves*, whose fair necks are grac'd
With Nuptial Rings their Ensigns chast;
Yet always, for some Cause unknown, 525
Sad pair unto the Elms they moan.
O why should such a Couple mourn,
That in so equal Flames do burn!

Then as I carless on the Bed
Of gelid *Straw-berryes* do tread, 530
And through the Hazles thick espy
The hatching *Thrastles* shining Eye,

The *Heron* from the Ashes top,
The eldest of its young lets drop,
As if it Stork-like did pretend   53.
That *Tribute* to *its Lord* to send.

But most the *Hewel's* wonders are,
Who here has the *Holt-felsters* care.
He walks still upright from the Root,
Meas'ring the Timber with his Foot;   54(
And all the way, to keep it clean,
Doth from the Bark the Wood-moths glean.
He, with his Beak, examines well
Which fit to stand and which to fell.

The good he numbers up, and hacks;   54!
As if he mark'd them with the Ax.
But where he, tinkling with his Beak,
Does find the hollow Oak to speak,
That for his building he designs,
And through the tainted Side he mines.   55(
Who could have thought the *tallest Oak*
Should fall by such a *feeble Strok'*!

Nor would it, had the Tree not fed
A *Traitor-worm,* within it bred.
(As first our *Flesh* corrupt within   55!
Tempts impotent and bashful *Sin.*
And yet that *Worm* triumphs not long,
But serves to feed the *Hewels young.*
While the Oake seems to fall content,
Viewing the Treason's Punishment.   56(

Thus I, *easie Philosopher,*
Among the *Birds* and *Trees* confer:
And little now to make me, wants
Or of the *Fowles,* or of the *Plants.*
Give me but Wings as they, and I   56!
Streight floting on the Air shall fly:
Or turn me but, and you shall see
I was but an inverted Tree.

Already I begin to call
In their most learned Original: 570
And where I Language want, my Signs
The Bird upon the Bough divines;
And more attentive there doth sit
Then if She were with Lime-twigs knit.
No Leaf does tremble in the Wind   575
Which I returning cannot find.

Out of these scatter'd *Sibyls* Leaves
Strange *Prophecies* my Phancy weaves:
And in one History consumes,
Like *Mexique Paintings*, all the *Plumes*.   580
What *Rome, Greece, Palestine*, ere said
I in this light *Mosaick* read.
Thrice happy he who, not mistook,
Hath read in *Natures mystick Book*.

And see how Chance's better Wit   585
Could with a Mask my studies hit!
The Oak-Leaves me embroyder all,
Between which Caterpillars crawl:
And Ivy, with familiar trails,
Me licks, and clasps, and curles, and hales.   590
Under this *antick Cope* I move
Like some great *Prelate of the Grove*,

Then, languishing with ease, I toss
On Pallets swoln of Velvet Moss;
While the Wind, cooling through the Boughs,   595
Flatters with Air my panting Brows.
Thanks for my Rest ye *Mossy Banks*,
And unto you *cool Zephyr's* Thanks,
Who, as my Hair, my Thoughts too shed,
And winnow from the Chaff my Head.   600

How safe, methinks, and strong, behind
These Trees have I incamp'd my Mind;
Where Beauty, aiming at the Heart,
Bends in some Tree its useless Dart;

And where the World no certain Shot   605
Can make, or me it toucheth not.
But I on it securely play,
And gaul its Horsemen all the Day.

Bind me ye *Woodbines* in your 'twines,
Curle me about ye gadding *Vines*,   610
And Oh so close your Circles lace,
That I may never leave this Place:
But, lest your Fetters prove too weak,
Ere I your Silken Bondage break,
Do you, *O Brambles*, chain me too,   615
And courteous *Briars* nail me through.

Here in the Morning tye my Chain,
Where the two Woods have made a Lane;
While, like a *Guard* on either side,
The Trees before their *Lord* divide;   620
This, like a long and equal Thread,
Betwixt two *Labyrinths* does lead.
But, where the Floods did lately drown,
There at the Ev'ning stake me down.

For now the Waves are fal'n and dry'd,   625
And now the Meadows fresher dy'd;
Whose Grass, with moister colour dasht,
Seems as green Silks but newly washt.
No *Serpent* new nor *Crocodile*
Remains behind our little *Nile*;   630
Unless it self you will mistake,
Among these Meads the only Snake.

See in what wanton harmless folds
It ev'ry where the Meadow holds;
And its yet muddy back doth lick,   635
Till as a *Chrystal Mirrour* slick;
Where all things gaze themselves, and doubt
If they be in it or without.
And for his shade which therein shines,
Narcissus like, the *Sun* too pines.   640

Oh what a Pleasure 'tis to hedge
My Temples here with heavy sedge;
Abandoning my lazy Side,
Stretcht as a Bank unto the Tide;
Or to suspend my sliding Foot 645
On the Osiers undermined Root,
And in its Branches tough to hang,
While at my Lines the Fishes twang!

But now away my Hooks, my Quills,
And Angles, idle Utensils. 650
The *young Maria* walks to night:
Hide trifling Youth thy Pleasures slight.
'Twere shame that such judicious Eyes
Should with such Toyes a Man surprize;
She that already is the *Law* 655
Of all her *Sex*, her *Ages Aw*.

See how loose Nature, in respect
To her, it self doth recollect;
And every thing so whisht and fine,
Starts forth with to its *Bonne Mine*. 660
The *Sun* himself, of *Her* aware,
Seems to descend with greater Care;
And lest *She* see him go to Bed;
In blushing Clouds conceales his Head.

So when the Shadows laid asleep 665
From underneath these Banks do creep,
And on the River as it flows
With *Eben Shuts* begin to close;
The modest *Halcyon* comes in sight,
Flying betwixt the Day and Night; 670
And such an horror calm and dumb,
Admiring Nature does benum.

The viscous Air, wheres'ere She fly,
Follows and sucks her Azure dy;
The gellying Stream compacts below, 675
If it might fix her shadow so;

The stupid Fishes hang, as plain
As *Flies* in *Chrystal* overt'ane;
And Men the silent *Scene* assist,
Charm'd with the *Saphir-winged Mist*.   68

Maria such, and so doth hush
The *World*, and through the *Ev'ning* rush.
No new-born *Comet* such a Train
Draws through the Skie, nor Star new-slain.
For streight those giddy Rockets fail,   68
Which from the putrid Earth exhale,
But by her *Flames*, in *Heaven* try'd,
Nature is wholly *vitrifi'd*.

'Tis *She* that to these Gardens gave
That wondrous Beauty which they have;   69
She streightness on the Woods bestows;
To *Her* the Meadow sweetness owes;
Nothing could make the River be
So Chrystal-pure but only *She*;
She yet more Pure, Sweet, Streight, and Fair,   69
Then Gardens, Woods, Meads, Rivers are.

Therefore what first *She* on them spent,
They gratefully again present.
The Meadow Carpets where to tread;
The Garden Flow'rs to Crown *Her* Head;   70
And for a Glass the limpid Brook,
Where *She* may all *her* Beautyes look;
But, since *She* would not have them seen,
The Wood about *her* draws a Skreen.

For *She*, to higher Beauties rais'd,   70
Disdains to be for lesser prais'd.
She counts her Beauty to converse
In all the Languages as *hers*;
Nor yet in those *her self* imployes
But for the *Wisdome*, not the *Noyse*;   71
Nor yet that *Wisdome* would affect,
But as 'tis *Heavens Dialect*.

Blest Nymph! that couldst so soon prevent
Those *Trains* by Youth against thee meant;
Tears (watry Shot that pierce the Mind;)   715
And *Sighs* (Loves Cannon charg'd with Wind;)
True Praise (That breaks through all defence;)
And *feign'd complying Innocence;*
But knowing where this *Ambush* lay,
She scap'd the safe, but roughest Way.   720

This 'tis to have been from the first
In a *Domestick Heaven* nurst,
Under the *Discipline* severe
Of *Fairfax,* and the starry *Vere;*
Where not one object can come nigh   725
But pure, and spotless as the Eye;
And *Goodness* doth it self intail
On *Females,* if there want a *Male.*

Go now fond Sex that on your Face
Do all your useless Study place,   730
Nor once at Vice your Brows dare knit
Lest the smooth Forehead wrinkled sit:
Yet your own Face shall at you grin,
Thorough the Black-bag of your Skin;
When *knowledge* only could have fill'd   735
And *Virtue* all those *Furrows till'd.*

Hence *She* with Graces more divine
Supplies beyond her *Sex* the *Line;*
And, like a *sprig of Misleto,*
On the *Fairfacian Oak* does grow;   740
Whence, for some universal good,
The *Priest* shall cut the sacred Bud;
While her *glad Parents* most rejoice,
And make their *Destiny* their *Choice.*

Mean time ye Fields, Springs, Bushes, Flow'rs,   745
Where yet She leads her studious Hours,
(Till Fate her worthily translates,
And find a *Fairfax* for our *Thwaites)*

Employ the means you have by Her,
And in your kind your selves preferr; 750
That, as all *Virgins* She preceds,
So you all *Woods, Streams, Gardens, Meads.*

For you *Thessalian Tempe's Seat*
Shall now be scorn'd as obsolete;
Aranjuez, as less, disdain'd; 755
The *Bel-Retiro* as constrain'd;
But name not the *Idalian Grove,*
For 'twas the Seat of wanton Love;
Much less the Dead's *Elysian Fields,*
Yet nor to them your Beauty yields. 760

'Tis not, what once it was, the *World*;
But a rude heap together hurl'd;
All negligently overthrown,
Gulfes, Deserts, Precipices, Stone.
Your lesser *World* contains the same. 765
But in more decent Order tame;
You Heaven's Center, Nature's Lap.
And Paradice's only Map.

But now the *Salmon-Fishers* moist
Their *Leathern Boats* begin to hoist; 770
And, like *Antipodes* in Shoes,
Have shod their *Heads* in their *Canoos.*
How *Tortoise like,* but not so slow,
These rational *Amphibii* go?
Let 's in: for the dark *Hemisphere* 775
Does now like one of them appear.

Fleckno, *an English Priest at* Rome

Oblig'd by frequent visits of this man,
Whom as Priest, Poet, and Musician,
I for some branch of *Melchizedeck* took,
(Though he derives himself from *my Lord Brooke*)
I sought his Lodging; which is at the Sign 5
Of the sad *Pelican*; Subject divine

For Poetry: There three Stair-Cases high,
Which signifies his triple property,
I found at last a Chamber, as 'twas said,
But seem'd a Coffin set on the Stairs head.   10
Not higher then Seav'n, nor larger then three feet;
Only there was nor Seeling, nor a Sheet,
Save that th' ingenious Door did as you come
Turn in, and shew to Wainscot half the Room.
Yet of his State no man could have complain'd;   15
There being no Bed where he entertain'd:
And though within one Cell so narrow pent,
He'd *Stanza's* for a whole Appartement.
    Straight without further information,
In hideous verse, he, and a dismal tone,   20
Begins to exercise; as if I were
Possest; and sure the *Devil* brought me there.
But I, who now imagin'd my self brought
To my last Tryal, in a serious thought
Calm'd the disorders of my youthful Breast,   25
And to my Martyrdom prepared Rest.
Only this frail Ambition did remain,
The last distemper of the sober Brain,
That there had been some present to assure
The future Ages how I did indure: 30
And how I, silent, turn'd my burning Ear
Towards the Verse; and when that could not hear,
Held him the other; and unchanged yet,
Ask'd still for more, and pray'd him to repeat:
Till the Tyrant, weary to persecute,   35
Left off, and try'd t' allure me with his Lute.
    Now as two Instruments, to the same key
Being tun'd by Art, if the one touched be
The other opposite as soon replies,
Mov'd by the Air and hidden Sympathies;   40
So while he with his gouty Fingers craules
Over the Lute, his murmuring Belly calls,
Whose hungry Guts to the same streightness twin'd
In Echo to the trembling Strings repin'd.
    I, that perceiv'd now what his Musick ment,   45
Ask'd civilly if he had eat this Lent.

He answered yes; with such, and such an one.
For he has this of gen'rous, that alone
He never feeds; save only when he tryes
With gristly Tongue to dart the passing Flyes.   50
I ask'd if he eat flesh. And he, that was
So hungry that though ready to say *Mass*
Would break his fast before, said he was Sick,
And th' *Ordinance* was only Politick.
Nor was I longer to invite him Scant: 55
Happy at once to make him Protestant,
And Silent. Nothing now Dinner stay'd
But till he had himself a Body made.
I mean till he were drest: for else so thin
He stands, as if he only fed had been   60
With consecrated Wafers: and the *Host*
Hath sure more flesh and blood then he can boast.
This *Basso Relievo* of a Man,
Who as a Camel tall, yet easly can
The Needles Eye thread without any stich,   65
(His only impossible is to be rich)
Lest his too suttle Body, growing rare,
Should leave his Soul to wander in the Air,
He therefore circumscribes himself in rimes;
And swaddled in's own papers seaven times,   70
Wears a close Jacket of poetick Buff,
With which he doth his third Dimension Stuff.
Thus armed underneath, he over all
Does make a primitive *Sotana* fall;
And above that yet casts an antick Cloak,   75
Worn at the first Counsel of *Antioch*;
Which by the *Jews* long hid, and Disesteem'd,
He heard of by Tradition, and redeem'd.
But were he not in this black habit deck't,
This half transparent Man would soon reflect   80
Each colour that he past by; and be seen,
As the *Chamelion,* yellow, blew, or green.
   He drest, and ready to disfurnish now
His Chamber, whose compactness did allow
No empty place for complementing doubt,   85
But who came last is forc'd first to go out;

I meet one on the Stairs who made me stand,
Stopping the passage, and did him demand:
I answer'd he is here *Sir*; but you see
You cannot pass to him but thorow me.   90
He thought himself affronted; and reply'd,
I whom the Pallace never has deny'd
Will make the way here; I said *Sir* you'l do
Me a great favour, for I seek to go.
He gathring fury still made sign to draw;   95
But himself there clos'd in a Scabbard saw
As narrow as his Sword's; and I, that was
Delightful, said there can no Body pass
Except by penetration hither, where
Two make a crowd, nor can three Persons here   100
Consist but in one substance. Then, to fit
Our peace, the Priest said I too had some wit:
To prov't, I said, the place doth us invite
By its own narrowness, Sir, to unite.
He ask'd me pardon; and to make me way   105
Went down, as I him follow'd to obey.
But the propitiatory Priest had straight
Oblig'd us, when below, to celebrate
Together our attonement: so increas'd
Betwixt us two the Dinner to a Feast.   110
    Let it suffice that we could eat in peace;
And that both Poems did and Quarrels cease
During the Table; though my new made Friend
Did, as he threatned, ere 'twere long intend
To be both witty and valiant: I loth,   115
Said 'twas too late, he was already both.
    But now, Alas, my first Tormentor came,
Who satisfy'd with eating, but not tame
Turns to recite; though Judges most severe
After th'Assizes dinner mild appear,   120
And on full stomach do condemn but few:
Yet he more strict my sentence doth renew;
And draws out of the black box of his Breast
Ten quire of paper in which he was drest.
Yet that which was a greater cruelty   125
Then *Nero*'s Poem he calls charity:

And so the *Pelican* at his door hung
Picks out the tender bosome to its young.
   Of all his Poems there he stands ungirt
Save only two foul copies for his shirt: 130
Yet these he promises as soon as clean.
But how I loath'd to see my Neighbour glean
Those papers, which he pilled from within
Like white fleaks rising from a Leaper's skin!
More odious then those raggs which the *French* youth   135
At ordinaries after dinner show'th,
When they compare their *Chancres* and *Poulains*.
Yet he first kist them, and after takes pains
To read; and then, because he understood
Not one Word, thought and swore that they were good. 140
But all his praises could not now appease
The provok't Author, whom it did displease
To hear his Verses, by so just a curse
That were ill made condemn'd to be read worse:
And how (impossible) he made yet more   145
Absurdityes in them then were before.
For he his untun'd voice did fall or raise
As a deaf Man upon a Viol playes,
Making the half points and the periods run
Confus'der then the atomes in the Sun.   150
Thereat the Poet swell'd, with anger full,
And roar'd out, like *Perillus* in's own *Bull*;
Sir you read false. That any one but you
Should know the contrary. Whereat, I, now
Made Mediator, in my room, said, Why?   155
To say that you read false *Sir* is no Lye.
Thereat the waxen Youth relented straight;
But saw with sad dispair that 'twas too late.
For the disdainful Poet was retir'd
Home, his most furious Satyr to have fir'd   160
Against the Rebel; who, at this struck dead,
Wept bitterly as disinherited.
Who should commend his Mistress now? Or who
Praise him? both difficult indeed to do
With truth. I counsell'd him to go in time,   165
Ere the fierce Poets anger turn'd to rime.

He hasted; and I, finding my self free,
As one scap't strangely from Captivity,
Have made the Chance be painted; and go now
To hang it in *Saint Peter's* for a Vow.   170

An Horatian *Ode upon* Cromwel's *Return from* Ireland

The forward Youth that would appear
Must now forsake his *Muses* dear,
    Nor in the Shadows sing
    His Numbers languishing.
'Tis time to leave the Books in dust,   5
And oyl th' unused Armours rust:
    Removing from the Wall
    The Corslet of the Hall.
So restless *Cromwel* could not cease
In the inglorious Arts of Peace,   10
    But through adventrous War
    Urged his active Star.
And, like the three-fork'd Lightning, first
Breaking the Clouds where it was nurst,
    Did thorough his own Side   15
    His fiery way divide.
For 'tis all one to Courage high
The Emulous or Enemy;
    And with such to inclose
    Is more then to oppose.   20
Then burning through the Air he went,
And Pallaces and Temples rent:
    And *Cæsars* head at last
    Did through his Laurels blast.
'Tis Madness to resist or blame   25
The force of angry Heavens flame:
    And, if we would speak true,
    Much to the Man is due.
Who, from his private Gardens, where
He liv'd reserved and austere,   30
    As if his highest plot
    To plant the Bergamot,

Could by industrious Valour climbe
To ruine the great Work of Time,
    And cast the Kingdome old   35
    Into another Mold.
Though Justice against Fate complain,
And plead the antient Rights in vain:
    But those do hold or break
    As Men are strong or weak.   40
Nature that hateth emptiness,
Allows of penetration less:
    And therefore must make room
    Where greater Spirits come.
What Field of all the Civil Wars,   45
Where his were not the deepest Scars?
    And *Hampton* shows what part
    He had of wiser Art.
Where, twining subtile fears with hope,
He wove a Net of such a scope,   50
    That *Charles* himself might chase
    To *Caresbrooks* narrow case.
That thence the *Royal Actor* born
The *Tragick Scaffold* might adorn:
    While round the armed Bands   55
    Did clap their bloody hands.
He nothing common did or mean
Upon that memorable Scene:
    But with his keener Eye
    The Axes edge did try: 60
Nor call'd the *Gods* with vulgar spight
To vindicate his helpless Right,
    But bow'd his comely Head,
    Down as upon a Bed.
This was that memorable Hour   65
Which first assur'd the forced Pow'r.
    So when they did design
    The *Capitols* first Line,
A bleeding Head where they begun,
Did fright the Architects to run;   70
    And yet in that the *State*
    Foresaw it's happy Fate.

And now the *Irish* are asham'd
To see themselves in one Year tam'd:
   So much one Man can do, 75
    That does both act and know.
They can affirm his Praises best,
And have, though overcome, confest
   How good he is, how just,
    And fit for highest Trust: 80
Nor yet grown stiffer with Command,
But still in the *Republick's* hand:
   How fit he is to sway
    That can so well obey.
He to the *Commons Feet* presents 85
A *Kingdome*, for his first years rents:
   And, what he may, forbears
    His Fame to make it theirs:
And has his Sword and Spoyls ungirt,
To lay them at the *Publick's* skirt. 90
   So when the Falcon high
    Falls heavy from the Sky,
She, having kill'd, no more does search,
But on the next green Bow to pearch;
   Where, when he first does lure, 95
    The Falckner has her sure.
What may not then our *Isle* presume
While Victory his Crest does plume!
   What may not others fear
    If thus he crown each Year! 100
A *Cæsar* he ere long to *Gaul*,
To *Italy* an *Hannibal*,
   And to all States not free
    Shall *Clymacterick* be.
The *Pict* no shelter now shall find 105
Within his party-colour'd Mind;
   But from this Valour sad
    Shrink underneath the Plad:
Happy if in the tufted brake
The *English Hunter* him mistake; 110
   Nor lay his Hounds in near
    The *Caledonian* Deer.

But thou the Wars and Fortunes Son
March indefatigably on;
   And for the last effect 115
   Still keep thy Sword erect:
Besides the force it has to fright
The Spirits of the shady Night,
   The same *Arts* that did *gain*
   A *Pow'r* must it *maintain*. 120

Tom May's Death

As one put drunk into the Packet-boat,
Tom May was hurry'd hence and did not know't.
But was amaz'd on the Elysian side,
And with an Eye uncertain, gazing wide,
Could not determine in what place he was, 5
For whence in Stevens ally Trees or Grass?
Nor where the Popes head, nor the Mitre lay,
Signs by which still he found and lost his way.
At last while doubtfully he all compares,
He saw near hand, as he imagin'd *Ares*. 10
Such did he seem for corpulence and port,
But 'twas a man much of another sort;
'Twas *Ben* that in the dusky Laurel shade
Amongst the Chorus of old Poets laid,
Sounding of ancient Heroes, such as were 15
The Subjects Safety, and the Rebel's Fear.
But how a double headed Vulture Eats,
Brutus and *Cassius* the Peoples cheats.
But seeing *May* he varied streight his Song,
Gently to signifie that he was wrong. 20
Cups more then civil of *Emathian* wine,
I sing (said he) and the *Pharsalian* Sign,
Where the Historian of the Common-wealth
In his own Bowels sheath'd the conquering health.
By this *May* to himself and them was come, 25
He found he was translated, and by whom.
Yet then with foot as stumbling as his tongue
Prest for his place among the Learned throng.

But *Ben,* who knew not neither foe nor friend,
Sworn Enemy to all that do pretend,   30
Rose more then ever he was seen severe,
Shook his gray locks, and his own Bayes did tear
At this intrusion. Then with Laurel wand,
The awful Sign of his supream command.
At whose dread Whisk *Virgil* himself does quake,   35
And *Horace* patiently its stroke does take,
As he crowds in he whipt him ore the pate
Like *Pembroke* at the Masque, and then did rate.
　　Far from these blessed shades tread back agen
Most servil' wit, and Mercenary Pen.   40
Polydore, Lucan, Allan, Vandale, Goth,
Malignant Poet and Historian both.
Go seek the novice Statesmen, and obtrude
On them some Romane cast similitude,
Tell them of Liberty, the Stories fine,   45
Until you all grow Consuls in your wine.
Or thou *Dictator* of the glass bestow
On him the *Cato,* this the *Cicero.*
Transferring old *Rome* hither in your talk,
As *Bethlem's* House did to *Loretto* walk.   50
Foul Architect that hadst not Eye to see
How ill the measures of these States agree.
And who by *Romes* example *England* lay,
Those but to *Lucan* do continue *May.*
But the nor Ignorance nor seeming good   55
Misled, but malice fixt and understood.
Because some one than thee more worthy weares
The sacred Laurel, hence are all these teares?
Must therefore all the World be set on flame,
Because a Gazet writer mist his aim?   60
And for a Tankard-bearing Muse must we
As for the Basket *Guelphs* and *Gibellines* be?
When the Sword glitters ore the Judges head,
And fear has Coward Churchmen silenced,
Then is the Poets time, 'tis then he drawes,   65
And single fights forsaken Vertues cause.
He, when the wheel of Empire, whirleth back,
And though the World's disjointed Axel crack,

Sings still of ancient Rights and better Times,
Seeks wretched good, arraigns successful Crimes.   70
But thou base man first prostituted hast
Our spotless knowledge and the studies chast.
Apostatizing from our Arts and us,
To turn the Chronicler to *Spartacus*.
Yet wast thou taken hence with equal fate,   75
Before thou couldst great *Charles* his death relate.
But what will deeper wound thy little mind,
Hast left surviving *Davenant* still behind
Who laughs to see in this thy death renew'd,
Right Romane poverty and gratitude.   80
Poor Poet thou, and grateful Senate they,
Who thy last Reckoning did so largely pay.
And with the publick gravity would come,
When thou hadst drunk thy last to lead thee home.
If that can be thy home where *Spencer* lyes   85
And reverend *Chaucer*, but their dust does rise
Against thee, and expels thee from their side,
As th' Eagles Plumes from other birds divide.
Nor here thy shade must dwell, Return, Return,
Where Sulphrey *Phlegeton* does ever burn.   90
The *Cerberus* with all his Jawes shall gnash,
Megœra thee with all her Serpents lash.
Thou rivited unto *Ixion's* wheel
Shalt break, and the perpetual Vulture feel.
'Tis just what Torments Poets ere did feign,   95
Thou first Historically shouldst sustain.
    Thus by irrevocable Sentence cast,
    May only Master of these Revels past.
    And streight he vanisht in a Cloud of pitch,
    Such as unto the Sabboth bears the Witch.   100

To his worthy Friend Doctor Witty upon his Translation of the Popular Errors

Sit further, and make room for thine own fame,
Where just desert enrolles thy honour'd Name

The good Interpreter. Some in this task
Take off the Cypress vail, but leave a mask,
Changing the Latine, but do more obscure   5
That sence in *English* which was bright and pure.
So of Translators they are Authors grown,
For ill Translators make the Book their own.
Others do strive with words and forced phrase
To add such lustre, and so many rayes,   10
That but to make the Vessel shining, they
Much of the precious Metal rub away.
He is Translations thief that addeth more,
As much as he that taketh from the Store
Of the first Author. Here he maketh blots   15
That mends; and added beauties are but spots.
    Cælia whose English doth more richly flow
Then *Tagus*, purer then dissolved snow,
And sweet as are her lips that speak it, she
Now learns the tongues of *France* and *Italy*;   20
But she is *Cælia* still: no other grace
But her own smiles commend that lovely face;
Her native beauty's not Italianated,
Nor her chast mind into the *French* translated:
Her thoughts are *English*, though her sparkling wit   25
With other Language doth them fitly fit.
    Translators learn of her: but stay I slide
Down into Error with the Vulgar tide;
Women must not teach here: the Doctor doth
Stint them to Cawdles, Almond-milk, and Broth.   30
Now I reform, and surely so will all
Whose happy Eyes on thy Translation fall,
I see the people hastning to thy Book,
Liking themselves the worse the more they look,
And so disliking, that they nothing see   35
Now worth the liking, but thy Book and thee.
And (if I Judgment have) I censure right;
For something guides my hand that I must write.
You have Translations statutes best fulfil'd.
That handling neither sully nor would guild.   40

The Character of Holland

Holland, that scarce deserves the name of *Land,*
As but th'Off-scouring of the *Brittish Sand*;
And so much Earth as was contributed
By *English Pilots* when they heav'd the Lead;
Or what by th' Oceans slow alluvion fell,   5
Of shipwrackt Cockle and the Muscle-shell;
This indigested vomit of the Sea
Fell to the *Dutch* by just Propriety.

    Glad then, as Miners that have found the Oar,
They with mad labour fish'd the *Land* to S*hoar*;   10
And div'd as desperately for each piece
Of Earth, as if't had been of *Ambergreece,*
Collecting anxiously small Loads of Clay,
Less then what building Swallows bear away;
Or then those Pills which sordid Beetles roul,   15
Tranfusing into them their Dunghil Soul.

    How did they rivet, with Gigantick Piles,
Thorough the Center their new-catched Miles;
And to the stake a strugling Country bound,
Where barking Waves still bait the forced Ground;   20
Building their *watry Babel* far more high
To reach the *Sea,* then those to scale the *Sky.*

    Yet still his claim the Injur'd Ocean laid,
And oft at Leap-frog ore their Steeples plaid:
As if on purpose it on Land had come   25
To shew them what's their *Mare Liberum.*
A daily deluge over them does boyl;
The Earth and Water play at *Level-coyl*;
The Fish oft-times the Burger dispossest,
And sat not as a Meat but as a Guest;   30
And oft the *Tritons* and the *Sea-Nymphs* saw
Whole sholes of *Dutch* serv'd up for *Cabillau*;
Or as they over the new Level rang'd
For pickled *Herring,* pickled *Heeren* chang'd.
Nature, it seem'd, asham'd of her mistake,   35
Would throw their Land away at *Duck* and *Drake.*

    Therefore *Necessity,* that first made *Kings,*
Something like *Government* among them brings.

For as with *Pygmees* who best kills the *Crane*,
Among the *hungry* he that treasures *Grain*,   40
Among the *blind* the one-ey'd *blinkard* reigns,
So rules among the *drowned* he that *draines*.
Not who first see the *rising Sun* commands,
But who could first discern the *rising Lands*.
Who best could know to pump an Earth so leak   45
Him they their *Lord* and *Country's Father* speak.
To make a *Bank* was a great *Plot of State*;
Invent a *Shov'l* and be a *Magistrate*.
Hence some small *Dyke-grave* unperceiv'd invades
The *Pow'r*, and grows as 'twere a *King of Spades*.   50
But for less envy some *joynt States* endures,
Who look like a *Commission of the Sewers*.
For these *Half-anders*, half wet, and half dry,
Nor bear *strict service*, nor *pure Liberty*.
    'Tis probable *Religion* after this   55
Came next in order; which they could not miss.
How could the *Dutch* but be converted, when
Th' *Apostles* were so many Fishermen?
Besides the Waters of themselves did rise,
And, as their Land, so them did re-baptize.   60
Though *Herring* for their *God* few voices mist,
And *Poor-John* to have been th' *Evangelist*.
Faith, that could never Twins conceive before,
Never so fertile, spawn'd upon this shore:
More pregnant then their *Marg'ret*, that laid down   65
For *Hans-in-Kelder* of a whole *Hans-Town*.
    Sure when *Religion* did it self imbark,
And from the *East* would *Westward* steer its Ark,
It struck, and splitting on this unknown ground,
Each one thence pillag'd the first piece he found: 70
Hence *Amsterdam, Turk-Christian-Pagan-Jew*,
Staple of Sects and Mint of Schisme grew;
That *Bank of Conscience*, where not one so strange
Opinion but finds Credit, and Exchange.
In vain for *Catholicks* our selves we bear;   75
The *universal Church* is onely there.
Nor can Civility there want for *Tillage*,
Where wisely for their *Court* they chose a *Village*.

How fit a Title clothes their *Governours*,
Themselves the *Hogs* as all their Subjects *Bores*!   8
   Let it suffice to give their Country Fame
That it had one *Civilis* call'd by Name,
Some Fifteen hundred and more years ago;
But surely never any that was so.
   See but their *Mairmaids* with their *Tails of Fish*,   8
Reeking at *Church* over the *Chafing-Dish*.
A vestal Turf enshrin'd in Earthen Ware
Fumes through the loop-holes of a wooden Square.
Each to the *Temple* with these *Altars* tend,
But still does place it at her *Western End*:   9
While the fat steam of *Female Sacrifice*
Fills the *Priests Nostrils* and puts out his *Eyes*.
   Or what a Spectacle the *Skipper gross*,
A *Water-Hercules Butter-Coloss*,
Tunn'd up with all their sev'ral *Towns of Beer*;   9
When Stagg'ring upon some Land, *Snick and Sneer*,
They try, like Statuaries, if they can,
Cut out each others *Athos* to a Man:
And carve in their large Bodies, where they please,
The Armes of the *United Provinces*.   10
   But when such Amity at home is show'd;
What then are their confederacies abroad?
Let this one court'sie witness all the rest;
When their whole Navy they together prest,
Not Christian Captives to redeem from Bands: 105
Or intercept the Western golden Sands:
No, but all ancient Rights and Leagues must vail,
Rather then to the *English* strike their sail;
To whom their weather-beaten *Province* ows
It self, when as some greater Vessel tows   110
A Cock-boat tost with the same wind and fate;
We buoy'd so often up their *sinking State*.
   Was this *Jus Belli & Pacis*; could this be
Cause why their *Burgomaster of the Sea*
Ram'd with Gun-powder, flaming with Brand wine,   115
Should raging hold his Linstock to the Mine?
While, with feign'd *Treaties,* they invade by stealth
Our sore new circumcised *Common wealth*.

Yet of his vain Attempt no more he sees
Then of *Case-Butter* shot and *Bullet-Cheese*. 120
And the torn Navy stagger'd with him home,
While the Sea laught it self into a foam,
'Tis true since that (as fortune kindly sports,)
A wholesome Danger drove us to our Ports.
While half their banish'd keels the Tempest tost, 125
Half bound at home in Prison to the frost:
That ours mean time at leizure might careen,
In a calm Winter, under Skies Serene.
As the obsequious Air and Waters rest,
Till the dear *Halcyon* hatch out all its nest. 130
The *Common wealth* doth by its losses grow;
And, like its own Seas, only Ebbs to flow.
Besides that very Agitation laves,
And purges out the corruptible waves.

And now again our armed *Bucentore* 135
Doth yearly their *Sea-Nuptials* restore.
And now the *Hydra of seaven Provinces*
Is strangled by our *Infant Hercules*.
Their Tortoise wants its vainly stretched neck;
Their Navy all our Conquest or our Wreck: 140
Or, what is left, their *Carthage* overcome
Would render fain unto our better *Rome*.
Unless our *Senate*, lest their Youth disuse,
The War, (but who would) Peace if begg'd refuse.

For now of nothing may our *State* despair, 145
Darling of Heaven, and of Men the Care;
Provided that they be what they have been,
Watchful abroad, and honest still within.
For while our *Neptune* doth a *Trident* shake,
Steel'd with those piercing Heads, *Dean, Monck and Blake.*
And while *Jove* governs in the highest Sphere, [150
Vainly in *Hell* let *Pluto* domineer.

The First
Anniversary
Of the Government under O. C.

Like the vain Curlings of the Watry maze,
Which in smooth streams a sinking Weight does raise;
So Man, declining alwayes, disappears
In the weak Circles of increasing Years;
And his short Tumults of themselves Compose,   5
While flowing Time above his Head does close.
    Cromwell alone with greater Vigour runs,
(Sun-like) the Stages of succeeding Suns:
And still the Day which he doth next restore,
Is the just Wonder of the Day before.   10
Cromwell alone doth with new Lustre spring,
And shines the Jewel of the yearly Ring.
    'Tis he the force of scatter'd Time contracts,
And in one Year the work of Ages acts:
While heavy Monarchs make a wide Return,   15
Longer, and more Malignant then *Saturn*:
And though they all *Platonique* years should raign,
In the same Posture would be found again.
Their earthy Projects under ground they lay,
More slow and brittle then the *China* clay: 20
Well may they strive to leave them to their Son,
For one Thing never was by one King don.
Yet some more active for a Frontier Town
Took in by Proxie, beggs a false Renown;
Another triumphs at the publick Cost,   25
And will have Wonn, if he no more have Lost;
They fight by Others, but in Person wrong,
And only are against their Subjects strong;
Their other Wars seem but a feign'd contest,
This Common Enemy is still opprest;   30
If Conquerors, on them they turn their might;
If Conquered, on them they wreak their Spight:
They neither build the Temple in their dayes,
Nor Matter for succeeding Founders raise;
Nor sacred Prophecies consult within,   35
Much less themselves to perfect them begin;

No other care they bear of things above,
But with Astrologers divine, and *Jove,*
To know how long their Planet yet Reprives
From the deserved Fate their guilty lives: 40
Thus (Image-like) an useless time they tell,
And with vain Scepter, strike the hourly Bell;
No more contribute to the state of Things,
Then wooden Heads unto the Viols strings.

    While indefatigable *Cromwell* hyes,   45
And cuts his way still nearer to the Skyes,
Learning a Musique in the Region clear,
To tune this lower to that higher Sphere.

    So when *Amphion* did the Lute command,
Which the God gave him, with his gentle hand,   50
The rougher Stones, unto his Measures hew'd,
Dans'd up in order from the Quarreys rude;
This took a Lower, that an Higher place,
As he the Treble alter'd, or the Base:
No Note he struck, but a new Story lay'd,   55
And the great Work ascended while he play'd.

    The listning Structures he with Wonder ey'd,
And still new Stopps to various Time apply'd:
Now through the Strings a Martial rage he throws,
And joyning streight the *Theban* Tow'r arose;   60
Then as he strokes them with a Touch more sweet,
The flocking Marbles in a Palace meet;
But, for he most the graver Notes did try,
Therefore the Temples rear'd their Columns high:
Thus, ere he ceas'd, his sacred Lute creates   65
Th'harmonious City of the seven Gates.

    Such was that wondrous Order and Consent,
When *Cromwell* tun'd the ruling Instrument;
While tedious Statesmen many years did hack,
Framing a Liberty that still went back;   70
Whose num'rous Gorge could swallow in an hour
That Island, which the Sea cannot devour:
Then our *Amphion* issues out and sings,
And once he struck, and twice, the pow'rful Strings.

    The Commonwealth then first together came,   75
And each one enter'd in the willing Frame;

All other Matter yields, and may be rul'd;
But who the Minds of stubborn Men can build?
No Quarry bears a Stone so hardly wrought,
Nor with such labour from its Center brought;   8
None to be sunk in the Foundation bends,
Each in the House the highest Place contends,
And each the Hand that lays him will direct,
And some fall back upon the Architect;
Yet all compos'd by his attractive Song,   8
Into the Animated City throng.

   The Common-wealth does through their Centers all
Draw the Circumf'rence of the publique Wall;
The crossest Spirits here do take their part,
Fast'ning the Contignation which they thwart;   9
And they, whose Nature leads them to divide,
Uphold, this one, and that the other Side;
But the most Equal still sustein the Height,
And they as Pillars keep the Work upright;
While the resistance of opposed Minds,   9
The Fabrick as with Arches stronger binds,
Which on the Basis of a Senate free,
Knit by the Roofs Protecting weight agree.

   When for his Foot he thus a place had found,
He hurles e'r since the World about him round;   10
And in his sev'ral Aspects, like a Star,
Here shines in Peace, and thither shoots a War.
While by his Beams observing Princes steer,
And wisely court the Influence they fear;
O would they rather by his Pattern won.   10
Kiss the approaching, nor yet angry Son;
And in their numbred Footsteps humbly tread
The path where holy Oracles do lead;
How might they under such a Captain raise
The great Designes kept for the latter Dayes!   11
But mad with Reason, so miscall'd, of State
They know them not, and what they know not, hate.
Hence still they sing Hosanna to the Whore,
And her whom they should Massacre adore:
But Indians whom they should convert, subdue;   11
Nor teach, but traffique with, or burn the Jew.

Unhappy Princes, ignorantly bred,
By Malice some, by Errour more misled;
If gracious Heaven to my Life give length,
Leisure to Time, and to my Weakness Strength,   120
Then shall I once with graver Accents shake
Your Regal sloth, and your long Slumbers wake:
Like the shrill Huntsman that prevents the East,
Winding his Horn to Kings that chase the Beast.

Till then my Muse shall hollow far behind   125
Angelique *Cromwell* who outwings the wind;
And in dark Nights, and in cold Dayes alone
Pursues the Monster thorough every Throne:
Which shrinking to her *Roman* Den impure,
Gnashes her Goary teeth; nor there secure.   130

Hence oft I think, if in some happy Hour
High Grace should meet in one with highest Pow'r,
And then a seasonable People still
Should bend to his, as he to Heavens will,
What we might hope, what wonderful Effect   135
From such a wish'd Conjuncture might reflect.
Sure, the mysterious Work, where none withstand,
Would forthwith finish under such a Hand:
Fore-shortned Time its useless Course would stay,
And soon precipitate the latest Day.   140
But a thick Cloud about that Morning lyes,
And intercepts the Beams of Mortal eyes,
That 'tis the most which we determine can,
If these the Times, then this must be the Man.
And well he therefore does, and well has guest,   145
Who in his Age has always forward prest:
And knowing not where Heavens choice may light,
Girds yet his Sword, and ready stands to fight;
But Men alas, as if they nothing car'd,
Look on, all unconcern'd, or unprepar'd;   150
And Stars still fall, and still the Dragons Tail
Swinges the Volumes of its horrid Flail.
For the great Justice that did first suspend
The World by Sin, does by the same extend.
Hence that blest Day still counterpoysed wastes,   155
The Ill delaying, what th'Elected hastes;

Hence landing Nature to new Seas is tost,
And good Designes still with their Authors lost.
    And thou, great *Cromwell*, for whose happy birth
A Mold was chosen out of better Earth;   16
Whose Saint-like Mother we did lately see
Live out an Age, long as a Pedigree;
That she might seem, could we the Fall dispute,
T'have smelt the Blossome, and not eat the Fruit;
Though none does of more lasting Parents grow,   16
But never any did them Honor so;
Though thou thine Heart from Evil still unstain'd,
And always hast thy Tongue from fraud refrain'd;
Thou, who so oft through Storms of thundring Lead
Hast born securely thine undaunted Head,   17
Thy Brest through ponyarding Conspiracies,
Drawn from the Sheath of lying Prophecies;
Thee proof beyond all other Force or Skill,
Our Sins endanger, and shall one day kill.
    How near they fail'd, and in thy sudden Fall   17
At once assay'd to overturn us all.
Our brutish fury strugling to be Free,
Hurry'd thy Horses while they hurry'd thee.
When thou hadst almost quit thy Mortal cares,
And soyl'd in Dust thy Crown of silver Hairs.   18
Let this one Sorrow interweave among
The other Glories of our yearly Song.
Like skilful Looms which through the costly thred
Of purling Ore, a shining wave do shed:
So shall the Tears we on past Grief employ,   18
Still as they trickle, glitter in our Joy.
So with more Modesty we may be True,
And speak as of the Dead the Praises due:
While impious Men deceiv'd with pleasure short,
On their own Hopes shall find the Fall retort.   19
But the poor Beasts wanting their noble Guide,
What could they more? shrunk guiltily aside.
First winged Fear transports them far away,
And leaden Sorrow then their flight did stay.
See how they each his towring Crest abate,   19
And the green Grass, and their known Mangers hate,

Nor through wide Nostrils snuffe the wanton air,
Nor their round Hoofs, or curled Mane's compare;
With wandring Eyes, and restless Ears they stood,
And with shrill Neighings ask'd him of the Wood.   200
Thou *Cromwell* falling, not a stupid Tree,
Or Rock so savage, but it mourn'd for thee:
And all about was heard a Panique groan,
As if that Natures self were overthrown.
It seem'd the Earth did from the Center tear;   205
It seem'd the Sun was faln out of the Sphere:
Justice obstructed lay, and Reason fool'd;
Courage disheartned, and Religion cool'd.
A dismal Silence through the Palace went,
And then loud Shreeks the vaulted Marbles rent.   210
Such as the dying Chorus sings by turns,
And to deaf Seas, and ruthless Tempests mourns,
When now they sink, and now the plundring Streams
Break up each Deck, and rip the Oaken seams.

But thee triumphant hence the firy Carr,   215
And firy Steeds had born out of the Warr,
From the low World, and thankless Men above,
Unto the Kingdom blest of Peace and Love:
We only mourn'd our selves, in thine Ascent,
Whom thou hadst left beneath with Mantle rent.   220

For all delight of Life thou then didst lose,
When to Command, thou didst thy self Depose;
Resigning up thy Privacy so dear,
To turn the headstrong Peoples Charioteer;
For to be *Cromwell* was a greater thing,   225
Then ought below, or yet above a King:
Therefore thou rather didst thy Self depress,
Yielding to Rule, because it made thee Less.

For, neither didst thou from the first apply
Thy sober Spirit unto things too High,   230
But in thine own Fields exercisedst long,
An healthful Mind within a Body strong;
Till at the Seventh time thou in the Skyes,
As a small Cloud, like a Mans hand didst rise;
Then did thick Mists and Winds the air deform,   235
And down at last thou pow'rdst the fertile Storm;

Which to the thirsty Land did plenty bring,
But though forewarn'd, o'r-took and wet the King.
    What since he did, an higher Force him push'd
Still from behind, and it before him rush'd, 240
Though undiscern'd among the tumult blind,
Who think those high Decrees by Man design'd.
'Twas Heav'n would not that his Pow'r should cease,
But walk still middle betwixt War and Peace;
Choosing each Stone, and poysing every weight, 245
Trying the Measures of the Bredth and Height;
Here pulling down, and there erecting New,
Founding a firm State by Proportions true.
    When *Gideon* so did from the War retreat,
Yet by the Conquest of two Kings grown great, 250
He on the Peace extends a Warlike power,
And *Is'rel* silent saw him rase the Tow'r;
And how he *Succoths* Elders durst suppress,
With Thorns and Briars of the Wilderness.
No King might ever such a Force have done; 255
Yet would not he be Lord, nor yet his Son.
    Thou with the same strength, and an Heart as plain,
Didst (like thine Olive) still refuse to Reign;
Though why should others all thy Labor spoil,
And Brambles be anointed with thine Oyl, 260
Whose climbing Flame, without a timely stop,
Had quickly Levell'd every Cedar's top.
Therefore first growing to thy self a Law,
Th'ambitious Shrubs thou in just time didst aw.
    So have I seen at Sea, when whirling Winds, 265
Hurry the Bark, but more the Seamens minds,
Who with mistaken Course salute the Sand,
And threat'ning Rocks misapprehend for Land;
While baleful *Tritons* to the shipwrack guide.
And Corposants along the Tacklings slide. 270
The Passengers all wearyed out before,
Giddy, and wishing for the fatal Shore;
Some lusty Mate, who with more careful Eye
Counted the Hours, and ev'ry Star did spy,
The Helm does from the artless Steersman strain, 275
And doubles back unto the safer Main.

What though a while they grumble discontent,
Saving himself he does their loss prevent.
   'Tis not a Freedome, that where All command;
Nor Tyranny, where One does them withstand: 280
But who of both the Bounders knows to lay
Him as their Father must the State obey.
   Thou, and thine House, like *Noah's* Eight did rest,
Left by the Wars Flood on the Mountains crest:
And the large Vale lay subject to thy Will,   285
Which thou but as an Husbandman wouldst Till:
And only didst for others plant the Vine
Of Liberty, not drunken with its Wine.
   That sober Liberty which men may have,
That they enjoy, but more they vainly crave: 290
And such as to their Parents Tents do press,
May shew their own, not see his Nakedness.
   Yet such a *Chammish* issue still does rage,
The Shame and Plague both of the Land and Age,
Who watch'd thy halting, and thy Fall deride,   295
Rejoycing when thy Foot had slipt aside;
That their new King might the fifth Scepter shake,
And make the World, by his Example, Quake:
Whose frantique Army should they want for Men
Might muster Heresies, so one were ten.   300
What thy Misfortune, they the Spirit call,
And their Religion only is to Fall.
Oh *Mahomet*! now couldst thou rise again,
Thy Falling-sickness should have made thee Reign,
While *Feake* and *Simpson* would in many a Tome,   305
Have writ the Comments of thy sacred Foame:
For soon thou mightst have past among their Rant
Wer't but for thine unmoved Tulipant;
As thou must needs have own'd them of thy band
For prophecies fit to be *Alcorand*.   310
   Accursed Locusts, whom your King does spit
Out of the Center of th'unbottom'd Pit;
Wand'rers, Adult'rers, Lyers, *Munser's* rest,
Sorcerers, Atheists, Jesuites, Possest;
You who the Scriptures and the Laws deface   315
With the same liberty as Points and Lace;

Oh Race most hypocritically strict!
Bent to reduce us to the ancient Pict;
Well may you act the *Adam* and the *Eve*;
Ay, and the Serpent too that did deceive.   32

But the great Captain, now the danger's ore,
Makes you for his sake Tremble one fit more;
And, to your spight, returning yet alive
Does with himself all that is good revive.

So when first Man did through the Morning new   32⋅
See the bright Sun his shining Race pursue,
All day he follow'd with unwearied sight,
Pleas'd with that other World of moving Light;
But thought him when he miss'd his setting beams,
Sunk in the Hills, or plung'd below the Streams.   33⋅
While dismal blacks hung round the Universe,
And Stars (like Tapers) burn'd upon his Herse:
And Owls and Ravens with their screeching noyse
Did make the Fun'rals sadder by their Joyes.
His weeping Eyes the doleful Vigils keep,   33⋅
Not knowing yet the Night was made for sleep:
Still to the West, where he him lost, he turn'd,
And with such accents, as Despairing, mourn'd:
Why did mine Eyes once see so bright a Ray;
Or why Day last no longer then a Day?   340
When streight the Sun behind him he descry'd,
Smiling serenely from the further side.

So while our Star that gives us Light and Heat,
Seem'd now a long and gloomy Night to threat,
Up from the other World his Flame he darts,   345
And Princes shining through their windows starts;
Who their suspected Counsellors refuse,
And credulous Ambassadors accuse.

' Is this, saith one, the Nation that we read
' Spent with both Wars, under a Captain dead?   350
' Yet rig a Navy while we dress us late;
' And ere we Dine, rase and rebuild their State.
' What Oaken Forrests, and what golden Mines!
' What Mints of Men, what Union of Designes!
' Unless their Ships, do, as their Fowle proceed   355
' Of shedding Leaves, that with their Ocean breed.

' Theirs are not Ships, but rather Arks of War,
' And beaked Promontories sail'd from far;
' Of floting Islands a new Hatched Nest;
' A Fleet of Worlds, of other Worlds in quest;   360
' An hideous shole of wood-Leviathans,
' Arm'd with three Tire of brazen Hurricans;
' That through the Center shoot their thundring side
' And sink the Earth that does at Anchor ride.
' What refuge to escape them can be found,   365
' Whose watry Leaguers all the world surround?
' Needs must we all their Tributaries be,
' Whose Navies hold the Sluces of the Sea.
' The Ocean is the Fountain of Command,
' But that once took, we Captives are on Land.   370
' And those that have the Waters for their share,
' Can quickly leave us neither Earth nor Air.
' Yet if through these our Fears could find a pass;
' Through double Oak, & lin'd with treble Brass;
' That one Man still, although but nam'd, alarms   375
' More then all Men, all Navies, and all Arms.
' Him, all the Day, Him, in late Nights I dread,
' And still his Sword seems hanging o're my head.
' The Nation had been ours, but his one Soul
' Moves the great Bulk, and animates the whole.   380
' He Secrecy with Number hath inchas'd,
' Courage with Age, Maturity with Hast:
' The Valiants Terror, Riddle of the Wise;
' And still his Fauchion all our Knots unties.
' Where did he learn those Arts that cost us dear?   385
' Where below Earth, or where above the Sphere?
' He seems a King by long Succession born,
' And yet the same to be a King does scorn.
' Abroad a King he seems, and something more,
' At Home a Subject on the equal Floor.   390
' O could I once him with our Title see,
' But let them write his Praise that love him best,
' It grieves me sore to have thus much confest.
     Pardon, great Prince, if thus their Fear or Spight
More then our Love and Duty do thee Right.   395

I yield, nor further will the Prize contend;
So that we both alike may miss our End:
While thou thy venerable Head dost raise
' So should I hope yet he might Dye as wee.
As far above their Malice as my Praise. 400
And as the *Angel* of our Commonweal,
Troubling the Waters, yearly mak'st them Heal.

On the Victory obtained by Blake over the Spaniards, in the Bay of Sanctacruze, in the Island of Teneriff. 1657

Now does *Spains* Fleet her spatious wings unfold,
Leaves the new World and hastens for the old:
But though the wind was fair, they slowly swoome
Frayted with acted Guilt, and Guilt to come:
For this rich load, of which so proud they are,
Was rais'd by Tyranny, and rais'd for War;
Every capatious Gallions womb was fill'd,
With what the Womb of wealthy Kingdomes yield,
The new Worlds wounded Intrails they had tore,
For wealth wherewith to wound the old once more. 1
Wealth which all others Avarice might cloy,
But yet in them caus'd as much fear, as Joy.
For now upon the Main, themselves they saw,
That boundless Empire, where you give the Law,
Of winds and waters rage, they fearful be, 1
But much more fearful are your Flags to see.
Day, that to those who sail upon the deep,
More wish't for, and more welcome is then sleep,
They dreaded to behold, Least the Sun's light,
With *English* Streamers, should salute their sight: 2
In thickest darkness they would choose to steer,
So that such darkness might suppress their fear;
At length theirs vanishes, and fortune smiles;
For they behold the sweet Canary Isles;
One of which doubtless is by Nature blest 2
Above both Worlds, since 'tis above the rest.
For least some Gloominess might stain her sky,
Trees there the duty of the Clouds supply;

O noble Trust which Heaven on this Isle poures,
Fertile to be, yet never need her showres. 30
A happy People, which at once do gain
The benefits without the ills of rain.
Both health and profit, Fate cannot deny;
Where still the Earth is moist, the Air still dry;
The jarring Elements no discord know, 35
Fewel and Rain together kindly grow;
And coolness there, with heat doth never fight,
This only rules by day, and that by Night.
Your worth to all these Isles, a just right brings,
The best of Lands should have the best of Kings. 40
And these want nothing Heaven can afford,
Unless it be, the having you their Lord;
But this great want, will not a long one prove,
Your Conquering Sword will soon that want remove.
For *Spain* had better, Shee'l ere long confess, 45
Have broken all her Swords, then this one Peace,
Casting that League off, which she held so long,
She cast off that which only made her strong.
Forces and art, she soon will feel, are vain,
Peace, against you, was the sole strength of *Spain*. 50
By that alone those Islands she secures,
Peace made them hers, but War will make them yours
There the indulgent Soil that rich Grape breeds,
Which of the Gods the fancied drink exceeds;
They still do yield, such is their pretious mould, 55
All that is good, and are not curst with Gold.
With fatal Gold, for still where that does grow,
Neither the Soyl, nor People quiet know.
Which troubles men to raise it when 'tis Oar,
And when 'tis raised, does trouble them much more. 60
Ah, why was thither brought that cause of War,
Kind Nature had from thence remov'd so far.
In vain doth she those Islands free from Ill,
If fortune can make guilty what she will.
But whilst I draw that Scene, where you ere long, 65
Shall conquests act, your present are unsung.

    For *Sanctacruze* the glad Fleet takes her way,
And safely there casts Anchor in the Bay.

Never so many with one joyful cry,
That place saluted, where they all must dye.   70
Deluded men! Fate with you did but sport,
You scap't the Sea, to perish in your Port.
'Twas more for *Englands* fame you should dye there,
Where you had most of strength, and least of fear.
    The Peek's proud height, the *Spaniards* all admire,   75
Yet in their brests, carry a pride much higher.
Onely to this vast hill a power is given,
At once both to Inhabit Earth and Heaven.
But this stupendious Prospect did not neer,
Make them admire, so much as they did fear.   80
    For here they met with news, which did produce,
A grief, above the cure of Grapes best juice.
They learn'd with Terrour, that nor Summers heat,
Nor Winters storms, had made your Fleet retreat.
To fight against such Foes, was vain they knew,   85
Which did the rage of Elements subdue.
Who on the Ocean that does horror give,
To all besides, triumphantly do live.
    With hast they therefore all their Gallions moar,
And flank with Cannon from the Neighbouring shore.   90
Forts, Lines, and Sconces all the Bay along,
They build and act all that can make them strong.
    Fond men who know not whilst such works they raise,
They only Labour to exalt your praise.
Yet they by restless toyl, became at Length,   95
So proud and confident of their made strength,
That they with joy their boasting General heard,
Wish then for that assault he lately fear'd.
His wish he has, for now undaunted *Blake*,
With winged speed, for *Sanctacruze* does make.   100
For your renown, his conquering Fleet does ride,
Ore Seas as vast as is the *Spaniards* pride.
Whose Fleet and Trenches view'd, he soon did say,
We to their Strength are more oblig'd then they.
Wer't not for that, they from their Fate would run,   105
And a third World seek out our Armes to shun.
Those Forts, which there, so high and strong appear,
Do not so much suppress, as shew their fear.

Of Speedy Victory let no man doubt,
Our worst works past, now we have found them out.   110
Behold their Navy does at Anchor lye,
And they are ours, for now they cannot fly.
  This said, the whole Fleet gave it their applause,
And all assumes your courage, in your cause.
That Bay they enter, which unto them owes,   115
The noblest wreaths, that Victory bestows.
Bold *Stainer* Leads, this Fleets design'd by fate,
To give him Lawrel, as the Last did Plate.
  The Thund'ring Cannon now begins the Fight,
And though it be at Noon, creates a Night.   120
The Air was soon after the fight begun,
Far more enflam'd by it, then by the Sun.
Never so burning was that Climate known,
War turn'd the temperate, to the Torrid Zone.
  Fate these two Fleets, between both Worlds had brought.
Who fight, as if for both those Worlds they fought.   [125
Thousands of wayes, Thousands of men there dye,
Some Ships are sunk, some blown up in the skie.
Nature ne'r made Cedars so high aspire,
As Oakes did then, Urg'd by the active fire.   130
Which by quick powders force, so high was sent,
That it return'd to its own Element.
Torn Limbs some leagues into the Island fly,
Whilst others lower, in the Sea do lye.
Scarce souls from bodies sever'd are so far,   135
By death, as bodies there were by the War.
Th' all-seeing Sun, neer gaz'd on such a sight,
Two dreadful Navies there at Anchor Fight.
And neither have, or power, or will to fly,
There one must Conquer, or there both must dye.   140
Far different Motives yet, engag'd them thus,
Necessity did them, but Choice did us.
  A choice which did the highest worth express,
And was attended by as high success.
For your resistless genious there did Raign,   145
By which we Laurels reapt ev'n on the Mayn.
So prosperous Stars, though absent to the sence,
Bless those they shine for, by their Influence. ·

Our Cannon now tears every Ship and Sconce,
And o're two Elements Triumphs at once. 150
Their Gallions sunk, their wealth the Sea does fill,
The only place where it can cause no Ill.
    Ah would those Treasures which both Indies have,
Were buryed in as large, and deep a grave,
Wars chief support with them would buried be, 155
And the Land owe her peace unto the Sea.
Ages to come, your conquering Arms will bless,
There they destroy, what had destroy'd their Peace.
And in one War the present age may boast,
The certain seeds of many Wars are lost. 160
    All the Foes Ships destroy'd, by Sea or fire,
Victorious *Blake,* does from the Bay retire,
His Seige of *Spain* he then again pursues,
And there first brings of his success the news;
The saddest news that ere to *Spain* was brought, 165
Their rich Fleet sunk, and ours with Lawrel fraught.
Whilst fame in every place, her Trumpet blowes,
And tells the World, how much to you it owes.

Two Songs at the Marriage of the Lord Fauconberg *and the Lady* Mary Cromwell

FIRST

CHORUS. ENDYMION. LUNA

Chorus.   Th' *Astrologers* own Eyes are set,
         And even Wolves the Sheep forget;
         Only *this Shepheard,* late and soon,
         Upon this Hill outwakes the *Moon.*
         Heark how he sings, with sad delight, 5
         Thorough the clear and silent Night.

Endymion. Cynthia, O Cynthia, turn thine Ear,
         Nor scorn *Endymions* plaints to hear.
         As we our Flocks, so you command
         The fleecy Clouds with silver wand. 10

Cynthia.	If thou a *Mortal,* rather sleep;
	Or if a *Shepheard,* watch thy Sheep.

Endymion.	The *Shepheard,* since he saw thine Eyes,	
	And *Sheep* are both thy *Sacrifice.*	
	Nor merits he a *Mortal's* name,	15
	That burns with an *immortal Flame.*	

Cynthia.	I have enough for me to do,
	Ruling the Waves that Ebb and flow.

Endymion.	Since thou disdain'st not then to share	
	On Sublunary things thy care;	20
	Rather restrain these double Seas,	
	Mine Eyes uncessant deluges.	

Cynthia.	My wakeful Lamp all night must move,
	Securing their Repose above.

Endymion.	If therefore thy resplendent Ray	25
	Can make a Night more bright then Day;	
	Shine thorough this obscurer Brest,	
	With shades of deep Despair opprest.	

Chorus.	Courage, *Endymion,* boldly Woo,	
	Anchises was a *Shepheard* too;	30
	Yet is *her younger Sister* laid	
	Sporting with him in *Ida's shade*:	
	And *Cynthia,* though the strongest,	
	Seeks but the honour to have held out longest.	

Endymion.	Here unto *Latmos Top* I climbe:	35
	How far below thine *Orbe* sublime?	
	O why, as well as Eyes to see,	
	Have I not Armes that reach to thee?	

Cynthia.	'Tis needless then that I refuse,	
	Would you but your own Reason use.	40

Endymion.	Though I so high may not pretend,
	It is the same so you descend.

Cynthia.   *These Stars* would say I do them wrong,
       Rivals each one for thee too strong.

Endymion. *The Stars* are fix'd unto their *Sphere,*   45
       And cannot, though they would, come near.
       Less Loves set of each others praise,
       While *Stars* Eclipse by mixing Rayes.

Cynthia.   That Cave is dark.

Endymion.   Then none can spy: 50
       Or shine Thou there and 'tis the Sky.

Chorus.   Joy to *Endymion,*
     For he has *Cynthia's* favour won.
      And *Jove* himself approves
   With his serenest influence their Loves.   55
      For he did never love to pair
       His Progeny above the Air;
     But to be honest, valiant, wise,
  Makes *Mortals* matches fit for *Deityes.*

SECOND SONG

HOBBINOL.   PHILLIS.   TOMALIN

Hobbinol. *Phillis, Tomalin,* away:
       Never such a merry day.
       For *the Northern Shepheards Son.*
       Has *Menalca's daughter* won.

Phillis.   Stay till I some flow'rs ha' ty'd   5
       In a Garland for the Bride.

Tomalin.   If thou would'st a Garland bring,
       Phillis you may wait the Spring:
       They ha' chosen such an hour
       When *She* is the only flow'r.   10

Phillis.   Let's not then at least be seen
       Without each a Sprig of Green.

Hobbinol.   Fear not; at *Menalca's Hall*
There is Bayes enough for all.
He when Young as we did graze,   15
But when Old he planted Bayes.

Tomalin.   Here *She* comes; but with a Look
Far more catching then my Hook.
'Twas those Eyes, I now dare swear,
Led our Lambs we knew not where.   20

Hobbinol.   Not our Lambs own Fleeces are
Curl'd so lovely as her Hair:
Nor our Sheep new Wash'd can be
Half so white or sweet as *She.*

Phillis.   *He* so looks as fit to keep   25
Somewhat else then silly *Sheep.*

Hobbinol.   Come, lets in some Carol new
Pay to Love and Them their due.

All.   Joy to that *happy Pair,*
Whose Hopes united banish our Despair.   30
   What *Shepheard* could for Love pretend,
Whil'st all the *Nymphs* on *Damon's* choice
       attend?
   What *Shepherdess* could hope to wed
Before *Marina's* turn were sped?   35
Now lesser Beauties may take place,
And meaner Virtues come in play;
       While they,
       Looking from high,
       Shall grace   40
Our Flocks and us with a propitious Eye.
   But what is most, the gentle Swain
   No more shall need of Love complain;
   But Virtue shall be Beauties hire,
And those be equal that have equal Fire.   45
   Marina yields. Who dares be coy?
Or who despair, now *Damon* does enjoy?

Joy to that happy Pair,
Whose Hopes united banish our Despair.

A Poem upon the Death of O. C.

That Providence which had so long the care
Of *Cromwell's* head, and numbered ev'ry hair,
Now in its self (the Glass where all appears)
Had seen the period of his golden Years:
And thenceforth onely did attend to trace,
What death might least so fair a Life deface.
    The People, which what most they fear esteem,
Death when more horrid so more noble deem;
And blame the last *Act*, like *Spectators* vain,
Unless the *Prince* whom they applaud be slain. 10
Nor Fate indeed can well refuse that right
To those that liv'd in War, to dye in Fight.
    But long his *Valour* none had left that could
Indanger him, or *Clemency* that would.
And he whom Nature all for Peace had made, 15
But angry Heaven unto War had sway'd,
And so less useful where he most desir'd,
For what he least affected was admir'd,
Deserved yet an End whose ev'ry part
Should speak the wondrous softness of his Heart. 20
    To *Love* and *Grief* the fatal Writ was sign'd;
(Those nobler weaknesses of humane Mind,
From which those Powers that issu'd the Decree,
Although immortal, found they were not free.)
That they, to whom his Breast still open lyes, 25
In gentle Passions should his Death disguise:
And leave succeeding Ages cause to mourn,
As long as Grief shall weep, or Love shall burn.
    Streight does a slow and languishing Disease
Eliza, Natures and his darling, seize. 30
Her when an infant, taken with her Charms,
He oft would flourish in his mighty Arms;
And, lest their force the tender burthen wrong,
Slacken the vigour of his Muscles strong;

Then to the Mothers brest her softly move,   35
Which while she drain'd of Milk she fill'd with Love.
But as with riper Years her Virtue grew,
And ev'ry minute adds a Lustre new;
When with meridian height her Beauty shin'd,
And thorough that sparkled her fairer Mind;   40
When She with Smiles serene and Words discreet
His hidden Soul at ev'ry turn could meet;
Then might y' ha' daily Affection spy'd,
Doubling that knot which Destiny had ty'd.
While they by sence, not knowing, comprehend   45
How on each other both their Fates depend.
With her each day the pleasing Hours he shares,
And at her Aspect calms his growing Cares;
Or with a Grandsire's joy her Children sees
Hanging about her neck or at his knees.   50
Hold fast dear Infants, hold them both or none;
This will not stay when once the other's gone.
  A silent fire now wasts those Limbs of Wax,
And him within his tortur'd Image racks.
So the Flowr with'ring which the Garden crown'd,   55
The sad Root pines in secret under ground.
Each Groan he doubled and each Sigh he sigh'd,
Repeated over to the restless Night.
No trembling String compos'd to numbers new,
Answers the touch in Notes more sad more true.   60
She lest He grieve hides what She can her pains,
And He to lessen hers his Sorrow feigns:
Yet both perceiv'd, yet both conceal'd their Skills,
And so diminishing increast their ills:
That whether by each others grief they fell,   65
Or on their own redoubled, none can tell.
  And now *Eliza's* purple Locks were shorn,
Where She so long her *Fathers* fate had worn:
And frequent lightning to her Soul that flyes,
Devides the Air, and opens all the Skyes: 70
And now his Life, suspended by her breath,
Ran out impetuously to hasting Death.
Like polish'd Mirrours, so his steely Brest
Had ev'ry figure of her woes exprest;

And with the damp of her last Gasps obscur'd,   75
Had drawn such staines as were not to be cur'd.
Fate could not either reach with single stroke,
But the dear Image fled the Mirrour broke.
  Who now shall tell us more of mournful Swans,
Of Halcyons kind, or bleeding Pelicans?   80
No downy breast did ere so gently beat,
Or fan with airy plumes so soft an heat.
For he no duty by his height excus'd,
Nor though a *Prince* to be a *Man* refus'd:
But rather then in his *Eliza's* pain   85
Not love, not grieve, would neither live nor reign:
And in himself so oft immortal try'd,
Yet in compassion of another dy'd.
  So have I seen a Vine, whose lasting Age
Of many a Winter hath surviv'd the rage.   90
Under whose shady tent Men ev'ry year
At its rich bloods expence their Sorrows chear,
If some dear branch where it extends its life
Chance to be prun'd by an untimely knife,
The Parent-Tree unto the Grief succeeds,   95
And through the Wound its vital humour bleeds;
Trickling in watry drops, whose flowing shape
Weeps that it falls ere fix'd into a Grape.
So the dry Stock, no more that spreading Vine,
Frustrates the Autumn and the hopes of Wine.   100
  A secret Cause does sure those Signs ordain
Fore boding Princes falls, and seldom vain.
Whether some Kinder Pow'rs, that wish us well,
What they above cannot prevent, foretell;
Or the great World do by consent presage,   105
As hollow Seas with future Tempests rage:
Or rather Heav'n, which us so long foresees,
Their fun'rals celebrates while it decrees.
But never yet was any humane Fate
By nature solemniz'd with so much state.   110
He unconcern'd the dreadful passage crost;
But oh what pangs that Death did Nature cost!
First the great *Thunder* was shot off, and sent
The Signal from the starry Battlement.

The *Winds* receive it, and its force out-do,   115
As practising how they could thunder too:
Out of the Binders Hand the Sheaves they tore,
And thrash'd the Harvest in the airy floore;
Or of huge Trees, whose growth with his did rise,
The deep foundations open'd to the Skyes.   120
Then heavy *Showres* the winged Tempests lead,
And pour the Deluge ore the *Chaos* head.
The Race of warlike *Horses* at his Tomb
Offer themselves in many an *Hecatomb*;
With pensive head towards the ground they fall,   125
And helpless languish at the tainted Stall.
Numbers of *Men* decrease with pains unknown,
And hasten not to see his Death their own.
Such Tortures all the Elements unfix'd,
Troubled to part where so exactly mix'd.   130
And as through Air his wasting Spirits flow'd,
The Universe labour'd beneath their load.

    Nature it seem'd with him would Nature vye;
He with *Eliza*, It with him would dye.

    He without noise still travell'd to his End,   135
As silent Suns to meet the Night descend.
The *Stars* that for him fought had only pow'r
Left to determine now his fatal Hour;
Which, since they might not hinder, yet they cast
To chuse it worthy of his *Glories* past.   140

    No part of time but bore his mark away
Of honour; all the Year was *Cromwell's* day:
But this, of all the most auspicious found,
Twice had in open field him Victor crown'd:
When up the armed Mountains of *Dunbar*   145
He march'd, and through deep *Severn* ending war.
What day should him *eternize* but the same
That had before *immortaliz'd* his *Name*?
That so who ere would at his Death have joy'd,
In their own Griefs might find themselves imploy'd;   150
But those that sadly his departure griev'd,
Yet joy'd remembring what he once atchiev'd.
And the last minute his victorious *Ghost*
Gave chase to *Ligny* on the *Belgick Coast*.

Here ended all his mortal toyles: He lay'd 15
And slept in Peace under the *Lawrel shade*.
  O Cromwell, Heavens Favorite! To none
Have such high honours from above been shown:
For whom the Elements we Mourners see,
And *Heav'n* it self would the great *Herald* be; 16
Which with more Care set forth his Obsequies
Then those of *Moses* hid from humane Eyes;
As jealous only here lest all be less,
That we could to his Memory express.
    Then let us to our course of Mourning keep: 16
Where *Heaven* leads, 'tis *Piety* to weep.
Stand back ye Seas, and shrunk beneath the vail
Of your Abysse, with cover'd Head bewail
Your *Monarch*: We demand not your supplies
To compass in our *Isle*; our Tears suffice; 17
Since him away the dismal Tempest rent,
Who once more joyn'd us to the Continent;
Who planted *England* on the *Flandrick shoar*,
And stretch'd *our frontire* to the *Indian Ore*;
Whose greater *Truths* obscure the *Fables* old, 17
Whether of *British Saints or Worthy's* told;
And in a valour less'ning *Arthur's* deeds,
For Holyness the *Confessor* exceeds.
    He first put Armes into *Religions* hand,
And tim'rous *Conscience* unto *Courage* man'd: 18
The Souldier taught that inward Mail to wear,
And *fearing God* how they should *nothing fear*.
Those Strokes he said will pierce through all below
Where those that strike from Heaven fetch their Blow.
Astonish'd armyes did their flight prepare, 18
And cityes strong were stormed by his prayer;
Of that for ever Preston's field shall tell
The story, and impregnable Clonmell.
And where the sandy mountain Fenwick scal'd,
The sea between, yet hence his pray'r prevail'd. 19
What man was ever so in Heav'n obey'd
Since the commanded sun o're Gibeon stay'd?
In all his warrs needs must he triumph, when
He conquer'd God, still ere he fought with men:

Hence, though in battle none so brave or fierce, 195
Yet him the adverse steel could never pierce.
Pity it seem'd to hurt him more that felt
Each wound himself which he to others delt;
Danger itself refusing to offend
So loose an enemy, so fast a friend. 200
Friendship, that sacred virtue, long dos claime
The first foundation of his house and name:
But within one its narrow limits fall,
His tendernesse extended unto all.
And that deep soule through every channell flows, 205
Where kindly nature loves itself to lose.
More strong affections never reason serv'd,
Yet still affected most what best deserv'd.
If he Eliza lov'd to that degree,
(Though who more worthy to be lov'd than she?) 210
If so indulgent to his own, how deare
To him the children of the Highest were?
For her he once did nature's tribute pay:
For these his life adventur'd every day:
And 'twould be found, could we his thoughts have cast, 215
Their griefs struck deepest, if Eliza's last.
What prudence more than humane did he need
To keep so deare, so diff'ring minds agreed?
The worser sort, so conscious of their ill,
Lye weak and easy to the ruler's will; 220
But to the good (too many or too few)
All law is uselesse, all reward is due.
Oh! ill advis'd, if not for love, for shame,
Spare yet your own, if you neglect his fame;
Least others dare to think your zeale a maske, 225
And you to govern only Heaven's taske.
Valour, religion, friendship, prudence dy'd
At once with him, and all that's good beside;
And we death's refuse nature's dregs confin'd
To loathsome life, alas! are left behind. 230
Where we (so once we us'd) shall now no more,
To fetch day, presse about his chamber-door;
From which he issu'd with that awfull state,
It seem'd Mars broke through Janus' double gate;

Yet always temper'd with an aire so mild,   235
No April sunns that e'er so gently smil'd;
No more shall heare that powerful language charm,
Whose force oft spar'd the labour of his arm:
No more shall follow where he spent the dayes
In warre, in counsell, or in pray'r, and praise;   240
Whose meanest acts he would himself advance,
As ungirt David to the arke did dance.
All, all is gone of ours or his delight
In horses fierce, wild deer, or armour bright;
Francisca faire can nothing now but weep,   245
Nor with soft notes shall sing his cares asleep.
   I saw him dead, a leaden slumber lyes,
And mortal sleep over those wakefull eyes:
Those gentle rays under the lids were fled,
Which through his looks that piercing sweetnesse shed;   250
That port which so majestique was and strong,
Loose and depriv'd of vigour, stretch'd along:
All wither'd, all discolour'd, pale and wan,
How much another thing, no more that man?
Oh! humane glory, vaine, oh! death, oh! wings,   255
Oh! worthlesse world! oh transitory things!
Yet dwelt that greatnesse in his shape decay'd,
That still though dead, greater than death he lay'd;
And in his alter'd face you something faigne
That threatens death, he yet will live again.   260
Not much unlike the sacred oak, which shoots
To Heav'n its branches, and through earth its roots:
Whose spacious boughs are hung with trophies round,
And honour'd wreaths have oft the victour crown'd.
When angry Jove darts lightning through the aire,   265
At mortalls sins, nor his own plant will spare;
(It groanes, and bruises all below that stood
So many years the shelter of the wood.)
The tree ere while foreshortned to our view,
When fall'n shews taller yet than as it grew: 270
So shall his praise to after times encrease,
When truth shall be allow'd, and faction cease,
And his own shadows with him fall; the eye
Detracts from objects than itself more high:

But when death takes them from that envy'd state,   275
Seeing how little we confess, how greate;
Thee, many ages hence, in martial verse
Shall th' English souldier, ere he charge, rehearse;
Singing of thee, inflame themselves to fight,
And with the name of Cromwell, armyes fright.   280
As long as rivers to the seas shall runne,
As long as Cynthia shall relieve the sunne,
While staggs shall fly unto the forests thick,
While sheep delight the grassy downs to pick,
As long as future time succeeds the past,   285
Always thy honour, praise and name, shall last.
  Thou in a pitch how farre beyond the sphere
Of humane glory tow'rst, and raigning there
Despoyl'd of mortall robes, in seas of blisse,
Plunging dost bathe and tread the bright abysse: 290
There thy great soule at once a world does see,
Spacious enough, and pure enough for thee.
How soon thou Moses hast, and Joshua found,
And David, for the sword and harpe renown'd;
How streight canst to each happy mansion goe?   295
(Farr better known above than here below;)
And in those joyes dost spend the endlesse day,
Which in expressing, we ourselves betray.
  For we, since thou art gone, with heavy doome,
Wander like ghosts about thy loved tombe;   300
And lost in tears, have neither sight nor mind
To guide us upward through this region blinde.
Since thou art gone, who best that way could'st teach,
Onely our sighs, perhaps, may thither reach.
  And Richard yet, where his great parent led,   305
Beats on the rugged track: he, vertue dead,
Revives; and by his milder beams assures;
And yet how much of them his griefe obscures.
He, as his father, long was kept from sight
In private, to be view'd by better light;   310
But open'd once, what splendour does he throw?
A Cromwell in an houre a prince will grow.
How he becomes that seat, how strongly streigns,
How gently winds at once the ruling reins?

Heav'n to this choice prepar'd a diadem,   3?
Richer than any eastern silk, or gemme;
A pearly rainbow, where the sun inchas'd
His brows, like an imperiall jewell grac'd.
   We find already what those omens mean,
Earth ne'er more glad, nor Heaven more serene.   3?
Cease now our griefs, calme peace succeeds a war,
Rainbows to storms, Richard to Oliver.
Tempt not his clemency to try his pow'r,
He threats no deluge, yet foretells a showre.

On Mr. Milton's *Paradise lost*

When I beheld the Poet blind, yet bold,
In slender Book his vast Design unfold,
Messiah Crown'd, *Gods* Reconcil'd Decree,
Rebelling *Angels*, the Forbidden Tree,
Heav'n, Hell, Earth, Chaos, All; the Argument
Held me a while misdoubting his Intent,
That he would ruine (for I saw him strong)
The sacred Truths to Fable and old Song,
(So *Sampson* groap'd the Temples Posts in spight)
The World o'rewhelming to revenge his Sight.
   Yet as I read, soon growing less severe,
I lik'd his Project, the success did fear;
Through that wide Field how he his way should find
O're which lame Faith leads Understanding blind;
Lest he perplext the things he would explain,
And what was easie he should render vain.
   Or if a Work so infinite he spann'd,
Jealous I was that some less skilful hand
(Such as disquiet alwayes what is well,
And by ill imitating would excell)
Might hence presume the whole Creations day
To change in Scenes, and show it in a Play.
   Pardon me, *mighty Poet*, nor despise
My causeless, yet not impious, surmise.
But I am now convinc'd, and none will dare
Within thy Labours to pretend a Share.

Thou hast not miss'd one thought that could be fit,
And all that was improper dost omit:
So that no room is here for Writers left,
But to detect their Ignorance or Theft.   30
    That Majesty which through thy Work doth Reign
Draws the Devout, deterring the Profane.
And things divine thou treatst of in such state
As them preserves, and Thee inviolate.
At once delight and horrour on us seize,   35
Thou singst with so much gravity and ease;
And above humane flight dost soar aloft,
With Plume so strong, so equal, and so soft.
The *Bird* nam'd from that *Paradise* you sing
So never Flags, but alwaies keeps on Wing.   40
    Where couldst thou Words of such a compass find?
Whence furnish such a vast expense of Mind?
Just Heav'n Thee, like *Tiresias,* to requite,
Rewards with *Prophesie* thy loss of Sight.
    Well mightst thou scorn thy Readers to allure   45
With tinkling Rhime, of thy own Sense secure;
While the *Town-Bays* writes all the while and spells,
And like a Pack-Horse tires without his Bells.
Their Fancies like our bushy Points appear,
The Poets tag them; we for fashion wear.   50
I too transported by the *Mode* offend,
And while I meant to *Praise* thee, must Commend.
Thy verse created like thy *Theme* sublime,
In Number, Weight, and Measure, needs not *Rhime.*

An
Elegy upon the Death of my
Lord *Francis Villiers*

Tis true that he is dead: but yet to chuse,
Methinkes thou Fame should not have brought the news
Thou canst discourse at will and speak at large:
But wast not in the fight nor durst thou charge.
While he transported all with valiant rage   5
His Name eternizd, but cut short his age;

On the safe battlements of Richmonds bowers
Thou wast espyd, and from the guilded Towers
Thy silver Trumpets sounded a Retreat,
Farre from the dust and battails sulphry heat.   1
Yet what couldst thou have done? 'tis alwayes late
To struggle with inevitable fate.
Much rather thou I know expectst to tell
How heavy *Cromwell* gnasht the earth and fell.
Or how slow Death farre from the sight of day   1
The long-deceived *Fairfax* bore away.
But untill then, let us young *Francis* praise:
And plant upon his hearse the bloody bayes,
Which we will water with our welling eyes.
Teares spring not still from spungy Cowardize.   2
The purer fountaines from the Rocks more steep
Destill and stony valour best doth weep.
Besides Revenge, if often quencht in teares,
Hardens like Steele and daily keener weares.
   Great *Buckingham*, whose death doth freshly strike   2
Our memoryes, because to this so like;
Ere that in the Eternall Court he shone,
And here a Favorite there found a throne;
The fatall night before he hence did bleed,
Left to his *Princess* this immortall seed.   3
As the wise *Chinese* in the fertile wombe
Of Earth doth a more precious clay entombe,
Which dying by his will he leaves consignd:
Til by mature delay of time refind
The christall metall fit to be releast   3
Is taken forth to crowne each royall feast:
Such was the fate by which this Postume breathd,
Who scarcely seems begotten but bequeathd.
   Never was any humane plant that grew
More faire then this and acceptably new.   4
'Tis truth that beauty doth most men dispraise:
Prudence and valour their esteeme do raise.
But he that hath already these in store,
Can not be poorer sure for having more.
And his unimitable handsomenesse   4
Made him indeed be more then man, not lesse.

We do but faintly Gods resemblance beare
And like rough coyns of carelesse mints appeare:
But he of purpose made, did represent
In a rich Medall every lineament.   50
  Lovely and admirable as he was,
Yet was his Sword or Armour all his Glasse.
Nor in his Mistris eyes that joy he tooke,
As in an Enemies himselfe to looke.
I know how well he did, with what delight   55
Those serious imitations of fight.
Still in the trialls of strong exercise
His was the first, and his the second prize.
  Bright Lady, thou that rulest from above
The last and greatest Monarchy of Love: 60
Faire *Richmond* hold thy Brother or he goes.
Try if the Jasmin of thy hand or Rose
Of thy red Lip can keep him alwayes here.
For he loves danger and doth never feare.
Or may thy tears prevaile with him to stay?   65
  But he resolv'd breaks carelesly away.
Onely one argument could now prolong
His stay and that most faire and so most strong:
The matchlesse *Chlora* whose pure fires did warm
His soule and only could his passions charme.   70
  You might with much more reason go reprove
The amorous Magnet which the North doth love.
Or preach divorce and say it is amisse
That with tall Elms the twining Vines should kisse
Then chide two such so fit, so equall faire   75
That in the world they have no other paire.
Whom it might seeme that Heaven did create
To restore man unto his first estate.
Yet she for honours tyrannous respect
Her own desires did and his neglect.   80
And like the Modest Plant at every touch
Shrunk in her leaves and feard it was too much.
  But who can paint the torments and that pain
Which he profest and now she could not faigne?
He like the Sun but overcast and pale: 85
Shee like a Rainbow, that ere long must faile,
Whose rosiall cheek where Heaven it selfe did view

Begins to separate and dissolve to dew.
　　At last he leave obtaines though sad and slow,
First of her and then of himselfe to goe.　　　　　　　　90
How comely and how terrible he sits
At once and Warre as well as Love befits!
Ride where thou wilt and bold adventures find:
But all the Ladies are got up behind.
Guard them, though not thy selfe: for in thy death　　95
Th' Eleven thousand Virgins lose their breath.

　　So *Hector* issuing from the Trojan wall
The sad *Iliades* to the Gods did call
With hands displayed and with dishevell'd haire
That they the Empire in his life would spare.　　　　100
While he secure through all the field doth spy
Achilles for *Achilles* only cry.
Ah ignorant that yet e're night he must
Be drawn by him inglorious through the dust.

　　Such fell young *Villiers* in the chearfull heat　　105
Of youth: his locks intangled all with sweat
And those eyes which the Sentinell did keep
Of love closed up in an eternall sleep.
While *Venus* of *Adonis* thinks no more
Slaine by the harsh tuske of the Savage Boare.　　110
Hither she runns and hath him hurried farre
Out of the noise and blood, and killing warre:
Where in her Gardens of Sweet myrtle laid
Shee kisses him in the immortall shade,

　　Yet dyed he not revengelesse: Much he did　　115
Ere he could suffer. A whole Pyramid
Of Vulgar bodies he erected high:
Scorning without a Sepulcher to dye.
And with his steele which did whole troopes divide
He cut his Epitaph on either Side.　　　　　　　　120
Till finding nothing to his courage fit
He rid up last to death and conquer'd it.

　　Such are the Obsequies to *Francis* own:
He best the pompe of his owne death hath showne.
And we hereafter to his honour will　　　　　　　125
Not write so many, but so many kill.
Till the whole Army by just vengeance come
To be at once his Trophee and his Tombe.

SATIRES
OF THE REIGN OF
CHARLES II

Clarindon's *House-Warming*

When *Clarindon* had discern'd beforehand,
  (As the Cause can eas'ly foretel the Effect)
At once three Deluges threatning our Land;
  'Twas the season he thought to turn Architect.

Us *Mars*, and *Apollo*, and *Vulcan* consume;   5
  While he the Betrayer of *England* and *Flander*,
Like the King-fisher chuseth to build in the Broom,
  And nestles in flames like the Salamander.

But observing that Mortals run often behind,
  (So unreasonable are the rates they buy-at)   10
His Omnipotence therefore much rather design'd
  How he might create a House with a *Fiat*.

He had read of *Rhodope*, a Lady of *Thrace*,
  Who was dig'd up so often ere she did marry;
And wish'd that his Daughter had had as much grace   15
  To erect him a Pyramid out of her Quarry.

But then recollecting how the Harper *Amphyon*
  Made *Thebes* dance aloft while he fidled and sung,
He thought (as an Instrument he was most free on)
  To build with the Jews-trump of his own tongue.   20

Yet a President fitter in *Virgil* he found,
    Of *African Poultney,* and *Tyrian Did'*
That he begg'd for a Pallace so much of his ground,
    As might carry the measure and name of an *Hyde.*

Thus dayly his Gouty Inventions he pain'd,   2
    And all for to save the expences of Brickbat,
That Engine so fatal, which *Denham* had brain'd,
    And too much resembled his Wives Chocolatte.

But while these devices he all doth compare,
    None sollid enough seem'd for his Thong *Caster*;   3
He himself would not dwell in a Castle of air,
    Though he had built full many a one for his Master.

Already he had got all our Money and Cattel,
    To buy us for Slaves, and purchase our Lands;
What *Joseph* by Famine, he wrought by Sea-Battel;   3
    Nay scarce the Priests portion could scape from his hands.

And hence like *Pharoah* that *Israel* prest
    To make Mortar and Brick, yet allow'd them no straw,
He car'd not though *Egypt's* Ten Plagues us distrest,
    So he could to build but make Policy Law.   4

The *Scotch* Forts & *Dunkirk*, but that they were sold,
    He would have demolisht to raise up his Walls;
Nay ev'n from *Tangier* have sent back for the mold,
    But that he had nearer the Stones of St. *Pauls.*

His Wood would come in at the easier rate,   4
    So long as the Yards had a Deal or a Spar:
His Friends in the Navy would not be ingrate,
    To grudge him some Timber who fram'd them the War.

To proceed in the Model he call'd in his *Allens,*
    The two *Allens* when jovial, who ply him with gallons,   5
The two *Allens* who serve his blind Justice for ballance,
    The two *Allens* who serve his Injustice for Tallons.

They approve it thus far, and said it was fine;
    Yet his Lordship to finish it would be unable;
Unless all abroad he divulg'd the design,   55
    For his House then would grow like a Vegetable.

His Rent would no more in arrear run to *Worster;*
    He should dwell more noble, and cheap too at-home,
While into a fabrick the Presents would muster;
    As by hook and by crook the world cluster'd of Atome. 60

He lik'd the advice, and then soon it assay'd;
    And Presents croud headlong to give good example:
So the Bribes overlaid her that *Rome* once betray'd:
    The Tribes ne'er contributed so to the Temple.

Straight Judges, Priests, Bishops, true sons of the Seal,   65
    Sinners, Governors, Farmers, Banquers, Patentees.
Bring in the whole Milk of a year at a meal,
    As all Chedder Dairys club to the incorporate Cheese.

Bulteales, Beakns, Morley, Wrens fingers with telling
    Were shriveled, and *Clutterbuck, Eagers & Kips*;   70
Since the Act of Oblivion was never such selling,
    As at this Benevolence out of the Snips.

'Twas then that the Chimny-Contractors he smoakd,
    Nor would take his beloved Canary in kind:
But he swore that the Patent should ne'er be revok'd;   75
    No, would the whole Parliament kiss him behind.

Like *Jove* under *Aetna* o'erwhelming the Gyant,
    For foundation he *Bristol* sunk in the Earth's bowel;
And *St. John* must now for the Leads be compliant,
    Or his right hand shall else be cut off with the Trowel. 80

For surveying the building, *Prat* did the feat,
    But for the expence he rely'd upon *Worstenholm,*
Who sate heretofore at the King's Receipt;
    But receiv'd now and paid the Chancellours Custome.

By Subsidies thus both Clerick and Laick,   8
    And with matter profane, cemented with holy,
He finish'd at last his Palace Mosaick,
    By a Model more excellent than *Lesly's* Folly.

And upon the *Tarras*, to consummate all,
    A Lanthorn, like *Faux's* surveys the burnt Town,   9
And shews on the top by the Regal Gilt Ball,
    Where you are to expect the Scepter and Crown.

Fond City, its Rubbish and Ruines that builds,
    Like vain Chymists, a flower from its ashes returning;
Your Metropolis House is in St. *James's* Fields,   9
    And till there you remove, you shall never leave burning

This Temple, of War and of Peace is the Shrine;
    Where this Idol of State sits ador'd and accurst:
And to handsel his Altar and Nostrils divine,
    Great *Buckingham's* Sacrifice must be the first.   10

Now some (as all Buildings must censure abide)
    Throw dust in its Front, and blame situation:
And others as much reprehend his Backside,
    As too narrow by far for his expatiation,

But do not consider how in process of times,   10
    That for Name-sake he may with *Hyde* Park it enlarge,
And with that convenience he soon for his Crimes
    At Tybourn may land, and spare the Tower-Barge.

Or rather how wisely his Stall was built near,
    Lest with driving too far his Tallow impair;   11
When like the good Oxe, for publick good chear,
    He comes to be roasted next St. *James's* Fair.

Upon his House

Here lies the sacred Bones
Of *Paul* late gelded of his Stones.

Here lie Golden Briberies,
The price of ruin'd Families:
The Cavaliers Debenter-Wall,   5
Fixt on an Eccentrick Basis;
Here 's *Dunkirk-Town* and *Tangier-Hall,*
The Queens Marriage and all;
The Dutchman's *Templum Pacis.*

Upon his Grand-Children

Kendal is dead, and *Cambridge* riding post.
What fitter Sacrifice for *Denham's* Ghost?

The last Instructions to a Painter

After two sittings, now our *Lady State,*
To end her Picture, does the third time wait.
But er'e thou fal'st to work, first *Painter* see
It be'nt too slight grown, or too hard for thee.
Canst thou paint without Colours? Then 'tis right: 5
For so we too without a Fleet can fight.
Or canst thou dawb a Sign-post, and that ill?
'Twill suit our great debauch and little skill.
Or hast thou mark't how antique Masters limn
The Aly roof, with snuff of Candle dimm,   10
Sketching in shady smoke prodigious tools,
'Twill serve this race of Drunkards, Pimps, and Fools.
But if to match our Crimes thy skill presumes,
As th' *Indians,* draw our Luxury in Plumes.
Or if to score out our compendious Fame,   15
With *Hook* then, through the *microscope,* take aim
Where, like the new *Controller,* all men laugh
To see a tall Lowse brandish the white Staff.
Else shalt thou oft thy guiltless Pencil curse,
Stamp on thy Pallat, nor perhaps the worse.   20
The Painter so, long having vext his cloth,
Of his Hound's Mouth to feign the raging froth,
His desperate Pencil at the work did dart,
His Anger reacht that rage which past his Art;

Chance finisht that which Art could but begin, 25
And he sat smiling how his Dog did grinn.
So may'st thou perfect, by a lucky blow,
What all thy softest touches cannot do.
    Paint then St. *Albans* full of soup and gold,
The new *Courts* pattern, Stallion of the old. 30
Him neither Wit nor Courage did exalt,
But Fortune chose him for her pleasure salt.
Paint him with *Drayman's* Shoulders, butchers *Mien,*
Member'd like Mules, with Elephantine chine.
Well he the Title of St. *Albans* bore, 35
For never *Bacon* study'd Nature more.
But Age, allaying now that youthful heat,
Fits him in *France* to play at Cards and treat.
Draw no Commission lest the *Court* should lye,
That, disavowing Treaty, ask supply. 40
He needs no Seal, but to St. *James*'s lease,
Whose Breeches were the Instrument of Peace.
Who, if the *French* dispute his Pow'r, from thence
Can straight produce them a *Plenipotence.*
Nor fears he *the most Christian* should trepan 45
Two Saints at once, St. *German,* St. *Alban.*
But thought the Golden Age was now restor'd,
When Men and Women took each others Word.
    Paint then again *Her Highness* to the life,
Philosopher beyond *Newcastle*'s Wife. 50
She, nak'd, can *Archimedes* self put down,
For an Experiment upon the *Crown.*
She perfected that Engine, oft assay'd,
How after Childbirth to renew a Maid.
And found how *Royal Heirs* might be matur'd, 55
In fewer months than Mothers once indur'd.
Hence *Crowder* made the rare Inventress free,
Of's *Highnesses Royal Society.*
Happy'st of Women, if she were but able
To make her glassen *D——s* once *malleable!* 60
Paint her with Oyster Lip, and breath of Fame,
Wide Mouth that Sparagus may well proclaim:
With *Chanc'lor's* Belly, and so large a Rump,
There, not behind the Coach, her Pages jump.

Express her studying now, if *China*-clay,   65
Can without breaking venom'd juice convey.
Or how a mortal Poyson she may draw,
Out of the cordial meal of the *Cacao*.
Witness ye stars of Night, and thou the pale
Moon, that o'rcome with the sick steam did'st fail;   70
Ye neighb'ring Elms, that your green leaves did shed,
And Fawns, that from the womb abortive fled.
Not unprovok'd she trys forbidden Arts,
But in her soft Breast Loves hid Cancer smarts.
While she revolves, at once, *Sidney's* disgrace,   75
And her self scorn'd for emulous *Denham's* Face;
And nightly hears the hated Guards away
Galloping with the *Duke* to other Prey.
    Paint *Castlemaine* in Colours that will hold,
Her, not her Picture, for she now grows old.   80
She through her Lacquies Drawers as he ran,
Discern'd Love's Cause, and a new Flame began.
Her wonted joys thenceforth and *Court* she shuns,
And still within her mind the Footman runs:
His brazen Calves, his brawny Thighs, (the Face   85
She slights) his Feet shapt for a smoother race.
Poring within her Glass she re-adjusts
Her looks, and oft-try'd Beauty now distrusts:
Fears lest he scorn a Woman once assay'd,
And now first, wisht she e're had been a Maid.   90
Great Love, how dost thou triumph, and how reign,
That to a Groom couldst humble her disdain!
Stript to her Skin, see how she stooping stands,
Nor scorns to rub him down with those fair Hands;
And washing (lest the scent her Crime disclose)   95
His sweaty Hooves, tickles him 'twixt the Toes.
But envious Fame, too soon, begun to note
More gold in's Fob, more Lace upon his Coat
And he, unwary, and of Tongue too fleet,
No longer could conceal his Fortune sweet.   100
Justly the Rogue was whipt in Porter's Den:
And *Jermyn* straight has leave to come agen.
Ah *Painter*, now could *Alexander* live,
And this *Campaspe* thee *Apelles* give!

Draw next a Pair of Tables op'ning, then 105
The *House of Commons* clatt'ring like the Men.
Describe the *Court* and *Country,* both set right,
On opposite points, the black against the white.
Those having lost the Nation at *Trick track,*
These now advent'ring how to win it back. 110
The Dice betwixt them must the Fate divide,
As Chance does still in Multitudes decide.
But here the *Court* does its advantage know,
For the Cheat *Turnor* for them both must throw.
As some from Boxes, he so from the Chair 115
Can strike the Die, and still with them goes share.
　　Here *Painter* rest a little, and survey
With what small Arts the publick game they play.
For so too *Rubens,* with affairs of State,
His lab'ring Pencil oft would recreate. 120
　　The close *Cabal* mark'd how the Navy eats,
And thought all lost that goes not to the Cheats:
So therefore secretly for Peace decrees,
Yet as for War the *Parliament* should squeeze;
And fix to the Revenue such a Summ, 125
Should *Goodrick* silence and strike *Paston* dumb;
Should pay Land Armies, should dissolve the vain
Commons, and ever such a *Court* maintain,
Hyde's Avarice, *Bennet's* Luxury should suffice,
And what can these defray but the *Excise?* 130
Excise, a Monster worse than e're before
Frighted the Midwife, and the Mother tore.
A thousand Hands she has and thousand Eyes,
Breaks into Shops, and into Cellars prys.
With hundred rows of Teeth the Shark exceeds, 135
And on all Trade like *Casawar* she feeds:
Chops off the piece where e're she close the Jaw,
Else swallows all down her indented maw.
She stalks all day in Streets conceal'd from sight,
And flies like Batts with leathern Wings by Night. 140
She wastes the Country and on Cities preys.
Her, of a female Harpy, in Dog Days:
Black *Birch,* of all the Earth-born race most hot,
And most rapacious, like himself begot.

And, of his Brat enamour'd, as't increast,   145
Bugger'd in Incest with the mungrel Beast.
    Say Muse, for nothing can escape thy sight,
(And Painter, wanting other, draw this Fight.)
Who, in an *English* Senate, fierce debate,
Could raise so long for this new Whore of State.   150
    Of early Wittals first the Troop march'd in,
For Diligence renown'd, and Discipline:
In Loyal haste they left young Wives in Bed,
And *Denham* these by one consent did head.
Of the old Courtiers next a Squadron came,   155
That sold their Master, led by *Ashburnham*.
To them succeeds a despicable Rout,
But knew the Word and well could face about;
Expectants pale, with hopes of spoil allur'd,
Thought yet but Pioneers, and led by *Steward*.   160
Then damming Cowards rang'd the vocal Plain,
Wood these commands, Knight of the Horn and Cane.
Still his Hook-shoulder seems the blow to dread,
And under's Armpit he defends his Head.
The posture strange men laught at of his Poll,   165
Hid with his Elbow like the Spice he stole.
Headless St. *Dennis* so his Head does bear;
And both of them alike *French* Martyrs were.
Court-Officers, as us'd, the next place took,
And follow'd *Fox,* but with disdainful look.   170
His Birth, his Youth, his Brokage all dispraise,
In vain, for always he commands that pays.
Then the Procurers under *Progers* fil'd,
Gentlest of men, and his Lieutenant mild,
Bronkard Loves Squire; through all the field array'd,   175
No Troop was better clad nor so well pay'd.
Then march't the Troop of *Clarendon,* all full,
Haters of Fowl, to *Teal* preferring *Bull*.
Gross Bodies, grosser Minds, and grossest Cheats;
And bloated *Wren* conducts them to their seats.   180
C——n advances next, whose Coife dos awe
The Miter Troop, and with his looks gives Law.
He March'd with Beaver cock'd of Bishop's brim,
And hid much Fraud under an aspect grim.

Next th' Lawyers Mercenary Band appear: 18
Finch, in the Front, and *Thurland* in the Rear.
The Troop of Priviledge, a Rabble bare
Of Debtors deep, fell to *Trelawny's* Care.
Their Fortune's error they supply'd in rage,
Nor any further would then these ingage.   19
Then marcht the Troop, whose valiant Acts before,
(Their publick Acts) oblig'd them still to more.
For Chimney's sake they all Sir *Pool* obey'd,
Or in his absence him that first it lay'd.
Then comes the thrifty Troop of Privateers,   19
Whose Horses each with other enterfeers.
Before them *Higgins* rides with brow compact,
Mourning his *Countess,* anxious for his Act.
Sir *Frederick* and Sir *Salomon* draw Lotts
For the command of Politicks or Sotts.   20
Thence fell to Words, but, quarrel to adjourn,
Their Friends agreed they should command by turn.
Carteret the rich did the Accomptants guide,
And in ill *English* all the World defy'd.
The *Papists,* but of those the *House* had none: 20
Else *Talbot* offer'd to have led them on.
Bold *Duncombe* next, of the Projectors chief:
And old *Fitz-Harding* of the Eaters Beef.
Late and disorder'd out the Drinkers drew;
Scarce them their Leaders, they their Leaders knew.   21
Before them enter'd, equal in Command,
Apsley and *Brotherick,* marching hand in hand.
Last then but one, *Powell,* that could not ride,
Led the *French* Standard, weltring in his stride,
He, to excuse his slowness, truth confest   21
That 'twas so long before he could be drest.
The *Lords Sons,* last, all these did reinforce:
Cornbury before them manag'd Hobby-horse.
     Never, before nor since, an Host so steel'd
Troop't on to muster in the *Tuttle-field.*   22
Not the first Cock-horse, that with Cork were shod
To rescue *Albemarle* from the Sea-Cod:
Nor the late Feather-men, whom *Tomkins* fierce
Shall with one Breath like thistle-down disperse.

All the two *Coventrys* their Gen'rals chose: 225
For one had much, the other nought to lose.
Nor better choice all accidents could hit;
While Hector *Harry* steers by *Will* the Wit:
They both accept the Charge with merry glee,
To fight a Battel, from all Gun-shot free.   230
    Pleas'd with their Numbers, yet in Valour wise,
They feign a parly, better to surprize:
They, that e're long shall the rude *Dutch* upbraid,
Who in a time of Treaty durst invade.
Thick was the Morning, and the *House* was thin,   235
The *Speaker* early, when they all fell in.
Propitious Heavens, had not you them crost,
Excise had got the day, and all been lost.
For th' other side all in loose Quarters lay,
Without Intelligence, Command, or Pay: 240
A scatter'd Body, which the Foe ne'r try'd,
But oftner did among themselves divide.
And some ran o're each night while others sleep,
And undescry'd return'd e're morning peep.
But *Strangeways*, that all Night still walk'd the round,   245
(For Vigilance and Courage both renown'd)
First spy'd the Enemy and gave th' Alarm:
Fighting it single till the rest might arm.
Such *Roman Cocles* strid: before the Foe,
The falling Bridge behind, the Stream below.   250
    Each ran, as chance him guides, to sev'ral Post:
And all to pattern his Example boast.
Their former Trophees they recal to mind,
And to new edge their angry Courage grind.
First enter'd forward *Temple*, Conqueror   255
Of *Irish*-Cattel and *Sollicitor*.
Then daring *Seymour*, that with Spear and Shield,
Had strecht the monster *Patent* on the Field.
Keen *Whorwood* next, in aid of Damsel frail,
That pierc't the Gyant *Mordant* through his Mail.   260
And surly *Williams*, the Accomptants bane:
And *Lovelace* young, of Chimney-men the Cane.
Old *Waller*, Trumpet-gen'ral swore he'd write
This Combat truer than the Naval Fight.

Of Birth, State, Wit, Strength, Courage, *How'rd* presumes,
And in his Breast wears many *Montezumes*.   [26
These and some more with single Valour stay
The adverse Troops, and hold them all at Bay.
Each thinks his Person represents the whole,
And with that thought does multiply his Soul: 27
Believes himself an Army, theirs one Man,
As eas'ly Conquer'd, and believing can.
With Heart of Bees so full, and Head of Mites,
That each, tho' Duelling, a Battel fights.
Such once *Orlando,* famous in *Romance,*   27
Broach'd whole Brigades like Larks upon his Lance.
    But strength at last still under number bows,
And the faint sweat trickled down *Temples* Brows.
Ev'n Iron *Strangeways*, chafing yet gave back,
Spent with *fatigue*, to breath a while Toback.   28
When, marching in, a seas'nable recruit
Of Citizens and Merchants held dispute:
And, charging all their Pikes, a sullen Band
Of *Presbyterian Switzers*, made a stand.
    Nor could all these the Field have long maintain'd,   285
But for th'unknown Reserve that still remain'd:
A *Gross* of *English Gentry*, nobly born,
Of clear *Estates,* and to no Faction sworn;
Dear Lovers of their King, and Death to meet,
For Countrys Cause, that Glorious think and sweet: 290
To speak not forward, but in Action brave;
In giving Gen'rous, but in Counsel Grave;
Candidly credulous for once, nay twice;
But sure the *Devil* cannot cheat them thrice.
The Van and Battel, though retiring, falls   295
Without disorder in their Intervals:
Then closing, all in equal Front fall on,
Led by great *Garrway,* and great *Littleton*.
Lee, equal to obey or to command,
Adjutant-General was still at hand.   300
The martial Standard *Sands* displaying, shows
St. *Dunstan* in it, tweaking *Satan's* Nose.
See sudden chance of War! To Paint or Write,
Is longer Work, and harder than to fight.

At the first Charge the Enemy give out;   305
And the *Excise* receives a total Rout.
Broken in Courage, yet the Men the same,
Resolve henceforth upon their other Game:
Where force had fail'd with Stratagem to play,
And what haste lost, recover by delay.   310
St. *Albans* straight is sent to, to forbear,
Lest the sure Peace, forsooth, too soon appear.
The Seamens Clamour to three ends they use;
To cheat their Pay, feign want, the *House* accuse.
Each day they bring the Tale, and that too true,   315
How strong the *Dutch* their Equipage renew.
Mean time through all the Yards their Orders run
To lay the Ships up, cease the Keels begun.
The Timber rots, and useless Ax does rust,
The unpractis'd Saw lyes bury'd in its Dust;   320
The busie Hammer sleeps, the Ropes untwine;
The Stores and Wages all are mine and thine.
Along the Coast and Harbours they take care
That Money lack, nor Forts be in repair.
Long thus they could against the *House* conspire,   325
Load them with Envy, and with Sitting tire:
And the lov'd *King*, and never yet deny'd,
Is brought to beg in publick and to chide.
But when this fail'd, and Months enough were spent,
They with the first days proffer seem content: 330
And to *Land-tax* from the *Excise* turn round,
Bought off with *Eighteen hundred thousand pound*.
Thus, like fair Thieves, the *Commons* Purse they share,
But all the *Members* Lives, consulting, spare.

    Blither than Hare that hath escap'd the Hounds,   335
The *House* Prorogu'd, the *Chancellor* rebounds.
Not so decrepid *Æson*, hash'd and stew'd
With *Magic* Herbs, rose from the Pot renew'd:
And with fresh Age felt his glad Limbs unite;
His Gout (yet still he curst) had left him quite.   340
What Frosts to Fruit, what Ars'nick to the Rat,
What to fair *Denham* mortal *Chocolat*;
What an Account to *Carteret*; that and more
A *Parliament* is to the *Chancellor*.

So the sad Tree shrinks from the Mornings Eye;   345
But blooms all Night, and shoots its branches high.
So, at the Suns recess, again returns,
The Comet dread, and Earth and Heaven burns.
    Now *Mordant* may, within his Castle Tow'r,
Imprison Parents, and the Child deflowre.   350
    The *Irish*-Herd is now let loose, and comes
By Millions over, not by *Hecatombs*.
And now, now, the *Canary-Patent* may
Be Broach'd again, for the great Holy-day
    See how he Reigns in his new Palace *culminant*,   355
And sits in State Divine like *Jove* the *fulminant*!
First *Buckingham*, that durst to him Rebel,
Blasted with Lightning, struck with Thunder fell.
Next the *Twelve Commons* are condemn'd to groan,
And roul in vain at *Sisyphus*'s Stone.   360
But still he car'd, while in Revenge he brav'd,
That Peace secur'd, and Money might be sav'd.
Gain and Revenge, Revenge and Gain are sweet:
United most, else when by turns they meet.
France had St. *Albans* promis'd (so they sing)   365
St. *Albans* promis'd him, and he the *King*.
The *Count* forthwith is order'd all to close,
To play for *Flanders*, and the stake to lose.
While Chain'd together two *Ambassadors*
Like Slaves, shall beg for Peace at *Hollands* doors.   370
This done, among his *Cyclops* he retires,
To forge new Thunder, and inspect their Fires.
    The *Court*, as once of War, now fond of Peace,
All to new Sports their wanton fears release.
From *Greenwich* (where Intelligence they hold)   375
Comes news of Pastime, Martial and old:
A Punishment invented first to awe
Masculine Wives, transgressing Natures Law.
Where when the brawny Female disobeys,
And beats the Husband till for peace he prays: 380
No concern'd *Jury* for him Damage finds,
Nor partial *Justice* her Behaviour binds;
But the just Street does the next House invade,
Mounting the neighbour Couple on lean Jade.

The Distaff knocks, the Grains from Kettle fly,   385
And Boys and Girls in Troops run houting by;
Prudent Antiquity, that knew by Shame,
Better than Law, Domestick Crimes to tame
And taught Youth by Spectacle Innocent!
So thou and I, dear *Painter*, represent   390
In quick *Effigy*, others Faults, and feign
By making them ridiculous to restrain.
With homely sight, they chose thus to relax
The Joys of State, for the new Peace and Tax.
So *Holland* with us had the Mast'ry try'd,   395
And our next neighbours *France* and *Flanders* ride.
    But a fresh News, the great designment nips,
Off, at the Isle of *Candy*, *Dutch* and ships.
Bab May and *Arlington* did wisely scoff,
And thought all safe if they were so far off.   400
Modern *Geographers,* 'twas there they thought,
Where *Venice* twenty years the *Turk* had fought:
While the first year our Navy is but shown,
The next divided, and the third we've none.
They, by the Name, mistook it for that Isle,   405
Where Pilgrim *Palmer* travell'd in Exile,
With the Bulls Horn to measure his own Head,
And on *Pasiphae*'s Tomb to drop a Bead.
But *Morrice* learn'd demonstrates, by the Post,
This Isle of *Candy* was on *Essex* Coast.   410
    Fresh Messengers still the sad News assure,
More tim'rous now we are, than first secure.
False Terrors our believing Fears devise:
And the *French* Army one from *Calais* spies.
Bennet and *May*, and those of shorter reach,   415
Change all for Guinea's, and a Crown for each:
But wiser Men, and well foreseen in chance,
In *Holland* theirs had lodg'd before, and *France*.
White-hall's unsafe, the *Court* all meditates
To fly to *Windsor*, and mure up the Gates.   420
Each does the other blame, and all distrust;
But *Mordant* new oblig'd, would sure be just.
Not such a fatal stupefaction reign'd
At *London*'s Flame, nor so the *Court* complain'd.

The *Bloodworth-Chanc'lor* gives, then does recal   425
Orders, amaz'd at last gives none at all.
   St. *Albans* writ to that he may bewail
To Master *Lewis,* and tell Coward tale,
How yet the *Hollanders* do make a noise,
Threaten to beat us, and are naughty Boys.   430
Now *Doleman's* disobedient, and they still
Uncivil: His unkindness would us kill.
Tell him our Ships unrigg'd, our Forts unman'd,
Our Money spent; else 'twere at his command.
Summon him therefore of his Word, and prove   435
To move him out of Pity, if not Love.
Pray him to make *De-Witte,* and *Ruyter* cease,
And whip the *Dutch,* unless they'l hold their peace.
But *Lewis* was of Memory but dull,
And to St. *Albans* too undutiful;   440
Nor Word, nor near Relation did revere;
But ask'd him bluntly for his *Character.*
The gravell'd *Count* did with the Answer faint:
(His *Character* was that which thou didst paint)
And so enforc'd, like Enemy or Spy,   445
Trusses his baggage, and the Camp does fly.
Yet *Lewis* writes, and lest our Hearts should break,
Consoles us morally out of *Seneque.*
   Two Letters next unto *Breda* are sent,
In Cipher one to *Harry* Excellent.   450
The first instructs our (Verse the Name abhors)
Plenipotentiary Ambassadors,
To prove by *Scripture,* Treaty does imply
Cessation, as the look Adultery.
And that by Law of Arms, in Martial strife,   455
Who yields his Sword has Title to his Life.
Presbyter Hollis the first point should clear;
The second *Coventry* the *Cavalier.*
But, would they not be argu'd back from Sea,
Then to return home straight *infecta re.*   460
But *Harry's* Order, if they won't recal
Their Fleet, to threaten, we will give them all.
   The *Dutch* are then in *Proclamation* shent,
For Sin against th' *Eleventh Commandment.*

Hyde's flippant Stile there pleasantly curvets;   465
Still his sharp Wit on States and Princes whets.
(So *Spain* could not escape his Laughters Spleen:
None but himself must chuse the *King* a *Queen*.)
But when he came the odious Clause to Pen,
That summons up the *Parliament* agen;   470
His Writing-Master many a time he bann'd,
And wish'd himself the Gout, to seize his hand.
Never old Letcher more repugnance felt,
Consenting, for his Rupture, to be Gelt;
But still in hope he solac'd, e're they come,   475
To work the Peace, and so to send them home.
Or in their hasty Call to find a flaw,
Their Acts to vitiate, and them over-awe.
But most rely'd upon this *Dutch* pretence,
To raise a two-edg'd Army for's defence.   480
    First, then he march'd our whole *Militia's* force,
(As if, alas, we Ships or *Dutch* had Horse.)
Then, from the usual *Common-place*, he blames
These; and in Standing-Armies praise declaims.
And the wise *Court*, that always lov'd it dear,   485
Now thinks all but too little for their Fear.
Hyde Stamps, and straight upon the ground the swarms
Of current *Myrmidons* appear in Arms.
And for their Pay he writes as from the *King*,
With that curs'd Quill pluck'd from a Vulture's Wing: 490
Of the whole Nation now to ask a Loan.
(The *Eighteen hundred thousand pound* was gone.)
    This done, he Pens a *Proclamation* stout,
In rescue of the *Banquiers Banquerout*:
His minion Imps that, in his secret part,   495
Lye nuzz'ling at the *Sacramental* wart;
Horse-leeches circling at the Hem'roid Vein;
He sucks the King, they him, he them again.
The Kingdoms Farm he lets to them bid least:
Greater the Bribe, and that 's at Interest.   500
Here Men induc'd by Safety, Gain, and Ease,
Their Money lodge; confiscate when he please.
These can, at need, at instant, with a scrip,
(This lik'd him best) his Cash beyond Sea whip.

When *Dutch* Invade, when *Parliament* prepare, 505
How can he Engines so convenient spare?
Let no Man touch them, or demand his own,
Pain of Displeasure of great *Clarendon*.
The State Affairs thus Marshall'd, for the rest
Monk in his Shirt against the *Dutch* is prest. 510
Often, dear *Painter*, have I sate and mus'd
Why he should still b'on all adventures us'd.
If they for nothing ill, like *Ashen-wood*,
Or think him, like *Herb-John*, for nothing good.
Whether his Valour they so much admire, 515
Or that for Cowardice they all retire.
As Heav'n in Storms, they call, in gusts of State,
On *Monk* and *Parliament*, yet both do hate.
All Causes sure concur, but most they think
Under *Herculean* Labours he may sink. 520
Soon then the *Independent* Troops would close,
And *Hyde*'s last Project would his Place dispose.
  Ruyter the while, that had our Ocean curb'd,
Sail'd now among our Rivers undisturb'd:
Survey'd their Crystal Streams, and Banks so green, 525
And Beauties e're this never naked seen.
Through the vain sedge the bashful *Nymphs* he ey'd;
Bosomes, and all which from themselves they hide.
The Sun much brighter, and the Skies more clear,
He finds the Air, and all things, sweeter here. 530
The sudden change, and such a tempting sight,
Swells his old Veins with fresh Blood, fresh Delight.
Like am'rous Victors he begins to shave,
And his new Face looks in the *English* Wave.
His sporting Navy all about him swim, 535
And witness their complaisence in their trim.
Their streaming Silks play through the weather fair,
And with inveigling Colours Court the Air.
While the red Flags breath on their Top-masts high
Terrour and War, but want an Enemy. 540
Among the Shrowds the Seamen sit and sing,
And wanton Boys on every Rope do cling.
Old *Neptune* springs the Tydes, and Water lent:
(The Gods themselves do help the provident.)

And, where the deep Keel on the shallow cleaves,   545
With *Trident*'s Leaver, and great Shoulder heaves.
Æolus their Sails inspires with *Eastern* Wind,
Puffs them along, and breathes upon them kind.
With Pearly Shell the *Tritons* all the while
Sound the Sea-march, and guide to *Sheppy Isle*.   550
   So have I seen in *April*'s bud, arise
A Fleet of Clouds, sailing along the Skies:
The liquid Region with their Squadrons fill'd,
The airy Sterns the Sun behind does guild;
And gentle Gales them steer, and Heaven drives,   555
When, all on sudden, their calm bosome rives
With Thunder and Lightning from each armed Cloud;
Shepherds themselves in vain in bushes shrowd.
Such up the stream the *Belgick* Navy glides,
And at *Sheerness* unloads its stormy sides.   560
   Sprag there, tho practic'd in the Sea command,
With panting Heart, lay like a fish on Land,
And quickly judg'd the Fort was not *tenable*,
Which, if a House, yet were not *tenantable*.
No man can sit there safe, the Cannon pow'rs   565
Through the Walls untight, and Bullet show'rs:
The neighbr'hood ill, and an unwholesome seat.
So at the first Salute resolves Retreat,
And swore that he would never more dwell there
Until the *City* put it in repair.   570
So he in Front, his Garrison in Rear,
March straight to *Chatham*, to increase the fear.
   There our sick Ships unrigg'd in Summer lay,
Like molting Fowl, a weak and easie Prey.
For whose strong bulk Earth scarce could Timber find,   575
The Ocean Water, or the Heavens Wind.
Those Oaken Gyants of the ancient Race
That rul'd all Seas, and did our Channe' grace.
The conscious Stag, so once the Forest dread,
Flies to the Wood, and hides his arm'ess Head.   580
Ruyter forthwith a Squadron does intack,
They sail securely through the Rivers track.
An *English* Pilot too, (O Shame, O Sin!)
Cheated of Pay, was he that show'd them in.

Our wretched Ships within their Fate attend, 585
And all our hopes now on frail Chain depend:
Engine so slight to guard us from the Sea,
It fitter seem'd to captivate a Flea.
A *Skipper* rude shocks it without respect,
Filling his Sails, more force to recollect. 590
Th' *English* from shore the Iron deaf invoke
For its last aid: Hold Chain or we are broke.
But with her Sailing weight, the *Holland* Keel
Snapping the brittle links, does thorow reel;
And to the rest the open'd passage shew. 595
    Monk from the bank the dismal sight does view.
Our feather'd *Gallants,* which came down that day
To be Spectators safe of the *new Play,*
Leave him alone when first they hear the Gun;
(*Cornbry* the fleetest) and to *London* run. 600
Our Seamen, whom no Dangers shape could fright,
Unpaid, refuse to mount our Ships for spight:
Or to their fellows swim on board the *Dutch,*
Which show the tempting metal in their clutch.
Oft had he sent, of *Duncombe* and of *Legg* 605
Cannon and Powder, but in vain, to beg:
And *Upnor*-Castle's ill-deserted Wall,
Now needful, does for Ammunition call.
He finds wheresoe're he succour might expect,
Confusion, folly, treach'ry, fear, neglect. 610
    But when the *Royal Charles,* what Rage, what Grief,
He saw seiz'd, and could give her no Relief!
That sacred Keel, which had, as he, restor'd
His exil'd *Sov'raign* on its happy Board;
And thence the *Brittish* Admiral became; 615
Crown'd, for that Merit, with their Masters Name.
That Pleasure-boat of War, in whose dear side
Secure so oft he had this Foe defy'd:
Now a cheap spoil, and the mean Victor's Slave,
Taught the *Dutch* Colours from its top to wave; 620
Of former Glories the reproachful thought,
With present shame compar'd, his mind distraught.
Such from *Euphrates* bank, a Tygress fell,
After the Robbers, for her Whelps does yell:

But sees, inrag'd, the River flow between.   625
Frustrate Revenge, and Love, by loss more keen,
At her own Breast her useless claws does arm;
She tears herself since him she cannot harm.
The Guards, plac'd for the Chains and Fleets defence,
Long since were fled on many a feign'd pretence.   630
Daniel had there adventur'd, Man of might;
Sweet *Painter* draw his Picture while I write.
Paint him of Person tall, and big of bone,
Large Limbs, like Ox, not to be kill'd but shown.
Scarce can burnt Iv'ry feign an Hair so black,   635
Or Face so red thine Oker and thy Lack.
Mix a vain Terrour in his Martial look,
And all those lines by which men are mistook.
But when, by shame constrain'd to go on Board,
He heard how the wild Cannon nearer roar'd;   640
And saw himself confin'd, like Sheep in Pen;
Daniel then thought he was in *Lyons* Den.
But when the frightful Fire-ships he saw,
Pregnant with Sulphur, to him nearer draw
Captain, Lieutenant, Ensign, all make haste,   645
E're in the Firy Furnace they be cast.
Three Children tall, unsing'd, away they row,
Like *Shadrack, Mesheck,* and *Abednego.*
Not so brave *Douglas*; on whose lovely chin
The early Down but newly did begin;   650
And modest Beauty yet his Sex did Veil,
While envious Virgins hope he is a Male.
His yellow Locks curl back themselves to seek,
Nor other Courtship knew but to his Cheek.
Oft has he in chill *Eske* or *Seine,* by night,   655
Harden'd and cool'd his Limbs, so soft, so white,
Among the Reeds, to be espy'd by him,
The *Nymphs* would rustle; he would forward swim.
They sigh'd and said, Fond Boy, why so untame,
That fly'st Love Fires, reserv'd for other Flame?   660
Fixt on his Ship, he fac'd that horrid Day,
And wondred much at those that run away:
Nor other fear himself could comprehend,
Then, lest Heav'n fall, e're thither he ascend.

But entertains, the while, his time too short   660
With birding at the *Dutch,* as if in sport:
Or Waves his Sword, and could he them conjure
Within its circle, knows himself secure.
The fatal Bark him boards with grappling fire,
And safely through its Port the *Dutch* retire: 670
That precious life he yet disdains to save,
Or with known Art to try the gentle Wave.
Much him the Honours of his ancient Race
Inspire, nor would he his own deeds deface.
And secret Joy, in his calm Soul does rise,   675
That *Monk* looks on to see how *Douglas* dies.
Like a glad Lover, the fierce Flames he meets,
And tries his first embraces in their Sheets.
His shape exact, which the bright flames infold,
Like the Sun's Statue stands of burnish'd Gold.   680
Round the transparent Fire about him glows,
As the clear Amber on the Bee does close:
And, as on Angels Heads their Glories shine,
His burning Locks adorn his Face Divine.
But, when in his immortal Mind he felt   685
His alt'ring Form, and soder'd Limbs to melt;
Down on the Deck he laid himself, and dy'd,
With his dear Sword reposing by his Side.
And, on the flaming Plank, so rests his Head,
As one that's warm'd himself and gone to Bed.   690
His Ship burns down, and with his Relicks sinks,
And the sad Stream beneath his Ashes drinks.
Fortunate Boy! if either Pencil's Fame,
Or if my Verse can propagate thy Name;
When *Œta* and *Alcides* are forgot,   695
Our *English* youth shall sing the Valiant *Scot.*
    Each doleful day still with fresh loss returns;
The *Loyal-London,* now a third time burns.
And the true *Royal-Oak,* and *Royal-James,*
Ally'd in Fate, increase, with theirs, her Flames.   700
Of all our Navy none should now survive,
But that the Ships themselves were taught to dive:
And the kind River in its Creek them hides,
Fraughting their pierced Keels with Oosy Tides.

Up to the *Bridge* contagious Terrour strook: 705
The *Tow'r* it self with the near danger shook.
And were not *Ruyters* maw with ravage cloy'd,
Ev'n *London*'s Ashes had been then destroy'd.
Officious fear, however, to prevent
Our loss, does so much more our loss augment.   710
The *Dutch* had robb'd those Jewels of the Crown:
Our Merchant-men, lest they should burn, we drown.
So when the Fire did not enough devour,
The Houses were demolish'd near the *Tow'r*.
Those Ships, that yearly from their teeming Howl,   715
Unloaded here the Birth of either Pole;
Furrs from the *North*, and Silver from the *West*,
From the *South* Perfumes, Spices from the *East*;
From *Gambo* Gold, and from the *Ganges* Gems;
Take a short Voyage underneath the *Thames*.   720
Once a deep River, now with Timber floor'd,
And shrunk, lest Navigable, to a Ford.
  Now (nothing more at *Chatham* left to burn)
The *Holland* Squadron leisurely return:
And spight of *Ruperts* and of *Albemarles*,   725
To *Ruyter*'s Triumph lead the captive *Charles*.
The pleasing sight he often does prolong:
Her Masts erect, tough Cordage, Timbers strong,
Her moving Shape; all these he does survey,
And all admires, but most his easie Prey.   730
The Seamen search her all, within, without:
Viewing her strength, they yet their Conquest doubt.
Then with rude shouts, secure, the Air they vex;
With Gamesome Joy insulting on her Decks.
Such the fear'd *Hebrew*, captive, blinded, shorn,   735
Was led about in sport, the publick scorn.
  Black Day accurs'd! On thee let no man hale
Out of the Port, or dare to hoise a Sail,
Or row a Boat in thy unlucky hour:
Thee, the Year's monster, let thy Dam devour.   740
And constant Time, to keep his course yet right,
Fill up thy space with a redoubled Night.
When aged *Thames* was bound with Fetters base,
And *Medway* chast ravish'd before his Face,

And their dear Off-spring murder'd in their sight;   74
Thou, and thy Fellows, held'st the odious Light.
Sad change, since first that happy pair was wed,
When all the Rivers grac'd their Nuptial Bed;
And Father *Neptune* promis'd to resign
His Empire old, to their immortal Line!   75
Now with vain grief their vainer hopes they rue,
Themselves dishonour'd, and the *Gods* untrue:
And to each other helpless couple moan,
As the sad Tortoise for the Sea does groan.
But most they for their Darling *Charles* complain: 75
And were it burnt, yet less would be their pain.
To see that fatal Pledge of Sea-Command,
Now in the Ravisher *De-Ruyter*'s hand,
The *Thames* roar'd, swouning *Medway* turn'd her tide,
And were they mortal, both for grief had dy'd.   76

   The *Court* in Farthing yet it self does please,
And female *Stewart*, there, *Rules the four Seas*.
But Fate does still accumulate our Woes,
And *Richmond* here commands, as *Ruyter* those.

   After this loss, to rellish discontent,   76
Some one must be accus'd by Punishment.
All our miscarriages on *Pett* must fall:
His Name alone seems fit to answer all.
Whose Counsel first did this mad War beget?
Who all Commands sold thro' the Navy? *Pett.*   77
Who would not follow when the *Dutch* were bet?
Who treated out the time at *Bergen*? *Pett.*
Who the *Dutch* Fleet with Storms disabled met,
And rifling Prizes, them neglected? *Pett.*
Who with false News prevented the *Gazette*?   77
The Fleet divided? Writ for *Rupert*? *Pett.*
Who all our Seamen cheated of their Debt?
And all our Prizes who did swallow? *Pett.*
Who did advise no Navy out to set?
And who the Forts left unrepair'd? *Pett.*   780
Who to supply with Powder, did forget
Languard, Sheerness, Gravesend, and *Upnor*? *Pett.*
Who all our Ships expos'd in *Chathams* Net?
Who should it be but the *Phanatick Pett.*

Pett, the Sea Architect, in making Ships,   785
Was the first cause of all these Naval slips:
Had he not built, none of these faults had bin;
If no Creation, there had been no Sin.
But, his great Crime, one Boat away he sent;
That lost our Fleet, and did our Flight prevent.   790
Then that Reward might in its turn take place,
And march with Punishment in equal pace;
Southampton dead, much of the Treasure's care,
And place in Counsel fell to *Duncombes* share.
All men admir'd he to that pitch could fly: 795
Powder ne're blew man up so soon so high.
But sure his late good Husbandry in *Peeter*,
Show'd him to manage the *Exchequer* meeter:
And who the Forts would not vouchsafe a corn,
To lavish the *King*'s Money more would scorn.   800
Who hath no Chimneys, to give all is best,
And ablest Speaker, who of Law has least;
Who less Estate, for *Treasurer* most fit;
And for a *Couns'llor*, he that has least Wit.
But the true cause was, that, in 's Brother *May*,   805
The *Exchequer* might the *Privy-purse* obey.
    But now draws near the *Parliament*'s return;
Hyde and the *Court* again begin to mourn.
Frequent in Counsel, earnest in Debate,
All Arts they try how to prolong its Date.   810
Grave *Primate Shelden* (much in Preaching there)
Blames the last Session, and this more does fear.
With *Boynton* or with *Middleton* 'twere sweet;
But with a *Parliament* abhors to meet,
And thinks 'twill ne're be well within this Nation,   815
Till it be govern'd by a *Convocation*.
But in the *Thames* mouth still *de Ruyter* laid,
The Peace not sure, new Army must be paid.
Hyde saith he hourly waits for a Dispatch;
Harry came Post just as he shew'd his Watch.   820
All to agree the Articles were clear,
The *Holland* Fleet and *Parliament* so near.
Yet *Harry* must job back and all mature,
Binding, e're th' *Houses* meet, the Treaty sure.

And 'twixt Necessity and Spight, till then,   828
Let them come up so to go down agen.
Up ambles *Country Justice* on his Pad,
And Vest bespeaks to be more seemly clad.
Plain *Gentlemen* are in Stage-Coach o'rethrown,
And *Deputy-Lieutenants* in their own.   830
The portly *Burgess*, through the Weather hot,
Does for his Corporation sweat and trot.
And all with Sun and Choler come adust;
And threaten *Hyde* to raise a greater Dust.
    But, fresh as from the *Mint*, the *Courtiers* fine   835
Salute them, smiling at their vain design.
And *Turner* gay up to his Pearch does march,
With Face new bleacht, smoothen'd and stiff with starch.
Tells them he at *Whitehall* had took a turn,
And for three days, thence moves them to adjourn.   840
Not so, quoth *Tomkins*; and straight drew his Tongue,
Trusty as Steel, that always ready hung;
And so, proceeding in his motion warm,
Th'Army soon rais'd, he doth as soon disarm.
True *Trojan*! while this Town can Girls afford,   845
And long as Cider lasts in *Hereford*;
The Girls shall always kiss thee, though grown old,
And in eternal Healths thy Name be trowl'd.
    Mean while the certain News of Peace arrives
At *Court*, and so reprieves their guilty Lives.   850
Hyde orders *Turner* that he should come late,
Lest some new *Tomkins* spring a fresh debate.
The *King*, that day rais'd early from his rest,
Expects as at a Play till *Turner's* drest.
At last together *Eaton* come and he: 855
No Dial more could with the Sun agree.
The *Speaker*, Summon'd, to the *Lords* repairs,
Nor gave the *Commons* leave to say their Pray'rs:
But like his Pris'ners to the Bar them led,
Where mute they stand to hear their Sentence read;   860
Trembling with joy and fear, *Hyde* them Prorogues,
And had almost mistook and call'd them Rogues.
    Dear *Painter*, draw this *Speaker* to the foot:
Where Pencil cannot, there my Pen shall do't;

That may his Body, this his Mind explain.   865
Paint him in Golden Gown, with Mace's Brain:
Bright Hair, fair Face, obscure and dull of Head;
Like Knife with Iv'ry haft, and edge of Lead.
At Pray'rs, his Eyes turn up the Pious white,
But all the while his *Private-Bill's* in sight.   870
In Chair, he smoaking sits like Master-Cook,
And a *Poll-Bill* does like his Apron look.
Well was he skill'd to season any question,
And make a sawce fit for *Whitehall's* digestion:
Whence ev'ry day, the Palat more to tickle;   875
Court-mushrumps ready are sent in in pickle.
When *Grievance* urg'd, he swells like squatted Toad,
Frisks like a Frog to croak a *Taxes* load.
His patient Piss, he could hold longer then
An Urinal, and sit like any Hen.   880
At Table, jolly as a Country-Host,
And soaks his Sack with *Norfolk* like a Toast.
At night, than *Canticleer* more brisk and hot,
And Serjeants Wife serves him for *Partelott*.
Paint last the King, and a dead shade of Night,   885
Only dispers'd by a weak Tapers light;
And those bright gleams that dart along and glare
From his clear Eyes, yet these too dark with Care.
There, as in the calm horrour all alone,
He wakes and Muses of th' uneasie Throne: 890
Raise up a sudden Shape with Virgins Face,
Though ill agree her Posture, Hour, or Place:
Naked as born, and her round Arms behind,
With her own Tresses interwove and twin'd:
Her mouth lockt up, a blind before her Eyes,   895
Yet from beneath the Veil her blushes rise;
And silent tears her secret anguish speak,
Her heart throbs, and with very shame would break.
The Object strange in him no Terrour mov'd:
He wonder'd first, then pity'd, then he lov'd: 900
And with kind hand does the coy Vision press,
Whose Beauty greater seem'd by her distress;
But soon shrunk back, chill'd with her touch so cold,
And th' airy Picture vanisht from his hold.

In his deep thoughts the wonder did increase,   90
And he Divin'd 'twas *England* or the *Peace*.
    Express him startling next with listning ear,
As one that some unusual noise does hear.
With Canon, Trumpets, Drums, his door surround,
But let some other Painter draw the sound: 91
Thrice did he rise, thrice the vain Tumult fled,
But again thunders when he lyes in Bed;
His mind secure does the known stroke repeat,
And finds the Drums *Lewis*'s March did beat.
    Shake then the room, and all his Curtains tear,   91
And with blue streaks infect the Taper clear:
While, the pale Ghosts, his Eye does fixt admire
Of Grandsire *Harry*, and of *Charles* his Sire.
Harry sits down, and in his open side
The grizly Wound reveals, of which he dy'd.   92
And ghastly *Charles*, turning his Collar low,
The purple thread about his Neck does show:
Then, whisp'ring to his Son in Words unheard,
Through the lock'd door both of them disappear'd.
The wondrous Night the pensive *King* revolves,   92
And rising, straight on *Hyde*'s Disgrace resolves.
    At his first step, he *Castlemain* does find,
Bennet and *Coventry*, as't were design'd.
And they, not knowing, the same thing propose,
Which his hid mind did in its depths inclose.   93
Through their feign'd speech their secret hearts he knew;
To her own Husband, *Castlemain*, untrue.
False to his Master *Bristol*, *Arlington*,
And *Coventry*, falser than any one,
Who to the Brother, Brother would betray;   93
Nor therefore trusts himself to such as they.
His Fathers Ghost too whisper'd him one Note,
That who does cut his Purse will cut his Throat.
But in wise anger he their Crimes forbears,
As Thieves repriev'd for Executioners;   94
While *Hyde* provok'd his foaming tusk does whet,
To prove them Traytors, and himself the *Pett*.
    Painter adieu, how will our Arts agree;
Poetick Picture, Painted Poetry.

But this great work is for our *Monarch* fit,   945
And henceforth *Charles* only to *Charles* shall sit.
His Master-hand the Ancients shall out-do
Himself the *Poet* and the *Painter* too.

To the King

So his bold Tube, Man, to the Sun apply'd,
And Spots unknown to the bright Star descry'd;
Show'd they obscure him, while too near they please,
And seem his Courtiers, are but his disease.
Through Optick Trunk the Planet seem'd to hear,   5
And hurls them off, e're since, in his Career.
    And you, *Great Sir*, that with him Empire share,
Sun of our World, as he the *Charles* is there.
Blame not the *Muse* that brought those spots to sight,
Which, in your Splendor hid, Corrode your Light;   10
Kings in the Country oft have gone astray,
Nor of a Peasant scorn'd to learn the way.
    Would she the unattended Throne reduce,
Banishing Love, Trust, Ornament and Use;
Better it were to live in Cloysters Lock,   15
Or in fair Fields to rule the easie Flock.
She blames them only who the *Court* restrain,
And, where all *England* serves, themselves would reign.
    Bold and accurs'd are they, that all this while
Have strove to Isle the *Monarch* from his *Isle*:   20
And to improve themselves, on false pretence,
About the Common *Prince* have rais'd a Fence;
The *Kingdom* from the *Crown* distinct would see,
And peal the Bark to burn at last the Tree.
(But *Ceres* Corn, and *Flora* is the Spring,   25
Bacchus is Wine, the Country is the *King*.)
    Not so does Rust insinuating wear,
Nor Powder so the vaulted Bastion tear;
Nor Earthquake so an hollow Isle overwhelm,
As scratching *Courtiers* undermine a *Realm*:   30
And through the Palace's Foundations bore,
Burr'wing themselves to hoard their guilty Store.

The smallest Vermin make the greatest waste,
And a poor Warren once a City ras'd.
But they whom born to Virtue and to Wealth, 3
Nor Guilt to flatt'ry binds, nor want to stealth;
Whose gen'rous Conscience and whose Courage high
Does with clear Counsels their large Souls supply;
That serve the *King* with their Estates and Care,
And, as in Love, on *Parliaments* can stare: 4
(Where few the number, choice is there less hard)
Give us this *Court,* and rule without a *Guard.*

Further Advice to a Painter

Painter once more thy Pencell reassume,
And draw me in one Scene London and Rome,
There holy Charles, here good Aurelius Sate,
Weeping to see their Sonns degenerate,
The Roman takeing up the fencers trade, 5
The Brittain Jigging it in Mascarade;
Whilest the brave youths tired with the work of State
Their wearied Limbs and minds to recreate,
Do to their more belov'd delights repair,
One to his Pathic, th' other to his Player. 10

Then change the scene and let the next present
A Landskip of our Mottly Parliament;
Where draw Sir Edward mounted on his throne,
Whose life does scarce one Generous Action own,
Unless it be his late Assumed grief 15
To keep his own and loose his sergeants wife.
And place me by the Barr on the left hand
Circean Clifford with his charming Wand,
Our Pig-eyed Duncomb in his Dover Fashion
Sate by the worst Attorney of the Nacion, 20
This great triumvirate that can devide
The spoyls of England; and along that side
Place Falstaffs Regement of Thread-bare Coates
All looking this way how to give their votes,
Their new made Band of Pentioners 25
That give their votes more by their eyes than ears:

And of his dear Reward let none dispair,
   For money comes when Seymour leaves the Chair.
Change once again and let the next afford
The figure of a Drunken Councell board   30
At Arlingtons, and round about it sate
Our mighty Masters in a warme debate;
Capacious Bowles with Lusty wine repleat
To make them th' other Councell board forgett.
Thus whilst the King of France with powerfull Armes   35
Frightens all Christendome with fresh Alarms,
Wee in our Glorious Bacchanals dispose
The humble fate of a Plebeian nose;
Which to effect when thus it was decreed
Draw me a Champion mounted on his steed,   40
And after him a brave Bregade of Hors
Arm'd at all points ready to reinforce
The body of foot that was to have the van
In this Assault upon a single man.
   Tis this must make Obryan great in Story,   45
   And add new Beams to Sands's former Glory.

Draw our Olimpia next in Councell Sate
With Cupid Seymour and the Tool of State,
Two of the five recanters of the Hous
That aime at mountains and bring forth a Mous,   50
Who make it by their mean retreat appear
Five members need not be demanded here.
These must assist her in her countermines
To overthrow the Darby Hous designes,
Whilst Positive walks Woodcock in the dark,   55
Contriving Projects with a Brewers Clerk.
Thus all imploy themselves, and without pitty
Leave Temple Single to be beat in the Citty.
What Scandal's this! Temple, the wise, the Brave,
To be reproacht with Tearm of Turncoat knave;   60
Whom France Esteem'd our Chiefe in Parliament,
To be at home made such a presedent!
   Tis hard; yet this he has for safe retreat:
   Tis by afflictions passive men grow great.

The Loyall Scot
Upon the occasion of the death of Captain Douglas burnt in one of his Majesties shipps at Chatham

Of the old Heroes when the Warlike shades
Saw Douglass Marching on the Elisian Glades,
They streight Consulting gather'd in a Ring
Which of their Poets shold his Welcome sing,
And (as a favourable Pennance) Chose
Cleavland on whom they would the Task Impose.
Hee Understood and Willingly Addrest
His ready muse to Court the Warlike Guest.
Much had hee Cur'd the Humor of his vein:
Hee Judg'd more Clearly now and saw more plain.   1
For those soft Airs had temper'd every thought,
And of wise Lethe hee had took a draught.
    Abruptly he began disguising art,
    As of his Satyr this had been a part.

Not so brave Douglass, on whose Lovely Chin   1
The Early down but newly did begin,
And modest beauty yet his sex did vail,
Whilst Envious virgins hope hee is a Male.
His shady locks Curl back themselves to seek
Nor other Courtship knew but to his Cheek.   2
Oft as hee in Chill Eske or Seyne by night
Hardned and Cool'd those Limbs soe soft, soe white,
Among the Reeds to bee espy'd by him
The Nymphs would Rustle, hee would forward swim:
They sigh'd and said 'fond boy why soe Untame,   2
That flyst loves fires reserv'd for other flame?'
Fix'd on his ship hee fac'd the horrid day
And wonder'd much at those that Runne away,
Nor other fear himself cold Comprehend
Then least Heaven fall ere thither hee Ascend.   3
With birding at the Dutch, as though in sport,
Hee entertains the while his life too short,
Or waves his sword and, Cou'd hee them Conjure,
Within its Circle knows himselfe secure.
The fatall bark him boards with Grapling fire   3
And safely through its ports the Dutch retire.

That pretious life hee yet disdaines to save
Or with known art to try the Gentle Wave.
Much him the glories of his Antient Race
Inspire, nor cold hee his own Deeds deface;   40
And secrett Joy in his own soul doth Rise
That Monk lookes on to see how Douglass dies.
Like a glad lover the fierce Flames hee meets
And tries his first Imbraces in their sheets.
His shape Exact which the bright flames enfold   45
Like the sun's Statue stands of burnisht Gold:
Round the Transparent fire about him Glowes
As the Clear Amber on the bee doth Close;
And as on Angells head their Glories shine
His burning Locks Adorn his face divine.   50
But when in his Imortall mind hee felt
His Altred form and sodred Limbs to Melt,
Down on the Deck hee laid him down and dy'd
With his dear sword reposing by his side,
And on his flaming Planks soe rests his head   55
As one that Huggs himself in a Warm bed.
The ship burnes down and with his reliques sinks,
And the sad stream beneath his Ashes drinks.
Fortunate Boy, if ere my verse may Claim
That Matchless grace to propagate thy fame,   60
When Oeta and Alcides are forgott,
Our English youth shall sing the valiant Scott.
Skip Sadles: Pegasus thou needst not Bragg,
Sometimes the Gall'way Proves the better Nagg.
Shall not a death soe Generous now when told   65
Unite our distance, fill the breaches old?
Such in the Roman forum Curtius brave
Galloping down Clos'd up the Gaping Cave.
Noe more discourse of Scotch or English Race
Nor Chaunt the fabulous hunt of Chivy Chase: 70
Mixt in Corinthian Mettall at thy Flame
Our nations Melting thy Colossus Frame,
Shall fix a foot on either neighbouring Shore
And Joyn those Lands that seemed to part before.

Prick down the point whoever has the Art   75
Where Nature Scotland doth from England part.

Anatomists may Sooner fix the Cells
Where life resides or Understanding dwells:
But this wee know, tho' that Exceed their skill,
That whosoever separates them doth kill.   80
What Ethick River is this Wondrous Tweed
Whose one bank vertue, th' other vice doth breed?
Or what new perpendicular doth rise
Up from her Stream Continued to the Sky's,
That between us the Common Air shold bar   85
And split the Influence of Every star?

When daring Blood to have his rents regain'd
Upon the English Diadem distrain'd,
Hee Chose the Cassock Circingle and Gown,
The fittest Mask for one that Robs a Crown.   90
But his Lay pitty underneath prevailed
And while hee spared the keepers life hee fail'd.
With the preists vestments had hee but put on
A Bishops Cruelty, the Crown had gone.

The world in all doth but two Nations bear,   95
The good, the bad, and those mixt every where.
Under each pole place either of the two,
The good will bravely, bad will basely doe;
And few indeed can paralel our Climes
For Worth Heroick or Heroick Crimes.   100
The Tryell would however bee too nice
Which stronger were, a Scotch or English vice,
Or whether the same vertue would reflect
From Scotch or English heart the same effect.
Nation is all but name as Shibboleth,   105
Where a Mistaken accent Causeth death.
In Paradice Names only Nature Shew'd,
At Babel names from pride and discord flow'd,
And ever since men with a female spite
First call each other names and then they fight.   110
Scotland and England cause of Just uproar!
Does man and wife signifie Rogue and Whore?
Say but a Scot and streight wee fall to sides:
That syllable like a Picts wall devides.

Rationall mens words pledges are of peace,   115
Perverted serve dissentions to increase.
For shame extirpate from each loyall brest
That senseless Rancour against Interest.
One King, one faith, one Language and one Ile:
English and Scotch, 'tis all but Crosse and Pile.   120
    Charles our great soul this onely Understands:
Hee our Affection both and will Comands,
And, where twin Simpathies cannot atone,
Knowes the last secret how to make them one.
Just soe the prudent Husbandman who sees   125
The Idle tumult of his factious bees,
The morning dews and flowers Neglected grown,
The hive a comb case, every bee a drone,
Powders them ore till none discern their foes
And all themselves in meal and friendship close.   130
The Insect Kingdome streight begins to thrive
And Each works hony for the Common Hive.
    Pardon, Young Heroe, this soe long Transport;
Thy death more noble did the same Extort.
My former satyr for this verse forget,   135
The hare's head 'gainst the goose gibletts sett.
I single did against a Nation write,
Against a Nation thou didst singly fight.
My differing Crime doth more thy vertue raise.
And such my Rashness best thy valour praise.   140

Here Douglas smileing said hee did Intend
After such Frankness shown to bee his friend,
Forwarn'd him therefore lest in time he were
Metemsicosd to some Scotch Presbyter.

The Statue in Stocks-Market

As cities that to the fierce conquerors yield
Do at their own charge their citadels build,
So Sir Robert advanced the King's statue, in token
Of bankers defeated and Lombard-street broken.

Some thought it a knightly and generous deed,
Obliging the city with a king and a steed,
When with honour he might from his word have gone back;
He that vows for a calm is absolved by a wreck.

But now it appears from the first to the last
To be all a revenge and a malice forecast,
Upon the King's birthday to set up a thing
That shews him a monster more like than a king.

When each one that passes finds fault with the horse,
Yet all do affirm that the king is much worse,
And some by the likeness Sir Robert suspect
That he did for the King his own statue erect.

To see him so disfigured the herbwomen chide,
Who upon their panniers more decently ride,
And so loose in his seat that all men agree
Even Sir William Peake sits much firmer than he.

But a market, they say, does suit the king well,
Who the Parliament buys and revenues does sell,
And others to make the similitude hold
Say his Majesty himself is bought too and sold.

This statue is surely more scandalous far
Than all the Dutch pictures that caused the war,
And what the exchequer for that took on trust
May be henceforth confiscate for reasons more just.

But Sir Robert to take all the scandal away
Does the fault upon the artificer lay,
And alleges the workmanship was not his own
For he counterfeits only in gold, not in stone.

But, Sir Knight of the Vine, how came't in your thought
That when to the scaffold your liege you had brought
With canvas and deals you e'er since do him cloud,
As if you had meant it his coffin and shroud?

Hath Blood him away (as his crown once) conveyed?
Or is he to Clayton's gone in masquerade?
Or is he in cabal in his cabinet set?
Or have you to the Compter removed him for debt?   40

Methinks by the equipage of this vile scene
That to change him into a Jack-pudding you mean,
Or else thus expose him to popular flouts,
As if we'd as good have a king made of clouts.

Or do you his beams out of modesty veil   45
With three shattered planks and the rags of a sail
To express how his navy was shattered and torn
The day that he was both restored and born?

Sure the king will ne'er think of repaying his bankers,
Whose loyalty now all expires with his spankers.   50
If the Indies and Smyrna do not him enrich,
They will scarce afford him a rag to his breech.

But Sir Robert affirms we do him much wrong;
For the graver's at work to reform him thus long.
But alas! he will never arrive at his end,   55
For 'tis such a king as no chisel can mend.

But with all his faults restore us our King,
As ever you hope in December for Spring,
For though the whole world cannot shew such another,
Yet we'd better by far have him than his brother.   60

The Statue at Charing Cross

What can be the Mistery why Charing Cross
This five moneths continues still blinded with board?
Dear Wheeler impart, for wee're all at a loss
Unless Puchinello be to be restor'd.

'Twere to Scaramuchio too great disrespect   5
To Limitt his troop to this Theatre small,
Besides the injustice it were to eject
The Mimick so legally seiz'd of Whitehall.

For a Diall the place is too unsecure
Since the privy garden could not it defend,   10
And soe near to the Court they will never indure
Any monument how their time they mispend.

Were these Deales kept in store for sheathing our fleet
When the King in Armado to Portsmouth should saile,
Or the Bishops and Treasurer did they Agree't   15
To repair with such riffe raffe our Churches old Pale?

No, to comfort the hearts of the poor Cavaleer
The late King on Horsback is here to be shown:
What a doe with the Kings and the Statues is here:
Have wee not had enough already of one?   20

Does the Treasurer think men so Loyally tame
When their Pensions are stopt to be fool'd with a sight?
And 'tis fourty to one if he Play the old Game
Hee'l shortly reduce us to fourty and eight.

The Trojan Horse, tho' not of Brass but of wood,   25
Had within it an Army that burnt up the Town:
However tis ominous if understood,
For the old King on Horseback is but an Halfecrown.

But his brother-in-law's horse had gain'd such repute
That the Treasurer thought prudent to Try it again,   30
And instead of that markett of herbs and of fruit
He will here keep a market of Parliament men.

But why is the worke then soe long at a stand?
Such things you should never or Suddainly doe.
As the Parliament twice was prorogued by your hand,   35
Will you venture soe far to Prorogue the King too?

Let 's have a King then, be he new be he old;
Not Viner delayed us so, tho' he was brooken
Tho' the King be of Copper and Danby of Gold,
Shall a Treasurer of Guinny a Prince Grudge of Token?   40

The Huswifely Treasuress sure is grown nice
That so liberally treated the members at supper.
She thinks not convenient to goe to the price,
And wee've lost both our King, our Hors and our Crupper.

Where for so many Barties there are to provide,   45
To buy a King is not so wise as to sell,
And however, she said, it could not be denyed
That a Monarch of Gingerbread would doe as well.

But the Treasurer told her he thought she was mad
And his Parliament List withall did produce,   50
Where he shew'd her that so many voters he had
As would the next tax reimburse them with use.

So the Statue will up after all this delay,
But to turn the face to Whitehall you must Shun;
Tho of Brass, yet with grief it would melt him away,   55
To behold every day such a Court, such a son.

A Dialogue between the Two Horses

INTRODUCTION

Wee read in profane and Sacred records
Of Beasts that have uttered Articulate words:
When Magpyes and Parratts cry 'walke Knave walk',
It is a clear proofe that birds too may talke;
Nay Statues without either windpipe or Lungs   5
Have spoken as plainly as men doe with Tongues:
Livy tells a strang story can hardly be fellow'd
That a sacraficed ox, when his Gutts were out, Bellow'd:
Phalaris had a Bull which grave Authors tell ye
Would roar like a Devill with a man in his belly: 10

Fryar Bacon had a head that spoke made of Brass,
And Balam the Prophet was reprov'd by his Asse:
At Delphos and Rome Stocks and Stones now and then, sirs,
Have to Questions return'd oracular Answers:
All Popish beleivers think something divine,   15
When Images speak, possesses the shrine:
But they that faith Catholick ne're understood,
When Shrines give Answers, say a knave 's in the Roode;
Those Idolls ne're speak, but the miracle 's done
By the Devill, a Priest, a Fryar, or Nun.   20
If the Roman Church, good Christians, oblige yee
To beleive men and beasts have spoke in effigie,
Why should wee not credit the publique discourses
Of a Dialogue lately between the two Horses,
The Horses I mean of Woolchurch and Charing,   25
Who have told many truths well worth a mans hearing,
Since Viner and Osburn did buy and provide 'um
For the two mighty Monarchs that doe now bestride 'um.
The stately Brass Stallion and the white marble Steed
One night came togeather by all is agreed,   30
When both the Kings weary of Sitting all day
Were stolne of Incognito each his own way,
And that the two Jades after mutuall Salutes
Not onely discoursed but fell to disputes.

DIALOGUE

W. Quoth the marble white Hors: 'twould make a stone
        speak
      To see a Lord Major and a Lumbard Street break,
      Thy founder and mine to Cheat one another,
      When both knaves agreed to be each others brother.   5
Ch. Here Charing broke silence and thus he went on:
      My Brass is provok't as much as thy stone
      To see Church and state bow down to a whore
      And the King's Chiefe minister holding the doore:
W. To see dei Gratia writ on the Throne,   10
      And the Kings wicked life say God there is none;
Ch. That he should be styled defender o' th faith,
      Who beleives not a word, the word of God saith;

W. That the Duke should turne Papist and that Church
        defy   15
        For which his own Father a Martyr did dye.
Ch. Tho he chang'd his Religion I hope hee's so civill
        Not to think his own Father is gone to the Devill.
W. That Bondage and Begery should be brought on the
        Nacion   20
        By a Curst hous of Commons and a blest Restauracion;
Ch. To see a white staffe make a Beggar a Lord
        And scarce a wise man at a long Councell board;
W. That the bank should be seiz'd yet the Chequer so poor;
        Lord a Mercy and a Cross might be set on the doore; 25
Ch. That a Million and half should be his revenue,
        Yet the King of his debts pay no man a penny;
W. That a King should consume three Realms whole
        Estates
        And yet all his Court be as poore as Church Ratts;   30
Ch. That of four Seas dominion and Guarding
        No token should appear but a poor Copper farthing;
W. Our worm-eaten Navy be laid up at Chatham,
        Not our trade to secure but foes to come at 'um,
Ch. And our few ships abroad become Tripoly's scorn   35
        By pawning for Victualls their Guns at Legorne;
W. That makeing us slaves by hors and foot Guards
        For restoring the King should be our Rewards.
Ch. The basest Ingratitude ever was heard;
        But Tyrants ingratefull are always afeard.   40
W. On Seventh Harry's head he that placed the Crown
        Was after rewarded with losing his own.
Ch. That Parliament men should rail at the Court,
        And get good preferment Imediately for't.
W. To the bold talking members if the Bastards you adde, 45
        What a rabble of Rascally Lords have been made.
Ch. That Traitors to their Country in a Brib'd Hous of
        Commons
        Should give away Millions at every Summons.
W. Yet some of those givers such beggerly Villains   50
        As not to be trusted for twice fifty shillings.
Ch. No wonder that Beggers should still be for giving
        Who out of what 's given do get a good living.

W. Four Knights and a Knave, who were Publicans made,
    For selling their Conscience were Liberally paid.

Ch. Yet baser the souls of those low priced Sinners,
    Who vote with the Court for drink and for Dinners.

W. 'Tis they who brought on us the Scandalous Yoak
    Of Exciseing our Cups and Taxing our Smoak.

Ch. But thanks to the whores who have made the King
        Dogged
    For giving noe more the Rogues are prorogued.

W. That a King shou'd endavour to make a warr cease
    Which Augments and secures his own profitt and peace.

Ch. And Plenipotentiaryes send into France
    With an Addleheaded Knight and a Lord without
        Brains.

W. That the King should send for another French whore,
    When one already hath made him soe poor.

Ch. Enough, dear Brother, for tho' we have reason,
    Yet truth many times being punisht for Treason,
    Wee ought to be wary and Bridle our Tongue;
    Bold speaking hath done both man and beast wrong.
    When the Asse so bouldly rebuked the Prophet,
    Thou knowest what danger was like to come of it;
    Tho' the beast gave his Master ne're an ill word,
    Insted of a Cudgell Balam wish't for a Sword.

W. Truth's as Bold as a Lyon, I am not afraid;
    I'le prove every tittle of what I have said.
    Our riders are absent; who is't that can hear?
    Letts be true to ourselves; whom then need wee fear?
    Where is thy King gone?

Ch.   To see Bishop Laud.

W. To Cuckold a Scrivener mine's in Masquerade.
    On ocasions like these he oft steals away
    And returns to remount about break of Day.
    In every dark night you are sure to find him
    With an Harlot go up on my Crupper behind him.

Ch. Pause, Brother, a while and calmly consider:
    What hast thou to say of my Royall Rider?

W. Thy Priest-ridden King turn'd desperate Fighter
    For the Surplice, Lawn-Sleeves, the Cross and the mitre,
    Till at last on a Scaffold he was left in the lurch
    By Knaves who cry'd themselves up for the Church,

Arch-Bishops and Bishops, Arch-Deacons and Deans   95
Ch. Thy King will ne're fight unless't be for Queans.
W.   He that dyes for Ceremonies dyes like a fool.
Ch. The King on thy Back is a Lamentable Tool.
W.   The Goat and the Lyon I Equally hate,
       And Free men alike value life and Estate.   100
       Tho Father and Sonne are different Rodds,
       Between the two Scourges wee find little odds.
       Both Infamous Stand in three Kingdoms votes,
       This for picking our Pocketts, that for cutting our
           Throats.   105
Ch. More Tolerable are the Lion Kings Slaughters
       Than the Goats making whores of our wives and our
           Daughters.
       The Debauch'd and the Bloody since they Equally
           Gall us,   110
       I had rather Bare Nero than Sardanapalus.
W.   One of the two Tyrants must still be our case
       Under all that shall Reign of the false Scottish race.
Ch. De Witt and Cromwell had each a brave soul.
W.   I freely declare it, I am for old Noll.   115
       Tho' his Government did a Tyrants resemble,
       Hee made England great and it's enemies tremble.
Ch. Thy Ryder puts no man to death in his wrath,
W.   But hee 's buryed alive in lust and in sloath.
Ch. What is thy opinion of James Duke of York?   120
W.   The Same that the Froggs had of Jupiters Stork.
       With the Turk in his head and the Pope in his heart
       Father Patricks Deciple will make England smart.
       If e're he be King I know Brittains Doome;
       Wee must all to the Stake or be Converts to Rome. 125
       A Tudor a Tudor! wee've had Stuarts enough;
       None ever Reign'd like old Besse in the Ruffe.
Ch. Her Walsingham could dark Councells unriddle,
W.   And our Sir Joseph write news-books, and fiddle.
Ch. Troth, Brother, well said, but thats somewhat bitter: 130
W.   His perfum'd predecessor was never much fitter.
Ch. Yet have wee one Secretary honest and wise:
W.   For that very reason hee 's never to rise.
Ch. But canst thou Divine when things shall be mended?

W.   When the Reign of the Line of the Stuarts is ended. 135
Ch.   Then, England, Rejoyce, thy Redemption draws nigh;
      Thy oppression togeather with Kingship shall dye.
W.   A Commonwealth a Common-wealth wee proclaim to
      the Nacion;
      The Gods have repented the Kings Restoration.   140

CONCLUSION

If Speech from Brute Animals in Romes first age
Prodigious events did surely presage,
That shall come to pass all mankind may swear
Which two inanimate Horses declare.
But I should have told you, before the Jades parted,   5
Both Gallopt to Whitehall and there Horribly farted,
Which Monarchys downfall portended much more
Than all that the beasts had spoken before.
If the Delphick Sybills oracular speeches,
As learned men say, came out of their breeches,   10
Why might not our Horses, since words are but wind,
Have the spirit of Prophecy likewise behind?
Tho' Tyrants make Laws which they strictly proclaim
To conceal their own crimes and cover their shame,
Yet the beasts of the field or the stones in the wall   15
Will publish their faults and prophesy their fall.
When they take from the people the freedome of words,
They teach them the Sooner to fall to their Swords.

Let the Citty drink Coffee and Quietly groan
They that Conquered the Father won't be slaves to the Son:
'Tis wine and Strong drink makes tumults increase;   [20
Chocolet Tea and Coffee are liquors of peace.
No Quarrells or oathes amongst those that drink 'um;
Tis Bacchus and the Brewer swear Dam 'um and sink 'um.
Then, Charles, thy edict against Coffee recall;   25
Theres ten times more Treason in Brandy and ale.

BIBLIOGRAPHIES

prepared by Milton Miller and Beverly Goldberg

The following bibliographies are selective. They try to combine a judicious mixture of criticism which has held its own over the years with helpful recent commentary. Some of the best discussion of individual poets and poems (even when these are not pointed out) is to be found in books listed under the headings "General" and "Metaphysical Poetry."

An asterisk (*) precedes books in the bibliographies known to exist in paperback editions.

1. BIBLIOGRAPHIES:

Annual Bibliography of English Language and Literature. Published in Great Britain by The Modern Humanities Research Association.

Berry, L. E. (*See under* Spencer.)

Bush, Douglas. *English Literature in the Earlier Seventeenth Century, 1600–1660.* London: Oxford, 1945; republished with revisions in a second edition, 1962.

MLA International Bibliography of Books and Articles on the Modern Languages and Literatures. New York: New York University Press. (Annual Bibliography of *PMLA* since 1922.)

Pinto, Vivian de Sola. *The English Renaissance, 1510–1688.* London: Cresset Press, 1951. (Second revised edition; first published 1938.)

Seventeenth-Century News. Edited since 1950 by J. Max Patrick of New York University.

Spencer, T. and Mark Van Doren. *Studies in Metaphysical Poetry.* New York: Columbia University Press, 1939. (Bibliography for 1912–1938.) Continued by L. E. Berry, *A Bibliography of Studies in Metaphysical Poetry, 1939–1960.* Madison, Wisconsin: University of Wisconsin Press, 1964.

Studies in Philology. Chapel Hill, North Carolina: Universit
of North Carolina Press. (Annual bibliography since 1922 o
"Recent Literature of the English Renaissance.")

The Year's Work in English Studies. London: John Murra
(for the English Association).

2. GENERAL:

Adams, R. M. *Strains of Discord: Studies in Literary Open
ness.* Ithaca, New York: Cornell University Press, 1958.

Allen, Don Cameron. *Image and Meaning: Metaphoric Tradi
tions in Renaissance Poetry.* Baltimore, Maryland: John
Hopkins Press, 1960.

Baker, Herschel. *The Wars of Truth.* Cambridge, Massachu
setts: Harvard University Press, 1952.

Bethell, Samuel Leslie. *The Cultural Revolution of the Sev
enteenth Century.* London: D. Dobson, 1951.

Bush, Douglas. *English Literature of the Earlier Seventeenth
Century, 1600–1660.* London: Oxford, 1962. (Revised edi
tion.)

Campbell, Lily B. *Divine Poetry and Drama in Sixteenth
Century England.* Berkeley, California: University of Cali
fornia Press, 1959.

* Cruttwell, P. *The Shakespearean Moment and its Place i
the Poetry of the Seventeenth Century.* London: Chatt
and Windus, 1954.

Davies, Godfrey. *The Early Stuarts 1603–1660.* London: Ox
ford, 1937.

Freeman, Rosemary. *English Emblem Books.* London: Chatt
and Windus, 1948.

* Grierson, H. J. C. *Cross-Currents in Seventeenth Centur
English Literature.* London: Chatto and Windus, 1927.

* Haller, William. *The Rise of Puritanism.* New York: Colum
bia University Press, 1938.

Hardison, O. B., Jr. *The Enduring Monument: A Study in th
Idea of Praise in Renaissance Literary Theory and Practice
Chapel Hill, North Carolina: University of North Carolin
Press, 1962.

* Hill, Christopher. *The Century of Revolution, 1603–1714
London: Nelson, 1961.

Hollander, John. *The Untuning of the Sky: Ideas of Music in English Poetry 1500–1700*. Princeton, New Jersey: Princeton University Press, 1961.

Keast, William, ed. *Seventeenth Century English Poetry: Modern Essays in Criticism*. New York: Galaxy Books, 1962.

Mahood, M. M. *Poetry and Humanism*. New Haven, Connecticut: Yale University Press, 1950.

Martz, L. L. *The Poetry of Meditation*. New Haven, Connecticut: Yale University Press, 1962. (Revised edition.)

Mazzeo, J. A., ed. *Reason and the Imagination: Studies in the History of Ideas, 1600–1800*. New York: Columbia University Press, 1962.

More, P. E. and F. L. Cross. *Anglicanism: The Thought and Practice of the Church of England. Illustrated from the Religious Literature of the Seventeenth Century*. Milwaukee, Wisconsin: Morehouse, 1935.

Nicolson, M. H. *The Breaking of the Circle: Studies in the Effect of the "New Science" upon Seventeenth Century Poetry*. New York: Columbia University Press, 1960. (Revised edition.)

Peterson, D. L. *The English Lyric from Wyatt to Donne*. Princeton, New Jersey: Princeton University Press, 1967.

Richmond, Hugh M. *The School of Love: The Evolution of the Stuart Love Lyric*. Princeton, New Jersey: Princeton University Press, 1964.

Ross, M. M. *Poetry and Dogma: Transfiguration of Eucharistic Symbols in Seventeenth Century English Poetry*. New Brunswick, New Jersey: Rutgers University Press, 1954.

Swardson, H. R. *Poetry and the Fountain of Light*. Columbia, Missouri: University of Missouri Press, 1962.

Sypher, Wylie. *Four Stages of Renaissance Style*. New York: Doubleday, 1955.

Wallerstein, Ruth C. *Studies in Seventeenth-Century Poetic*. Madison, Wisconsin: University of Wisconsin Press, 1950.

Wedgewood, C. V. *Poetry and Politics under the Stuarts*. Cambridge: Cambridge University Press, 1960.

Wiley, M. L. *The Subtle Knot: Creative Scepticism in Seventeenth-Century England*. London: George Allen, 1952.

Willey, Basil. *The Seventeenth Century Background*. London: Chatto and Windus, 1934.

Williamson, G. *The Proper Wit of Poetry.* Chicago: Unive
sity of Chicago Press, 1961.

————. *Seventeenth-Century Contexts.* London: Faber an
Faber, 1960.

3. METAPHYSICAL POETRY:

Alvarez, A. *The School of Donne.* New York: Pantheon Book
1961.

* Bennett, Joan. *Five Metaphysical Poets.* Cambridge: Can
bridge University Press, 1964.

Duncan, J. E. *The Revival of Metaphysical Poetry: The Histor
of a Style, 1800 to the Present.* Minneapolis, Minnesota
University of Minnesota Press, 1959.

Eliot, T. S. *Homage to John Dryden.* London: Hogarth Press
1924.

————. *Selected Essays.* London: Faber and Faber, 1934. (Se
especially "The Metaphysical Poets, Andrew Marvell, Joh
Dryden.")

Ellrodt, R. *Les poètes métaphysiques anglais.* Paris: Librairi
José Corti, 1960. (3 vols.)

Esch, Arno. *Englische religiose Lurik des 17. Jahrhundrets
Tübingen: Max Niemeyer, 1955.

* Ford, B., ed. *From Donne to Marvell.* London: Pengui
Books, 1956.

* Gardner, Helen. *Metaphysical Poets.* London: Oxford Uni
versity Press, 1967. (Second edition.) See Introduction.

* Grierson, H. J. C. *Metaphysical Lyrics and Poems of th
Seventeenth Century.* New York: Galaxy Books, 1959
(First published 1921.) See Introduction.

Husain, Itrat. *The Mystical Element in the Metaphysical Poet
of the Seventeenth Century.* London: Oliver and Boyd, 1948

Johnson, Samuel. *The Lives of the Poets.* (See especially th
Lives of Cowley, Denham, and Waller in any of the man
editions available.)

Leishman, J. B. *The Metaphysical Poets.* New York: Russel
and Russell, 1963. (Revised edition.)

* Leavis, F. R. *Revaluation: Tradition and Development i
English Poetry.* London: Chatto and Windus, 1936.

Mazzeo, J. A. *Renaissance and Seventeenth Century Studies
New York: Columbia University Press, 1964.

Mourgues, Odette de. *Metaphysical, Baroque, and Précieux Poetry.* Oxford: Clarendon Press, 1953.

Praz, Mario. *Studies in Seventeenth Century Imagery.* London: Warburg Institute, 1939. (2 vols.)

Sharp, Robert L. *From Donne to Dryden: The Revolt Against Metaphysical Poetry.* Chapel Hill, North Carolina: University of North Carolina Press, 1940.

* Tuve, Rosemond. *Elizabethan and Metaphysical Imagery.* Chicago: University of Chicago Press, 1947.

Walton, Geoffrey. *Metaphysical to Augustan: Studies in Tone and Sensibility in the Seventeenth Century.* London: Bowes and Bowes, 1955.

Warnke, Frank, ed. *European Metaphysical Poetry.* New Haven, Connecticut: Yale University Press, 1961. See Introduction.

* White, Helen C. *The Metaphysical Poets: A Study in Religious Experience.* New York: Collier Books, 1962. (First published 1936.)

* Williamson, G. *The Donne Tradition.* Cambridge, Massachusetts: Harvard University Press, 1930. (Reprinted New York, 1958.)

THE POETS:

JOHN DONNE

Bibliography:

Keynes, Geoffrey. *A Bibliography of Dr. John Donne.* Cambridge: Cambridge University Press, 1958.

Concordance:

Combs, H. C. and Z. R. Sullens. *A Concordance to the English Poems of John Donne.* Chicago: University of Chicago Press, 1940.

Biography:

Bald, Robert C. *Donne and the Drurys.* Cambridge: Cambridge University Press, 1959.

Fausset, H. I. *John Donne: A Study in Discord.* London: J. Cape, 1924.

Gosse, Sir Edmund. *The Life and Letters of John Donne.* London, 1899. (Reprinted Gloucester, Massachusetts, 1959.)

Hardy, E. *John Donne: A Spirit in Conflict.* London: Constable, 1942.

Le Comte, Edward. *Grace to a Witty Sinner: A Life of Donne.* New York: Walker, 1965.

Simpson, E. M. *A Study of the Prose Works of John Donne.* London: Oxford, 1948. (Revised edition.)

Walton, Izaak. *Lives.* . . . London: Oxford, 1927. (World's Classics edition, contains 1675 version.)

Texts:

Gardner, Helen, ed. *John Donne: The Divine Poems.* London: Oxford, 1952.

————. *The Elegies and the Songs and Sonnets of John Donne.* London: Oxford, 1965.

Grierson, H. J. C., ed. *The Poems of John Donne.* London: Oxford, 1912. (2 vols.)

Manley, Frank, ed. *John Donne: The Anniversaries.* Baltimore, Maryland: Johns Hopkins Press, 1963.

Redpath, T., ed. *The Songs and Sonets of John Donne.* London: Methuen, 1956.

Criticism:

Andreasen, N. J. C. "Theme and Structure in Donne's *Satyres*," *Studies in English Literature*, III (1963), 59–75.

Chambers, A. B. " 'Goodfriday, 1613. Riding Westward': The Poem and the Tradition," *Journal of English Literary History*, XXVIII (1961), 31–53.

* Clements, A. L., ed. *John Donne's Poetry: Authoritative Texts, Criticism.* New York: W. W. Norton, 1966.

Coffin, C. M. *John Donne and the New Philosophy.* New York: Columbia University Press, 1958. (First published 1937.)

Colie, R. L. "John Donne's Anniversary Poems and the Paradoxes of Epistemology," *Philological Quarterly*, XLIII (1964), 159–170. (Part II of "The Rhetoric of Transcendence.")

Freccero, John. "Donne's 'Valediction Forbidding Mourning,' " *Journal of English Literary History*, XXX (1963), 335–376.

Gardner, Helen. "The Argument about 'The Ecstasy,' " *Elizabethan and Jacobean Studies*, Oxford: Clarendon Press, 1959, 279–306.

————, ed. *John Donne: A Collection of Critical Essays.* Englewood Cliffs, New Jersey: Spectrum, 1962.

Gransden, K. W. *John Donne.* London: Longmans, 1954.

Guss, D. L. *John Donne, Petrarchist.* Detroit, Michigan: Wayne State University Press, 1966.

* Kermode, Frank, ed. *Discussions of John Donne.* Boston: D. C. Heath, 1962.

* Leishman, J. B. *The Monarch of Wit.* London: Hutchinson's University Library, 1951.

Louthan, Doniphan. *The Poetry of John Donne.* New York: Bookman Associates, 1951.

Martz, L. L. "John Donne: The Meditative Voice," *Massachusetts Review,* I (1960), 326–342.

Rooney, W. J. " 'The Canonization' — the Language of Paradox Reconsidered," *Journal of English Literary History,* XXIII (1956), 36–47. (See Cleanth Brooks, "The Language of Paradox: 'The Canonization,'" in **The Well Wrought Urn.* New York: Harcourt, Brace & World, 1956.)

Smith, A. J. *John Donne: The Songs and Sonets.* London: E. Arnold, 1964.

Spencer, T., ed. *A Garland for John Donne, 1631–1931.* Oxford: Oxford University Press, 1931. (Reprinted Gloucester, Massachusetts, 1958.)

Stein, Arnold. "Donne's Prosody," *PMLA,* LIX (1944), 373–397.

————. *John Donne's Lyrics: The Eloquence of Action.* Minneapolis, Minnesota: University of Minnesota Press, 1962.

————. "Meter and Meaning in Donne's Verse," *Sewanee Review,* LII (1944), 288–301.

Unger, Leonard. *Donne's Poetry and Modern Criticism.* Chicago: Regnery, 1950.

Warren, Austin. "Donne's 'Extasie,'" *Studies in Philology,* LV (1958), 472–480.

Williamson, G. "The Design of Donne's Anniversaries," *Modern Philology,* LX (1963), 183–191.

GEORGE HERBERT

Bibliography:

Tannenbaum, S. A. and D. R. *George Herbert: A Concise Bibliography.* New York: S. A. Tannenbaum, 1946.

Concordance:

Mann, Cameron. *A Concordance to the English Poems of George Herbert.* Boston: Houghton Mifflin, 1927.

Biography:

Chute, Marchette. *Two Gentle Men.* New York: E. P. Dutton, 1959.

Hyde, A. G. *George Herbert and His Times.* London: Methuen, 1906.

Walton, Izaak. (*See under* DONNE, Bibliography.)

Texts:

Hutchinson, F. E., ed. *George Herbert: The Works.* Oxford: Oxford University Press, 1945. (Revised edition.)

McCloskey, M. and P. R. Murphy, eds. *The Latin Poetry of George Herbert: A Bilingual Edition.* Athens, Ohio: Ohio University Press, 1965.

Criticism:

Bottrall, Margaret. *George Herbert.* London: John Murray, 1954.

Bowers, Fredson. "Herbert's Sequential Imagery: 'The Temper,' " *Modern Philology*, LIX (1962), 202–213.

Colie, R. L. "Logos in *The Temple*, George Herbert and the Shape of Content," *Journal of the Warburg and Courtauld Institutes*, XXVI (1963), 327–342.

Gardner, Helen. See Introduction to World's Classics edition, 1961.

* Knights, L. C. *Explorations.* New York: New York University Press, 1964. (First published 1947.)

Ostriker, Alicia. "Song and Speech in the Metrics of George Herbert," *PMLA*, LXXX (1965), 62–68.

Rickey, M. E. "Herbert's Technical Development," *Journal of English and Germanic Philology*, LXII (1963), 745–760.

————. *Utmost Art: Complexity in the Verse of George Herbert.* Lexington, Kentucky: University of Kentucky Press, 1966.

Summers, J. *George Herbert, His Religion and Art.* Cambridge, Massachusetts: Harvard University Press, 1954.

Tuve, Rosemond. "George Herbert and *Caritas*," *Journal of the Warburg and Courtauld Institutes*, XXII (1959), 303–331.

————. *A Reading of George Herbert*. Chicago: University of Chicago Press, 1952.

————. "Sacred 'Parody' of Love Poetry, and Herbert," *Studies in the Renaissance*, New York: Renaissance Society of America, 1961, VIII, 249–290.

* Warren, Austin. *Rage for Order*. Ann Arbor, Michigan: University of Michigan Press, 1959. (First published 1938.)

RICHARD CRASHAW

Texts:

Martin, L. C., ed. *Poems English, Latin and Greek of Richard Crashaw*. London: Oxford University Press, 1957. (Revised edition.)

* (No editor). *The Verse in English of Richard Crashaw*. New York: Grove Press, 1949.

Criticism:

Eliot, T. S. *For Lancelot Andrewes, Essays on Style and Order*. London: Faber and Gwyer, 1927.

Madsen, W. G. "A Reading of 'Musicks Duell,'" *Studies in Honor of John Wilcox*, A. D. Wallace and W. O. Ross, eds. Detroit, Michigan: Wayne State University Press, 1958.

Pettoello, L. "A Current Misconception Concerning the Influence of Marino's Poetry on Crashaw's," *Modern Language Review*, LII (1957), 321–328.

* Praz, Mario. *The Flaming Heart: Essays on Crashaw, Macchiavelli and Other Studies*. Garden City, New York: Anchor Books, 1958.

Rickey, M. E. *Rhyme and Meaning in Crashaw*. Lexington, Kentucky: University of Kentucky Press, 1961.

* Wallerstein, Ruth C. *Richard Crashaw: A Study in Style and Poetic Development*. Madison, Wisconsin: University of Wisconsin Press, 1959. (First published 1935.)

* Warren, A. *Richard Crashaw: A Study in Baroque Sensibility*. Ann Arbor, Michigan: University of Michigan Press, 1957. (First published 1939.)

Willey, Basil. *Richard Crashaw, A Memorial Lecture*. Cambridge: Cambridge University Press, 1949.

* Williams, G. W. *Image and Symbol in the Sacred Poetry of Richard Crashaw*. Columbia, South Carolina: University of South Carolina Press, 1963.

ANDREW MARVELL

Biographies:

Bradbrook, M. C. and M. G. Lloyd Thomas. *Andrew Marvell.* Cambridge: Cambridge University Press, 1940.

Legouis, Pierre. *André Marvell, poète, puritain, patriote.* Paris: H. Didier, 1928.

————. *Andrew Marvell: Poet, Puritan, Patriot.* New York: Oxford University Press, 1965. (The standard biography, above, compressed and brought up to date.)

Texts:

MacDonald, Hugh, ed. *The Poems of Andrew Marvell.* Cambridge, Massachusetts: Harvard University Press, 1956. (Second edition.)

Margoliouth, H. M., ed. *The Poems and Letters of Andrew Marvell.* New York: Oxford University Press, 1952. (Revised edition.)

Criticism:

Allen, D. C. (*See under* "General." Two chapters on Marvell poems: "The Nymph Complaining" and "Upon Appleton House.")

Colie, R. L. "Marvell's 'Bermudas' and the Puritan Paradise," *Renaissance News,* X (1957), 75–79.

* Hill, Christopher. *Puritanism and Revolution.* New York: Humanities Press, 1959.

Hyman, L. W. *Andrew Marvell.* New York: Grosset and Dunlap, 1964.

Klonsky, Milton. "A Guide Through 'The Garden,'" *Sewanee Review,* LVIII (1950), 16–35.

Legouis, P. "Marvell and the New Critics," *Review of English Studies* (new series), VIII (1957).

Leishman, J. B. *The Art of Marvell's Poetry.* London: Hutchinson, 1966.

Poggioli, R. "The Pastoral of the Self," *Daedalus,* LXXXVIII (1959), 686–699.

* Press, John. *Andrew Marvell.* London: (British Council), 1958.

Rosenberg, J. D. "Marvell and the Christian Idiom," *Boston University Studies in English,* IV (1960), 152–161.

Røstvig, Maren-Sofie. "Andrew Marvell's 'The Garden': A Hermetic Poem," *English Studies,* XL, 2 (1959), 65–76.

————. *The Happy Man: Studies in the Metamorphoses of a Classical Ideal, 1600–1700*. Oxford: Basil Blackwell and Mott, 1955.

Scoular, Kitty. *Natural Magic: Studies in the Presentation of Nature in English Poetry from Spenser to Marvell*. New York: Oxford University Press, 1965.

Stewart, Stanley. *The Enclosed Garden*. Madison, Wisconsin: University of Wisconsin Press, 1966.

Summers, J. H. "Marvell's 'Nature,'" *Journal of English Literary History*, XX (1953), 121–135.

Tayler, E. W. *Nature and Art in Renaissance Literature*. New York: Columbia University Press, 1964.

Toliver, H. E. *Marvell's Ironic Vision*. New Haven, Connecticut: Yale University Press, 1965.

Wallerstein, Ruth C. (See under "General." The second part discusses Marvell's poetry.)

INDEX OF FIRST LINES

A broken Altar, Lord, thy servant reares   337

A Brooke whose streame so great, so good   590

A drop, one drop, how sweetly one faire drop   525

A Plant of noble stemme, forward and faire   583

A Sheafe of Snakes used heretofore to be   317

A wreathed garland of deserved praise   482

Æternall loue! what 'tis to loue thee well   697

After those reverend papers, whose soule is   190

After two sittings, now our Lady State   827

Ah my deare angrie Lord   469

Alas, how pleasant are their dayes   730

Alas, poore Death, where is thy glorie?   468

All after pleasures as I rid one day   385

All haile sweet Poët, more full of more strong fire   182

All Hybla's honey, all that sweetnesse can   524

All Kings, and all their favorites   52

All Trees, all leavy Groves confesse the Spring   575

All we have is God's, and yet   525

Almightie Judge, how shall poore wretches brook   484

Almightie Lord, who from thy glorious throne   486

Although thy hand and faith, and good workes too   95

And art thou grieved, sweet and sacred Dove   436

And is he gone, whom these armes held but now?   695

And let thy Patriarches Desire   292

And now th'art set wide ope, The Speare's sad Art   520

And since this life our nonage is   291

And since thou so desirously   293

And thy illustrious Zodiake   292

As cities that to the fierce conquerors yield   857

As due by many titles I resigne   277

As he that sees a dark and shadie grove   352

As he that sees a starre fall, runs apace   136

As I one ev'ning sat before my cell   439

As if the storme meant him   518

As men, for fear the starres should sleep and nod   435

As on a window late I cast mine eye   418

As one put drunk into the packet-boat   784

As the sweet sweat of Roses in a Still   101

As virtuous men passe mildly away   70

At once, from hence, my lines and I depart   184

At th' Iuory Tribunall of your hand   701

At the round earths imagin'd corners, blow   280

Awake sad heart, whom sorrow
ever drowns   413
Away despair! my gracious Lord
doth heare   450
Away thou fondling motley hu-
morist   141

Batter my heart, three person'd
God; for, you   282
Before I sigh my last gaspe, let
me breath   75
Blasted with sighs, and sur-
rounded with teares   55
Beyond th'old Pillers many have
travailed   90
Blest are your North parts, for all
this long time   190
Blest be the God of love   370
Blest Order, which in power dost
so excell   459
Blest payre of Swans, Oh may
you interbring   135
Both rob'd of aire, we both lye in
one ground   89
Brave rose, (alas!) where art
thou? in the chair   440
Bright BABE! Whose awfull
beautyes make   624
Bright Goddesse, (whether Joue
thy father be   699
Bright spark, shot from a
brighter place   379
Brittaine, the mighty Oceans
lovely Bride   591
Broken in pieces all asunder
393
Busie enquiring heart, what
wouldst thou know?   444
Busie old foole, unruly Sunne
43
But now, to Thee, faire Bride, it
is some wrong   134
But that thou art my wisdome,
Lord   398
But undiscerning Muse, which
heart, which eyes   133
Bvt there were Rocks would not
relent at This   636
But you are over-blest. Plenty
this day   136

By childrens births, and death, I
am become   89
By miracles exceeding power of
man   276
By our first strange and fatall
interview   115

Canst be idle? canst thou play
414
Casting the times with their
strong signes   537
Christ bids the dumbe tongue
speake, it speakes, the
sound   516
Climb at Court for me that will
751
Clora come view my Soul, and
tell   732
Come and let us live my Deare
604
Come away   483
Come, braue soldjers, come, &
see   696
Come, bring thy gift. If blessings
were as slow   447
Come death, come bands, nor do
you shrink, my eares   527
Come little Infant, Love me now
728
Come live with mee, and bee my
love   68
Come Lord, my head doth burn,
my heart is sick   409
Come, Madam, come, all rest my
powers defie   121
Come, my Way, my Truth, my
Life   455
Come wee Shepheards who have
seene   534
Come we shepheards whose
blest Sight   619
Come ye hither All, whose taste
477
Compassion in the world againe
is bred   92
Content thee, greedie heart   438
Could not once blinding me,
cruell, suffice   531
Courage my Soul, now learn to
wield   714

Damon *come drive thy flocks this way* 721

Daphnis *must from* Chloe *part* 736

Dear, heaun-designed SOVL! 678

Dear hope! earth's dowry, & heaun's debt! 689

Dear Reliques of a dislodg'd SOVL, *whose lack* 686

Deare Friend, sit down, the tale is long and sad 430

Deare love, for nothing lesse then thee 61

Deare reliques of a dislodg'd soule, whose lacke 590

Death be not proud, though some have called thee 281

Death I recant, and say, unsaid by mee 249

Death, thou wast once an uncouth hideous thing 483

Death, what dost? ô hold thy Blow 584

Deigne at my hands this crown of prayer and praise 274

Do not beguile my heart 443

Each blest drop, on each blest limme 514

Enough: and leave the rest to Fame 752

Eternall God, (for whom who ever dare 298

Even as lame things thirst their perfection, so 186

Faire, great, and good, since seeing you, wee see 202

Faire soule, which wast, not onely, as all soules bee 241

Faithlesse and fond Mortality 582

False glozing pleasures, casks of happinesse 465

Father of Heaven, and him, by whom 290

Father, part of his double interest 283

First was the World as one great

Cymbal made 748

Fond woman, which would'st have thy husband die 93

For every houre that thou wilt spare mee now 45

For Godsake hold your tongue, and let me love 45

For that faire blessed Mothermaid 291

For the first twenty yeares, since yesterday 84

Foure Teeth thou had'st that ranck'd in goodly state 600

Full of rebellion, I would die 353

Go, intercept some Fountain in the Vein 712

God grant thee thine own wish, and grant thee mine 318

Goe, and catche a falling starre 41

Goe now; and with some daring drugg 687

Goe now with some dareing drugg 576

Goe smiling soules, your new built Cages breake 517

Good wee must love, and must hate ill 58

Had we but World enough, and Time 729

Hail, sister springs! 659

Hail, most high, most humble one! 656

Haile Bishop Valentine, whose day this is 127

Haile Sister Springs 508

Happy me! ô happy sheepe! 531

Hark! she is call'd, the parting houre is come 657

Harke newes, ô envy, thou shalt heare descry'd 110

Harke shee is called, the parting houre is come 564

Hast thee harsh verse, as fast as thy lame measure 183

881

Hath aged winter, fledg'd with
    feathered raine   700
Hath onely Anger an Omni-
    potence   519
Having been tenant long to a
    rich Lord   349
He is starke mad, who ever sayes
    69
He that cannot chuse but love
    88
He that is one   497
He that is weary, let him sit   383
Heark, how the birds do sing
    431
Heark how the Mower Damon
    Sung   744
Hears't thou, my soul, what seri-
    ous things   653
Her eyes flood lickes his feets
    faire staine   526
Her of your name, whose fair
    inheritance   273
Here lies the sacred Bones   826
Here's no more newes, then ver-
    tue, 'I may as well   169
Here take my Picture; though I
    bid farewell   98
Here where by All All Saints in-
    voked are   199
Here, where our Lord once laid
    his Head   515
Here where our LORD once lay'd
    his Head   638
High mounted on an Ant Nanus
    the tall   581
Holinesse on the head   472
Holland, that scarce deserves the
    name of Land   788
Honour is so sublime perfection
    193
Hope, whose weak being ruin'd
    is   567
Hope, whose weake beeing
    ruin'd is   688
How fit our well-rank'd Feasts
    doe follow   598
How fresh, O Lord, how sweet
    and clean   464
How is the gold becomme so
    dimme? How is   310

How Life and Death in Thee
    522
How Life & death in Thee   640
How over Sions daughter hath
    God hung   305
How should I praise thee, Lord!
    how should my rymes   362
How sits this citie, late most
    populous   302
How soon doth man decay!
    401
How sweetly doth My Master
    sound! My Master!   473
How vainly men themselves
    amaze   749
How well her name an Army
    doth present   382
How wisely Nature did decree
    718

I am a little world made cun-
    ningly   279
I am the man which have afflic-
    tion seene   307
I am two fooles, I know   47
I am unable, yonder begger cries
    90
I blesse thee, Lord, because I
    GROW   433
I can love both faire and browne
    44
I cannot ope mine eyes   369
I cannot skill of these thy wayes
    399
I fixe mine eye on thine, and
    there   68
I gave to Hope a watch of mine:
    but he   423
I have consider'd it, and finde
    347
I have done one braver thing   42
I Joy, deare Mother, when I view
    411
I know it is my sinne, which
    locks thine eares   372
I'll tell thee now (deare Love)
    what thou shalt doe   56
I know the wayes of Learning;
    both the head   392
I late the roman youth's lou'd

prayse & pride 680

I long to talke with some old lovers ghost 74

I made a posie, while the day ran by 397

I never stoop'd so low, as they 83

I paint so ill, my peece had need to bee 576

I saw the Vertues sitting hand in hand 375

I scarce beleeve my love to be so pure 59

I sing no harme good sooth to any wight 111

I sing the NAME *which None can say* 613

I sing the progresse of a deathlesse soule 258

I struck the board, and cry'd, No more 452

I threatned to observe the strict decree 443

I travell'd on, seeing the hill, where lay 442

I wonder by my troth, what thou, and I 40

I would be married, but I'de have no Wife 596

Iesu, no more, it is full tide 529

Iesu, no more! It is full tide 646

If as a flowre doth spread and die 364

If, as mine is, thy life a slumber be 187

If as the windes and waters here below 433

If ever Pitty were acquainted 586

If faithfull soules be alike glorifi'd 280

If in his Studie he hath so much care 91

If poysonous mineralls, and if that tree 280

If thou chance for to find 501

If thou dost find an house built to thy mind 501

If we could see below 474

If yet I have not all thy love 47

If you from spoyle of th'old worlds farthest end 90

Image of her whom I love, more then she 104

Immensitie cloysterd in thy deare wombe 275

Immortall Heat, O let thy greater flame 361

Immortall Love, authour of this great frame 361

In shade of death's sad TREE 643

In what torne ship soever I embarke 301

Is murther no sin? or a sin so cheape 523

Is not thy sacred hunger of science 189

It cannot be. Where is that mightie joy 363

Joy, I did lock thee up: but some bad man 429

JESU is in my heart, his sacred name 414

Iesu, no more, it is full tide 529

Iesu, no more! It is full tide 646

Kendal is dead, and Cambridge riding post 827

Kill me not ev'ry day 368

Kinde pitty chokes my spleene; brave scorn forbids 147

Kindly I envy thy songs perfection 188

King of Glorie, King of Peace 446

King of Glorie, King of Peace 493

Klockius so deeply hath sworne, ne'r more to come 91

Know you faire, on what you looke 556

Know'st thou this, Souldier? 'tis a much chang'd plant, which yet 525

Know'st thou this, Souldier? 'Tis a much-chang'd plant which yet 648

883

Language thou art too narrow, and too weake   251

Let all the world in ev'ry corner sing   360

Let forrain nations of their language boast   466

Let hoary Time's vast Bowels be the Grave   602

Let it no longer be a forlorne hope   514

Let mans Soule be a Spheare, and then, in this   288

Let me powre forth   62

Let wits contest   480

Like Esops fellow-slaves, O Mercury   91

Like one who' in her third wid-dowhood doth professe   168

Like the vain Curlings of the Watry maze   792

Listen sweet Dove unto my song   366

Little think'st thou, poore flower   78

Live Jesus, Live, and let it bee   508

Lo here a little volume, but great Book!   675

Lo here the faire Chariclia! in whom strove   596

Loe here a little volume, but large booke   552

Loe where a WOVNDED HEART with Bleeding EYES con-spire   659

Look vp, languishing Soul! Lo where the fair   639

Looke to mee faith, and looke to my faith, God   238

Lord, by thy Sweet & Sauing SIGN   632

Lord, how can man preach thy eternall word?   373

Lord, how couldst thou so much appease   357

Lord, how I am all ague, when I seek   348

Lord, I confesse my sinne is great   356

Lord, I will mean and speak thy praise   457

Lord, in my silence how do I despise   376

Lord, let the Angels praise thy name   402

Lord, make me coy and tender to offend   397

Lord, my first fruits present themselves to thee   323

Lord, thou art mine, and I am thine   456

Lord, what is man? why should he coste thee   641

Lord, when the sense of thy sweet grace   674

Lord, who createdst man in wealth and store   352

Lord, who hast form'd me out of mud   373

Lord, with what bountie and rare clemencie   386

Lord, with what care hast thou begirt us round   354

Lord, with what glorie wast thou serv'd of old   408

Love, any devill else but you   60

Love bade me welcome: yet my soul drew back   485

Love, brave vertues younger Brother   598

Love built a stately house; where Fortune came   388

Love is lost, nor can his Mother   579

Love now no fire hath left him   602

Loue, thou art Absolute sole Lord   665

Love thou art absolute, sole Lord   556

Luxurious Man, to bring his Vice in use   743

Mad paper stay, and grudge not here to burne   192

MADAME, / Here where by All All Saints invoked are   199

MADAME, / Man to Gods image;

Eve, *to mans was made*
180

MADAME, / *'Mongst those long
rowes of crownes that guild
your race* 631

MADAME, / *Reason is our Soules
left hand, Faith her right*
171

MADAME, / *That I might make
your Cabinet my tombe*
255

MADAME, / *You have refin'd
mee, and to worthyest
things* 172

*Man is a lumpe, where all beasts
kneaded bee* 174

*Man is the World, and death
th'Ocean* 247

*Man to Gods image; Eve, to
mans was made* 180

*Mark you the floore? that square
& speckled stone* 372

*Marke but this flea, and marke in
this* 64

Marry, and love thy Flavia, *for,
shee* 94

*Meeting with Time, Slack thing,
said I* 424

*Midst all the darke and knotty
Snares* 521

*Money, thou bane of blisse, &
sourse of wo* 382

*'Mongst those long rowes of
crownes that guild your
race* 631

Moyst with one drop of thy
blood, my dry soule 276

*Mvse not that by thy mind thy
body is led* 185

*My comforts drop and melt away
like snow* 467

*My Fortune and my choice this
custome break* 255

My God, a verse is not a crown
375

My God, I heard this day 394

My God, I read this day 400

My God, if writings may 406

*My God, the poore expressions of
my Love* 499

*My God, where is that ancient
heat towards thee* 500

*My heart did heave, and there
came forth, O God!* 378

My joy, my life, my crown! 466

My Love is of a birth as rare
739

*My Mind was once the true
survey* 747

My name engrav'd herein 53

*My stock lies dead, and no
increase* 367

*My words & thoughts do both
expresse this notion* 389

*Nature had long a Treasure
made* 741

*Natures lay Ideot, I taught thee
to love* 100

*No Lover saith, I love, nor any
other* 85

*No roofes of gold o're riotous
tables shining* 684

No Spring, nor Summer Beauty
hath such grace 102

*Not in rich furniture, or fine
aray* 359

*Not that in colour it was like thy
haire* 105

*Nothing could make me sooner
to confesse* 224

*Now, as in Tullias tombe, one
lampe burnt cleare* 137

Now does Spains *Fleet her spa-
tious wings unfold* 802

*Now from your Easts you issue
forth, and wee* 135

*Now is The noon of sorrow's
night* 635

*Now Lord, or never, they'll be-
leeve on thee* 517

*Now thou hast lov'd me one
whole day* 41

Now Westward Sol *had spent
the richest Beames* 571

*O blessed bodie! Whither art
thou thrown?* 350

O Blessed glorious Trinity 291

O day most calm, most bright 380

O do not use me 387

O Dreadfull Justice, what a fright and terrour 441

O gratious Lord, how shall I know 495

O Holy Ghost, whose temple I 290

O might those sighes and teares returne againe 278

O Mighty Nothing! unto thee 520

O my chief good 348

O Sacred Providence, who from end to end 418

O Sonne of God, who seeing two things 290

O spitefull bitter thought 454

O that I could a sinne once see! 369

O these wakefull wounds of thine! 528

O thou the span of whose Omnipotence 703

O Thou which to search out the secret parts 188

O what a cunning guest 427

O who shall, from this Dungeon, raise 724

O who will give me tears? Come all ye springs 462

O who will show me those delights on high? 485

Oblig'd by frequent visits of this man 776

Of that short Roll of friends writ in my heart 188

Of the old Heroes when the Warlike shades 854

Of what an easie quick accesse 405

Oh, all ye, who passe by, whose eyes and minde 337

Oh Book! infinite sweetnesse! let my heart 365

Oh doe not die, for I shall hate 50

Oh glorious spirits, who after all your bands 382

Oh King of grief! (a title strange, yet true 345

Oh, let mee not serve so, as those men serve 99

Oh my blacke Soule! now thou art summoned 278

Oh that I knew how all thy lights combine 365

Oh, to vex me, contraryes meet in one 285

Oh to what height will love of greatnesse drive 158

Oh, what a thing is man! how farre from power 428

On the proud bankes of great Euphrates flood 533

Once, and but once found in thy company 96

One Eye? a thousand rather, and a Thousand more 522

Others at the Porches and entries of their Buildings . . . 257

Our storme is past, and that storms tyrannous rage 163

Our times are much degenerate from those 711

Out of a fired ship, which, by no way 89

Painter once more thy Pencell reassume 852

Pallas saw Venus arm'd, and streight she cry'd 581

Passenger who e're thou art 587

Peace mutt'ring thoughts, and do not grudge to keep 374

Peace pratler, do not lowre 407

Phillis, Tomalin, away 808

Philo, with twelve yeares study, hath beene griev'd 91

Philosophers have measur'd mountains 347

Poore heart, lament 434

Poore nation, whose sweet sap and juice 452

Poore silly soul, whose hope and head lies low 413

Praised be the God of love 396

Prayer the Churches banquet,

Angels age 359
Pregnant again with th'old twins
  Hope, and Feare 184
Presse me not to take more
  pleasure 475

Reason is our Soules left hand,
  Faith her right 171
Remember, O Lord, what is
  fallen on us 313
Rich, churlish LAND! *that hid'st*
  so long in thee 682
Rich Lazarus! *richer in those*
  Gems, thy Teares 518
Rise heart; thy Lord is risen. Sing
  his praise 351
Rise, Heire of fresh Eternity
  529
Rise, Royall SION! *rise & sing*
  651
Rise then, immortall maid! Reli-
  gion *rise!* 563
Rise, thou best & brightest
  morning! 623
Rise thou first and fairest
  morning 566

Salute the last and everlasting
  day 276
Salvation to all that will is nigh
  274
See here an easie Feast that
  knowes no wound 515
See how the arched Earth does
  here 752
See how the Orient Dew 716
See Sir, how as the Suns hot
  Masculine flame 273
See with what simplicity 740
Seene? and yet hated thee? they
  did not see 525
Send home my long strayd eyes
  to mee 66
Send me some token, that my
  hope may live 87
Shame of thy mother soyle! ill-
  nurtur'd tree! 698
Shee'is dead; And all which die
  82
Show me deare Christ, thy

spouse, so bright and clear
  284
Show me himselfe, himselfe
  (bright Sir) O show 517
Since Christ embrac'd the Crosse
  it selfe, dare I 285
Since I am coming to that Holy
  roome 315
Since, Lord, to thee 353
Since she must go, and I must
  mourn, come Night 108
Since she whom I lov'd hath
  payd her last debt 284
Sir, more then kisses, letters
  mingle Soules 164
Sir, / Our times are much de-
  generate from those 711
Sir; though (I thanke God for it)
  I do hate 144
Sit further, and make room for
  thine own fame 786
Sleep sleep old Sun, thou canst
  not have repast 287
So his bold Tube, Man, to the
  Sun apply'd 851
So, so, breake off this last la-
  menting kisse 84
Soe I may gaine thy death, my
  life I'le giue 696
Some man unworthy to be pos-
  sessor 61
Some that have deeper digg'd
  loves Myne then I 63
Sorrie I am, my God, sorrie I am
  423
Sorrow, who to this house scarce
  knew the way 252
Souls joy, when thou art gone
  480
Spit in my face you Jewes, and
  pierce my side 281
Stand still, and I will read to
  thee 87
Svppose he had been Tabled at
  thy Teates 523
Sure, Lord, there is enough in
  thee to dry 500
Sweet day, so cool, so calm, so
  bright 391
Sweet Peace, where dost thou

dwell? I humbly crave
426

Sweet were the dayes, when
thou didst lodge with Lot
402

Sweetest love, I do not goe 48

Sweetest of sweets, I thank you:
when displeasure 371

Sweetest Saviour, if my soul
416

T'have written then, when you
writ, seem'd to mee 175

Take heed of loving mee 83

Take these, times tardy truants,
sent by me 609

Tamely, fraile body, 'abstaine to
day; to day 287

Teach me, my God and King
481

Tell me bright Boy, tell me my
golden Lad 515

Th' Astrologers own Eyes are
set 806

Th' have left thee naked Lord,
O that they had 528

That I might make your Cabinet
my tombe 255

That on her lap she casts her
humble Eye 518

That Providence which had so
long the care 810

That unripe side of earth, that
heavy clime 195

The Bell doth tolle 498

The bird, that's fetch't from
Phasis floud 697

The cold white snowie Nunnery
293

The Complin hour comes last, to
call 637

The Day is spent, & hath his will
on mee 498

The early PRIME blushes to say
633

The fleet Astronomer can bore
389

The forward Youth that would
appear 781

The God of love my shepherd is
470

The harbingers are come. See,
see their mark 474

The heavens rejoyce in motion,
why should I 117

The merrie world did on a day
412

The modest front of this small
floore 603

The ninth will awfull horror
hearkened to those groanes
636

The smiling Morne had newly
wak't the Day 578

The Sun-beames in the East are
spred 137

The Third hour's deafen'd with
the cry 634

The wanton Troopers riding by
725

The worlds light shines, shine as
it will 526

Therefore to THEE & thine Aus-
pitious ray 630

Therefore with thee triumpheth
there 293

These Houres, & that which
houer's o're my END 638

They'haue left thee naked, LORD,
O that they had! 648

Think'st Thou that this Love can
stand 748

This is my playes last scene, here
heavens appoint 279

This reverend shadow cast that
setting Sun 581

This twilight of two yeares, not
past nor next 178

Thou art not so black, as my
heart 82

Thou art repriv'd old yeare, thou
shalt not die 133

Thou art too hard for me in Love
496

Thou cheat'st us Ford, mak'st
one seeme two by Art 595

Thou hast made me, And shall
thy worke decay? 277

888

Thou hast the art on't Peter; and
  canst tell   527
Thou in the fields walkst out thy
  supping howers   92
Thou shalt not laugh in this
  leafe, Muse, nor they   156
Thou speak'st the word (thy
  word's a Law)   520
Thou that hast giv'n so much to
  me   425
Thou trim'st a Prophets Tombe,
  and dost bequeath   524
Thou water turn'st to Wine (faire
  friend of Life)   521
Thou which art I, ('tis nothing
  to be soe)   161
Thou who condemnest Jewish
  hate   468
Thou who dost dwell and linger
  here below   468
Thou, whom the former precepts
  have   336
Thou, whose diviner soule hath
  caus'd thee now   299
Thou, whose sweet youth and
  early hopes inhance   323
Though All the ioyes I had fleed
  hence with Thee   581
Though I be dead, and buried,
  yet I have   199
Though it be some divorce to
  thinke of you   134
Though now 'tis neither May nor
  June   702
Throw away thy rod   476
Thus have I back againe to thy
  bright name   561
Thus haue I back again to thy
  bright name   670
Thus thou descend'st to our in-
  firmitie   135
Thy Eagle-sighted Prophets too
  292
Thy father all from thee, by his
  last Will   91
Thy flattering picture, Phryne, is
  like thee   91
Thy friend, whom thy deserts to
  thee enchaine   186

Thy God was making hast into
  thy roofe   519
Thy hands are washt, but ô the
  waters spilt   517
Thy sacred Academie above
  294
Thy sinnes and haires may no
  man equall call   90
Till I have peace with thee, warr
  other men   123
'Tis lost, to trust a Tombe with
  such a guest   219
'Tis not the work of force but
  skill   611
Tis the yeares midnight, and it
  is the dayes   66
Tis true that he is dead: but yet
  to chuse   819
'Tis true, 'tis day; what though it
  be?   52
To make a final conquest of all
  me   734
To make the doubt cleare, that
  no woman's true   113
To see both blended in one flood
  524
To thee these first fruits of my
  growing death   527
To these, Whom Death again did
  wed   589
To these, whom DEATH again did
  wed   685
To thy Lover   600
To what a combersome unwield-
  inesse   74
To write a verse or two is all the
  praise   367
Twice or thrice had I loved thee
  51
Two, by themselves, each other,
  love and feare   89
Two Devills at one blow thou
  hast laid flat   522
Two Mites, two drops, (yet all
  her house and land)   515
Two soules move here, and mine
  (a third) must move   223
Two went to pray? ô rather say
  519

889

Vnder an undermin'd, and shot-
   bruis'd wall   90
Vnder thy shadow may I lurke a
   while   516
Vnseasonable man, statue of ice
   130
Vpon this Primrose hill   79

Wee read in profane and Sacred
   records   861
Welcome deare feast of Lent:
   who loves not thee   390
Welcome my Griefe, my Ioy;
   how deare's   524
Welcome sweet and sacred cheer
   478
Well dy'd the World, that we
   might live to see   206
Well; I may now receive, and
   die; My sinne   149
Well meaning readers! you that
   come as freinds   671
Well Peter dost thou wield thy
   active sword   526
Went you to conquer? and have
   so much lost   170
What bright soft thing is this?
   513
What can be the Mistery why
   Charing Cross   859
What doth this noise of thoughts
   within my heart   437
What ever story of their crueltie
   516
What Heav'n-besieged Heart is
   this   692
What heau'n-intreated HEART is
   This   611
What if this present were the
   worlds last night?   282
What is this strange and uncouth
   thing?   463
What? Mars his sword? faire Cy-
   therea say   581
What mean'st thou Bride, this
   companie to keep   136
What succour can I hope the
   Muse will send   596
When blessed Marie wip'd her
   Saviours feet   471

When by thy scorne, O mur-
   dresse I am dead   69
When Clarindon had discern'd
   beforehand   823
When Death, shall part us from
   these Kids   722
When first my lines of heav'nly
   joyes made mention   405
When first thou didst entice to
   thee my heart   354
When first thy sweet and gra-
   cious eye   470
When for the Thorns with which
   I long, too long   717
When God at first made man
   458
When I am dead, and Doctors
   know not why   81
When I beheld the Poet blind,
   yet bold   818
When I dyed last, and, Deare, I
   dye   49
When my devotions could not
   pierce   384
When my grave is broke up
   againe   80
When that rich Soule which to
   her heaven is gone   207
When you are Mistresse of the
   song   591
Where art thou Sol, while thus
   the blind-fold Day   595
Where is that holy fire, which
   Verse is said   124
Where, like a pillow on a bed
   72
Where the remote Bermudas ride
   720
Whether that soule which now
   comes up to you   253
While that my soul repairs to her
   devotion   371
Whilst yet to prove   85
Whither away delight?   453
Whither, O, Whither art thou
   fled   460
Who ere shee bee   605
Who ever comes to shroud me,
   do not harme   77
Who ever guesses, thinks, or

dreames he knowes 65
Who ever loves, if he do not pro-
    pose 119
Who is the honest man? 377
Who makes the Past, a patterne
    for next yeare 166
Who reade a chapter when they
    rise 399
Who sayes that fictions onely
    and false hair 363
Why are wee by all creatures
    waited on? 282
Why do I languish thus, droop-
    ing and dull 417
Why dost Thou wound my
    wounds, ô Thou that pass-
    est by 523
Why this man gelded Martiall I
    muse 91
Wilt thou forgive that sinne
    where I begunne 316
Wilt thou love God, as he thee!
    then digest 283
With all the powres my poor

Heart hath 649
With his kinde mother who par-
    takes thy woe 275
With sick and famisht eyes 448
Within this sober Frame expect
    755
Would any one the true cause
    find 602
Wounded I sing, tormented I in-
    dite 458

Ye living Lamps, by whose dear
    light 746
You have refin'd mee, and to
    worthyest things 172
You that are she and you, that's
    double shee 204
You, that decipher out the Fate
    734
Your mistris, that you follow
    whores, still taxeth you 90

Zealously my Muse doth salute
    all thee 185

INDEX OF TITLES AND AUTHORS

Aaron   472

Act. 5. The sicke implore St. Peter's shadow   516

Act. 8. On the baptized Æthiopian   514

Act. 21. I am ready not onely to be bound but to dye   527

Affliction (I)   354

Affliction (II)   368

Affliction (III)   378

Affliction (IV)   393

Affliction (V)   400

Against Irresolution and Delay in Matters of Religion   692

Agonie, The   347

Aire and Angels   51

Ales Phasiacis petita Colchis &c. R. Cr. [Out of Petronius]   697

Alexias The Complaint of The Foresaken Wife of Sainte Alexis   680

Altar, The   337

Ametas and Thestylis making Hay-Ropes   748

Anagram, The [Elegie II]   94

Ana-{ MARY   { ARMY }gram   382

Anatomie of the World, An   206

And a certaine Priest comming that way looked on him and passed by [Luke 10]   523

And he answered them nothing [Matthew 27]   520

Angels, The   291

Anniversarie, The   52

Annvnciation   274

Annunciation and Passion, The   287

Answer, The   467

Antiphon (I)   360

Antiphon (II)   396

Antiquary   91

Apologie For The Fore-Going Hymne as hauing been writt when the author was yet among the protestantes, An   670

Apologie for the precedent Hymne, An   561

Apostles, The   292

Apparition, The   69

Artillerie   439

Ascention   276

Assurance   454

Authors Motto, The   508

Autumnall, The [Elegie IX]   102

Avarice   382

Bag, The   450

Baite, The   68

Banquet, The   478

Beginning of Heliodorus, The   578

Benediction, The   135

Bermudas   720

Bitter-sweet   469

Blessed be the paps which Thou hast sucked [Luke 11]   523

blind cured by the word of our Saviour, The [Matthew 9]   520

Blossome, The   78

Bracelet, The. Vpon the losse of his Mistresses Chaine, for which he made satisfaction [Elegie XI]   105

Breake of day   52

Bridegroomes comming, The   136

Brides going to bed, The 136
British Church, The 411
broken heart, The 69
Bunch of Grapes, The 429
burnt ship, A 89
Businesse 414
But men loved darknesse rather then light [Joh. 3] 526
But now they have seen, and hated 525

Cales and *Guyana* 90
Call, The 455
Calme, The 163
Canonization, The 45
Carmen Deo Nostro 611
Change [Elegie III] 95
Character of Holland, *The* 788
Charitas Nimia, or The Dear Bargain 641
Charms and Knots 399
Christmas 385
Church, The 337
Church-floore, The 372
Church-lock and key 372
Church Militant, The 486
Church-monuments 371
Church-musick 371
Church-porch, The 323
Church-rents and schisms 440
Clarindon's *House-Warming* 823
Clasping of hands 456
Clorinda and Damon 721
Close, The 630
Collar, The 452
Coloss. 3.3. Our Life is hid with Christ in God 389
Come see the place where the Lord lay [Mat. 28] 517
Communitie 58
Comparison, The [Elegie VIII] 101
Complaining 443
Compline 637
Computation, The 84
Confession 427
Confessors, The 293
Confined Love 61
Conscience 407

Constancie 377
Content 374
Coronet, The 717
CRASHAW, RICHARD 505–705
Crosse, The 285
Crosse, The 463
Crvcifying 276
Curse, The 65

Damon the Mower 744
Dampe, The 81
Daphnis and *Chloe* 736
Dawning, The 413
Death 483
Death [Elegie] 251
Death's Lectvre at the Funeral of a Yovng Gentleman 686
Decay 402
Dedication, The [to *The Temple*] 323
Definition of Love, The 739
Delights of the Muses, The 571
Deniall 384
Description of A Religiovs Hovse and Condition of Life (Ovt of Barclay) 684
Dialogue 416
Dialogue-Antheme, A. CHRISTIAN DEATH 468
Dialogue Between The Resolved Soul, and Created Pleasure, A 714
Dialogue between the Soul and Body, A 724
Dialogue between the Two Horses, A 861
Dialogue between Thyrsis *and* Dorinda, *A* 722
Dies Irae Dies Illa. The Hymn of the Chvrch, In Meditation of The Day of Ivdgment 653
Discharge, The 444
Discipline 476
Disinherited 91
Dissolution, The 82
Dives asking a drop [Luke 16] 525

893

Divine Epigrams   514
Divine Poems   273
Divinitie   435
Doctors, The   294
DONNE, JOHN   37–318
Dooms-day   483
Dotage   465
Dreame, The   61
Dreame, The [Elegie X]   104
Dulnesse   417
Dumbe healed, and the people
   enjoyned silence, The
   [Mar. 7]   516

Easter   351
Easter day   529
Easter-wings   352
Ecclogve. 1613. December 26
   130
Elegie I. Jealousie   93
Elegie II. The Anagram   94
Elegie III. Change   95
Elegie IV. The Perfume   96
Elegie V. His Picture   98
Elegie VI.   99
Elegie VII   100
Elegie VIII. The Comparison
   101
Elegie IX. The Autumnall   102
Elegie X. The Dreame   104
Elegie XI. The Bracelet   105
Elegie XII. His parting from her
   108
Elegie XIII. Julia   110
Elegie XIV. A Tale of a Citizen
   and his Wife   111
Elegie XV. The Expostulation
   113
Elegie XVI. On his Mistris   115
Elegie XVII. <Variety>   117
Elegie XVIII. Loves Progress
   119
Elegie XIX. Going to Bed   121
Elegie XX. Loves Warre   123
Elegie. Death   251
Elegie on Mris Boulstred   249
Elegie on the Lady Marckham
   247
Elegie on the L.C.   252

Elegie upon the untimely death
   of the incomparable Prince
   Henry   238
Elegy upon the death of Mr Stan-
   ninow fellow of Queenes
   Colledge, An   700
Elegy upon the Death of my
   Lord Francis Villiers, An
   819
Elixir, The   481
Employment (I)   364
Employment (II)   383
English Poems Not Included in
   The Temple   495
Ephes. 4.30. Grieve not the Holy
   Spirit, &c.   436
Epigrams   89
Epicedes and Obseqvies. Vpon
   the Deaths of Sundry Per-
   sonages   238
Epitaph, An. Upon Doctor
   Brooke   590
Epitaph, An. Upon Husband
   and Wife, which died, and
   were buried together   589
Epitaph, An. Vpon Mr. Ashton
   a conformable Citizen   603
Epitaph upon — —, An   752
Epitaph Vpon a Yovng Married
   Couple Dead and Bvried
   Together, An   685
Epitaphs   255
Epithalamion. The time of the
   Mariage   133
Epithalamion made at Lincolnes
   Inne   137
Epithalamion, Or mariage Song
   on the Lady Elizabeth and
   Count Palatine being mar-
   ried on St. Valentines day
   127
Epithalamions, or Marriage
   Songs   127
Equality of persons   133
Even-song   370
Euen-song   498
Evensong   636
Expiration, The   84
Expostulation, The [Elegie XV]
   113

894

Extasie, The 72
Eyes and Tears 718

Fair Singer, The 734
Faith 357
Fall of a wall 90
Familie, The 437
Farewell to love 85
Father, *The* 290
Feasts and Revells 136
Feaver, A 50
first Anniversary, The 207
First Anniversary of the Government under O.C., The 792
First Elegie, The [Alexias The Complaint of The Forsaken Wife of Sainte Alexis] 680
First Song [The Progresse of the Soule] 258
Flaming Heart Vpon the Book and Picture of the seraphicall saint Teresa, The 671
Flea, The 64
Fleckno, an English Priest at Rome 776
Flower, The 464
Foil, The 474
For the Hour of Matines 632
For the Hovr of Prime 633
Forerunners, The 474
Frailtie 376
Funerall, The 77
Funerall ELEGIE, *A* 219
Further Advice to a Painter 852

Gallery, The 732
Garden, The 749
Giddinesse 428
(Give to Caesar———) (And to God———) [Marke 12] 525
Glance, The 470
Glimpse, The 453
Going to Bed [Elegie XIX] 121
Going to the Chappell 135
Good Friday 348
Goodfriday, 1613. *Riding Westward* 288

good-morrow, The 40
Good-night, The 137
Grace 367
Gratefulnesse 425
Grief 462

H. Baptisme (I) 352
H. Baptisme (II) 353
H. Communion, The 359
H. Communion, The 495
H. Scriptures, The (I and II) 365
H: W: in Hiber: belligeranti 170
Harbinger to the Progresse, The 223
Heaven 485
Her Apparrelling 135
HERBERT, GEORGE 321–501
Hero and Leander 89
Heroicall Epistle 124
Himne for the Circumcission day of our Lord, An 566
Himn, The. O Gloriosa Domina 656
His Epitaph 587
His parting from her [Elegie XII] 108
His Picture [Elegie V] 98
Holdfast, The 443
Holy Ghost, The 290
Holy Sonnets 274, 277
Home 409
Hope 423
Hope 688
Horatian Ode upon Cromwel's Return from Ireland, *An* 781
Howres, The [The Office of the Holy Crosse] 632
Hymn of Sainte Thomas in Adoration of the Blessed Sacrament, The. Adoro Te 649
Hymn To The Name and Honor of The Admirable Sainte Teresa, A 665
Hymne of the Nativity, sung by the Shepheards, A 534
Hymne to Christ, at the Authors

last going into Germany, A
301

Hymne to God my God, in my
sicknesse 315

Hymne to God the Father, A
316

hymne to the Saints, and to Mar-
quesse Hamylton, A [To Sir
Robert Carr] 253

Humilitie 375

I am not worthy that thou
should'st come under my
roofe [Matthew 8] 519

I am ready not onely to be bound
but to dye [Act. 21] 527

I am the Doore 520

Ille & nefasto te posuit die &c.
R. Cr. [Out of Horace] 698

In amorem divinum (Hermannus
Hugo) 697

In cicatrices Domini Jesu 696

In memory of the Vertuous and
Learned Lady Madre de
Teresa that sought an early
Martyrdome 556

In praise of Lessius his rule of
health 576

In the Gloriovs Assumption of
Our Blessed Lady. The
Hymn 657

In the Glorious Epiphanie of Our
Lord God. A Hymn Svng
as by the three Kings 624

In the Holy Nativity of Our Lord
God. A Hymn Sung as by
the Shepheards 619

Indifferent, The 44

Infinitati Sacrum, 16. Augusti
1601. Metempsychosis
257

Invitation, The 477

It is better to go into Heaven
with one eye, &c. 522

Jealosie [Elegie I] 93

Jeat Ring sent, A 82

Jesu 414

Jews, The 452

Joh. 3. But men loved darknesse

rather then Light 526

Joh. 15. Vpon our Lords last
comfortable discourse with
his Disciples 524

Joh. 16. Verily I say unto you,
yee shall weep and lament
524

Jordan (I) 363

Jordan (II) 405

Josephs coat 458

Judgement 484

Julia [Elegie XIII] 110

Justice (I) 399

Justice (II) 941

Klockius 91

Knell, The 498

La Corona 274

lame begger, A 90

Lamentations of Jeremy, for the
most part according to Tre-
melius 302

Last Instructions to a Painter,
The 827

Lavda Sion Salvatorem. The
Hymn for the Bl. Sacrament
651

Lecture upon the Shadow, A
87

Legacie, The 49

Lent 390

L'Envoy 493

Letter from Mr. Crashaw To the
Countess of Denbigh.
Against Irresolution and
Delay in matters of Religion
692

Letters to Severall Personages
161

Letter to the Lady Carey, and
Mrs Essex Riche, From
Amyens 199

licentious person, A 90

Lier, The 92

Life 397

Litanie, The 290

Longing 448

Love 496

Love (I and II) 361

896

Love (III) 485
Love-joy 418
Love unknown 430
Lovers infinitenesse 47
Loves Alchymie 63
Loves Deitie 74
Loves diet 74
Loves exchange 60
Loves growth 59
Loves Horoscope 598
Loves Progress [Elegie XVIII] 119
Loves Vsury 45
Loves Warre [Elegie XX] 123
Loyall Scott, The. Upon the occasion of the death of Captain Douglas burnt in one of his Majesties shipps at Chatham 854
Luk. 7. She began to wash his feet with teares and wipe them with the haires of her head 526
Luk. 11. Vpon the dumbe Devill cast out, and the slanderous Jewes put to silence 522
Luk. 15. On the Prodigall 515
Luke 2. Quaerit Jesum suum Maria 695
Luke 10. And a certaine Priest comming that way looked on him and passed by 523
Luke 11. Blessed be the paps which Thou hast sucked 523
Luke 16. Dives asking a drop 525

M. Crashaws Answer For Hope 689
Man 394
Mans medley 431
Mar. 7. The dumbe healed, and the people enjoyned silence 516
Marie Magdalene 471
Marke 4. Why are yee afraid, O yee of little faith? 518
Marke 12. (Give to Caesar——) (And to God——) 525

Martyrs 293
MARVELL, ANDREW 709–866
Mat. 28. Come see the place where the Lord lay 517
Match, The 741
Math. 16.25. Whosoeuer shall loose his life &c. 696
Mattens 369
Matthew 8. I am not worthy that thou should'st come under my roofe 519
Matthew 9. The blind cured by the word of our Saviour 520
Matthew 22. Neither durst any man from that Day aske him any more Questions 521
Matthew 23. Yee build the Sepulchres of the Prophets 524
Matthew 27. And he answered them nothing 520
Mercurius Gallo-Belgicus 91
Message, The 66
Method, The 434
Miserie 402
Mortification 401
Mourning 734
Mower against Gardens, The 743
Mower to the Glo-Worms, The 746
Mower's Song, The 747
Musicks Duell 571
Musicks Empire 748

Nativitie 275
Nature 353
Negative love 83
Neither durst any man from that Day aske him any more Questions [Matthew 22] 521
New Year's Day 623
Ninth, The 636
Niobe 89
nocturnall upon S. Lucies day, Being the Shortest day, A 66

897

Nymph complaining for the
    death of her Faun, The
    725

O dea syderei seu to stirps alma
    Tonantis &c. [Out of Bar-
    clay's Euphormion]   699
Obedience   406
obscure writer, An   91
Obsequies to the Lord Harring-
    ton, brother to the Lady
    Lucy, Countesse of Bedford
    241
Odour, The. 2. Cor. 2.15   473
Of the Progresse of the Soule
    223
Offering, An   447
Office of the Holy Crosse, The.
    The Howres   632
Omnibus   255
On a Drop of Dew   716
On a foule Morning, being then
    to take a journey   595
On a prayer booke sent to Mrs.
    M.R.   552
On a Treatise of Charity   563
On his Mistris [Elegie XVI]
    115
On Hope, By way of Question
    and Answer, between A.
    Cowley, and R. Crashaw
    567
On Marriage   596
On Mr. G. Herberts booke inti-
    tuled the Temple of Sacred
    Poems, sent to a Gentle-
    woman   556
On Mr. Milton's Paradise lost
    818
On Nanus mounted upon an Ant
    581
On our crucified Lord Naked,
    and bloody   528
On St. Peter casting away his
    Nets at our Saviours call
    527
On St. Peter cutting of Malchus
    his eare   526
On the Assumption of the Virgin
    Marie   564

On the baptized Æthiopian
    [Act. 8]   514
On the bleeding wounds of our
    crucified Lord   529
On the Blessed Virgins bashful-
    nesse   518
On the Frontispiece of Isaacsons
    Chronologie explained   602
On the Miracle of Loaves   517
On the miracle of multiplyed
    loaves   515
On the Prodigall [Luk. 15]   515
On the still surviving markes of
    our Saviours wounds   516
On the Victory obtained by
    Blake over the Spaniards, in
    the Bay of Sanctacruze, in
    the Island of Teneriff. 1657.
    802
On the water of our Lords
    Baptisme   514
On the wounds of our crucified
    Lord   528
Our life is hid with Christ in God
    [Coloss. 3.3]   389
Our Lord in his Circumcision to
    his Father   527
Out of Barclay's Euphormion
    699
Out of Catullus   604
Out of Grotius his Tragedy of
    Christes sufferinges   703
Out of Horace   698
Out of Martiall   600
Out of Petronius   697
Out of the Greek Cupid's Cryer
    579
Out of the Italian   602
Out of the Italian   602
Out of the Italian. A Song   600
Out of Virgil. In the praise of
    the Spring   575

Paradise   433
Paradox, The   85
Parodie, A   480
Patriarches, The   292
Peace   426
Pearl, The. Matth. 13.45   392
Perfume, The (Elegie IV)   96

Perirrhanterium (The Church-
   porch) 323
Perseverance 499
Phryne 91
Picture of little T.C. in a Prospect
   of Flowers, The 740
Pilgrimage, The 442
Poem upon the Death of O.C., A
   810
Poems 711
Poems from Manuscripts 695
Poems from Walton's Lives 500
Posie, The 480
Praise (I) 367
Praise (II) 446
Praise (III) 457
Prayer (I) 359
Prayer (II) 405
Prayer. An Ode, Which Was
   Praefixed to a Little Prayer-
   book Given to a Young
   Gentle-Woman 675
Priesthood, The 459
Primrose, being at Mountgomery
   Castle, upon the hill, on
   which it is situate, The 79
Prohibition, The 83
Prophets, The 292
Providence 418
Psalme 23 531
Psalme 137 533
Pulley, The 458
Pyramus and Thisbe 89

Quaerit Jesum suum Maria
   [Luke 2] 695
Quidditie, The 375
Quip, The 412

Raderus 91
Raising of the Bride 134
Ralphius 92
Raysing of the Bridegroome
   134
Recommendation, The 638
Redemption 319
Relique, The 80
Repentance 356
Reprisall, The 347

Resvrrection 276
Resurrection, imperfect 287
Rose, The 475

Sacrifice, The 337
Sainte Mary Magdalene or The
   Weeper 659
Sampson to his Dalilah 531
Sancta Maria Dolorvm or The
   Mother of Sorrows. A
   Patheticall descant vpon the
   deuout Plainsong of Stabat
   Mater Dolorosa 643
Sapho to Philænis 124
Satires of the Reign of Charles II
   823
Satyre I 141
Satyre II 144
Satyre III 147
Satyre IIII 149
Satyre V 156
Search, The 460
Second Anniversary, The 224
Seconde Elegie, The [Alexias
   The Complaint of The For-
   saken Wife of Sainte Alexis]
   681
selfe accuser, A 90
Self-condemnation 468
<Selfe Love> 88
Senec. Traged. ex Thyeste Chor.
   2 751
Sepulchre 350
She began to wash his feet with
   teares and wipe them with
   the haires of her head [Luc.
   7] 525
sicke implore St. Peter's shadow,
   The [Act. 5] 516
Sighs and Grones 387
Sinne (I) 354
Sinne (II) 369
Sinner, The 348
Sinnes round 423
Sion 408
Sir John Wingefield 90
Sixt, The 635
Size, The 438
Song, A 674
Song 41, 48

899

Songs and Sonnets　40
Sonne, The　466
Sonne, *The*　290
Sonnet. The Token　87
Sonnets　500
Sospetto d' Herode　537
Starre, The　379
Statue at Charing Cross, *The*　859
Statue in Stocks-Market, The　857
Steps to the Temple　508
Storm, The　433
Storme, The. To Mr. *Christopher Brooke*　161
Submission　398
Sunday　380
Sunne Rising, The　43
Superliminare [*The Church-porch*]　336

Tale of a Citizen and his Wife, A [*Elegie XIV*]　111
Teare, The　513
Temper, The (I)　362
Temper, The (II)　363
Temperance, or the Cheap Physitian. Vpon the Translation of Lessius　687
Temple　275
Temple, The　323
Thanksgiving, The　345
Third, The　634
Third Elegie, The [*Alexias The Complaint of The Forsaken Wife of Sainte Alexis*]　682
Time　424
time of the Mariage, The [*Epithalamion*]　133
To all Angels and Saints　382
To *E.* of *D.* with six holy Sonnets　273
To His Coy Mistress　729
To his Noble Friend Mr. Richard Lovelace, *upon his Poems*　711
To his worthy Friend Doctor Witty upon his Translations of the Popular Errors　786
To Mr *B.B.*　189

To Mr *C.B.*　186
To Mr *Christopher Brooke* [*The Storme*]　161
To Mr *E. G.*　186
To Mr *George Herbert*, with one of my Seals, of the Anchor and Christ　317
To Mr *I. L.*　190
To Mr *I. L.*　188
To Mr *R. W.*　187
To Mr *R. W.*　188
To Mr *R. W.*　185
To Mr *R. W.*　185
To Mr *Rowland Woodward*　168
To Mr *S. B.*　188
To Mr *T. W.*　182
To Mr *T. W.*　184
To Mr *T. W.*　183
To Mr *T. W.*　184
To Mr Tilman *after he had taken orders*　299
To Mrs *M. H.*　192
To my Successor　501
To Our B. Lord Vpon the Choice of his Sepulcher　640
To our Lord, upon the Water made Wine　521
To Pontius *washing his blood-stained hands*　523
To Pontius *washing his hands*　517
To Sir *H.W.* at his going Ambassador to *Venice*　190
To Sir Robert Carr [*An hymne to the Saints, and to Marquesse Hamylton*]　253
To Sr *Edward Herbert* at *Julyers*　174
To Sr Henry Goodyere　166
To Sr Henry Wotton　164
To Sr Henry Wootton　169
To the Countesse of Bedford　171, 172, 175, 193
To the Countesse of Bedford. *Begun in France but never perfected*　199
To the Countesse of Bedford [*Epitaph on Himselfe*]　255
To the Countesse of Bedford. *On*

New-yeares day   178
To the Countesse of Huntingdon
   180, 195
To the Countesse of Salisbury.
   August. 1614   202
To the Infant Martyrs   517
To the King   851
To the Lady Bedford   204
To the Lady Magdalen Herbert:
   of St. Mary Magdalen   273
To the Morning. Satisfaction for
   sleepe   596
To the Name Above Every Name,
   The Name of Jesus. A
   Hymn   613
To the Noblest & best of Ladyes,
   the Countess of Denbigh
   611
To the praise of the dead, and the
   Anatomie   206
To the Queen An Apologie for
   the Length of the following
   Panegyrick   591
To the Queen. Vpon the Duke
   of Yorke his Birth. A Pane-
   gyricke   591
To the Queen's Majesty   631
To the Same Party Councel Con-
   cerning Her Choise   678
Tom May's Death   784
Translations from Latin Poems
   317, 318
Trinitie Sunday   323
Trinity, The   291
Trinity Sunday   497
triple Foole, The   47
true Hymne, A   466
23d Psalme, The   470
Twicknam garden   55
Two Dedicatory Poems   701
Two Songs at the Marriage of
   the Lord Fauconberg and
   the Lady Mary Cromwell
   806
Two went up into the Temple to
   pray   519

undertaking, The   42
unfortunate Lover, The   730

Ungratefulnesse   386
Unkindnesse   397
Upon Appleton House, to my
   Lord Fairfax   755
Vpon Bishop Andrewes his Pic-
   ture before his Sermons
   581
Vpon Doctor Brooke [An Epi-
   taph]   590
Vpon Ford's two Tragedyes
   Loves Sacrifice and The
   Broken Heart   595
Upon his Grand-Children   827
Upon his House   826
Vpon Husband and Wife, which
   died, and were buried to-
   gether [An Epitaph]   589
Vpon Lazarus his Teares   518
Vpon Mr. Ashton a comformable
   Citizen [An Epitaph]   603
Vpon Mr. Staninough's Death
   590
Vpon Mr. Thomas Coryats Cru-
   dities   158
Vpon our Lords last comfortable
   discourse with his Disciples
   [Joh. 15]   524
Vpon our Saviours Tombe where-
   in never man was laid   522
Vpon the Asse that bore our
   Saviour   519
Vpon the Bleeding Crucifix. A
   Song   646
Vpon the Body of Our Bl. Lord,
   Naked and Bloody   648
Vpon the Crowne of Thorns Tak-
   en Downe From the head of
   our Bl. Lord, all Bloody
   648
Vpon the Death of a Gentleman
   582
Vpon the Death of Mr. Herrys
   583
Upon the Death of the Lord
   Hastings   712
Vpon the Death of the most de-
   sired Mr. Herrys   584, 586
Vpon the Deaths of Sundry Per-
   sonages [Epicedes and Ob-
   seqvies]   238

Vpon the dumbe Devill cast out, and the slanderous Jewes put to silence (Luk. 11) 522

Vpon the faire Ethiopian sent to a Gentlewoman 596

Vpon the H. Sepulcher 638

Upon the Hill and Grave at Bill-borow. To the Lord Fairfax 752

Vpon the Infant Martyrs 524

Vpon the Powder Day 598

Vpon the Sepulchre of our Lord 515

Vpon the Thornes taken downe from our Lords head bloody 525

Vpon the translation of the Psalmes by Sir Philip Syd-ney, and the Countesse of Pembroke his Sister 298

Vpon two greene Apricockes sent to Cowley by Sir Crashaw 609

Vpon Venus putting on Mars his Armes 581

Valediction: forbidding mourn-ing, A 70

Valediction: of my name, in the window, A 53

Valediction: of the booke, A 56

Valediction: of weeping, A 62

Vanitie (I) 389

Vanitie (II) 413

<Variety> [Elegie XVII] 117

Verily I say unto you, yee shall weep and lament [Joh. 16] 524

Vertue 391

Vexilla Regis, the Hymn of the Holy Crosse 639

Virgin Mary, The 291

Virgins, The 293

Water-course, The 468

Weeper, The 508

Whitsunday 366

Whosoever shall loose his life &c. [Math. 16.25] 696

Why are yee afraid, O yee of lit-tle faith? [Marke 4] 518

Widowes Mites, The 515

Will, The 75

Windows, The 373

Wishes. To his (supposed) Mis-tresse 605

Witchcraft by a picture 68

With a Picture sent to a Friend 576

Womans constancy 41

World, The 388

Wreath, A 482

Yee build the Sepulchres of the Prophets [Matthew 23] 524

Young Love 728